The
Great Migration

Volume I

A-B

Other NEHGS Titles by
Robert Charles Anderson, FASG

The Great Migration Directory
Immigrants to New England,
1620–1640
6 x 9, hdcvr, 480 pp., $64.95

The Great Migration Begins
Immigrants to New England,
1620–1633 (first series)
6 x 9, 2,386 pp. in 3 vols.
hdcvr, $125; pbk, $79.95

The Pilgrim Migration
Immigrants to Plymouth Colony, 1620–1633
6 x 9 pbk, 708 pp., $29.95

The Winthrop Fleet
Massachusetts Bay Company Immigrants to New England,
1629–1630
6 x 9 hdcvr, 912 pp., $64.95

Available from shop.AmericanAncestors.org/collections/great-migration

The
Great Migration

Immigrants to New England
1634 - 1635

Volume I

A-B

Robert Charles Anderson
George F. Sanborn Jr.
Melinde Lutz Sanborn

Great Migration Study Project
NEW ENGLAND HISTORIC GENEALOGICAL SOCIETY
Boston, Massachusetts

ISBN: 978-0-88082-332-6
Library of Congress Control Number: 2015951893

Cover design by Carolyn Sheppard Oakley
Printed by Yurchak Printing, Landisville, Pennsylvania
Paperback edition printed November 2015

NEW ENGLAND HISTORIC
GENEALOGICAL SOCIETY
Boston, Massachusetts
www.AmericanAncestors.org

Dedicated to

Dean Crawford Smith and Roberta Stokes Smith

in gratitude for
forty years of friendship and ten years support of the
Great Migration Study Project

TABLE OF CONTENTS

Volume One

LIST OF SKETCHES

PREFACE & ACKNOWLEDGEMENTS

This fourth volume to be published by the Great Migration Study Project begins a second series, which will cover the years 1634 and 1635. The number of immigrants to New England during these years was about fifty percent greater than the number who arrived in the previous fourteen years, and so six volumes will be required for these two years.

The plan of research and the sketch format adopted for the first three volumes have stood up to four years of usage and criticism, and so this second series will not differ from the first in appearance or in the nature of the contents.

The principal change in the conduct of the Project in the last three years is that George F. Sanborn Jr. and Melinde Lutz Sanborn have joined me as full participants in research and writing.

Many people have given me assistance of all varieties over the past few years. I hope that I have included here all those who have helped, but if I have omitted anyone, it is only by inadvertence.

My parents, Albert E. and Frances H. Anderson, have supported me unstintingly throughout this Project. Even through the obstacles created by his stroke of some years ago, my father continued to demonstrate interest in the Project right up to his death last November.

Dean Crawford Smith and Roberta Stokes Smith have continued their enthusiastic advocacy and support for this Project, as further evidenced by the Dedication of this volume.

Ralph J. Crandall, Executive Director of NEHGS, and the Officers and Board have also continued their strong support.

Aileen Novick, following in Margaret Costello's footsteps, has assisted in producing the *Great Migration Newsletter*, and has also done the proofreading for this volume.

Jane F. Fiske, F.A.S.G., editor of the *New England Historical and Genealogical Register*, has continued to supply valued advice on Rhode Island families and on editorial practices.

David L. Greene, Roger D. Joslyn and Robert S. Wakefield, all Fellows of the American Society of Genealogists, have read the entire manuscript, making valuable suggestions and saving me from numerous errors. Roger has provided the indexes, and Bob has been especially helpful on the families of Plymouth Colony, on which he is the undisputed expert of our times.

Gordon L. Remington of Salt Lake City, Utah, has assisted greatly in seeking out records of importance to the Project in the vast holdings of the Family History Library.

Harry Macy, F.A.S.G., Editor of the *New York Genealogical and Biographical Record,* has helped me with those immigrants who resided for a time in New Amsterdam or on Long Island.

David Curtis Dearborn, F.A.S.G., and Jerome E. Anderson at the Society supplied much reference material. Peter Drummey provided access to important research materials at the Massachusetts Historical Society.

On some sketches I have benefited greatly from data supplied by various individuals who have not yet had the opportunity to publish their finds elsewhere, and I am most grateful to them for allowing the inclusion of that material here.

- John Brandon for information on Thomas Bell.
- Don C. Stone for information on Thomas Boylston.

Special acknowledgement is made of the generous bequest received in 1993 from the estate of Dorothy Pickering Bartlett Pearce for the support of the Great Migration Study Project, made in memory of her father, J. Gardner Bartlett, director of the Society's Committee on English Research, 1906-1917. In the first years of this century, Mr. Bartlett and his second wife, Elizabeth French, made major contributions to the identification of early immigrants, part of the foundation on which these volumes build.

Even with all this help, there will still be errors here, and they are all attributable to the authors. Please send any suggested corrections to Great Migration Study Project, 101 Newbury Street, Boston MA 02116.

Robert Charles Anderson
Derry, New Hampshire
17 June 1999

SCOPE

For the user of this set of volumes to understand what is being presented, we must define carefully the scope of the Great Migration Study Project. Who were the participants in the Great Migration? What information is being collected on these people?

CRITERIA FOR INCLUSION IN
THE GREAT MIGRATION:
IMMIGRANTS TO NEW ENGLAND, 1634-1635

The first phase of the Great Migration Study Project attempted to identify and describe all those Europeans who settled in New England prior to the end of 1633. The date was chosen because of the steep increase in migration beginning in 1634 and continuing for the rest of that decade (see Robert Charles Anderson, "A Note on the Pace of the Great Migration," *The New England Quarterly* 59[1986]:406-7). As a rough estimate, fifteen percent or more of the immigrants to New England arrived in the fourteen years from 1620 to 1633, with the remaining eighty-five percent coming over in half as many years, from 1634 to 1640.

The second phase attempts to carry out the same program for the years 1634 and 1635. As noted above, migration to New England accelerated in 1634, with something on the order of two thousand to twenty-five hundred immigrants in that year. Migration remained at that level for the remainder of the decade. About thirteen-hundred individuals or families are known to have come to New England in 1634 and 1635, amounting probably to twenty percent or more of the entire Great Migration. Six volumes will be needed to cover the immigrants of these years, and at the end this second series close to forty percent of the Great Migration immigrants will have been treated.

As discussed below, we have for 1634 and 1635 more surviving passenger lists than for any other part of the Great Migration. Even so, there are many hundreds who arrived in these two years who do not appear on the passenger lists. We have, therefore, compiled our list of immigrants by employing three broad sets of criteria beyond the passenger lists:

      1) appearance in a record generated after 14 May 1634 and before 25 May 1636,

      2) direct or indirect implication of arrival by the end of 1635 included in a record of later date, and

>   3) appearance as a member of the immediate family of a
>   person known to have arrived in 1634 or 1635.

Let us examine each of these categories a little more closely.

First, we have examined all available records generated in New England, or elsewhere about New England, between 14 May 1634 and 25 May 1636, and have extracted the names of all persons in those records who appear as residing in New England by that time. These records are described in more detail in the various subheadings under SOURCES below. The dates in May of 1634 and 1636 are chosen because of some features of the migration process. Most passenger ships did not leave England until spring, because of the bad weather in the North Atlantic earlier in the year. Thus it would be impossible for a passenger on one of these ships to have joined a church and then applied for freemanship in time for the annual General Court of Election, which in 1634 took place on 14 May and in 1636 on 25 May. Thus it is assumed that all the men who appeared in the list of freemen on 25 May 1636 must have arrived in New England no later than 1635.

Second, many records exist which were generated after 1635, but which clearly imply that a person named in that document was in New England in 1635 or earlier. Most frequently this will be a deposition, made as late as half a century after the arrival of the immigrant, in which the immigrant would recall some event in which he or she was involved in New England before 1636. Another record of this sort might be a grant of land to a man in 1639, for example, stating that he had been a servant to a New England resident for the previous five years. (These delayed statements must be handled with care, for they are sometimes at odds with other, more reliable evidence.)

Third, although there were many single men and women in the Great Migration, the vast majority of the immigrants came in family groups. For the purposes of this study we will adopt the somewhat arbitrary rule that a married man arrived in New England with his wife and all his children, unless there is evidence to the contrary (and in like manner a widowed woman would be assumed to arrive with all her children). If any more distant relatives of an immigrant, such as a sibling or niece or nephew, are known to have come to New England, they will not be assumed to have arrived at the same time; independent evidence will be required for such kinsmen. As an example, Henry Woolcott is known to have left two sons behind when he came to Dorchester, but all his other children are assumed to have come with him on the *Mary & John* in 1630. On the other hand, the three children of Emanuel Downing by his first wife (James, Mary and Susan) came to New England in 1630 and 1633, but their father, with his second wife and children by that wife, did not arrive until 1637.

Having studied the available records with these criteria in mind, we have compiled a list of slightly more than thirteen hundred families or unattached men and women who arrived in New England in 1634 or 1635. There exist claims for many hundreds more who had also arrived by this time, but most of these claims are demonstrably false. These claims have been rejected when they are not consistent with one or more of the three tests described above. Undoubtedly some immigrants who did arrive in 1635 or earlier have been omitted because of this strict exclusion, but we deem this preferable to the arbitrary and ungrounded inclusion of many persons who did not in fact come until some years later.

GOAL

The goal of the Great Migration Study Project may be stated very simply: to provide a concise, reliable summary of past research on the early immigrants to New England, which will reduce the amount of time which must be spent in discovering this past work, and will therefore serve as a foundation for future research.

The Project may be viewed, then, as an immense literature search, a scouring of the journals and books that have been published in the last century and a half. This is not to say that the Great Migration volumes contain no new research and no new discoveries. A number of English origins for immigrants are presented here for the first time, and many previously unidentified spouses have now been revealed.

A researcher interested in immigration to New England in the quarter-century after the arrival of the Mayflower has had, until now, to look in dozens of places to learn what is known about any one immigrant. After 135 years, the first place to go is still James Savage's *Genealogical Dictionary of New England*. This set was a marvel of its time and remains the only source which attempts to cover all families in New England for the seventeenth century. But there have been many genealogical advances since the days of Savage, and we must also look in thousands of other books and periodicals when researching these early immigrants.

The purpose of this set of books is to summarize and, to a limited extent, evaluate what we know about the immigrants to New England in

1634 and 1635. Modern researchers should not have to waste large amounts of time in searching out or, worse, redoing the research of earlier genealogists. With the current state of the genealogical literature this can be very difficult. The Great Migration volumes aim to provide a solid base which researchers of the future can use as a stepping-off point for doing new research on a given immigrant.

The primary goal is to document each life as completely as possible. In some cases this is a relatively easy task, since there may be only one or two records for the person in New England, and no clues to trace him or her back to England, or forward into a later career. In the majority of cases, however, an abundance of evidence exists, and a way must be found to bring it under control. After some experimentation, a standard format was developed to organize what is known about these participants in the Great Migration.

The standard sketch consists of three formatted sections: migration, biographical detail, and genealogical detail. This is followed by a section of COMMENTS, which allows discussion of material not accommodated elsewhere, and also discussion of discrepancies or matters of dispute between various authorities. The contents of the standard sketch are demonstrated in more detail in the Sample Sketch below.

There are several things, though, that the standard sketch, and the Great Migration Study Project as a whole, does not attempt to accomplish.

> If the parentage of the immigrant is known, that will be included. If a reasonably close relation to another immigrant is known, that will also be stated, perhaps naming other relatives who remained in England. But if the ancestry of the immigrant is known beyond his parents, it will usually not be presented or discussed, although a citation to anything published on the subject will be included.

> Not every detail of the life of the immigrant will be incorporated into each sketch. If the subject of the sketch was one of the leaders of a colony, his lesser offices and day-to-day activities, as recorded in official records, will not be recorded here. If the immigrant was a land speculator, not every deed or land grant will be noted. In general, the more obscure and the more poorly recorded

the immigrant in question, the greater will be the effort to find and include every known record.

The children of immigrants will not be traced until their deaths. We will attempt, of course, to identify every child, and to find the best evidence for that child's date and place of birth. After that we will look only for enough documentation to place that child beyond infancy, to distinguish him or her from others of the same name. Thus we will attempt to document the marriages of all children (although occasionally this may only be a first marriage). A death date will be sought for those who lived to adulthood and did not marry, and in these instances we may also include a probate record of the deceased, as it will frequently help in establishing the complete list of children of the immigrant. A death date may also be sought if it includes an age at death, and thus establishes an approximate year of birth.

CONSTRUCTING A SKETCH

In most instances, the construction of a sketch begins with consultation of Savage and Pope (both *Pioneers of Massachusetts* and *Pioneers of Maine and New Hampshire*). The information from these brief accounts of the immigrants is entered into the appropriate categories in the sketches with the clear understanding that many changes and additions will be necessary before the sketch may be called complete. Sometimes problems in the presentations by Savage and Pope arise immediately, especially if the two sources are in clear contradiction. On other occasions problems appear only at a later stage in the process.

For the majority of the immigrants who were married, the next step is to consult Clarence Almon Torrey's "New England Marriages Prior to 1700." For this purpose, the complete manuscript of the index, available at the New England Historic Genealogical Society in Boston, is examined. This manuscript includes for each marriage one or more citations to sources in which some mention of the married couple may be found. These citations may be to contemporary source documents or to secondary sources of many varieties. Torrey ceased work on his index in 1960, shortly before his death, and for the period after 1960 his work is supplemented by a privately generated card index, mostly to the periodical literature, covering the years from 1961 to the present.

As many as possible of the sources cited by Torrey are then collected and examined. At this point additional material from these sources may be added to the growing sketch. As the sketch continues to develop in this way, a number of things may happen. Points of dispute or controversy between two or more sources may appear, and they are noted so that they may be investigated and, if possible, resolved. Ideas for additional places to search may also come to light, and these are also added to the list of additional avenues of research.

Once the basic outline of the sketch has been created in this way, and many of the outstanding problems have been defined, research in primary sources begins. The vital records and church records are examined, deeds and wills are abstracted, and court records are surveyed. As will be explained in more detail in the next section, the best source possible is sought for each fact and for each genealogical connection.

The form of a sketch, in which a defined set of categories is filled in for each immigrant, forces research into the necessary areas, so that the same documents which are used to answer the genealogical questions or to complete the information on *ESTATE* are also examined for evidence of *EDUCATION*.

The last step is to review the work done on the sketch, and return to Savage, Pope and any other secondary sources of value to the immigrant under study. The COMMENTS section is then used to discuss the problem areas, in which two or more earlier researchers are in conflict. In many instances the conflict can be resolved, but, as this is not always possible, one can do no more than state the dispute, and perhaps suggest a path of research which might lead to a resolution.

This is also the stage at which the immigrant himself or herself may be evaluated. If the subject of the sketch was unusually contentious, or unusually innocuous, it might be reason for comment. The sketch should now be complete, with the immigrant's life outlined, using the best sources, and taking note of any remaining problems or of any unusual features of the person's life.

CHRONOLOGICAL ANALYSIS

CRITERIA FOR APPROXIMATING DATES

When we do not have an exact date for a vital event, such as a birth, baptismal, marriage or death date, we will in all instances create an approximated date for that event. We do this for a number of reasons. Sometimes this type of chronological analysis will reveal an unsuspected contradiction in previous treatments of a family, indicating perhaps that not all the children of a man could have been born to his only known wife. Even when the analysis does not reveal anything of immediate import, it may help to narrow the parameters within which future research must be conducted.

The approximation of dates may be done in a variety of ways. The most desirable manner of approximating dates is from a piece of evidence which states an age, or in some other way describes a specific span of years. If an age at death, or an age at the time of a deposition available, then a year of birth may be estimated, and in such a case the entry will read "b. about 1634," indicating a date that is reliable within a relatively narrow span of years, perhaps just two years above or below the estimated date.

More frequently the evidence for estimating an age will be less precise, and we will have to state an age in a different way: saying that someone was "b. say 1634," meaning that this is our best estimate, but that it may be some years off in either direction. We may only have a date of first marriage, from which we will state a likely birth date based on the usual age at first marriage. There are many other indicators which help us to establish these broad ranges.

Although some of the dates approximated in this study will in the future be found to be wide of the mark, we believe that it is important to provide some context for future research, and at least try to get a feel for what is chronologically possible with some of these immigrants. As will be seen, when a birthdate is estimated through a long string of other estimations, the date arrived at will generally be the latest date that the birth could have taken place, or close to it. Thus, in examining English records we will ignore candidates of that name who were born some years after the suggested birth date.

The criteria for producing "say" dates are many and varied, and only a few will be mentioned here. As noted above, a likely time for first marriage will be assumed. In a large number of cases men married for the first time in their early to mid twenties, and so an age of twenty-five will be used in this study. Women married for the first time in their late teens or early twenties, so an arbitrary age at first marriage of twenty will be assumed for women in the absence of evidence to the contrary.

"Say" dates may also be generated by reliance on other milestones in life, such as the age at which one could choose a guardian, or sell real estate, or become a freeman. The particular criterion used in a given case will generally be stated explicitly.

ORDERING FAMILIES

The next step in chronological analysis is the examination of whole families for the purpose of establishing birth-order for the children. This task poses no great problems when we have a complete set of birth or baptismal records, and when there are no internal inconsistencies among them.

When there are children without any precise date of birth, we begin, if possible, with those that do. This provides a framework around which we can attempt to place the others. We then look for those who have been assigned an "about" date of birth, based usually on age at death or age as given in a dated deposition. (If it happens that we do not have any children with known birth or baptismal dates, then we must erect our basic framework from those with "about" dates.)

We wish to fit the children with well-estimated years of birth into the framework at the most likely intervals. The first rule that we observe is that the births come about two years apart (unless we have strong evidence for multiple births, or for the employment of a wet nurse, which would allow the mother to conceive again soon after childbirth). We look, then, for gaps of three years or more into which a child might be placed (not enforcing the two-year interval rule too strictly).

At this point we will be left with children who have been assigned only "say" dates (based, perhaps, on a known date of first marriage, or on some other age-constrained life event), or for whom no clues on age are yet available. Those with "say" dates can be fitted into any remaining places. Those without any age information at all, perhaps children who died young with a known death date but no age at death, or unmarried children who died at a more advanced age, will now be placed into any plausible available slots.

Throughout this process we try to make the sequence of births as continuous as possible, for reasons that will emerge in a moment. We must be on the lookout for conflicts and contradictions, which may be indications that we have made an error in estimating or recording one of the dates. Also, by placing some of those without any age information into available gaps in the sequence, we should be able to assign "say" dates to most of the remaining children.

By making it our goal to place all the children in a single, compact sequence, we may obtain some useful information about other matters. If after all our efforts, there remains a large gap, or more than one, in the list of children, we may wish to seek for an explanation. Such a gap may indicate nothing more than a string of stillbirths or deaths in infancy, but other possible explanations may direct our research into new channels.

One explanation for the gap might be that the immigrant had more than one wife, with an early group of children by a first wife, a gap before a second marriage, and then a second wife. Even without a gap, a second wife would be indicated if the sequence of children was spread out over much more than twenty years.

Another explanation, usually more difficult to verify, would be that the couple were separated for a number of years. Sometimes the immigrant head of household came to New England alone, while his wife was still of child-bearing age, and did not send for her or return to fetch her until some years later.

This process of determining the order of birth of the children in a family, although time-consuming, frequently provides some of the best new data on that family. While some of the positions assigned to the children may turn out to be incorrect, the value of this process in pointing out conflicts and contradictions and in directing further research is worth the effort.

DOCUMENTATION AND CITATION

Although the terms documentation and citation are sometimes used interchangeably, they are employed here to describe two distinct but related steps in the process of supplying evidence to support one's conclusions.

DOCUMENTATION is the inclusion of complete or partial copies of the records in a sketch, whether as lengthy extracts or brief abstracts.

CITATION is the presentation of that information that identifies a source or a record, and allows the reader to find that source for himself or herself easily.

DOCUMENTATION

In some instances an abstract of a document or record may be sufficient. Perhaps only a small portion of the document is relevant to the matter at hand, or perhaps the document is burdened with much formulaic or legalistic language which does not in itself advance the argument. When an abstract is made, those portions of the record that have been used without change of verbiage are included in quotation marks, while the portions not in quotation marks have been abbreviated or paraphrased.

In other cases a complete document, or large uninterrupted portions of a document, may be incorporated in the sketch. This may be because the entire document is important for making a specific point, or simply because it is intrinsically interesting, and gives an insight into the life and times of the immigrants we are studying. In some cases the language of a document is so convoluted and complex that it is simply safer to produce a lengthy extract, as an attempted paraphrase might be just as long as the original, and not convey the point so well.

Whether a document is abstracted or transcribed in full, the Modernized Method of transcription is employed. In this technique, modern spelling, punctuation and capitalization are used, and abbreviations are expanded. In the case of personal and place names, however, the spellings of the document itself are retained, and abbreviations are expanded in square brackets. The original author or scribe's choice and sequence of words are not disturbed. The edition of William Bradford's history of Plymouth Colony which we are most often using here, prepared by Samuel Eliot Morison, employs the Modernized Method. (See Frank Freidel, ed., *Harvard Guide to American History*, revised edition, two volumes in one, pp. 27-36 for a complete discussion of this subject with examples.)

CITATION

Most citations will be given in an abbreviated form in the text, with the expansion of these short forms presented in the **Key to Titles,** to be found in the front of each volume of this set. If a source is used in only a few sketches, the full citation may be given at each occurrence, in which case no entry will appear in the **Key to Titles.** In some cases, generally a single-family genealogy, a source will be used, but the full citation will also appear in that sketch, and nowhere else.

Vital records may sometimes appear without citation. In the case of entries from English parish registers, this means that the item has been taken directly from the original or a microfilm copy of the register, which has been examined in the course of preparing the sketches. When an English parish register entry has been taken from another source, that source will be given.

When citing New England town vital records, especially from Massachusetts, no citation will appear if the entry has been taken from a volume published in alphabetic order (unless the entry appears in an unlikely part of the alphabet).

FORM OF DATES

Since England and the English colonies were still using the Julian calendar, a date which fell between 1 January and 24 March of the year could be ambiguous as to the year of the date. We employ various conventions in presenting these dates. If the double-dating is given explicitly in the record, or if the double-dated year can be deduced with confidence from the sequence of chronologically arranged records, the date will be given in the form "28 February 1636/7." If the double-dating can be deduced with reasonable but not complete confidence, the form will be "28 February 1637[/8]." If the double-dating cannot be determined with much assurance, the date will be given as "28 February 1637[/8?]." And in some cases no attempt will be made to resolve the date, and it will be presented simply as "28 February 1637."

The use of "[NS]" to indicate New Style dates will be employed only for records created in jurisdictions already using the Gregorian calendar. Most of these will be from Leiden or New Amsterdam. In no case will a date created under the Julian calendar be adjusted to the Gregorian calendar.

SOURCES

Hundreds of sources were consulted for this study, in libraries, archives and courthouses. Some were viewed in the original, some on microfilm, and some only in printed versions. We cannot describe in detail here every source consulted, but rather we will comment briefly on some of the more important documents employed in constructing these sketches. Many of these sources have been discussed in the pages of the *Great Migration Newsletter*, and where appropriate reference will be made to that publication.

PASSENGER LISTS

ORIGINAL AND RECONSTRUCTED LISTS

Most genealogists have a special interest in the ship on which their immigrant sailed when migrating to New England, but unfortunately there are very few authentic passenger lists surviving from the time of the Great Migration. However, we are especially fortunate for the years 1634 and 1635, most importantly because of the survival of the London Port Book for 1635. Passenger lists will again become scarce in 1636 and later years.

The passenger ships which came to New England in 1634 and 1635 have been discussed in detail in the *Great Migration Newsletter*. For 1634 we have more information than for any Great Migration year other than 1635, but still for a minority of the immigrants [GMN 6:9-10, 16, 17-18, 24]. For 1635 we probably have records of two-thirds to three-quarters of the immigrants to New England [GMN 7:1-2, 8-10, 16-18, 24-26, 32, 8:1-2, 8].

PUBLISHED PASSENGER LISTS

Over the last two centuries American and British genealogists have diligently searched the Public Record Office in London, and many other repositories, and have published many lists from the 1630s. Our discussion here will be based on three of the most important and most readily available volumes: John Camden Hotten, *The Original Lists of Persons of Quality...* (New York 1880; rpt. Baltimore 1962, 1968); Charles Edward Banks, *The Planters of the Commonwealth* (Boston 1930; rpt. Baltimore 1961 and later); and Peter Wilson Coldham, *The Complete Book of Emigrants: 1607-1660* (Baltimore 1987).

One matter to be noted immediately is that the lists that we find for the early seventeenth century are nothing like the passenger lists that we are accustomed to from two centuries later. In the nineteenth century, we frequently have lists made up by the shipping company or the ship's captain, and also lists made upon embarkation in England or Europe and debarkation in America. Because of this we have a good check on who actually sailed on a given vessel, and who actually arrived at the American port.

For the seventeenth century the records are different. We have absolutely no official lists generated in the New World upon the arrival of a ship. What does survive was created at dockside in England, in two closely related sets of documents - the Port Books and the Licenses to Pass Overseas. Examples of the lists from Port Books are found in the material recently uncovered by Coldham for some of the West Country ports; this material has been incorporated in *The Complete Book of Emigrants,* as for example the Weymouth list on page 183. The most extensive record of passengers we have for any year is for London in 1635, and this consists entirely of the Licenses to Pass Overseas granted for that year.

Of the three volumes cited above, the oldest, by Hotten, remains the most valuable, since he retained the original sequence of the lists, and in general remained most faithful to the original. Banks, on the other hand, took vast liberties with the records, rearranging them to suit his judgments, and adding extensive editorial notations in a manner not easy to distinguish from the records themselves. Coldham, for the 1635 list, is less useful than Hotten, since he gathered all entries for a given ship, and omitted the day-by-day groupings of arrivals at dockside. However, Coldham surveyed many sources not used by Hotten, such as Admiralty cases and the various series of State Papers. For this reason, Coldham's collection is more broadly valuable for the whole period of the Great Migration.

Until someone undertakes the preparation of a complete edition of passengers lists according to modern editorial standards, the best results will be obtained by a careful correlation of Hotten and Coldham, with a cautious dash of Banks.

LISTS OF FREEMEN

The status of freeman was primarily of political importance, for it gave one the right to vote for colony officers. In some colonies, though, freemanship was tied to church membership, and so the meaning was somewhat different. Massachusetts Bay and New Haven, the most Puritan of the Puritan colonies, made church membership a prerequisite for freemanship, while the rest of the New England colonies did not.

Lists of freemen may be used for a number of purposes beyond providing biographical information about an immigrant. Like tax lists at a later time, a list of freemen provides basic information about the presence or absence of a person on a given date. And, as noted above, freemanship in Massachusetts Bay and New Haven supplies information about church membership, from which we can learn not just whether this or that individual was a church member at a given time; we can also reconstruct some of the history of churches whose records have been lost by studying the lists over a period of years.

MASSACHUSETTS BAY

Because Massachusetts Bay Colony started out legally as a chartered trading company, freemanship was in a sense limited to the stockholders, those who had contributed financially to the company. But when the charter and the government were transferred to New England in 1630 the nature of the corporation began to evolve, and so did the nature of freemanship.

As a result more than one hundred men requested on 18 October 1630 to be made free. Winthrop and his fellow Assistants presumably took the winter to think this over, and on 19 May 1631, just before the General Court in that year, more than a hundred men were admitted as freemen, the list being not quite the same as that of the previous fall. Once this group had been made free, the General Court ordered that henceforth one had to be a church member to become a freeman, and so it remained until the Restoration.

Freemen were admitted several times a year, usually at the opening of a court session, with the largest number being admitted each year at the May General Court, the court at which the colony officers were elected. Each town (and church) apparently sent in a list of those who qualified at a given time, and these were frequently (but not always) entered into the colony lists grouped in this way, so that one can often place an individual's residence at the time of receiving freemanship by reference to his neighbors in the list. (See GMN 1:17 for more discussion of the Massachusetts Bay lists of freemen and how they may be interpreted.)

PLYMOUTH COLONY

The Plymouth Colony lists of freemen are quite different from those of Massachusetts Bay. As noted above, freemanship was not connected with church membership in this colony. Although admissions to freemanship are sometimes recorded as part of the colony court proceedings, many of the admissions were not recorded.

The lists that we do have were compiled at specific dates, and then revised for a period of years, until they became sufficiently outdated that a completely new list was deemed necessary. Such lists exist for 1633, 1637, 1639, 1658, 1670 and 1684, and the 1639 and 1658 lists were accompanied by parallel compilations of those who had taken the oath of fidelity. (See GMN 5:17 for a more detailed discussion of the Plymouth records of freemen.)

RHODE ISLAND

When Portsmouth was established in 1638, and again when Newport broke away in 1639, lists of inhabitants were drawn up which functioned as lists of freemen. When the two towns recombined as one government in 1640 a brief attempt was made to compile a list of freemen, but this practice did not last long [RICR 1:52, 70, 91-92].

The only other early attempt to maintain such a compilation for this colony was a list of those in each of the four Rhode Island towns as of 1655 [RICR 1:299-300]. There may be some doubt as to the date assigned to this list, for it includes for the town of Newport both a John Coggeshall and a John Coggeshall Jr., when there should have been only one adult of that name in town. This list should be analyzed further to determine whether the date of 1655 is correct or not.

CONNECTICUT

In Connecticut freemanship was not tied to church membership, and perhaps partly for this reason there does not appear to have been an effort to compile regular lists of those who were freemen. An accounting was made in 1669 for all the Connecticut Colony towns [CCCR 2:518-26], but by this date many of the immigrants of interest to us were already deceased.

NEW HAVEN

New Haven was even more stringent than Massachusetts Bay in linking church membership and the political franchise, and so in the earliest days admission as an inhabitant of the town and the church were almost the same event. In the earliest New Haven records are two lists of freemen which are similar but not identical [NHCR 1:9-10, 17-18]. These lists were not created on one date, but were begun in 1639 at the settlement of New Haven and then augmented regularly as new individuals were admitted.

COLONY AND COURT RECORDS

In the early colonies the full separation of executive, legislative and judicial powers had not been attained, and the records of the General Court of the colony could encompass business of all varieties. The colonial records for Massachusetts Bay, Plymouth, Rhode Island, Connecticut and New Haven have all been transcribed and published, in volumes that are cited frequently here. (Full bibliographic detail for these sets may be found in the Key to Titles under MBCR, PCR, RICR, CCCR and NHCR.) The regions that are now Maine and New Hampshire were not separate jurisdictions during the years of the Great Migration and immediately after, and they do not have records equivalent to those of the other colonies, but court records and other official documents relating to these areas have been published. (See MPCR and NHPP in Key to Titles.)

In some instances the colony records incorporate court proceedings on a level below that of the full colony. The Massachusetts Bay colony records, for example, include in the early years not only the proceedings of the General Court and the Court of Assistants, but records of sittings of what would properly be called the Suffolk County Quarter Court.

The most important of the lower-level court records that have survived and been published are those of Essex County, Massachusetts. The extraordinary detail of some of these records (including material in the unpublished files) has allowed the inclusion of interesting biographical matter in the sketches of Essex residents that has not been possible for the settlers in other parts of New England.

Another important group of records that could not be fully utilized was the Middlesex Court Files, now in the custody of the Commonwealth of Massachusetts Archives. These loose files of court documents are no longer in a sequence which allows them to be easily retrieved, and so it has not always been possible to cite directly documents that are known to exist. Some scholar will do the genealogical and historical world a great favor by subjecting these files to modern archival techniques.

NOTARIAL RECORDS

During the first two decades of the Massachusetts Bay Colony, two Boston residents acted as notaries, and their records are some of the most valuable we have for this period. Because the duties of notaries included the drafting of powers of attorney, which frequently were required when a New England settler was deputizing someone else to receive a legacy or settle other business in England, these records provide many clues for determining the English origins of some of the immigrants.

LECHFORD

Thomas Lechford arrived in New England on 27 June 1638 and immediately began to ply his trade. He was an adherent of the Church of England, and for this and other reasons he was often at odds with the colony authorities and returned to England to stay in 1641. (See Thomas G. Barnes, "Thomas Lechford and the Earliest Lawyering in Massachusetts, 1638-1641," in Daniel R. Coquillette, *Law in Colonial Massachusetts, 1630-1800*, Publications of the Colonial Society of Massachusetts, Volume 62 [Boston 1984], pp. 338.)

Lechford's notarial records were first published in 1885 by the American Antiquarian Society, and were reprinted in 1988: *Thomas Lechford, Note-Book Kept by Thomas Lechford, Esq., Lawyer, In Boston, Massachusetts Bay, from June 27, 1638, to July 29, 1641* (Cambridge 1885; rpt. Camden, Maine, 1988). The 1885 edition included an index in which the citations were to the original pagination and not to the pages as printed; the reprint includes that index and also a newly created index which refers directly to the printed pagination, and our citations herein use the new index.

ASPINWALL

William Aspinwall arrived with the Winthrop Fleet in 1630. At the time of the Antinomian Controversy he took the side of the adherents of Anne Hutchinson and John Wheelwright, and departed for Rhode Island in 1638. By 1642 he had rehabilitated himself with the Boston authorities, and he soon began to acquire employment in many jobs which involved the recording of official documents. On 13 November 1644 the court ordered that he "shall be a public notary for this jurisdiction" [MBCR 2:86], and he continued at this post until 1651 when he too returned to England (see *WILLIAM ASPINWALL* sketch in the previous series and the sources cited there [GMB 1:55-60]).

Aspinwall's notarial records were published in 1903 by the Boston Record Commissioners, and have not been reprinted: *A Volume Relating to the Early History of Boston Containing the Aspinwall Notarial Records from 1644 to 1651* (Boston 1903). The transcriber of this volume did not always understand the legal abbreviations used, and a new edition would be welcome.

TOWN RECORDS

The earliest towns of New England apparently did not begin to keep records of their meetings from the day of settlement. This was probably because Winthrop and other leaders believed in 1630 that the dispersal around the Bay was only temporary, and that they would eventually be gathering the whole population together in one place very soon.

This of course never came to pass, partly because of personality differences between men such as Winthrop and Dudley, and partly because of the greatly increased population of Massachusetts Bay in 1633, making it impossible to bring everyone together in one settlement.

This may be a partial explanation for the fact that most of the records for the earliest towns begin in 1633 or 1634 (although in some cases the first few leaves of the volume may have been lost). The records for most of these towns have been published, and are used here in that form. (See BTR, CaTR, ChTR, DTR, PTR, RTR, STR and WaTR in the **Key to Titles**.) As with so many other record categories the early Lynn town records are lost, and our only evidence for this town in the early years comes from colony records, private correspondence and a very few items of town records that were later recorded in the Essex Court records.

The records of two towns require some additional comments. The Dorchester town records as published begin early in 1633, but clearly the first two leaves of the volume have been lost. An old index to this volume gives some entries from the lost pages, and these were published in a footnote on the family of John Greenway of Dorchester [NEHGR 32:58].

The Charlestown town records are a special problem because, like the church records of that town, they were recopied in the 1660s. The copyist omitted some of the early records, added a lengthy historical narrative at the beginning and inserted documents pertaining to Charlestown from colony records and elsewhere. In addition he misread many of the names, especially given names. The user of the Charlestown town records needs to be very cautious. A careful, annotated edition of the town records of Charlestown would be an excellent addition to the literature.

VITAL RECORDS

Most New England towns began the recording of vital records from the earliest days, and a great majority of these record books have come down to us intact. The records for many of the Massachusetts towns were published in the systematic series a century ago, with the events being arranged in alphabetic order. For other towns throughout New England vital records have been published in many formats, citations to which may be found in the **Key to Titles**.

There is an unusual volume of vital records that was generated in the early days of Massachusetts Bay Colony which deserves special attention. When published in the *Register*, beginning with the first issue of the second volumes they were referred to as the "Early Records of Boston," but they have only a limited connection with Boston.

The document in question is in fact a compilation of those vital records submitted to the county court by the towns of Suffolk County, beginning in 1644. Massachusetts Bay Colony established counties in 1643, two of them being Suffolk and Middlesex, but Middlesex did not take on an independent existence until 1649. Thus for the years prior to 1649 this book of records includes submissions from the towns of Boston, Roxbury, Dorchester, Braintree, Weymouth and Dedham (which then made up Suffolk County), and Cambridge, Charlestown, Watertown, Concord, Woburn and Sudbury (then Middlesex). Hingham, which should have begun sending in its records in 1644, did not in fact do so until 1649. Even then, it did not include items retrospectively, as did the other towns. Also in 1649, Springfield sent in some vital records; it was for the moment part of Middlesex County, prior to the establishment of Hampshire County.

The probable reason for calling these the "Early Records of Boston" is that they are now, and have long been, in the custody of the Boston City Registrar. They are properly records of Suffolk County and should be returned to that jurisdiction. This volume was transcribed in the last century by David Pulsifer, and, as noted above, published in the *Register*.

For several of the towns the record tells us that the register of births and deaths runs "until the first of the first month 1644." Given the problems with the calendar at this time, we want to know just what is meant by this limit on the first group of records, which supposedly includes everything back to the "first founding of their towns."

Examination of several of the towns shows that in this record the year began on the first of March, and not on the 25th, as in many other records. One specific example which helps in this determination comes from the entries from Dedham, in which Mary Aldridge, daughter of Henry and Mary, was born on the tenth of the first month (March) 1643, and died on the 24th of the second month (April) 1643. This sequence is possible only if the first of March is New Year's Day. Thus, the announced terminus for this first set of records, in the notation of double-dating, would be 1 March 1643/4.

The clerks of the writs for the towns did not report all births and deaths which had occurred in each town prior to 1 March 1643/4, but only those for families which still resided in the town at that later date. And for those families, only events which had taken place while the family actually resided there were recorded.

The records in this volume are beset by another problem as well. Since they were obtained from the town clerks by the county clerk, they have been copied over a number of times, which has allowed many errors to creep in. In the best of circumstances, the county clerk might have copied directly from the original record prepared by the town clerk. But more frequently it is likely that the town clerk made a copy of his records, which was then carried to Boston to be copied again by the county clerk into the single volume for the whole county. And there may have been other steps of which we are unaware. The opportunities for scribal errors were abundant.

In general, then, the county copy, as represented by the misnamed "Early Records of Boston," is much inferior to the copy retained by the town. Savage makes this point frequently in his *Genealogical Dictionary of New England*, when comparing this county copy (which is all that exists for Boston of civil vital records at this date) with the record of church baptisms. If there is an existing alternative to the county copy for this period down to 1644, and a discrepancy appears, the first thing to do is to check the originals. If the discrepancy persists, the alternative source should be preferred to the county copy.

LAND RECORDS

The earliest land records in New England are found for the most part at the local rather than the county level. The land was granted to groups of settlers who were willing to establish a new town, and they in turn parcelled out the land to individual landholders. The group that controlled the land eventually became known as the proprietors, and grew into an institution separate from the town itself.

Even after the original grant from the town to the individual, sales from one person to another were frequently recorded by the town rather than the county. Search in the town records, published or unpublished, will frequently reveal a record of a land transaction which one might otherwise expect to find recorded at the county courthouse.

Each of the towns had its own methods of dividing up the land available to each of them, but the general principles were similar from town to town. The first grant was usually of a houselot, about five acres or so, and the right to additional proprietary shares attached to this lot. This grant would be followed by a few small grants of meadow land (also called marsh or swamp), then some arable land, and finally some woodland or upland, usually the least valuable and desirable land in town.

More detailed discussions of town landgranting practices have been published in the *Great Migration Newsletter*: Boston 3:3-4; Cambridge 1:12-13; Charlestown 2:6; Dedham 4:6; Dorchester 1:28-29; Hartford 3:29-30; Hingham 7:28; Ipswich 3:22; Lynn 1:21; New Haven 6:4-5; Roxbury 2:13-14; Salem 2:19-22; Southampton 5:5-6; Springfield 5:20-21; Watertown 1:4-6; Wethersfield 4:29-30; Weymouth 5:30.

The Massachusetts Bay General Court ordered that each town prepare an inventory of the landholding in that town, and most complied. Such inventories, frequently referred to as the Book of Possessions, have survived for Boston, Cambridge, Charlestown, Hingham, Roxbury and Watertown. (See **Key to Titles** under BBOP, CaBOP, ChBOP, HiBOP, RBOP and WaBOP.)

CHURCH RECORDS

Because religious conviction was the primary motivation for migration for most of those who came to New England during the Great Migration, establishing a church in each new settlement was one of the first matters attended to. Although the survival of records from these churches is spotty, what does survive provides some of the most important evidence we have for the immigrants to New England during this period.

The Boston records begin with the foundation of the church in 1630 and are continuous for the period of interest to us. There is a listing of admissions to church membership, which for the first few years does not have the date of admission. This list was however maintained in chronological order, and by correlating the list with our knowledge of other events, such as deaths or the dates of arrival of immigrants, we can roughly date an admission from this period. By 1633 the admissions are dated, and soon this part of the church records also contains much disciplinary matter, and records of letters of dismissal and recommendation. There is also a separate listing of baptisms. (See BChR in **Key to Titles**, and GMN 3:4-6, 7:3-6.)

The Salem church records before December 1636 consist only of a rough list of church members, which includes only those persons who were members in later 1636; all those who had joined at an earlier date, but had died or moved away, are omitted from this list. There are also some who were still resident in Salem in 1636 and were known to be church members who were omitted. From late 1636 there is a continuous record for several years of baptisms and admissions. (See SChR in **Key to Titles**, and GMN 2:19-21).

The church records of Lynn do not exist prior to 1792. A few facts about the early church may be gleaned from such sources as Winthrop's writings and the lists of freemen [GMN 1:20].

Charlestown church records survive from the founding of the church in 1631, and include both admissions to membership and baptisms. As with other Charlestown records, the church book was recopied about 1660, and much of the data was corrupted. (See ChChR in **Key to Titles**, and GMN 2:4.)

Although the ordinary church records of Cambridge do not survive for the ministries of Thomas Hooker or Thomas Shepard, there are copies of some of the so-called "confessions" made by church members upon admission to membership [GMN 5:9], and these frequently provide information about the church members found nowhere else.

The Watertown church records prior to 1686 have been lost, but, as with Lynn, some information can be obtained from other sources, again including Winthrop's writings and the lists of freemen.

Roxbury church was founded in 1632, and Rev. John Eliot maintained a set of records that are a hybrid of proper church records and a private diary. The list of admissions frequently goes beyond the basic data of the admission, and gives the spouse and children of the member, as well as other biographical detail. There are also separate lists of baptisms and of deaths and burials (one is not always sure which was intended). (See RChR in **Key to Titles**, and GMN 2:12-13, 6:19-25.)

The first Dorchester church removed to Windsor when Warham and most of his flock left for that town. All that remains for Dorchester is what was kept by Rev. Richard Mather for the second church which he founded. This has both a list of admissions and a list of baptisms, the latter being annotated in a later hand, giving the fate decades later of some of those baptized in Dorchester. (See DChR in **Key to Titles**, and GMN 1:29.)

Plymouth did not have a minister for most of its early history, and lay leaders such as William Brewster carried out many of the pastoral duties. The earliest Plymouth church records include a history of the early church, written many decades later; death records for a few of the early immigrants appear here, but it is otherwise not very helpful for the years of the Great Migration. (See PChR in **Key to Titles**.)

When Rev. John Lathrop arrived at Scituate, he organized a church, and kept records of that church during its few years at Scituate, and then for many more years after he and the church removed to Barnstable [NEHGR 9:279-87, 10:37-43; GMN 5:12].

Similarly, Rev. Peter Hobart maintained a record of births, baptisms, marriages, deaths and burials at Hingham during the years when he was minister there; as with the journals kept by Eliot and Lathrop, this was not strictly speaking a church record [GMN 7:28-29].

JOURNALS AND LETTERS

The sources discussed in the sections above are almost entirely official documents, which are generally of a formal nature and do not provide as much insight into individual character and behavior as we might like. There do exist a number of private documents, generally in the form of letters and diaries, which help to give us a more complete picture of the lives of the immigrants. The discussion here does not exhaust the list of diaries and correspondence created during the seventeenth century, but merely highlights those that have been used most frequently in the sketches in these volumes.

WINTHROP JOURNAL

The most important diary is more than a diary - John Winthrop's History of New England (also known as Winthrop's Journal, and referred to hereinafter as WJ). This lengthy record includes private items, matters relating to the development of Massachusetts Bay and all the other early New England colonies, events at court which did not make it into the official court records, and much more. (In the *Newsletter*, and elsewhere in the work of the Great Migration Study Project, we use the 1853 edition prepared by James Savage, which contains many useful annotations. The 1908 edition, part of the Original Narratives of Early American History series, was heavily bowdlerized, and should not be relied on. In 1996 Richard S. Dunn and Laetitia Yeandle published an updated version of *The Journal of John Winthrop, 1630-1649*, in which the readings are more accurate than those of Savage, but the annotations not as interesting [Cambridge 1996].)

In one brief line Winthrop could provide a morsel of biographical detail available nowhere else, as, for example, under date of 7 April 1636 when he records that "Mr. Benjamin's house burnt, and 100 pounds in goods lost" (WJ 1:220). This refers to John Benjamin of Watertown, and from this short entry we learn about his social status, the possibility that he was involved in trade, and a setback in his affairs.

Acting as magistrate, Winthrop recorded various misdemeanors in the back of his journal, such as the 20 July 1637 confession of John Hobby, apparently of Dorchester, that he had stolen some beaver skins from Samuel Cole of Boston (WJ 2:425-26). Entries of this sort are the equivalent of extracts from records of a magistrate's court, which otherwise do not exist this early.

Winthrop maintained his journal right up until his death in 1649, and so for the first two decades of Massachusetts Bay Colony this is an essential source for information about individuals and about the growth and change of New England communities and institutions.

WINTHROP PAPERS

Just as John Winthrop's journal is the most important diary for the earliest years in Massachusetts, so the vast archive of correspondence collected by the Winthrop family is the largest collection of letters for the period. The Massachusetts Historical Society has published the papers of the Winthrop family from 1498 through 1654 in six volumes, with more to come (*Winthrop Papers*, 6 volumes [Boston, 1925-1992], hereinafter WP). The Winthrop correspondence was also published much earlier in the *Massachusetts Historical Society Collections*, Fourth Series, Vol. 6 & 7, and Fifth Series, Vol. 1 & 8. In this version the letters were arranged by correspondent rather than chronologically, and so far some purposes may be a more convenient source.

Many extracts from the letters appear in the sketches of individual immigrants. Frequently the Winthrop correspondence provides direct evidence of the English origin of an immigrant, especially of those who had lived in the neighborhood of Winthrop's old home in Groton. In a letter to John Winthrop of 17 January 1636/7, Robert Ryece described a dispute that had arisen in Lavenham, Suffolk, and had been carried over into New England. In support of his story Ryece stated that "the widdow Onge, now of Waterton in N:E but then of Lavenham," had witnessed one stage of the dispute in her own shop and could testify to the same (WP 3:347-48).

BRADFORD LETTERBOOK

William Bradford kept a letterbook, into which he copied both incoming and outgoing correspondence. As with so many of Bradford's manuscripts, this volume had an unusual history, and only a small portion has been preserved, covering the years 1624 through 1630, the surviving portion begins on page 339 of the original. Even this small remnant is filled with useful information.

These letters were first published in 1794, accompanied by an account of how they were rescued [MHSC 1:3:27-76]. George Ernest Bowman reprinted them more than a century later, and in the interim the original pages had been mislaid again [MD 5:5-16, 75-81, 164-71, 198-201, 6:16-17, 141-47, 207-15, 7:5-12, 79-82]. These several installments were then gathered into a separate publication in 1906 [*Governor William Bradford's Letter Book* (Boston 1906)].

HULL DIARY

John Hull was born in 1624 and came to New England in 1635 with his family. For most of his adult life he maintained a diary, not as complete or discursive as those of Winthrop before him or Sewall after, but still of great value, and the only thing we have to fill the gap between those two. Hull includes some entries regarding New England events predating his arrival; these were presumably written down some years after the fact. The entries begin in earnest in the mid-1640s and continue until 1682, the year before his death.

Hull divided his diary into two sections, "Some Passages of God's Providence About Myself and in Relation to Myself..." and "Some Observable Passages of Providence Toward the Country ...," which were published together in 1857 [*Transactions and Collections of the American Antiquarian Society*, Volume III, pp. 141-250].

SEWALL DIARY

Overlapping with John Hull's diary is that of Samuel Sewall, who began his entries in 1674 and continued until just before his death in 1729 (M. Halsey Thomas, ed., *The Diary of Samuel Sewall, 1674-1729*, 2 volumes [New York, 1973]). Sewall's diary also focusses on the Boston gentry, but is more inclusive and expansive than Hull's. Even though Sewall began his diary almost half a century after the arrival of Winthrop, there were still many immigrants from the 1630s living, the closing years of whose lives are documented by Sewall. On 18 December 1685, for example, Sewall reported that "Father John Odlin, one of the very first inhabitants of Boston, dies" (p. 88).

WILLIAMS CORRESPONDENCE

The celebrated Roger Williams also left behind much correspondence (Glenn W. LaFantasie, ed., *The Correspondence of Roger Williams*, 2 volumes, 1629-1682 [Providence 1988]). The majority of these letters were to or from the Winthrops, and so much of this material had already been published in the *Winthrop Papers*. But there are some items unique to this collections, such as a letter from George Ludlow to Williams written not long before 26 October 1637. Ludlow did not leave many traces during his brief stay in New England, and this letter is valuable in outlining his life.

LETTERS FROM NEW ENGLAND

Many more letters have survived from other collections. Some years ago Everett Emerson gathered all letters he could find that had been sent from Massachusetts back home in the decade from 1629 to 1638 (Everett Emerson, ed., *Letters from New England: The Massachusetts Bay Colony, 1629-1638* [Amherst, 1976]).

One of the most interesting items in this compendium is the long letter from Thomas Dudley to the Countess of Lincoln, written in the latter half of March 1630/1 (pp. 67-83). This letter, composed in a style similar to some of the published pamphlets of the period, provided much detail on the dispersal of the Winthrop Fleet passengers around Massachusetts Bay, and even beyond, taking note of some immigrants who had removed to the Piscataqua or had even returned to England. Dudley also described the sequence of settlement of the Massachusetts Bay towns in 1630 and 1631.

Of more particular interest are the reports Dudley made of the deaths of various individuals. We are told that "about the beginning of September died Mr. [William] Gager, a right godly man, a skillful chirurgeon, and one of the deacons of our congregation" (p. 72). "Amongst those who died about the end of this January, there was a girl of eleven years old, the daughter of one John Ruggles, of whose family and kindred died so many that for some reason it was matter of observation amongst us" (p. 77). Both Gager and Ruggles had been neighbors of Winthrop in England.

Also of interest from this volume is the December 1634 letter from James Cudworth of Scituate to his stepfather, Dr. John Stoughton (pp. 139-42). Cudworth relates much detail on the churches of Plymouth and Massachusetts Bay colonies which had been founded by that date (and their ministers), and on others that were in the process of being established. He also informs Stoughton that "my uncle Thomas is to be married shortly, to a widow that has good means and has five children." This would be the second marriage for both Thomas Stoughton (brother of Dr. John Stoughton), at that time of Dorchester, and Margaret (Baret)

Huntington, the widow of Simon Huntington, who had come to New England in 1633.

MISCELLANEOUS

Among the sources which don't fit into any of the categories above are the records of two private institutions, Harvard College and the Ancient and Honorable Artillery Company.

HARVARD COLLEGE

After one or two false starts, a college was established in 1636 in Cambridge, which soon took on the name of Harvard College in consequence of a bequest of books by John Harvard who died at Charlestown in 1638. The first class graduated in 1642, consisting of only nine men, and for the rest of the century about this many graduated each year, although in some years there were no graduates.

We have several sources of information about the students and faculty at Harvard. First are the records of Harvard College itself, which for the years from 1636 through 1750 have been published by the Colonial Society of Massachusetts: *Harvard College Records*, Parts I through V, Publications of the Colonial Society of Massachusetts, Volumes 15, 16, 31, 49, 50 (Boston 1925, 1935, 1975).

John Langdon Sibley began in 1873 the practice of compiling brief biographies of each graduate of Harvard, arranged first by class and then by rank within the class. Sibley completed three volumes, carrying the project down to the class of 1689: *Biographical Sketches of Graduates of Harvard University, in Cambridge, Massachusetts*, Volumes I through III (Cambridge 1873, 1881, 1885). After a hiatus of forty-eight years Clifford K. Shipton resumed where Sibley had left off, and produced fourteen additional volumes, through the class of 1770. (See Marcus A. McCorison, "Clifford Kenyon Shipton: A Checklist of his Publications," in *Sibley's Heir: A Volume in Memory of Clifford Kenyon Shipton*, Publications of the Colonial Society of Massachusetts, Volume 59 [Boston 1982], pp. 17-35.) No further volumes have been published since Shipton's death, but the Massachusetts Historical Society has reactivated the project and further volumes should be appearing soon.

Of most direct concern to us are Sibley's three volumes, which include brief accounts of sons of many of the immigrants within our period. While these volumes occasionally contain a date or other piece of information not easily confirmed elsewhere, they have been cited here principally as a biographical resource.

At the time of the Tercentenary celebrations of Harvard College in 1936 Samuel Eliot Morison wrote several volumes on the history of Harvard College. Of most importance to us is *The Founding of Harvard College* (Cambridge 1935), which includes an appendix titled "English University Men Who Emigrated to New England Before 1646" (pages 359 through 410). Many of the men discussed in this appendix, of course, came before 1634, and so fall within our ambit. (Other volumes by Morison that cover this period are *Harvard College in the Seventeenth Century*, 2 volumes [Cambridge 1936].)

Finally, one specialized study on the economic aspects of the college has broader interest than might be obvious: Margery Somers Foster, "*Out of Smalle Beginnings...*" [:] *An Economic History of Harvard College in the Puritan Period (1636 to 1712)* (Cambridge 1962).

ANCIENT AND HONORABLE ARTILLERY COMPANY

In 1637 a group of prominent residents of Massachusetts Bay, mostly Boston merchants and magistrates, founded the Ancient and Honorable Artillery Company of Massachusetts, in clear imitation of the like-named organization in London. Although this body did have some military importance, it may be viewed also as the seventeenth-century equivalent of a men's eating club.

The records of the Company itself have not been published, but Oliver Ayer Roberts compiled four volumes of the *History of The Military Company of the Massachusetts Now Called the Ancient and Honorable Artillery Company of Massachusetts, 1637-1888* (Boston 1895-1901). This compilation is somewhat like Sibley in that it treats the members of the Company year by year, as they were admitted.

There may be some reason to question the accuracy of some of these records, as there are a number of people admitted who do not seem to appear elsewhere in New England records, or who appear as members of the Company at much too young an age. Nevertheless, this source is cited, usually along with other evidence of military service in the *OFFICES* section, simply to let interested readers know what is claimed about these people.

HOW TO USE THIS BOOK

This second series of Great Migration volumes consists of sketches of more than thirteen hundred families or unattached individuals who came to New England in 1634 or 1635. Each sketch follows a regular format, which is described below in more detail in the section entitled KEY TO SKETCH HEADINGS. Every statement in each sketch is supported by citation to a document. Most of the citations appear in an abbreviated form, the abbreviations being expanded in the section below entitled KEY TO TITLES.

Two additional conventions which are employed in these sketches will help the reader navigate through this book:

When a name is given all in capital letters, this means that that person also came to New England in 1634 or 1635, and is the subject of a sketch elsewhere in this second series of volumes. When a name is given all in capital letters and in italics, this means that that person came to New England in 1633 or earlier, and is the subject of a sketch in *The Great Migration Begins*.

A string of citations of the form "[Dawes-Gates 1:74, citing Perley 1:254, citing ELR 20:12]" or "[MD 16:181-82, citing PCLR 2:2:73]" may serve one of two purposes. It may indicate a secondary source which cites a document, when the document itself has not been examined; or it may indicate a published transcript of a document, followed by the citation of the document itself.

KEY TO SKETCH HEADINGS

Except for that minority of persons who left behind one or two records in New England, each of the persons treated in these three volumes is presented according to a fixed format, which forces research to answer a series of questions. There are three sections which are rigidly formatted, and then a more informal section.

The first section asks questions related directly to the movements of the family or individual from the date of the last known residence in England to the end of his, her or their lives. Entries in this section will generally be very brief, without documentation; the evidence for the statements made here will be found under headings in later sections of the sketch.

The second group of questions is of a biographical nature, attempting to provide answers about education, officeholding, wealth and so on.

The third formatted section presents the specifically genealogical material: birth, death, spouses and children.

These three sections are followed by a free-form space, in which a variety of matters may be discussed, and finally, in some cases, a bibliographic note for those families which have been treated in print several times.

The rest of this section proceeds through the parts of a sketch, pointing out what is likely to be found under each heading, and what is not.

PRESERVED PURITAN

ORIGIN: The origin for our purposes is the last known residence in England before migration. This will frequently be different from the place of birth, and knowledge of this difference can be important in assessing the motivation for migration, and connecting the immigrant with others who made the move about the same time. The place of birth will be given as the place of origin only when no other residence in England is known.

If any residence in England other than the place of birth is known, it will be given here even if it was many years before the date of migration. For example, Bigod Eggleston, who was born at Settrington, Yorkshire, lived at a later date in Norwich, Norfolk, but was last seen there in 1614, sixteen years before he came to New England. Presumably he lived somewhere else in England in the 1620s, but for now we give his origin as Norwich.

An origin will be given only when there is solid evidence. If someone in the past has made a plausible suggestion, or if there is a leading clue, the entry here will be "Unknown," and there will be discussion of the possibilities in the *COMMENTS* section. (Information on place and date of birth, if known, will be given in the genealogical portion of the sketch, under *BIRTH.*)

MIGRATION: In this section we attempt to determine the year in which this person or family migrated to New England. If we are fortunate enough to have an entry on a passenger list, the year will be given, along with the name of the vessel. Where there is no passenger list entry (the majority of the cases), the year of migration is estimated from the evidence available. For example, it will frequently be the case that the first evidence we have for the presence of a person in New England is on the list of freemen of 25 May 1636. Since most of the passenger ships arrived in May and June in these years, and since freemanship presupposed church membership, a status not instantly attained, we assume that anyone made free on that date must have arrived no later than 1635, and that year will be given at this point. Thus, in some cases the year given here will be precise, and in other cases it will be the latest possible date of arrival; in either case, if no citation is given here, the year chosen may be deduced from information given in a later section.

FIRST RESIDENCE: The evidence on first residence in New England will usually come from the surviving town or church records, although it may also be learned from court or literary sources. In many instances the evidence on first residence will be from several years after arrival in New England, and so the possibility remains that the immigrant settled in one place for a short time without leaving a record, and then moved on to another settlement. The entry here will simply be based on the best surviving evidence.

REMOVES: If the subject of the sketch resided in more than one New England settlement, that information is given here. When the year of removal is known or can be deduced, the entry would say, for example, "Hartford 1635"; in this example, we would probably not have a record which explicitly stated that the person made the move in that year, but we would learn from the Cambridge records that the person had received land grants in 1633 and 1634, but did not appear in the land inventory taken in the fall of 1635, indicating early removal to Hartford, in advance of the main party. In many instances we will not be able to fix the date of migration so precisely, and the entry might then read "Windsor by 1648," indicating that the person was of record in Windsor in that year, but his or her last record in the prior place of residence was two or more years earlier. In some cases a family might reside in one of those towns that subdivided itself early, and so a date of "removal" might be impossible to determine. In Charlestown, for instance, many families soon established homes on the opposite side of the Mystic River from Charlestown proper. When this area was set off some years later as Malden, it cannot be said that the family moved, only that the town line had shifted around them. Similar situations arise with Beverly and Braintree. In these instances the new town will be included in the list of *REMOVES,* but without a date attached.

RETURN TRIPS: This section encompasses movements in which the sometime New England resident returned to England temporarily or permanently, or moved on to a colony outside New England, whether on the mainland or in the Caribbean.

OCCUPATION: This heading will frequently be blank, as many of the early New Englanders left no direct evidence of occupation. In a few instances when a detailed inventory allows a deduction that the person was a subsistence farmer, the occupation will be stated as husbandman. In most instances when no evidence is available and this section is omitted, we may assume that the person could be described as yeoman or husbandman.

CHURCH MEMBERSHIP: When we have direct evidence from surviving church records of membership in a given church, that knowledge will appear here. In addition, when church membership can be deduced from other records, most commonly from admission to freemanship in Massachusetts Bay after 1 May 1631, that will be included here as well. For many settlements we have no surviving church records and no information on church membership. Most importantly, since no records exist for the early Plymouth church, and since no minister was settled there for a long period of time, we will only enter data on membership in Plymouth church for a few people who are mentioned directly in that context by Bradford or some other contemporary writer.

FREEMAN: Most of our evidence on freemanship comes from Massachusetts Bay Colony, where, after 18 May 1631 and until the Restoration, church membership was a prerequisite for freemanship. This was also the case in New Haven Colony, but not in the other colonies. With the exception of the 19 October 1630 list of those wishing to be made free, all of our records for Massachusetts Bay are for admission. In other colonies we have both records of admission (far less complete than those of Massachusetts Bay), and lists of those who were freemen at a specific date.

EDUCATION: The most direct evidence for education will be for those men, mostly ministers, who attended one of the universities in England - Cambridge or Oxford. Our source for these institutions will be Venn and Foster. Some immigrants also attended a grammar school in England (preparatory to university in some cases).

Beyond evidence of this sort, we will rely principally on three other sources to get some idea of the level of education and literacy reached by a given immigrant: holding an office which required reading and writing ability, such as town clerk; ownership of books, usually found in probate inventories; and ability to sign one's name.

OFFICES: This section includes both civil service, whether at the town, county or colony level, and also military service. In most sketches we attempt to include all discoverable service, with the limitation that much of the evidence, especially for town offices, remains in manuscript form, not all of which has been searched. For those community leaders who held many higher offices, no attempt has been made here to collect evidence on all lesser offices.

ESTATE: Most of the material included under this heading will be from land and probate records. At this early period much of the evidence on landholding (not limited to proprietorial grants) is to be found in town records, even for Massachusetts; since much of this material remains unpublished, not all records of land transactions for the persons of interest to us have been included here.

Much of the evidence for the identities of the children of the immigrants, and the birth order, will be found here. When more detailed argumentation on these points is needed, it will be found under *COMMENTS* below.

BIRTH: When we know the English origin of the immigrant, and have the baptismal record, that will be entered here, along with the names of the parents of the immigrant. More frequently, we will not have this information; nevertheless, in almost all cases, an attempt will be made to estimate a year of birth for the immigrant, however crudely. This will be based largely on certain assumptions about the minimum or average age at which certain life events occurred: fourteen to witness a document or choose a guardian; sixteen to become a church member; twenty-one to become a freeman; twenty-five as the approximate age of first marriage for most men.

DEATH: In the absence of a specific record of death, an estimate will be made based on the appearance of the subject in other records. This will frequently be based on probate documents, but there are many other possibilities. In such cases there may be no direct citation of the relevant documents here, as they will almost always be cited more directly under some other heading.

MARRIAGE: For each spouse data on date and place of marriage, when known, is given, as well as the parents of the spouse, any previous or later spouses of that spouse, and a date of death.

CHILDREN: Evidence which allows us to compile a list of children born to a given couple, and to deduce their birth order, will be found mostly under *ESTATE, COMMENTS,* or both.

When we do not have a specific date of birth of baptism from primary sources, we attempt to assign an approximate date, in order to bring the family into better focus. In some cases that date will be relatively precise, and will be entered as, for example, "about 1638." Such a date will generally be derived from an age at death or an age given in a deposition, but may also be imposed by our knowledge of the structure of the rest of the family. An "about" date should be considered to be accurate within a year or two on either side of the stated year. Dates which are known less precisely will be entered as, for example, "say 1638." These dates may be assigned somewhat arbitrarily, based on our knowledge of other dates in the family, on birth order, and on a number of assumptions, including the expectation of a two-year interval between births (unless the earlier child died very soon) and the exclusion of multiple births without specific evidence for such events.

We do not attempt here to outline the full career of each child. We wish only to determine whether the child died young, and if not, whether the child eventually married. Thus, although all known marriages of the child will usually be given, in some cases we may only present the first marriage, just to differentiate this child from others of the same name in other families. We do not make a special effort to determine the date of death, although this may be included if it assists in estimating the year of birth.

ASSOCIATIONS: Two different types of information may appear here. First, when the subject of the sketch is related, whether by marriage or by blood, to some other immigrant to New England prior to 1643, and when that relationship existed prior to migration, that information will be shown here. This may simply demonstrate the influence of kinship on migration, or it may provide clues for further research in England. Second, if no such tie to another participant in the Great Migration is known, this will be the place to point out persistent associations with other immigrants, which may provide clues to English origins and group or chain migrations.

COMMENTS: This section provides an opportunity for discussing any matter which does not fit neatly into one of the sections described above. It may include, but is not restricted to, the following:

- Specific records which do not fall into any of the narrowly-defined categories above, but which are thought to be of interest. The most common of these will be court appearances, whether in civil or criminal proceedings.
- Various activities which fall outside the categories of the biographical section, such as William Aspinwall's trading and exploratory expedition up the Delaware River, or the evidence for George Alcock as a butcher.
- Discussion of errors or discrepancies, whether in primary or secondary sources. If possible the discrepancy will be corrected; if not, the arguments in favor of various positions will be presented. Errors in obscure sources may be ignored, but all problems in Savage and Pope will be discussed.
- Evidence and arguments for specific genealogical conclusions will be given in this section. In some cases the records given under the ESTATE section above will be sufficient, without further interpretation, to establish the list of children. But when this is not the case, further evidence and argumentation will be given here.
- Suggestions for further research may be presented here. This will be the case when not all available records have been searched, or when some likely line of research suggests itself.

BIBLIOGRAPHIC NOTE: For some families, there has been sufficient material published to require separate discussion. This will especially be the case when a late-nineteenth century genealogy has been corrected by more recent articles in the periodical literature, or when there are two or more published genealogies of greatly different value. This note will attempt to point out the relative value of what is in print, in hopes of deterring the continued reliance on outdated and incorrect claims.

KEY TO TITLES

This listing includes all titles employed in more than one sketch in *The Great Migration Begins* and the present series. If a source is used in only one sketch, the full bibliographic details are given in that sketch.

Abel Lunt Anc
Walter Goodwin Davis, *The Ancestry of Abel Lunt, 1769-1806, of Newbury, Massachusetts* (Portland, Maine, 1963)

Ackley-Bosworth
Nathan Grier Parke II, *The Ancestry of Lorenzo Ackley & His Wife, Emma Arabella Bosworth*, Donald Lines Jacobus, ed. (Woodstock, Vermont, 1960)

Ancestral Roots
Frederick Lewis Weis, *Ancestral Roots of Sixty Colonists Who Came to New England between 1623 and 1650*, 6th ed. (Baltimore 1988)

Angell Anc
Dean Crawford Smith, *The Ancestry of Emily Jane Angell, 1844-1910* (Boston 1992).

Annis Spear Anc
Walter Goodwin Davis, *The Ancestry of Annis Spear, 1775-1858, of Litchfield, Maine* (Portland, Maine, 1945)

Aspinwall
"A Volume Relating to the Early History of Boston Containing the Aspinwall Notarial Records from 1644 to 1651," in *Reports of the Record Commissioners of the City of Boston*, Volume 32 (Boston 1903)

Austin
John Osborne Austin, *The Genealogical Dictionary of Rhode Island* ... (Albany 1887; rpt. Baltimore 1969 [with *addenda et corrigenda* as published in TAG])

Backus Anc   Mary E.N. Backus, comp. and ed., *The New England Ancestry of Dana Converse Backus* (Salem 1949)

Badger Gen   Alice W. Badger, comp., *Four Ancestral Lines and Descendants of Erastus Beethoven and Fanny Babcock (Campbell) Badger* (Chestnut Hill, Massachusetts, 1982)

Bailey   Frederic W. Bailey, *Early Massachusetts Marriages Prior to 1800 ... with the Addition of Plymouth County Marriages, 1692-1746* (Baltimore 1979 [a reprint of three separate volumes published in 1897, 1900 and 1914, along with Plymouth County marriages published in *The Genealogical Advertiser* in 1898 and 1899])

Bangs   *The Pilgrims in The Netherlands, Recent Research, Papers Presented at a Symposium held by The Leiden Pilgrim Documents Center and The Sir Thomas Browne Institute*, Jeremy D. Bangs, ed. (Leiden, The Netherlands, 1984)

BarbMR   Joanne McRee Sanders, comp., *Barbados Records, Marriages, 1643-1800*, 2 volumes (1982)

BarbPR   Joanne McRee Sanders, comp., *Barbados Records, Wills and Administrations, 1639-1680*, Volume 1 (1979)

BarnChR   Barnstable, Massachusetts, Church Records

BarnPR   Barnstable County, Massachusetts, Probate Records

Bassett Gen   Buell Burdett Bassett, *One Bassett Family in America ...* (Springfield, Massachusetts, 1926)

Bassett-Preston   Belle Preston, *Bassett-Preston Ancestors* (New Haven 1930)

Batchelder Gen

Frederick Clifton Pierce, *Batchelder, Batcheller Genealogy. Descendants of Rev. Stephen Bachiler, of England, a Leading Nonconformist, Who Settled the Town of New Hampton, N.H. and Joseph, Henry, Joshua and John Batcheller of Essex Co., Massachusetts* (Chicago 1898)

BBOP

"The Book of Possessions" for Boston, in *Second Report of the Record Commissioners of the City of Boston; containing the Boston Records, 1634-1660, and the Book of Possessions*, 2nd ed. (Boston 1881)

BChR

The Records of the First Church in Boston, 1630-1868, Publications of the Colonial Society of Massachusetts, Volumes 39, 40 and 41, Richard D. Pierce, ed. (Boston 1961)

Bethia Harris Anc

Walter Goodwin Davis, *The Ancestry of Bethia Harris, 1748-1833, Wife of Dudley Wildes of Topsfield, Massachusetts* (Portland, Maine 1934)

Boardman Anc

William F. J. Boardman, *The Ancestry of William Francis Joseph Boardman* (Hartford 1906)

Bodge

George Madison Bodge, *Soldiers in King Philip's War being A Critical Account of That War with A Concise History of the Indian Wars of New England From 1620-1677* (Leominster, Massachusetts, 1896; rpt. Baltimore 1967)

Bond

Henry Bond, *Genealogies of the Families and Descendants of the Early Settlers of Watertown, Massachusetts ...*, two volumes in one, second edition (Boston 1860)

Boston PR   Charles Wilmer Foster, *The Parish Registers of Boston in the County of Lincoln,* 2 volumes, in The Publications of the Lincoln Record Society, Parish Register Series, Volumes 1 and 3 (Lincoln, England, 1914, 1915)

Boston Second   Chandler Robins, *History of the Second Church, or Old North, in Boston* (Boston 1852)

Bosworth Gen   Mary Bosworth Clarke, *Bosworth Genealogy...* (San Francisco 1926)

Bradford   William Bradford, *Of Plymouth Plantation, 1620-1647,* Samuel Eliot Morison, ed. (New York 1952)

Bradford LB   *Governor William Bradford's Letter Book* (Boston, 1906; rpt. from *Mayflower Descendant,* 1904-06)

Brady Anc   L. Effingham deForest and Anne Lawrence deForest, *James Cox Brady and His Ancestry* (New York 1933)

Brainerd Anc   Thomas Chalmers Brainerd, *Ancestry of Thomas Chalmers Brainerd,* Donald Lines Jacobus, ed. (Montreal 1948)

BranLR   Branford, Connecticut, Land Records

BrChR   Brooklyn Church Records, in *Holland Society Yearbook,* 1897

BridTR   Bridgewater, Massachusetts, Town Records

Briggs Gen   L. Vernon Briggs, *History and Genealogy of the Briggs Family, 1254-1937, In Three Volumes* (Boston 1937)

Brown-Parker	Blanche Brown Bryant, *The Progenitors and Descendants of Thomas Page Brown and Sarah (Sally) Parker* (Springfield, Vermont, 1938)
BrPR	Bristol County, Massachusetts, Probate Records
BrTR	*Records of the Town of Braintree, 1640 to 1793*, Samuel A. Bates, ed. (Randolph 1886), pp. 1-625
BrVR	*Records of the Town of Braintree, 1640 to 1793*, Samuel A. Bates, ed. (Randolph 1886), pp. 627-940
BTR	"Boston Town Records," in *Second Report of the Record Commissioners of the City of Boston; containing the Boston Records, 1634-1660, and the Book of Possessions*, 2nd ed. (Boston 1881)
BTR2	*A Report of the Record Commissioners of the City of Boston Containing the Boston Records from 1660 to 1701* (Boston 1881)
Bulkeley Gen	Donald Lines Jacobus, *The Bulkeley Genealogy, Rev. Peter Bulkeley* (New Haven 1933)
Burrage	Champlin Burrage, *The Early English Dissenters, 1550-1641* (Cambridge, England, 1912)
Bushnell Anc	J. Gardner Bartlett, *The Ancestry of Daniel Bushnell* ... (Boston 1918)
Button Gen	R. Glen Nye, *Button Families of America* (n.p. 1971)
BVR	*Boston Births, Baptisms, Marriages, and Deaths, 1630-1699*, Ninth Report of the Boston Record Commissioners (Boston 1883; rpt. Baltimore 1978)

CaBOP   *The Register Book of the Lands and Houses in the "New Towne" and the Town of Cambridge...* (Cambridge 1896)

CaChR   Stephen Paschall Sharples, ed., *Records of The Church of Christ at Cambridge in New England, 1632-1830* (Boston 1906)

CaTR   *The Records of the Town of Cambridge (Formerly Newtowne) Massachusetts, 1630-1703...* (Cambridge 1901)

CCCR   *The Public Records of the Colony of Connecticut, 1636-1776*, 15 volumes (Hartford 1850-1890)

CCL   Leonard H. Smith Jr., comp., *Cape Cod Library of Local History and Genealogy*, 2 vols. (Baltimore 1992)

Chapin   Howard M. Chapin, *Documentary History of Rhode Island*, 2 vols. (Providence 1916, 1919)

Chase-Wigglesworth   Alicia Crane Williams, *Chase-Wigglesworth Genealogy: The Ancestors and Descendants of Philip Putnam Chase and His Wife Anna Cornelia Wigglesworth* (Baltimore 1990)

ChBOP   *Charlestown Land Records, 1638-1802*, Third Report of the Boston Record Commissioners, 2nd ed. (Boston 1883)

ChChR   *Records of the First Church in Charlestown, Massachusetts, 1632-1789*, James Frothingham Hunnewell, ed. (Boston 1880)

Chelsea Hist   Mellen Chamberlain, *A Documentary History of Chelsea, Including the Boston Precincts of Winnisimmet, Rumney Marsh, and Pullen Point, 1624-1824*, 2 volumes (Boston 1908)

ChTR	Charlestown Town Records (see "Sources: Town Records: Charlestown")
ChVR	*Vital Records of Charlestown, Massachusetts, to the Year 1850*, Volume I, Roger D. Joslyn, ed. (Boston 1984)
Clap	Roger Clap, *Memoirs of Capt. Roger Clap* (Boston 1731; rpt. Boston 1844)
Coldham	Peter Wilson Coldham, *The Complete Book of Emigrants, 1607-1660* (Baltimore 1987)
Coltman Anc	Edith Bartlett Sumner, *Ancestry and Descendants of James Hensman Coltman and Betsey Tobey* (Los Angeles 1957)
Conant Gen	Frederick Odell Conant, *A History ... of the Conant Family* (Portland, Maine, 1887)
Converse Gen	Charles Allen Converse, *Some of the Ancestors and Descendants of Samuel Converse, Jr. ... Major James Convers ... Hon. Heman Allen ... Captain Jonathan Bixby, Sr. ...* (Boston 1947)
Copp's Hill	Thomas Bridgman, *Epitaphs from Copp's Hill Burial Ground, Boston* (Boston 1851; rpt. Bowie, Maryland, 1989)
Corbin	Corbin Manuscript Collection at New England Historic Genealogical Society (Call #SG COR 5, being "historical and genealogical material, generally pertaining to central and western Massachusetts for the period 1650-1850")
Council NE	"Records of the Council for New England," *Proceedings of the American Antiquarian Society*, Meeting of April 24, 1867, pp. 53-131

CoVR   *Concord, Massachusetts[:] Births, Marriages, and*
                           Deaths[:] 1635-1850 (Concord, n.d.)

CP   *The Complete Peerage of England, Scotland, Ireland,*
                           Great Britain and the United Kingdom, The
                           Hon. Vicary Gibbs, ed., 13 volumes in 14
                           (London 1910-1940)

CSM   *Publications of the Colonial Society of Massachusetts*,
                           Volume 1 to present (1895+)

CSPD   Calendar of State Papers, Domestic

CT Civil List   *List of Officials Civil, Military, and Ecclesiastical of*
                           Connecticut Colony... and New Haven Colony...,
                           Donald Lines Jacobus, comp. (New Haven
                           1935)

CTVR   *Births Marriages and Deaths Returned from*
                           Hartford, Windsor and Fairfield and Entered in
                           the Early Land Records of the Colony of
                           Connecticut..., Edwin Stanley Welles, ed.
                           (Hartford 1898)

DAB   *Dictionary of American Biography*

Davenport   Isabel MacBeath Calder, *Letters of John Davenport,*
                           Puritan Divine (New Haven 1937)

Davis Fam   Samuel Forbes Rockwell, *Davis Families of Early*
                           Roxbury and Boston (North Andover 1932)

Dawes-Gates   Mary Walton Ferris, *Dawes-Gates Ancestral Lines*,
                           2 vols. (n.p., 1943, 1931)

DChR   *Records of the First Church at Dorchester in New*
                           England, 1636-1734 (Boston 1891)

DeChR   *The Record of Baptisms, Marriages and Deaths... from the Church Records in the Town of Dedham, Massachusetts, 1638-1845...,* Don Gleason Hill, ed. (Dedham 1888)

DeHR   *The Dedham Historical Register,* 14 volumes (Dedham 1890-1903)

DeTR   *The Early Records of the Town of Dedham, Massachusetts. 1636-1659 ... being Volume Three of the Printed Records of the Town,* Don Gleason Hill, ed. (Dedham 1892)

DeVR   *The Record of Births, Marriages and Deaths... in the Town of Dedham, Volumes 1 & 2...,* Don Gleason Hill, ed. (Dedham 1886)

Dewey Gen   Adelbert M. Dewey and Louis Marinus Dewey, *Life of George Dewey, Rear Admiral, U.S.N., and Dewey Family History* (Westfield, Massachusetts, 1898)

Dexter   Henry Martyn Dexter and Morton Dexter, *The England and Holland of the Pilgrims* (London, 1906; rpt. Baltimore 1978)

DNB   *Dictionary of National Biography*

Doc Hist ME   *Documentary History of the State of Maine,* 24 vols. in *Collections of the Maine Historical Society, Second Series* (Portland, 1869-1916)

Doc Hist NY   *The Documentary History of the State of New York,* 4 vols., E.B. O'Callaghan, ed. (Albany 1849)

Doggett Gen   Samuel Bradlee Doggett, *A History of the Doggett-Daggett Family* (Boston 1894)

Dommerich Anc   Louis Effingham deForest, *Our Colonial and Continental Ancestors: The Ancestry of Mr. and Mrs. Louis William Dommerich* (New York 1930)

Dorset Marr   *Dorset Parish Registers, Marriages*, W.P. Phillimore and Edmund Nevill, eds.

Dover Hist   John Scales, *History of Dover, New Hampshire* (Dover 1923; rpt. Bowie, Maryland, 1977)

DoVR   *Vital Records of Dover, New Hampshire, 1686-1850* (Bowie, Maryland, 1977) (reprint of *Collections of the Dover, N.H., Historical Society*, Volume 1 [Dover 1894])

Drake's Boston   Samuel G. Drake, *The History and Antiquities of Boston, the Capital of Massachusetts and Metropolis of New England From its Settlement in 1630 to the Year 1770* (Boston 1856)

Drake's Founders   Samuel G. Drake, *Result of Some Researches Among the British Archives for Information Relative to the Founders of New England: Made in the Years 1858, 1859 and 1860* (Boston 1860)

DSGRM   *Detroit Society for Genealogical Research Magazine*, Volume 1 to present (Detroit, Michigan, 1937+)

DTR   *Fourth Report of the Record Commissioners of the City of Boston. 1880. Dorchester Town Records* (Boston 1883)

Dudley   Thomas Dudley, Letter to Lady Bridget, Countess of Lincoln, 12 and 28 March 1630/1, in *Letters from New England: The Massachusetts Bay Colony, 1629-1638*, Everett Emerson, ed. (Amherst, Massachusetts, 1976), pp. 66-83

Dudley Wildes Anc   Walter Goodwin Davis, *The Ancestry of Dudley Wildes, 1759-1820, of Topsfield, Massachusetts* (Portland, Maine, 1959)

DukesLR   Dukes County, Massachusetts, Deeds

DuVR   *Vital Records of Duxbury, Massachusetts, to the Year 1850* (Boston 1911)

DVR   *Dorchester Births, Marriages, and Deaths to the End of 1825*, Twenty-first Report of the Boston Record Commissioners (Boston 1890)

Early Rehoboth   Richard LeBaron Bowen, *Early Rehoboth: Documented Historical Studies of Families and Events in This Plymouth Colony Township*, 4 volumes (Rehoboth 1945-1950)

Easthampton TR   Easthampton, Long Island, New York, Town Records

Eddy Gen   Ruth Story Devereux Eddy, comp., *The Eddy Family in America* (Boston 1930)

Edgartown TR   Edgartown, Massachusetts, Town Records

EIHC   *Essex Institute Historical Collections*, Volume 1 to present (1859+)

Eliot Gen   Wilimena Hannah Emerson, *...Genealogy of the Descendants of John Eliot* (New Haven 1905)

ELR   Essex County, Massachusetts, Deeds, microfilm copies

Enfield Hist   Francis Olcott Allen, *The History of Enfield, Connecticut*, 3 vols. (Lancaster, Pennsylvania, 1900)

English Adventurers   Peter Wilson Coldham, *English Adventurers and Emigrants, 1609-1660* (Baltimore 1984)

English Homes   Charles Edward Banks, *The English Ancestry and Homes of the Pilgrim Fathers* ... (New York c1929)

EPR   *The Probate Records of Essex County, Massachusetts, 1635-1681*, 3 volumes (Salem 1916-1920; rpt. Newburyport, Massachusetts, 1988). Citations to the unpublished probate records are to case numbers, or to register volumes (which begin with volume 301).

EQC   *Records and Files of the Quarterly Courts of Essex County, Massachusetts, 1636-1686*, 9 volumes (Salem 1911-1975)

Essex Ant   *The Essex Antiquarian*, Volume 1 through 13, Sidney Perley, ed. (Salem 1897-1909)

Evans Festschrift   *Studies in Genealogy and Family History in Tribute to Charles Evans On the Occasion of His Eightieth Birthday*, Lindsay L. Brook, ed. (Salt Lake City 1989)

Exeter Hist   Charles H. Bell, *History of the Town of Exeter, New Hampshire* (Exeter 1888; rpt. Bowie, Maryland, 1979)

Fairfield LR   Fairfield, Connecticut, Deeds

Fairfield PR   Fairfield County, Connecticut, Probate Records

FANH   Donald Lines Jacobus, *Families of Ancient New Haven*, 9 volumes in 3 (Baltimore 1974; originally published as *New Haven Genealogical Magazine*, Volumes 1 through 8 [New Haven 1922-1932]; these were the first 8 volumes of TAG, which see)

Farmington LR   Farmington, Connecticut, Deeds

Farm VR Barbour   Farmington Vital Records, Barbour Collection, Connecticut State Library, Hartford, Connecticut

Farwell Gen   John Dennis Farwell, Jane Harter Abbott and Lillian M. Wilson, *The Farwell Family*, 2 volumes (n.p. 1929)

Felt   Joseph B. Felt, *Annals of Salem*, 2nd edition, 2 volumes (Salem 1845, 1849)

Fiske Notebook   *The Notebook of the Reverend John Fiske, 1644-1675*, Publications of the Colonial Society of Massachusetts, Volume 47 (Boston 1974)

Flagg   Ernest Flagg, *Genealogical Notes on the Founding of New England, My Ancestors' Part in that Undertaking* (n.p. 1926; rpt. Baltimore 1973)

FOOF   Donald Lines Jacobus, comp. and ed., *History and Genealogy of the Families of Old Fairfield*, 3 volumes (Fairfield, Connecticut, 1930; rpt. Baltimore 1976, 1991)

Ford   William Bradford, *History of Plymouth Plantation, 1620-1647*, Worthington Chauncey Ford, ed., 2 volumes (Boston 1912)

Foster   Joseph Foster, *Alumni Oxonienses: The Members of the University of Oxford, 1500-1714 ...*, 4 volumes (Oxford 1891-1892)

Frothingham   Richard Frothingham, Jr., *The History of Charlestown, Massachusetts* (Boston 1845)

GDMNH — Sybil Noyes, Charles Thornton Libby and Walter Goodwin Davis, *Genealogical Dictionary of Maine and New Hampshire* (Portland, Maine, 1928-1939; rpt. Baltimore 1972)

Gen Adv — *The Genealogical Advertiser*, v. 1-4 (Cambridge, 1898-1901; rpt. Baltimore, GPC, 1974)

Gen Bull — *The Genealogical Bulletin*

Gen Mag — *The Genealogical Magazine* (Salem, Massachusetts 1810-1915)

Gilbert Gen — Homer Worthington Brainard, Harold Simeon Gilbert and Clarence Almon Torrey, *The Gilbert Family, Descendants of Thomas Gilbert, 1582(?)-1659* (New Haven 1953)

Gilberts of New England — George Gordon Gilbert and Geoffrey Gilbert, *Gilberts of New England. Part I: Descendants of John Gilbert of Dorchester*, and Homer W. Brainard and Clarence A. Torrey, *Gilberts of New England. Part II: Descendants of Mathew Gilbert of New Haven, Humphrey Gilbert of Ipswich, and William Gilbert of Boston, from the Gilbert Family Manuscript Genealogy* (Victoria, British Columbia, 1959)

Gillespie Anc — Paul W. Prindle, *Ancestry of Elizabeth Barrett Gillespie (Mrs. William Sperry Beinecke)* (New Orleans 1976)

Gleaner — *Gleaner Articles*, Fifth Report of the Boston Record Commissioners (Boston revised 1887)

GMB — Robert Charles Anderson, *The Great Migration Begins: Immigrants to New England, 1620-1633*, 3 volumes (Boston 1995)

GMC26

John Brooks Threlfall, *Twenty-Six Great Migration Colonists To New England & Their Origins* (Madison, Wisconsin, 1993)

GMC50

John Brooks Threlfall, *Fifty Great Migration Colonists To New England & Their Origins* (Madison, Wisconsin, 1990)

GMN

Great Migration Newsletter, Volume 1 through present (1990+)

GMNJ

Genealogical Magazine of New Jersey, Volume 1 through present (1925+)

Good News

"Good Newes From New England: or a true Relation of things very remarkable at the Plantation of Plimoth in New England..." by E[dward] W[inslow], in Alexander Young, *Chronicles of The Pilgrim Fathers of The Colony of Plymouth, From 1602 to 1625...*, 2nd edition (Boston 1844; rpt. Baltimore 1974); pp. 271-375

Goodwin Anc

Frank Farnsworth Starr, *Various ancestral lines of James Goodwin and Lucy (Morgan) Goodwin, Hartford, Connecticut*, 2 vols. (Hartford 1915)

Goodwin Gen

James Junius Goodwin, *The Goodwins of Hartford, Connecticut, Descendants of William and Ozias Goodwin* (Hartford 1891)

Goodwin Papers

Frank Farnsworth Starr, *English Goodwin Family Papers* (Hartford 1921)

Gorges

The Letters of Thomas Gorges, Deputy Governor of the Province of Maine, 1640-1643, Robert E. Moody, ed. (Portland 1978)

Granary   *Gravestone Inscriptions and Records of Tomb Burials*
                                in the Granary Burying Ground, Boston, Mass.
                                (Salem 1918)

Granberry   Donald Lines Jacobus, *The Granberry Family and*
                                Allied Families (Hartford 1945)

Grant   "Matthew Grant Record, 1639-1681" in *Some Early*
                                Records and Documents of and Relating to The
                                Town of Windsor, Connecticut, 1639-1703
                                (Hartford 1930)

Gravesend TR   Gravesend, New York, Town Records

Gregory Stone Gen   J. Gardner Bartlett, *Gregory Stone Genealogy,*
                                Ancestry and Descendants of Dea. Gregory
                                Stone of Cambridge, Mass., 1320-1917 (Boston
                                1918)

Guilford Anc   Joan S. Guilford, *The Ancestry of Dr. J.P. Guilford*
                                (Orange, California, 1990)

HaBOP   *Original Distribution of the Lands in Hartford*
                                Among the Settlers, 1639, Collections of the
                                Connecticut Historical Society, Volume 14
                                (Hartford 1912; rpt. Bowie, Maryland, 1989)

Hadley Hist   Sylvester Judd, *The History of Hadley,*
                                Massachusetts (1905; rpt. Somersworth, New
                                Hampshire, 1976)

HadVR   Hadley, Massachusetts, Vital Records

HAHAC   Oliver Ayer Roberts, *History of... the Ancient and*
                                Honorable Artillery Company of Massachusetts,
                                1637-1888, 4 volumes (Boston 1895-1901)

Hale, House	Donald Lines Jacobus and Edgar Francis Waterman, *Hale, House and Related Families, Mainly of the Connecticut River Valley* (Hartford 1952; rpt. Baltimore 1978)
Hall-Baldwin	Edith Bartlett Sumner, *Ancestry and Descendants of Amaziah Hall and Betsey Baldwin* (Los Angeles 1954)
HamCCR	Hampshire County, Massachusetts, Court Records
HamLR	Hampshire County, Massachusetts, Deeds, Springfield, Massachusetts
Hammatt Papers	Abraham Hammatt, *The Hammatt Papers. Early Inhabitants of Ipswich, Massachusetts. 1633-1700* (Ipswich 1880-1899; rpt. Baltimore 1980)
HamPR	Hampshire County, Massachusetts, Probate Records, Northampton, Massachusetts (and on microfilm)
HamVR	Manuscript volume of vital records kept at Hadley Town Hall; same hand, same format and similar time span as Pynchon VR; covers Hadley, Hatfield, Deerfield and Northampton
Hampton Hist	Joseph Dow, *History of the Town of Hampton, New Hampshire: From Its Settlement in 1638, To The Autumn of 1892* (Salem 1893)
HampVR	*Vital Records of Hampton, New Hampshire To The End of the Year 1900*, Vol. 1, George Freeman Sanborn Jr. and Melinde Lutz Sanborn, eds. (Boston 1992)

HaPR   Hartford County, Connecticut, Probate Registers
                        (two sets of records in some volumes,
                        "probate" side and "court" side)

Hartford PD   Hartford Probate District, original files,
                        Connecticut State Archives (and on
                        microfilm)

HarVR   Louise H. Kelley and Dorothy Straw, *Vital
                        Records Town of Harwich, Massachusetts,
                        1694-1850* (Harwich 1982)

HaTR   "Hartford Town Votes, Volume I. 1635-1716" in
                        Collections of the Connecticut Historical Society,
                        Volume 6 (Hartford 1897)

HaVR   "Early Hartford Vital Records" in *Collections of the
                        Connecticut Historical Society*, Volume 14, pp.
                        575-632 (Hartford 1912; rpt. Bowie,
                        Maryland, 1989)

HaVR Barbour   Hartford Vital Records, Barbour Collection,
                        Connecticut State Library, Hartford,
                        Connecticut.

HempTR   *Records of the Towns of North and South Hempstead,
                        Long Island, New York, 1654-1880*, 8 volumes,
                        Benjamin D. Hicks, ed. (Jamaica, New York,
                        1896-1904)

Henry Adams   J. Gardner Bartlett, *Henry Adams of Somersetshire,
                        England and Braintree, Mass. His English
                        Ancestry and Some of His Descendants* (New
                        York 1927)

Hewes Gen   Eben Putnam, *Lieutenant Joshua Hewes* (New
                        York 1913)

HiBOP   Hingham, Massachusetts, Book of Possessions
                        (original)

Higginson — Francis Higginson, *New-Englands Plantation with The Sea Journal and Other Writings* (Salem 1908)

Hingham Hist — George Lincoln, *History of the Town of Hingham, Massachusetts*, 3 volumes (Hingham 1893; rpt. Somersworth, New Hampshire, 1982)

Hinshaw — William Wade Hinshaw and Thomas Worth Marshall, *Encyclopedia of American Quaker Genealogy*, Volume III, New York and Long Island (Ann Arbor, Michigan, 1940)

History of Grants — Samuel F. Haven, *History of Grants under the Great Council For New England* ... (Boston 1869)

HiTR — Hingham, Massachusetts, Town Records (original)

HiVR — Hingham, Massachusetts, Vital Records (original)

Holden Gen — Eben Putnam, *The Holden Genealogy* (Boston 1923-26)

Hotten — *The Original Lists of Persons of Quality...*, John Camden Hotten, ed. (London 1874; rpt. Baltimore 1974)

Hoyt — David Webster Hoyt, *The Old Families of Salisbury and Amesbury, Massachusetts*, 3 vols. (Providence, R.I., 1897-1919)

Hubbard — William Hubbard, *A General History of New England from the Discovery to MDCLXXX* (Cambridge 1815)

Hull   "Diary of John Hull" in *Transactions and
                        Collections of the American Antiquarian Society*,
                        Volume 3 (Worcester 1857)

Hutchinson   Thomas Hutchinson, *The History of the Colony and
                        Province of Massachusetts Bay*, 3 volumes, ed.
                        Lawrence Shaw Mayo (Cambridge 1936)

ILR   Ipswich Land Records, manuscript, Essex
                        County Courthouse, Salem, Massachusetts

Ipswich Hist   Thomas Franklin Waters, *Ipswich In the
                        Massachusetts Bay Colony*, 2 vols. (Ipswich
                        1905, 1917)

ITR   Ipswich, Massachusetts, Town Records (both the
                        originals and the limited records that have
                        been published are muddled and
                        unpaginated, so no volume or page
                        citations are given with this citation)

JIC   *A Tribute to John Insley Coddington on the Occasion
                        of the Fortieth Anniversary of The American
                        Society of Genealogists*, Neil D. Thompson
                        and Robert Charles Anderson, eds. (New
                        York 1980)

John White   Frances Rose-Troup, *John White, The Patriarch of
                        Dorchester [Dorset] and The Founder of
                        Massachusetts, 1575-1648...* (New York 1930)

Johnson   Edward Johnson, *Johnson's Wonder-Working
                        Providence, 1628-1651*, J. Franklin Jameson,
                        ed. (New York 1910)

Joseph Neal Anc   Walter Goodwin Davis, *The Ancestry of Joseph
                        Neal, 1769-c.1835* (Portland, Maine, 1945)

Kempton Anc Dean Crawford Smith, *The Ancestry of Eva Belle Kempton, 1878-1908, Part I: The Ancestry of Warren Francis Kempton, 1817-1879* (Boston 1996)

Kingsbury Gen Frederick John Kingsbury and Mary Kingsbury Talcott, *The Genealogy of the Descendants of Henry Kingsbury of Ipswich and Haverhill, Mass.* (Hartford 1905)

King's Chapel Thomas Bridgman, *Memorials of The Dead In Boston, Containing Select Transcripts of Inscriptions...in the King's Chapel Burial Ground, in the City of Boston* (Boston 1853)

King's County Settlers Teunis G. Bergen, *Register in Alphabetical Order of the Early Settlers of Kings County, Long Island, N.Y. ...* (rpt. Cottonport, Louisiana, 1973)

Kittery Hist Everett S. Stackpole, *Old Kittery and Her Families* (Lewiston, Maine, 1903; rpt. Somersworth, New Hampshire, 1981)

KitVR Joseph Crook Anderson II and Lois Ware Thurston, *Vital Records of Kittery, Maine, To The Year 1892*, Maine Genealogical Society Special Publication No. 8 (Camden, Maine, 1991)

Lachaire *The Register of Salomon Lachaire, Notary Public of New Amsterdam, 1661-1662*, New York Historical Manuscripts Dutch, ed. Kenneth Scott and Kenn Stryker-Rodda (Baltimore 1978)

Lancaster Records Henry S. Nourse, *The Early Records of Lancaster, Massachusetts. 1643-1752* (Lancaster, Massachusetts, 1884; rpt. Bowie, Maryland, 1993)

LanVR   Henry S. Nourse, ed., *The Birth, Marriage and
                               Death Register, Church Records and Epitaphs of
                               Lancaster, Massachusetts. 1643-1850*
                               (Lancaster 1890; rpt. Bowie, Maryland, 1993)

LCVR   James N. Arnold, *Vital Record of Rhode Island,
                               1636-1850*, First Series, Volume 4, Part VI,
                               Little Compton (Providence 1893)

Lechford   *Note-book Kept by Thomas Lechford, Esq., Lawyer, in
                               Boston, Massachusetts Bay, from June 27, 1638,
                               to July 29, 1641*, Edward Everett Hale, Jr., ed.
                               (Cambridge 1885; rpt. Camden, Maine,
                               1988). Citations herein refer to the
                               pagination as printed (and not to the
                               manuscript pagination) and will therefore
                               differ from the index entries of the 1885
                               edition.

Letters of NE   *Letters from New England. The Massachusetts Bay
                               Colony, 1629-1638*, Everett Emerson, ed.
                               (Amherst, Massachusetts, 1976)

Loomis Rec   Copy of Windsor Vital Records prepared by
                               Town Clerk and included in Barbour Index

Lydia Harmon Anc   Walter Goodwin Davis, *The Ancestry of Lydia
                               Harmon, 1755-1836, Wife of Joseph Waterhouse
                               of Standish, Maine* (Boston 1924)

Lyme VR   Verne M. Hall and Elizebeth B. Plimpton,
                               comps., *Vital Records of Lyme, Connecticut to
                               the End of the Year 1850* (Lyme 1976)

Lynn Hist   Alonzo Lewis and James Newhall, *History of
                               Lynn...* (Lynn 1890)

LynnHSR   *The Register of the Lynn Historical Society*,
                               Numbers 1 through 23, 1897-1926

M&JCH   *Search for the Passengers of the Mary & John 1630,* Volume 1 through present (Toledo, Ohio, 1985+)

MA Arch   "Massachusetts Archives," being bound volumes of loose papers at the Commonwealth Archives of Massachusetts, Boston, Massachusetts

MA Civil List   William H. Whitmore, *The Massachusetts Civil List for the Colonial and Provincial Periods, 1630-1774* (Albany 1870; rpt. Baltimore 1969)

Macdonough-Hackstaff   Rodney MacDonough, *The MacDonough-Hackstaff Ancestry* (Boston 1901)

Magna Chart Sureties   Frederick Lewis Weis, *The Magna Charta Sureties, 1215, The Barons Named in the Magna Charta, 1215 and Some of Their Descendants Who Settled in America During the Early Colonial Years,* 4th ed. (Baltimore 1991)

Magnalia   Cotton Mather, *Magnalia Christi Americana...,* 2 volumes (Hartford 1855)

Maine PR   John Eldridge Frost, *Maine Probate Abstracts,* 2 volumes (Camden, Maine, 1991)

Maine Wills   William M. Sargent, *Maine Wills, 1640-1760* (Portland 1887; rpt. Baltimore 1972)

Malden Hist   Deloraine Pendre Corey, *The History of Malden, Massachusetts, 1633-1785* (Malden 1899)

Mansfield VR   Susan W. Dimock, *Births, Baptisms, Marriages and Deaths From the Records of the Town and Churches in Mansfield, Connecticut, 1703-1850* (New York 1898)

ManVR   *Vital Records of Manchester, Massachusetts, to the End of the Year 1849* (Salem 1903)

Manwaring   *A Digest of the Early Connecticut Probate Records,* Volume One, Hartford Probate District, 1635-1700, Charles William Manwaring, comp. (Hartford 1904)

Marsh Gen   Dwight Whitney Marsh, *Marsh Genealogy. Giving Several Thousand Descendants of John Marsh of Hartford, Ct., 1636-1895* (Amherst, Massachusetts, 1895)

MarVR   *Vital Records of Marshfield, Massachusetts, to the year 1850,* Robert M. Sherman and Ruth Wilder Sherman, eds. (n.p. 1970)

Martha's Vineyard Hist   Charles Edward Banks, *The History of Martha's Vineyard, Dukes County, Massachusetts in Three Volumes* (Edgartown 1966)

MBCR   *Records of the Governor and Company of the Massachusetts Bay in New England, 1628-1686,* Nathaniel B. Shurtleff, ed., 5 volumes in 6 (Boston 1853-1854)

McArthur-Barnes   Selim Walker McArthur, *McArthur-Barnes Ancestral Lines,* Donald Lines Jacobus, ed. (Portland, Maine, 1964)

McCormick-Hamilton   Leander McCormick-Goodhart, *Genealogical Tables of the Descendants of John Hamilton of "Locust Hill"*... (n.p., 1933)

MCF   Middlesex County Court Files, deposited at the Commonwealth Archives of Massachusetts, Boston, Massachusetts (and on microfilm)

MCR   Middlesex County, Massachusetts, Court Record Books (microfilm)

MD	*Mayflower Descendant,* Volume 1 through present (1899-1937, 1985+)
MF	*Mayflower Families* (the "silver" books)
MFIP	*Mayflower Families in Progress* (the "pink" books)
MHGR	*Maine Historical & Genealogical Recorder*
MHSC	Collections of the Massachusetts Historical Society, Volume 1 through present (1792+). This serial is divided into a number of series, so the citations will sometimes be in three parts, designating series, volume and page.
MHSP	Proceedings of the Massachusetts Historical Society, Volume 1 through present (1791+). This serial is divided into a number of series, so the citations will sometimes be in three parts, designating series, volume and page.
MidChR	Middletown, Connecticut, Church Records
MiddleVR	*Middleborough, Massachusetts Vital Records,* Barbara Lambert Merrick and Alicia Crane Williams, eds., 2 vols. (Boston 1986, 1990)
MidLR	Middletown, Connecticut, Deeds
MidVR	Middletown, Connecticut, Vital Records
MidVR Barbour	Middletown, Connecticut, Vital Records, Barbour transcript
Milford LR	Milford, Connecticut, Land Records
Minor Diary	*The Diary of Thomas Minor, Stonington, Connecticut. 1653 to 1684* (n.p. 1899; rpt. n.p. 1993 [with the diary of Manasseh Minor, 1696 to 1720])

Minot Gen   Joseph Grafton Minot, *A Genealogical Record of the Minot Family...* (Boston 1897)

MLR   Middlesex County, Massachusetts, Deeds

Monnette   Orra Eugene Monnette, *First Settlers of Ye Plantations of Piscataway and Woodbridge, Olde East New Jersey, 1664-1714*, parts 1-7 (Los Angeles 1930-1935)

Moore Anc   L. Effingham deForest and Anne Lawrence deForest, *Moore and Allied Families: The Ancestry of William Henry Moore* (New York 1938)

Morison   Samuel Eliot Morison, *The Founding of Harvard College* (Cambridge 1935) [especially for Appendix B, "English University Men Who Emigrated to New England Before 1646," pp. 359-410]

Morton   Nathaniel Morton, *The New-England's Memorial ...* (Plymouth 1826)

Mourt   *A Journal of the Pilgrims at Plymouth. Mourt's Relation. A Relation or Journal of the English Plantations Settled at Plymouth in New England, by Certain English Adventurers Both Merchants and Others*, Dwight B. Heath, ed. (New York 1963)

MPCR   *Province and Court Records of Maine*, 6 volumes (Portland 1928-1975; volumes 1-3 rpt. Newburyport, Massachusetts, 1991)

MPR   Middlesex County, Massachusetts, Probate Records

MQ   *Mayflower Quarterly*, Volume 1 to present (1935+)

Mulford Anc	Charles H. Cory, Jr., *Lineal Ancestors of Susan (Kitchell) Mulford, Mother of Mrs. Susan (Mulford) Cory*, 4 vols. (n.p. 1937)
Munsey-Hopkins	D.O.S. Lowell, *A Munsey-Hopkins Genealogy ...* (Boston 1920)
Nantucket Land	Henry Barnard Worth, *Nantucket Lands and Land Owners* (Bowie, Maryland, 1992)
NanVR	Nantucket, Massachusetts, Vital Records
NEHGR	*New England Historical and Genealogical Register*, Volume 1 through present (1847+)
Newbury Hist	Joshua Coffin, *A Sketch of the History of Newbury, Newburyport & West Newbury* (Hampton, New Hampshire, 1845)
Newell Anc	William M. Emery, *Newell Ancestry: The Story of the Antecedents of William Stark Newell* (n.p. 1944)
New English Canaan	Thomas Morton, *New English Canaan* (Amsterdam 1637; rpt. Boston 1883)
New London Hist	Frances Mannering Caulkins, *History of New London, Connecticut* (New London 1852)
New London PD	New London County, Connecticut, Probate District
Newport Gleanings	Jane Fletcher Fiske, *Gleanings from Newport Court Files, 1659-1783* (Boxford, Massachusetts, 1998)
New York Wills	Original wills of New York (microfilm)
NGSQ	*National Genealogical Society Quarterly*, Volume 1 through present (1912+)

NHChR	New Haven, Connecticut, Church Records
NHCR	*Records of the Colony and Plantation of New Haven, 1638-1649, 1653-1664*, 2 volumes, Charles J. Hoadly, ed. (Hartford 1857-1858)
NHGR	*New Hampshire Genealogical Record*, Volume 1 through present (1903-1910; 1990+)
NHLR	New Haven, Connecticut, Land Records
NHPCR	New Hampshire Province Court Records, manuscript records at New Hampshire Division of Records Management and Archives, Concord, New Hampshire
NHPLR	New Hampshire Provincial Deeds, New Hampshire Division of Records Management and Archives, Concord, New Hampshire
NHPP	*Provincial Papers, Documents and Records Relating to the Province of New Hampshire from 1686 to 1722*, 40 volumes, Nathaniel Boulton, ed. (Manchester, N.H., 1867-1943)
NHPR	New Haven, Connecticut, Probate Records
NHTR	*New Haven Town Records*, 3 volumes, Franklin Bowditch Dexter, ed. (New Haven 1917-1962)
NHVR	*Vital Records of New Haven, 1649-1850*, 2 volumes (Hartford 1917, 1924)
NJArch	New Jersey Archives
NJHSP	*New Jersey Historical Society Proceedings*, four series, 1845 to present

NLCR   New London County, Connecticut, Court Records

NLLR   New London, Connecticut, Deeds

NLR   (Old) Norfolk County, Massachusetts, Deeds

NLVR Barbour New London Vital Records, Barbour Collection, Connecticut State Library, Hartford, Connecticut

Noble Gen   Lucius M. Boltwood, *History and Genealogy of the Family of Thomas Noble of Westfield, Massachusetts* (Hartford 1878)

Northampton Hist James Russell Trumbull, *History of Northampton, Massachusetts, From its Settlement in 1654* (Northampton 1902)

NorthVR   Northampton, Massachusetts, Vital Records

Norwalk Hist   Charles M. Selleck, *Norwalk* (Norwalk 1896)

Norwich Cem   George S. Porter, *Inscriptions from Gravestones in the Old Burying Ground, Norwich Town, Connecticut* (Norwich 1933)

NoVR   *Vital Records of Norwich, 1659-1848*, 2 volumes (Hartford 1913)

Noyes-Gilman   Charles Phelps Noyes, *Noyes-Gilman Ancestry* (St. Paul, Minnesota, 1907)

NYChR   *Marriages from 1639 to 1801 in the Reformed Dutch Church, New York*, Collections of the New York Genealogical and Biographical Society, Volume I (New York 1890), and *Baptisms from 1639 to 1730 in the Reformed Dutch Church, New York*, Collections of the New

York Genealogical and Biographical Society, Volume II (New York 1901)

NYCM   *New York Council Minutes*

NYGBR   *The New York Genealogical and Biographical Record,* Volume through present (1869+)

NYHM:D   New York Historical Manuscripts: Dutch

NYHM:E   New York Historical Manuscripts: English

NYMarr   *New York Marriages Previous to 1784 ...* (Baltimore 1868, 1984)

Old Dover   John Scales, *Historical Memoranda concerning Persons and Places in Old Dover, N.H.* (Dover 1900)

Ordway Anc   Dean Crawford Smith, *The Ancestry of Samuel Blanchard Ordway, 1844-1916* (Boston 1990)

Otis   Amos Otis, *Genealogical Notes of Barnstable Families...*, 2 volumes (Barnstable, Massachusetts, 1888, 1890; rpt. Baltimore 1979, in 1 volume)

Parke-Gildersleeve   Nathan Grier Parke II, *The Ancestry of Rev. Nathan Grier & his Wife, Ann Elizabeth Gildersleeve,* Donald Lines Jacobus, ed. (Woodstock 1959)

Parker-Ruggles   John William Linzee, Jr., *The History of Peter Parker and Sarah Ruggles of Roxbury, Mass., and Their Ancestors and Descendants* (Boston 1913)

PCC   Prerogative Court of Canterbury, England

PChR

Plymouth Church Records, 1620-1859, Part 1 and Part 2 in Publications of the Colonial Society of Massachusetts, volumes 22 and 23 (Boston 1920, 1923)

PCLR

Plymouth Colony Deeds (from microfilm; Volume 1 has been published as Volume 12 of PCR)

PCR

Records of the Colony of New Plymouth in New England, Nathaniel B. Shurtleff and David Pulsifer, eds., 12 volumes in 10 (Boston 1855-1861)

PCPR

Plymouth Colony Probate Records (from microfilm)

Pemaquid Papers

"Pemaquid Papers," in *Collections of the Maine Historical Society,* vol. 5 (Portland 1857), pp. 1-138

Penobscot Pioneers

Philip Howard Gray, *Penobscot Pioneers,* 6 volumes (Camden, Maine, 1992-96)

Perley

Sidney Perley, *The History of Salem, Massachusetts,* 3 volumes (Salem 1924-1928)

Philip Sherman

Roy V. Sherman, *Some of the Descendants of Philip Sherman, The First Secretary of Rhode Island* (Akron 1968)

Phoebe Tilton Anc

Walter Goodwin Davis, *The Ancestry of Phoebe Tilton, 1775-1847, The Wife of Capt. Abel Lunt of Newburyport, Massachusetts* (Portland 1947)

Pillsbury Anc

Mary Lovering Holman, *Ancestry of Charles Stinson Pillsbury and John Sargent Pillsbury ...* 2 vols. (Concord, 1938)

Plain Dealing — Thomas Lechford, *Plain Dealing: or, Newes From New-England* (London 1642)

Planters — Charles Edward Banks, *The Planters of the Commonwealth, 1620-1640* (Boston 1930; rpt. Baltimore 1972)

PLR — Plymouth County, Massachusetts, Deeds (from microfilm)

Plymouth Wills — C.H. Simmons, Jr., *Plymouth Colony Records, Volume 1, Wills and Inventories, 1633-1669* (Camden, Maine, 1996)

PoLE — Portsmouth, Rhode Island, Land Evidences

Pope — Charles Henry Pope, *The Pioneers of Massachusetts...* (Boston 1900; rpt. Baltimore 1965)

Pope MNH — Charles Henry Pope, *The Pioneers of Maine and New Hampshire, 1623 to 1660...* (Boston 1908; rpt. Baltimore 1973)

PoTR — *The Early Records of the Town of Portsmouth* (Providence 1901)

PoVR — Portsmouth, Rhode Island, Vital Records

PPR — Plymouth County, Massachusetts, Probate Records (from microfilm)

Prince — Thomas Prince, *A Chronological History of New England ...*, Samuel G. Drake, ed., third edition (Boston 1852)

PRO — Public Record Office, London, England

PrTR — *The Early Records of the Town of Providence*, 21 volumes (Providence 1892-1915)

PTR
Records of the Town of Plymouth, Volume 1, 1636 to 1705 (Plymouth 1889)

Pulsifer
David Pulsifer, manuscript transcription of the Middlesex County, Massachusetts, County Court records, vol. 1, 1653-

Putnam's Mag
Putnam's Monthly Historical Magazine, Volumes 1-7 (1892-99)

PVR
Vital Records of Plymouth, Massachusetts, to the Year 1850, Lee D. van Antwerp, comp., and Ruth Wilder Sherman, ed. (Camden, Maine, 1993)

Pynchon Court
Colonial Justice in Western Massachusetts (1639-1702), The Pynchon Court Record. An Original Judges' Diary of the Administration of Justice in the Springfield Courts in the Massachusetts Bay Colony, Joseph H. Smith, ed. (Cambridge, Massachusetts, 1961)

Pynchon Papers
The Pynchon Papers, Volume I: Letters of John Pynchon, 1654-1700 and *Volume II: Selections from the Account Books of John Pynchon, 1651-1697*, Publications of the Colonial Society of Massachusetts, Volumes 60 and 61, Carl Bridenbaugh, ed. (Boston 1982)

Pynchon VR
Manuscript volume of vital records kept by John Pynchon, at Connecticut Valley Historical Museum

Rambles
Charles Brewster, *Sketches of Persons, Localities and Incidents of Two Centuries, Rambles About Portsmouth*, 2 series (Portsmouth, New Hampshire, 1869-1873; rpt. 1967)

RBOP
Roxbury Book of Possessions in Sixth Report of the Boston Record Commissioners (Boston 1884), pp. 11-51

RCA   *Records of the Court of Assistants*, 3 volumes
               (Boston 1901-1928)

RChR   *Roxbury Land and Church Records*, Sixth Report of
               the Boston Record Commissioners (Boston
               1884), pp. 74-191

ReVR   James N. Arnold, *Vital Record of Rehoboth, 1642-
               1896...* (Providence 1897)

RICR   *Records of the Colony of Rhode Island and Providence
               Plantations...*, 1636-1692, 10 volumes, John
               Russell Bartlett, ed. (Providence 1856-1865)

RICT   *Rhode Island Court Records: Records of the Court of
               Trials of the Colony of Providence Plantations,
               1647-1662*, Volume I (Providence 1920)
               [RICT 1]; *Rhode Island Court Records: Records
               of the Court of Trials of the Colony of Providence
               Plantations, 1662-1670*, Volume II
               (Providence 1922) [RICT 2]; Jane Fletcher
               Fiske, trans., *Rhode Island General Court of
               Trials, 1671-1704* (Boxford, Massachusetts,
               1998) [RICT 3]

RIGR   *Rhode Island Genealogical Register*, Volume 1
               through present (1978+)

RIHSC   *Rhode Island Historical Society Collections*, Volume
               1 through present (1827+)

RILE   *Rhode Island Land Evidences, Volume I, 1648-1696*
               (Providence 1921; rpt. Baltimore 1970)

RIRoots   *Rhode Island Roots*, Volume 1 through present
               (1975+)

RIVR   James N. Arnold, *Vital Record of Rhode Island,
               1636-1850*, Volumes 1 through 21
               (Providence 1891-1912)

Robert Rose Gen   Christine Rose, *Descendants of Robert Rose of Wethersfield and Branford, Connecticut* ... (San Jose, California, 1983)

Rowlandson's Narrative *The Narrative of the Captivity and Restoration of Mrs. Mary Rowlandson* (Lancaster, Massachusetts, 1903)

Rowley Fam   George Brainard Blodgette, comp., *Early Settlers of Rowley, Massachusetts* (Rowley 1933)

RPCC   *Records of the Particular Court of Connecticut, 1639-1663*, Collections of the Connecticut Historical Society, Volume 22 (Hartford 1928; rpt. Bowie, Maryland, 1987)

RTR   Robert J. Dunkle & Ann S. Lainhart, *The Town Records of Roxbury, Massachusetts, 1647 to 1730, Being Volume One of the Original* (Boston 1997)

RVR MS   Roxbury Vital Records, manuscript copy at New England Historic Genealogical Society, Boston

RWCorr   *The Correspondence of Roger Williams, Volume One 1629-1653, Volume Two 1654-1682*, Glenn W. LaFantasie, ed. (Providence 1988)

Saints   George F. Willison, *Saints and Strangers*... (New York 1945)

Salisbury Fam   Edward Elbridge Salisbury and Evelyn McCurdy Salisbury, *Family Histories and Genealogy*, 3 vols. in 5 (New Haven 1892)

Salisbury Mem   Edward Elbridge Salisbury, *Family Memorials. A Series of Genealogical and Biographical Monographs* ... (New Haven 1885)

Saltonstall Papers   Robert E. Moody, *The Saltonstall Papers, 1607-1815, Volume 1: 1607-1789*, Collections of the Massachusetts Historical Society, Volume 80 (Boston 1972)

SandVR   Caroline Lewis Kardell and Russell A. Lovell, Jr., *Vital Records of Sandwich, Massachusetts, to 1885*, 3 volumes (Boston 1996)

Sarah Hildreth Anc   Walter Goodwin Davis, *The Ancestry of Sarah Hildreth, 1773-1857, Wife of Annis Spear of Litchfield, Maine* (Portland, Maine, 1958)

Sarah Johnson Anc   Walter Goodwin Davis, *The Ancestry of Sarah Johnson, 1775-1824, Wife of Joseph Neal of Litchfield, Maine* (Portland 1960)

Sarah Miller Anc   Walter Goodwin Davis, *The Ancestry of Sarah Miller, 1755-1840, Wife of Lieut. Amos Towne of Arundel (Kennebunkport), Maine* (Portland 1939)

Sarah Stone Anc   Walter Goodwin Davis, *The Ancestry of Sarah Stone, Wife of James Patten of Arundel (Kennebunkport) Maine* (Portland 1930)

Savage   James Savage, *A Genealogical Dictionary of the First Settlers of New England*, 4 volumes (Boston 1860-1862; rpt. Baltimore 1965)

SayVR   *The Vital Records of Saybrook Colony, 1635-1860*, ed. Elizebeth Bull Plimpton (Old Saybrook, Connecticut, 1985)

SChR   *The Records of the First Church in Salem, Massachusetts, 1629-1736*, Richard D. Pierce, ed. (Salem 1974)

SCC   *Records of the Suffolk County Court, 1671-1680*, 2 vols., in *Publications of The Colonial Society of Massachusetts*, vols. 29 and 30 (Boston, 1933)

SCHSR   *Suffolk County Historical Society Register*

ScitTR   Jeremy Dupertuis Bangs, *The Seventeenth-Century Town Records of Scituate, Massachusetts,* Volume One (Boston 1997)

Scott Gen   Mary Lovering Holman, *The Scott Genealogy....* (Boston 1919)

Scrapbook   *The Plymouth Scrap Book, The Oldest Original Documents Extant In Plymouth Archives...,* Charles Henry Pope, ed. (Boston 1918)

ScVR   *Vital Records of Scituate, Massachusetts, to the Year 1850*, 2 volumes (Boston 1909)

Seversmith   Herbert Furman Seversmith, *Colonial Families of Long Island, New York and Connecticut Being the Ancestry & Kindred of Herbert Furman Seversmith ...,* typescript (Washington DC 1939-1958)

Sewall   *The Diary of Samuel Sewall*, Volume One 1674-1708, Volume Two 1709-1729, M. Halsey Thomas, ed. (New York 1973)

Shepard   *Thomas Shepard's Confessions*, Publications of the Colonial Society of Massachusetts, Volume 58, George Selement & Bruce C. Woolley, eds. (Boston 1981)

Sibley   John Langdon Sibley, *Biographical Sketches of Graduates of Harvard University, 1642-1689*, 3 volumes (Cambridge 1873-1885)

Simon Stone Gen	J. Gardner Bartlett, *Simon Stone Genealogy ...* (Boston 1926)
Shattuck	Lemuel Shattuck, *A History of the Town of Concord...* (Boston 1835)
SimsLR	Simsbury, Connecticut, Deeds
SimsVR Barbour	Simsbury Vital Records, Barbour Collection, Connecticut State Library, Hartford, Connecticut
SJC	Supreme Judicial Court, Massachusetts
SLR	*Suffolk Deeds*, Volumes 1 through 14 (Boston 1880-1906). Citations to later volumes are from the microfilm copies of the originals.
Small Gen	Lora Altine Woodbury Underhill, *Descendants of Edward Small of New England and the Allied Families with Tracings of English Ancestry*, revised edition, 3 volumes (Boston and New York, 1934)
Snow-Estes	Nora E. Snow, *The Snow-Estes Ancestry*, 2 volumes (Hillburn, New York, 1939)
SoTR	*The First Book of Records of the Town of Southampton...* (Sag-Harbor, New York, 1874)
Spencer	Wilbur D. Spencer, *Pioneers on Maine Rivers with Lists to 1651...* (Portland, Maine, 1930; rpt. Bowie, Maryland, 1990)
SPR	Suffolk County, Massachusetts, Probate Records
SPR NS	Suffolk County, Massachusetts, Probate Records, New Series

Spragues of Malden   George Walter Chamberlain, *The Spragues of Malden, Massachusetts* (Boston 1923)

Springfield Fam   Thomas B. Warren, *Springfield Families*, 3 vols. (Springfield 1934-1935)

Springfield Hist   Henry M. Burt, *The First Century of the History of Springfield. The Official Records from 1636 to 1736*, 2 volumes (Springfield 1898 & 1899)

SpTR   Springfield, Massachusetts, Town Records

Stevens-Miller Anc   Mary Lovering Holman (and Winifred Lovering Holman), *Ancestry of Colonel John Harrington Stevens and his wife Frances Helen Miller*, 2 volumes (n.p. 1948, 1951)

Stillwell   John E. Stillwell, *Historical and Genealogical Miscellany: Data Relating to the Settlement and Settlers of New York and New Jersey*, 5 vols. (n.p. 1903-32; rpt. Baltimore 1970)

StLR   Stamford, Connecticut, Deeds

Stonington Hist   Richard Anson Wheeler, *History of the Town of Stonington, County of New London, Connecticut, From Its First Settlement in 1649 to 1900, With a Genealogical Register of Stonington Families* (1900; rpt. Mystic 1966)

StonVR Barbour   Stonington Vital Records, Barbour Collection, Connecticut State Library, Hartford, Connecticut

STR   *Town Records of Salem, Massachusetts*, 1634-1691, 3 volumes (Salem 1868, 1913, 1934)

Stratton   Eugene Aubrey Stratton, *Plymouth Colony: Its History & People, 1620-1691* (Salt Lake City 1986)

StrLR	Stratford, Connecticut, Vital Records
StrVR Barbour	Stratford Vital Records, Barbour Collection, Connecticut State Library, Hartford, Connecticut
StTR	Stamford, Connecticut, Town Records
SuBOP	Sudbury, Massachusetts, Book of Possesions
SuTR	Sudbury, Massachusetts, Town Records
SVR	*Vital Records of Salem, Massachusetts, to the End of the Year 1849*, 6 volumes (Salem 1916-1925; rpt. Newburyport, Massachusetts, 1988)
SwVR	*Vital Records of Swansea, Massachusetts To 1850*, transcribed by H.L. Peter Rounds (Boston 1992)
TAG	*The American Genealogist*, Volume 9 to present (1932+)
Talmage Gen	Arthur White Talmadge, *The Talmadge, Tallmadge and Talmage Genealogy, Being the Descendants of Thomas Talmadge of Lynn, Massachusetts, With An Appendix Including Other Families* (New York 1909)
Taunton Hist	Samuel Hopkins Emery, *History of Taunton, Massachusetts, from Its Settlement to the Present Time* (Syracuse 1893)
TEG	*The Essex Genealogist*, Volume 1 to present (1981+)
TG	*The Genealogist*, Volume 1 to present (1980+)
Thomas Cooke Gen	Jane Fletcher Fiske, *Thomas Cooke of Rhode Island*, 2 volumes (Boxford, Massachusetts, 1987)

Three Episodes   Charles Francis Adams, *Three Episodes of Massachusetts History*, 2 volumes (Boston and New York, 1903)

Three Visitors   Sydney V. James, Jr., *Three Visitors to Early Plymouth* (Plymouth 1963)

Tingley-Meyers   Raymon Meyers Tingley, *Some Ancestral Lines* (Rutland, Vermont, 1935)

Topo Dict   Charles Edward Banks, *Topographical Dictionary of 2885 English Emigrants to New England, 1620-1650*, Elijah Ellsworth Brownell, ed. (Philadelphia 1937; rpt. Baltimore 1957)

TopsHC   *The Historical Collections of the Topsfield Historical Society*, Volume 1 to present (1895+)

Torrey   Clarence Almon Torrey, *New England Marriages Prior to 1700*, 12 volumes, original manuscript, New England Historic Genealogical Society

Tracy Gen   Sherman Weld Tracy, comp., *The Tracy Genealogy, Being Some of the Descendants of Stephen Tracy of Plymouth Colony, 1623* (Rutland 1936)

Transatlantic Shermans   Bertha L. Stratton, comp., *Transatlantic Shermans* (New York 1969)

Trelawny Papers   *The Trelawny Papers*, James Phinney Baxter, ed., in *Collections of the Maine Historical Society, 2nd Series*, Volume 3 (Portland, Maine, 1884)

Two Voyages   *John Josselyn, Colonial Traveler. A Critical Edition of Two Voyages to New England*, Paul J. Lindholdt, ed. (Hanover and London, 1988)

UGM   *Utah Genealogical and Historical Magazine*, 31
                             volumes (Salt Lake City 1910-1940)

Venn   John Venn and J.A. Venn, *Alumni Cantabrigienses,
                             Part I (From the Earliest Times to 1751)*, 4
                             volumes (Cambridge 1922-1927)

WaBOP   "Lands, Grants, Divisions, Allotments,
                             Possessions and Proprietors' Book," Section
                             Two in *Watertown Records Comprising the
                             First and Second Books of Town Proceedings ...*
                             (Watertown 1894)

WaChR   Watertown Church Records, Watertown Town
                             Records, volume 4

WarLE   Warwick, Rhode Island, Land Evidences

WarTR   *The Early Records of the Town of Warwick*
                             (Providence 1926)

Warner-Harrington   Frederick Chester Warner, *The Ancestry of Samuel,
                             Freda and John Warner*, typescript (Boston
                             1949-55)

Waterhouse Anc   Walter Goodwin Davis, *The Ancestry of Joseph
                             Waterhouse, 1754-1837, of Standish, Maine*
                             (Portland 1949)

Waterman Gen   E.F. Waterman, *The Waterman Family*, Donald
                             Lines Jacobus, ed., 3 volumes (New Haven
                             1939-1954)

Waters   Henry FitzGilbert Waters, *Genealogical Gleanings
                             In England*, 2 volumes (Boston 1901)

WaTR   "Records of Town Proceedings - First and Second
                             Books," Section One in *Watertown Records
                             Comprising the First and Second Books of Town
                             Proceedings ...* (Watertown 1894)

WaVR · · · · · · · · · "Records of Births, Deaths and Marriages - First Book and Supplement," Section Three in *Watertown Records Comprising the First and Second Books of Town Proceedings* ... (Watertown 1894)

Welles Gen · · · · · · · · · Donna Holt Siemiatkoski, *The Descendants of Governor Thomas Welles of Connecticut, 1590-1658 and his wife Alice Tomes* (Baltimore 1990)

Wentworth Gen · · · · · · · · · John Wentworth, *The Wentworth Genealogy: English and American*, 3 volumes (Boston 1878)

Westchester Court · · · · · · · · · Dixon Ryan Fox, ed., *The Minutes of the Court of Sessions (1657-1696), Westchester County, New York*, Publications of the Westchester County Historical Society, Volume II, Source Series, Volume I (White Plains, New York, 1924)

Westchester TR · · · · · · · · · Westchester, New York, Town Records

Westminster Abbey PR *The Marriage, Baptismal, and Burial Registers of the Collegiate Church or Abbey of St. Peter, Westminster,* Joseph Lemuel Chester, ed. (London 1876)

WetLR · · · · · · · · · Wethersfield, Connecticut, Land Records

Wethersfield Hist · · · · · · · · · Henry Reed Stiles, *The History of Ancient Wethersfield*, 2 vols. (New York 1904; rpt. Somersworth, New Hampshire, 1987)

WetVR Barbour · · · · · · · · · Wethersfield Vital Records, Barbour Collection, Connecticut State Library, Hartford, Connecticut

WeVR · · · · · · · · · *Vital Records of Weymouth, Massachusetts, to the Year 1850*, 2 volumes (Boston 1910)

Weymouth Hist   George Walter Chamberlain, *History of Weymouth, Massachusetts*, Volumes Three and Four, Genealogy of Weymouth Families (Weymouth 1923; rpt. Baltimore 1984, 2 volumes in 1)

WeyTR   Weymouth, Massachusetts, Town Records, original manuscript at town hall, Weymouth, Massachusetts

Whiteway   *William Whiteway of Dorchester His Diary 1618 to 1635* (Dorchester, Dorsetshire, 1991)

WiLR   Windsor, Connecticut, Deeds (microfilm of original at Connecticut State Library, Hartford, Connecticut)

Windsor Hist   Henry Reed Stiles, *The History and Genealogies of Ancient Windsor, Connecticut ...*, 2 vols. (Hartford, 1891-92)

WiVR   Windsor Vital Records, typescript, Connecticut State Library (1918-29)

WiVR Barbour   Windsor Vital Records, Barbour Collection, Connecticut State Library, Hartford, Connecticut

WJ   John Winthrop, *The History of New England from 1630 to 1649*, James Savage, ed., 2 volumes (Boston 1853). Citations herein refer to the pagination of the 1853 and not the 1826 edition, even though the index to the 1853 edition continues to use the 1826 pagination.

WMJ   Medical Journals of John Winthrop Jr., 1657-1669, manuscript, Massachusetts Historical Society, Boston, Massachusetts

Wolcott Gen   Chandler Wolcott, *Wolcott Genealogy[:] The Family of Henry Wolcott* (Rochester 1912)

Wood   William Wood, *New England's Prospect*, Alden T. Vaughan, ed. (Amherst 1977)

Worthley   Harold Field Worthley, *An Inventory of the Records of the Particular (Congregational) Churches of Massachusetts Gathered 1620-1805*, in *Harvard Theological Studies*, volume 25 (Cambridge 1970)

WoVR   Edward F. Johnson, *Woburn Records of Births, Deaths, and Marriages, from 1640 to 1873*, 4 parts (Woburn 1890-1894)

WP   *Winthrop Papers, 1498-1654*, 6 volumes, various editors (Boston 1925-1992)

WPR   Worcester County, Massachusetts, Probate Records

WWP   *Johnson's Wonder-Working Providence, 1628-1651*, J. Franklin Jameson, ed. (New York 1910; rpt. 1952)

Wyllys Papers   "The Wyllys Papers. Correspondence and Documents Chiefly of Descendants of Gov. George Wyllys of Connecticut. 1590-1796" in *Collections of the Connecticut Historical Society*, Volume 21 (Hartford 1924)

Wyman   Thomas Bellows Wyman, *The Genealogies and Estates of Charlestown, Massachusetts: 1629-1818*, 2 volumes (Boston 1879; rpt. in 1 volume Somersworth, New Hampshire, 1982)

YarVR   Robert M. Sherman and Ruth Wilder Sherman,
                              *Vital Records of Yarmouth, Massachusetts To
                              The Year 1850*, 2 vols. (Warwick, Rhode
                              Island, 1975)

YLR   *York Deeds*, 18 volumes (Portland, Maine, 1887-
                              1910)

York Hist   Charles Edward Banks, *History of York, Maine*, 2
                              volumes (Boston 1931, 1935)

Young's First Planters   *Chronicles of the First Planters of the Colony of
                              Massachusetts Bay ...*, Alexander Young, ed.
                              (Boston 1846; rpt. Baltimore 1975)

Young's Pilgrim Fathers *Chronicles of the Pilgrim Fathers of the Colony of
                              Plymouth ...*, Alexander Young, ed. (Boston
                              1844; rpt. Baltimore 1974)

JOHN ABBOTT
MARY ABBOTT

"Jo[hn] Abbott," aged 16, and "Marie Abbott," aged 16, were enrolled on 6 April 1635 at London as passengers for New England on the *Hopewell* [Hotten 49].

COMMENTS: Eleven passengers were accepted for passage on the *Hopewell* on 6 April 1635, all between the ages of twelve and twenty-one, and all apparently single and without other family, suggesting that they were all servants. John Abbott was third in this group of eleven, and Mary Abbott was seventh.

This John Abbott may be the one whose death on 22 May 1637 was reported by Winthrop: "Math[hew] Bridge, for killing, by careless discharging a pistol at Concord, one John Abbot, John Bridge his father of Newton undertook in £40 for his appearance at next court" [WJ 1:425].

On 6 June 1637, "Mathewe Bridg being accused to be guilty of the untimely death of John Abbot, the said Mathewe, & John Bridge, his father, were bound in £40 for his appearance at the next Quarter Court" [MBCR 1:198]. On 19 September 1637, "Mathew Bridge appearing, & no evidence coming in against him, he was quit by proclamation" [MBCR 1:203].

No record of Mary Abbott has been found in New England.

ROBERT ABBOTT

ORIGIN: Unknown
MIGRATION: 1634
FIRST RESIDENCE: Watertown
REMOVES: Wethersfield 1636, New Haven 1642, Branford 1646

CHURCH MEMBERSHIP: Admission to Watertown church prior to 3 September 1634 implied by freemanship. Admission to New Haven church prior to 6 August 1642 implied by freemanship.

FREEMAN: 3 September 1634 (as "Rob[er]te Abbitt," ninth in a sequence of eleven Watertown men) [MBCR 1:369]. On 6 August 1642 "Brother Abbott ... received the charge of freeman" at New Haven [NHCR 1:76; see also NHCR 1:10, 138].

EDUCATION: His inventory included "books" valued at 12s. On 6 July 1658, "Matthew Roe lay my claim to a Bible that he saith his father Abbut gave to his wife; Debora Abbut saith that she heard her father tell the children that they should not spoil that Bible for it was their sister Roe's" [BranLR 1:324].

OFFICES: Connecticut jury, 2 July 1640, 2 September 1641 [CCCR 1:55, 66].

"[B]rother Abbott ... freed from training [at New Haven], by reason of ... bodily infirmities," 5 April 1643 [NHCR 1:86].

ESTATE: On 25 July 1636 granted a Great Dividend of thirty-five acres at Watertown [WaBOP 5]. In the Inventory of Grants held three parcels: homestall of ten acres; three acres of meadow; and Great Dividend of thirty-five acres [WaBOP 101-2].

On 24 February 1644[/5], "Rob[er]t Abbott and Will[iam] Paine desired that their land might be laid out on the East side, in such a form as may be convenient for them to fence it and improve it" [NHCR 1:156].

The undated inventory of Robert Abbott, "who deceased September 30 1658," was untotalled; the only real estate included was "the house and land," valued at £20 [BranLR 1:195-96].

On 29 May 1659, "Robert Abbott, late of Branford deceased, who died intestate, being possessed of an estate amounting to £120 or £130, or thereabouts, a question was brought to the court whether the 2 youngest children should not be considered above their proportion, being not duly provided for considering their years, which the court having considered, it was declared that £10 shall be taken out of the estate for the help of the widow for the bringing up of these two children, which being done, the estate is to be divided, according to the true intent of the law in that case, between the widow & children, which is referred to the court at Branford" [NHCR 2:302].

On 4 November 1659, "John Robins of Branford weaver" bound himself to "pay or cause to be paid to the children of the deceased Robert Abut their several portions appointed by the court": to "Petter Abut the eldest son," £1 5d.; to "Matthew Roe," £5 9s. 1d.; to "Debora Abbut," £7 9s.; and to "all the rest of the children their several portions as they come to age" £10 9s. apiece - "John Abut," "Joship Abbut," "Danill Abbut," "Abigal Abbut," and "Marie Abbut" [BranLR 1:197].

On 17 March 1670/1, John Abbot gave a receipt to Robert Foot of Branford for £10 9s., the portion due him from John Robbins; on 3 November 1676 Daniel Abbot gave a receipt to Robert Foot of Branford for £10 9s. "left me by my father Robert Abbot which aforesaid sum was due from my father-in-law John Robbins"; on 2 April 1677, Joseph Abbot gave a receipt to Robert Foot of Branford for £10 9s. "which is the full of my due from my father-in-law John Robbins for my portion" [BranLR 2:41]. On 5 September 1684, "William Robberds" gave a receipt to "widow Sarah Foot of Branford (with what I received of her husband Robert Foot now deceased) the full and just sum of ten pounds nine shillings which was the full of my wife's portion due to her from her father Robert Abbot's estate" [BranLR 2:42].

BIRTH: By about 1605 based on estimated date of marriage.
DEATH: Branford 30 or 31 September 1658 [BranLR 1:170, 195-96].
MARRIAGE: (1) By about 1630 _____ _____. She died before 1649.

(2) By 1649 Mary _____. She married (2) Branford 4 November 1659 John Robbins [BranLR 1:173].
CHILDREN:
With first wife
  i   SARAH, b. say 1630; m. by 1650 Matthew Rowe (eldest child b. New Haven 10 August 1650 [NHVR 1:4]).
  ii   PETER, b. by about 1632 ("Petter Abut" was granted land in Branford on 16 February 1652[/3?] [BranLR 1:169]); m. by an unknown date Elizabeth Evarts, daughter of John Evarts (his estate papers "named the four sons, and the child of their sister Elizabeth Abbott" [FOOF 1:193, citing an unknown source]); on 16 October 1667 he was hanged for murdering her and attempting to murder their child [see COMMENTS below].
  iii DEBORAH, b. say 1641; m. New Haven "in October 1661" Nathan Andrews [NHVR 1:19].
With second wife
  iv   JOHN, b. 23 September 1649 (calc.) (apprenticed to William Lewis Sr. on 28 December 1658, aged 9 years, 3 months, 5 days [BranLR 1:196]); bp. New Haven 7 October 1649

[NHChR 15]; living 17 March 1670/1 [BranLR 2:41]; no further record.

v	ABIGAIL, b. Branford 2 October 1650 [BranLR 1:171]; bp. New Haven 1 June 1651 "by virtue of communion of churches" [NHChR 16]; living 1670, when Jonathan Rose sold her a horse [BranLR 1:138]; no further record (but see MARY below).

vi	ROBERT, bp. New Haven 1 June 1651 "by virtue of communion of churches" [NHChR 16]; no further record.

vii	JOSEPH, b. Branford 20 April 1652 [BranLR 1:171]; m. by 1700 Anna Sanford (probably), daughter of Thomas Sanford (eldest child b. East Haven 15 August 1700 [FOOF 1:7]; in 1721 Thomas Sanford deeded land to his sons Samuel and John and grandson William, with a provision that son John "pay at my death to daughter Anna Abbot £4" [Carlton E. Sanford, *Thomas Sanford* ... (Rutland, Vermont, n.d.), p. 93]).

viii	BENJAMIN, b. Branford 10 January 1653[/4] [BranLR 1:171]; d. Branford 27 March 1654 [BranLR 1:170].

ix	DANIEL, b. Branford 12 February 1654[/5] [BranLR 1:172]; m. by 1694 Hannah Brooks, daughter of John Brooks (eldest child b. New Haven 22 April 1694 [NHVR 1:74]; "[before] the Court 1693 with Hannah Brooks, dau[ghter] of John, whom apparently he married" [FOOF 1:7]).

x	MARY, b. Branford 13 March 165[6/]7 [BranLR 1:172]; on 11 July 1665 "Mary Abut" became "an apprentice by the consent of my father-in-law John Robins and the Church of Brandfoord to George Clarke of Milfoord ... until I be of eighteen years of age" [BranLR 1:221]; m. by 1681 William Roberts (if he had only one wife, then she had children born from 1681 to 1697, which would make this the only daughter of Robert Abbott available as his wife; but if only the earlier children of William Roberts were by the daughter of Robert Abbott, then Mary's elder sister Abigail might have been the wife of Roberts [FANH 6:1510]).

ASSOCIATIONS: The involvement of Robert Foote and his widow in the settlement of Robert Abbott's estate may indicate some relationship.

COMMENTS: The three parcels of land granted to Robert Abbott in Watertown appear in the hands of Roger Wellington in the Inventory of Possessions, and form the basis of the latter's proprietary right, under which he began to receive grants from Watertown on 28 February 1636/7 [WaBOP 8, 51-52, 101, 136]. Robert Abbott must have sold his Watertown holdings in 1636, which would have been at the time of his removal to Wethersfield.

Although there are no dates of birth for the first three children of Robert Abbot, they seem to be some years older than the other six, and on this basis we have assumed that Robert Abbot had two wives. In the case of sons Joseph and Daniel, Jacobus gives them the marriages as above, "despite late marriage age" [FANH 4:943].

On 2 January 1644[/5], "Brother Abbott demanded satisfaction of Mr. Lamberton for damage done by his hogs in the Oyster Shell Field, but respited" [NHCR 1:152, 162].

On 29 May 1659, the "magistrate and deputies of Branford informed that Peter Abbott coming thither the last year to help his father to weed corn, was taken the same day with a lunacy, which occasioned much charge & exercise to their town, which they conceived should be borne by the public, he being no settled inhabitant there, but had lived sometimes in one plantation & sometimes in another, and that if it should please God again so to exercise him, they saw not how the people of Branford (having been under the afflicting hand of God) could be able to supply him with such things as his condition would call for, to which the court answered, that they saw not but that Branford, to whom he did belong, must in justice bear it, but withal it was promised that if God should so again afflict them in Peter Abbot, they will have a brotherly respect to them &, if there be cause, help them in a way of mercy, as this court shall think meet" [NHCR 2:300-1].

On 8 October 1667, "Peter Abbott late of Fayrefeild thou art here indicted by the name of Peter Abbott so that thou not having the fear of God before thine eyes thou hast committed murder which is manslaughter by murdering thy wife & for endeavoring to murder thy child for which according to the law of God & the law of this corporation thou deservest to die. The prisoner at the bar having heard the indictment read to him being demanded whether guilty or not: Answered he was guilty of the death of his wife & for endeavoring to kill his child. The jury return they find the prisoner guilty of murder according to the indictment. The court having considered of the verdict of the jury approved thereof & passed sentence of death upon the prisoner, which is that he should be on the sixteenth of this instant carried to the place of execution & there be hanged by the neck until he is dead & then be cut down & buried. The secretary is in the name of this court by warrant to require the public officer to see this sentence executed" [HaPR 3(court):71].

BIBLIOGRAPHIC NOTE: The best treatments of Robert Abbott are brief ones prepared by Donald Lines Jacobus in 1922 and 1930 [FANH 1:8, 4:943; FOOF 1:5-6].

MATTHEW ABDY

ORIGIN: London
MIGRATION: 1635 on the *Abigail*
FIRST RESIDENCE: Boston

OCCUPATION: Fisherman [SLR 12:176].
EDUCATION: Made his mark to a 1682 deed, as did his second wife.
ESTATE: On 5 April 1682, "Matthew Abdey," Sr., of Boston, fisherman, and wife Alice sold for £64 to "Savil Sympson" of Boston, cordwainer, "all that their messuage or tenement ... lying and being in Boston abovesaid near unto the third meetinghouse," bounded on the east, south and north by Nathaniel Reynolds [SLR 12:176-77].

BIRTH: About 1620 (aged 15 in July 1635 [Hotten 98]; aged "about 28" on 17 May 1654 [SJC Case #236]; deposed "aged forty-eight years" on 25 June 1669 [EQC 4:157]).
DEATH: After 5 April 1682 [SLR 12:176-77].
MARRIAGE: (1) By 1648 Tabitha Reynolds, daughter of Robert Reynolds [SPR Case #213]. She died at Boston [blank] [May] 1661 [BVR 80].
   (2) Boston 24 May 1662 Alice Cox [BVR 86], who was living 5 April 1682 [SLR 12:176-77].
CHILDREN:
   With first wife
         i   MARY, b. Boston 24 May 1648 [BVR 27]; living 20 April 1658 when named in the will of grandfather Robert Reynolds [SPR Case #213]; no further record.

ii   TABITHA, b. Boston 24 November 1652 [BVR 36]; perhaps
     married George Tankersley, who, with wife Tabitha, had
     children recorded in Boston, 24 September 1673 and 17
     September 1674 [BVR 129, 134].

iii MATTHEW, b. by April 1658 (named in will of grandfather
     Robert Reynolds [SPR Case #213]); m. (1) Cambridge 10
     April 1688 as her second husband Deborah (Stimson)
     Wilson, widow of Robert [MLR 13:99]; m. (2) by 25
     February 1727/8 Ruth _____ [CaChR 95], who d.
     Cambridge 10 December 1762, aged 93 years.

ASSOCIATIONS: In his 20 April 1658 will, Robert Reynolds bequeathed to
"my daughter Tabitha Abdy and her son Mathew Abdy, and if he should
die, to her two daughters either of them alike" a share in his house and
lands if his only son, Nathaniel, died without children. Otherwise, each
of Robert's daughters was to have £20 [SPR Case #213].

COMMENTS: On 1 July 1635, "Mathew Abdy," aged 15, was enrolled at
London on the *Abigail* as a passenger for New England [Hotten 98].
   "Matth[ew] Abdee" took the Oath of Allegiance at Boston 11 November
1678 [SCC 963] and "Math[ew] Abdee" took the Oath of Allegiance as a
resident of Roxbury 1679 [SCC 969]. (One of these may be the son of the
immigrant.)
   The 1653 deposition of George Croskum indicated that in 1650
         he fished at Munhegen with Mr. Hill, and stayed upon the island
         after John Devorix went away; the latter left upon the island two
         swine and entreated deponent and William Liloby to put them
         aboard John Wilkeson's, who promised to bring them into the
         bay, and so Mathue Abdie and William Eavens killed one of them
         and spent it in their voyage [EQC 1:325].
   In the 1655-6 fishing voyage trial of Rev. Robert Jordan vs. John
Ridgway, Matthew Abdy, aged "about 28," deposed on 17 May 1654 that
"the fish were taken in to Charlestown and delivered to Capt. Breden for
John Ridgway and to Robert Corben for Mr. Jordan" [SJC Case #236].
   In a deposition sworn on 25 June 1669, Matthew Abdy, aged forty-eight
years, and John Downes, aged forty years, deposed in the case of Ellis vs.
Clearke [EQC 4:157].
   Matthew Abdy appears to have lived a subsistence level existence as a
fisherman. He is not of record as a freeman, nor did he ever hold public
office. The Abdys had no church affiliation, and their children were not
baptized. Son Matthew was finally baptized in Cambridge in his late 60s

[CaChR 95]. Matthew Sr.'s only lands appear to have come to him from his first father-in-law, and he did not obtain other properties during his career.

BIBLIOGRAPHIC NOTE: Noyes, Libby, and Davis take too literally the humorous verse "Father Abbey's Will" penned by young John Seccombe [*Cyclopaedia of American Literature* 1:126]. Seccombe's impolite parody featured a fabricated will enumerating the pathetic belongings of Matthew Abdy, Jr., Harvard College's humble janitor of many decades, and an amorous ode directed to Abdy's aged and unattractive widow from his "brother" sweeper at New Haven. After reading this, to suggest that it meant Matthew Abdy Jr. had a brother "living in New Haven in 1732" demonstrates a deficiency in someone's sense of humor [GDMNH 58].

DOROTHY ADAMS

"Dorothie Adams," aged 24, was enrolled at London on 18 July 1635 as a passenger for New England on the *Defence* [Hotten 107].

COMMENTS: No record of Dorothy Adams has been found in New England.

RICHARD ADAMS

ORIGIN: Batcombe, Somerset
MIGRATION: 1635
FIRST RESIDENCE: Weymouth
REMOVES: Malden by about 1650

OCCUPATION: Planter.
CHURCH MEMBERSHIP: Admission to a Massachusetts Bay church, probably Dorchester, prior to 2 September 1635 implied by freemanship.
FREEMAN: 2 September 1635 (third in a sequence of six Weymouth men [MBCR 1:371]).
EDUCATION: Signed his deed and will. Drafted several semiliterate petitions to Middlesex court [MCF Folios #45, 53].

OFFICES: Grand jury, 19 September 1637 [MBCR 1:203]. Deputy to General Court for Weymouth, 2 November 1637, 12 March 1637/8 [MBCR 1:205, 220]. Weymouth member of Massachusetts Bay committee to levy a tax on each town, 12 March 1637/8 [MBCR 1:225]. Commissioner to end small causes at Weymouth, 6 September 1638 [MBCR 1:239].

On 19 June 1665, Middlesex Court excused Richard Adams from further training, based on his petition that he was "of the age of threescore or thereabout, also being lame" [MCF Folio #45].

ESTATE: On 18 August 1674, "Richard Addams" of Malden, planter, "with the assent & consent of Elizabeth my wife," sold to Thomas Linde of Malden, yeoman, "a certain parcel of marsh meadow land ... in Malden ... containing four acres" [MLR 6:27-28; TAG 22:199].

In his will, dated 21 March 1673/4 and proved 15 December 1674, "Richard Addams of Maulden" bequeathed to "my beloved wife all the land and meadow that is [in] mine hands so long as she doth live a widow [and] in case she shall dispose herself in marriage again she shall have but two-third parts in the land and housing"; to "my daughter Mary Clowe of Charlestowne one acre of land ... below the swamp and one acre of saltmarsh that joineth to the three acres of saltmarsh that I have sold to Thomas Lynde of Mauldon that joineth to Phineas Upham saltmarsh"; to "my daughter Sarah Counts of Charlestowne one acre and half of land lying in Charlestowne ... and one acre saltmarsh lying next to my daughter Clowe saltmarsh"; to "my daughter Ruth Grover the house pasture next to Phineas Upham land ... and three acres of saltmarsh lying in Charlestowne ... the said my daughter Ruth to pay to my younger daughter Hannah Addams three pounds when she shall enter on the possession of the land"; to "my younger daughter Hannah Adames the other part of the house pasture and housing and the rest of the planting land & two acres of saltmarsh lying to my daughter Sarah Counts saltmarsh"; moveables to "my daughter Ruth" and "my daughter Hannah"; "my son Lazarus Grover" to be executor; moveables to "my wife"; "my will is that the three acres of saltmarsh lying to Phinies Upham saltmarsh sold and set over to Thomas Lind shall be confirmed according to law by my lawful executors and measured out"; witnessed by John Upham, Thomas Linde and Philip Atwood [MPR 4:99-100, Case #221].

The inventory of the estate of "Richard Adams deceased of Malden," taken 9 December 1674, was untotalled and listed £78 in real estate: "three acres saltmarsh in Charleston lands," £15; "five acres saltmarsh in Malden lands," £20; "one acre and half acre land planting," £3; and "[illegible] acres planting land in Mauldon and housing," £40 [MPR 4:101, Case #221].

BIRTH: About 1606 (aged 29 in 1635 [Hotten 284]).
DEATH: Malden 6 October 1674.
MARRIAGE: (1) By 1635 Mary (_____) Cheame. She died in 1642 or later.
  (2) After 1642 Elizabeth _____. She died at Malden in November 1656.
  (3) By 1662 Elizabeth _____ [MLR 6:27].

CHILDREN:
  With first wife
      i   SARAH, b. Weymouth 3 July 1637 [NEHGR 8:348, 9:171]; m.
           Malden 25 February 1662 Edward Counts.
      ii   SAMUEL, b. Weymouth 6 June 1639 [NEHGR 8:348, 9:171];
           apparently living in 1653 (see *ASSOCIATIONS* below); no
           further record.
      iii RUTH, b. Weymouth 3 June 1642 [NEHGR 8:348, 9:171]; m. by
           1665 Lazarus Grover (eldest known child b. Malden
           [blank] December 1665) [Dawes-Gates 1:338-42].
      iv   Child, b. by 21 July 1653 (implied by will of John Bibble [see
           ASSOCIATIONS below]); possibly child of his second
           wife; no further record.
  With third wife
      v   HANNAH, b. Malden [blank] January 1662; m. Lynn 13 March
           1678/9 Isaac Wellman. On 27 May 1679 "Isaac Wellman of
           Lynn with the assent & consent of Hannah my wife" sold
           land in Malden being "the moiety ... of the pasture land
           sometime Richard Adams" [Joshua Wyman Wellman,
           Descendants of Thomas Wellman of Lynn, Massachusetts
           (Boston 1918), 84-89, especially 86, citing MLR 17:633].
ASSOCIATIONS: JOHN UPHAM and Richard Adams sailed to New
England on the same ship and resided in Weymouth until about 1650
when both moved to Malden. They or their children held adjoining land,
and John Upham witnessed the will of Richard Adams.
  In his will of 21 July 1653, John Bibble bequeathed to "Richard Adames
of Maldon and his wife and five children twelve pence apiece" [MPR Case
#1667; NEHGR 9:306-7; see also TAG 31:91], suggesting a possible
relation. (Three of the five children of Richard Adams would have been
his stepdaughter, Mary Cheame, and his own daughters Sarah and Ruth,
and a fourth was presumably his son Samuel, who would have been
fourteen at the time of John Bibble's will, but is otherwise unrecorded
after his birth. A fifth child, for whom there is no other record, must have

been born by 1653, and is here, because of the vagueness of dates for the wives of Richard Adams, ascribed arbitrarily to his first wife.)

COMMENTS: "Rich[ard] Adams," aged 29, "Mary his wife," aged 26, and "Mary Cheame his daughter," aged one, sailed for New England on 20 March 1634/5 as passengers on a vessel from Weymouth; Adams was servant of WILLIAM READ of Batcombe, Somerset [Hotten 284].

In his will Richard Adams names "my daughter Mary Clowe" of Charlestown, and most sources identify her as Mary Adams, daughter of Richard. William Clough was married to Mary by 9 August 1656, when she was admitted to Charlestown church [NEHGR 23:282], pointing to the conclusion that this was "Mary Cheame," Richard's stepdaughter.

Pope intermingled records for this man and for RICHARD ADAMS of Salem.

RICHARD ADAMS

ORIGIN: Unknown
MIGRATION: 1635 on the *Abigail*
FIRST RESIDENCE: Salem

OCCUPATION: Bricklayer. On 15 January 1637[/8], 12s. 4d. was paid to "Adams for daubing the meeting house" at Salem [STR 1:64]. On 12 November 1660 "Rich[ard] Adams" was paid 16s. for "mending [the] meeting house" [STR 2:8]. On 10 November 1668, Salem selectmen ordered that "Mathew Woodwell have liberty granted to make bricks near Rich[ard] Adams's fence, near where Thomas Trusler made bricks formerly" [STR 2:95].
EDUCATION: On 20 June 1679, Richard Adams, as one of the appraisers of the estate of Alester Mackmallen, signed the inventory by mark [EQC 7:320].
OFFICES: Salem fenceviewer, 23 April 1657, 22 April 1661, 21 March 1663/4 [STR 1:199, 2:14, 45].

On 26 November 1672, "[w]hereas Richard Adams was formerly to pay two bushels of corn per annum to the use of the company, court now released him from common training, he paying one bushel of Indian corn yearly" [EQC 5:122]. On 30 June 1674, "Richard Adams was released from common training, paying 2s. yearly to the use of the company"; the same order was entered on 21 July 1674 [EQC 5:362, 379].

ESTATE: On 25 September 1637, "Richard Addams demands 5s. due from Isack Davis, and also desires some house ground" [STR 1:58]. On 24 February 1637/8, "Rich[ar]d Adams hath his 5 acres changed and to have it at the mill and to have a proportion to set a house near Lt. Davenport's" [STR 1:67].

On 29 January 1637/8, the town lent "Adams" 24s. (which was accounted for on 20 March 1647/8), and on 3 March 1637/8, there "was lent to Richard Addams by agreement of the town six bushels of corn" [STR 1:65, 68, 154].

On 25 June 1638, it was ordered that four persons, including "[Rich] Adams," "all which were forgotten in the division shall have their half acres apiece of marsh land" [STR 1:70].

On 7 January 1661/2, Salem selectmen ordered that "upon the request of Rich[ard] Adams for land formerly granted not entered, that it shall now be entered to the value of twenty acres of upland, & order be taken for the laying of it out to him" [STR 2:20].

On 26 June 1678, Richard Adams was one of the petitioners regarding the Salem commons. Along with this action was the resolution of a dispute between Richard Adams and Bray Wilkins, in which Adams was referred to as "old Goodman Adams" [EQC 7:74-76].

BIRTH: About 1606 (aged 29 in 1635 [Hotten 91]).
DEATH: After November 1679 (when Lt. John Pickering was chosen tythingman for a district that included Richard Adams [STR 2:311]).
MARRIAGE: By 1635 Susan ____.
CHILDREN: None recorded.

COMMENTS: "Richard Adams," bricklayer, aged 29, and "Suzan Adams," aged 26, enrolled at London on 26 June 1635 as passengers for New England on the *Abigail*, with certificates of conformity from Northampton [Hotten 91].

On 22 March 1657/8, Richard Adams and twelve other men were assigned to "the fore seat in the South Gallery" in the meetinghouse [STR 1:214].

For unstated service, Richard Adams was paid £1 4s. by the town on 12 May 1647, and 12s. on 14 December 1658 [STR 1:152, 222].

On 29 January 1677/8, "Elizabeth Wilkins, servant of Richard Adams," was presented for theft [EQC 6:387]. On 30 April 1678, Elizabeth Wilkins was found guilty, and in the course of the proceedings "Richard Addams and wife Susanah" made depositions [EQC 6:438-39].

WILLIAM ADAMS

"W[illia]m Adams," aged 15, was enrolled at London on 6 May 1635 as a passenger for New England on the *Elizabeth & Ann* [Hotten 76].

COMMENTS: This William Adams was too young to be the landholder at Cambridge in 1636 (see next sketch) or the freeman of 22 May 1639 [MBCR 1:375]. Savage suggests that this passenger was son of William Adams of Ipswich, but this seems only a guess.

WILLIAM ADAMS

ORIGIN: Unknown
MIGRATION: 1635
FIRST RESIDENCE: Cambridge

OCCUPATION: Planter.
ESTATE: In the accounting of houses in Cambridge of 8 February 1635/6, "Will Addams" is included "by the Fresh Pond" [CaTR 19].
   On the "12th of the first month [March]," apparently in 1637, "William Adams, planter," was shown as holding two parcels of land at Cambridge: "one house and lot containing half an acre"; and "9 acres of planting ground at the Fresh Pond" [CaBOP 44].

BIRTH: By about 1614 based on ownership of land.
DEATH: After 1637.
MARRIAGE: None recorded.
CHILDREN: None recorded.

COMMENTS: The two parcels of land ascribed to William Adams soon passed through the hands of a Thomas Adams. The "house and lot" of William Adams were described as having Robert Parker as an abutter on the east, and as being on "the highway that leads unto Watertowne"; in 1639 Robert Parker's house is entered as being "in the lane to Watertowne," and as having "Thomas Addams" as an abutter on the west [CaBOP 58]. In a Cambridge land inventory of about 1639 the holdings of Nathaniel Sparhawk include "[b]ought of Thomas Addams one house at the Fresh Ponde with nine acres of upland" [CaBOP 51].

The land at Fresh Pond is especially interesting. In the listing of houses of 8 February 1635/6 there are only five names, the first three of which are Gilbert Crackbone, Walter Nichols and William Adams [CaTR 19]. Crackbone and Nichols both came from Great Coggeshall, Essex, and were both admitted freemen on 7 December 1636 [MBCR 1:372]. By 1639 Nathaniel Sparhawk had obtained all three of these parcels at Fresh Pond, the parcel of William Adams said to have been bought from Thomas Adams, and the parcel of Walter Nichols from Thomas Nichols [CaBOP 51]. This last circumstance suggests that these early Cambridge records for Thomas Adams and Thomas Nichols are simple scribal errors, rather than evidence for calling Thomas Adams a son or brother of William Adams.

As noted in the sketch above, this William Adams who held land in Cambridge in 1635 could not, by reason of age, be the fifteen-year-old passenger of 1635. Both Savage and Pope (whose sketch under the name of William Adams is especially muddled) ascribe to the Cambridge man the freemanship record of 22 May 1639 [MBCR 1:375], and make him the same as the William Adams of Ipswich. They have been followed in this assumption by a number of other authors [Seversmith 1:93-104, and the other secondary sources cited there].

The portion of the list of freemen of 22 May 1639 in which William Adams appears is not organized by town, so we cannot say where this man resided at that date. Nothing in the Cambridge records indicates that this William Adams had a family. The identification of the Cambridge William Adams with the Ipswich man of the same name is possible, but need not be true, and nothing other than identity of names points in that direction.

ALICE ALBON

"Alice Albon," aged 25, was enrolled on 11 September 1635 at London as a passenger for New England on the *Hopewell* [Hotten 131].

COMMENTS: No record for Alice Albon in New England has been found.

Pope thinks that she is the same as a "sister Olbon (lately Cole)" mentioned in the Cambridge church records in 1658 [CaChR 9], but this is probably a different person.

JOHN ALBRO

ORIGIN: Unknown
MIGRATION: 1634 on the *Francis*
FIRST RESIDENCE: Boston
REMOVES: Portsmouth by 1639

OCCUPATION: Magistrate.
CHURCH MEMBERSHIP: Since his death record appears in the Friends' records, John Albro apparently became a Quaker at some time in his life.
FREEMAN: In Portsmouth section of 1655 Rhode Island list of freemen [RICR 1:299].
EDUCATION: Signed his will. Bequeathed "my great Bible" to his grandson John Anthony.
OFFICES: Assistant, 16 May 1671, 2 May 1677, 1 May 1678, 7 May 1679, 5 May 1680, 4 May 1681, 2 May 1683, 7 May 1684, 6 May 1685 [RICR 2:386, 565, 3:5, 30, 85, 99, 122, 151, 168; Newport Court Book A:1, 6, 8, 55, 57, 61, 74, 82, 87, 95, 100, 103, 105, 107, 112, 122, 126, 132, 134]. Councillor for Governor Andros, 1687 [PoTR 237].

Committee to go to "Mrs. Arnold, widow to the deceased Governor Arnold, and from her demand and receive His Majesty's Charter of this Colony, and all other parchments and writings that were in the said deceased Governor's custody," 28 August 1678 [RICR 3:17]. Committee to go to "Mrs. Ann Coddington, widow to our late deceased Honored Governor, and of her demand and receive the Charter and all other writings that were in the late Governor's custody," 8 November 1678 [RICR 3:24-25]. Committee to go to "our late Honored Governor, Major Peleg Sanford, and of him demand and receive the Charter and other papers, &c., in his custody," 2 May 1683 [RICR 3:123].

Deputy to General Court for Portsmouth, 22 May 1660, 21 May 1661, 1 March 1663/4, 2 May 1666, 4 September 1666, 6 May 1668, 29 October 1668, 22 March 1669/70, 4 May 1670, 29 June 1670, 4 May 1675, 2 May 1683 [RICR 1:428, 437, 2:22, 146, 150, 222, 236, 301, 336, 527, 3:121-22; PoTR 92, 104, 124, 132, 135, 139, 143, 151, 154, 183, 216].

Grand jury, 24 February 1661[/2], 11 March 1661/2, 13 October 1663 [PoTR 108; RICR 1:78, 2:19]. Jury, 26 May 1649, 16 July 1650 [RICR 1:5; PoTR 46; Newport Court Book A:24, 26]. Rate maker, 1651, 1662, 1675, 1681 [PoTR 53, 109, 185, 212]. Auditor, 1661, 1668, 1681, 1683 [PoTR 106, 144, 211, 219]. Coroner's jury, 1661 [PoTR 107].

Portsmouth clerk of the weights and measures, June 1649, 1650 [PoTR 43-45]. Town councillor, June 1656-84 [PoTR 71, 76, 85, 89, 93, 106, 111, 118, 129, 131, 138, 142, 148, 209-10, 214]. Moderator, 12 October 1675, 14 January 1675[/6], 21 April 1676, 5 August 1678, 11 October 1678, 31 December 1678, 2 June 1679, 23 June 1679, 14 February 1679/80, 7 June 1680, 30 August 1680, 27 December 1680, 14 March 168[0/]1, 9 July 1681, 6 March 168[1/]2, 4 June 1683, 14 August 1683, 4 January 1683/4, 10 March 1683/4, 2 June 1684, 15 August 1684, 12 December 1684, 16 March 1684/5, 1 June 1685, 14 August 1685, 30 November 1685, 19 March 1685/6, 2 April 1686, 14 January 1686/7, 7 April 1687, 20 June 1693 [PoTR 186-87, 190, 197-200, 202, 204, 206-7, 209-10, 212-13, 218-20, 222-27, 229-31, 234-35, 250]. Committee to determine the suitability of future freemen, June 1674 [PoTR 181]. Recorder of highways, 1660 [PoTR 97]. Committee to settle accounts with Newport, 31 December 1678 [PoTR 198]. Committee to run the Portsmouth line, 1660[/1] [PoTR 99]. Committee to lease Hog Island, 27 December 1680 [PoTR 207]. Committee to set site for water mill, February 1682[/3] [PoTR 217]. Committee to enlarge town, 12 January 1684[/5] [PoTR 225, 228]. Viewer of cattle going to the island, 1649-50 [PoTR 43, 45]. Lot-layer and surveyor, 1657-1678, 1693-94 [PoTR 81, 140, 154, 161, 166, 170, 194, 252, 255]. Committee to prevent destruction of common timber, 23 April 1667 [PoTR 137]. Committee appointed to go to Boston to "rightly inform his excellency concerning the affairs of Hog Island," 12 August 1687 [PoTR 237-38]. Committee to control the common lands, 2 June 1690 [PoTR 242].

On 2 December 1679, Rhode Island court ordered that "[u]pon the presentation of Captain John Albro, Assistant, for the sum of three pounds, twelve shillings, four pence, in or as money, by him disbursed, being arrested as an Assistant of this Colony, at the complaint of Mr. John Saffin, of Boston, to the Court at Boston, 28th of October, 1679, this assembly do own the said demand" [RICR 3:75].

Elected sergeant at Portsmouth, 13 March 1644[/5] [RICR 1:127]. Sergeant "in Thomas Gorton's place," 21 November 1649 [PoTR 43]. Lieutenant by 1 April 1653 [PoTR 59]. Captain by May 1677 [Newport Court Book A:55]. Major by 27 December 1680 [PoTR 207]. Elected major for the Colony, 3 May 1682 [RICR 3:108]. Portsmouth commissioner to secure Indians, 13 March 1675/6 [RICR 2:534].

ESTATE: The town of Portsmouth granted him land in 1639 on the condition that he build on it [PoTR 5]. On 19 January 1651[/2], the town granted him six acres in the swamp "in lieu of what the town oweth the said John" [PoTR 57]. On 3 July 1656, the town voted that "John Albro shall have his gun again and be acquitted of his rate for service done for the town" [PoTR 72]. On 20 November 1657, "Lieut. John Albro" had his grant of thirty-two acres laid out [PoTR 79]. In spring of 1661, after the death of Thomas Cornell, the grass at Dyer's Island was granted to John Albro and William Corry [PoTR 100].

On 24 November 1656, Ralph Earl Senior of Portsmouth sold to "Daniell Greenell" of Portsmouth thirty acres in Portsmouth, which "was given & granted by the town of Portsmouth aforesaid unto Nathaniel Potter deceased, & sold and conveyed by John Albro to James Sands, & by Jeames Sands the aforesaid land was sold to Samuell Wilson and by Samuel Wilson the said land was sold & conveyed unto William Shearman, and by William Shearman the said land was sold & conveyed unto Ralph Earle of Portsmouth Senior" [PoTR 331-32]. (This deed is apparently the only evidence for the claim that John Albro married the widow of Nathaniel Potter.)

In his will, dated 28 December 1710 and proved 12 January 1712/3, "Major John Albro of the Town of Portsmouth" ordered that "there shall be a straight line beginning at a white thorn bush standing at the circuit corner so running upon a straight line to Henry Brightman's fence where his and mine join together" and bequeathed to "my son John Albro" "all my land lying on the southeastward side of said line"; to "my two grandsons (viz:) Albro Anthony and John Anthony" equally "all the remaining part of my land lying on the northwestwardly side of the abovesaid line" in Portsmouth "containing by estimation thirty acres of land ... with all and singular the buildings, orchards, fencings, commons, liberties and privileges thereunto belonging"; to "my granddaughter Sarah Anthony daughter of my daughter Susanna Anthony" £80, half at age eighteen and half at twenty-five, or to her issue if she die before then, to be paid by Albro and John Anthony; "if my daughter Susanna should outlive her husband then she shall have equal privilege with her sons in the said house and land during her natural life"; to "my grandson Albro Anthony" moveables; to "my grandson John Anthony" moveables, including "my great Bible"; to "my granddaughter Sarah Anthony" £80 and moveables; to "my son John Albro" moveables and to "his children" 40s. "to be equally divided between them"; to "my son Samuel Albro" 50s.; to "my daughter Mary Hicks" moveables; to "my daughter Elisabeth Congdon" 50s. and moveables; to "my daughter Susanna Anthony" moveables; to "my granddaughter Dorothy Bentley daughter of my son Samuel" 16s.; "and as for what right I have in Misquamacuk Purchase I give equally between my two sons John Albro and Samuel Albro"; to "my

daughter Susanna Anthony" the residue of the moveables; "my loving
son-in-law John Anthony and my loving daughter Susanna Anthony"
executor and executrix; "my loving friends William Sanford and Giles
Slocum both of Portsmouth" to be overseers [Portsmouth Town Council
Book 2:216].

On 15 January 1712/3, "John Albro of Portsmouth" gave a receipt to
"John Anthony of Portsmouth aforesaid executor and his wife my sister
Susanna Anthony executrix" for the moveables received under his
father's will [Portsmouth Town Council Book 2:217]. On 24 January
1712/3, "Mary Hicks of Plymouth ... widow" gave a receipt to "my brother-
in-law John Anthony of Portsmouth ... and his wife my sister Susanna
Anthony" for her legacies under her father's will [Portsmouth Town
Council Book 2:217]. On 7 April 1713, "Samuel Albro of Kingstown ...
yeoman" gave a receipt to "my brother-in-law John Anthony and his wife
Susanna Anthony my sister" for the bequest to him of 50s., and "also one
legacy of sixteen shillings ... which was given unto my daughter Dorothy
Bently by my father John Albro" [Portsmouth Town Council Book 2:217].
On 13 April 1713, "John Albro of Portsmouth" gave a receipt to "John
Anthony of Portsmouth ... and his wife my sister Susanna Anthony" for
the legacy of 40s. "my father John Albro ... gave unto my children ...
several of them not being of age according to law" [Portsmouth Town
Council Book 2:217]. On 15 June 1714, "Elisabeth Condun of Kingstown"
gave a receipt to "my brother-in-law John Anthony of Portsmouth ... and
his wife my sister Susanna Anthony" for the legacies under her father's
will [Portsmouth Town Council Book 2:218]. On 23 December 1719,
"Sarah Anthony of Portsmouth ... a singlewoman" gave receipts to "my
brother Albro Anthony of Portsmouth" and to "my brother John Anthony
of Portsmouth" for the legacy under her grandfather's will [Portsmouth
Town Council Book 2:218].

BIRTH: About 1620 (aged 14 in 1634 [Hotten 278]; aged 95 or 96 at death
in 1712 [RIVR 4:Portsmouth:49, 7:84]).
DEATH: Portsmouth 1 December 1712 "in his 96th year" [RIVR
4:Portsmouth:49] or 17 December 1712, aged 96 years [RIVR 7:84].
MARRIAGE: By about 1645 Dorothy (____) Potter, widow of Nathaniel
[PoTR 331]. She died at Portsmouth 19 February 1696/7 [RIVR
4:Portsmouth:49].
CHILDREN:
      i   SAMUEL, b. say 1645 (in his 95th year at death, April 1739
           [Austin 234, citing Narragansett Church records]; at least

21 at receipt of cattle earmark, 30 November 1667 [PoTR 271]); m. say 1670 (or soon thereafter) Isabel Lawton (in her will of 8 January 1725[/6] Ruth Wodell, widow of William Wodell, made a bequest to "cousin Ruth Sweet, daughter to my sister Isabel Albro" [Austin 435, citing Portsmouth probate records]; she was Ruth (Lawton) Wodell, daughter of George and Elizabeth (Hazard) Lawton [Austin 121-22]).

ii ELIZABETH, b. say 1650; m. say 1670 Benjamin Congdon (William, apparently their eldest son, was probably born in the early 1670s, as he had children born in the late 1690s [Austin 53]).

iii MARY, b. say 1653; m. by about 1673 Thomas Hicks (their daughter Sarah married on 1 May 1693 [RIVR 4:Portsmouth:5]).

iv JOHN, b. by 1655 (chosen for the jury of trials 21 April 1676 [PoTR 190]); charged May 1679 with "begetting a child on the body of Margaret Hall" [Newport Court Book A:84; RICR 3:51-52, 74-75]; m. Portsmouth 27 April 1693 Mary Stokes [RIVR 4:Portsmouth:3].

v SUSANNA, b. probably in late 1650s or early 1660s (her first child born 25 September 1694 and her last child born 16 February 1698/9 [RIVR 4:Portsmouth:53]); m. Portsmouth 3 January 1693/4 John Anthony [RIVR 4:Portsmouth:3].

ASSOCIATIONS: Despite the ten-year gap between John's presence on the passenger list and his first appearance in Rhode Island colony records, we assume this is the same man based on his connection to WILLIAM FREEBORN, who also came to Portsmouth. This association with Freeborn is also the reason for placing Albro in Boston for his first few years in New England.

COMMENTS: On 30 April 1634, "John Aldburgh aged 14" was enrolled at Ipswich as one of "those which did not take the Oath of Allegiance or Supremacy being under aged" shipped on the *Francis* bound for New England as a servant of William Freeborn [Hotten 278].

Both Pope and Savage fail to mention any of the children but Susanna.

Many responsibilities were placed in John Albro's hands, as witness his long list of public offices. Lieut. John Albro also presented a bill of debt about work done at the fort, 5 January 1666[/7] [PoTR 136], and was one of the first men sent for upon the discovery of the burnt remains of

Rebecca Cornell in her Portsmouth home, a death for which her son, Thomas Cornell, was tried and convicted of murder [Newport Court Book A:27].

AGNES ALCOCK

"Annis Aldcock," aged 18, was enrolled at London on 1 July 1635 as a passenger for New England on the *Abigail* [Hotten 98].

COMMENTS: She appears in the list of passengers at the end of the enrollments for that date, along with a number of other young, unmarried men and women. She has not been found in any New England record.

JOHN ALDERMAN

ORIGIN: Unknown
MIGRATION: 1634 on the *Recovery*
FIRST RESIDENCE: Dorchester
REMOVES: Salem by 1636

CHURCH MEMBERSHIP: Admitted to Salem church in January 1636/7 [SChR 6]. Later annotated as "Dead."
FREEMAN: 22 May 1639 [MBCR 1:376].
EDUCATION: Signed a bill of presentments [EQC 1:160] and his will. In 1647/8 he was ordered to teach his apprentice to read and write [EQC 1:132].
OFFICES: Constable of Salem, 8 July 1639 [EQC 1:1]. Essex grand jury, 26 December 1643, 9 July 1644, 26 January 1648[/9], 26 June 1649 [EQC 1:57, 62, 153, 169; STR 1:104, 120]. Petit jury, 25 June 1639, 29 September 1640, 29 December 1640, 29 June 1641, 15 December 1645, 28 December 1646, 28 December 1648, 25 December 1650 [EQC 1:11, 21, 24, 28, 129, 181; STR 1:139, 146]. Salem fenceviewer, 4 April 1641 [STR 1:111].
ESTATE: In the 1636 Salem land grant "Mr. Jno. Alderman" received fifty acres "above Mr. Cole" [STR 1:21]. In the 25 December 1637 grant of undivided marsh and meadow "Mr. Alderman" received half an acre, for a household of two [STR 1:103].

In his will, dated 3 July 1657 and proved 3 September 1657, John Alderman of Salem, "being weak in body," bequeathed cattle to Mr. "Norice," Mr. Eliot, Mr. Eliot's Indians, Mr. Thatcher, Mr. Whiting of Lynn, Mr. "Waltom" of Marblehead, Mr. "Cobat," and John Horne of Salem; to "Ezera Clape the son of Edward Clape and Nathaniell Clape the son of Nicholas Clape" his house and land and to pay for it as follows: to "Israell Mason daughter of Major Mason ten pounds to be paid two years after my decease, the rest to be paid at three year's end by three pounds a year to Mr. Norice so long as he lives to enjoy it"; to "John Pickiring" moveables; to "Elizibeth Pickirin" clothing; to "Jonathan Pickirin my arms & all my nursery of apple trees at my ten acre lot"; to "goodwife Bufam" 20s.; to "Josuah Bufam" 10s.; and "to the rest of her children 5s. apiece"; to "Edward Clape" clothing; to "Prudence Clape her two daughters, to Barbara Stoder her two daughters & to Nicholas Clape his two daughters all the household stuff I have bedding & linen"; to "brother Marshall" old clothes; to "Mistress Fellton" 10s.; to "widow Denis" 10s.; and to "Goody Curtice" 10s. Overseers Edward Clap and John Horne. Edward Clap executor [EPR 1:256-57].

The inventory of the estate of "Mr. John Alderman," taken on 23 July 1657, totalled £105 17s. (against which were £4 10s. in debts), of which £40 was real estate: "one dwelling house with two acres of ground adjoining and ten acres of land lying in the north neck & an outlot containing about fifty acres ... with the meadow belonging to it" [EPR 1:257].

On 24 July 1663, "Ezra Clap son of Edmond Clapp of Dorchester ..., yeoman, and Nathaniell Clapp son of Nicholas Clap of the said town of Dorchester" sold to "Giles Coree of Salem ..., husbandman, one dwelling house with the appurtenances thereunto belonging & two acres upland, also fifty acres of upland with the meadow thereto belonging ..., also ten acres of upland lying in the north neck ..., which said house & several parcels of land aforespecified was given & bequeathed unto them the said Ezra & Nathaniell Clapp by the last will & testament of Mr. John Alderman, late of Salem, deceased" [ELR 4:108].

BIRTH: About 1584 (if he was "about fifty" when he got lost in 1634 [WJ 1:144]).
DEATH: Salem between 3 July 1657 (date of will) and 23 July 1657 (date of inventory).
MARRIAGE: By 1636 Jane _____ (quite possibly Jane Clapp, daughter of Nicholas Clapp of Sidbury, Devon; see ASSOCIATIONS below). "Jane Alderman" appears in the list of Salem church members compiled late in

1636 [SChR 6]. It is evident that she predeceased her husband, since she is not named in his 1657 will.

CHILDREN: None recorded.

ASSOCIATIONS: John Alderman's very interesting will bequeathed the bulk of his estate to the children and grandchildren of Nicholas Clapp of Sidbury, Devonshire, leading to the suggestion that John's wife may have been Jane, the eldest daughter of Nicholas [Stevens-Miller Anc 1:278], thus connecting John Alderman to the vast Clapp kinship network.

There are three more groupings of legatees who may also have been closely related to John Alderman or his wife, whoever she may have been. Israel Mason was Major *JOHN MASON's* only daughter with his unknown first wife [GMB 2:1227-28], and this is presumably an important clue to her identity. The Pickerings and the Buffums may also have been related in some way.

COMMENTS: "John Elderman" was a passenger for New England in 1634 on the *Recovery*, sailing from Weymouth, Dorset [NGSQ 71:171-72, 77:251].

In an entry dated 30 September 1634, Winthrop notes that

> About this time one Alderman, of Bear Cove, being about fifty years old, lost his way between Dorchester and Wessaguscus, and wandered in the woods and swamps three days and two nights, without taking any food, and, being near spent, God brought him to Scituate; but he had torn his legs much, etc. Other harm he had none [WJ 1:144].

In July 1647 John Alderman sued Henry Cook over fourteen goats, and Cook countersued for defamation [EQC 1:115]. In 1648, when Richard Hollingsworth was admonished for sleeping in church, John Alderman and Edmund Batter were witnesses [EQC 1:159]. He witnessed again in December 1649, against Mary Oliver, who had been convicted of stealing goats [EQC 1:182]. In June 1652, Thomas Scudder sued John Alderman for saying "he would lie like a dog." "Mr. Alderman confessed that he was sorry" [EQC 1:256].

In January 1647/8 Richard Graves of Salem apprenticed his son, John, to Mr. John Alderman of Salem, for ten years, the boy being between seven and eight. Alderman was to teach him to read and write, and at the end of his time to give him two good suits of apparel and a two-year-old heifer when he was seventeen [EQC 1:132].

With John Bullfinch, John Alderman took the 1 January 1644[/5] inventory of Margaret Pease of Salem [EPR 1:40] and, with Michael

Shaflinge, took the 3 January 1644[/5] inventory of Robert Pease of the same [EPR 1:42]. In 1655 John Alderman and Robert Buffum took the inventory of the estate of Robert Moulton Sr. of Salem [EPR 1:210].

WILLIAM ALFORD

ORIGIN: St Lawrence Pountney, London
MIGRATION: 1634
FIRST RESIDENCE: Salem
REMOVES: Boston by 1647

OCCUPATION: Skinner [WP 3:163]; merchant [Aspinwall 411].
CHURCH MEMBERSHIP: "Mary Alford" was among those who joined the Salem church before December 1636 [STR 1:6], but William does not appear on the Salem list. He was received into the Boston Church on 9 April 1654 [BChR 70]. His second wife, Ann, may not have been a member of the Boston Church, for baptisms of their children were credited only to William.
EDUCATION: Sufficient to carry on a correspondence with Winthrop [WP 6:398-99].
OFFICES: Salem committee to locate shops, 22 August 1635 [STR 1:10].
   Boston constable, 12 March 1659/60 [BTR 2:154].
ESTATE: In 1636 "Mr Alford" received 200 acres at Salem "where it is allotted to him provided that in case he depart to leave it desiring no advantage by it" [STR 1:22 (this grant was in the non-freeman's part of the list, indicating that Alford was not a church member at this time)]. Mr. Alford received one acre in the 25 December 1637 division of marsh and meadow, with a household of ten persons [STR 1:103].
   On 30 June 1664, William Alford of Boston, merchant, purchased from John and Mary Evered *alias* Webb of Boston, merchant, the wharf, warehouses and rights owned by Evered *alias* Webb [SLR 4:322-23]. On 10 September 1673, William Alford was one of the largest subscribers to build a new wharf at Boston [BTR 2:84].
   In his will, dated 13 April 1676 and proved 23 January 1676/7, "William Alford of Boston ... merchant ... grown aged and weak of body" bequeathed to "my loving daughter Mary Usher" £100 and "my Bible"; to "my grandchild Peter Butler" £50; to "my grandchild Hannah Butler" £50 at 18 or marriage; to "my grandchild Samuel Butler" £50 at 21; to "my

grandchild Mary Butler" £50 at 18 or marriage; if any die, their share to be divided equally among the survivors; to "my daughter Hudson" £100; to "my grandchild Elisabeth Hudson" £50 at 18 or marriage; to "my daughter Bethiah" £50; to "my son Nathaniel's child (if it be now living)" £10; to "the wife of my son Elisha" £10; to the First Church of Christ in Boston "whereof I am now member" £10; to the poor of said church £10; released all debts owed by Mr. Hudson Leverett; released Goodman Salisbury and Goodman Willis of Bridgewater and "all other my debtors who are poor one moiety of the debt they owe me"; to Mr. Peter Lidgett and his wife 20s. for rings; to Mr. Hezekiah Usher Jr., Mr. John Usher and Elizabeth his wife 10s. each; to Elizabeth Usher "daughter of said John Usher" 20s.; named "loving son-in-law Mr. Hezekiah Usher of Boston," executor, and "loving friends Mr. Anthony Stoddard and Mr. Peter Lidget," overseers; residue to be proportionally divided among Peter Butler, Hannah Butler, Samuel Butler, Mary Butler, Elizabeth Hudson "my daughter," Elizabeth Hudson "my grandchild," and "my daughter Bethiah" [SPR 6:171-72]. He followed this will with a codicil dated 9 June 1676 because Hezekiah Usher and Peter Lidgett were "both already taken away by death." He named his "loving daughter Mrs. Mary Usher and Mr. Anthony Stoddard and Deacon Henry Allen," executors. Stoddard and Allen renounced their executorship, leaving Mary Usher sole executrix.

The inventory of the estate of William Alford, taken 27 January 1676[/7], totalled £758 19s. 8d., of which £674 was real estate: "the outmost warehouse next the sea with the land or wharf whereon it standeth," £200; "three old warehouses on the north side of the land being old and not tenantable, these 3 without the land," £50; a "small warehouse on the east side of Mr. Usher's dwelling house," £10; "fourteen feet of land on the north side of said dwelling house and equal in breadth," £14; and "the remaining part of the land and wharf as it lies in broken parcels including the land and wharf that the old warehouse stands upon," £400. Mary Usher presented an adjustment to the inventory of "her late father Mr. William Alford" showing another hundred pounds of assets and over £200 in debts as well as £557 in legacies [SPR 12:136-37].

BIRTH: About 1605 (aged about 25 in 1630 [marriage allegation]; deposed aged 62 years in 1667 [SJC Case #821]).
DEATH: Buried Boston 13 January 1676/7 [NEHGR 7:207].
MARRIAGE: (1) St John, Hackney, Middlesex, 10 June 1630 Mary Draper. On 8 June 1630 a marriage allegation was entered with the Bishop of London, describing the groom as "William Alford of the parish of St.

Stephen Walbrooke, London, skinner & a bachelor, aged about 25 years,"
and the bride as "Mary Draper of Hackney in the County of Middlesex,
maiden, aged about 22 years and at the dispose of George Harwood of
London, merchant, her uncle" [Bishop of London Marriage Allegations,
Volume 13, 1629-1631, folio 49v]. On the Salem church member list, Mary
is annotated later as "dead," indicating that she probably died in the mid-
1650s.

(2) By 1658 Ann _____ (when she was mother of their son born at
Boston [BVR 65]).

CHILDREN:

With first wife

i MARY, bp. St Lawrence Pountney, London, 1 June 1631
("Mary the daughter of William Alforde skinner and
Mary his wife lying at Edward Godfrey's house in this
parish"); m. (1) by 1654 Peter Butler (eldest known child
of "Peter and Mary Buttler" b. Boston 21 January 1654[/5?]
[BVR 46]); m. (2) by 13 April 1676 Hezekiah Usher (when
her father names him in his will [SPR 12:136-37]); m. (3)
after 9 June 1676 and before 8 December 1682 Samuel
Nowell, son of *INCREASE NOWELL* (in his codicil of 9
June 1676 her father still calls her Mary Usher, but
indicates Hezekiah has died [SPR 12:136-37]; on 8
December 1682, "Samuel Nowell of Boston ... planter and
Mary his wife late relict one of the executors of Mr.
Hezekiah Usher Sr. of said Boston merchant deceased"
fulfilled one of Usher's legacies [SLR 12:311]) [Sewall 94].

ii ELIZABETH, b. say 1634; m. Boston 1 December 1659
Nathaniel Hudson [BVR 72], son of *WILLIAM HUDSON*.
(The sketch of William Hudson failed to identify this
marriage for Nathaniel [GMB 2:1036].)

iii NATHANIEL, bp. Salem 21 March 1636/7 [SChR 16]; m. by
1676 _____ _____ (father's will [SPR 12:136-37]).

iv SAMUEL, bp. Salem 17 February 1638/9 [SChR 17]; no further
record.

v BETHIAH, bp. Salem 26 June 1642 [SChR 19]; living
unmarried in April 1676 and presumably in 1679 (father's
will and codicil [SPR 12:136-37]).

vi JONATHAN ("the son of Mrs. Mary Alford a recommended
member of the church at Salem and wife to Mr. Willyam

Alford"), bp. Boston 5 December 1647 "being about 6 days old" [BChR 309]; apparently died soon.

vii   ELISHA, b. say 1651; m. by April 1676 _____ _____ (father's will [SPR 12:136-37]). (Pope incorrectly abstracts the will of William Alford by combining two separate items, thus creating a non-existent bequest to "dau[ghter] Bethia, wife of his son Elisha" [Pope 13], and this has been picked up by Torrey. We do not know the given name of Elisha's wife.)

With second wife

viii   JOHN, b. Boston 29 November 1658 [BVR 65]; bp. Boston 5 December 1658 ("son of our brother William Alford") [BChR 333]; d. Boston 29 January 1658/9 [BVR 65].

ix   JONATHAN, bp. Boston 17 May 1663 [BChR 340]; d. Boston 24 May 1663 [BVR 90].

ASSOCIATIONS: On 20 May 1659, William Alford had the power to sell land for John and Sarah Leverett of Boston and London [SLR 11:55-57, 64-66].

COMMENTS: On 11 April 1634 Francis Kirby wrote from London to John Winthrop Jr. at Agawam that

The bearer hereof Mr. William Alford, skinner, is an honest man well known to me and also to Mr. Cotton of Boston. I desire you to be acquainted with him and to show him what kindness you can without prejudice to yourself. He is come with his family to plant amongst you [WP 3:163].

On 20 November 1637, "Mr. Alfoot" was among five men of Salem to be disarmed for their support of Wheelwright and Hutchinson, and to deliver their arms to Lt. Davenport [MBCR 1:212].

Alford and John Winthrop Jr. settled into an uneasy association, trading in goats and sheep until 1653 [WP 6:342], when they fell out over payment and dealings with third parties, as we learn from a series of letters that extend into 1654 [WP 6:398-99]. Alford's trading spread south down the coast to New London [RPCC 201].

The two-hundred acre land grant in Salem was contingent upon his remaining in town, suggesting that he had some pressing reason to relocate to Boston and leave such a large parcel behind.

Benjamin Alford of Boston, merchant, is called "prob. s. of William" and "a prisoner in Barbary" by Savage, but no evidence connecting the two men was seen.

GEORGE ALLEN

ORIGIN: Unknown
MIGRATION: 1635
FIRST RESIDENCE: Weymouth
REMOVES: Sandwich 1638

FREEMAN: Propounded for freeman of Plymouth Colony 5 March 1638/9 [PCR 1:117] and admitted 3 September 1639 [PCR 1:130].

OFFICES: Sandwich constable, 3 September 1639 (replacing Thomas Armitage in mid-term) [PCR 1:125, 130]. Surveyor of highways, 3 March 1639/40, 2 June 1640 [PCR 1:141, 156]. Committee to divide meadow at Sandwich, 16 April 1640 [PCR 1:147]. Deputy for Sandwich to Plymouth General Court, 2 June 1640, 1 June 1641, 7 June 1642, 20 August 1644 [PCR 1:155, 2:16, 40, 75].

ESTATE: In the inventory of Weymouth land made about 1642, Ralph Allen and John Allen held land "first granted to George Allin" [Weymouth Hist 1:184, 188].

Received 6½ acres in the division of meadow at Sandwich, 16 April 1640 [PCR 1:149].

In his undated will, proved 7 June 1649, "Georg[e] Allen the elder late of Sandwidge" bequeathed to "all my children" 12p. apiece; to "my son Matth[e]w" one calf and 5s.; to "my wife" the old cow; "my house & household stuff to my wife during the time that she continueth unmarried but in case she marries again my will is that they shall be disposed of to be divided amongst my five least children"; to "my five least children" a cow apiece; to "my son Will[i]am the meadow I bought of Peeter Gaunt being in the second division"; "for my land & the rest of my meadow I give unto my sons Henry & Samuell"; "my adventure in the bark I leave to my wife & the five least children"; wife "Katheren Allen" to be executrix and Ralph Allen and Richard Bourne to be overseers [PCPR 1:1:84; Plymouth Wills 175; MD 9:224-25].

The inventory of the estate of "Georg[e] Allen of Sandwidg lately deceased," taken 22 September 1648, totalled £44 16s., with no real estate included; his share in the Plymouth bark was £3 [PCPR 1:1:84; Plymouth Wills 176; MD 9:225].

On 10 July 1656, "Henery and Samuell Allin of Boston ... joint heirs of a piece of land ... in the bounds of Sandwich ... with certain meadow ground thereunto adjoining and appertaining, which was the proper possession of our father George Allin deceased, and by him given to us ... with the consent of our mother, to say now Katheren Collins who hath interest therein during her life," sold this land "unto Gorge Alline of Sandwich aforesaid" [MD 25:136-37, citing PCLR 3:7].

BIRTH: By about 1585 based on estimated date of first marriage. (By the argument in *COMMENTS* below, he, and not his son of the same name, was the George Allen in the 1643 Sandwich list of men able to bear arms, and so was not yet sixty in that year and thus was born after 1583. If this estimate of 1585 is correct, then we can suggest that the age given for George on the 1635 passenger list is wildly inaccurate, and remains without any satisfactory explanation.)

DEATH: Buried at Sandwich 2 May 1648 [SandVR 1:4].

MARRIAGE: (1) By about 1610 _____.

(2) By 1627 Katherine _____ (assuming that William was her oldest Allen child). She married (2) by 1656 John Collins of Boston [MD 25:136-37, citing PCLR 3:7]. On 27 July 1670, Gideon Allen was granted administration on the estate of "John Collins late of Boston deceased" [SPR NS 1:480]. (John K. Allen noted the marriage in London on 5 November 1624 of "George Allen of London, clothworker, and Katherine Starkes of Woking," Surrey, and noted that this was a good chronological fit for the New England couple [JKA:George 5-6]. Since George Allen was very likely from Somerset, and is not known to have been in London, this suggestion seems unlikely, but, pending further research, not impossible.)

CHILDREN:

With first wife

    i   JOHN, b. about 1610 (in his will of 12 March 1689[/90], "John Allen of Swanzey" said he was "in the eighty year of my age" [Gen Adv 3:121, citing BarnPR 1:19]); m. by an unknown date Christian _____ (in his will of 12 March 1689[/90] John Allen bequeathed to "wife Christian Allen" [Gen Adv 3:121, citing BarnPR 1:19]).

    ii   ROBERT, b. say 1614; d. before 10 June 1661 [PCR 3:221-22, 4:9, 12], apparently unmarried.

   iii   RALPH, b. say 1617; m. by about 1642 Susanna[?] _____ (eldest certain child, Joseph, b. about 1642 [GMNJ 16:7]; her forename given in many sources as Susanna, but without record evidence cited).

   iv   GEORGE, b. about 1619 (aged 16 in 1635 [Hotten 283]); m. (1) by 1648 Hannah _____ (eldest child b. Sandwich 24 June

1648 [MD 14:168]) [GMNJ 16:8-10]; m. (2) after 1682 Sarah
_____, who survived him [MD 18:136].

v   ROSE, b. say 1621; m. (1) by about 1639 Joseph Holway/
Holloway/ Holley (son Joseph married by 1664 [MD
14:167]); m. (2) Sandwich 19 May 1648 William Newland
[PCR 8:6; SandVR 1:4 (a footnote to this entry tells us
"`Allen' was first written, but it was crossed out in the
same ink, and the entry completed as printed")]. (In his
will, dated 26 August 1690, William Newland named as
one of his overseers "my brother-in-law William Allen"
[MD 24:61-63, citing BarnPR 1:4-5].)

With second wife

vi   WILLIAM, b. about 1627 (aged 8 in 1635 [Hotten 283]); m.
Sandwich 21 March 1649 Priscilla Browne [MD 16:122;
SandVR 1:5; PCR 8:9], daughter of *PETER BROWNE*
[GMB 1:261].

vii   MATHEW, b. about 1629 (aged 6 in 1635 [Hotten 283]); m.
Sandwich 6 June 1657 Sarah Kirby [MD 14:169; SandVR
1:19].

viii   HENRY, b. say 1631; m. (1) by 1663 Sarah Hill (eldest child b.
Milford 21 October 1663 [FOOF 1:13]; Sarah Allen, wife
of Henry, admitted to Milford church and baptized, 7
[worn] 1666 [TAG 16:33, citing Milford church records];
Jacobus called her daughter of John Hill of Guilford,
without citing evidence [TAG 20:Supplement:3; see also
NEHGR 57:251]); m. (2) in 1685 Rebecca (_____) Rose,
widow of Robert Rose, son of *ROBERT ROSE* of
Wethersfield [FOOF 1:506; Robert Rose Gen 16-17].

ix   SAMUEL, b. say 1633; living 1656 [MD 25:136-37, citing PCLR
3:7]; no further record.

x   GIDEON, b. say 1635; m. by 1671 Sarah Prudden, daughter of
Rev. Peter Prudden (eldest child b. Boston 9 August 1671
[BVR 117]; in a deed of 16 May 1686, John Prudden, son
of Peter Prudden, calls Gideon Allen his brother [i.e.,
brother-in-law] [NEHGR 84:63-64, abstracting Milford LR
3:9]).

ASSOCIATIONS: George Allen was probably related in some way to
Ralph Allen, mason, of Sandwich (see *COMMENTS* below).

COMMENTS: "George Allyn," aged 24 [*sic*], "Katherin Allyn his wife," aged 30, " George Allyn his son," aged 16, "Will[ia]m Allyn his son," aged 8, "Mathew Allyn his son," aged 6, and "Edward Poole his servant," aged 26, sailed for New England on 20 March 1634/5 in an unnamed ship from Weymouth, Dorsetshire [Hotten 283].

A number of claims have been made regarding the English origin of George Allen, deriving him from London, Somerset or Leicester, but none of these has been more than a suggestion [GMNJ 16:3-4; TAG 36:64]. The known origins of all of his fellow passengers are in the West Country, mostly from Batcombe or Broadway in Somerset, so George Allen's origin should be sought in that area.

Savage and others, presumably following the misguided lead of the author of the history of Lynn, say that George Allen was first at Lynn, in 1636. The origin of this statement would be the belief that all the earliest settlers of Sandwich were from Lynn. But George Allen was first at Weymouth, and there is no reason to believe that he ever resided at Lynn.

At one time or another just about every young Allen male in southeastern New England has been placed as a son of George Allen. The following discussion examines some of those who are known to be sons of George, and others for whom there are claims of various likelihood. Since one of the Ralph Allens of Sandwich was not a son of George Allen, we assume that not all Allens of Sandwich were sons of George, and so have included among the children of George only those for whom there is some evidence. We have not resolved all problems here, and have not even considered all published claims. We hope, however, that we have cleared away some of the confusion.

JOHN: In the Weymouth land inventory of about 1643, both "John Allin" and "Ralph Allin" held land "first granted to George Allin" [Weymouth Hist 1:184, 188]. The most likely explanation of this arrangment is that these two men were both older sons of George Allen. Many of the early settlers of Weymouth removed to Rehoboth soon after 1643, and a John Allen is found there, who we have assigned as this son of George.

ROBERT: "Rob[er]te Allen" was one of five men from Sandwich who were sent against the Narragansetts in 1645. Pope, citing Sandwich Town Records, stated that Robert "revolted from the covenant of his father" [Pope 14]. On 10 June 1661, "John Allin, of Rehoboth, came into Court, and informed concerning his proceedings about his late deceased brother, Robert Allin, who was found dead in his house on his bed" [PCR 3:221-22,

4:9, 12]. On the basis of these records, John and Robert are placed as the two oldest children of George Allen, the immigrant.

GEORGE: George Allen, son of the immigrant, sailed to New England with his father in 1635, his age given as 16, and so born about 1619. Most authors say that he "spent all of his adult life in Sandwich, and in 1643 his name appears in a list of males living there aged between 16 and 60" [GMNJ 16:8]. Since only one George Allen appears in the 1643 list, it is therefore assumed by some that the immigrant was not included because he had already passed his sixtieth birthday.

At the same time, most authors claim that the George Allen who began having children in Boston in 1645 had earlier been in Weymouth [Savage 1:30]. There are at least three records for the name George Allen in Weymouth in the early 1640s, at a time when the immigrant had already moved to Sandwich. In March 1640 (probably 1640/1) "Tho[mas] Apellgate of Waymouth" sold to "George Allen of Waymouth my house and homelot in Waymouth accounted seven acres, also two acres of salt marsh, also eight acres of planting land at Smelt Brook & also a great lot" [SLR 1:17]. Early in 1641 "George Allen of Weymouth in New England, planter, aged about twenty-one years," deposed with regard to a dispute about lading a ship [Lechford 392]. In the Weymouth land inventory taken about 1643 is an entry for "The Land of George Allin": "Three acres in Kingoke Hill first granted to Robert Lovell" [Weymouth Hist 1:190].

The deposition would make this George Allen born about 1620, in very close agreement with the age of the son of the immigrant George Allen. Two other men with the same surname, Ralph Allen and John Allen, also held land in Weymouth in 1643, in both cases including parcels "first granted to George Allen." This set of circumstances makes it likely that George Allen, the immigrant, left three of his older sons behind in Weymouth when he moved to Sandwich, and that all three of the Weymouth records noted above pertain to George Allen, the son of the immigrant. This would further imply that the George Allen who began having children in Boston in 1645 had no earlier connection with Weymouth and was not a member of the family of George Allen, the passenger of 1635.

George Allen, son of the immigrant, must have moved to Sandwich sometime after 1643 and before 1648, when his son Caleb was born at Sandwich. Pope, in his sketch of the elder George Allen, states that "the following are not specified of George, Sen. or Jun.: Caleb b. June 27, 1648, Hester b. Dec. 8, 1648, Ebenezer, b. Feb. 10, 1649" [Pope 14]. When the younger George Allen died "Caleb Allin of Sandwich ... and others his natural brethren and sisters" and "Sarah Allin, relict of George Allin late of Sandwich aforesaid, deceased," entered an agreement in 1693 with regard to the settlement of the estate [MD 18:136, citing BarnPR 1:79]. Caleb was, then, of the third generation. Hester, born on 8 December 1648, was a daughter of Ralph Allen, mason, and Ebenezer was son of Ralph Allen, wheelwright (see below).

That this George Allen of Sandwich was the son of the immigrant George Allen is clinched by the will of William Allen of Sandwich, who was undoubtedly a son of the immigrant George Allen. William Allen, in his will dated 17 February 1697/8, left his entire estate (after the death of "Priscilla my now wife") to "my nephew Daniel Allen of Sandwich aforesaid son of my brother George Allen deceased" [MD 32:26-27, citing BarnPR 2:210]. George Allen of Sandwich had son Daniel born 22 May 1663 [SandVR 2:1238].

RALPH: For about a decade there were two Ralph Allens residing in Sandwich, whose records are difficult to disentangle. On 4 March 1650/1, "Anthony Wright commenced suit ... against Ralph Allen, Junior" [PCR 7:52, 54]. On 4 August 1651, a warrant was "directed to require Ralph Allen, Senior, personally to appear, to answer unto such misdemeanors as whereof he is accused" [PCR 2:171]. With two exceptions to be discussed later, distinctions between Senior and Junior were not seen after 7 June 1659, when "Ralph Allin, Senior," appeared in a list of men summoned to appear at court for refusing to take the oath of fidelity [PCR 3:168]. The name Ralph Allen appeared again on 6 October 1659 and several subsequent occasions in late 1659 and through 1660, in similar circumstances, without a marker for seniority [PCR 3:176, 181, 191, 201, 209], suggesting that one of the Ralph Allens died in the fall of 1659.

We may begin to make some progress in unravelling the tangle of records by examining those which state an occupation. "Experience Allin the daughter of Ralphe Allin mason" was born at Sandwich on 14 March 1651 [MD 14:109; SandVR 1:12]. Two other births for children of a Ralph Allen at about this time were "Jediah Allen," born 3 January 1646, and "Epherim Allin," born 20 March 1656 [MD 14:109, 166; SandVR 1:12, 16]. On 12 October 1662, "Jone Swift of Sandwich" (widow of William) included in her will bequests to "my grandchild Experience Allen" and "unto Jedediah Allen and Experience Allen" [MD 16:21-22, citing PCPR 2:2:16]. As noted by Charles Carroll Gardner, the entries in a fragmentary Bible record for this family may be interpreted to imply that Ralph Allen, father of Jedediah Allen, died before "Jane Swift," the testator of 1662 and grandmother of Jedediah [NEHGR 25:146; GMNJ 16:52]. Thus, Ralph

Allen, mason, whose wife was a Swift, and who had children Jedediah, Experience and Ephraim, would be the one who died in or about late 1659.

On 29 June 1663, Constant Southworth sold to "Ralph Allin of the town of Sandwich ... wheelwright ... all that my portion or lot of land lying and being at the place or places commonly called Acushena, Coaksett and places adjacent" [MD 18:171-72, citing PCLR 2:2:129]. On 15 October 1663, "Allis Bradford" sold to "Ralph Allin of the town of Sandwich ... wheelwright ... the one half of my whole entire part, portion or share of land being the one half of a purchaser's share of land ... at the place or places commonly called and known by the names of Acushena, Coaksett and places adjacent" [MD 18:176-77, citing PCLR 2:2:131b-c]. In his will of 18 December 1691, "Ralph Allin of Sandwich" made bequests to children John, Joseph, Increase, Ebenezer, Zachariah and Patience (to the last of whom he gave "one quarter part of that share of land which I bought of Constant Southward"), and named as his overseers "my brother William Allen and Edward Perry" [MD 32:166, citing BarnPR 2:75]. Thus, Ralph Allen, wheelwright, who lived far past 1659, was the son of the immigrant George Allen.

We now return to the two records which refer to Ralph Allen Senior after 1659. On 5 June 1671, "Ralph Allin, Senior," was made a surveyor of highways at Sandwich [PCR 5:58]. On 18 April 1675, "Meary Allen, the daughter of Ralph Allen Senior," was buried at Sandwich [MD 14:169; SandVR 1:19]. From 1660 until the end of the century, no Ralph Allen of Sandwich is known other than the testator of 1691. The second of these records does not necessarily refer to a living Ralph Allen, but the first certainly does.

In summary, Ralph Allen, Senior, wheelwright, son of the immigrant George Allen, died in the 1690s, and Ralph Allen, Junior, mason, of undetermined kinship, died in or about 1659.

Ralph Allen, the son of the immigrant, was apparently born about 1617, so Ralph Allen Junior, whatever his relation, must have been younger. Some of the accounts of the Ralph Allen who was not son of the immigrant had an earlier wife than the one discussed above, and by this supposed wife he had older children [JKA:Ralph 19-20; GMNJ 16:52]. John K. Allen reported the marriage at St Mary-le-Bow, London, on 6 May 1619 of Ralph Allen and Hester English, and suggested this was a first marriage for Ralph Allen Junior [JKA:Ralph 20]. Given the chronology stated above, this marriage cannot have been for Ralph Allen

Junior of Sandwich, and the earlier children ascribed to him by these authors must not be considered part of his family.

SAMUEL: Guilford (among others) thought that Samuel Allen of Braintree might be a son of George, but the Samuel Allen who acted in 1656 with Henry Allen was apparently one of George Allen's younger sons, and therefore would be two young to be Samuel of Braintree. Samuel, son of George, disappears after his deed of 1656.

GIDEON: Gideon is placed as one of the younger sons of George because he was administrator of the estate of John Collins, who would have been his father-in-law, and because he is later found in association with Henry Allen in Connecticut.

FRANCIS: Francis Allen married at Sandwich on 20 July 1662 Mary Barlow [SandVR 2:1249]; this suggests a birth for Francis about 1637. He had children Rachel, Abigail, Abia, Rebecca and Hannah [SandVR 2:1239]. These names do not suggest any connection with George or Ralph Allen, nor does any other evidence. (Pope has an entry for Francis Allen of Sandwich, noting that he was in the list of men able to bear arms in 1643, and then goes on to present records of a completely unrelated Francis of Roxbury [Pope 13].)

JAMES: James Allen of Sandwich had daughter Amy born at Sandwich in 1663, daughter Mary born in 1665, and daughter Abigail born in 1667 [SandVR 1:17]. If Amy were his eldest child, then we can estimate his birth about 1638. George Allen, son of the immigrant George Allen, had a son James born in 1658 [SandVR 1:17]. As with Francis Allen, there is no evidence beyond this to suggest a connection with George or Ralph Allen. For both Francis and James Allen, coincidence of surname appears to be the only reason for including them among the children of George Allen.

BIBLIOGRAPHIC NOTE: In 1924 John Kermott Allen prepared typescript accounts of "George Allen of Weymouth, Mass., 1635 ..." and of "Ralph Allen of Sandwich, Massachusetts," copies of which were deposited in major genealogical libraries; these volumes are cited above as JKA:George and JKA:Ralph.

In 1941, as part of his serialized "Genealogical Dictionary of New Jersey," Charles Carroll Gardner compiled accounts of both George Allen and Ralph Allen of Sandwich [GMNJ 16:1-4, 49-52]; although there are some errors in these accounts, Gardner's treatment remains the best in print on these families.

In 1990 Joan S. Guilford prepared an unreliable account of George Allen which ascribed to him fifteen children, some of whom were actually his grandchildren and others of whom were not related at all [Guilford Anc 1-10].

JOHN ALLEN

ORIGIN: Unknown
MIGRATION: 1634
FIRST RESIDENCE: Dorchester
REMOVES: Springfield by 1636

OCCUPATION: Carpenter [DTR 7].
ESTATE: On 1 September 1634, the town of Dorchester "ordered that Bray Clarke and John Allen shall build an house upon the Rock by John Holman" [DTR 7]. On the same day, John Allen was one of ten men (mostly young and single) who were granted "3 acres apiece up Naponset" [DTR 7]. On 22 November 1634, "John Alline" was one of thirteen men who were to "have six acres of land granted them [for] their small and great lots at Naponset betwixt the Indian field and the mill" [DTR 8].

COMMENTS: This is probably the same man who witnessed the Indian deed to William Pynchon dated 15 July 1636 at Springfield, and the one who was paid £3 on an undated account [possibly 1636]: "John Allen he to undertake the getting of the thatch and all other things belonging to it with lathing and nails, only the carriage of thatch excepted" for the meetinghouse [Springfield Hist 1:160]. It would not be surprising if the John Allen building a house in Dorchester in 1634 was helping to build the Springfield meetinghouse in 1636.

There are no New England records subsequent to 1636 that can be attributed to this man.

Pope would have him marry in 1651, but this marriage is for Mr. John Allyn of Hartford [GMB 3:1691-92].

He is not the "Mr. Allen" whose "strong water" was delivered into the hands of the deacons of Dorchester for the benefit of the poor "for his selling of it divers times to such as were drunk with it, he knowing thereof," on the basis of which record, Savage makes an entry for "John Allen" in Dorchester as an innkeeper in 1632 [MBCR 1:99]. John was never called "Mr."

JOHN ALLEN

ORIGIN: Hernehill, Kent
MIGRATION: 1635 on the *Abigail*
FIRST RESIDENCE: Plymouth
REMOVES: Scituate by 1645

OCCUPATION: Husbandman, planter.

FREEMAN: "John Allen" is included in the 1639 list of those at Plymouth who took the oath of fidelity, but his name was later crossed out [PCR 8:181]. Propounded for Plymouth freemanship, 3 March 1645/6 [PCR 2:95], and admitted 1 June 1647 [PCR 2:114]. ("John Allen" is the last name in the Scituate section of the "1639" list of Plymouth freemen, and was presumably appended to that list in 1647 [PCR 8:175].) In Scituate section of 1655 list of Plymouth Colony freemen [PCR 8:198].

OFFICES: Scituate constable, 4 June 1645 [PCR 2:83]. Petit jury, 1 June 1647 [PCR 2:117]. Grand jury, 7 June 1648, 4 October 1648 [PCR 2:124, 134].

ESTATE: On 5 March 1637/8, Plymouth Court granted to John Allen "six acres & half of lands more, lying on Woberry Plain, ... to be added to that he hath at Wellingsley, by Mr. Weeks, which is three acres and a half, or thereabouts, so that the whole is ten acres granted him" [PCR 1:78].

On 16 September 1641, "John Allen of Plym[outh], planter," sold to Ezra Covell, for £20, "all that his dwelling house and buildings thereunto belonging with all those his ten acres of lands where his house is and at Woebury Plain," unless Covell should fail of payment, in which case the property should revert to Allen [PCR 12:75]. On 7 March 1642[/3], "John Allen" sold to Samuel Eddy, "in consideration of one cow," "all that his house, barns & buildings with the lands thereunto belonging lying at Willingsly and Woeberry Plain" [PCR 12:90].

On 1 December 1646, "John Allin, planter," of Scituate, was purchaser of a one-thirtieth share at Conihasset from Timothy Hatherly [PCR 12:158-60].

The inventory of the estate of "John Allinge," taken 25 September 1662, totalled £168 14s. 6d., with no real estate included [PCPR 2:2:77].

On 3 October 1662, "Ann Allin, widow, and Mr. Timothy Hatherley, both of Scittuate, do hereby stand bound and are engaged unto the Governor and Court of Plymouth in the sum of four hundred pounds" and "letters of administration [were] granted by them unto the said Ann Allin to administer the estate of John Allin, deceased" [PCR 4:28].

On 5 May 1663, "[i]n answer unto a petition preferred to the Court by Judith, the wife of Will[i]am Peakes, of Scittuate, in reference unto her son Josias Leichfeld, the adopted son of John Allin, deceased, the Court have ordered and do hereby give liberty unto the said Josias Leichfeild to choose two guardians, and to present them unto the next General Court" [PCR 4:35]. On the same day, "[i]n answer unto a particular in a letter directed to the Court from Mr. Hatherley, wherein he desired the Court would take other security for the estate of John Allin, there being no other appearing to give in security, do hereby signify that they look at him as standing bound and engaged unto them in that behalf, and are not willing to a release until some other do appear to be engaged, and therefore do advise him to take the best course he can to secure himself" [PCR 4:35].

On 1 June 1663, "[w]hereas John Allin, of Scittuate, and Anna, his wife, long since took Josias Leichfeild as their adopted child, with purpose to bring him up, and to do for him as their child, and so faithfully performed during the said Allin his life, and not long before his death was mindful of him; yet being suddenly taken away, left not his mind so full and particular concerning him as he intended and might have been desired; yet so much appeared to the Court upon oath as in their apprehensions carried the true intent and force of a will. The said Josias having chosen Lieutenant James Torrey and Cornet Robert Studson his guardians, it was at this Court agreed between Anna, the relict of the said Allin, and the boy's abovenamed guardians, with the Court's approbation and liking, that the said Josias should have twenty pounds sterling paid into the hands of his guardians about Michaelmas next, by them to be improved for him, and soon after that time to be freed & to be put forth to a trade, and conveniently fitted out with suitable apparel and necessaries; and when he shall come to the age of twenty-one years, to be possessed of the farm and appurtenances given him by the said John Allin, deceased" [PCR 4:39].

On 2 June 1663, "Nicholas Baker of Scittuate aged 53 years" deposed that "I and Mr. Hatherley, being desired by John Allin of Scittuate to come to him to help him in making his will, were with him but two days before he died, and Mr. Hatherley being gone forth, and not returning so soon as he was expected, the said John Allin told me that he had sent for us to write his will and that his intent was to give Josias Leichfeild that house and land where he then lived, when he came of age, and that his wife should have the other house and land of his where Jonas Pittles then lived and that for the rest of his estate it should be in his wife's power to give to the said boy as she did see him carry himself, for said he I would have the boy beholden to my wife, and not my wife to the boy" [PCPR 2:2:76].

On 7 March 1664/5, "Mr. Micael Peirse came before this Court, and desired that an order passed by the Court in reference unto the disposing of the estate of John Allin, deceased, with special reference unto the portion of Josias Leichfeild, might be considered by the Court, and amended in respect that some detriment is likely to accrue unto him by the said order, it standing as it doth; in answer whereunto the Court returned, that forasmuch as diverse of the magistrates were absent, whose help is very requisite for the right regulating thereof, it is referred unto a more full Court for the doing of it" [PCR 4:81-82].

On 9 June 1665, "[w]hereas there was an agreement made between the Court and Lieutenant James Torrey and Cornet Robert Studson, as guardians unto Josias Leichfeild and Anna, sometimes the wife of John Allen, bearing date June, 1663, and stands upon record particularly to be seen, we do hereby declare and testify, that the said agreement we did and do clearly understand was for a full and final issue and settlement of what pertained unto the said Leichfeild from Goodman Allen's estate" [PCR 4:89]. On 5 November 1663, "Cornet Robert Stetson and James Torrey, of Scituate," gave a receipt to "Micaell Peirse, of Hingham," for £20 "the said Micaell Peirse was appointed to pay unto us for the use of Josias Leichfeild" [PCR 4:89].

BIRTH: About 1605 (aged 30 in 1635 [Hotten 90]).
DEATH: By 25 September 1662 (date of inventory).
MARRIAGE: By 1635 Anne _____. She married (2) by 1664 Michael Pierce of Hingham [PCR 4:81-82, 89].
CHILDREN: None recorded.

COMMENTS: On 22 June 1635, "Jo[h]n Allen," aged 30, husbandman, and "his wife Anne," aged 30, were enrolled as passengers at London, with certificates of conformity from the minister at Herne Hill, Kent, as passengers for New England on the *Abigail* [Hotten 90].

Examination of the Hernehill parish registers for the 1620s and 1630s reveals no Allen entries.

The Plymouth John Allen is assumed to be the man who appeared in Scituate because of the short gap between his disappearance from Plymouth and his appearance in Scituate. In Scituate we find him with wife Anne, which matches the couple that arrived in 1635. This chain of inference could well be overturned. Savage claims the Plymouth man was in that town by 1633, but no record for the name in Plymouth earlier than 1637 has been found.

Savage suggests that the 1635 passenger settled in Charlestown [Savage 1:32], but the John Allen of Charlestown did not appear in that town until 1639, and at that date had wife Sarah [Wyman 17].

John Allen does not appear in the 1643 Plymouth Colony list of men able to bear arms, indicating that he may have been physically incapacitated.

In 1889 Frederick Clifton Pierce identified the second wife of Michael Pierce as "Mrs. Annah James," who resided in Marshfield and "had a son Mark, and her daughter Abigail m. Charles Stockbridge" [Frederick Clifton Pierce, *Pierce Genealogy, No. IV, Being the Record of the Posterity of Capt. Michael, John and Capt. William Pierce* ... (Albany 1889), p. 33]. The evidence given above shows that the second wife of Michael Pierce was the widow of John Allen, and that she had no connection with the James family. More careful work done by Mary E.N. Backus in 1949 gives a more reliable picture of the James family of Marshfield, with no indication of a connection to Michael Pierce [Backus Anc 94-95]. This sort of confusion is typical of the work of Frederick Clifton Pierce.

SAMUEL ALLEN

"Sam[ue]ll Allen" was admitted to freemanship of Massachusetts Bay Colony on 6 May 1635 [MBCR 1:370].

COMMENTS: This record tells us that a man by the name of Samuel Allen had arrived in Massachusetts Bay by 1634 and that he had been admitted to one of the churches in existence at that time, as a consequence of which he was made a freeman just before the election court of 1635. But what was his later history?

We should first note that there have been claims that this Samuel Allen arrived in 1630 on the *Mary & John,* but these have no basis [GMB 3:2097].

No other New England record for a Samuel Allen has been found between this single item in 1635 and several for 1639, the latter of which represent three individuals.

1) Braintree: On 24 February 1639/40, the town of Boston granted a great lot at Mount Wollaston [later Braintree] to "Samuel Allen, of the

same [Mount Wollaston], for 7 heads, 28 acres" [BTR 1:49]. If this Samuel Allen had lived in Boston for some years before this land grant, and if he was the freeman of 1635, then he should appear before the date of the freemanship as a member of Boston church, but no record of any Samuel Allen appears so early in Boston church records. We cannot connect the Braintree man with the record of freemanship.

2) Windsor: Reference was made on 18 March 1638/9 to the house of Samuel Allen at Windsor [Windsor Hist 1:150]. He resided at Windsor until his death in 1648 [GMB 2:1038; Hale, House 447-49], and nothing connects him with the 1635 Massachusetts Bay record of freemanship.

3) Newport: In the list of those admitted to freemanship at Newport in early 1639 we find the following three consecutive names: Samuel Allen, George Allen, Ralph Allen [RICR 1:92]. These men do not appear in any other Rhode Island record, but in this list they appear among a number of others who were from Weymouth in Massachusetts Bay, and all three of these Allen names are also connected with Weymouth [see sketch of GEORGE ALLEN]. Nothing connects this Samuel Allen with the record of freemanship.

We cannot state with finality that the record of freemanship does not pertain to any one of these three men, but neither does anything in the lives of these three men lean toward identifying any one of them as the freeman of 1635.

HUGH ALLEY

ORIGIN: Stepney, Middlesex
MIGRATION: 1635 on the *Abigail*
FIRST RESIDENCE: Lynn

EDUCATION: Made his mark to his will. His inventory included "books" valued at 5s.
ESTATE: In his will, dated 2 January 1673[/4] and proved 1 July 1674, "Hugh Ally Senior" bequeathed to "my son John Ally" a sheep and lamb for his wife and children to use until the children come of age; to "my grandchild John Linsey" a ewe and the first lamb to "his [John's] brother Eleazer Linsey"; to "Samuell Linsey" the increase of the sheep, to be kept until they are all of age; to "my grandchildren Eleazer Linsy's children" lambs; to "Martha Mills and her child Martha Mills" sheep; residue to "my

wife" to dispose at her death to "my children as she sees most need" [EPR 2:407-8, 301:53-54].

The inventory of the estate of Hugh Alley, taken on 7 February 1673[/4], totalled £60 17s. 4d., of which £10 was real estate: "one house and one acre of land & half" [EPR 2:408, 301:54].

BIRTH: About 1608 (aged 27 in 1635 [Hotten 97]; deposed 1662 "aged about 53" [SJC Case #448; EQC 2:394-95]).
DEATH: Lynn 25 January 1673[/4].
MARRIAGE: By 1641 Mary _____. She survived to administer his estate on 1 July 1674 [EPR 2:408].
CHILDREN (all born Lynn):
   i   MARY, b. 6 January 1641[/2]; m. Lynn 6 June 1667 John Lindsay.
   ii   JOHN, b. 30 November 1646; m. Lynn "middle" August 1670 Joanna Furnell.
   iii MARTHA, b. 31 July 1649; m. Lynn 1 April 1671 James Mills.
   iv   SARAH, b. 15 April 1651; m. Lynn [blank] August 1668 Eleazer Lindsay.
   v   HUGH, b. 15 October 1653; m. Lynn 9 December 1681 Rebecca Hood.
   vi   SOLOMON, b. 2 August 1656; killed with Thomas Lothrop, one of the "flower of Essex" to die at Bloody Brook on 18 September 1675 [Bodge 137-38].
   vii HANNAH, b. 1 June 1661; almost certainly the unnamed daughter of "Hugh, sr." who d. Lynn 30 October 1674.
   viii JACOB, b. 5 August 1663; no further record.

COMMENTS: On 30 June 1635, "Hugh Alley," aged 27, servant of HENRY COLLINS, was enrolled at London, with a certificate of conformity from the minister at Stepney, Middlesex, as a passenger for New England on the *Abigail* [Hotten 97]. Hugh Alley did not receive land in the 1638 Lynn land division, indicating that he may then still have been in service to Henry Collins.

On 26 June 1655, Hugh Alley sued "Mr. Jon. Beckes & Company, undertakers of the ironworks at Lynn, and Mr. Gifford, their late agent," for debt [EQC 1:394].

On 31 March 1657, Hugh Alley was presented for "being drunk at John Hathorn's," and on 1 July 1657, he was fined 10s. for being drunk (perhaps the same offense) [EQC 2:36, 50].

In 1662, Hugh Alley, giving his age as 53, deposed in the dispute over JOHN HUMPHREY's farm [SJC Case #448; EQC 2:394-95].

In his will Hugh Alley named explicitly only his four eldest children, who were already married by that time. The remaining, younger children were referred to only indirectly, and so we have no way of knowing whether son Jacob was still alive in 1674 or not.

BIBLIOGRAPHIC NOTE: In 1899 Sidney Perley published a brief, undocumented account of Hugh Alley and his agnate descendants [Essex Ant 3:49-52]. Perley gave 25 January 1674 as the date of death of Jacob, the youngest child of the immigrant; but this date does not appear in the published Lynn vital records, and it is the same as the date given for the death of the immigrant himself.

In 1990 Alicia Crane Williams prepared an account of a line of descent from Hugh Alley through his son Hugh [Chase-Wigglesworth 49-54].

WILLIAM ALMY

ORIGIN: South Kilworth, Leicestershire
MIGRATION: 1635 on the *Abigail*
FIRST RESIDENCE: Lynn
REMOVES: Sandwich 1637, Portsmouth 1642

OCCUPATION: Planter.
FREEMAN: Oath of fidelity at Sandwich, 1639 [PCR 8:184]. In Portsmouth section of 1655 Rhode Island list of freemen [RICR 1:299].
EDUCATION: Signed his deed of 22 June 1642. Signed his will.
OFFICES: Deputy for Portsmouth to Rhode Island General Court, 16 May 1648, 23 May 1650, 11 March 1655/6, 17 March 165[5/]6, 19 May 1657, 14 October 1663, 24 November 1663 [RICR 1:210, 326, 327, 354, 504, 508; PoTR 44, 75]. Rhode Island petit jury, 16 July 1650, 11 March 1655/6, 2 March 1660/1, 1 October 1661, 25 April 1666, 7 May 1666, 28 April 1668 [PoTR 46, 69, 102, 108, 133, 140; RICR 1:326; RICT 2:43, 48-49]. Grand jury, 28 February 1662/3, 13 October 1663, 13 October 1665, 9 May 1670 [PoTR 116, 130; RICT 2:19, 91]. Committee to "agitate and bring in their result of four bills delivered to them," 19 May 1657 [RICR 1:355-56]. Colony assessor for Portsmouth, 19 October 1663 [RICR 1:507]. Portsmouth delegate to "join with Newport in the purchase of Cunnuniquut Island ... and Dutch Island with it" [PoTR 66].

Portsmouth town meeting moderator, 7 March 1659/60 [PoTR 91]. Portsmouth assessor, 15 September 1659 [PoTR 91]. Portsmouth deputy warden, 4 June 1660 [PoTR 93].

ESTATE: On 3 April 1637, "Will[ia]m Almey" was one of the "ten men of Saugust" who "shall have liberty to view a place to sit down & have sufficient lands for three score families," thus establishing the town of Sandwich [PCR 1:57]. On 16 April 1640, "Mr. Almey" received eight and a half acres in the division of meadow at Sandwich [PCR 1:149]. On 22 June 1642, "Will[ia]m Almy late of Sandwich" sold to "Edmond Freeman of Sandwich the younger ... one dwelling house in Sandwich aforesaid with all appurtenances together with all the lands whatsoever to me belonging lying within the bounds of Sandwich aforesaid and also all such lands or moneys which either now do belong or hereafter shall accrue to me the said Will[ia]m Almy by way of satisfaction for sundry charges by me disbursed in my undertakership for the laying out of the lands in Sandwich aforesaid" [PCLR 1:84].

On 28 November 1643, "Mr. Almy" received eight acres of planting ground in Portsmouth [PoTR 23]. On 5 January 1656[/7?], "William Almy ... of Portsmouth" sold to Richard Bulgar of Portsmouth "a grant of eight acres of land granted to me the said William Almy within the common fence" [PoTR 342-43].

On 14 November 1644, William Almy was one of three men "to have land at the wading river" at Portsmouth [RICR 1:82]. On 29 April 1650, "[i]t is granted unto Mr. Will[iam] Almy to have that land that lyeth at the head of his farm to come to the same height that Phillip Shearman his land now runneth viz: to leave two rod between Newport path and the said land" [PoTR 45, 65].

On 17 October 1659, "William Almy ... of Portsmouth ... plant[er]" deeded to "my son John Almy dwelling ... with me a part of my farm whereon I now dwell, on the south side thereof ... the said land being about fifty acres" [PoTR 372].

In his will, dated "the last of February 1676" [i.e., 28 February 1676/7] and proved 23 April 1677, "William Almy" ordered "my body to be buried by my son John if I die here upon my farm"; "if my wife outlive me she shall have all during her natural life and after her death Christopher shall have half my farm ... which is next to the land which I gave to my son John Almy," the malthouse to be shared between Christopher and John; "the other half of my farm ... to my son Job Almy with my dwelling house and two orchards"; "for my cattle and the moveables what is remaining at our deaths I give to my daughter An and my daughter Catharen each of them two parts and to my son Christopher Almy and my son Job Almy each of them one part"; to "my grandchild Bartholomew West" £20 when he comes of age; "my two sons Christopher Almy and Job Almy" to be executors [PoLE 1:144].

BIRTH: About 1601 (aged 34 in 1635 [Hotten 93]), son of Christopher and _____ (Clarke) Almy of South Kilworth, Leicestershire [NEHGR 71:320].
DEATH: Between 28 February 1676/7 (date of will) and 23 April 1677 (probate of will).
MARRIAGE: By license dated 17 July 1626 Audrey Barlow ("Williamus Almie de South Kilworth," gent., "etatis 26 annorum," and "Audream Barlowe de Lutterworth ... etatis 26 annorum," with the consent of Stafford Barlowe of Lutterworth, gent., father of the said Audrey [Archdeaconry of Leicester Marriage Licenses, 1621-1632, folio 28v; NEHGR 71:318]. She died after 28 February 1676/7, when she was named in her husband's will.
CHILDREN:

i   ANNIS, bp. South Kilworth 26 February 1626/7 [NEHGR 71:317]; m. by 1649 John Greene (eldest child b. Warwick 10 August 1649 [RIVR 1:Warwick:165]; in a letter of 5 November 1690, John Greene referred to brother Christopher Almy [RIHSC 21:132]; Ann, widow of Captain John Greene, d. Warwick 6 May 1709, aged 82 [RIVR 1:Warwick:166]).

ii CATHERINE, b. say 1630; m. about 1652 Bartholomew West (see COMMENTS below).

iii CHRISTOPHER, b. about 1632 (aged 3 in 1635 [Hotten 93]; "under the age of twenty-one years old" on 8 December 1652 [PrTR 15:59]; in his will of 4 September 1708 "Christopher Almy of Portsmouth" declared himself to be "in the seventy-seventh year of my age" [Portsmouth Town Council Book 2:213]); m. 9 July 1661 Elizabeth Cornell (date of marriage given in secondary sources [e.g., NEHGR 71:322], but not found in published Portsmouth vital records), daughter of Thomas and Rebecca (Briggs?) Cornell [TAG 19:230, 35:107, 36:16-18; RIHSC 21:126-27].

iv JOHN, b. say 1637; m. by 1668 Mary Cole, daughter of *JAMES COLE* of Plymouth [PCLR 3:326; GMB 1:423; Austin 238]. (As this couple had no children, the estimate of marriage date derives from their appearance in a deed of 1668. Mary Cole's date of birth was estimated as 1632, and the marriage may well have taken place some years earlier, so John's date of birth is estimated to fit into a convenient gap in the list of children of the immigrant. Both these estimated dates of birth may be off by some years.)

v   JOB, b. say 1639; m. by 1664 Mary Unthank, daughter of Christopher Unthank (eldest known child b. 20 January 1664 [Austin 211, citing an unknown source]; on 1 September 1677, "Christopher Unthank, inhabitant of Portsmouth," with "Susan Unthank," made a deed of gift to "my son-in-law Job Almy of the same town" [Warwick LE A2:310-11]).

COMMENTS: The 1618-9 heralds' visitation of Northamptonshire includes a pedigree of "Almey of Badby," which shows William Almy, his parents, uncles, cousins, and paternal grandparents and great-grandparents [Walter C. Metcalfe, *The Visitations of Northamptonshire Made in 1564 and 1618-19* ... (London 1887), p. 61].

In 1625 "Edward Clement, clerk, sued William Almey, yeoman, son and executor of Christopher Almey, deceased, about the parsonage of Lutterworth [co. Leicester] and a bond connected therewith" [NEHGR 71:318, citing Court of Requests, James I, Bundle 397].

Massachusetts Bay records contain three entries which apply to another WILLIAM ALMY, present in Massachusetts in 1631 and 1634 [GMB 1:44-45, citing MBCR 1:88, 122, 244]. These records have been employed to argue that the subject of the present sketch came to New England in 1630, returned to England in 1634, and came a second time to New England in 1635. But as these are two different men, we have only the evidence that the William Almy currently under consideration arrived in 1635, with no evidence of an earlier presence in New England.

On 17 June 1635, "W[illia]m Almond," aged 34, "Awdry Almond," aged 32, "Annis Almy," aged 8, and "Chri[stopher] Almie," aged 3, were enrolled at London as passengers for New England on the *Abigail* [Hotten 93].

The immigrant of 1635 does appear in Massachusetts Bay records within months after his arrival. On 1 March 1635/6, it was "ordered, that all the bills & writings about one Rob[er]te Way shall be delivered into the Court, & that Ensign Jennison, Edward Burton, & Sam[ue]ll Hosier, shall pay 20s. apiece to Will[ia]m Almy, as also that the said Rob[er]te Way shall be taken from Mr. Stoughton, where now he is, & put to the said Will[ia]m Almy, & him shall serve till he hath satsfied the sum of £3, which if he do, he shall pay 20s. thereof back again to Sam[ue]ll Hosier" [MBCR 1:163-64].

On the same day the same court ordered that "[w]hereas, in a suit betwixt David Johnson & Will[ia]m Almy, concerning one James Ludam, sometimes servant to either of them, there was a judgment of £5 granted to Will[ia]m Almy against David Johnson, but upon some consideration execution was respited, & now, by consent of all parties, it was agreed that the said £5 shall be borne equally betwixt them, that is to say, that the widow Johnson shall pay five nobles, & James Ludam the sum of five nobles to the said Will[ia]m Almy, & he to lose the rest" [MBCR 1:164].

On 4 December 1638, "W[illia]m Almy" was one of several Sandwich men fined "for keeping swine unringed" [PCR 1:107]. On 1 June 1641, "Georg[e] Allen, of Sandwich, became party to the action that Edward Dotey prefers against Will[ia]m Alney [*sic*] of Sandwich" [PCR 2:18]. On 7 December 1641, "attachment of a calf (in the hands of Rob[er]te Boatefish, of Sandwich) of the goods of Will[ia]m Almey, was made, ... to answer the jury 6s. 6d., and 3s. to the clerk for charges of a suit he left unpaid when he left the town of Sandwich" [PCR 2:28].

In a letter of estimated date 23 May 1650 to John Winthrop Jr., Roger Williams, in describing the activities of the crew of a French prize vessel, reported that "one of them (having lain with Mr. Amie's daughter of Portsmouth) is like now to marry her. The parents and the English are troubled greatly" [RWCorr 313-14]. This cannot be daughter Annis, who had married John Greene by 1649, so, unless there is a third daughter otherwise unrecorded, this record must refer to daughter Catherine. She does not appear on the 1635 passenger list with her parents and two siblings. If she was born in New England, then, it could be no earlier than the latter half of 1635, which would make her no more than fourteen at the time of the incident noted above. The probable resolution is that Catherine was born in England just before or after her brother Christopher, and either was omitted from the passenger list or came at a later time. We therefore estimate her date of birth as about 1630, although a date around 1634 would also be consistent with the other evidence. Furthermore, if this record does apply to Catherine, then she could not have been married to Bartholomew West in 1650. Pending more detailed investigation of the family of Bartholomew West, we estimate that the marriage took place about 1652.

In November 1652 "William Almy of Rhode Island" sued John Smith of Warwick, merchant, claiming that Smith and his partner William Field "doth detain & keep from the said William Almy ... the quantity of five anchors & a half of liquors," worth £40; the town of Providence first dismissed the case, but early in 1652 reexamined the evidence and found for Almy [PrTR 2:67, 69, 15:50-53, 57-61; RWCorr 382, 384; WarTR 79].

On 27 June 1654 at Ipswich, Captain Kempo Sebada sued Christopher Almy "for detaining his bark ten or eleven months" [EQC 1:347]. On 26 September 1654, Christopher Almy sued William Dyer "for selling him a vessel valued at £56 10s., which was unjustly taken from Captain Sebada. As both parties belonged to another jurisdiction and the case concerned the state, plaintiff withdrew" [EQC 1:363]. On 17 March 1655/6, the case was brought before Rhode Island court, which gave "Christopher Almie, or his father in his behalf, ... authority hereby to demand of Mr. Nicho[las] Easton" the state's share of the value of the vessel [RICR 1:330]. The case dragged on for several years, without a clear resolution [RICR 1:350, 387-9, 425, 430, 440].

On 16 October 1669, the town of Portsmouth voted to institute a suit against William Almy for throwing a fence across a highway which "doth lead to one of the most principal watering places for cattle in this town," and Almy began a countersuit; the town won the suit in the court of trials and began on 6 July 1671 to try to enforce their victory [PoTR 150-52, 155-56, 164; RICT 2:94-95].

BIBLIOGRAPHIC NOTE: In 1887 Austin published a substantial account of the family of William Almy [Austin 236-39]. In 1913 George Andrews Moriarty published a limited selection of records showing the immigrant's immediate ancestry [EIHC 49:172-76]. In 1917 George Walter Chamberlain published a number of English wills and parish register entries, from which he compiled three generations of the paternal ancestry of the immigrant (in agreement with Moriarty's work) [NEHGR 71:310-24]. Moriarty also published some briefer notes on the Almy family [RIHSC 21:131; TAG 20:119-20].

JOSEPH ALSOP

ORIGIN: London
MIGRATION: 1635 on the *Elizabeth & Ann*
FIRST RESIDENCE: Unknown

REMOVES: New Haven by 1644

OCCUPATION: Ship master. In spring of 1652/3, Joseph Alsop was freed from training and watching because he was master of a vessel above 15 tons [NHTR 1:164]. In 1681 the possibility that a bell for the New Haven meetinghouse be brought from Massachusetts Bay in Joseph Alsop's vessel was lengthily discussed [NHTR 2:415]. He was called "Skipper Alsop" in the proceedings of 20 June 1687 [NHTR 3:52].

In 1644 Joseph Alsop of New Haven affirmed in court that

> he had sailed for John Evance two years, & it was long ere he could get him to account, and that being come to account, & he was to have his money, he said he was merely cheated by him as at last [NHCR 1:299-300].

From 1681 to 1690 Joseph Alsop annually signed a receipt for goods transported on his vessel [NHLR 1:78, 92, 141, 256, 268, 353, 401, 453, 477]. (This was not the son assuming the occupation of the father. The son Joseph died 12 January 1690/1 [TAG 35:251], whereas the father was still referred to as "Skipper Alsop" as late as 10 December 1694 [NHTR 3:111].)

CHURCH MEMBERSHIP: By the early 1660s, Joseph Alsop was sitting in the short seats at the upper end of the meetinghouse, with other men ranked as sergeants, and his wife sat in the side seats above the door [NHTR 1:511, 513].

FREEMAN: New Haven oath of fidelity, 1644 [NHCR 1:139]. Admitted a freeman at New Haven on 8 June 1657 [NHTR 1:316].

EDUCATION: Signed receipts as ship master.

OFFICES: New Haven jury, 6 February 1665/6, 6 March 1665/6, 5 March 1666/7, 6 August 1667, 5 April 1670, 8 April 1670, 3 January 1670/1 (as "Joseph Alsup Sen[io]r") [NHTR 2:169, 171, 200, 206, 259, 274].

New Haven constable, 28 December 1674 [NHTR 2:326]. Rate collector, 15 January 1682/3 [NHTR 2:428]. Fence viewer, 25 April 1693 [NHTR 3:103].

ESTATE: In 1648 Joseph Alsop was a tenant in Mrs. Eldred's out lots, being one of those who "are to have 6 acres within the two mile in 3 parts" [NHCR 1:94]. On 3 April 1649, Joseph Alsop told the court "that he desired to leave the six acres of land the town gave him and Christopher Todd was willing to have it" [NHCR 1:450].

On 6 March 1654/5, land, including a house, once owned by John Livermore, Theophilus Higginson and Thomas Willitt, was passed to Joseph Alsop [NHTR 1:232].

On 14 February 1669/70, Joseph Alsop requested a piece of ground "against his house" [NHTR 2:255]. On 13 February 1670/1, the town granted him thirty feet by two rods, 4 feet from the upper side of his house [NHTR 2:286-7]. In the 1680 third division on the west side of New Haven, Joseph Alsop Sr. was granted 56 acres based on 9 heads and £100 of estate [NHTR 2:408]; this land was laid out on 7 March 1683/4 [NHLR 1:222].

On 9 June 1684, "Joseph Alsup senior of New Haven" recorded his landholdings in New Haven: "one houselot containing half an acre and twenty rods ... with two dwelling houses that standeth on the said homelot and other outhouses"; "one warehouse standing near the creek between the warehouses of Mr. Thomas Trowbridge and John Prout"; ten acres of meadow "which he had by way of exchange with Sergeant John Winston"; four acres at the Beaver Pond; twenty-eight acres of upland "lying in the second division of the suburbs quarter"; six acres and a half and twenty-five rods of upland in "the first division which belonged at first to John Livermore"; three acres of meadow "belonging to the allotment of the aforesaid John Livermore being in the Solitary Cove"; and "one parcel of land in the third division lately laid out by the town order containing fifty-six acres bounded as is described by the bill under the surveyor's hand recorded in the page 222" [NHLR 1:209-10].

On 3 February 1686/7, "Joseph Allsup senior ... enters caution concerning a certain house and land belonging to it, which house and land was sold by Eleazer Morris of New Haven unto the said Joseph Allsup and the said Morris refuseth to make conveyance thereof according to law" [NHLR 1:320]. On 16 February 1693/4, "Joseph Alsup of New Haven do, in the behalf of my son Daniell Alsup of said place now absent, protest against the sale of the house, warehouse and homelot of my son Joseph Alsup late of New Haven deceased and do by these presents forbid any person or persons to buy the same with any other lands belonging to the said Joseph Alsup deceased" [NHLR 1:587].

On 10 December 1694, "Skipper Alsop's" motion to exchange his meadow and land at Beaver Pond for two acres of meadow was granted [NHTR 3:111]; on 30 March 1696, Joseph Alsop and the town of New Haven exchanged land, Alsop receiving two acres of salt meadow on the Great Island in East River, and the town receiving four acres of meadow or swamp at Beaver Pond [NHLR 1:667]. On 8 March 1696/7, "Joseph Allsop propounded to the town to see if they could help him to his meadow lying in Solitary Cove" and at the next town meeting they ordered that the town surveyor lay out the meadow [NHTR 3:135-36].

On 29 [torn] 1699, "Hannah Alsop of New Haven," singlewoman, made bond to act as administrator of the estate of Joseph Alsop Senior of New Haven, deceased [NHPR Case #198].

BIRTH: About 1621 (aged 14 years in 1635 [Hotten 58]).

DEATH: New Haven 8 November 1698 [NHVR 1:80].

MARRIAGE: By 1647 Elizabeth Preston, daughter of WILLIAM PRESTON (in his will of 9 July 1647, William Preston made a bequest to "Joseph Alsop's wife my daughter" [NHVR 1:104n (published); NHVR 1:166-68 (original)]).

CHILDREN:

   i   JOSEPH, b. say 1648; m. New Haven 25 November 1672 Abigail Thompson [NHVR 1:31], daughter of John Thompson [TAG 35:251]. Joseph Alsop d. 12 January 1690/1 and she m. (2) John Miles [TAG 35:247-54].

   ii ELIZABETH, b. 22 June 1650 [NHVR 1:2]; on 29 April 1657, John Winthrop Jr. treated "Joseph Alsop's daughter of 7 years" [WMJ 38]; m. by 1677 Thomas Talmadge (first known child b. 2 December 1677 [New Haven VR 1:46]) [TAG 35:251].

   iii SARAH, b. 8 September 1652 [NHVR 1:8]; d. New Haven 24 January 1698/9 [NHVR 1:80], unmarried.

   iv MARY, b. 3 October 1654 [NHVR 1:11]; m. New Haven 2 November 1680 John Miles [NHVR 1:48; TAG 35:247-54].

   v   ABIGAIL, b. 4 November 1656 [NHVR 1:13]; m. New Haven 14 July 1681 John Rowe [NHVR 1:48; TAG 35:251].

   vi HANNAH, b. 2 December 1659 [NHVR 1:18]; d. by 9 August 1722, unmarried [NHPR Case #197; TAG 35:251].

   vii JOHN, b. 3 January 1661/2 [NHVR 1:18]; no further record.

   viii LYDIA, b. 26 July 1665 [NHVR 1:22]; m. New Haven 8 November 1688 James Trowbridge [NHVR 1:63].

   ix DANIEL, b. 13 August 1667 [NHVR 1:27]; d. New Haven 11 January 1698/9 [NHVR 1:80], unmarried.

   x   JEMIMA, b. 10 February 1670/1 [NHVR 1:33]; m. New Haven 24 March 1691/2 John Paine [NHVR 1:65].

ASSOCIATIONS: On 4 February 1650/1, Joseph Alsop requested letters of administration on the estate of his brother THOMAS ALSOP [NHTR 1:58].

COMMENTS: On 13 April 1635, "Joseph Alsopp," aged 14, was enrolled at London on the *Elizabeth & Ann* as a passenger to New England [Hotten 58].

On 7 February 1653/4, Joseph Alsop acted as agent for "Mistress Evance" in the matter of money due her from the estate of Henry Bishop [NHTR 1:199]. In January 1656/7 he was again an attorney, this time for Robert Graye of Salem in the matter of a claim against the estate of John Roberts [NHTR 1:294]; this case dragged on into 1659 [NHTR 1:385]. He represented Mrs. Sheafe of Boston in a matter of a bark owned by John Tompson [NHTR 1:422-23].

Alsop was fined, with two others, for failing to rebuild his fence ten days after it had been burned down. The court remitted the fine on 14 May 1649 [NHCR 1:459].

As a mariner, Joseph Alsop had contact up and down the coast, and often carried news with him [NHTR 2:4]. He was a victim of Zubah Lampson's pilfering in 1664 [NHTR 2:91].

In his will, dated 16 January 1643[/4] and proved 10 February 1646[/7], "John Allsopp" of Bonsall, Derbyshire, gentleman, made bequests to "my two brothers and sister now living in New England" as well as "Sister Jane Jackson now wife to Mr. Roger Jackson of Ashburne," Derbyshire, "my eldest brother Mr. Anthony Allsopp of Allsopp in the Dale," and "my grandmother Mrs. Jane Allsopp" [Waters 425-27, citing PCC Fines 34]. In 1892, Charles Baldwin suggested that the two brothers and sister were George Alsop, Timothy Alsop and Elizabeth (Alsop) Baldwin, wife of Richard Baldwin, and that they were cousins of Joseph and Thomas Alsop of Connecticut [NEHGR 46:366-69]. Jacobus also thought that all these Alsops were related [Ackley-Bosworth 187-88]. Further research must be undertaken to confirm or refute these guesses.

THOMAS ALSOP

ORIGIN: Unknown
MIGRATION: 1635 on the *Elizabeth & Ann*
FIRST RESIDENCE: Unknown
REMOVES: Stratford by 1650

ESTATE: On 4 February 1650[/1], "Joseph Alsop desired the [New Haven] court to grant him letters of administration upon some estate of his

brother's which is in the hands of Moses Wheeler at Stratford, but the
Court, understanding that his brother was a planter at Stratford, told him
that it belonged not to this Court to do it, but to the Court at
Connecticote because his brother was a planter in that jurisdiction"
[NHTR 1:58]. There is no record of a probate for Thomas at Hartford, so
perhaps Joseph did not follow the town's advice.

BIRTH: About 1615 (aged 20 in 1635 [Hotten 78]).
DEATH: Stratford by 4 February 1650/1.
MARRIAGE: None recorded. (The request by Joseph to administer his
brother's goods suggests that there was no widow to perform this duty.)
ASSOCIATIONS: His brother, JOSEPH ALSOP, asked for administration
of his estate in 1650/1 [NHTR 1:58].

COMMENTS: "Tho[mas] Alsopp," aged 20, was enrolled at London on 14
May 1635 as a passenger for New England on the *Elizabeth & Ann* [Hotten
78].

ROBERT ANDREWS

ORIGIN: Unknown
MIGRATION: 1634
FIRST RESIDENCE: Ipswich

OCCUPATION: Innkeeper, licensed to keep an ordinary by the General
Court on 3 September 1635 [MBCR 1:159], and again, was allowed on 13
May 1640 to "draw wine at Ipswich," according to town regulations
[MBCR 1:292].
CHURCH MEMBERSHIP: Admission to Ipswich church prior to 6 May
1635 implied by freemanship.
FREEMAN: 6 May 1635 [MBCR 1:370].
EDUCATION: He signed his will, and was concerned enough with the
higher education of his son, Thomas, to make provision therein for his
continued schooling and possible university attendance.
ESTATE: On 13 January 1637[/8], the town of Ipswich granted to
"Goodman Andrewes and Goodman Haffield 2 acres of ground in the
place where Mr. Tuttell['s] hayricks stand" [ITR]. About 1637 there was
granted "to Robert Andrewes one hundred acres of land having Chebacco

Creek on the northwest ..., likewise ten acres of meadow lying upon Labour-in-vayne Creek ..., likewise twelve acres of land lying on the north side of the town ..., likewise six acres on the hill lying on the north side of town ..., also an houselot in town near the river" [ITR].

In his will, dated 1 March 1643[/4] and proved 26 March 1644, "Robert Andrewes of Ipsw[i]ch" named "eldest son John Andrews" executor, and bequeathed "unto my wife Elizabeth Andrews" £40; to "John Griffin the son of Humfry Griffin" £16 to be paid to him when he turns 21, "& if he shall die before he comes to that age it shall return to my two sons John & Thomas Andrews"; "concerning my son Thomas Andrews my will is that he shall live with his brother John Andrews three years two of which he shall be helpful to his brother John Andrews in his husbandry and the last of the three years he shall go to school to recover his learning and if he shall go to the university or shall set himself upon some other way of living his brother John shall allow him ten pounds by the year for four years & then fifteen pounds by the year for two years succeeding after"; "concerning the fourscore pounds which is to be paid unto my son-in-law Francklin's daughter Elizabeth Francklin my grandchild my will is that if she die before the debt is due it shall be thus disposed ten pounds of it shall go to my son Daniell Hovie's child Daniell Hovey my grandchild and the other seventy pounds shall be divided between my two sons John & Thomas Andrews and if those my two sons should die then thirty pounds should be divided between my kinsmen John, Thomas, & Robert Burnum by equal portions & twenty more should go to Humphry Gryffin's two other sons & the other twenty shall go to Daniell Hovey. And because my son John Andrews is yet under age I do commend him unto Thomas Howlet as his guardian until he shall come of age" [EPR 1:27-28].

BIRTH: By about 1593 based on estimated date of marriage.
DEATH: Between 1 March 1643/4 (date of will) and 26 March 1644 (probate of will).
MARRIAGE: By about 1618 Elizabeth _____ (probably a widow).
CHILDREN:

i   ALICE, b. say 1618; m. by 1638 William Franklin (eldest known child b. Boston 3 October 1638 [BVR 6]). She died before 2 April 1641 on which date her father and William Franklin, her husband, agreed that £40 of her marriage portion, still unpaid, should remain in her father's hands until her daughter, Elizabeth Franklin, should marry or

reach age 18, whereupon an additional £40 should be
added to it and £80 should be turned over to her; careful
provisions were made for Elizabeth's upbringing and
education by her grandfather or her stepmother, Phebe
Franklin, in the event William Franklin died during her
minority [Annis Spear Anc 152-53, citing EQC 3:162-66].

ii   ABIGAIL, b. say 1623; m. by 1643 Daniel Hovey, and had one
child at the time her father made his will.

iii JOHN, b. about 1628 (deposed 29 March 1659, as "John
Andrews Jr.," "aged about thirty-one years" [EQC 2:145];
deposed 28 November 1659 "aged about thirty-one years"
[EQC 2:185]; deposed 1 May 1661 "aged about thirty-two
years" [EQC 2:284]); m. Sarah Holyoke, daughter of
Edward Holyoke, Esq., and his first wife, Prudence
Stockton, of Lynn, baptized at Tanworth, Warwickshire,
on 18 September 1623 [Hale, House 643-44; NEHGR
147:20-21].

iv   THOMAS, b. say 1630, under age on 1 March 1643/4 when his
father provided for him in his will, and clearly younger
than his brother, John, was a school-master in Ipswich
and d. there unm. on 10 July 1683 [EQC 9:120]. The
inventory of the estate of "Mr. Thomas Andrews," schoolmaster, was "proved" on 16 September 1683, and
included "goods & books, £38 9s.," "debts, as appears by
his book of accounts, £356 2s. 6d.," a lot at Hogg Island,
£8, and other debts and expenses [EQC 9:120-21]. John
Ward, sometime resident of Ipswich, in his will dated 28
December 1652 and proved on 25 March 1656, stated,
"My books I do give to Thomas Andrews of Ipswich and
also my chirurgeon chest and all that is now in it" [EQC
1:420-21].

ASSOCIATIONS: Robert Andrews, in his will, speaks of his "kinsmen
John, Thomas & Robert Burnum," without specifying the relationship.
People have invented parents for the Burnham boys, making their father
one Robert Burnham, and their mother one "Mary Andrews," an alleged
sister of Robert Andrews, thereby making the boys nephews of Robert
Andrews, all without any evidence whatsoever [Warner-Harrington 17].

COMMENTS: Robert Andrews has been placed by various writers as a
passenger on the ill-fated *Angel Gabriel* in 1635 [e.g., Dommerich Anc 43],

but this is a physical impossibility. Andrews was admitted to Massachusetts Bay freemanship on 6 May 1635, an event which implies his arrival in New England by 1634 and which required his presence in New England on 6 May 1635. The *Angel Gabriel* was riding at anchor near Bristol, England, on 26 May 1635, and did not sail for New England until 4 June [Young's First Planters 450-53].

Robert Andrews of Ipswich owed the late Rev. Joseph Avery £2 at the time of the latter's death on 15 August 1635 [MBCR 1:154]. Robert also signed a petition of the inhabitants of Ipswich, dated 21 June 1637, in which the petitioners opposed the recall of John Winthrop Jr. [WP 3:432-33].

Estimating the years of birth of Robert Andrews's children is a challenge. It would appear that Elizabeth, the purported stepdaughter, was born by 1619; she was undoubtedly married by 1639, and likely before that, as she had three sons by the time Robert Andrews made his will. ELIZABETH, b. England by 1619; m. (1) say 1639 Humphrey Griffin of Ipswich; m. (2) Hugh Sherratt of Haverhill. In his will, Robert Andrews left bequests to the three sons of Humphrey Griffin, but did not state any relationship to them, although the amounts were similar to that left to his stated grandson, Daniel Hovey. On 30 March 1647, Elizabeth, widow of Robert Andrews, was admonished by the court for cursing and reviling her son-in-law, Humphrey Griffin. Likewise, Humphrey Griffin of Ipswich was presented "for reviling his wife's mother" [EQC 1:113]. Referring to a stepmother as "mother" was common, and does not prove an umbilical connection. Later, when the estate of Thomas Andrews, unmarried son of Robert Andrews, was administered, Daniel Hovey, husband of Abigail Andrews, wrote to the court listing the nieces and nephews of the deceased, so as to show the names of the heirs. All were named but Elizabeth's five children, and they did not petition the court to be recognized as heirs, either. Moreover, the court ordered distribution of the estate of Thomas Andrews to the children of his "only brother," and to "the children now living who descended from the two sisters" [EQC 9:120]. It is, therefore, clear that Elizabeth was not a sibling of the whole blood to the rest. The question then is whether she was a daughter of Robert Andrews from a previous marriage, or a daughter of Elizabeth, wife of Robert Andrews, from a previous marriage. Because Robert Andrews did not name Elizabeth in his will, though she was still living, and because her mother and her husband were in court later for calling each other names, and because her children are not named as heirs to Thomas Andrews's estate, we conclude that Elizabeth was more likely a daughter of Elizabeth (_____) Andrews from a previous marriage than she was a daughter of Robert Andrews himself, and in that we concur with Walter Goodwin Davis who also considered this problem [Annis Spear Anc 152].

Alice, whose daughter Elizabeth Franklin was born in Boston on 3 October 1638, could not have been born herself much later than our suggested birth year for Elizabeth. And Abigail, who had a son by the time her father made his will, was probably not born later than 1623. There is then a gap of approximately five years before John's birth. We know that Thomas was younger than John, since John was asked in his father's will to look out for Thomas, hence the estimated year of birth of 1630 for the son Thomas. All of these, with the possible exception of John, are estimated dates, and some tolerance in either direction must be allowed for in the absence of more substantial evidence.

Pope, in error, states that Capt. Andrews made his will on 2 April 1641, and that it was proved on "22 (8) 1647." Pope took the erroneous date from the agreement between Robert Andrews and William Franklin [Pope 18; Annis Spear Anc 152-53].

SAMUEL ANDREWS

ORIGIN: London
MIGRATION: 1635 on the *Increase*
FIRST RESIDENCE: Saco

OCCUPATION: Dyer.
CHURCH MEMBERSHIP: On 7 September 1636, "Samuell Andrewes" paid £3 towards the minister's rate in Saco [MPCR 1:facing page 1].
EDUCATION: Jane Mackworth's inventory included "one Bible & another book" valued at 10s.
ESTATE: On 20 November 1638, Richard Vines of Saco, Esq., leased to John West "now of Saco," husbandman, for one thousand years, one mansion or dwelling house with the appurtenances, and 100 acres of land, lying on the south side of Saco River, "heretofore in the tenure or occupation of Thomas Coole, or Samuel Andrews, or one of them," in consideration of the payment of two shillings and "one fat capon in the feast of the nativity of our Saviour" [YLR 1:34-35, 79-80], but this land was leased by Vines on 1 August 1638 to Jane Andrews of Saco, widow, the

indenture mentioning that it consisted of "one hundred acres of land together, and next adjoining unto that parcel of land whereon her late deceased husband Samuel Andrews had built an house, & fenced in about four acres of ground, being part of the said hundred acres," reference to the mansion house being conspicuously absent [YLR 1:42-43]. The property seemed to be in the hands of Mr. Joseph Bolles in 1654, the record describing it as being "next Mr. Mackworth's lot," and subsequent to that Vines evidently sold it to Richard Hitchcock of Saco, planter [YLR 1:43].

In her will, dated 20 May 1676 and proved 24 October 1676, "Jane Mackworth of Boston ... widow" bequeathed to "my loving sons-in-law Abraham Addams & William Rogers all my housing, lands & meadows ... at Casco Bay ... during the term of their natural lives" and after their decease to be divided equally among their living children (a note at the end of the will directs that the potential division include "the children Rebecca had by Nathaniel Wharfe & what Sarah hath by her now husband"); to "my said sons-in-law Abraham Addams and William Rogers" two oxen; to "each of my children a pewter platter"; to "my daughter Rebecca Rogers" moveables; to "my daughter Sarah Addams wife of the said Abraham Addams" moveables; to "my daughter Purchase my great iron pot"; "all my clothes and household linen shall be equally divided amongst my four daughters"; residue to "my dear children to be equally divided between them"; "my said sons-in-law Abraham Addams & William Rogers" to be executors [SPR 6:131].

The inventory of the estate of Jane Mackworth, taken 25 May 1676 and 2 June 1676, totalled £123 4s. [SPR 12:98].

BIRTH: About 1598 (aged 37 in 1635 [Hotten 60]).
DEATH: Before 1 August 1638 when Jane is called a widow in a deed [TG 3:50, 81, citing YLR 1:42-43].
MARRIAGE: By 1625 Jane _____. She married (2) by about 1641 Arthur Mackworth of Falmouth and resided there and at Boston, where she died between 20 May 1676 and 24 October 1676 [TG 3:50-51].
CHILDREN [TG 3:50-56]:

> i   JAMES, b. 21 February 1625/6, bp. St James, Garlickhithe, London, 5 March 1625/6; m. (1) Dorcas Mitton; m. (2) Boston (int.) 6 August 1696 Margaret (Phips) Halsey [TG 3:59-67; *Twenty-eighth Report of the Boston Record Commissioners, Boston Marriages from 1700 to 1751* (Boston 1898), p. 349].

   ii   REBECCA, b. 1 April 1628, bp. St Peter, Paul's Wharf, London, 16 April 1628; bur. St James, Garlickhithe, London, 6 October 1629.

   iii   JANE, b. 21 February 1629/30, bp. St James, Garlickhithe, 7 March 1629/30 (called 3 years old at emigration [Hotten 60]); m. by 1658 Francis Neale [TG 351-52].

   iv   ELIZABETH, b. 4 May 1632, bp. St James, Garlickhithe, 13 May 1632 (called 2 years old at emigration [Hotten 60]); m. (1) by about 1653 Richard Pike; m. (2) by about 1657 *THOMAS PURCHASE* [GMB 3:1532]; m. (3) Lynn [blank] November 1678 John Blaney [TG 3:52-54].

   v   SAMUEL, bp. St James, Garlickhithe, 16 August 1634; bur. there 16 September 1634.

   vi   PHILIPPA, b. about 1636; m. (1) Falmouth 25 November 1662 George Felt, son of *GEORGE FELT* [GMB 1:663]; m. (2) Rowley 19 December 1682 Samuel Platts; m. (3) Rowley 9 April 1690 Thomas Nelson [TG 3:54-56].

ASSOCIATIONS: Samuel Andrews brought with him in his family a servant named "Ellyn Longe" [Hotten 60], misread as "Ellyn Loucje," aged 20 [TG 50], and as "Elen Lougie" [GDMNH 65]. Also on board the *Increase* with the Andrews family were ROBERT NANNEY [Naney], aged 22 years, ROBERT SANKEY, aged 30 years, and JAMES GIBBONS, aged 21 years, who also settled in Saco [Hotten 60]. All four of the adult males in this list have next to their names the annotation "Robert Cordell goldsmith in Limbert Street [probably Lombard Street] sent them away."

COMMENTS: "Samuell Andrewes, aged 37 years," was examined on 14 April 1635 at London for passage to New England on the *Increase*, along with "Jane the wife of the abovesaid Sam[uel] Andrewes, 30 years, Ellyn Longe her servant aged 20 years, Jane Andrewes her daughter aged 3 years, [and] Elizabeth Androwes her daughter aged 2 years" [Hotten 60].

Savage did not name the daughter Philippa, and believed James was born here, evidently because his name does not appear on the list of those examined for passage [Savage 1:53-55]. Pope confuses this Samuel Andrews with a man of the same name who resided in Charlestown.

Samuel Andrews was called "citizen of London" by George Cleeve [GDMNH 65], which may have been true, but also may have been a product of Cleeve's fertile imagination.

BIBLIOGRAPHIC NOTE: The most comprehensive treatment of this extended family was published in 1982 by Robert J. Dunkle [TG 3:45-95]. This article was motivated by the entries in an old family Bible, which provided much information not available elsewhere.

THOMAS ANDREWS

ORIGIN: Unknown
MIGRATION: 1634
FIRST RESIDENCE: Dorchester

OCCUPATION: Mason. On 9 September 1661, Thomas Andrews was warned "to daub the meeting house or else to take the fines that is due for not training of him" [DTR 107]. (On at least two other occasions he did work for the town, which may also have called on his masonry skills. On 9 November 1657 "Goodman Andrus" was paid 8s. for "work about [the] meeting house," and in 1670 "Tho[mas] Andrews for work at the meeting house" was paid 8s. [DTR 81, 173].)

CHURCH MEMBERSHIP: Although they were not members in full communion, both Thomas and his wife Ann signed the covenant of the Dorchester church, by virtue of which their daughter Hannah was granted letters of dismission to Roxbury in 1660 [DChR 33].

EDUCATION: Signed Dorchester petition of 1641 with his mark [DTR 106]. Signed his will with his mark.

OFFICES: Dorchester fenceviewer, 13 February 1653/4, 9 February 1656/7, 12 March 1659/60, 12 March 1665/6 ["senior"], 8 March 1668/9 [DTR 67, 85, 100, 132, 158]. Dorchester bailiff, 3 December 1660 [DTR 102].

ESTATE: On 22 November 1634, Thomas Andrews was granted two acres in Dorchester [DTR 8]. On 17 December 1635, he was granted three acres in lieu of a great lot [DTR 13]. In the division of the Neck on 18 March 1637/8, he received 2 acres 1 quarter and 30 rods of land and in the other land 2 acres 3 quarters and 10 rods [DTR 31].

In his will, dated 6 April 1667 and proved 4 August 1673, Thomas Andrews of Dorchester, "being aged and the same accompanied with many infirmities," bequeathed to "my dear wife Anne ... the use of my whole estate" to become the property of "my son Thomas Andrews" upon her death; son Thomas to pay "my daughter Hanna Hopkins" £7, and 20s. apiece to "her children as they come of age ... my daughter shall accept of it as the full of her portion with what she hath already had"; "dear wife and my son Thomas Andrews," executors; "loving friends James Blake and Samuel Clap," overseers; "the legacies of 20s. apiece extend no further than to the children born before the date hereof" [SPR 7:318].

The inventory of Thomas Andrews Sr. of Dorchester, taken 20 May 1673 at the request of the widow and son, totalled £181 7s. 5d., of which £147 10s. was real estate: "house, barn, orchards, arable land, pasture land and meadow"; the inventory also included £1 9s. 7d. in "mason's tools and other implements" [SPR 7:318].

William Hopkins, having formerly "put in caution against the will," had composed his differences with the other heirs by the time of the proving [SPR 7:318].

BIRTH: By about 1611 based on estimated date of marriage.
DEATH: Dorchester 20 May 1673 [DVR 28].
MARRIAGE: By about 1636 Ann _____. She died at Dorchester on 13 January 1684[/5] [DVR 120].
CHILDREN:

> i   HANNAH, b. say 1636; m. say 1656 William Hopkins (three children of William Hopkins were baptised on the same day at Roxbury, 6 May 1660 [RChR 123]).
> ii   THOMAS, bp. Dorchester 23 June 1639 [DChR 151]; m. Dorchester 31 December 1667 Phebe Goard [DVR 22].

ASSOCIATIONS: He called James Blake and Samuel Clap "loving friends" when he appointed them his overseers [SPR 7:318].

COMMENTS: Pope misinterpreted the Dorchester church records which say: "Hannah the wife of Henery Garnesy admitted the 22 of the (2) 60 The day above said Hannah the daughter of Thomas Andrews desired letters of dismission to join to the church of Roxbury" [DChR 33]. Pope declared that Thomas Andrews's daughter Hannah was the wife of Henry Garnsey based on this record. Garnsey's wife was actually Hannah Munning. Clearly what was meant was that Hannah, daughter of Thomas Andrews, petitioned the church the same day that Hannah Garnsey was admitted, not that they were the same person.

THOMAS ANDREWS

ORIGIN: Unknown
MIGRATION: 1635
FIRST RESIDENCE: Hingham

ESTATE: "The several parcels of land & meadow legally given unto Thomas Andrews by the town of Hingham": 18 September 1635, "for a houselot five acres of land, two acres of it butting upon the town street ... the other three acres of it lyeth at the further end of the same neck"; 1635, "for a planting lot five acres lying upon the Old Planters' Hill in the Plain Neck"; 1635, "for a Great Lot twelve acres called by the name of Ward Hill"; 1635, "two acres being the one half of a little island that is compassed about with the Home Meadow"; and, 1647 [*sic*], "six acres of salt marsh at Conyhassett, it is the third lot in the first division ... which said meadow was given in satisfaction for six acres of meadow which he should have at Nantascutt" [HiBOP 17]. ("The several parcels of land & meadow legally given unto Joseph Andrews by the town of Hingham" included "for a houselot five acres of land, two acres of it butting upon the town street southward and upon part of his own land and upon part of Richard Betscome's land northward, bounded with the land of Thomas Andrews his father eastward and with the land of Mr. William Walton westward, the other three acres of it lying at the further end of the same neck bound with the land of Thomas Andrews his father eastward and with the land of Richard Betscome westward and butting upon Broad Cove northward and upon his own land and upon his father's Thomas Andrews land southward" [HiBOP 18].)

BIRTH: By about 1572 based on estimated date of marriage.
DEATH: "Old Thomas Andruce" died at Hingham on 21 August 1643 [NEHGR 121:16].
MARRIAGE: By about 1597 _____ _____. She is not seen in any New England record.
CHILD:

    i   JOSEPH, b. about 1597 (d. Hingham 1 January 1679/80, aged 83 [Hingham Hist 11]); m. by 1632 Elizabeth _____ (eldest child b. 1632 [Small Gen 859]).

COMMENTS: In his entry for this man Pope says to "See Plaisto," which leads to the entry for *JOSIAS PLASTOWE*, which includes a reference to Plaistow's servant *THOMAS ANDREWS* [Pope 364]. The servant would be much too young to be the immigrant to Hingham in 1635, and father of Joseph Andrews of Hingham, so this must be a different man [GMB 1:45, 3:1481-82].

The entire chronological structure of this family is based on the age at death given for Joseph Andrews. As this would make him about thirty-five at marriage, this age may be somewhat inflated, which would move the estimated birth date and marriage date for Thomas Andrews some years later.

BIBLIOGRAPHIC NOTE: A brief account of the immigrant, with a much longer account of his son Joseph, has been prepared by Lora A. W. Underhill [Small Gen 852-60]. On the basis of earlier accounts she included THOMAS ANDREWS of Dorchester as a second son of the immigrant, but with a clear acknowledgement that there is no evidence for this.

Alicia Crane Williams has also traced a line of descent from this immigrant [Chase-Wigglesworth 55].

WILLIAM ANDREWS

On 5 April 1635, "William Andrews of Hampsworth, carpenter," was enrolled at Southampton in the *James* of London for New England [Drake's Founders 56].

COMMENTS: This William Andrews cannot be connected with records for any of the men by that name in early New England. There was a William Andrews who in 1638 assaulted his master, Mr. Henry Coggan, and as a result was placed as servant to John Endicott [MBCR 1:246, 269]. These two records cannot be connected to any of the other known men by the name, but there is also nothing to connect the 1638 William Andrews with the passenger of 1635.

WILLIAM ANDREWS

ORIGIN: Unknown
MIGRATION: 1634
FIRST RESIDENCE: Cambridge
REMOVES: Hartford 1637

OCCUPATION: Schoolmaster at Hartford, 1643, 1648, 1650, 1655 (and probably other years) [HaTR 65, 87, 94, 108].
CHURCH MEMBERSHIP: Admission to Cambridge church prior to 4 March 1634/5 implied by freemanship.
FREEMAN: 4 March 1634/5 (as "Mr. Will[ia]m Andrewes," first in a sequence of nineteen Cambridge men [MBCR 1:370]).
EDUCATION: Sufficient to be schoolmaster and town recorder at Hartford. His inventory included "1 ring, 3 spoons & books" valued at £3 10s.
OFFICES: Cambridge selectman, 23 November 1635 [CaTR 14]. Constable, 23 November 1635 [CaTR 14].
  Connecticut jury, 5 March 1644/5 [CCCR 1:122].
  On 12 January 1651[/2], "Mr. William Andrewes was chosen recorder for the town of Hartford" [HaTR 97].
ESTATE: On 1 December 1634, William Andrews was granted five acres in the Westend Field in Cambridge [CaTR 10]. On 20 August 1635, he received a proportional share of 2½ in the undivided meadow [CaTR 13].
  In the Cambridge land inventory on 10 October 1635, "William Andrewes" held two parcels: "in the town one house with backside about half a rood"; and "in Westend Field about five acres" [CaBOP 29]. In the 8 February 1635/6 listing of those with houses in Cambridge, William Andrews was credited with two in the town [CaTR 18]. On 25 September 1637, "Mr. Samuell Sheeperd ... bought of Mr. Will[iam] Andrews his house & all his land & rights in the common that lay in Newtowne" [CaBOP 41].
  Granted thirty acres at Hartford on 3 January 1639/40 [HaTR 23]. In the Hartford land inventory he held eleven parcels: one acre and one rood "on which his dwelling house now standeth with other outhouses, yards & gardens"; two acres of upland; eighteen acres and two roods of upland (annotated "four acres of this sold to J: Ensigne"); two roods and twenty-five perches in the Little Meadow; eight acres in the South Meadow; four acres, three roods and twenty perches of "meadow lying in Hockanum";

six acres of swamp in the Great Swamp; six acres and three roods of "swamp lying in Hockanum"; one acre and one rood of "Indian Ground lying in the South Meadow which he had of John Crow" (annotated "March 7th 1657," presumably indicating the date of purchase); "[o]ne parcel of upland (which he had of Mr. Thomas Wells, magistrate) containing 40 acres ... and is in exchange for all his upland on the east side of the Great River"; and "one parcel of upland which he received of the town containing thirteen acres" [HaBOP 388-90].

On 8 April 1645, the earmark of "Will[ia]m Andrewes" was recorded at Hartford [HaTR 336].

In his will, dated 1 April 1659 and proved on an unknown date, William Andrews bequeathed to "Abigail, my wife, my house, barn and homelot as it is enclosed between my son Edward Grannis and me," also "all my meadow and swamp lying in the South Meadow and that lyeth in the place called Hockanum, and all my upland elsewhere, during the time of her natural life," also some cattle and all other moveables so long as she remains unmarried; if she marry again, "such of the moveables as she can conveniently spare shall be disposed of among our children as she seeth meet"; to "my son John one working steer"; "Abigail, my wife, shall dispose of my land, meadow, swamp, housing and homelot among our children, to every one of them some, as she shall think fit"; "I hereby do make Abigail, my wife, my sole executrix ... and I do also entreat my friend Edward Stebbing and my brother George Grave to assist my wife and to see this my will executed & performed" [HaPR 2:129; Manwaring 1:92].

The inventory of the estate of "William Andrewes of Hartford," taken 8 August 1659, totalled £211 14s. 11d., of which £90 was real estate: "his house, barn and homelot," £22; "meadow land, 9 acres 3 roods," £42; "swamp land, 3 acres 1 rood," £13; and "upland ground, 49 acres," £13 [HaPR 2:130; Manwaring 1:92].

On 20 January 1674/5, "Abigail Berding of Hartford ... widow for and in consideration of my natural love unto my son John Andrews & my son Thomas Andrews & my son Sam[ue]ll Andrews & my son-in-law Thomas Spencer Junior & in pursuance of the last will & testament of my loving husband William Andrews sometimes of Hartford deceased" deeded "unto them the said John Andrews, Thomas Andrews & Thomas Spencer Junior all that houselot & the buildings & fences thereon that sometimes pertained to my said husband William Andrews situate & being in Hartford as it is now divided, possessed & enjoyed by them, and unto him the said John Andrews one piece of land lying in the south meadow of the aforenamed Hartford, containing by estimation three roods, ... as also one acre of woodland on the west side of Rocky Hill, & unto them the said John Andrews, Thomas Andrews & Sam[ue]ll Andrews all other my lands whatsoever" in Hartford, "provided that none of the abovenamed grantees or their heirs shall or may make any alienation of the premises during the natural life of me the said Abigail Berding without my special allowance & consent in writing, & also that during the term of the natural life of me the said Abigail Berding the said John Andrews, Thomas Andrews & Samuell Andrews shall well & truly pay or cause to be paid from each of them every year yearly, the full sum of two pounds ten shillings" [HaPR 1:25; Hartford PD Case #478].

On 4 April 1683, "the widow Bearding's last will & inventory of her estate was exhibited in court & proved & ordered to be recorded" [HaPR 4(court):68]. The will was nuncupative, consisting of two depositions. "George Graves aged about 52 years and Samuell Andrewes aged about 36 years" testified "that we were with widow Abigail Bardin about three weeks before she died and she did before us declare that her will was that after her death the said Samuell Andrewes should have what was due to her from Gherrard Spencer and that the said Samuell should pay her debts and funeral charges, also that her daughter Hester Spencer should have all her other goods excepting some few things she had given away before; Samuel Andrewes excepteth only of the above written that he remembers not his grandmother's words that he should pay her debts and funeral charges but owneth that he will do it" [Hartford PD Case #478]. "Paul Peck Senior aged about 60 years testifieth that a day or two before widow Bardin died she told him that her will was that Samuell Andrewes should have what was due to her from Gherrard Spencer and that the rest of her goods she gave to her daughter Hester Spencer except some few small things she had given away before" [Hartford PD Case #478]. The inventory of "the estate of the widow Beardin deceased March 26 1682/3" totalled £19 10s. [Hartford PD Case #478].

BIRTH: By about 1607 based on estimated date of marriage (but possibly earlier [TAG 35:56]).

DEATH: Between 1 April 1659 (date of will) and 8 August 1659 (date of inventory).

MARRIAGE: By about 1632 Abigail _____. (She may have been sister of George Graves of Hartford [TAG 35:56].) She married (2) Nathaniel Barding [Manwaring 1:182-83; TAG 35:56] and died 26 March 1682/3

(unless this is the date the inventory was taken, in which case she probably died somewhat earlier) [Hartford PD Case #478].
CHILDREN:

 i JOHN, b. say 1632; m. (1) by 1669 _____ Lilly; m. (2) by 1675 Mary _____ [TAG 35:58 (for discussion of both marriages)].

 ii ABIGAIL, b. say 1634; bur. Fairfield [blank] May 1653 [CTVR 30].

 iii ELIZABETH, b. say 1636; m. Hartford 3 May 1655 Edward Grannis [CTVR 32].

 iv THOMAS, b. Hartford 4 May 1638 [CTVR 31]; m. by about 1670 Hannah Kirby, daughter of John Kirby (in the settlement of the estate of John Kirby in 1677 in the list of children is "Hannah, wife of Thomas Andrews, age 27 years" [Manwaring 1:212; TAG 35:58]).

 v ESTHER, b. Hartford [blank] September 1641 [CTVR 31]; m. by about 1666 Thomas Spencer, son of *THOMAS SPENCER* [TAG 27:166-67, 35:57; GMB 3:1720].

 vi SAMUEL, b. Hartford 20 October 1645 [CTVR 31; HaVR 576 (omits day of birth)]; m. about 1668 Elizabeth Spencer, daughter of *THOMAS SPENCER* [TAG 27:163, 35:59; GMB 3:1720].

ASSOCIATIONS: Francis Andrews of Hartford and Fairfield and John Andrews of Farmington may have been younger half-brothers of William Andrews [TAG 35:57, 59].

COMMENTS: In our earlier discussion of *WILLIAM ANDREWS* of Lynn, we gave reasons for believing that the first Cambridge William Andrews, the subject of the present sketch, was the freeman of 4 March 1634/5 [GMB 1:46]. In his discussion of the present William Andrews, Jacobus distinguishes carefully between the two men of the name at Cambridge, and concludes that the Mary Andrews, wife of William, who died at Cambridge on 19 January 1640 was wife of the second man of that name, and not of the Hartford man [TAG 35:55].

On 6 June 1636, the town of Cambridge agreed "with Mr. Andrewse for his man to keep the calves for 12s. a week so long as we think good only we are to provide him a man for the present if he shall require it of us" [CaTR 23].

On 26 October 1636, the Massachusetts Bay General Court acknowledged that "Newe Towne presented a book of their records under the hands of Will[iam] Andrews, constable, John Beniamin, & Will[iam] Spencer" [MBCR 1:182].

Barbour claimed that the Christian Andrews who married John Birchard, son of THOMAS BIRCHARD, was a daughter of this William Andrews [*Families of Early Hartford, Connecticut* (Baltimore 1977), pp. 9-10], but she was daughter of the widow Catherine Andrews [TAG 64:88-89].

BIBLIOGRAPHIC NOTE: In 1958 Donald Lines Jacobus compiled an account of this William Andrews and his sons, carefully distinguishing him from other men by the name of William Andrews [TAG 35:55-59].

In 1991 Edward H. Little prepared a summary of the life and family of William Andrews [*Colonial Ancestors* ... (Camden, Maine, 1991), 1-7].

JOHN ANTHONY

On 24 March 1633/4, "John Anthony" is included in the passenger list of the *Mary & John* of London, preparing to depart from Portsmouth, with the annotation "left behind"; a later annotation indicates that he was one of six men who had intended to sail on the *Mary & John*, but stayed behind with intent to sail on the *Hercules* [Drake's Founders 70-71].

COMMENTS: As the name John Anthony does not appear in New England for many years after 1634, there is no assurance that this man did come on the *Hercules*. The claim has been made that he did come in 1634, and is the same as the John Anthony seen in Portsmouth, Rhode Island, in 1640 and later, but the Rhode Island man may just as well have been a second man of the same name.

JOAN ANTROBUS

ORIGIN: St Albans, Hertfordshire
MIGRATION: 1635
FIRST RESIDENCE: Unknown

ESTATE: On 16 May 1614, administration on the estate of Walter Antrobus of St Albans was granted to "Jane Antrobus, his widow" [Archdeaconry of St Albans, Diocese of London, Admon Act Book, 1574-1638].

BIRTH: About 1567 based on date of marriage.

DEATH: 1635 or later, perhaps in New England.

MARRIAGE: Joan Arnold married at St Albans 8 February 1586/7 Walter Antrobus [St Albans PR 135]. He was buried at St Albans 5 April 1614 [St Albans PR 204].

CHILDREN (all baptized St Albans, Hertfordshire):

    i   WILLIAM, bp. 25 June 1587 [St Albans PR 25]; m. St Albans 6 July 1607 Alice Denton [St Albans PR 140].

    ii   WALTER, bp. 1 June 1589 [St Albans PR 28]; no further record.

    iii   ROBERT, bp. 21 February 1590/1 [St Albans PR 29]; no further record.

    iv   JOAN, bp. 25 June 1592 [St Albans PR 30]; m. (1) St Albans 23 October 1609 Thomas Lawrence [St Albans PR 141]; m. (2) by 1628 JOHN TUTTLE [TAG 51:173].

    v   ELIZABETH, bp. 6 August 1598 [St Albans PR 35]; presumably she who m. St Albans 5 May 1617 John Cowley [St Albans PR 144].

    vi   HENRY, bp. 25 April 1600 [St Albans PR 36]; bur. St Albans 14 June 1602 [St Albans 196].

ASSOCIATIONS: Through her daughter, Joan (Antrobus) (Lawrence) Tuttle, this immigrant was ancestress of several members of the Tuttle, Lawrence and Giddings families (see sketches of JOHN TUTTLE, GEORGE GIDDINGS, JOHN LAWRENCE, THOMAS LAWRENCE and WILLIAM LAWRENCE).

In his will of 27 January 1664[/5], "William Antrobus of London Esq." bequeathed to "William Antrobus in New England the sum of forty shillings for a legacy and that is all he shall have out of my estate" [PCC 11 Hyde]. Sir Reginald Antrobus suggests that this may be the William Antrobus baptized at St Albans 7 April 1611, son of William Antrobus [St Albans PR 46; Antrobus Pedigrees 34, 108], and therefore nephew of Joan (Arnold) Antrobus [Antrobus Pedigrees 12-13, 96]. But the testator of 1665 and the William baptized in 1611 were third cousins once-removed, so the legatee may be another William more closely related to the testator.

COMMENTS: On 2 April 1635, "Joan Antrobuss," aged 65, was enrolled at London, with a certificate of conformity "from the minister of St Albans, Hertfordshire," as a passenger for New England on the *Planter* [Hotten 45].

No record of Joan Antrobus has been found in New England. She may have chosen at the last minute not to make the trip, or she may have died aboard ship. If she did make the passage to New England, she probably resided in Ipswich with her daughter and son-in-law.

BIBLIOGRAPHIC NOTE: In 1929 Sir Reginald L. Antrobus published extensive information on the Antrobus families of England, including data relating to the branch of interest to us here [Sir Reginald L. Antrobus, *Antrobus Pedigrees: The Story of a Cheshire Family* (London 1929), 12-13, 96-97 (cited above as Antrobus Pedigrees)].

In 1941 Mary Walton Ferris published a brief account of Joan Antrobus [Dawes-Gates 1:64-65].

THOMAS ANTRUM

ORIGIN: Salisbury, Wiltshire
MIGRATION: 1635 in the *James*
FIRST RESIDENCE: Salem

OCCUPATION: Weaver.
CHURCH MEMBERSHIP: Admitted to Salem church on 24 March 1638/9 [SChR 8].
FREEMAN: 18 May 1642 [MBCR 2:291].
EDUCATION: Made his mark as witness to the 1659 will of John Woodis, and to his own will [EPR 1:290, 414].
OFFICES: Essex grand jury, 27 June 1643, 29 November 1659 [EQC 1:53, 2:182, 194]. Petit jury, June 1651, 25 September 1660 [EQC 1:229, 2:225].

Salem tax collector "for the ten acre lots & from the bridge to Michael Shaflin's house," 1657 [STR 1:210].
ESTATE: In the 1636 Salem land grant "Thos: Antram" received 30 acres, not in the "freeman's land" [STR 1:22]. In the 25 December 1637 grant of meadow and marsh "Tho: Anthom" received three-quarters of an acre based on five persons in his household [STR 1:103].

On 3 April 1637, Edmund Batter was granted ten acres of marsh "in lieu of twenty acres which he should surrender out of his farm for his brother Antram" [STR 1:43]. On 3 December 1649, there was "[g]ranted to Thomas Antrum 50 acres of land whereof 20 was before granted" [STR 1:161].

On 5 April 1653, Edmund Batter of Salem sold to "Thomas Anthrop" "his farm at Brooksby, excepting what was sold to Richard Way and excepting a parcel of meadow and land called Cranberry Pond" [ELR 1:25]. On 15

December 1658, Thomas Antrum of Salem mortgaged to "Isaack Burnap of the same town (son-in-law to the said Tho[mas]) ... all that my farm with a dwelling house thereon with outhouses, barn, fences, with all appurtenances thereto belonging, which farm with housing is that which I the said Tho[mas] Antrum formerly bought of my brother Edmond Batter ... only reserving unto myself & proper use while I live the lower fire room to the east of the dwelling house & the chamber over the parlor to the west" [ELR 1:58].

On 28 February 1653/4, "Thomas Antrop" of Salem sold to "Rob[ert] Goodhall ... forty acres of land lying near the said Rob[ert]'s land" [ELR 1:22]. On 13 June 1660, Thomas Antrum sold a farm to Isaac Burnap, but Burnap failed to pay the full price, and Antrum took him to court, but withdrew the suit [EQC 2:209]. In an undated document (recorded among others from early 1662), "Edmond Batter, executor of the estate of Thomas Antrum deceased," acquitted Isaac Burnap of further payments [ELR 2:36].

In his will, dated 24 January 1662[/3] and proved 3 July 1663, Thomas Antrum bequeathed to "Isaack Burnape the son of my daughter Burnape" £10 at 21; to "Thomas Spooner" a colt; to "Helyard Verin" £5; to "Obadiah Antrum my son all the remainder of my estate," but if Obadiah die before the will is proved, then "the child or children of my daughter Hannah Burnape: (who hath had her full portion already)" to have it at eighteen; Edmond Batter, executor, and Thomas Spooner and Helyard Veren, overseers [EPR 1:413-14].

The inventory of the estate of Thomas Antrum of Salem, taken 17 February 1662[/3], totalled £263 6s., of which £86 was real estate: "due for a farm he sold in his lifetime," £80; and "2 pieces of marsh containing 1¼ acres," £6 [EPR 1:414-15].

BIRTH: Probably the Thomas Antrum baptized St Edmunds, Salisbury, Wiltshire, 31 December 1601, son of Thomas Antrum.
DEATH: Between 24 January 1662[/3] (date of will) and 17 February 1662[/3] (date of inventory).
MARRIAGE: St Edmunds, Salisbury, 24 May 1630 Jane Batter. She evidently predeceased him.
CHILDREN:

    i   THOMAS, bp. St Edmunds, Salisbury, 6 April 1634; no further record.

    ii   HANNAH, bp. Salem 8 July 1638 [SChR 16]; m. Salem 8 November 1658 Isaac Burnap.

iii OBADIAH, bp. Salem 7 June 1640 [SChR 18]; m. by 1664 Martha Baker (on 27 June 1665, Salem court noted that "Obadiah Antrum, late of Salem, ... embarked upon a voyage, about a year ago, intending to go to Nevis, since which time neither he nor the vessel he went in had been heard from" [EQC 3:265; EPR 2:13]; in March of 1666/7 "Martha Anthru, aged about twenty-three years," deposed about events that had taken place at "her father's house," the house of "Mr. Baker" [EQC 3:395]); she m. (2) Topsfield 22 June 1670 Thomas Andrews.

iv MARY, bp. Salem 16 July 1643 [SChR 19]; evidently died unmarried before 1663.

v JOHN, bp. Salem 29 March 1646 [SChR 21]; evidently died unmarried before 1663.

ASSOCIATIONS: Jane Batter, wife of Thomas Antrum, was sister of EDMUND BATTER of Salem.

On 27 November 1666, Obadiah Antrum's widow, Martha, was ordered to pay £30 to John Phelps, son of Henry Phelps, "kinsman," and £30 to "Hana, wife of Isaack Burnap, sister of the deceased" [EPR 2:13]. The Bakers came to court to depose that Obadiah feared his "Uncle Batter would cozen his wife of all that he had" so he made his will and made the Baker brothers overseers [EPR 2:14]. In 1660 Edmund Batter was called uncle of John Phelps [EQC 2:262], implying that Henry Phelps had married another of Batter's sisters.

COMMENTS: "Thomas Antram, weaver," was a passenger on the *James* of London, sailing from Southampton in April 1635 [NEHGR 14:333]. Along with nine others, he was said to be "late of New England"; this may be an error for "late of New Sarum [i.e., Salisbury]," the known origin of some of these men.

On 9 September 1645, "Thomas Antram [is] exempted from training, and is to pay 10s. a year" [EQC 1:84]. If the baptism given above for the immigrant is correct, then this exemption could not have been based on advanced age.

A very troublesome Giles Corey is called "Antram's boy" in 1644 and steals from him in 1649 [EQC 1:68, 172]. (In 1666 Giles Corey was an appraiser of the estate of Obadiah Antrum [EPR 2:13].)

THOMAS APPLEGATE

ORIGIN: Unknown
MIGRATION: 1635
FIRST RESIDENCE: Weymouth
REMOVES: Newport 1641, Gravesend 1646

OCCUPATION: Ferryman [MBCR 1:156, 165, 246, 249]. Planter [Lechford 392-93]. Weaver [Chapin 2:141].
EDUCATION: Signed his bond of 11 January 1651 [NS] [Gravesend TR 1:59].
ESTATE: On 11 November 1646 [NS], John Ruckman sold to "Thomas Applegate" his plantation in Gravesend [Stillwell 3:2, citing an unknown source (but possibly Gravesend TR 1:4, which is damaged and contains an incomplete 1646 entry involving John Ruckman)]. (The other Gravesend land transactions of the immigrant cited by Stillwell were actually made by Thomas Applegate Junior.)

On 8 January 1651 [NS], "Thomas Aplegate Senior" was fined for not keeping his fence in proper repair [Gravesend TR 1:55].

On 23 May 1662 [NS], Salomon Lachaire "drew up a power of attorney in English for Bartholomeus Appel [*sic*] to Henry Timberlake of Road Island, to take up and use for the constituent's benefit a certain piece of land there called Appelgat's Plain formerly belonging to his the constituent's deceased father" [Lachaire 155].

BIRTH: By about 1598 based on estimated date of marriage.
DEATH: Between 18 January 1656 [NS] (when "Thomas Aplegate Senior" appraised the estate of John Morris [Gravesend TR 3:3]) and 1657 (when "Elizabeth Applgate" had 11 acres in the "list of what land every man hath in tillage" in Gravesend in 1657 [Gravesend TR 3:4]).
MARRIAGE: By about 1623 Elizabeth _____ (assuming she was the mother of all his children).
CHILDREN:

     i   HELENA, b. say 1623; m. (1) by about 1644 Thomas Farrington (on 31 August 1654 [NS] "Thomas Appelgat" sued William Harck, requesting "as grandfather of the surviving child of Thomas Farrington" that the defendant "deliver up to him the goods and cattle, which he as curator of said child has in his possession" [Fernow 1:235]); m. (2) (as

"Helena Appelgat, wede van Thomas Farrington") New Amsterdam 15 August 1646 [NS] Louis Hulet [NYChR 14]; m. (3) (as "Helena Appelgat") New Amsterdam 9 February 1648 [NS] Carle Morgyn [NYChR 15].

ii   BARTHOLOMEW, b. say 1625; m. [blank] October 1650 Hannah/Anneken Patrick [Gravesend TR 1:44], daughter of *DANIEL PATRICK* [GMB 3:1405].

iii   THOMAS, b. say 1628 (adult by 20 December 1650 [NS], when "Thomas Aplegate Junior" purchased land in Gravesend from Randall Huett [Gravesend TR 1:50]); m. Johanna Gibbons, daughter of Richard Gibbons. (On 9 October 1678, "Richard Gibbons of Midletowne, freeholder," deeded to "Thomas Aplegate Senior of the Falls, inhabitant," "one hundred acres in or upon a certain place called the Nutt Swamp" [East Jersey Deeds AII:142]. In his will of 1 February 1698/9, "Thomas Appell[gate] of Midlton in East Jersey" bequeathed to "my son Benjamine fifty acres of land" and to "my son Richard & his heirs fifty acres of land which aforementioned hundred acres I had of my father-in-law Richard Gibbons"; he also bequeathed to "my loving wife Johanna" [East Jersey Deeds G:1]. On the basis of this will, Stillwell concluded that Johanna was a second wife, and only Benjamin and Richard were her children, a possible but not a necessary conclusion.)

iv   JOHN, b. about 1630 (d. 1712 aged 82 [FOOF 1:21, citing Fairfield gravestone]); m. by 1662 Avis Goulding, daughter of William Goulding of Gravesend (on 17 June 1662 [NS], "William Goulder of Gravesend" secured a debt "for the appearer's son-in-law Johan Appelgate" (signed as "William Goulder *alias* Goulding") [Lachaire 161-62]). (On an unknown date "John Applegate of Fairefeild in the County of Coneticote" sold to "Will[iam] Goulding Junior of Gravesend" a parcel of land in Gravesend, but on 28 October 1673, this sale was made null and void [Gravesend TR 2:208].) (See also FOOF 1:21-22 and Fairfield PD Cases #155 and 156.)

COMMENTS: On 2 September 1635, "Thomas Aplegate was licensed to keep a ferry betwixt Wessaguscus & Mount Woolliston, for which he is to have 1d. for every person, & iiid. a horse" [MBCR 1:156]. On 3 March 1635/6, "Thomas Aplegate was discharged of keeping the ferry of Waymothe, & Henry Kingman licensed to keep the said ferry during the pleasure of the Court" [MBCR 1:165].

On 4 December 1638, "William Blanton, appearing, was enjoined to appear at the next Court, with all the men that were in the canoe with him, & [blank] Aplegate, which owned the canoe out of which the 3 persons were drowned; & it was ordered, that no canoe should be used at any ferry upon pain of £5, nor no canoe to be made in our jurisdiction before the next General Court, upon pain of £10" [MBCR 1:246]. On 5 March 1638/9, William Blanton, Thomas Applegate and four other men "appearing, were discharged, with an admonition not to adventure too many into any boat," and on the same day "Thomas Aplegate was appointed to have 29s. for his canoe, when the arms which he borrowed are returned back as good as they were when he borrowed them" [MBCR 1:249].

On 6 September 1636, "Elisabeth, the wife of Thomas Aplegate, was censured to stand with her tongue in a cleft stick, for swearing, railing, & reviling" [MBCR 1:177].

In October 1640, Thomas Applegate of Weymouth, planter, hired John King of Weymouth, seaman, to be master of Applegate's boat on a voyage both for fishing and for carrying freight. A dispute arose early in 1641 because King had allowed the boat to be overladen [Lechford 392-93].

On 1 June 1641, "Will[ia]m Newland complains against Thomas Applegate, in an action of trespass upon the case, to the damage of £20. The jury find for the plaintiff, and assess him £8 damages, and the charges of the suit" [PCR 7:19]. On 1 June 1641, "Richard Burne undertook & promised to make good & pay all such damages as might happen if Thomas Applegate should by bringing the suit about again recover anything against W[illia]m Newland, who this Court hath recovered against the said Applegate £8 damages, and the charges of the suit" [PCR 2:18]. On 6 September 1641, "Thomas Applegate complains against Will[ia]m Newland, in an action of trespass for detaining certain swine. The jury find for the defendant, & give him the charges of the suit" [PCR 7:23]. On 7 September 1641, "George Allen & Mr. Edward Dillingham are nominated, by consent of both parties, to apprize the swine Will[ia]m Newland hath in execution of Thom[as] Applegate, and what the want in value of eight pounds & charges the said Applegate is to give his bill to the said Newland for payment thereof" [PCR 2:24]. (All of the participants in this dispute except for Applegate resided in Sandwich. Applegate may have resided there briefly between his years in Weymouth and Newport, but there is no direct evidence for this.)

On 1 December 1641, "[Thomas] Applegate of Nuport" sued John Roome of the same town [Chapin 2:133, 135]. On 7 June 1643, William Dyer of Newport sued "Thomas Applegate, weaver, of the same town," and at the same court session Henry Bull sued Applegate [Chapin 2:141]. On 5 September 1643, "Thomas Applegat of Nuport" sued Edward Andrews, and on the same day he sued "W[illia]m Heavens of Portsmo[uth] upon a mortgage of house & land consigned by Sam[uel] Willbore to the said Thomas" [Chapin 2:147]. On 3 December 1643, a dispute between Nicholas Cotterell and Thomas Applegate was sent to arbitration [Chapin 2:149]; this dispute, or another between the same two men, was still alive in 1646 [Chapin 2:161].

Teunis G. Bergen stated that Thomas Applegate was "in N[ew] A[msterdam] as early as 1641" [Kings County Settlers 14], but no record has been found to support this claim.

Thomas Applegate was one of the patentees of Flushing on 10 October 1645 [NS] [Frederick Van Wyck, *Select Patents of New York Towns* (Boston 1938), pp. 4-8], but he does not seem to have settled there, as he had land at Gravesend very soon after this date.

While a resident of Gravesend, Thomas Applegate was frequently before the court for uncivil behavior. On 14 February 1650 [NS], he was censured for making a disturbance at court, so that the court could not go on with its business [Gravesend TR 1:35].

His greatest problem apparently arose from his claim that "the Governor had done him wrong about the orphan [presumably the child his daughter Helena had with Thomas Farrington]," as a result of which he was prosecuted on 8 January 1651 [NS] for slandering the Governor and some residents of Gravesend. For his claim that the Governor had taken a bribe in the case, Applegate was sentenced to have his tongue bored, but after his confession this sentence was apparently reversed [Gravesend TR 1:53-54]. On 11 January 1651 [NS], "Thomas Applegate Senior" was required to post a bond of five hundred guilders to ensure his good behavior, and on 7 July 1652 [NS], this bond was voided [Gravesend TR 1:59].

BIBLIOGRAPHIC NOTE: The best published account of Thomas Applegate and his family was prepared by John E. Stillwell in 1914 [Stillwell 3:1-6].

THOMAS ARMITAGE

ORIGIN: Unknown (but see *ASSOCIATIONS* below)
MIGRATION: 1635 on the *James* of Bristol
FIRST RESIDENCE: Plymouth
REMOVES: Sandwich 1638, Stamford 1641, Hempstead by 1644, Oyster Bay by 1659

OCCUPATION: Yeoman. Planter.
FREEMAN: Admitted freeman of Plymouth Colony on 2 January 1637/8 [PCR 1:74] (and then added to the list of freemen of 7 March 1636/7 [PCR 1:53]).
EDUCATION: Signed his deeds by mark.
OFFICES: Plymouth grand jury, 5 June 1638 [PCR 1:87]. Sandwich constable, 5 March 1638/9, 4 June 1639 [PCR 1:116, 125]. Deputy for Sandwich to Plymouth Court, 4 June 1639 [PCR 1:126].
ESTATE: On 2 October 1637, Plymouth Court ordered "that Mr. John Atwood, Thomas Armitage, and John Shawe ... have enlargement of lands next unto the lands abutting above their lots at Playne Dealeing" [PCR 1:65].

On 7 December 1641, the town of Stamford granted a houselot to "Tho[mas] Armitag" [TAG 10:41, citing Stamford TR 1:6]. On 7 January 1642, "[Tho] Armitag" was on the Stamford rate list [TAG 10:43, citing Stamford TR 1:15].

Thomas Armitage received 28 acres at Merock in Hempstead [HempTR 1:115]. In 1658 there was "given and granted by Francis Weekes of Hamsteede the half of the meadow that lies at Marecok the meadow that was formerly Thomas Arymitage's unto William Jacoakes and Thomas Ellison"; Ellison gave to "my father-in-law Tho[mas] Chamin ... all that my right and title of meadow lying at the aforesaid Marcok which quarter part containing seven acres" [HempTR 1:171-72; see also HempTR 1:227, 261].

Thomas Armitage was included among the purchasers of Oyster Bay in 1653 [Oyster Bay TR 1:354-55, 670-71].

On 13 December 1660, Nicholas Wright sold to Thomas Armitage "my lot of meadow being the sixth in number and lying between his own and Francis Wilckes" in Oyster Bay [Oyster Bay TR 1:3]. On 14 September 1663, Thomas Armitage was granted ten acres of land at Oyster Bay [Oyster Bay TR 1:7].

On 26 May 1659, "Thomas Armitage of Oyster Bay, yeoman," stated that any "will or deed-of-gift, made by me unto my son Mannasseth Armitage at present in the College at Cambridge in New England, whereby I should have made over my estate unto him, only to be allowed a competent maintenance during my life, or what else therein may seem to appear, I do hereby declare and protest against any such writings or deeds-of-gift by me ever signed or sealed, and if any such appear now or hereafter, it is a false and forged one never by me made, signed, sealed nor consented unto; and I do hereby utterly disavow [and] disown any such act or deed ... and do further declare that my said son Mannasseth Armitage hath fraudulently taken from me several bills, bonds and writings of concernment and conveyed them out of my custody where and whither I know not, but with a purpose I believe to convert them to his own use, wherefore I do hereby likewise desire all persons to me indebted not to pay or satisfy unto my said son any debt or debts due to me" [HempTR 1:108-9].

On 3 June 1659, five persons made depositions about this dispute. Robert Ashman said "that in & about nine years last past, he was then bound for James Pine unto Thomas Armitage his father-in-law for the sum of thirty pounds" which "he did intend to give unto his son Manasseth and this he did, because his wife should not have his estate after his death, and deprive his son; also he said that he had an estate in the hands of Daniell Whitehead of seventy pounds; and that he did intend for his son Mannaseth, and being at Hemsteede the winter last past in Anno 1658, the said Tho[mas] Armitage was at the house of this deponent, and he said that James Pine had been with him at the house of Robert Jackson the night before and being in some debate about Manasseth aforesaid, and he told this deponent that James Pine were best be quiet or else he would make such work with him and his son Manasseth that would make them better be quiet, and then this deponent replied I know that you said you would give him, that estate in goodman Whitehead and goodman Pine's hands, and now I hope you will not deprive him, of what you told me you would give him, then said Thomas Armitage, I have now married a young wife and may have other children, and therefore may have need of that myself, that Mannasseth taken away to be at my own disposing" [HempTR 1:109-10].

"William Smith inhabitant in Hemsteede" stated that "in and about nine years last past, that Tho[mas] Armitage proffered him some cattle to keep for the use of his son Mannasseth Armitage, and that at the end of 11 years time he should return both the cattle and the profit unto the use of his son aforesaid, and in some time afterward, this deponent speaking with Tho[mas] Armitage, he told him that he had put the cattle into Daniell Whitehead for the sum of £70 sterling to be paid unto the use of his sonn Mannasseth aforesaid, and his reason was (as he said) it was because at his death, his wife should not deprive his son of it, but that he might have a comfortable maintenance" [HempTR 1:110-11].

"Jeremy Wood inhabitant of Hemsteede" deposed that "upon some conference had with Thomas Armitage in and about 2 or 3 days after that he had passed a deed of gift unto his son Mannasseth Armitage, he told him that he had taken an opportunity being Mr. Moore and Mr. Wood had been in the town, and that he had gotten them to make a deed of gift of the £70 sterling, the which this deponent and Henry Persall stood bound for Daniell Whitehead, he had given it unto his son Mannasseth Armitage, that at the end of 10 or 11 years, he should have both the same, and the moneys due from James Pine, when the time was expired" [HempTR 1:111].

"Ellizabeth the wife of Jeremy Wood" deposed that "in and about seven years last past, that Martha the late wife of Tho[mas] Armitage, being at her house, she told this deponent, that Mr. Moore and Mr. Wood were both of them, as she supposed, then at her house, and that they were about making a deed of gift from her husband unto her son-in-law Manasseth Armitage, and thereupon this deponent going forth of doors with the said Martha Armitage they did see both Mr. Moore and Mr. Wood come out of the house of Mr. Armitage aforesaid, and then said she unto this deponent Now I suppose they have done it: and this deponent having some discourse with Thomas Armitage concerning the matter, he did acknowledge that he had made a deed of gift of some part of his estate unto his son Manasseth, and that his children should enjoy his estate, lest the children of this woman meaning their stepmother, should deprive his own children" [HempTR 1:112].

In an undated document "Thomas Armatage of Oyster Bay on Long Iland, planter, ... notwithstanding any act of mine already passed by me in my last will and testament which will and testament I do hereby declare void" deeded by gift to "And [sic] Lyllestone likewise of Oyster Bay aforesaid whom by God's permission I intend to make my wedded wife" a horse and, at his death, two cows and "my now dwelling house situated in Oyster Bay aforesaid with all my whole lot of orchard and garden thereunto belonging" for life, then to revert to his heirs, "unless there remain issue of my body begotten of the said Ann Lillestone then the said house, orchard, garden and land to remain unto the said issue forever" [Oyster Bay TR 1:7-8]. On 30 January 1663[/4?], "Thomas Armitage of Oyst[e]rbay on Long Island and my wife Ann Lillysone according to her maiden name with the advice & consent of my son Daniel Whitehead" sold to John Townsend of Oyster Bay "all our housing & lands both meadow & upland that do any ways belong to me or us here in Oysterbay notwithstanding any deed of gifts or jointures that did pass or was made amongst us ... namely, the two meadow lots in the Great Meadow on the north side of the town of Oysterbay ... and our housing that we now enjoy & houselot or land fenced in, with half a share of meadow at the south" [Oyster Bay TR 1:591].

BIRTH: By about 1601 based on estimated date of marriage.
DEATH: By 1667 (if "Anne Hermitage" who married Samuel Barret in that year was his widow).
MARRIAGE: (1) By about 1626 _____ _____; she died by 1650.
  (2) By 1650 Martha _____; she died by 1659.
  (3) By 1659 Anne Lillestone. (Seversmith thought she "was probably the Anne Hermitage who married Samuel Barrett by a license issued 18 December 1667" [Seversmith Armitage:115].)
CHILDREN:
  With first wife
    i   Daughter, b. say 1626; m. by about 1646 Daniel Whitehead (eldest son adult by 1667) [NYGBR 118:154-55].
    ii Daughter, b. say 1630; m. by about 1650 James Pine (apparently already son-in-law of Thomas Armitage in 1650 [HempTR 1:109]; their eldest child was probably Susan who married on 10 May 1671 John Searing [Seversmith Armitage:115-16, 121-23]).
    iii MANASSEH, b. say 1640; Harvard College 1660 [Sibley 2:67-68]; witnessed a deed at Newtown, Long Island, on 1 April 1662 [NYGBR 63:360, citing Newtown Town Records, 1659-1688, p. 21]; no further record.
ASSOCIATIONS: Thomas Armitage would seem to have been associated with several immigrants from Halifax, Yorkshire, to New England, including Matthew Mitchell, Edmund Wood and John Lum, who were probably passengers with him on the *James* in 1635, and who settled at Stamford at the same time he did [NYGBR 120:1-4]. On 27 September 1625, a Thomas Armitage married Susan Michell at Bradford, Yorkshire, and Seversmith and others have thought that this might be the immigrant, and that Susan Michell might be in some way related to

Matthew Mitchell, but no one has been able to prove this [Seversmith Armitage:115; NYGBR 120:101].

COMMENTS: On 27 May 1635, Thomas Armitage was one of the passengers on the *James*, then still at anchor in Bristol harbor, who accompanied RICHARD MATHER on a visit to the *Angel Gabriel* [Young's First Planters 450].

Thomas Armitage does not appear in New England records until 2 October 1637 [PCR 1:65]. (His addition to the list of freemen of 7 March 1636/7 was made only after his admission to freemanship on 2 January 1637/8 [PCR 1:53, 74].) Where did he reside during these two years?

Some sources say he was at Lynn, but there is no record of him there, and this is apparently an unsupported attempt to attach him to Godfrey Armitage and Joseph Armitage, who did appear in Lynn at about this same time.

There is no record of Thomas Armitage in Dorchester, where Rev. RICHARD MATHER and some of the other passengers on the *James* settled.

Pope says that Thomas Armitage "settled at Ipswich," but no record has been found to support this statement.

On 4 September 1638, "Thom[as] Armitage" of Sandwich was fined 2s. for having "2 swine unringed" [PCR 1:98]. Armitage was elected to two offices on 4 June 1639, constable and deputy, and in each case he was replaced in mid-term [PCR 1:125, 126], indicating that he left Sandwich in late 1639 or early 1640, a year or more before he appeared at Stamford.

The inventory of the estate of William Swift of Sandwich, dated 29 January 1642[/3?], showed that at his death Swift owed a debt of £5 to "Goodman Armitage" [MD 4:171, citing PCPR 1:45].

Late in his life Thomas Armitage became embroiled in an intrafamilial dispute, the records of which provide us much of our information about his marriages and his children [HempTR 1:108-12; Oyster Bay TR 1:7-8, 591 (extracted at length above)]. The depositions of 1659 refer to events that had taken place in or about 1650, by which time Thomas Armitage was married to his second wife, Martha, who had children with an earlier husband, but who had no children with Thomas. The maneuvers undertaken by Armitage in 1650 were aimed at protecting the rights of the children of his first wife.

By 1659 Martha had died and Thomas had married Anne Lillestone, a much younger woman. He had hopes of fathering more children, and so wished to provide for them, should they materialize. Whether his son

Manasseh had already made efforts to seize what he thought was his share of the estate, or whether the actions of Thomas in 1659 triggered these efforts, we cannot tell.

Since the transactions of 1650 were to be in effect for ten or eleven years, we conclude that Manasseh was born in about 1640, and would reach his maturity in about 1661, which is consistent with his dates at Harvard College.

JASPER ARNOLD
ANN ARNOLD

"Jesper Arnold," aged 40, and "Ann Arnold," aged 39, were enrolled at London on 2 July 1635 as passengers for New England on the *Abigail* [Hotten 98].

COMMENTS: Jasper and Ann Arnold were listed with five other intended passengers on this date, these seven persons having received their certificates of conformity "from the minister of Shorditch parish & Stepney parish" [Hotten 98]. Jasper and Ann were probably husband and wife, but this is not certain. There is no record for either of them in New England.

JOHN ARNOLD

ORIGIN: Unknown
MIGRATION: 1634
FIRST RESIDENCE: Cambridge
REMOVES: Hartford

CHURCH MEMBERSHIP: Admission to Cambridge church prior to 6 May 1635 implied by freemanship.
FREEMAN: 6 May 1635 (as "John Arnoll," third in a sequence of eight Cambridge men) [MBCR 1:370].
EDUCATION: The inventory included "books" valued at £1 10s.
ESTATE: Granted five acres in the Westend Field in Cambridge, 4 August 1634 [CaTR 9]. Received a proportionate share of one in the undivided meadow, 20 August 1635 [CaTR 13]. In the 8 February 1635/6 listing of houses, credited with one house in the town [CaTR 18].

In the Cambridge land inventory on 10 October 1635 held two parcels: "in the town one house with garden and backside about half a rood"; and "in Westend Field about five acres" [CaBOP 28].

In the Hartford land inventory of February 1639/40, he held eight parcels: two acres "on which his dwelling house now standeth"; three acres of upland; ten acres and two roods of upland; one rood and three perches in the Little Meadow; four acres in the South Meadow; two acres in the forty acres of meadow; one acre and three roods in the Great Swamp; and two acres and one rood in the swamp by the Great River [HaBOP 282-83].

In his will, dated 22 August 1664 and proved 2 March 1664/5, "John Arnold of Hartford" bequeathed to "my dear and loving wife Susana Arnold the sole & full use of my now dwelling house and houselot, the barn & all appurtenances belonging" during her natural life, and also all moveables, she to pay the following legacies "unto my dear and loving children": to "my son Josias Arnold one cow and my two acres of land in the clayboard swamp after the death of my wife"; "my other upland lot near the town's end if my son Joseph Arnold return to dwell again in Hartford within two years after the date hereof I give the one half of the said lot to him & his heirs forever, the other half part of it I give to my son Daniell & his heirs forever"; to "my son Daniell after the decease of my aforesaid wife my now dwelling house, houselot & barn with all appurtenances thereunto belonging"; "my will is that if my son Daniell shall live and be married & have a child or children that the aforesaid premises shall be his and his heirs forever but if he shall marry and die without issue my will is that his wife shall enjoy the aforesaid premises during her natural life and after her decease my will is that all those premises I have herein given to my son Daniell shall be the estate of my son Joseph Arnold & his heirs forever"; to "my dear & loving grandchild Mary Buck forty shillings to be paid at her age of eighteen years or within one full year after the decease of my aforesaid wife"; "my loving brethren Edward Stebbing and Lieutenant Bull to be overseers" [Hartford PD Case #202].

The inventory of the estate of John Arnold, taken 26 December 1664, totalled £106 2s. (against which were debts of £7), of which £55 was real estate: "his house & houselot, barn & some woodland" [Hartford PD Case #202].

BIRTH: By about 1603 based on estimated date of marriage.

DEATH: Hartford between 22 August 1664 (date of will) and 26 December 1664 (date of inventory).

MARRIAGE: By about 1628 Susanna _____. On 21 June 1666, John Winthrop Jr. treated "Arnoll, Susan, widow of Hartford, 68 y.," and again on 12 March 1666/7 "Arnol, [blank], widow above 70 y. of Hartford" [WMJ 666, 710].

CHILDREN:

    i   JOSIAH, b. about 1628 (on 5 April 1658, John Winthrop Jr. treated "Arnoll, Josyas, 30 y." [WMJ 100]); named in his father's will, 22 August 1664; no further record.

    ii   JOSEPH, b. say 1634; m. between 21 August 1659 and 11 February 1659/60 Elizabeth Wakeman, daughter of *SAMUEL WAKEMAN* (on 10 April 1659, and again from 17 through 21 August 1659, John Winthrop Jr. treated Elizabeth Wakeman, "G[oodman] Willett's daughter [i.e., stepdaughter]", and on 11 February 1659/60 he treated "Arnol, Joseph his wife, G[oodman] Willett's daughter" [WMJ 156, 167, 187]) [GMB 3:1901].

    iii   MARY, b. say 1636; m. Wethersfield 17 April 1658 Emanuel Buck [TAG 44:168-72].

    iv   DANIEL, b. say 1638; m. by 1676 (and probably some years before) Elizabeth Osborn; in his nuncupative will of 1676 James Osborn named "son-in-law Daniel Arnold," and in the inventory Elizabeth Arnold is included in the list of children [Manwaring 1:223-24]).

COMMENTS: Some sources assign to this immigrant a son John, but no evidence for this has been found. Such inventions usually derive from a misinterpretation of a record for the immigrant.

As a consequence of the schism in Hartford church, John Arnold was one of those who signed the 18 April 1659 agreement to leave Hartford and establish the town that would become Hadley [SJC Case #313]. Arnold was, however, "too weak to come to Hadley," and was voted a pension of £5 a year for life, while he lived at Hartford, with a further allocation of 50s. a year to his widow [Deerfield Hist 233, citing Hadley Town Records].

WILLIAM ARNOLD

ORIGIN: Ilchester, Somerset
MIGRATION: 1635
FIRST RESIDENCE: Hingham
REMOVES: Providence 1636

FREEMAN: In the Providence section of the 1655 list of Rhode Island freemen [RICR 1:299]. In a list of Providence freemen of 1665 [PrTR 15:73]. Swore allegiance to King Charles II, 31 May 1666 [PrTR 3:101].
EDUCATION: Sufficient to compose lengthy letters in support of his positions in land disputes.
OFFICES: Pawtuxet member of committee to run the line between Providence and Pawtuxet, 29 January 1668[/9] [PrTR 17:215]; report presented at Providence, 15 February 1668[/9] [PrTR 3:136].
ESTATE: On 18 September 1635, there was "[given] unto William Arnall by the Town of Hingham for a houselot two acres of land lying in the Town Street" [HiBOP 30].

On 8 October 1638, Roger Williams deeded the lands that he had earlier bought from the Indians, and which had become the settlement of Providence, to a large group of men, including William Arnold, who thereby became the proprietors of Providence [RICR 1:20; see also PrTR 5:306-9].

William Arnold had a half-right in the first lot of thatch beds in Providence [PrTR 9:19] and a half-right in the lower Bailey's Cove lot [PrTR 17:219].

On 29 August 1640, William Harris of Providence sold to William Arnold of Providence "all that meadow with the upland ground, which is the fifth part of that land or meadow which was laid out the last year unto us five persons, viz: Tho[mas] James, William Harris, William Carpenter, Tho[mas] Olney & William Field" [PrTR 1:107-8].

On 14 April 1641, the town of Providence confirmed unto "William Arnold one of the free inhabitants of the Town of Providence" the following pieces of land: "his house share," 112 poles by eight poles; "one plot of ground lying by the river," nine poles; six poles square on which "the said William Arnold have set up a wolf trap"; three acres of meadow "on the west side of the river called Wanasquattuckett"; a piece of land "which lieth upon the salt river at the furthermost side of the town," 48 poles by 80 poles; also "all the neck or point of land that lieth between the salt river and the aforesaid land"; and "another piece of land lying upon the neck of the town upon a point over against Wachamoquott to the land called Whatcheer" [PrTR 1:109-11].

On 2 April 1642, Thomas Olney of Providence "hath demised, granted and to farm letten unto William Arnold of Providence, or of Pautuxett, all the proper right and title that he hath or doth belong or appertain unto him in all the land that lieth between the great fresh river called Pautuxett (on the south) and the bounds that parteth the land of Providence aforesaid, and the land of Pautuxett aforesaid on the north, and the great salt river on the east, and the river called Pauchasett on the west, excepting the third share of land lying upon the neck near unto the fall at Pautuxett and his part in the vineyard which is near the end of the aforesaid share, and his part in the point or neck of land lying before the fall, and one share of meadow which he hath sold unto William Feild of Providence, and his part of fishing at the fall ... only he hath demised, granted and to farm letten unto the said William Arnold one acre and half of land at or in the west end of his share aforesaid" [PrTR 1:103-4].

On 11 January 1642/3, "William Arnold of Providence, or Pautuxett, ... hath demised, granted, and to farm let unto Thomas Olney of Providence the proper right and title that I have or do belong or appertain unto me in all the land that I have lying within the bounds of the Town of Providence aforesaid excepting my house or housing with my house share of land and my share of land lying upon the neck of the town before the point of Watchamoqut, being about six acres, and my right in all the commons of the town aforesaid, these four particulars before excepted I do reserve unto myself and for my use, only I have demised, granted and to farm letten unto the said Thomas Olney together with all the rest of my right and interest as aforesaid, the four particulars before mentioned of mine only excepted: two acres of land at or in the east end of my home share, all which land right and interest as aforesaid is now in the tenure, use or occupation of the said Thomas Olney"; "if it shall happen at any time hereafter that there be any more land within the bounds of the town aforesaid to be appropriated unto me ... by virtue of the same right which at this time belongeth to me, then I or mine heirs and assigns is to enjoy but one half of that new appropriated land, and the said Thomas Olney his heirs or assigns is to receive, possess and enjoy the other half of that new appropriated land"; "before these presents were agreed I William Arnold hath demised [and] granted unto my son Benedict Arnold a plot of ground which lyeth by Mooshaske River side before the house shares of Bennedict Arnold, aforesaid, and Frances

Weekes and the aforesaid plot of ground is all the ground that I William Arnold have sold or granted within this Town of Providence besides the grant abovesaid made to Thomas Olney aforesaid" [PrTR 1:64-66, 2:7].

On 17 October 1643, "William Arnold of Providence" deeded to "my son Benedict Arnold all my proper right & interest that do belong to me in a parcel, or share of land lying upon the neck near the fall called Pautuxet" [PrTR 14:251].

On 27 August 1645, "Osomequen, the chief sachem of Pokanocuk," sold to "William Arnold of Pautuxett ... all that land which lyeth on the west side of the Great Salt River which floweth up to Providence between the bounds of the land that was once in the tenure, use or occupation of Soconanoco on the south side of the same, and the Salt River on the east part and the north side of the great cove which cometh in on the north side of that neck of land called Saxefraxe, and from thence unto the north side of the pond called Massapague, and so within these bounds westward all and general" [PrTR 15:74].

On 7 March 1646[/7?], "William Arnold of Pautuxett" deeded to "my daughter Joane the wife of Zacariah Roades all that my proper right, title and interest that do belong to me in a part of that land or meadow that of late I bought of Thomas Olney Senior of Providence ... being on the west side of a small river called Papaquinapauge River" [PrTR 1:80-81].

On 30 January 164[worn], "William Arnold of Pautuxit" sold to "Arthour Feinner of Providence" his title to "all the land that lieth at or upon the neck or point that is near unto the place called Whatcheer" in Providence [PrTR 4:11-12].

In a Providence tax list of 2 September 1650, William Arnold was assessed £3 6s. 8d. [PrTR 15:33], and in a list of 3 June 1671 he was assessed £1 11s. 3d. [PrTR 15:136].

On 24 June 1652, Ralph Earle of Portsmouth sold to "William Arnold of Pautuxett all that proper right and title or interest that once he bought of Nathaniel Dickens in or of a certain parcel of meadow and upland containeth about the value of five acres more or less, all which said premises are situate, lying and being on the west side of the now dwelling house of the said Will[iam] Arnold" [PrTR 1:106-7]. On 25 March 1658, Henry Fowler of Providence sold to "Will[iam] Arnold of Pautuxett all his proper right title and interest in a certain parcel of land, which formerly did belong unto Mary Person wife unto Thomas Peerson of Providence," about two acres [PrTR 1:107].

On 31 August 1658, "William Arnold of Pautukett" deeded to "Jeremiah Roades my grandson all my proper right ... in that land that I set upon to close in by the consent of William Carpenter & Zachary Roades being a part of that land that fell to us by the order of our arbitrators, vide Eleaser Lusher, William Hauthorne, John Easton [and] Joseph Tory the which lyeth at the place called Pumgansett" and also "all that marsh, meadow or tussocks that lyeth on both sides of the river ... that run out of Massapague into the great river of Pautuxett" [PrTR 14:212].

On 27 April 1659, William Arnold petitioned the Court "that when the Town granted 60 acres of upland and 3 acres of meadow to every man to be appropriated then I made thereof an acre and half of meadow lying on the river that runneth out at the southwest end of Mashapague Pond the which is now conceived to be out of the Town bounds, my desire therefore to the Town is that the Town will be pleased to let me have an acre and half of meadow allowed me in the nearest place that can be found out to that place, the which the Town I hope will not deny me forasmuch that I was [one] that the very first day entered with some others upon the land of Providence and so laid out my money to buy and help pay for it, besides [much] hardship and danger I and mine with others did undergo to possess and keep the same a good while after & therefore I was one of the first in choice of any lands to be laid out to the Townsmen afterwards" [PrTR 15:77-78].

There was "laid out unto William Arnold of Pautuxett upon the 31 day of May in the year 1662 a parcel or neck of land near about Mashapauge (viz:) all the upland lying between the line lately run between the bounds of the Town of Providence, and Pautuxett, on the southwest, and nor[th]west parts of it, and to it the swampy and tussocky place lying on the west and northwest and north parts of it ... all the said land, swamp, or tussocks is near about the sum of thirty and two acres" [PrTR 1:78-79, 15:90]. On 19 February 1665[/6], William Arnold received Lot #75 in "the division of land on the east side of the seven mile line" [PrTR 3:73].

On 31 May 1670, "William Arnold of Pautuxett" sold to "Henry Fouler Senior all that land that was laid out to me by two of the town deputies, near to the place called Masshapauge, the place where it lyeth and the manner how the same lyeth is plainly expressed, and recorded in the town records" [PrTR 1:24, 113, 2:157-58, 15:131].

On 9 February 1673[/4], "William Arnold of Pautuxett" sold to John Sheldon of the same "all my right, title or claim which doth in anywise belong to me of commons belonging to me as a purchaser of the town of Providence" [PrTR 20:288].

On 12 April 1675, William Arnold drew Lot #89 "for the dividing of the land beyond or on the west side of the seven mile line," and on 24 May

1675, he drew Lot #50 "for the second dividing of the land between the seven mile line and the four mile line on the east side of the seven mile line" [PrTR 4:46, 48].

On 17 March 1683/4, William Arnold received a share in "the division of the lands on the west side of the seven-mile line" (presumably distributed to his estate) [PrTR 4:65]. In a deed of 18 May 1685, John Sheldon sold "one-third part of a full half-right of commoning lying on the east side of the four mile line, the which said half-right of commoning I the said John Sheldon obtained of William Arnold of Pautuxett (deceased)" [PrTR 14:121-22].

BIRTH: Born 24 June 1587 [NEHGR 33:427], son of Nicholas and Alice (Gully) Arnold [NEHGR 69:66-68].

DEATH: After "the beginning of [King Philip's] war [i.e., mid-1675]" [PrTR 15:182] and before 3 November 1677 (on which date Benedict Arnold described himself as "eldest son and heir of William Arnold late of Pautuxett in the said Colony deceased" [PrTR 14:5]).

MARRIAGE: By 1611 Christian Peak, born 15 February 1583, daughter of Thomas Peak [NEHGR 33:428].

CHILDREN:

    i   ELIZABETH, b. 23 November 1611 [NEHGR 33:428]; m. by about 1635 William Carpenter (son Joseph, apparently the eldest child of this couple, was not yet married in late 1658 [TAG 70:196, 204, citing PCPR 2:1:80-82; MD 14:231-33], but probably soon after [Austin 36]; in his will of 10 February 1679/80, William Carpenter bequeathed to his sons Silas and Benjamin "that part of a share of meadow that I bought of my brother Stephen Arnold" [PrTR 6:140-1]).

    ii   BENEDICT, b. 21 December 1615 [NEHGR 33:428]; m. 17 December 1640 Damaris Westcott [NEHGR 33:428], daughter of Stukely Westcott (in a letter of 18 October 1677, reference was made to testimony presented earlier by "Mr. W[illia]m Arnold father to our honored present Governor & Stukely Westcot (father to our Governor's wife)" [PrTR 15:163; RWCorr 2:741]).

    iii JOANNA, b. 27 February 1617 [NEHGR 33:428]; m. (1) by 7 March 1646[/7?] Zachariah Rhodes [PrTR 1:80-81] (on 13 January 1712/3, "John Roades of Warwick" sold land "that of late fell to me by virtue of a deed from my grandfather

William Arnold to my mother Joan Roades, as being eldest son living at her decease" [PrTR 21:70-71]); m. (2) Providence 11 January 1666[/7?] Samuel Reape [RIVR 2:Providence:155].

iv STEPHEN, b. 22 December 1622 [NEHGR 33:428], bp. Ilchester, Somerset, 26 December 1622 [NEHGR 69:67]; m. Providence 24 November 1646 "Sarah Smith, [daughter] of Edward of Rehoboth" [RIVR 2:Providence:7].

ASSOCIATIONS: Thomas Hopkins of Providence was son of William and Joan (Arnold) Hopkins, and therefore nephew of William Arnold [RIHSC 14:47].

COMMENTS: In 1879 Edwin Hubbard published a document which purported to give information on six generations of the Arnold family, the earliest entries of which were thought to be in the handwriting of William Arnold himself; as will be seen, later research has shown that many of the dates in this document are reliable, thus validating the entire document [NEHGR 33:427-32].

In the same issue of the *Register*, Henry T. Drowne published a pedigree of the Arnold ancestry, prepared by Horatio G. Somerby, carrying the line back sixteen generations into Wales [NEHGR 33:432-38].

In 1915 Edson Salisbury Jones published a brief account of his own research into the ancestry of William Arnold [NEHGR 69:64-69]. He first demonstrated the problems with the ancestry proposed by Somerby, and then presented records which showed that William Arnold was from Ilchester, Somerset, and that his father was Nicholas Arnold. Somerby did not even have the correct name for the immigrant's father. Jones also argued that Thomas Arnold of Watertown was not a brother or son of William Arnold.

In 1921 Fred A. Arnold placed in print a longer account of the researches of Edson S. Jones, demonstrating especially the large number of records from English parish registers which were in accord with the family document published by Hubbard in 1879 [RIHSC 14:33-49, 68-86].

In summary, the family document published by Hubbard in 1879 may be relied upon, the pedigree prepared by Somerby is completely erroneous, and William Arnold came from Ilchester, Somerset.

Somerby incorrectly stated that Elizabeth Arnold, daughter of the immigrant, married Thomas Hopkins [NEHGR 33:436], an error also printed by Savage [Savage 1:67, 2:462]. Savage and Somerby may have fallen into this error as a side effect of the known connection between the

Hopkins and Arnold families through the marriage of Joan Arnold, sister of William Arnold the immigrant, to Thomas Hopkins, father of the immigrant of the same name.

Benedict Arnold, in his continuation of the record begun by his father, included the following account of the migrations of his family: "Memorandum. My father and his family set sail from Dartmouth in Old England, the first of May, Friday & arrived in New England June 24 Anno 1635. Memorandum. We came to Providence to dwell the 20th of April, 1636" [NEHGR 33:428].

On 27 July 1640, William Arnold was one of those who signed the "constitution" of Providence [RICR 1:31; PrTR 15:5].

Over the years, William Arnold became involved in a number of controversies with his neighbors, consisting mostly of land disputes with Providence with regard to the Arnold family landholdings at Pawtuxet and of conflicts with the Gortonists at Warwick. (In addition to the documents in the next two paragraphs, see RICR 1:234; PrTR 4:73-76, 14:145-47, 273-76, 15:27-32, 94-95, 236-38, 20:359-61; RWCorr 189n, 212-14, 240n, 316, 318n, 402n, 444, 446n, 472, 472n, 473, 474n, 508-10.)

On 28 October 1642, John Winthrop, as governor, and three assistants of Massachusetts Bay wrote to "our neighbors of Providence" that "[w]hereas W[illia]m Arnold of Patuxet & Robert Cole & others have lately put themselves & their families, lands & estates under the protection & government of this jurisdiction & have since complained to us that you have since (upon pretense of a late purchase from the Indians gone about to deprive them of their lawful interest confirmed by 4 years' possession, & otherwise to molest them: We thought good therefore to write to you on their behalf to give you notice that they and their lands &c. being under our jurisdiction we are to maintain them in their lawful right" [SLR 1:33].

On 28 January 1655/6, at a court held at Providence, it was "ordered that Mr. Rog[er] Williams & Mr. Olnie draw a letter in answer to one from Will[iam] Arnold date the 4th of 10th [4 December] 1655" [PrTR 2:91]. On 27 April 1657, at a court held at Providence, it was "ordered that whereas the Town hath received two letters from W[illiam] Arnold of Pautuxet bearing date the 11th & 16th of April 1657 concerning deciding of differences by arbitrators it is ordered that the letter drawn up & read in this meeting be sent to him & the rest of Pautuxet under the Town Clerk's hand" [PrTR 2:103].

On 5 December 1658, "William Arnold of Pautuxett" reported to the town that he had landed "one anchor of liquors," and the same again on

21 May 1660 [PrTR 2:25-26]. On 9 March 1658/9, Rhode Island General Council took notice of "a robbery committed by several Indians at Pawtuxett upon William Arnold," and ordered that warrants be issued "to the sheriff to apprehend all or any of the offenders" [RICR 1:406].

On 16 October 1678, "William Hopkins aged thirty-one or thereabouts" deposed "that at the beginning of the war they heard at Providence, that William Arnold of Pautuxett would not leave his own house, then some neighbors desired this deponent to go to Pautuxett and persuade him to go to some garrison for safety, or go down to Rhode Island, then this deponent said he would go and did not question but to persuade him, and so this deponent went to Pautuxett to the house of William Arnold, and told the said William Arnold of the danger of the times, and did persuade him to go to some garrison, or down to Rhode Island to his son Benedict's, but he was very unwilling to leave his own house, and said he would not go down to Rhode Island, but if he must leave his own house he would go to Providence, yet after he said Providence was so far off he had rather be nearer home; then this deponent asked him if he would go to his son Stephen's garrison, and the said William Arnold said he did not care if he did go thither, and so desired this deponent to go to his son Stephen's and call him to come to him and then he would go with him to his garrison, then this deponent went to his son Stephen Arnold and called him, and so then presently his son Stephen [went] to his father and desired his father to go to his garrison, and the said William Arnold did go along with his son Stephen and this deponent to his son Stephen's garrison" [PrTR 15:182-83].

THOMAS ARROWSMITH

In a 1634 accounting of "hiredmen's wages," "Tho[mas] Arrosmith" was paid £3 3s. [Trelawny Papers 38].

COMMENTS: Thomas Arrowsmith has not been found in any other New England record, so he apparently was employed at Richmond Island for one season and then departed.

ALICE ASHBY

"Alice Ashbey," aged 20, maid servant to William Holman, was enrolled at London on 20 June 1635 as a passenger for New England on the *Defence* [Hotten 89].

COMMENTS: Not found in any New England record.

In the London port book, Alice Ashby's name comes between that of WILLIAM HOLMAN's wife and his five children. As a result the indexer of Hotten fell into the error of giving to the five Holman children the surname Ashby.

JOHN ASTWOOD

ORIGIN: Little Hadham, Hertfordshire
MIGRATION: 1635 on the *Hopewell*
FIRST RESIDENCE: Roxbury
REMOVES: Milford by 1639
RETURN TRIPS: To England by 1654

OCCUPATION: Husbandman [Hotten 46].
CHURCH MEMBERSHIP: Admitted to Roxbury church as member #132, among the 1635 arrivals [RChR 81].
FREEMAN: 3 March 1635/6 [MBCR 1:371]
EDUCATION: Signed his will [NEHGR 38:421, citing PCC Alchin 505]. The inventory of his widow's estate included two Bibles valued at £1 1s., "one parcel of books" valued at £1 7d. 6d., and a pair of spectacles.
OFFICES: Deputy for Milford, 27 October 1643, 3 April 1644 [NHCR 1:112, 129]. Arbiter, 8 October 1649 [NHCR 492].
    Captain, 1646-53 [NHCR 1:263, 332, 467; NHTR 1:169].
ESTATE: In the 1646 inventory of Milford land John Astwood held six parcels: a seven-and-a-half acre home lot, twenty-one acres and one rood at the west field in creek shot, twenty-one acres and one rood at west field in fence shot, ten acres at Stubby Plain, twenty-three acres at the Great Meadow and "for his half division twenty acres ... on Eseck Plain" [Milford LR 1:78, 82, 87, 92, 95, 100].

    In his will, dated 27 June 1654 and proved 31 August 1654, John Astwood of Milford bequeathed to "my loving wife Sarah Astwood" all the estate in New England; "of my estate here in England in Abutley" to "my brother William Astwood ten pounds"; to "my loving mother five pounds sterling and the use of two rooms of my house"; to "my brother Robert Astwood" five pounds; to "John Rute" 10s.; residue to executor "my son Samuel Astwood" [NEHGR 38:421, citing PCC 505 Alchin].

In her will, dated 9 November 1669 [no date of proving recorded], "Mrs. Sarah Astwood of Milford, widow," bequeathed to "my daughter-in-law Hannah Freeman wife of Stephen Freeman" a pair of sheets "formerly Capt. Astwood's"; to "my grandchild John Baldwin" livestock, pewter, household goods; to "my grandchild Mary Woodruffe" her choice of goods; to "Reverend Pastor Mr. Roger Newton" 20s.; to "my grandchild Sarah Burwell" 5s.; to "my grandchild Mehetabel Fien" 5s.; to "my grandchild Martha Newton" 5s.; to "my daughter Elizabeth Baldwin, widow," all household goods not spoken for; to "my grandchild Mathew Woodruffe my great Bible"; to "my son John Baldwin" 20s.; to "my grandchild Sarah Rigson" a pewter platter; to "my grandchild Temperence Baldwin" a hat; to "my grandchild Mary Baldwin" a petticoat; to "my great-grandchild Sarah Burwell" a pewter platter; to "my beloved daughter Mary Plumb" a book called *The Soul's Conflict*; "my beloved brothers Richard Platt & Thomas Wheeler" overseers [NHPR 1:2:33-34].

The inventory of the estate of "Mrs. Sarah Astwood of Milford" was taken 20 November 1669 and totalled £108 2s. 9d., of which £56 5s. 8d. was real estate: "10 acres of land in the Indian side in the old field" [NHPR 1:2:34].

BIRTH: About 1609 (aged 26 in 1635 [Hotten 46]).

DEATH: "Abutley," England, between 27 June 1654 (date of will) and 31 August 1654 (probate of will) [NEHGR 38:421]. ("Abutley" has not been satisfactorily identified.)

MARRIAGE: (1) 13 February 1633/4 Missenden, Hertfordshire, Dinis Stallworth. She was buried at Little Hadham, Hertfordshire, on 26 December 1634 (not long after the baptism of their only child).

(2) By 1635 Martha _____. "Martha Astwood the wife of John Astwood" was admitted to Roxbury church as member #135, among the arrivals of 1635, and shortly after the admission of her husband [RChR 81]. (Possibly she was the Martha Carter, aged 27, on the *Hopewell* with John in 1635 [Hotten 46].)

(3) By 2 August 1640 Sarah (_____) Baldwin, widow of Sylvester [TAG 16:29, citing Milford Church Records, p. 1]. She was buried at Milford on

13 November 1669 [TAG 16:29, citing Milford Church Records, p. 1].
CHILDREN:
  With first wife
    i   SAMUEL, bp. Little Hadham, Hertfordshire, 19 December
        1634; no further record.
  With second wife
    ii HANNAH, b. say 1636; m. (1) by 1653 Stephen Freeman
        [Parke-Gildersleeve 69, citing Milford church records in
        which Hannah is called "wife of brother Stephen
        Freeman and daughter of Capt. Astwood"]; m. (2) after
        1675 Robert Porter [Parke-Gildersleeve 69, citing Milford
        LR 1-2:58, 3:7 (correct date for which is 23 November
        1685)]; m. (3) after 1689 [John?] Clark (on 10 March
        1690[/1] Hannah Clark is called "now widow formerly the
        wife of Robert Porter" [Milford LR 3:57]).
ASSOCIATIONS: Brother James Astwood came a few years later and
settled in Roxbury, leaving a 1653 will bequeathing £5 to "brother John
Astwood" [SPR Case #132].
    On the same day and in the same parish, John Astwood married Dinis
Stallworth and William Fowler married Grace Stallworth. Astwood and
Fowler were long associated in New England, and it is apparent that
Parke and Jacobus, who noted this pairing of familiar names, but denied
they were the New England immigrants, did not see the baptism of
Astwood's son Samuel or the burial of his first wife Dinis in Little
Hadham [Parke-Gildersleeve 71].

COMMENTS: On 3 April 1635, "Husbandman Jo: Astwood," aged 26, was
enrolled at London on the *Hopewell* as a passenger for New England
[Hotten 46]. Enrolled at the same time were "Jo: Ruggells," aged 10,
"Martha Carter," aged 27, and "Marie Elliott," aged 13 [Hotten 46].
    "Captain Ashwood" performed the marriage between Joseph Pecke and
Widow Burrill at Milford 12 September 1650 and was still performing
marriages in 1652 [NHVR 1:2, 103].
    On 5 July 1653, Susan Clarke, daughter of James, charged Ellis Mew
with indecent assault. During the course of the case, Susan's mother
stated "that the girl should have gone to Milford to dwell with Capt.
Astwood," but her good disposition had caused John Jones to keep her in
his service instead [NHTR 1:182-83]. It is probable that John Astwood was
still in Connecticut at this date. It seems likely that he went to England,

planning to return after a brief visit, since he calls himself of Milford in his will, implying he had not changed his residence to "Abutley."

BIBLIOGRAPHIC NOTE: In 1959 Nathan Grier Parke and Donald Lines Jacobus compiled a brief account of the family of John Astwood [Parke-Gildersleeve 71-72].

JOHN ATHERSON

"Jo[hn] Atherson" was enrolled on 18 April 1635 at London as a passenger for New England on the *Susan & Ellen* [Hotten 63].

COMMENTS: Not seen in any New England record.

THEODORE ATKINSON

ORIGIN: Unknown
MIGRATION: 1634
FIRST RESIDENCE: Boston

OCCUPATION: Feltmaker, hatter, beavermaker [SLR 6:337-38]. On 17 December 1652, Theodore Atkinson recorded a number of legal documents, including deeds and debt instruments, most of which were probably related to his business activities. In one of these records, on 7 October 1652, "Thomas Webber, master of the good ship called the *Mayflower* ... now riding at anchor in the river at Boston" sold to "Theodore Atkinson of Boston feltmaker" one-sixteenth of the ship and its furnishings [SLR 1:258-59].
CHURCH MEMBERSHIP: "Theodorus Atkinson servant to our brother John Newgate" was admitted to Boston church on 11 January 1634/5 [BChR 19].
FREEMAN: 18 May 1642 [MBCR 2:291].
EDUCATION: Signed his deeds.
OFFICES: Boston constable, 12 March 1648/9 [BTR 1:94]. Clerk of the market, 12 March 1654/5 [BTR 1:122].
ESTATE: On 31 August 1640, "Theodor Atkinsone is granted his Great Lot, for two heads at Muddie River, if it be there to be had after others are served that had their grants before him" [BTR 1:55].

On 24 June 1645, "Thomas Hawkins of Boston ... baker" sold to "Theoder Atkinson of Boston ... feltmaker a certain house and garden" in Boston [SLR 1:255-56]. On 29 September 1645, "Increase Nowell, Will[ia]m Hibbins, Henry Dunster and George Coke, feoffees in trust for the estate of Mr. Josse Glover," sold to "Theodore Atkinson of Boston ... feltmaker" "a certain house & garden in Boston formerly the possession of Mr. Josse Glover ... together with three acres of land lying in the Newfield" [SLR 1:254-55].

On 28 June 1652, "Robert Moone late of Boston ... tailor, in consideration of a debt due to Theoder Atkinson of the same Boston hatter," mortgaged to "the said Theoder Atkinson my late dwelling house in the said Boston with the orchards & gardens" [SLR 1:222]. On 13 July 1652, "Sampson Shore of Boston" sold to "Theodora Atkinson of Boston aforesaid beavermaker my dwelling house in Boston aforesaid lately purchased of Will[ia]m Aspinwall together with all houses, outhouses, gardens, yards, orchards, meadows to the same belonging, be the same two acres more or less" [SLR 1:235, 256]. On 30 January 1653/4, "Theodore Adkenson of Boston ... merchant and Abigall his wife" sold to Edward Rawson of Boston "all that their cottage or tenement with the close, orchard or garden thereto belonging containing by estimation two acres & a half ... which he the said Theodore Atkeson lately purchased of William Aspinnall of Boston ... late in the tenure or occupation of Thomas Grubb and now of the said Edward Rawson" [SLR 2:1-4]. On 24 February 1653[/4], Thomas Boyden of Boston, planter, and Frances his wife and Theodore Atkinson of Boston, feltmaker, and Abigail his wife exchanged land, the Boydens receiving three acres of pasture in the New Field and the Atkinsons receiving two acres of pasture in Boston Field [SLR 5:192-94]. On 11 July 1654, "Sarah Fippenny of Boston ... widow" sold to "Theodor Atkinson of Boston aforesaid feltmaker ... all that dwelling house, orchard, garden & backside hereunto adjoining containing about half an acre of land & towards the old windmill in Boston" [SLR 2:39-40].

On 15 December 1655, "Theodore Atkinson of Boston, feltmaker," and "John Shaw of Boston, butcher," confirmed to Thomas Broughton three-quarters of an acre, being part of a three-acre parcel "upon the Mill Hill near Charles River" which John Shaw had sold to William Phillips and William Phillips sold to Thomas Broughton, with Atkinson claiming that he had separately purchased the three-quarters of an acre directly from Shaw, and Shaw admitting that he had done so [SLR 2:221-22].

On 27 January 1658[/9], "John Chandler of Portsmouth in Puscataque River shoemaker" sold to "Theoder Atkinson of Boston ... feltmaker a house & ground thereunto belonging standing and being on the south side of the said Boston near the waterside, opposite against Dorchester Neck, ... which said house & land was of old in the tenure & possession of Miles Reeding a cooper since purchased by the said Chandler of one Wilson a bricklayer" [SLR 3:198-99]. On 28 March 1659, "Theoder Atkinson of Boston ..., feltmaker, & Abigail Atkinson his wife" sold to Peter Warren of Boston, mariner, "one dwelling house & ground thereunto ... which said house and land was John Chandler's and purchased by the said Atkinson of the said Chandler as by a deed bearing date the twenty seventh of January" 1658 [SLR 4:235-36].

On 20 September 1661, "Captain James Oliver of Boston ... merchant & Mary his wife" sold to "Theoder Atkinson of the said Boston, merchant, ... a small warehouse in Boston aforesaid which is a thoroughfare or passageway to a bigger warehouse, the said small warehouse having a chamber overhead, & a garret over the said chamber ..., also a great warehouse" [SLR 3:456-58].

On 17 April 1663, "Theoder Atkinson of Boston ..., feltmaker, & Abigaile his wife" sold to Vincent Druce of Cambridge, yeoman, "all that their piece of upland ... at Muddy River ... being thirteen acres" [SLR 4:108-9].

On 15 April 1667, the deacons of the [First] Church of Christ in Boston sold to "Theoder Atkinson Senior of Boston ..., merchant," seven acres and seven rods at Fort Hill with the buildings thereon [SLR 5:190-92].

On 2 April 1670, "Theodor Atkinson Sen[io]r of Boston ..., feltmaker, ... with the free and full consent of Mary Atkinson his now wife" sold to Henry Ellis of Boston, mariner, a parcel of land "being at the southward end of Boston aforesaid containing forty and three foot in the front and forty and three foot in the rear" [SLR 7:187-89].

On 13 September 1671, Theodore Atkinson of Boston, feltmaker, deeded to "my son Ebenezar Atkinson and to my daughter Abigall Atkinson" land in Boston as an execution against the estate of Captain John Williams of Southwark in England [SLR 7:299; see also SLR 4:152, 8:335].

On 5 October 1671, "Theoder Atkinson of Boston ... senior, feltmaker" granted "unto Robert Sanders & Henry Allen both deacons of the First Church of Boston ... a piece or parcel of land ... at the southward end of the said town of Boston and near adjoining to the Fort Hill there, containing about twenty rods ... immediately after the decease of the said Theoder Atkinson from thenceforth forever" [SLR 10:330-1]. On 5 October 1671, Theodore Atkinson Senior of Boston, feltmaker, deeded to "John Rogers, son of Mr. John Rogers, minister in Ipswich," a piece of land "being in [the] southward end of Boston aforesaid near the Fort Hill there containing in breadth & length about ten rods" [SLR 8:256-57]. On 10 October 1671, "Theodore Atkinson Senior of Boston ... feltmaker" deeded to "Daniel Gookins son of Capt. Daniel Gookins of Cambridge ... a piece or parcel of land lying & being situate at the southward end of Boston aforesaid near the Fort Hill, containing by the breadth and length thereof ten rod of ground" [SLR 12:212-13]. On 20 October 1671, Theodore Atkinson Senior of Boston, feltmaker, sold "John Cotton, son of Seaborn Cotton of Hampton," New Hampshire, a parcel of land "at the southward end of Boston aforesaid containing by the breadth and length thereof ten rod of ground" [SLR 8:174-75]. On 4 December 1671, "Theoder Atkinson Senior of Boston ... feltmaker" deeded to "Jacob and Joseph Walker the sons of Robert Walker of Boston aforesaid, weaver, a piece or parcel of land ... at the southward end of Boston aforesaid, containing by the breadth and length thereof about ten rod of ground" [SLR 12:369].

On 30 January 1671[/2], Theodore Atkinson Senior of Boston, feltmaker, sold to Joseph Gridley of Boston a piece of land "at the southward end of Boston aforesaid, containing eleven foot & a half foot in breadth, at the front, forty-nine foot & a half foot or thereabouts in breadth in the rear, and fourscore foot on each side"; his wife Mary Atkinson signed [SLR 10:31-32]. On 5 April 1672, "Theoder Atkinson Senior of Boston ... feltmaker and Mary his wife" sold to Thomas Danforth of Cambridge "all that his dwelling house and land which he long since bought of Robert Moone with the two orchards on either side thereof ... being about half an acre" [SLR 11:304-6]. On 24 July 1672, Theodore Atkinson of Boston, senior, feltmaker, sold to John Marsh of Boston, currier, "a parcel of land ... in Boston aforesaid right over against the lands that late was John Pell's deceased lane or highway being between the said parcel of land containing ten rods in the whole"; on the same day "Mary now wife of the abovenamed Theodor Atkinson" consented [SLR 9:332-33].

On 16 May 1673, Theodore Atkinson Senior of Boston, feltmaker, sold to Thomas Davis of Haverhill a piece of land at "the southward end of Boston aforesaid near the Fort Hill there containing by the breadth & length thereof twenty rod of ground"; his wife Mary Atkinson signed [SLR 8:183-84]. On 30 March 1677, Theodore Atkinson Senior of Boston, feltmaker, deeded to Peter Bracket and Jacob Eliot, deacons of the Third Church in Boston, a piece of land "at the southward end of the town of Boston aforesaid containing by the breadth and length thereof twenty rod of ground" [SLR 10:130].

On 5 March 1674/5, "Theodor Atkinson Senior of Boston ... feltmaker and his wife Mary" sold to Joseph Baker of Boston, tailor, "a piece or parcel of land ... at the southward end of Boston aforesaid and is part of the land which was formerly the land of John Farebanx of Boston aforesaid containing forty and two foot in breadth ... to run back upon a straight line sixty foot in length" [SLR 9:188-90]. On 8 April 1675, "Theodore Atkinson Senior of Boston, ... feltmaker, and Mary his wife" sold to Thomas Kellond of Boston, merchant, "all that piece or parcel of land ... at the southward end of the town of Boston aforesaid near the Fort Hill and containing by the breadth and length thereof thirty-eight rod of ground" [SLR 9:178-79].

On 16 March 1676/7, "Theodore Atkinson of Boston ..., feltmaker, and Mary his wife" sold to James Webster of Boston, brewer, "a piece or parcel of land ... at the southward end of Boston containing forty and two foot in breadth at the front ... and so running back from the said street upon a straight line sixty foot in length" [SLR 10:205-6]. On 18 March [*recte* February] 1677/8, "Theodore Atkinson of Boston ..., feltmaker, and Mary his wife" sold to John Marsh of Boston, currier, "a piece or parcel of land ... at the southward end of Boston aforesaid and next adjoining to other of the land of the said John Marsh and containing twenty-four foot and nine inches in breadth at the front ... and so running back upon a straight line and the same breadth sixty-six foot in length" [SLR 10:271-72].

On 22 March 1676/7, Theodore Atkinson of Boston, feltmaker, for the "real love and parental affection that I bear unto my daughter Abigail Atkinson, deceased, and in consideration of the respects that I bear unto Abraham Spencer that married my said daughter Abigail," deeded to Abraham Spencer a piece of land "at the southward end of Boston aforesaid containing thirty foot in breadth at the front" [SLR 10:129-30]. On 16 September 1678, "Theodore Atkinson of Boston ..., feltmaker, with the free and full consent of my now wife Mary Atkinson" sold to Abraham Spencer a piece of land "at the southward end of Boston near to Fort Hill ... next adjoining to a piece of land formerly given by me the said Atkinson unto the said Abraham Spencer" [SLR 11:143-44].

On 1 July 1681, "Theodor Atkinson of Boston ... feltmaker ... with the free and full consent of his wife Mary Atkinson" sold to "John Fisher now in Boston aforesaid feltmaker ... a piece or parcel of land ... being at the south end of Boston aforesaid and next adjoining to other of the land of the said Atkinson and containing fifty foot at the front next the street" [SLR 12:85-86]; on the same day John Fisher mortgaged the land back to Theodore Atkinson [SLR 12:86-87]. On 18 October 1681, "Theodore Atkinson of Boston ... feltmaker ... and Mary his wife" mortgaged to "John Richards Esquire of Boston" attorney and agent for "Major Robert

Thomson of London" (to whom Atkinson owed £156) "all that their piece or parcel of land scituate near the southerly end of the town of Boston aforesaid, containing by estimation about three-quarters of an acre" [SLR 12:120-21]. On 17 December 1681, "Theodore Atkinson of Boston ... feltmaker" sold to "James Brading of said Boston, ironmonger, ... all those my three several lots or parcels of land lying and being upon Long Island within the Mattachusetts Bay and Township of Boston abovesaid, containing in the whole by estimation ten acres ..., four acres thereof more or less I purchased of William Ingraham late of said Boston, cooper, ..., a second parcel containing three acres more or less I purchased of William Causteen formerly of said Boston, ... the third lot or parcel hereby granted containing three acres more or less I purchased of William Lane of Boston, laborer"; "Mary my wife" consented to and signed the deed [SLR 12:136-37].

On 6 September 1682, "Theoder Atkinson of Boston ... feltmaker and Mary his wife" sold to "Jonathan Balston Senior of Boston aforesaid, shipwright, ... all that his dwelling house situate and standing at the southerly end of Boston and all the land it standeth upon and a piece of land thereto adjoining" [SLR 12:276-77].

On 28 December 1686, "Theodore Atkinson of Boston ..., feltmaker, & Mary his wife" sold to John Tower Sr. of Hingham, yeoman, "all that their piece or parcel of land situate, lying & being in Boston aforesaid containing by estimation fifty foot square" [SLR 14:116-18].

On 30 June 1697, "Theoder Atkinson of Boston ..., feltmaker, and Mary his wife" sold to Jeremiah Dummer of Boston "a certain piece or parcel of pasture land situate, lying and being at the southerly end of the town of Boston aforesaid containing in the whole twenty-eight rod and one-quarter" [SLR 14:357-59].

On 30 September 1701, "Mary Atkinson, relict widow of Theodore Atkinson late of Boston ..., feltmaker, deceased," refused administration on her husband's estate and asked that "the same may be granted unto his grandson Theodore Atkinson" [SPR NS 6:35-36]. On 3 October 1701, "Theodore Atkinson of New Castle in the Province of New Hampshire ..., feltmaker, grandson of Theodore Atkinson," was appointed administrator [SPR 14:403].

BIRTH: About 1614 (deposed 13 May 1676 "aged about sixty-two years" [EQC 6:155]; aged 90 in 1701 [Sewall 387]).
DEATH: Buried Boston 16 August 1701, aged 90 [Sewall 387].

MARRIAGE: (1) By about 1642 Abigail Chambers, daughter of Thomas Chambers [GMB 1:324-26; SLR 6:333]. On 15 October 1648 "Abigail Atkinson the wife of our brother Theodore Atkinson upon letters of dismission from the Church at Ipswich" was admitted to Boston church "having likewise declared her condition [to the Elders in their private meeting]" [BChR 51]. She died after 17 April 1663 [SLR 4:108] and before October 1667.

(2) Soon after 21 October 1667 Mary (Wheelwright) Lyde, daughter of Rev. JOHN WHEELWRIGHT and widow of Edward Lyde [BVR 77; SLR 8:422, 9:143]. On 21 October 1667, "Theoder Attkinson Senior of Boston ... merchant or feltmaker sendeth greeting that whereas their is a contract of marriage between me the said Atkinson & Mrs. Mary Lyde widow ... to the intent therefore that my said intended wife may not be left destitute in case of my decease" she is to have "a warehouse ... in Boston near adjoining unto Mr. Peter Oliver's ground together with a certain small tract of land lying & being between the aforesaid warehouse & Mr. Peter Oliver's land the said house & land in value being worth about two hundred & fifty pounds" [NLR 2:94]. On 4 January 1711/2 at Boston occurred "the funeral of Mrs. M. Atkinson, born in New-England, aged 73 years, buried in a tomb in the New-burying place, from her son, Mr. Lyde's house" [Sewall 675].

CHILDREN (all born and baptized at Boston):

With first wife

    i   THEODORE, b. 10 April 1644 [BVR 17], bp. 28 April 1644 "being about 9 days old" [BChR 295-96]; m. by 1668 Elizabeth Mitchelson (eldest child b. Boston 25 June 1668 [BVR 106]), daughter of EDWARD MITCHELSON. She m. (2) Henry Deering (administration on the estate of "Theodore Atkinson Jr. sometime of Boston deceased intestate" was granted to "Elizabeth Atkinson his widow and Mr. Samuel Shrimpton, merchant, a principal creditor to the said estate," and they carried out their duties, but the magistrates failed to record the grant of administration, so "at the instance of Mr. Henry Deering who married with Elizabeth the relict of said Atkinson," the grant of administration was belatedly recorded on 23 January 1678[/9] [SPR 5:352]; in his will of 27 April 1680, "Edw[ard] Mitchelson of Cambr[idge]" designated as his residuary legatees "my three daughters Ruth Green, Bethia Weld & Elizab[eth] Dearing" [MPR 5:332]). (The date of marriage between Henry Deering and Elizabeth (Mitchelson) Atkinson is given in secondary sources as 15 November 1676 [Wentworth Gen 1:115; NYGBR 52:41], but this marriage does not appear in Boston vital records, nor has it been found elsewhere.)

ii   NATHANIEL, b. 28 November 1645 [BVR 21], bp. 30 November 1645 "being about 4 days old" [BChR 300]; Harvard College 1667 [Sibley 2:221]; no further record.

iii   ABIGAIL, b. 24 August 1647 [BVR 25], bp. 29 August 1647 "being about 7 days old" [BChR 307]; d. soon.

iv   ELEAZER, bp. 3 February 1649/50 "being about 8 days old" [BChR 316]; presumably he is the "son Ebenezar Atkinson" who received land from his father on 13 September 1671 [SLR 7:299]; no further record.

v   THOMAS, bp. 22 October 1654 [BChR 329]; no further record.

vi   ABIGAIL, b. 9 December 1657 [BVR 60], bp. 13 December 1657 [BChR 333]; m. by 1676 Abraham Spencer [SLR 10:129-30].

With second wife

vii   JOHN, b. 13 June 1672 [BVR 122]; no further record.

viii   THEODORE, b. 28 February 1673[/4] [BVR 126]; no further record.

ASSOCIATIONS: Theodore Atkinson's first wife, Abigail Chambers, was younger sister of AMY CHAMBERS, wife of THOMAS MATSON [GMB 1:324-26].

In his unprobated will of 23 October 1638, JOHN NEWGATE bequeathed to "Theodore Atkinson my servant twenty pounds ... to be paid him when his time of service shall be expired" [Lechford 19].

John Atkinson of Newbury was nephew of Theodore Atkinson [NEHGR 98:288 and Pillsbury Anc 2:719-24, citing ELR 28:185; see also SLR 8:220, 274].

COMMENTS: Savage claims that Theodore Atkinson was "from Bury in Co. Lancaster," while Pope has him coming "from Bury St. Edmunds [Suffolk]." There is no solid evidence for either origin [Pillsbury Anc 2:719], but, since John Newgate, Atkinson's master, held land in Horningsheath [modern Horringer], Suffolk, Pope's suggestion is more likely than Savage's.

On 15 October 1640, Robert Mantell of Dorchester entered a bond to pay an unstated amount to "William Baker, citizen & haberdasher of

London," to the use of Thomas Atkinson [Lechford 326].

On 19 August 1644, "James Alexander servant to Theodore Atkinson" died at Boston [BVR 17].

THOMAS ATKINSON

ORIGIN: Unknown
MIGRATION: 1635
FIRST RESIDENCE: Plymouth

OCCUPATION: Yeoman [PCR 1:106].
FREEMAN: Thomas Atkinson appears in the "1633" list of Plymouth Colony freemen, just before those men made free on 5 January 1635/6 [PCR 1:4]. He is in the 7 March 1636/7 list of Plymouth freemen [PCR 1:53]. In Plymouth section of "1639" Plymouth Colony list of freemen (with name later crossed out, indicating death or departure) [PCR 8:174].
OFFICES: Plymouth coroner's jury, 5 June 1638 [PCR 1:88].
ESTATE: On 7 November 1636, Thomas Atkinson was one of eight men granted six acres apiece, "[all] which persons have or are to build in the town of Plym[outh], and these lands to belong to their dwelling houses there, & not to be sold from their houses" [PCR 1:46]. On 4 December 1637, "Thomas Atkinson is granted to enlarge his garden place at his now dwelling house towards the brook side" [PCR 1:70]. On 26 July 1638, "Thom[as] Atkinson" was one of three men who were to share "in the black heifer which was Henry Howlande['s]" [PTR 1:4].

BIRTH: By about 1614 based on date of freemanship.
DEATH: After 28 February 1639/40 [PCR 1:140].
MARRIAGE: None recorded. (The court-ordered placement of William Honeywell in the household of Thomas Atkinson may indicate that the latter was married [PCR 1:139-40], for it is unlikely that the court would place one single man with another.)
CHILDREN: None recorded.

COMMENTS: On 4 December 1638, Thomas Atkinson, yeoman, posted bond of £40 as surety for Samuel Gorton when the latter was brought before Plymouth Court [PCR 1:106].

On 28 February 1639/40, arrangements were made for William Honeywell, servant of Mr. Thomas Prence, to reside with Thomas Atkinson during part of the term of his service [PCR 1:139-40].

About the time that Thomas Atkinson disappeared from the Plymouth records, a Thomas Atkins began to appear [PTR 1:6; PCR 2:4]. In 1967 Florence Barclay treated Thomas Atkins of Kennebec, who may be this Thomas Atkins of Plymouth, without suggesting any connection with Thomas Atkinson [NEHGR 121:241-45].

PHILIP ATWOOD

ORIGIN: Unknown
MIGRATION: 1635
FIRST RESIDENCE: Charlestown
REMOVES: Malden, Quinsigamond (Worcester) 1675, Malden 1676, Bradford by 1700

OCCUPATION: Planter.
EDUCATION: Signed his deeds.
ESTATE: On 28 January 1673[/4?], "Philip Atwood of Maulden ... planter, with the assent & consent of Rachel my wife," sold to John Sprague of Malden "a certain nine-acre lot in Charlestown" [MLR 6:447]. On 1 October 1674, "Philip Atwood of Mauldon ... planter, with the assent & consent of Rachell my wife," sold to Jose Bucknam of Malden seven acres of land, partly in Malden and partly in Charlestown; Philip and Rachel Atwood acknowledged this deed on 24 October 1674, he signing and she making her mark [MLR 7:176].

In April 1675 "Philip Atwood of Concord" had fifty acres of land surveyed and recorded at the settlement that would become Worcester [Charles Nutt, *History of Worcester and Its People* (New York 1919), pp. 1-2, citing Worcester Proprietors' Records].

On 18 January 1680[/1?], "Philip Atwood Senior of Malden ... with the assent & consent of Elizabeth my wife" deeded to "my son Phillip Atwood ... all that moiety or one-half part of a certain dwelling house in Charlestown ... which Richard Austin now lives in with a garden plot containing sixteen foot of land one way & twelve foot the other way & one-half part of the yard thereto belonging all which was formerly given to me by my father-in-law Batchelor by his will" [MLR 9:530].

On 25 December 1685, "Phillip Atwood of Maldon ... planter, with the assent & consent of Elizabeth my wife," deeded to "Phillip Atwood my son ... all my lands as followeth: my houselot, 3 acres more or less ... with all my housing, dwelling house, barn, outhouses, stables & houses thereon contained, with my orchards therein contained or anyway belonging; also six acres of land" and "5 acres of land" [MLR 9:532]. On 17 February 1713/4, "whereas my honored father Philip Atwood late of Bradford deceased did by deed of gift bearing date the 25th day of December 1685 as more fully may appear on record at Charlestowne in Middlesex all his lands in the realm of England and part of said land lying in Worcester in New England which my father began to settle and did plant, but was forced to desert by reason of the war, for several reasons me there moving but more especially for a certain sum of money to me in hand paid by Oliver Atwood of Boston in the County of Suffolke, ferryman, ... I Phillip Atwood, son to the abovenamed Phillip Atwood, deceased," sell the land in Worcester to Oliver Atwood [MLR 16:448].

BIRTH: About 1620 (aged 12 or 13 in 1635 [Hotten 49, 59]; deposed 16 June 1663 "aged 45 or thereabouts" [MCF Folio #35]; in his 85th year at his death on 1 February 1700[/1] [Essex Ant 5:17]).
DEATH: Bradford 1 February 1700[/1] "in the 85 year of his age" [Essex Ant 5:17, transcribing tombstone inscriptions from Ancient Burying Ground at Bradford].
MARRIAGE: (1) By 1653 Rachel Bachelor, daughter of WILLIAM BACHELOR. She died at Malden on 7 November 1674. (Two death dates for Rachel, wife of Philip Atwood, were sent in by the town of Malden for recording by Middlesex County, 5 February 1673[/4] and 7 November 1674. Philip's wife Rachel was clearly alive on 24 October 1674, when she acknowledged her joint deed with her husband of 1 October 1674 [MLR 7:176], so only the latter of these two dates can be correct. The earlier death date may pertain to their daughter Rachel.)
(2) Malden 7 April 1675 Elizabeth Grover; she died at Malden on [blank] October 1676.
(3) Elizabeth _____ ; she died at Malden on 3 April 1688.
CHILDREN (all born Malden):
  With first wife
    i   RACHEL, b. [blank] August 1653; no further record; probably the "Rachel, wife [sic] of Philip Atwood," who died at Malden 5 February 1673[/4].
    ii   MARY, b. [blank] January 1655[/6?]; no further record.

iii   PHILIP, b. [blank] September 1658 (d. at Bradford 13 April
          1722 "in the 64th year of his age" [Essex Ant 5:17]); m.
          Salem 23 July 1684 Sarah Tenney (recorded at Bradford).
iv   ABIGAIL, b. [blank] December 1662; m. Charlestown 12
          November 1686 Andrew Mitchell [ChVR 1:26].
v   ELIZABETH, b. [blank] August 1669; m. Malden 16 November
          1688 Philip Covell.
vi   OLIVER, b. [blank] April 1671; m. Charlestown 30 March 1699
          Anna Betts [ChVR 1:173, 185].

COMMENTS: On 6 April 1635, "Phillipp Atwood," aged twelve, was
enrolled at London as a passenger for New England on the *Planter*, and
on 13 April 1635, "Phillip Atwood," aged thirteen, was enrolled at London
as a passenger for New England on the *Susan & Ellen* [Hotten 49, 59].
These two entries are probably for the same person, moving from one
vessel to another.

 Even though the name Philip Atwood does not appear in New England
records for eighteen years after 1635, we consider this to be the same man
because of the relative rarity of the name and the compatibility of his age
at death and other New England information on his age with his age as
given at embarkation in England.

 The record of Philip Atwood's grant of land at Worcester calls him "of
Concord," but no other record has been found which places him in that
town. Since he calls himself of Malden in his deeds of 1674, this record is
probably defective. When his son Philip conveys this Worcester land to
his brother Oliver, he refers to the deed of 25 December 1685 as passing
this right to him from his father; unless there was a second deed of this
same date, we must assume that the younger Philip construed the phrase
"all my lands" as broadly as possible.

JONAS AUSTIN

ORIGIN: Tenterden, Kent
MIGRATION: 1635 on the *Hercules* of Sandwich
FIRST RESIDENCE: Cambridge
REMOVES: Hingham 1636, Taunton 1651

OCCUPATION: Yeoman.

FREEMAN: Plymouth oath of fidelity, 3 June 1657 [PCR 3:117, 8:187]. In Taunton section of 29 May 1670 Plymouth Colony list of freemen [PCR 5:276].

EDUCATION: Signed deeds and coroner's jury reports by mark.

OFFICES: Coroner's jury at Taunton, 10 June 1651, 5 July 1664 [PCR 2:175, 4:71]. Taunton highway surveyor, 3 June 1657 [PCR 3:116].

ESTATE: On 20 August 1635, "[blank] Austin" received a proportional share of one-half in the undivided meadow at Cambridge [CaTR 13]. In the list of houses in Cambridge, dated 8 February 1635/6, "Jonnas Austine" was credited with one in the town [CaTR 18].

By 1639 THOMAS BLODGET of Cambridge had purchased from "Jonas Austen two acres of planting ground in the West End" [CaBOP 59].

"The several parcels of land and meadow legally given unto Jonas Austen by the Town of Hingham": 3 July 1636, "for a houselot five acres of land"; undated, "for a planting lot four acres of land"; 8 October 1637, "for a Great Lot twelve acres of land lying upon the Great Plain 28 Lot in the first furlong"; undated, "two acres of salt marsh lying in Layford's Liking Meadow"; undated, "four acres of land lying in Hockly Field ... which four acres of land was given him for satisfaction for a part of his houselot that was taken away for the highway which runs between John Beale's houselot and his own"; and, undated, "three acres of meadow at Conyehassett its the fifth lot over the river" [HiBOP 56].

On 1 February 1650[/1], "Jonas Austen of Hingham" sold to "John Beale the eldest of Hingham his home lot 4 acres more or less house & barn in Hingham ...; also eight acres land in Hockley Neck ...; also four acres in planting Broad Cove" [SLR 1:133]. (In his will of 30 June 1656 William Ripley of Hingham referred to "four acres of salt meadow, which I bought of Jonas Austen, lying at Lyford's Liking" [NEHGR 6:354].)

On 6 February 1650[/1], "W[illia]m Hollaway late of Taunton" sold to "Jonas Austen of Hingham all his land in Taunton, to say one home lot of six acres ... & three acres joining to the same late purchased of widow Randall ...; also the housing, outhousing, gardens, orchards, fencings, etc.; also one acre ... at the end of the said home lot lying in common with John Parker aforesaid; also a parcel of land called the Neck & lot containing eleven acres ...; also one parcel of meadow seven or eight acres ... lying at the Broad Cove ...; also his great lot containing twenty-six acres ... about two mile distant from the town, with all privileges & appurtenances" [SLR 1:133].

On 19 November 1652, "Jonas Austin of Taunton ..., yeoman," sold to Edward Bobbett of Taunton "a certain parcel of land ... [in] Taunton aforesaid on the south side of the Great River ... containing twelve pole in breadth and in quantity by estimation [six?] acres broad" [PCLR 4:71].

On 27 February 1676/7, "Jonas Austine Se[nio]r of Taunton ... having formerly for several years past freely given to my only son Jonas Austine Jun[io]r lately deceased certain parcel of land within the town of Taunton aforesaid, and having omitted giving my son a full and legal deed of the aforesaid lands during the time of his life, these are therefore to declare to all people whom it may concern that I the aforesaid Jonas Austine Sen[io]r do by these presents confirm the aforesaid lands to my aforesaid son's wife and children ...; the lands is [blank] acre lot with a small parcel of upland adjoining to the same whereon the now dwelling house of the said widow standeth, the three acres of land [described]; and secondly two acres of upland ... with an acre of swamp adjoining" [PCLR 4:84].

BIRTH: Baptized Staplehurst, Kent, 3 December 1598, son of Jarvis and Mary (Bassock) Austin [NEHGR 67:164-65].
DEATH: Taunton 30 July 1683 [MD 22:94].
MARRIAGE: (1) Tenterden, Kent, 22 January 1626/7 Constance (_____) Robinson, widow of William Robinson [NEHGR 67:162, 165]. She died at Taunton on 22 April 1667.

(2) Taunton 14 December 1667 Frances (_____) Hill, widow of John Hill of Dorchester [NEHGR 58:157-59]. On 28 June 1674, "Francis Hill that was, but now Francis Asten, was dismissed [from the church at Dorchester] to join the church at Tanton" [DChR 11]. She died at Dorchester on 18 November 1676 [DVR 29].
CHILDREN:
With first wife
    i   MARY, bp. Tenterden, Kent, 24 August 1628 and bur. there 18 December 1629 [NEHGR 67:162].
    ii   JONAS, bp. Tenterden 28 February 1629/30 [NEHGR 67:162]; m. by 1661 Esther _____ (eldest child b. 3 January 1662, which must have been 3 January 1661/2, since second child was b. 12 May 1663 [MD 18:168 (in which surname is incorrectly given as "Allin")]; on 22 November 1676 "Ester Austine widow" swore to the inventory of Jonas Austin Jr. [PCPR 3:2:26, 57]).
    iii   MARY, bp. Tenterden 5 August 1632 [NEHGR 67:162]; sailed for New England in 1635; no further record.
ASSOCIATIONS: Although no kinship relation has been found between Jonas Austin and NATHANIEL TILDEN, both of Tenterden, Kent, they

certainly knew one another in England, since Tilden witnessed the 1625 will of William Robinson, whose widow soon married Austin [NEHGR 67:161-62].

COMMENTS: On 2 and 4 March 1634[/5], "Jonas Austen of Tenterden & Constance his wife," along with "Jonas Austen," "Lidia Robinson," and "[blank] Austen, a little child," had their conformity certified by the vicar, the mayor, and another magistrate of Tenterden, and were enrolled as passengers for New England on the *Hercules* of Sandwich [NEHGR 75:218, 79:108]. LYDIA ROBINSON was stepdaughter of Jonas Austin, his first wife's daughter by her first husband. The "little child" was the Mary Austin baptized on 5 August 1632.

Savage entertains, but does not wholly accept the idea that it was the son of the immigrant who married the widow of John Hill, while Pope intermixes records for the immigrant and his son of the same name.

Savage claims that Jonas Austin was "found at Taunton 1643," presumably referring to the 1643 list of men able to bear arms. Austin does not appear in that list, and, as seen in the deed cited above, was still in Hingham as late as 1651 [SLR 1:133].

BIBLIOGRAPHIC NOTE: In 1913 Elizabeth French published her research into the English origin of Jonas Austin, including two generations of his paternal ancestry, as well as data on his mother's family, the Bassocks [NEHGR 67:161-69].

JOSEPH AVERY

ORIGIN: Romsey, Hampshire
MIGRATION: 1635 on the *James* of Southampton
FIRST RESIDENCE: Newbury
REMOVES: With 22 others, including his wife and children, he embarked at Ipswich 11 August 1635, and set sail the following day, intending to settle at Marblehead [Young's First Planters 486], but died on his way there, apparently in a hurricane.

OCCUPATION: Minister.
EDUCATION: Of Berkshire, matriculated at Queen's College, Oxford, 28 April 1615, aged 15; B.A. from St Edmund Hall 10 July 1618, M.A. 19 April 1621 [Foster 1:46; Morison 364].

ESTATE: On 1 September 1635, "There is administration graunted to Mr. Anthony Thacher of the goods and chattels of Mr. Joseph Avery, deceased, which he is to inventory, & return the same into the next Court; & the said goods are to remain in his hands till further order be taken therein.

An Inventory of the Goods and Chattels of Joseph Avery, deceased.

Due to him from John Emery, carpenter, £07 00s. 00d.

Item: from Robte. Andrewes, of Ipswich, which
    he confesseth to be due, & to be pd forthwith, 02 00 00

Item: from Mr. William Hilton, 02 16 00
    or a sow & pigs to that value. Testis, Rich: Kent.

From Rich: Kent, of Ipswich, ten bushels of Indian corn, which he
    acknowledgeth.

John Emery denies his debt, but Richard Knight, Nicholas Holte, & John Knight, all three of Newbury, can & will testify & prove it to be due, only he was, by condition, to pay the said £7 in his work, which he was to do as soon as Mr. Avery did call upon him for it, out of which said £7 there is something paid in labor already, as he can make to appear" [MBCR 1:154].

BIRTH: About 1600 (aged 15 in 1615 [Foster 1:46]).

DEATH: 15 August 1635 by drowning (Pope says 16 August, in error [Pope 24]).

MARRIAGE: By 1623 _____ _____. Died 15 August 1635 by drowning.

CHILDREN:

    i   JOHN, bp. Hursley, Hampshire, 31 July 1623; d. 15 August 1635 by drowning.

    ii   Child, d. 15 August 1635 by drowning.

    iii SUSANNA, bp. Romsey, Hampshire, 14 August 1627; d. 15 August 1635 by drowning.

    iv ELIZABETH, bp. Romsey 16 April 1629; d. 15 August 1635 by drowning.

    v   SARAH, bp. Romsey 12 August 1632; d. 15 August 1635 by drowning.

    vi Child, d. 15 August 1635 by drowning.

ASSOCIATIONS: He was called "cousin" by Anthony Thacher [Young's First Planters 485-495; Coldham 121].

COMMENTS: As Savage points out, Hubbard was in error in stating that Joseph Avery came in the *Angel Gabriel*, for Avery arrived in Boston the day before that ship left Bristol for New England [Savage 1:83]. Cotton

Mather refers to the minister in error as *John* Avery, which name was repeated by many writers thereafter [Magnalia 1:331]. Coldham wonders whether the Averys came on the *Reformation* in the spring of 1634 [Coldham 121], but he appears not to have seen Young. There it is stated that the Averys and others came on the *James* in 1635 from Southampton, arriving at Boston 3 June of that year [Young's First Planters 485].

In the course of reporting on a severe storm that hit New England in August of 1635, Winthrop stated that "[i]n the same tempest a bark of Mr. Allerton's was cast away upon Cape Ann, and twenty-one persons drowned; among the rest one Mr. Averye, a minister in Wil[t]shire, a godly man, with his wife and six small children, were drowned. None were saved but one Mr. Thacher and his wife.... One of the children was then cast dead on shore, and the rest never found" [WJ 1:196-197].

A much longer account than Winthrop's was that of Anthony Thacher, one of those who suffered through and survived the shipwreck. This narrative, in the form of a letter to his brother in England, has come down to us in two versions [Letters of NE 167]. First, Increase Mather obtained a copy of the letter for use in his *Essay for the Recording of Illustrious Providences*; nearly two centuries later Alexander Young reprinted the letter from Mather [Young's First Planters 485-95]. Second, most, but not all, of the letter survives in manuscript form in England; this was published in 1976 [Letters of NE 168-74], and Coldham has also prepared an abstract of it [Coldham 121]. The extracts below are taken form the Mather-Young version.

> There was a league of perpetual friendship between my cousin Avery and myself, never to forsake each other to the death, but to the partakers of each other's misery or welfare, as also of habitation, in the same place. Now upon our arrival in New-England, there was an offer made unto us. My cousin Avery was invited to Marble-head, to be their pastor in due time; there being no church planted there as yet, but a town appointed to set up the trade of fishing. Because many there (the most being fishermen,) were something loose and remiss in their behavior, my cousin Avery was unwilling to go thither; and so refusing, we went to Newberry, intending there to sit down. But being solicited so often both by the men of the place, and by the magistrates, and by Mr. Cotton, and most of the ministers, who alleged what a benefit we might be to the people there, and also to the country and commonwealth, at length we embraced it,

and thither consented to go. They of Marble-head forthwith sent a pinnace for us and our goods.

We embarked at Ipswich August 11, 1635, with our families and substance, bound for Marble-head, we being in all twenty-three souls, viz., eleven in my cousin's family, seven in mine, and one Mr. William Eliot, sometimes of New Sarum, and four mariners. The next morning, having commended ourselves to God, with cheerful hearts, we hoisted sail. But the Lord suddenly turned our cheerfulness into mourning and lamentations. For on the 14th of this August, 1635, about ten at night, having a fresh gale of wind, our sails being old and done, were split. The mariners, because that it was night, would not put to new sails, but resolved to cast anchor till the morning. But before daylight, it pleased the Lord to send so mighty a storm, as the like was never known in New-England since the English came, nor in the memory of any of the Indians. It was so furious, that our anchor came home. Whereupon the mariners let out more cable, which at last slipped away. Then our sailors knew not what to do; but we were driven before the wind and waves [Young's First Planters 485-87].

Now none were left in the bark, that I knew or saw, but my cousin, his wife and children, myself and mine, and his maid-servant ... by a mighty wave I was, with the piece of the bark, washed out upon part of the rock, where the wave left me almost drowned. But recovering my feet, I saw above me, on the rock, my daughter Mary. To whom I had no sooner gotten, but my cousin Avery and his eldest son came to us; being all four of us washed out by one and the same wave. We went into a small hole on the top of the rock, whence we called to those in the pinnace to come unto us ... But presently came another wave, and dashing the pinnace all to pieces, carried my wife away ... unto the shore ... All the rest that were in the bark were drowned in the merciless seas. We four by that wave were clean swept away from off the rock also into the sea; the Lord, in one instant of time, disposing of fifteen souls of us according to his good pleasure and will [Young's First Planters 489-90].

While Winthrop's account differs slightly, in the number of people on the vessel and in the apparent number of Avery's dependents, from the more detailed account provided by Thacher, it must be observed that Thacher was an eye-witness, as well as a relative of Avery's, and that

Thacher wrote his minutely-detailed account of the harrowing experience to his brother, Rev. Peter Thacher of the church of St Edmund's, Salisbury, Wiltshire, "within a few days" of the awful calamity [Young's First Planters 494]. Consequently, Thacher's date of their deaths must be the more reliable, and is used here. If we are to reconcile Winthrop's statement that Avery had six children with Thacher's comment that there were eleven in the family, then it is likely that the Averys had three servants in their household, although only a maid servant is mentioned by Thacher.

THOMAS AVERY

ORIGIN: Unknown
MIGRATION: 1634 on the *Mary & John*
FIRST RESIDENCE: Salem

OCCUPATION: Blacksmith.
CHURCH MEMBERSHIP: Admitted to Salem church 30 September 1638 [SChR 7].
FREEMAN: 28 February 1642/3 [EQC 1:50].
EDUCATION: Signed John Bridgman's (also called George Bridgman) undated and imperfect will with his mark "T," the will being presented for probate at Salem on 29 November 1655 [EPR 1:226; EQC 1:410].
ESTATE: At a Salem town meeting held on 26 January 1645/6, Thomas Avery desired a little meadow before his door [STR 1:141].

On 10 March 1657/8, "Thomas Avery of Salem ..., blacksmith, & Susanna his wife" sold to George Corwin, merchant, "his dwelling house, shop, barn or other outhousing thereto belonging, together with 16 acres of upland & 6 acres of meadow" [ELR 1:37]. (On 16 December 1717, apparently in reference to this land, Daniel Southwick and Samuel Aborne deposed about three parcels of land owned by John Trask tertius of Salem, husbandman, one of which was "near Ely Gyles, which he bought of Jonathan Curwin Esq., [where] there was erected and built a cottage or dwelling place at or before the time aforesaid [1661] by Thomas Avery of Salem aforesaid, blacksmith, deceased" [ELR 32:254-55].)

BIRTH: By 1622 (based on date of church membership and date of freemanship).
DEATH: Last seen on 20 July 1658 [EQC 2:109].

MARRIAGE: By 1654 Susanna _____ (assuming she is the "sister Avery" named in the 23 March 1654/5 will of Rebecca Bacon). She died after 10 March 1657/8, when she sold land with her husband.

CHILDREN: None recorded.

ASSOCIATIONS: Thomas Avery was mentioned in the will of widow Rebecca Bacon of Salem, dated 23 March 1654/5 and proved 29 November 1655, in which he was made overseer and was referred to as "Brother Thomas Avery" [EQC 1:411-413]. Rebecca Bacon named a large number of "brothers" and "sisters" in her will, which probably indicates that they were brethren in the church rather than actual relatives of hers. She left to "sister Avery and Hornis each of them a neck handkerchief" [EPR 1:228; see also TAG 73:23-32]. It is observed that the vast majority of the people named in the Bacon will are of known Quaker persuasion, giving rise to the possibility that the Averys became Friends.

COMMENTS: Thomas Avery's name appears on the passenger list of the *Mary & John*, Robert Sayres, master, which sailed from Southampton on 24 March 1633/4 [NEHGR 9:267]. Since a number of the individuals on that list are known to have settled in Salem, it seems likely that the Thomas Avery on the list is the man of that name being admitted to the Salem church four years later.

At a court held at Salem on 24 June 1656, Ezekiel Wathen, apprentice to Thomas Avery, was discharged, being 20 years old [EQC 1:428].

On 20 July 1658, Thomas Avery and Samuel Shattuck were summoned to court for absenting themselves from public worship, which again indicates that they were probably sympathetic to the Friends [EQC 2:109].

At a meeting of the selectmen of Salem, held on 27 December 1673, a distribution was made of land belonging to the town as common land that was claimed by anyone, and held by anyone, beyond what was their right, and it was found that "that land of Capt. Corwin's that was Avery's land" was among the parcels to be granted, probably indicating that the Averys had died or removed prior to Corwin's claiming the land [STR 2:180-81].

Indeed, next to Thomas Avery's name on the record of his admission to the Salem church is later written "removed." This might mean that he and his family had left the town of Salem, although we should not discount the possibility that he was "removed" from the list of church members because of his Quaker inclinations.

Whatever his fate, he is not the Thomas Avery of Portsmouth, New Hampshire, born about 1631, and a proprietor there in 1657, whose widow was named Joan [GDMNH 70], with whom Torrey has confused him.

MILES AWKLEY

ORIGIN: Unknown
MIGRATION: 1635
FIRST RESIDENCE: Boston

BIRTH: By about 1610 based on estimated date of marriage.
DEATH: Probably about 1638.
MARRIAGE: By 1635 Mary _____.
CHILDREN:

    i   ELIZABETH, b. Boston 1635 [BVR 3]; no further record.
    ii   MILES, b. Boston 1 April 1638 [BVR 6]; no further record.

COMMENTS: The two Boston birth records are the only evidence we have for this immigrant. Their inclusion in the records implies that some member of the family was still resident in Boston in 1644-5, so it may be that Miles Awkley died about the time of birth of his son Miles, and his widow Mary then remarried to some other Boston man.

FRANCIS BABER

On 20 March 1634/5, "Francis Baber," chandler, aged 36, was enrolled as a passenger for New England on the unnamed ship from Weymouth [Hotten 283].

On 4 September 1638, "Francis Baver, of Scituate, [was] presented for offering to lie with the wife of Will[ia]m Holmes, & to abuse her body with uncleanness" [PCR 1:98].

COMMENTS: No other record of this man has been found in New England.

JOHN BACHELOR

ORIGIN: Unknown
MIGRATION: 1634
FIRST RESIDENCE: Watertown
REMOVES: Dedham 1637, Reading 1648

OCCUPATION: Husbandman.
CHURCH MEMBERSHIP: Admission to Watertown church prior to 6 May 1635 implied by freemanship. Admitted to Dedham church, with his wife, 30 July 1641 [DeChR 25].
FREEMAN: 6 May 1635 (as "John Batchel[e]r," seventh in a sequence of eight Watertown men) [MBCR 1:370].
EDUCATION: His inventory included "a Bible and some other books" valued at 15s.
OFFICES: Watertown selectman, 1635 [WaTR 2]. Dedham selectman, 1639, 1640 [DeTR 1:53, 62]. Dedham tax collector, 30 March 1640 [DeTR 1:66].

ESTATE: Granted thirty-five acres as a Great Dividend in Watertown, 25 July 1636 [WaBOP 4]. Granted six acres in the Beaverbrook Plowlands, 28 February 1636/7 [WaBOP 7]. Granted six acres in the Remote Meadows, 26 June 1637 [WaBOP 9].

In the Inventory of Grants "John Batchilor" held six parcels: homestall of seven acres; two acres of marsh; six acres of plowland; six acres of Remote Meadows; thirty-five acres of upland; and three acres of upland [WaBOP 75]. By the time of the Composite Inventory (and probably some years earlier) he had sold this land to Jeremiah Norcross [WaBOP 20-21].

On 11 August 1637, the town of Dedham "granted that John Bacheler & John Roper may have lots with us" [DeTR 1:33]. On 14 July 1641, there was granted to "Jno. Batcheler one small parcel of land near the claypits on the island" [DeTR 1:80]. Granted two acres and one rood, 6 February 1642/3 [DeTR 1:95]. Granted seven acres of woodland, 4 February 1644/5 [DeTR 1:110]. Granted "one small parcel of upland being part of the common ground lying at the south end of part of his houselot, which parcel he desires to set a barn upon," 29 December 1647 [DeTR 1:117].

On 16 September 1647, "John Batchelor of Dedham," as security for "2 cows sold to him & John Plimton," mortgaged to Thomas Dudley "his dwelling house in Dedham with all the outhouses & ground thereto adjoining being 16 acres enclosed, of which 4 acres is meadow" [SLR 1:84].

In the country rate for 1648, "Joh[n] Batchelor" was assessed 5s. 11d., and his house was valued at £3 [DeTR 1:152, 154].

On 28 June 1648, Henry Feltch of Reading sold to "John Batchler of Dedham, husbandman, ... my lot at Reading with all the appurtenances and town right thereunto belonging" [MLR 1:21, 72].

On 11 February 1650/1, Dedham selectmen recorded (apparently some years after the fact) a grant to "Joh[n] Batchelor" of eight acres of meadow in Broad Meadow, and another grant of two acres of swamp [DeTR 1:174, 175]. (On 9 February 1665/6, the town of Dedham granted to Edward Hawes a piece of swamp "in full satisfaction for swamp formerly purchased of Joh[n] Batchelor as due to him in that swamp that was taken away by Cambridge" [DeTR 2:114].)

On 10 July 1654, Isaac Hart of Reading leased to "John Bachelder Senior & Junior" several parcels in Lynn for 21 years [MLR 2:199]. On 19 January 1657[/8?], Thomas Marshall of Lynn sold to "John Bachelder" forty acres of upland in Reading [MLR 2:117].

In his will, dated 2 July 1670 (with codicil of 3 April 1676) and proved 20 June 1676, "John Batchelour of Redding ... Senior" bequeathed "my

freehold or town privileges ... unto my sons John and David ... equally";
to "my son John Batchilour" "my dwelling house, outhouses, orchard,
yards, with all the lands, privileges and appurtenances to them
belonging, containing thirty acres," also "a parcel of meadow ground of
three acres," also "nine acres of meadow," also "my long meadow lying
toward Andover," also "my lot in the cedar swamp, reserving liberty for
my son David of timber necessary for or toward the building and
finishing his house, hereafter mentioned," also "one hundred and fifty
acres of my two hundred twenty six acres lot, in the farther end"; to "my
son David Batchilour" "the other part of my two hundred twenty six acres
of upland, the other part of my meadow ground joining to the long
meadow aforementioned," also "my three acres of meadow by the dark
swamp," also my three acres of meadow ground, purchased of John
Peirce, lying eastward of the Great Swamp, with my interest of
swampland, lately allotted to the inhabitants of Redding"; to "my
daughter Mary Cowdrey" "my ten acres of upland lying on the
Westplain"; one-fourth of cattle and swine to "my said daughter Mary
Cowdrey" and three-fourths to "my son David"; additional moveables to
John and David; "my son John Batchilour" to be sole executor; "my
beloved friends Francis Skerry of Salem, Joseph Hills of Nubury, John
Brown and Jonathan Poole of Redding" to be overseers. In his codicil of 3
April 1676, he directed that the three acres of meadow which he had
bought of "John Percon" go to son John rather than son David, and the
part of the swampland bequeathed to David go to John instead [MPR
Case #594, 4:229-34].

The inventory "of the estate of John Bacheller Senior who deceased the
third of May one thousand six hundred seventy six," taken 20 June 1676,
totalled £433 15s., of which £409 10s. was real estate: "The building with all
the land about it ... which containeth about thirty acres of land," £160;
"three acres of meadow," £9; "nine acres of meadow," £25; "three acres of
meadow," £6; "two hundred and twenty six acres of upland and seven
acres of meadow," £60; "a parcel of cedar swamp," £1 10s.; "six acre[s] and
a half of wet swamp," £6; "three acres of meadow," £12; "ten acres of
upland," £10; and "forty acres of land with the building," £120 [MPR Case
#594]. A note at the end of the inventory tells us that the "household
goods by the providence of God were the most of them taken away by
fire."

BIRTH: By about 1610 based on estimated date of marriage.
DEATH: Reading 3 May 1676 (inventory).

MARRIAGE: By about 1635 Rebecca _____. She died at Reading on 9 March 1661/2.

CHILDREN:

    i   JOHN, b. say 1635; m. (1) Reading 7 January 1662 Sarah Lunt, daughter of HENRY LUNT of Newbury [TAG 16:136, 138; Abel Lunt Anc 9] (she must be the Sarah who died at Reading 21 December 1685, miscalled "wid. of John"); m. (2) Reading 10 May 1687 Hannah (Boynton) Warner, daughter of John Boynton of Rowley and widow of Nathaniel Warner of Ipswich [TAG 16:136-37] (she d. Reading 5 October 1693); m. (3) Reading 12 June 1694 Hannah [blank] [TAG 16:136]. (See *COMMENTS* below for further discussion of this man's marriages.)

   ii   MARY, b. say 1637; m. Reading 22 November 1660 Nathaniel Cowdrey.

  iii   SAMUEL, b. Dedham 8 January 1639/40 [DeVR 1]; bp. Dedham 27 January 1639/40 ("Samuell the son of our brother Batchelour a member of the church of Watertowne") [DeChR 22]; d. Reading 25 March 1662.

  iv   JONATHAN (twin), b. Dedham 14 December 1643 [DeVR 2]; bp. Dedham 24 December 1643 [DeChR 27]; d. Reading 4 December 1653.

   v   DAVID (twin), b. Dedham 14 December 1643 [DeVR 2]; bp. Dedham 24 December 1643 [DeChR 27]; m. Reading 30 December 1679 Hannah Plummer.

ASSOCIATIONS: Some secondary sources claim that the wife of JOHN EATON of Dedham and Reading was sister of John Bachelor. No evidence has been found to support this claim, but a record does exist which may explain why some researchers have been led to this conclusion. On 30 July 1641, "brethren John Batchellour & John Eaton with their wives" were admitted to Dedham church [DeChR 25]. This record describes Bachelor and Eaton as brethren in the church, but may have been taken incorrectly by some researchers to indicate that they were brothers-in-law, assuming that Eaton had married Bachelor's sister. The maiden surname of John Eaton's wife remains unknown.

COMMENTS: Savage has divided this immigrant into two men, separating the Watertown and Dedham part of his life from his years in Reading, whereas Pope has combined records for the immigrant and for his son of the same name.

In the grants of the Beaverbrook Plowlands and the Remote Meadows at Watertown in 1637, John Bachelor each time received six acres, indicating that there may have been as many as six people in his household. Although we don't have dates of birth for the first two known children of John, they were probably both alive at the time of these grants, making a known family of four. The other two acres of each grant may be accounted for by additional, unknown persons, or by possession of cattle sufficient to justify the grant.

"John Bacheler" attended his first Dedham town meeting on 28 November 1637 [DeTR 1:35]. Since he had been granted land in Watertown just a few months before, his move to Dedham must have taken place in the latter part of 1637. And since the births of his two eldest children were not recorded in Dedham, they must both have been born before the move.

On 19 October 1658, Massachusetts Bay General Court "ordered, that the Treasurer for Suffolke discharge & pay Henry Wight, constable, late of Dedham, the sum of twenty shillings for his charges allowed him for bringing down Goody Batchiler with a cart, &c." [MBCR 4:1:354]. This may refer to the wife of John Bachelor, making a return visit to Dedham for some unexplained reason.

Since the three marriages of John Bachelor, son of the immigrant, took place over a period of more than thirty years, there may be some doubt that they all pertain to the same man. The evidence that all three are in fact the marriages of one man may be found in the will of this John Bachelor and in the vital records of Reading. In his will of 23 May 1705, "John Bacheller of Redding" bequeathed to "my loving wife Hannah Bacheller" and to "my son John Bacheller," to "my son Nathaniel Bacheller," to "my son David Hartshor[n]e and Rebeckah Hartshorne my daughter his wife," to "my son John Pratt and unto my daughter Sarah Pratt," to "my daughter Mary Bacheller ... at the age of eighteen years or at marriage," and to "my daughter Elizebeth Bacheller ... at marriage or at eighteen years of age" [MPR Case #595]. On 17 December 1705, guardianship papers were issued for "Mary Bacheller daughter of John Bacheller late of Redding deceased, a minor in the eighteenth year of her age" [MPR Case #597] and "Eliza[beth] Bacheler daughter of John Bacheler late of Redding deceased, a minor in the fifteenth year of her age" [MPR Case #596].

These records may be compared with the Reading birth records. John Bachelor and his wife Sarah had the following children: Rebecka, b. 30 October 1663; John, b. 23 February 1665/6; Henry, b. 29 July 1668 and d. 11

November 1668; Sarah, b. 9 July 1670; Samuel, b. 23 January 1671; and Nathaniel, b. 17 March 1674/5. John Bachelor and his wife Hannah had two children: Mary, b. 19 November 1688; and Elizebeth, b. 18 August 1691. The birthdates for these last two children match precisely the ages in the 1705 guardianships, and correspond to the last two children named in John Bachelor's will. The children born to John and Sarah match the rest of the children in John's will (with the assumption that the son Samuel had died without issue by 1705).

The demonstration is completed by noting that Hannah, the mother of the two younger children, died on 5 October 1693, and John named a wife Hannah in his will, showing that he married a third time.

WILLIAM BACHELOR

ORIGIN: Unknown
MIGRATION: 1634
FIRST RESIDENCE: Charlestown

OCCUPATION: Victualler.
CHURCH MEMBERSHIP: Admitted to Charlestown church 10 January 1634/5 [ChChR 8].
FREEMAN: 29 May 1644 [MBCR 2:293].
EDUCATION: He signed his deeds and his will.
ESTATE: Granted two acres of planting ground at Charlestown, 10 January 1634/5 (this grant later rescinded) [ChTR 12]. Granted an unknown number of acres [page damaged], 1635 [ChTR 15]. Granted one share of hayground, 1635, soon increased to two shares [ChTR 19,20]. Granted 3¼ cow commons, 1637 [ChTR 33]. In the Mysticside allotments of 23 April 1638, recorded with parcels of fifteen, thiry and zero acres [ChTR 36]. Had three cow commons in stinted common, 30 December 1638 [ChTR 42].

In the 1638 Charlestown Book of Possessions "William Batchelor" held six parcels: "four acres of arable land and meadow ... with a dwelling house upon it. (A piece of salt and fresh meadow having been sold to Robert Leach.)"; three milch cow comons; four acres of arable land in the Line Field; one acre of meadow in Mystic Marshes; fifteen acres of woodland in Mystic Field; and forty acres of land in Water Field [ChBOP 63-64].

On 3 July 1648, Robert Leach and "William Batchelour" exchanged land, Leach receiving "a piece of meadow land both salt and fresh, lying & situate in the west side" and Bachelor receiving "two acres of planting land ... in the east field" [MLR 8:92]. On 2 December 1654, "William Bachelor of Charlestown" sold to Henry Dunster four acres in Menotomy Field [MLR 1:104]. On 17 November 1656, William Brackenbury of Malden sold to "William Bacheldor" of Charlestown "one house ... with all the gardens, orchard or backside ... containing by estimation twenty rods of ground" in Charlestown [MLR 1:188]; on the following day, "William Bachelor of Charlestowne ... victualer" mortgaged this land back to Brackenbury [MLR 1:190].

In his will, dated 11th day of the twelfth month 1669 [i.e. 11 February 1669/70], with a codicil dated the following day, and proved on 21 June 1670, William Bachelor provided for his wife, Rachel, leaving her his current dwelling house as well as the house "my son Richard Austin lives in," and all his moveable estate and household goods, and he stated that his will was that "my son Richard" should continue to live in the house during the life of William's wife while paying rent to her according to the worth thereof, and further that William's moveables be at his wife's disposal during her life, and that, at her decease, "to be given unto her children," but she was free to sell any of the land, houses, or moveables, if required for her support and maintenance, there being an equal amount out of every child's portion; after her decease his now dwelling house and appurtenances were left to his son, Joseph; after his wife's decease, he left his two daughters, Rachel Atwood and Abigail Austin, the house "(if undisposed of by my wife)" that Richard Austin now lives in, "the yard to come within two feet of my now dwelling house with the use of the highway to come into the yard, & that highway to lie in common to both houses"; further "my son Richard should have this house and yard paying after the decease of my wife, to my son Atwood the value & worth of half of it" during the time of his non-payment, to pay valuable rent for it, and the said Richard shall have liberty to fetch water from the well of the said Joseph during Richard's lifetime and the lifetime of his child after him, the said Richard paying half the cost of maintaining the well while he makes use of it, with Richard and Joseph both having a garden plot; when son Joseph enters into possession of the house, following his mother's decease, he is to pay within one year or when they come of age £5 in equal portions to Joseph Cromwell and Benjamin Cromwell; further that "my three grandchildren now living with me, Joseph Cromwell, Benjamin Cromwell, & Susanna Lawrence," be left at my wife, Rachel's, disposal; and lastly that my woodlot on "Mystic Side" [Malden] be given to my son Joseph. The codicil, made the following day, and witnessed by John Cutler, stipulated that son Joseph was to have one cow common in the Stinted Common in Charlestown, he to pay unto John Cromwell ten shillings after the decease of William's wife, and also that daughter Abigail Austin was to have one cow common in the Stinted Common in Charlestown after the decease of William's wife, Abigail to pay unto John Cromwell ten shillings. William Bachelor, in a hand remarkably shakier than that of just the day before, signed his name.

The inventory, taken on 29 March 1670 by John Cutler and Richard Kettell, and exhibited on 21 June 1670, totalled £261 14s., of which £179 was real estate: "the house that Richard Austin does live in with the yard behind it," £80; "the dwelling house that W[illia]m Batchler did live in with the yard & garden & out houses," £85; "two cow commons," £12; and "1 wood lot at Mistick: Side," £2 [MPR Case #619].

In her undated will, proved 16 December 1668, "Susannah Laurance of Charlestowne ... widow" bequeathed her entire estate "unto my two daughters to Abigail and unto Susannah Laurance" to maintain them "till they be able to live of their own"; if they both die, then the remainder of the estate to "my honored father & mother Bachelder and after their death unto my two sisters Rachel Atwood & Abigail Asting"; "my father Bachelder and my brother Atwood of Maulden" to be executors [MPR 3:124].

BIRTH: About 1596 (aged 73 at death on 22 February 1669[/70] [ChVR 1:73]; aged about 72 years at death on 20 February 1669[/70] [Wyman 42, citing gravestone]).
DEATH: Charlestown 22 February 1669[/70] ("Aged 73" in margin) [ChVR 1:73]. His gravestone states he died 20 February 1669[/70], aged about 72 years [Wyman 42, citing gravestone].
MARRIAGE: (1) Jane _____, who evidently died soon after 1 July 1637.

(2) By late 1637 Rachel Bate (see COMMENTS below). She died in Charlestown 28 May 1676 (but marginal annotation says "28:7:76" [i.e., 28 September 1676]) [ChVR 1:97], aged 73 years [Wyman 1:42, citing gravestone].
CHILDREN:
  With first wife
    i   RACHEL, b. say 1633; m. by 1653 PHILIP ATWOOD.

ii SEABORN, bp. 12 January 1634/5 [ChChR 46]; m. (1) by 1657 John Cromwell [MA Arch 38B:240 (see *COMMENTS* below)]; m. (2) Charlestown 22 May 1663 Robert Paris [ChVR 1:43].

iii ABIGAIL, bp. 1 July 1637 [ChChR 47]; m. Charlestown 11 November 1659 Richard Austin [ChVR 1:38].

With second wife

iv SUSANNA, b. say 1642; m. Charlestown 2 November 1664 John Lawrence [ChVR 1:50].

v JOSEPH, b. 20 August 1644 [ChVR 1:8]; m. Charlestown 22 December 1670 Agnes (Wadland) Gillingham [ChVR 1:50, 77], widow of William Gillingham [Wyman 2:985].

COMMENTS: William Bachelor was admitted an inhabitant of Charlestown in 1634, and is included in the January 1634/5 list of Charlestown inhabitants [ChTR 11, 15].

Pope gives the date William Bachelor was made a freeman, but it is misentered in the sketch of Rev. *STEPHEN BACHILER,* which immediately precedes that for William Bachelor [Pope 26].

Frederick Clifton Pierce in his 1898 *Batchelder, Batcheller Genealogy* reproduces on page 39 the details of what appears to be an English Chancery Court deposition, although no reference to the original source is given. In this abstract it is claimed that one William Bacheler married Jane Cowper in October 1632, she having been at one time a servant of Henry Arthur of Standford Dingley, Berkshire, gentleman. Jane had subsequently lent Mr. Arthur some money left to her by her aunt, Katherine Smyth, and so on. While this deposition is interesting in the details and clues it provides, there is no way of telling whether it refers to the William Bachelor and wife Jane under discussion here. More research is required to identify the source of this document, and then to establish a link with our Charlestown settlers of these names.

Herbert F. Seversmith and John Insley Coddington argued that William Bachelor's second wife Rachel was the daughter of James and Mary (Martine) Bate, baptized at Lydd, Kent, on 5 February 160[3/]4 [NEHGR 51:269], and therefore sister of JAMES BATE and CLEMENT BATE [Seversmith 1:290-91, citing personal correspondence with Coddington]. The most important evidence is the will of Smallhope Bigg, dated 3 May 1638, which included a bequest to "James Bate, to Clement Bate, to the wife of William Batchelor my kinfolks, to John Compton, to Edward White and to Martha his wife all which are now resident in New

England" [Consistory Court of Canterbury 51:115; see also Waters 21].
The only William Bachelor known to be in New England was the subject
of this sketch, and Rachel's inclusion in the bequest immediately after
James and Clement Bate argues strongly for the conclusion reached by
Seversmith and Coddington. For Smallhope Bigg to know of this
marriage by 3 May 1638, William Bachelor's first wife must have died
soon after the baptism of their child on 1 July 1637, and the marriage to
Rachel Bate must then have occurred late in 1637. She would then have
been thirty-three years old, and apparently did not have any children
until she had been married for about four or five years. If her 1st child
was Joseph, she was forty years old at the time, and the age at death said
to be given on her tombstone is in accord with the date of baptism of
Rachel Bate.

The estimated date of birth for daughter Susanna could well be an
underestimate. If she were born in the gap between 1637 and 1642, she
could be a daughter of either of William's wives, and their dates would
need to be adjusted accordingly.

That Seaborn Bachelor married John Cromwell early in 1657 is evident
from a petition in her behalf submitted to the General Court. Eleven
Charlestown women ("four of these are midwives") "being desired thereto
have been with Seaborn Cromwell this day being the 12th day of the 3d
month [May] 1657 and having had conference with her to our best of
discernings, our apprehensions are that it is more probable by what we
find she is with child than other.... We humbly submit our thoughts to
the Honored Court yet we are jointly doubtful in our spirits that if
Seaborn have any bodily correction at present it may prove dangerous
and hurtful to her" [MA Arch 38B:240]. One of these eleven women was
"Rachell Bacheller," Seaborn's mother. Within a few days, both legislative
bodies appended to this petition their responses. "The magistrates know
no time fitter to whip her than what is appointed & therefore see no
cause on this motion to alter their judgment." "The Deputies on
consideration of what is here presented do not consent hereto but judge
it may be deferred without violation of justice to a more convenient
season if our honored magistrates consent thereto." The final outcome of
the case is not known.

GEORGE BACON

ORIGIN: Unknown
MIGRATION: 1635 on the *Increase*
FIRST RESIDENCE: Hingham

OCCUPATION: Mason.
ESTATE: "The several parcels of land and meadow legally given unto George Backon by the town of Hingham": 18 September 1635, "for a houselot five acres of land"; 1635, "for a planting lot four acres of land"; 8 October 1637, "for a greater lot fourteen acres of land lying upon the Great Plain in the first furlong to the eastward of the center"; and 10 June 1637, "two acres of salt marsh lying in Weymouth Meadow" [HiBOP 44r].

On 30 March 1670, "John Pollie of Roxbury ... having formerly had to wife one Susanna the daughter of one George Bacon of Hingham ... deceased which said George Bacon died possessed of houses and lands lying and being within the Township of Hingham aforesaid and one Edward Goold taking to wife the widow of the said Bacon," John Polley "and the aforesaid Susanna in the time of her life" sold to the said Edward Goold "all our right, title and interest had then or might have had hereafter in and unto all or any of the said houses and lands that the said George Bacon died possessed of" [SLR 12:357-58].

On 28 March 1672, "Samuel Bacon of Hingham ... housecarpenter" sold to "my brother Peter Bacon of the same town abovesaid a third part of the great lot and what other part thereof shall fall to my share after the decease of my mother Margaret Gold now living in the same town, the which lot lyeth between a great lot of Thomas Hubbard's and the lot where the dwelling house of Peter Bacon aforesaid now standeth" [SLR 11:393].

On 2 February 1683/4, Peter Bacon of Hingham petitioned for administration of the estate of his late father, George Bacon of Hingham, stating that "whereas your petitioner's father, George Bacon of Hingham, many years since died intestate and his widow, your petitioner's mother, soon after married again and has had the improvement of all his estate as well real as personal until the time of her decease which was the last year and your petitioner has been at charge in maintaining his aged mother for a considerable time before her decease, and your petitioner having purchased of the rest of his brethren many years since all the right in their father's estate so that now your petitioner is the true and rightful owner of all the remains of his said father's estate and your petitioner understanding that this honored court did in his absence grant administration upon the said estate to strangers, upon your petitioner's request did forbid any action by virtue of the same." The court decided the same day to hold a hearing on the said petition [SPR NS 3:9-10]. On 28 March 1684, adminstration was granted to Capt. John Smith and Capt. John Jacob of Hingham, on "the estate of George Bacon sometime of Hingham many years since deceased" [SPR NS 3:10-11].

BIRTH: About 1592 (aged 43 in 1635 [Hotten 55]).

DEATH: Buried at Hingham on 3 May 1642 [NEHGR 121:14].

MARRIAGE: (1) By about 1623 _____ _____; she died in England between 1627 and 1635.

(2) Between 1635 and 1640 Margaret _____; she married (2) EDWARD GOLD [SLR 12:357-58]. She died at Hingham on 6 or 7 February 1682/3 [HiVR 57; NEHGR 121:211]. (The first known child of Edward Gold was baptized at Hingham between 12 and 26 March 1642/3 [NEHGR 121:15], between ten and eleven months after the burial of George Bacon. This seems too early for the widow of George Bacon to have remarried, but no other wife of Edward Gold is known.)

CHILDREN:

With first wife

  i   SAMUEL, b. about 1623 (aged 12 in 1635 [Hotten 55]); living on 28 March 1672 [SLR 11:393]. (The Samuel Bacon who m. Hingham 17 December 1675 "Mary Jacob the daughter of John Jacob" [HiVR 36] was son of Nathaniel Bacon of Barnstable [SPR Case #1171].)

  ii   SUSAN[NAH], b. about 1625 (aged 10 in 1635 [Hotten 55]); m. about 1647 John Polley of Roxbury [TAG 41:206; SLR 12:357-58].

  iii JOHN, b. about 1627 (aged 8 in 1635 [Hotten 55]); no further record.

With second wife

  iv   PETER, b. say 1640, bp. Hingham 17 September 1654 [NEHGR 121:104]; m. (1) Hingham 25 May 1670 Sarah Jenkins [NEHGR 121:124 (surname of bride not given)], who d. at Hingham 21 July 1677 [HiVR 41] (in his will of 2 March 1699, Edward Jenkins of Scituate bequeathed 5s. to "my granddaughter Mary Bacon" [PPR 1:311-12]; Peter Bacon had daughter Mary b. Hingham 14 or 15 July 1677

[Hingham Hist 2:16; NEHGR 121:205 (four children born
to this couple, two of them known to have died young -
also Sarah b. 15 April 1675, who probably also died
young)]); m. (2) Hingham 19 February 1679/80 Martha
(Howland) Damon [NEHGR 121:205; HiVR 51½], widow
of John Damon of Scituate and daughter of Arthur
Howland of Marshfield; she d. at Hingham 19 December
1732, in her 94th year [NGSQ 71:89-90].

v   MARY, b. Hingham 30 March 1642 [NEHGR 121:14], bp. there
17 September 1654 [NEHGR 121:104]; no further record.
(Torrey's entry for Josiah Lane of Hingham gives his wife
as Mary Bacon, who could conceivably be this Mary, but
none of the references in the Torrey entry gives evidence
for this identification.)

COMMENTS: "Geo[rge] Bacon," mason, aged 43, and his children,
"Samuell," aged 12, "Jo[h]n," aged 8, and "Susan," aged 10, were enrolled at
London on 17 April 1635 as passengers for New England on the *Increase*
[Hotten 55].

Pope includes a "Ch. _____ bapt Nov. 27, 1640," but no such record
appears in the Hobart Journal.

On 12 September 1671, Samuel Bacon sued Edward Gold for £40 for
withholding and refusing to make satisfaction upon demand for a cow
and all her increase "about five & twenty years," with all due damages,
the jury finding for the plaintiff in the amount of £16 and costs of court
[SCC 1:12].

Samuel Bacon, "eldest son" of George Bacon, brought suit against
Edward Gold of Hingham for £45 on 23 October 1671 for withholding one
third part of a dwelling house and several parcels of land lying in
Hingham belonging to the said Samuel Bacon which were the lands of his
said father, deceased, and also for improving the said lands for more than
24 years. The court found in the plaintiff's favor, awarding him the one
third part of the "housing land & meadow," and £20 for the
improvements, together with costs of court [SCC 1:12].

If the one-third share held by Samuel represented his double share as
eldest son, then the implication is that there were five children to share in
the estate of George Bacon. If this is the case, then George's son John (or
an heir of John) was alive at the time of George's death, or there was
another child of George, not otherwise accounted for.

CHRISTOPHER BAILY

In a 1634 accounting of "hiredmen's wages," "Chr[istopher] Baily" was paid £3 [Trelawny Papers 38].

COMMENTS: Christopher Baily has not been found in any other New England record, so he apparently was employed at Richmond Island for one season and then departed.

ALEXANDER BAKER

ORIGIN: London
MIGRATION: 1635 on the *Elizabeth & Ann*
FIRST RESIDENCE: Boston

OCCUPATION: Ropemaker [BChR 45]. In his 1685 will, Alexander styles himself a collarmaker [SPR 6:489]. In a deed dated 7 March 1692/3 his granddaughters describe him as "our honored grandfather Alexander Baker, late of Boston in New England aforesaid, collarmaker, deceased" [SLR 14:220].
CHURCH MEMBERSHIP: On 4 October 1645, "Alexander Baker a ropemaker and Elizabeth Baker his wife" were admitted to Boston church [BChR 45, 299].
FREEMAN: 6 May 1646 [MBCR 2:294].
OFFICES: Boston clerk of the market, 11 March 1666/7 [BTR 2:34]. Constable, 24 April 1676 [BTR 2:100].
   On 30 April 1678, Alexander Baker of Boston was "freely discharged from attending upon ordinary trainings he keeping arms according to law" [SCC 911].
ESTATE: On 21 January 1674[/5], Capt. John Hull confirmed the sale of land adjoining Alexander Baker's property to John Man and Alexander Baker by Hudson and Sarah Leveret of Boston [SLR 6:225-26].
   In his will, dated 18 February 1684[/5] and proved 11 May 1685, "Alexander Baker of Boston," collarmaker, "being in the seventy ninth year of my age ... God having bestowed twelve children on me and my dearly beloved wife Elizabeth, and enabled me by his blessing of my labors in my calling to bring the most of them to trades and see them settled & disposed of into a married condition, seven of them being yet

alive," bequeathed to "my children, i.e., John, Joshua, William, Josiah, Elizabeth Watkins, Christian Roberts and Sarah Wales" 5s. each; residue (except the workshop, tools, and three or four feet of ground from the shop bequeathed to "my son William whom I have brought up to my trade") to "my well beloved wife Elizabeth Baker," she to be executrix [SPR 6:489].

BIRTH: About 1607 (aged 28 in 1635 [Hotten 69]; called himself "in his 79th year" in 1684/5 [SPR 6:489]).
DEATH: Between 18 February 1684/5 (date of will) and 11 May 1685 (date of probate).
MARRIAGE: By 1632 Elizabeth _____, born about 1612 (aged 23 in 1635 [Hotten 69]). She was alive on 18 February 1684/5 when her husband made his will [SPR 6:489].
CHILDREN:

- i   ELIZABETH, b. say 1632; m. by 1652 Thomas Watkins (first known child b. Boston 27 November 1652 [BVR 36]).
- ii   CHRISTIAN, b. say 1634; m. Boston 18 July 1654 Simon Roberts [BVR 48].
- iii ALEXANDER, b. Boston 15 January 1635[/6] [BVR 3]; bp. 5 October 1645 "being 9 years and about 9 months old" [BChR 299]; predeceased his father, unm.
- iv   SAMUEL, b. Boston 16 January 1637/8 [BVR 5]; bp. 5 October 1645 "being 7 years and about 9 months old" [BChR 299]; predeceased his father, unm.
- v   JOHN, b. Boston 20 June 1640 [BVR 9]; bp. 5 October 1645 "being 5 years and about 15 weeks old" [BChR 299]; living 1684/5; no further record. (Elizabeth, daughter of Jacob Waterhouse of New London, was in 1693 the widow of someone named Baker, possibly a John Baker, but whether this John Baker is unknown [TAG 47:100; Wethersfield Hist 2:752].)
- vi   JOSHUA, b. Boston 30 April 1642 [BVR 13]; bp. 5 October 1645 "being 3 years and about 5 months old" [BChR 299]; living 1684/5; m. New London 13 September 1674 Hannah, widow of Tristram Minter [TAG 47:100; NLVR Barbour 12, citing "1:9"].
- vii HANNAH, b. Boston 29 September 1644 [BVR 17]; bp. 5 October 1645 "being about a year and 6 days old" [BChR 299]; m. by 1679 John Aulgar of Boston (son John b.

Boston 13 August 1679 to "John & Hannah Aulgar" [BVR 147]; on 7 March 1692/3, Elizabeth Baker and Sarah Baker, daughters of William Baker and granddaughters of Alexander Baker, appointed "our trusty and beloved uncle Mr. John Algure of Boston" to be their attorney [SLR 14:220]) [NEHGR 31:101].

viii   WILLIAM, b. Boston 15 May [*sic*] 1647 [BVR 25]; bp. 18 April 1647 [BChR 306]; m. by 1669 Eleanor _____ (first known child Elizabeth born Boston 29 March 1669 [BVR 110; SLR 14:220]).

ix   JOSEPH, bp. Boston 8 April 1649 "being about 3 days old" [BChR 314]; predeceased his father, unm.

x   SARAH, bp. Boston 25 May 1651 [BChR 320]; m. by 1684/5 Jonathan Wales (eldest known child b. Boston 19 January 1687[/8] [BVR 177], three years after Sarah is called Wales in her father's will).

xi   BENJAMIN, b. Boston 16 March 1652[/3] [BVR 36]; bp. 14 August 1653 [BChR 325]; predeceased his father, unm.

xii   JOSIAH, b. Boston 26 February 1654[/5] [BVR 46]; bp. 4 March 1654/5 [BChR 327]; m. by 1680 Mary _____ (eldest known child born Boston 8 June 1680 [BVR 151]).

COMMENTS: On 17 April 1635 "Alexander Baker," aged 28, "Uxor Elizabeth," aged 23, "Elizabeth Baker," aged 3, and "Christian Baker," aged 1 year, were enrolled as passengers for New England on the *Elizabeth & Ann* [Hotten 69].

Pope and Savage missed son Joseph and daughter Sarah. Pope further erred when he said Alexander had twelve children living at the time he wrote his will; what Alexander said was that he had been blessed with twelve children, seven of whom were still living.

FRANCIS BAKER

On 2 April 1635, "A Taylor Francis Baker," aged 24, was enrolled to be transported to New England on the *Planter*, having "brought certificate from the Minister of St Albons in Hertfordshire" [Hotten 45].

COMMENTS: There is no evidence to connect this Francis Baker with the "Francis Baker, cooper," who was admitted to dwell at Yarmouth on 1 June 1641 [PCR 2:17]. The six-year gap with no records, coupled with the differing occupations, makes it extremely unlikely that this was the same man.

GEORGE BAKER

In a 1634 accounting of "hiredmen's wages," "Geo[rge] Baker" was paid £2 3s. [Trelawny Papers 38].

COMMENTS: George Baker has not been found in any other New England record, so he apparently was employed at Richmond Island for one season and then departed.

NATHANIEL BAKER

ORIGIN: Unknown
MIGRATION: 1635
FIRST RESIDENCE: Hingham

OCCUPATION: Yeoman [SLR 8:60-62].
CHURCH MEMBERSHIP: Nathaniel Baker or his wife was admitted to Hingham church by July 1639 when their daughter, Mary, was baptized [NEHGR 121:11].
FREEMAN: Took the Oath of Allegiance in Hingham 29 October 1678 [SCC 2:975].
EDUCATION: Signed his name to deeds [SLR 8:60-62, 11:335-37] and to his will. The inventory of his estate included "his books," valued at 30s.
OFFICES: Hingham selectman, 1 December 1650 [HiTR, 1642-1651, 25]. Constable, 8 March 1668[/9] [SLR 5:1].
ESTATE: "The several parcels of land and meadow legally given unto Nathaneell Baker by the town of Hingham": "for a house lot five acres of land," 18 September 1635; "for a planting lot two acres of land lying upon Pleasant Hill," 1635; "for a Great Lot ten acres of land lying upon the Great Plain," 8 October 1637; "one acre & half of salt marsh lying in Weymoth Meadow," 10 June 1637; "two acres of planting land lying at the

end of his own house lot," no date; "one acre and half of salt marsh at Conyehassett, it is the fifth lot in the first division ... which parcel of meadow was given him for satisfaction for meadow given him at Nantascott," 1647; "a piece of ground to set a barn upon at the southward of his home lot where he now dwells," [11?] January 1650; "four acres of salt marsh lying at Conyehassett it is the fourth lot in the third division," 1647; and "a parcel of land for the straightening of the fence of his Great Lot over the new bridge, provided it doth not exceed two acres, but the wood is to remain to the use of the town," 1 January 1654 [HiBOP 43].

Nathaniel Baker was admitted as a planter to the plantation at Nantasket [Hull] on 9 April 1642. He, like the others so admitted, was to have two acres of land located in the valley between the two hills next to Peddock's Island, as well as two acres of meadow, and four acres of planting land at Peddock's Island "to be laid out when the plantation shall be fuller," in the meantime to have liberty to plant wherever they wished, and reserving the beaches for anyone to set up fishing stages as desired [MBCR 2:5-6].

On 25 February 1655[/6?], "upon a request of Goodman Baker unto the Town concerning the running of his greater lot lying over the new bridge along by the fresh river it falling out that there was a neck of the town's land did fall into that greater lot if it run upon a straight line from a marked tree by a great rock to a little small tree by the side of a hill at the outside of his great lot the matter having been discussed by the town at a town meeting, the town did refer it to the townsmen to do in it according to their discretion and it is ordered by the selectmen that that nook of land which fell in his lot which doth amount to three acres and a rood, it is given him and he is to run upon a straight line, only the wood of that land is retained for the town's use, this three acres and a rood that the selectmen hath given him is besides that two acres of land that the town had given him before, both which doth amount to five acres of land and better" [HiBOP 43].

On 15 January 1648, John Porter of Salem granted unto Nathaniel Baker of Hingham his house and lot in Hingham, with the barns and outbuildings, and "several parcels of land in Hingham" [SLR 1:101]. On 16 December 1649, "Henery Chamberlin" sold to "Nathaneell Baker ... my Great Lot ... and my meadow at Conyhassett" [HiBOP 43].

On 17 June 1661, Nathaniel Baker of Hingham, together with Capt. Joshua Hubbard, Lt. John Smith and Sgt. John Leavitt, purchased a tract of land fifteen miles square from various Indians, which deed was acknowledged by Chish-thamuck Pumham-sem on 4 April 1661,

Wamsutta alias Alexander on 2 June 1662, and, in a separate release dated 8 June 1664, with a map of the tract attached thereunto, by "Pom-me-toc-come al[ia]s Philip," who speaks of "my brother Alexander alias Womsittah deceased" [SLR 7:161-64].

On 15 January 1672/3, "Nathaniell Baker of Hingham ..., yeoman, ... for the entire love & respect, that I have unto my son-in-law John Loring and to Mary his wife my daughter, of Hull," granted to them "one third part of that parcel of land, that lyeth between the highway leading to the land called the world's end and the Fresh River, namely that their part next to the highway that leadeth to John Pharas house or the bridge"; also "one third part of my great lot over the bridge, namely that third part next to Turkey Hill, next to the lot of John Pharo"; also "one great lot lying on the Great Plain that was formerly Henry Chamberlines the shoemaker, as bounded in the town book of Hingham"; also "one lot lying in the first division at Conihasset containing fifteen shares in the whole, lying next to Mathew Ganet's land, as bounded in town book"; also "one third part of my lot of land lying in the third division, which lot in the whole contains fifteen shares, bounded as in the town book"; also "one full third part of all the privilege of commons and common lands, wood, herbage, and feeding, to me in any wise due or appertaining, within the limits and bounds of Hingham"; also "all my meadow lands from the head of Porter's Cove downwards towards Lincornes Rocks, and all my meadow land at Turkey Meadow, bounded as in the town book"; these lands to be possessed by "them the said John Loring & Mary his wife from & immediately after the decease of me the said Nathaniell Baker & of Saray my now wife, during the time of the natural life of them the said John Loring & Mary his wife, or of the longer liver of them & after their decease to their children, namely, to John, Joseph, Thomas, Isaac, Nathaniell & Daniell Loring," with further provisions for carrying out this grant [SLR 8:60-62].

On 14 February 1673/4, Humphrey Johnson and his wife, Eleanor, of Hingham sold to Nathaniel Baker of Hingham, yeoman, Lot 44 of the second division of the Conihasset uplands in Hingham, containing 17¼ acres and 12 rods [SLR 9:44-45].

On 13 July 1680, Nathaniel Baker of Hingham, yeoman, granted unto "my wife's kinsman, Andrew Lane of Hingham ... wheelwright ... my lot of saltmarsh which I ... am now possessed of by virtue of the Town of Hingham their grant to me as may appear by the town record the said lot is the fifth lot in the first division of Conihasset saltmarshes in Hingham and the said lot contains one acre and half an acre of saltmarsh" [SLR 11:335-37].

In his will, dated 11 May 1682 and proved 25 July 1682, Nathaniel Baker of Hingham bequeathed "unto my beloved wife Sarah Baker all my household goods ... and also my Indians, man and woman servants, for their apprenticeships"; to "my beloved wife Sarah for ... her natural life my whole estate not already disposed of ... and at her decease my will is that Joseph Loring my grandchild shall have all my houses, orchards, and home land adjoining hereunto, and a piece of salt meadow adjoining to said land which said meadow was sometimes Nolton's, as also one piece of salt meadow in the home meadow sometimes Strong's, also my salt meadow at Porter's Cove from the head of said cove towards Bass Point, also that my lot of land at a place called the worlds end, also one lot next to the Ware River in the Neck, so called, also a grant of salt meadow I had of Henry Chamberlin at Cohasset, also ten shares of my common rights or privileges in the Town of Hingham, and also two-thirds of my land, both meadow and upland, that lyeth between the highway that leadeth into the Neck and the Fresh River, so called, also two-thirds of my great lot over said river on the left side of the way to Turkey Hill, also two-thirds of my third division lot so called, also my lot in the fourth division next Waymouth, also my cattle and moveables not already disposed," the abovesaid estate to "my said grandchild Joseph Loring to him and his heirs forever if he live to have any child, otherwise to be equally divided amongst his brothers after the said Joseph's decease, saving one-third of said estate to his widow, if he leave any, during her natural life, provided also the said Joseph Loring doth relinquish or give up his right to or interest in certain parcels of land given by me Nathanael Baker to his father John Loring to be divided amongst his sons ... as also that the said Joseph pay ... to his brother Jacob Loring and to his sisters Marah and Rachel Loring" £100, of which £50 to Jacob at age 21 or one year after the death of his grandmother Baker, and to Marah and Rachel £25 each at the age of 18, or one year after the death of their grandmother Baker, and if any of these three grandchildren died before receiving his or her legacy, then that person's share is to be divided among those surviving; to "my grandchild Nathaniel Loring all that my lot of land in the second division of Cohasset upland and a piece of salt meadow on the south side of the Great Neck at Cohasset of about four or five acres"; to "my grandsons Thomas Loring, Isaac Loring, Nathan[ie]ll Loring, and Jacob Loring all that my part share or interest in a parcel of land lying in the Narragansett Country in partnership with Capt. Hobart, Lt. Smith, and Deacon John

Levit, to be equally divided betwixt my said grandsons or the survivors of them when they come to age"; to "my grandchild Daniel Loring a great lot lying on the great plain which was formerly the lot of William Carsley, and unto the six children of my brother Nicholas Baker deceased ten shillings apiece"; to "my son-in-law John Loring my right in a lot of land with the deed for the same that I had of Humphrey Johnson in the second division of Cohasset upland"; "Sarah my beloved wife and Joseph Loring my grandson" to be executors; "Deacon John Leavitt, Capt. John Thaxter, Cornet Mathew Cushing, and John Jacob" to be overseers [SPR 6:386-88].

The inventory of Nathaniel Baker's estate, dated 23 June 1682, totalled £1273 19s., of which £1074 was real estate: "his housing, home lot, orchards & a piece of salt meadow adjoining thereunto about an acre," £210; "a piece of salt meadow in the home meadow," £60; "a piece of salt meadow at Porter's Cove," £80; "a parcel of land at the world's end, so called," £60; "one lot of land next the Ware River," £10; "the land at the going into the Neck next the Fresh River, being several small lots," £120; "the Great Lot over the River toward Turkey Hill," £300; "a lot on the Great Plain sometimes Carsley's," £12; "a lot on the Great Plain sometimes Chamberlyn's," £10; "a piece of fresh meadow in Turkey Meadow," £10; a piece of salt meadow at Cohasset about 4 acres," £22; "a lot in the first division of Cohasset upland," £25; "a lot in the second division of said upland," £80; "a lot in the third division of said upland," £15; "a lot in the fourth division," £10; "his shares or rights in the Commons," £30; and "a parcel of land to the west of Providence," £20 [SPR 9:87-88].

On 12 February 1696/7, letters of administration *cum testamento annexo* were granted to Thomas Loring of Hingham, sadler, on the remaining estate of his grandfather, Nathaniel Baker, sometime of Hingham, yeoman, both executors, Sarah Baker and Joseph Loring, being deceased [SPR 11:255, NS 4:212-14].

On 20 April 1697, a new inventory was made of the estate left remaining to be administered, totalling £714 4s., of which £706 14s. was real estate: "the housing & home lot, orchard, & a piece of saltmarsh adjoining thereunto," £210; "a piece of saltmarsh in the home meadows," £72; "a piece of salt meadow at Porter's Cove," £40; "a piece of land at the World's End," £60; "a piece of land lying as we go into the Neck," £70; "the pasture over the river as we go to Turkey Hill," £220; "the third division in Cohasset upland," £10; "the fourth division nigh Weymouth line," £4 14s.; and "ten shares of the undivided Commons," £20. Amounts due to be paid from the estate amounted to £98 7s., including 12d. due to Thomas

Loring, shipwright (evidently not Thomas Loring, sadler, the administrator of the estate) [SPR 11:275-76]. Sometime after 20 October 1697 "Thomas Loring of Hingham administrator *cum testamento annexo* ... of Nathan[ie]l Baker sometime of Hingham aforesaid, yeoman, deceased" filed an account in which he noted that the estate had increased in value to £719 4s. pursuant to "the sale of a piece of land at the world's end, more than it was appraised at in the inventory"; he charged the estate with expenses of £104 10s., most of which went to three legacies: to "Jacob Loring, grandchild of the deceased," £50; to "Mary Loring (now Jones)," £25; and to "Rachel Loring," £25 [SPR 16:229].

BIRTH: By about 1614, based on grant of land in 1635 and estimated date of marriage.
DEATH: Hingham 3 June 1682 [NEHGR 121:210; HiVR 56].
MARRIAGE: (1) By 1639 _____ Lane, daughter of William Lane of Dorchester, who left his "son Nath Baker of Hingham" £8 in his will dated 28 February 1650[/1], by which date Nathaniel Baker's wife was evidently deceased as she was not named in her father's will [NEHGR 5:304].

(2) After 28 February 1650[/1] Sarah _____, who died, a widow, at the home of her [step]daughter, Mary (Baker) Loring, on 19 August 1695 [Hingham Hist 411].
CHILD:
With first wife
    i   MARY, bp. Hingham [blank] July 1639 [NEHGR 121:11]; m. Hingham 16 December 1657 John Loring [NEHGR 121:107].
ASSOCIATIONS: He was a brother of Rev. NICHOLAS BAKER of Hingham, Hull and Scituate, naming the six children of his brother, Nicholas, in his will. Nicholas named his brother, Nathaniel, an overseer of his will.

COMMENTS: Nathaniel Baker unsuccessfully sued the town of Hingham, the General Court upholding the jury's verdict in the matter, 23 May 1650 [MBCR 3:197-198], mentioned again on 30 May 1650 [MBCR 4:1:14].

At the Suffolk County Court session of 27 January 1673/4, Nathaniel Baker of Hingham brought suit against Humphrey Johnson of Hingham in the amount of £20 for refusing to sign a deed of Lot 44 in the second division of "Conahasset upland" in Hingham, which land Baker had formerly bought of said Johnson and had paid him in full for it, the jury finding for the plaintiff [SCC 1:392].

Samuel Lincoln of Hingham was admonished by the Suffolk County Court during its session of 28 July 1674 for peeling an apple tree and cutting off the ears of a horse belonging to Nathaniel Baker [SCC 1:480].

In the Suffolk County Court session of 30 October 1677, Nathaniel Baker of Hingham complained against Simon Burr Jr. of Hingham for assailing and wounding him on the road as he was riding from Hingham to Scituate, for which Burr was found guilty and sentenced to be whipped thirty stripes, and to pay Baker £10 plus costs of court and prison, the corporal punishment being remitted upon payment of the fine [SCC 2:866-67].

A complaint was brought before the Suffolk County Court session of 30 July 1678 against Nathaniel Baker of Hingham for voting more than once at one time for a selectman, the court fining him 20s. and costs of court [SCC 2:939].

The inventory of Nathaniel Baker's estate included an Indian servant, valued at £6 [SPR 9:87-88].

Two wives are assigned to Nathaniel Baker solely on the basis of the will of William Lane, which names his son-in-law but not his daughter, which has been interpreted above to imply that his daughter was dead when he drew up his will. If this interpretation is not made, then it may be that Nathaniel Baker had only one wife, Sarah Lane, daughter of William.

NICHOLAS BAKER

ORIGIN: Unknown
MIGRATION: 1635
FIRST RESIDENCE: Hingham 1635
REMOVES: Hull about 1644, Scituate 1660

OCCUPATION: Planter. Minister.
CHURCH MEMBERSHIP: Nicholas Baker or his wife (or perhaps both) belonged to the Hingham church as early as 1638, as several of their children were baptized there.

In 1660 he was ordained the third minister of the first church of Scituate, and successfully brought together the first and the second churches which had quarrelled for twenty years [Savage 1:98; Morison 365-66]. Cotton Mather tells us that "I am content that there should be received (for the saints of this catalogue [of early New England ministers] already departed have received him) honest Mr. Nicholas Baker of Scituate; who, though he had but a private education, yet, being a pious and zealous man; or, as Dr. Arrowsmith expresses it, so good a logician, that he could offer up to God a reasonable service; so good an arithmetician, that he could wisely number his days; and so good an orator, that he persuaded himself to be a good Christian; and being also one of good natural parts, especially of a strong memory, was chosen pastor of the church there; and in the pastoral charge of that church he continued about eighteen years, until that horror of mankind, and reproach of medecine, the stone (under which he preached patience by a very memorable example of it; never letting fall any word worse than this, which was an usual word with him, `A mercy of God it is no worse!') put an end unto his days" [Magnalia 1:594-95].

FREEMAN: 3 March 1635/6 (sixth in a sequence of eight Hingham men) [MBCR 1:371].

EDUCATION: Although Mather tells us that Nicholas Baker "had but a private education [i.e., did not attend Oxford or Cambridge]" [Magnalia 1:594], there is a record of a man of this name who matriculated from St John's, Cambridge, Easter, 1628; B.A. 1631/2; M.A. 1635 [Venn 1:71], and this record has been attached to the immigrant by some.

The inventory of his portion of the estate at Hull included "books" valued at £8 18s. His widow's portion of the inventory included "1 trunk, one chest and books and other small things" valued at £2 5s. 10d.

OFFICES: Deputy to the General Court for Hingham, 25 May 1636, 2 May 1638 [MBCR 1:174, 227]. Commissioner to end small causes in Hingham, 4 November 1646 [MBCR 2:166, 3:83].

ESTATE: "The several parcels of land and meadow legally given unto Nicholas Baker by the town of Hingham": "for a houselot five acres of land," 18 September 1635; "for a planting lot two acres of land lying upon Pleasant Hill," 1635; "for a Great Lot sixteen acres of land, fourteen acres of it lying by Weymoth River ... the other two acres of it lying upon Squirrel Hill," 4 June 1636; "all that swamp ... at the end of his own lot and his brother Nathanaell's lot against the sea," no date; "an addition of planting land containing three acres lying partly against his own home lot and partly against the home lot of his brother Nathaneell Baker," no date; "for a small planting lot two acres of land lying by the fresh river," 20 November 1637; "whereas Nicholas Baker had one acre of meadow in

Weymoth Meadow he hath exchanged it with the town for three swamp pieces of meadow," no date; and "one acre of salt marsh lying in Broad Cove Meadow," 1635 [HiBOP 42].

In his will, dated 15 June 1678 and proved 29 October 1678, "Mr. Nicholas Baker, pastor of a Church of Christ at Scittuate," bequeathed "unto Grace my beloved wife, in the consideration of her singular and extraordinary love & faithfulness in the discharge of her duty unto me and my children, ... all that which was her own before marriage with me, everything only the Great Cyprus Chest which I give to her during her natural life only," also household goods and livestock for her maintenance, also "the one half of that my dwelling house which is in Hull ... with the full half of the orchard," stock, and gardens, and "all my homelot in Hull aforesaid, which lies upon the hill southwestward next adjoining to Thomas Jones his lot, together with that lot of salt meadow which lies in White Head meadows, and so much of the swamp at Allerton Hill as is or may be mowable, together with one lot upon Strawberry Hill, and one lot upon Sagamore Hill, one lot upon White Head, one lot upon Peducke's Island, and the one half of all my land upon any island belonging to Hull on which I have any land, together with one half of all common rights" during her natural life, also "all my estate of upland and meadow land ... in Hingham ... together with all the common rights ... during her natural life only," with provisions for the cutting of timber by the children; "also it is my will that my son Samuel shall pay unto my wife forty shillings in money per annum during her natural life in consideration of such lands as I shall put into his hands"; to "my eldest son Samuel I give the other part of my dwelling house ... and all my other lands ... before mentioned as given unto my wife during her natural life ... together with all the common rights both for wood and pasture belonging to one lot," also "after my wife her decease the other part of my said dwelling house ... before given unto my wife during her natural life, together with the other part of my land at Allerton Hill, and half all land and meadow, whether upon the main or upon the islands, and half the common right both for wood and pasture in the township of Hull," also "my first division of Conahasset lands in Hingham ... the half of my home lot next to Thomas Jones his lot excepted from these gifts," also "my home lot entirely which lies next to Thomas Jones his lot before given unto my wife ... together with the other half of all the land or meadow either on the islands or on the main, with the other half also of the common rights both of pasture and wood ... of my lands in Hull ... only," also "provided that my son Samuel pay ... unto my daughter Mary and my daughter Elizabeth ten pounds to each of them in silver money within one year after my wife's decease, or his entrance upon the above-given estate"; to "my son Nicholas ... all my estate in land and meadows, common right and whole estate in Hingham ... after my wife's decease ... excepting only the first division of Conihasset land before given unto my son Samuel, provided my son Nicholas pay ... unto my daughter Sarah ten pounds in silver money, and to my daughter Deborah ten pounds in silver money ... within one year after my wife's decease or his entrance upon the above given estate; but in case my son Nicholas should not live to come again then my mind and will is that all my estate in Hingham settled upon Nicholas ... do rest and settle upon my four daughters ... Mary, Elizabeth, Sarah and Deborah," and if this should come to pass then Samuel would be discharged from paying the legacies above mentioned to the daughters Mary and Elizabeth; "the land given me by a town vote in Scittuate ... unto my four daughters Mary, Elizabeth, Sarah and Deborah to be equally divided betwixt them"; to "my wife's grandchild Mary Webb after my wife's decease the Cyprus Chest"; to "my children sons and daughters by an equal division" "the brass andirons and the rest of my books not before disposed of"; to "my four daughters abovenamed by an equal division" "the rest of my moveables not before given"; "my wife" to pay "unto my grandchild Mercye Baker ten pounds"; "my beloved wife Grace executrix and my eldest son Samuell Baker as joint executor"; "my beloved brother Nathaniel Baker and my loving kinsman John Loren to be the overseers." In a nuncupative codicil Thomas Nicolls, aged about forty years, deposed on 29 October 1678 that "a little before Mr. Nicholas Baker of Scittuate died I was at his house and watched with him, and he called his son Samuell, and his wife, and said that it was his mind that his sons, Samuell and Nicholas, should have his wearing apparel, ... for he said that he had forgot to set it down in the will, but he said it was my real mind" [PCPR 3:2:133-35].

The inventory of the estate of "Mr. Nicholas Baker," taken 28 August 1678, totalled £84 10s. 6d.; one part listed "[t]he goods in the parlor that were his wife's before she married him," and another part itemized "the estate of Mr. Nicholas Baker which was his proper goods before he married her." The wife's possessions included "one Ciprus Chest" worth £5 [PCPR 3:2:136-37]. The inventory of "the estate of Mr. Nicholas Baker of Scittuate ... deceased the 22cond of August 1678 lying in Hull in the County of Sussex [sic] in New England," taken 8 October 1678, totalled £203 18s., of which £200 was real estate: "the home lot lying on the northeast hill ... with all the privileges," £115; and "the home lot lying on the southwest hill ... with all the privileges," £85 [PCPR 3:2:137]. On 11 October 1678, "all the lands and privileges of the late deceased Mr. Nicholas Baker, in Hingham are appraised at" £140 [PCPR 3:2:135]. The first of these three inventories was only for the property in Scituate, and, in typical Plymouth Colony style, did not list any real estate. The total for these three inventories was £428 8s. 6d., of which £340 was real estate.

BIRTH: About 1610 (deposed on 2 June 1663 aged 53 years [PCPR 2:2:76]).
DEATH: Scituate 22 or 29 August 1678 [PCPR 3:2:137; NEHGR 121:202]. (The inventory of Nathaniel Baker's estate at Hingham gives his date of death as 22 August, while Peter Hobart's journal says that he died on 29 August; neither gives his age at death, and no other contemporary record of his death has been found. Savage said that he died "22 Aug. 1678, aged 67" [Savage 1:67], but he does not state his source, and the age at death may simply be based on the deposition of 1663.)
MARRIAGE: (1) By 1638 _____ _____. She died at Scituate on 23 April 1661 [NEHGR 121:112].

(2) 29 April 1662 Grace (____) Dipple [Hingham Hist 2:17, citing an unknown source], who survived him. (Her daughter, Grace Dipple, married at Scituate on 16 April 1666 Joseph Webb of Boston.)
CHILDREN:
With first wife
  i SAMUEL, bp. Hingham 21 October 1638 [NEHGR 121:11]; m. (1) by 1664 Fear Robinson, daughter of *ISAAC ROBINSON* [GMB 3:1593]; m. (2) Abigail (Lathrop) Huntington [TAG 18:46].
  ii MARY, bp. Hingham [blank] December 1640 [NEHGR 121:13]; m. Scituate 26 February 1661/2 Stephen Vinal.
  iii JOHN, bp. Hingham 6 November 1642 [NEHGR 121:15]; on 1 May 1678, administration was granted on the estate of "John Baker, mariner, late deceased in Boston," to "Samuel Baker his brother (in right of the widow and children left by said Baker and others concerned therein)" [SPR 12:28]; the inventory of "John Baker son of Mr. Nicholas Baker who died April 19, 1678," was presented on 1 May 1678. (No records of a John Baker in Boston have been found which correspond with this man; his wife and children may perhaps be found in some other port, possibly in the Caribbean.)

    iv   ELIZABETH, bp. Hingham 10 November 1644 [NEHGR
         121:17]; m. Scituate 2 February 1664[/5] John Vinal.
    v   NICHOLAS, b. probably at Hull, about 1646 [NEHGR
         142:123]; m. by about 1687 Experience Collier, daughter
         of Thomas Collier (on 8 October 1695, administration was
         granted to "Jane Colyer of Hull" on the estate of "your
         son-in-law Nicholas Baker late of Boston" [SPR Case
         #2273, 13:680]; on 14 May 1696, "Jane Colyer widow
         administratrix" of the estate of "her son-in-law Nicholas
         Baker late of Boston, mariner," presented her account,
         which included "sickness and funeral charges of
         Experience Baker, widow of the deceased" [SPR Case
         #2273, 11:161]; on 19 May 1697, "Jane Collyer widow" was
         made guardian of "your granddaughters Jane Baker
         daughter of Nicholas Baker ... (being a minor about ten
         years of age) and Elizabeth Baker daughter of the said
         deceased (being a minor about seven years of age" [SPR
         11:288-89]) [NEHGR 142:356-59].
    vi   SARAH, b. say 1650; m. Scituate 22 February 1671[/2] Josiah
         Litchfield.
    vii DEBORAH, bp. at Hingham 6 June 1652 [NEHGR 121:25]; m.
         Scituate 25 April 1678 Israel Chittenden.
ASSOCIATIONS: Brother of NATHANIEL BAKER of Hingham, who
mentioned the six children of his late brother, Nicholas Baker of
Hingham, in his will dated 11 May 1682. Nicholas named his brother,
Nathaniel Baker, an overseer of his will.

COMMENTS: Nicholas Baker and others applied to the General Court on
2 August 1642 for liberty to plant at Seekonk [Rehoboth], but he does not
appear to have gone there [PCR 2:43].
    Nicholas Baker and Thomas Loring, both of Hull, together with John
Richards of Weymouth, were appointed by Thomas Richards of
Weymouth to be overseers of the latter's will in that instrument dated 17
December 1650, the testator being sick at the house of Thomas Loring in
Hull where he presumably died. Some writers have thought that
Nicholas Baker's first wife must have been a Richards, apparently
because of this reference, but there is no other evidence for this
assumption [NEHGR 7:232].
    On 10 April 1656, Nicholas Baker, together with Thomas Loring, John
Stone and Benjamin Bosworth, all planters of Hull, purchased from

Nauhawton of Ponkapoag in Dorchester all his interest in that neck of land known as Nantasket and now being the town of Hull, being a tract about five miles long [SLR 12:393].

On 2 June 1663, Nicholas Baker, aged 53 years, deposed to the terms of the nuncupative will of John Allen of Scituate, and was one of those taking the inventory of Allen's estate [PCPR 2:2:76].

It has been suggested that Nicholas Baker perhaps had a son, Thomas, who married Christian Beal [NEHGR 142:123]. Nicholas Baker in his will does not name a son Thomas, nor does he name any grandchildren who could have been children of Thomas. Thomas *Bacor* of Hingham married Christian Beal, daughter of Nathaniel Beal and granddaughter of John Beal of Hingham. She was presumably the child baptized on 9 November 1654 [NEHGR 121:104], and died at Boston on 20 September 1677 [NEHGR 121:200], leaving a small son, Thomas. This Thomas is mentioned in the will of his grandfather Beal, who died on 20 December 1708, the will being proved on 29 December that year [Savage 1:146]. If Thomas *Bacor* was Nicholas' son, and left a child named Thomas (even if he himself died as a young man), then why did the godly grandfather Baker not name grandson Thomas in his will, as grandfather Beal did? However, Thomas does not seem to be Nathaniel's son, and there are no other Bakers in Hingham. The possibility exists that Thomas *Bacor* was really Thomas *Bacon*, and perhaps a son of GEORGE BACON of Hingham, although a new reading of the original manuscript of Hobart's journal at the Massachusetts Historical Society shows conclusively that the surname is written *Bacor* in the original. It is doubtful that Thomas belongs in either the Baker or the Bacon families here mentioned, and he was probably from somewhere else.

BIBLIOGRAPHIC NOTE: In 1988 Ethel Farrington Smith published an interesting discussion of early Hull, with a map of the first houselot grants and a genealogical study of Nicholas Baker and his sons [NEHGR 142:121-25].

SAMUEL BAKER

On 12 May 1635, "Samuell Baker," aged 30, was enrolled at London as a passenger for New England on the *Elizabeth & Ann*, as part of a group which had its certificate of conformity from the minister of Benenden, Kent [Hotten 78].

COMMENTS: Savage places this immigrant as a resident of Lynn, dying there on 16 December 1666. This death is recorded at Lynn, but there are no earlier records for a Samuel in the town, and therefore no reason to connect this death with the immigrant of 1635.

JOHN BALDIN
WILLIAM BALDIN

"Jo[hn] Baldin," aged 13, and "W[illia]m Baldin," aged 9, were enrolled at London, on 18 July 1635 as passengers for New England on the *Pied Cow* [Hotten 106].

COMMENTS: The only other person entered for this ship on this day was "Will[ia]m Harrison," aged 55, with a "certificate from the minister of his conformity & from Sir Edward Spencer resident near Branford that he is no subsidy man" [Hotten 106]. The Baldin boys may have been kinsmen of Harrison, or servants.

Pope thought that the elder of these two might be "the John Balden who covenanted in 1648 to work four years for Wm. Collier of Duxbury" [Pope 29]. No record of this event has been found, and the gap of thirteen years makes the identification unlikely. Pope also suggests this John later resided in Woburn and Billerica, which is even more unlikely.

WILLIAM BALLARD

ORIGIN: Unknown
MIGRATION: 1635
FIRST RESIDENCE: Lynn

OCCUPATION: Husbandman.
CHURCH MEMBERSHIP: Admission to Lynn church prior to 24 May 1638 implied by freemanship.
FREEMAN: 24 May 1638 [MBCR 1:374].
EDUCATION: Sufficient to be appointed magistrate of county court.
OFFICES: Magistrate, Salem Quarterly Court, 26 June 1638, 27 July 1638 [MBCR 1:232; EQC 1:8, 9]. Committee to lay out land granted by colony, 6 September 1638 [MBCR 1:240]. Lynn representative on committee to

levy colony rate, 6 September 1638 [MBCR 1:242]. Committee to determine boundary between Salem and Lynn, 13 March 1638/9 [MBCR 1:253]. On 6 June 1639, Timothy Tomlins was appointed in place of "Mr. Ballard" to "view the place by Linn, to see if it be fit for a plantation" [MBCR 1:263].

Admitted to Ancient and Honorable Artillery Company, 1638 [HAHAC 1:53].

ESTATE: "Will[iam] Ballord" was granted sixty acres in Lynn in 1638 [EQC 2:270].

A deposition concerning William Ballard's failure to make a will is recorded in the first volume of Suffolk probates, but the right edge of the page has been damaged, and several words are now illegible. The version published in 1848 [NEHGR 2:183] and the version in the nineteenth-century manuscript copy of the original volume [SPR 1:15 (copy)] differ from one another, and both contain words no longer legible. The following transcript is taken from the original record volume, with the original line breaks [SPR 1:15 (original)]:

Nicholas Browne and Gearard Spencer [worn]
affirmeth that being with Mr. Will[ia]m Ballard of Linn [worn]
before his death, & persuading him to make his will [worn]
said Mr. Ballrd told them, he intended to do it the next [worn]
died before he could put it in writing, he would have [worn]
half his estate, & the other half to be divided among [worn]
children the said Will[ia]m Ballard being then of perfect [worn]
inge
taken upon oath 1 of 1st m[worn]

(The year this document was made is no longer legible, but in the published version and the nineteenth-century copy is given as 1639, a reasonable date given our estimate of William Ballard's date of death.)

On 27 June 1643, the inventory of "William Ballard of Lynn, deceased," was filed [EQC 1:54; EPR 1:24]. On 28 December 1647, Salem court noted that "Timothie Tomlins and Thomas Erington were appointed guardians of the children of William Ballard, deceased; and Timothie Tomlins having since deceased, Nicolas Batty of Lin was appointed in his place. Thomas Putnum of Lin and Thomas Laughton were appointed to divide the lands between the mother and children according to the will" [EQC 1:131; EPR 1:24].

On 2 September 1695, administration on "the estate of William Ballard, formerly of Linn, was granted to John Ballard son of deceased." The inventory of the estate of William Ballard deceased, taken 1 October 1695, totalled £173 10s., all in real estate: "upland in the neck 10 acres," £50; "salt marsh lying near the two trees in the town marsh being 5 acres," £25; "salt marsh in the neck 2½ acres," £11; "Noman's Swamp so-called," £25 10s.; "the houselot 6 acres," £30; and "one parcel of land lying in Reding," £32 [EPR Case #1605].

BIRTH: About 1603 (aged 32 in 1635 [Hotten 107]).

DEATH: Between 13 March 1638/9 (when he signed a committee report [MBCR 1:253]) and 6 June 1639 (when he was replaced on a committee [MBCR 1:263]). (DeForest made a slight error in estimating the date of death [Dommerich Anc 46].)

MARRIAGE: By about 1633 Elizabeth ____. She married (2) in 1640 or soon after William Knight (in his will of 2 December 1653 William Knight refers to "my four children which I had by my last wife Elizabeth," and makes bequests to "John Ballard" and "Nathaniel Ballard" [EPR 1:213; EQC 1:394]) and (3) Lynn 28 March 1656 Allen Bread.

CHILDREN:

   i   HESTER, b. about 1633 (aged 2 in 1635 [Hotten 107]); m. by 1652 Joseph Jenks Jr. (on 30 November 1652, "Ester, wife of Joseph Jenkes,Jr.," was one of four Lynn residents "fined for wearing silver lace" [EQC 1:271]; on 29 June 1655, John Ballard, brother of Hester, deposed that he "was his brother Jenckes's servant" [EQC 1:392]).

   ii   JOHN, b. about 1634 (aged 1 in 1635 [Hotten 107]; deposed aged twenty-one in 1655 [EQC 1:392]; deposed aged twenty-five in 1659 [EQC 2:193]); m. by 1669 Rebecca ____ (see *COMMENTS* below).

   iii   NATHANIEL, b. about 1636 (deposed in 1684 "aged forty-eight years" [EQC 9:341]); m. Lynn 16 December 1662 Rebecca Hutson.

COMMENTS: On 13 July 1635, "W[illia]m Ballard," aged 32, husbandman, "Elizabeth Ballard," aged 26, "Hester Ballard," aged 2 and "Jo[hn] Ballard," aged 1, were enrolled at London as passengers for New England on the *James* [Hotten 107].

Savage proposed that the William Ballard who came in 1634 was father of the William who came in 1635, and hopelessly intermixed William of Lynn and William of Andover.

A 1638 list of those in Suffolk, England, who were delinquent in their payments of ship money includes a few names that are annotated as having gone to New England; as published, these entries include William Ballard of Bradwell [NEHGR 61:69]. Examination of the Bradwell parish register shows no entries for the surname Ballard in the late 1620s and early 1630s, but there is a baptism on 21 February 1629/30 for "Marye, the daughter of William Bullard." William Bullard, an early inhabitant of Dedham, Massachusetts, had a daughter Mary who married in 1650, so the ship money entry would seem to be for William Bullard of Dedham, and not for William Ballard [TAG 72:135-36].

On 25 June 1639, "Mr. Holliock in behalf of the Lord Brooks, by Mr. Ballard's agreement ordered to pay 50s. per hire of a yoke of oxen for 3 months to Rich[a]r[d] Hutchenson" [EQC 1:11].

Most writers on this family claim that the immigrant had a son William [Ballard Gen 18; Dommerich Anc 46-47; TEG 16:71-72]. Very few records are ascribed to this alleged son: service on a grand jury in September 1665; baptism of a daughter Rebecca in 1668; a daughter Elizabeth who marries in 1684; and an administration and inventory of 1695, which names a son John.

Taking up these points in chronological order, examination of the published Essex court records shows that a court was held in Ipswich on 26 September 1665, but William Ballard does not appear in the grand jury or petit jury of this or any other Essex Court. This claimed record was given only by deForest, and may be an error in his own notes.

The birth of Rebecca Ballard, daughter of William, on 2 October 1669 does appear in the Lynn vital records, but no other birth of a child of William is found. There is a gap in the list of children of Nathaniel Ballard, whose first two recorded children were born in 1666 and 1670. Perley gives Nathaniel a daughter Rebecca, who married a Stace of Attleborough, and places her in this gap. We conclude that the Lynn clerk slipped in entering this birth, and gave the name of the grandfather rather than the father.

On 22 May 1684, "Allen Bread & Elizabeth Ballard of Linn" were married at Charlestown [ChVR 1:123]. This record does not mention William Ballard, and we shall set this aside for the moment.

To this point, then, we have no evidence for a William Ballard who was son of the immigrant, and we are left with the administration of 1695. This consists only of six parcels of real estate, which have the appearance of the collection of land that a first-generation immigrant would receive; in particular, the "parcel of land lying at Reading" is almost certainly the sixty acres received in 1638 by the immigrant William Ballard [EQC 2:270].

As noted above, Elizabeth, the widow of the immigrant, had a life interest in half the estate of William Ballard, and she later married William Knight and then Allen Bread. As the wife of Allen Bread she was still alive as late as 1681 [TEG 11:98, citing ELR 6:22]; Allen Bread disposed of his estate to his children during his lifetime, and so does not leave a will in which his wife might be named. The most likely solution to this puzzle is that Elizabeth outlived her third husband for a few years, and that upon her death the real estate of the immigrant William Ballard that had been in her hands for more than half a century had to be divided among her heirs. The "son John" would then be the son of the immigrant.

This leaves the 1684 marriage of "Elizabeth Ballard of Linn" as the only unresolved part of the puzzle, but as this record does not refer to William Ballard, it is not sufficient evidence to suppose that there was a William in the second generation, and so we conclude that William Ballard the immigrant did not have a son William.

On 29 June 1655, "John Ballad [sic], aged twenty-one years, deposed that when he was his brother Jenckes' servant he worked in that boat of Joseph Armitage's which was cast away" [EQC 1:392]. On 28 November 1659, "Jon. Ballard, aged twenty-five years, deposed that six months ago he saw John Chaxfield living in Barbadoes" [EQC 2:193].

Farlow claimed that John Ballard had two wives, Susanna Story and Rebecca _____ [Ballard Gen 18]. As evidence for the first wife, he gives only "Salem Rec.," the meaning of which is not evident. The only Story family which might have a daughter of the right age is that of William Story of Ipswich. Nora E. Snow does include a Susanna in this family, but without dates or any later history [Snow-Estes 1:107]; William Story, son of the immigrant, had wife Susanna Fuller, and there may exist a document in which some member of the family calls her "daughter" or "sister," from which an improper conclusion was drawn.

We are assisted in analyzing the alleged marriages of John by the details of the recording of the births of his children. First, there is no record of a son William born on 1 October 1667, as claimed by Savage and many later writers. Second, the first two known children, Sarah and Rebecca, were recorded in the county but not in the town records, with the mother's name not given, and these are claimed by Farlow to be children of Susanna Story. The remaining children were recorded in the town records, with the mother's name given as Rebecca. Note that one of the children supposed to be born to Susanna Story was named Rebecca, and no child was named Susanna. For these reasons, we conclude that

Susanna Story never existed and that John Ballard had only one wife, Rebecca, whom he married by 1669.

BIBLIOGRAPHICAL NOTE: In 1902 Sidney Perley published an outline sketch of William Ballard and five generations of descent in the male line [Essex Ant 6:39-40]. In 1911 Charles Frederic Farlow compiled an account of the descendants of this immigrant [*Ballard Genealogy: William Ballard (1603-1639) of Lynn, Massachusetts, and William Ballard (1617-1689) of Andover, Massachusetts, and Their Descendants* (Boston 1911), cited above as Ballard Gen]. In 1930 Louis Effingham deForest prepared a brief account of William Ballard, with excellent analyses on several points [Dommerich Anc 45-47]. In 1996 Marcia Lindberg Wiswall revised and updated the earlier account by Charles Frederic Farlow [TEG 16:71-74].

WILLIAM BALLARD

On 26 March 1634, William Ballard took the oath of supremacy to pass to New England on the *Mary & John* [Drake's Founders 70].

COMMENTS: Savage proposed that this man setted at Lynn, and may have been the father of the WILLIAM BALLARD who came in the following year and also settled at Lynn. The William Ballard of 1635 was most certainly the resident of Lynn, based on the names of the children, and there is no evidence for an elder generation there.

The only other early William Ballard resided in Andover, and Savage muddled the Andover and Lynn families. The earliest record of the William Ballard of Andover was on 25 March 1651 when he was made a freeman [EQC 1:218]. There is no reason to connect William Ballard of Andover with the passenger of 1634.

GUY BANBRIDGE

ORIGIN: Newcastle upon Tyne, Northumberland
MIGRATION: 1634
FIRST RESIDENCE: Cambridge

OCCUPATION: Butcher (in England). In 1632 "Bambrigg Guy butcher" was admitted as a freeman of Newcastle upon Tyne, Northumberland [*The Register of Freemen of Newcastle upon Tyne*, Newcastle upon Tyne Records Series, Vol. 3 (Newcastle upon Tyne 1923), p. 16].

CHURCH MEMBERSHIP: Admission to Cambridge church prior to 4 March 1634/5 implied by freemanship. In 1658 "Justice Bainbrick the widow of Guy Bainbrick deceased" was a member in full communion of Cambridge church [CaChR 10].

FREEMAN: 4 March 1634/5 (fourth in a sequence of nineteen Cambridge men) [MBCR 1:370].

OFFICES: Cambridge fenceviewer, 7 December 1635 (as "Mr. Bambrigg") [CaTR 15].

ESTATE: Granted one acre in the Westend in Cambridge, 4 August 1634 [CaTR 9]. Granted four acres "behind the Pine Swamp, 5 January 1634/5 [CaTR 11]. Granted a proportional share of 1½ in the undivided meadow ground, 21 April 1635 [CaTR 13]. In the list of houses, credited with one in the Westend, 8 February 1635/6 [CaTR 18].

In the Cambridge land inventory on 10 October 1635, "Guy Bambrig" held two parcels: in the "Westend one house with backside about one acre"; and "by the Pine Swamp about four acres" [CaBOP 33]. In the inventory of 1639 "Guy Banbridge" had two lots: in "the new lots next Manotomie six acres of planting ground"; and in "the new west field three acres of planting ground" [CaBOP 55]. In the inventory of 6 September 1642, "Guye Banbrige" held five parcels: in "West End one dwelling house, with about three roods of land"; in "the new west field three acres more or less"; "on the plain towards Menotamye six acres more or less"; in "the Freshpond Meadow seven acres & half more or less"; and in "Pine Swamp Field four acres more or less" [CaBOP 96-97].

By an unknown date Stephen Day had bought "of Guy Bandbrike & Samuell Greene 14 acres of planting ground" [CaBOP 70]. By an unknown date "Guye Benbrike" had received two lots on the south side of Charles River, three acres in the lower division and three acres 29 [poles?] in the upper division [CaBOP 331]. By an unknown date "Gie Banbrooke" had purchased lots of seven acres and one acre in Fresh Pond Meadow [CaBOP 333].

In 1645 "Guy Banbricke" was granted three acres and a half "on the west side of Monotamye River" [CaBOP 128].

In the division of Shawsheen on 4 June 1652, "widow Banbricke" received forty acres [CaTR 97]. In 1662 one acre and a half in the first division of the south side of Charles River was granted to "Widow

Banbricke" [CaBOP 140]. On 27 February 1664/5 and 27 March 1665, "Justin Banbricke" was granted Lot 56, ten acres and one common [CaBOP 146].

In her will, undated but proved 6 March 1672/3, "Justess Banbery" bequeathed to "my daughter Plume my feather bed & to Elisabeth Plume my silk cap, to my daughter Buttler my cloth gown & my blue watered petticoat & to Hanna Butler my silk hood and four pair of shoes, two pair to my daughter Buttol[s] children ... and to Debora Greene my bed[sted?]" and "for the five pound that Joseph Greene gave me I give twenty shillings of it to Mr. John Whiting" [TAG 46:8-10, with facsimile and full transcription of his will, also citing Manwaring 1:177].

BIRTH: By about 1595 based on estimated date of marriage.
DEATH: Buried at Cambridge 10 April 1645.
MARRIAGE: By about 1620 Justice ____. "Justice Banbricke widow aged about 64 years" deposed on 13 July 1664 [MCF Folio #34]. She had moved to Hartford by 1666 [TAG 46:9, citing WMJ 691, 837] and died there by 6 March 1672/3 (probate of will).
CHILD:

 i JANE, b. say 1620; m. by 1640 Samuel Green, son of *BARTHOLOMEW GREEN* [TAG 46:7-11]. (She had died by 1658, when the entry in the church records for her husband and family listed "Jane his wife (daughter to the foresaid Justice Bainbrick) now deceased" [CaChR 10].)

COMMENTS: In early 1639, the mayor and other officials of Newcastle upon Tyne, Northumberland, conducted an examination of Giles Bittleston of that place, who was clearly (and correctly) suspected of Puritan activities. One of the documents unearthed during the examination was a letter addressed to "Thomas Cheasman or Edward Winshop," dated 1 September 1638, which closes "Love to all I write to, which is Thomas Cheasman, William Cutter, Edward Winshop, and Guy Bainbridge" [CSPD Charles I, 1638-1639, p. 418]. (See sketch of THOMAS CHEESEHOLME for further details.)

BIBLIOGRAPHIC NOTE: In 1970 Donald Lines Jacobus published an article on the "Banbridge-Green-Plumb-Butler Connections," in which he transcribed and analyzed the will of Justice Banbury, and demonstrated that the two women she calls daughters were in fact her granddaughters [TAG 46:7-11].

MARTHA BANES

On 18 July 1635, "Martha Banes," aged 20, was enrolled at London as a passenger for New England on the *Defence* [Hotten 107].

COMMENTS: Martha Banes appears among a number of young, unmarried men and women, apparently servants. She has not been found in any New England record.

THOMAS BARBER

ORIGIN: St Mildred Breadstreet, London
MIGRATION: 1635 on the *Christian*
FIRST RESIDENCE: Windsor

OCCUPATION: Carpenter. On 28 March 1637, "it is ordered that Mr. Frances Stiles shall teach Geo. Chapple, Tho: Cooper & Thomas Barber his servants in the trade of a carpenter to his promise for their service of their term behind 4 days in a week only to saw & slit their own work that they are to frame themselves with their own hands together with himself or some other master workmen" [CCCR 1:8-9].
CHURCH MEMBERSHIP: Either he or his wife was a member of the Windsor church since their children were baptized there.
FREEMAN: Connecticut 10 April 1645 [CCCR 1:124].
EDUCATION: Company of Carpenters apprenticeship [TAG 71:111-12].
OFFICES: Connecticut Particular Court jury, December 1655, 1 December 1659 [RPCC 154, 205].
　Sergeant, 1649 [RPCC 74].
ESTATE: On 8 December 1640, Thomas Barber was granted a houselot of eight acres and twelve acres of woodland in Windsor. On the same day it was recorded that he had purchased from "Benjamin Nuberry" a three-mile tract, also twelve acres once "Thomas Cooppers" [WiLR 1:24].
　A will, written or not, is implied in the probate of Thomas Barber, but none has been found.
　On 4 February 1662[/3], the distribution of Thomas Barber's estate was as follows: "to John and Sarah jointly as their father willed," the house and barn and all the home lot, land over the river, half the 24-acre lot, half the marsh, and to John a cow, as well as £20 more to John and Sarah.

Thomas Barber's share comprised "a mare that he claims as a gift from his father," half his father's tools, the 14-acre upland lot, half the out lot, half the marsh, and his proportion, being £33 15s. "Sam[ue]ll Barber" received £33 15s., as did "Mercey" and "Josias." "And what the estate amounts to more than the inventory when debts are paid shall be distributed betwixt the four younger children Thomas, Sam[ue]ll, Mercey and Josias and if any child die before they come to age sons 21 years daughters 18 years the portion of the deceased shall be divided amongst the survivors equally" [RPCC 263]. (The land owned jointly by Sarah and John is more fully detailed in the holdings of Timothy Hall, Sarah's husband [WiLR 1:87].)

On 4 February 1662/3, "Samuell Barber manifesting his desire thereto was then placed an apprentice unto his brother Thomas until he accomplish the age of twenty-one years" [RPCC 262]. On the same day, "Mercey Barber with her consent and desire is placed with Lt. Walter Filer and his wife until she be eighteen years of age unless she marry before" [RPCC 262]. On the same day, "Josias Barber according to his desire is placed with Deacon John Moore until he accomplish the age of twenty-one years" [RPCC 262]. On 30 January 1664[/5?], "Mercy Barber made choice of Lt. Walter Fyler to be her guardian" [RPCC 264].

The inventory of the estate of Thomas Barber, taken 20 October 1662, was exhibited 4 February 1662[/3] and totalled £132 14s., of which £113 was real estate: "house, barn orchard, home lot," £80; "land over the great river," £15; "14 acres woodland," £4; "24 acres woodland," £4; and "10 acres marsh," £10 [RPCC 273-74].

BIRTH: Baptized Stamford, Lincolnshire, 25 December 1612, son of John and Elizabeth (Lumley) Barber [TAG 71:111-12].
DEATH: Windsor 11 September 1662 [CTVR 21; Grant 83].
MARRIAGE: Windsor 7 October 1640 Jane ____ [Grant 24]. She died at Windsor on 10 September 1662 as "[t]he wife of Thomas Bar Ber" [CTVR 21; Grant 83]. In the inventory of Thomas Barber, taken 20 October 1662, "his wives apparel deceased" was valued at £15 [RPCC 274].
CHILDREN:

    i   JOHN, bp. Windsor 24 July 1642 [Grant 24; CTVR 33]; m. Springfield 2 September 1663 Bathsheba Coggins [CTVR 10; Grant 25].

    ii   THOMAS, b. Windsor 14 July 1644 [Grant 24; CTVR 33]; m. Windsor 17 December 1663 Mary Phelps [Grant 25; CTVR 10], daughter of *WILLIAM PHELPS* [GMB 3:1446].

    iii   SARAH, bp. Windsor 19 July 1646 [Grant 24; CTVR 33]; m. Windsor 26 November 1663 Timothy Hall [Grant 62].

    iv   SAMUEL, bp. Windsor 1 October 1648 [Grant 25; CTVR 33]; m. (1) Windsor 1 December 1670 Mary Coggins [CTVR 12; Grant 25 (surname of bride not given)]; m. (2) Windsor 25 January 1676[/7] Ruth Drake [CTVR 14; Grant 25].

    v   MERCY, bp. Windsor 12 October 1651 (published as "Mary") [CTVR 33]; m. Windsor 8 July 1669 John Gillett [CTVR 12; Grant 40], son of *JONATHAN GILLETT* [GMB 2:768].

    vi   JOSIAH, b. Windsor 15 February 1653/4 [CTVR 40]; m. (1) Windsor 22 November 1677 Abigail Loomis [Grant 74; CTVR 14]; m. (2) by 12 March 1701/2 Sarah (____) Drake, widow of Enoch Drake [Manwaring 1:551].

ASSOCIATIONS: Barber's master, FRANCIS STILES, was a native of Milford, Bedfordshire, but like others on the *Christian*, he had his letter of conformity from St Mildred Breadstreet. In 1996, Donald S. Barber published London's Worshipful Company of Carpenters guildhall record of Thomas Barber's apprenticeship:

> Received of Francis Stiles for apprenticing Thomas Barber, son of John Barber of Stamford in the County of Lincoln, yeoman, deceased, from St Thomas's day next for 9 years. 2s. 2d. [TAG 71:111].

Thomas was 22 at this time and was probably recruited by Saltonstall for New England. Barber and some of Stiles's other servants were unusually old for apprenticeship, which caused difficulties as they attempted to fit into Windsor society.

COMMENTS: On 16 March 1634[/5], "Tho: Barber," aged 21 years, was enrolled as a passenger for New England on the *Christian*, having taken the oath of allegiance and supremacy [Hotten 42].

    Grant, in his list compiled 17 August 1677, reported that "Thomas Barber Snr." had six children born in Windsor [Grant 90].

    On 16 May 1649, Thomas Barber was sued by William Franklin and fined £4 2s. 6d. in wheat [RPCC 65]. Testimony offered by Robert Hayward and Thomas Barber showed that the debt in question had been left "with Thomas Forde to do in it with [Benjamin] Nuberry as he saw cause," but the appeal failed [RPCC 66-67; CCCR 1:183-84, 191].

    On 6 December 1649, the Particular Court ruled that "Sargeant Barber for his disorderly striking Lt. Cooke is adjudged to lay down his place, and is fined to the country £5" [RPCC 74; CCCR 1:203]. Barber repented, being "affected with his great evil and rash passionate carriage," and was freed from the fine, but evidently not re-established as sergeant [RPCC 81].

BIBLIOGRAPHIC NOTE: In 1996 Donald S. Barber published the English origin of Thomas Barber, including the identification of his parents [TAG 71:111-12].

WILLIAM BARKER

On 6 October 1635, "Will[ia]m Barker" was one of six men who "shall be whipped for running from their masters, & for stealing a boat & diverse other things with them, as also shall give satisfaction to the country for their charges in sending to fetch them home, & likewise shall serve their said masters twice so long at the end of their time, as they have been absent from their master's service, by reason of their running away" [MBCR 1:162].

On 5 April 1636, it is "[o]rdered, that Will[ia]m Barker shall be whipped for stealing bacon, cheese, &c., from Ralfe Tompkins" [MBCR 1:172].

COMMENTS: The six men who ran from their masters were William Barker, SIMON BIRD, CLEMENT COLE, WILLIAM DOWNES, PETER PYFORD and GEORGE WILBY. Three of these men (Bird, Cole and Wilby) were passengers to New England on the *Susan & Ellen* in 1635 [Hotten 59]. At least three of them (Bird, Cole and Downes) settled first at Boston. Ralph Tompkins resided at Dorchester. William Barker may have resided at one of these towns.

Pope states that this William Barker was "witness from Marblehead in Essex Court in 1642" [Pope 32]. No person of this name is found in the early Essex Court records, but a William Barber did witness against Thomas Gray of Marblehead in 1642 [EQC 1:48].

This William Barker is not found in any other New England record.

JOHN BARNARD

ORIGIN: Unknown
MIGRATION: 1634 on the *Francis*
FIRST RESIDENCE: Cambridge
REMOVES: Hartford 1636, Hadley 1659

CHURCH MEMBERSHIP: Admission to Cambridge church prior to 4 March 1634/5 implied by freemanship.
FREEMAN: 4 March 1634/5 (as "John Bernard," tenth in a sequence of nineteen Cambridge men) [MBCR 1:370].
EDUCATION: He signed his will. His inventory included "his books," valued at £1 13s.
OFFICES: Hadley sealer of weights and measures, 31 March 1663 [HamCCR 1:24]. Hampshire county petit jury, 29 March 1664 [HamCCR 1:30].
ESTATE: On 4 August 1634, granted five acres in the West End in Cambridge [CaTR 9]. Received a proportional share of one and a half in the division of meadow ground, 20 August 1635 [CaTR 13].

In the Cambridge land inventory on 10 October 1635, John Barnard held one parcel: "In the West End one dwelling house with other outhouses and planting ground about eight acres" [CaBOP 34]. By 1639 this piece of land was in the possession of John Bridge [CaBOP 55].

In the Hartford land inventory, in February 1639[/40], "John Barnord" held eleven parcels: three acres "on which his dwelling house now standeth with other outhouses, yards & gardens ... part whereof he bought of Arthur Smith"; three acres of upland; eleven acres and one rood of upland; seven acres in the South Meadow; one rood and twenty-nine perches in the Little Meadow; one acre on the east side of the Great River; two acres two roods in the Dead Swamp; four acres two roods in the Oxpasture; three acres two roods of swamp in the Great Swamp; five acres in the Great Swamp "which he bought of James Ensine"; and three acres of upland "which he bought of Robert Bartlet" (annotated "October 11th 1654") [HaBOP 217-19]. On 27 September 1663, John Barnard sold to Henry Hayward "all & whatsoever house or houses, malt house or malt houses, land or lands ... which do now unto him belong" in Hartford [HaBOP 219-20].

An undated entry in the Wethersfield land inventory enumerates "The lands of John Barnard of Hartford which he bought of Mr. Edward

Hopkins...: One piece in the great meadow containing four acres.... Other lands which he bought of Mr. Leet.... One piece lying in the great meadow," eight acres; "Another piece lying in the great meadow," four acres; "Another piece lying in the dry swamp," 8½ acres; and "Another piece lying in the wet swamp," four acres [WetLR 1:72].

In his will, dated 21 May 1664 and proved 27 September 1664, "John Barnard of Hadley" made "my loving wife Mary Barnard" sole executrix and bequeathed to her "all my house, houses, land or lands of what kind soever" at Wethersfield, and after her decease to "the children of Henry Hayward my kinsman which he now hath to be equally divided to each of them"; to "my loving wife Mary Barnard all my house, houses, land or lands of what kind soever" at Hadley, and after her decease "to the use & towards the maintenance of a school ... my piece of land lying in the [illegible] as also my piece of land that lies in Hockanum" and to "my kinsman Morgan Bedient ... my dwelling house & homelot with my malthouse & all other outhouses upon my lot as also my piece of land that lieth homeward in the nook or aquavita bottle" and to "Thomas Bedient ... all other parcels of land that do or shall belong to me in Hadley, and in case my wife shall die before the said Morgan & Thomas shall be one & twenty years of age then my overseers" to improve the land until they come of age; to "my cousin Steele's two daughters Mary Steele & Sarah Steele," £3 apiece; to "John Russell my pastor five pounds & to his son John five pounds"; to "Mr. John Whiting, minister at Hartford," £4; to "my maid that was Mary Beckwith all my part of cattle that is in her father's hands"; to "Francis Barnard," £2 and to "John Barnard his son," £3; residue to "my loving wife aforesaid"; "and in case my sister Mary Bedient come over to New England I do give unto her five pounds" [HamCCR 1:35-37].

The inventory of the estate of "John Barnard late deceased in Hadley," taken 10 June 1664, totalled £600 9s. 8d., of which £365 10s. was real estate: "his house, homelot, malthouse & all his other land," £215 10s.; and "his house & homelot & malthouse & other lands lying in Wethersfeild in Connecticut," £150 [HamCCR 1:37].

On 28 March 1665, "Mary Barnard of Hadley being deceased who was executrix of the last will & testament of her husband John Barnard deceased, this court appoints Francis Barnard & Rich[ard] Goodman administrators" [HamCCR 1:51].

In her will, dated 7 February 1664[/5] and proved 28 March 1665, "Mary Barnard of Hadley" bequeathed to "my sister Mary Bedient now resident at Hartford" moveables "for her use until her son Morgan Bedient shall be one and twenty years of age"; to "my cousin Henry Hayward the bill of twenty pounds that is in my hand"; to "my cousin his wife," moveables; to "my cousin Mary Hayward their daughter," moveables; to "Mr. Russell my pastor," £2; to "Mrs. Russell his wife," moveables; "to & for the use of the church one pewter basin & one pewter platter"; "to the use & furtherance of learning in the town of Hadley," £4; to "my loving friend Richard Goodman two pounds & one glass of strong water & to his wife I give two suits of my wearing linen"; "the rest of my wearing linen" to "my nurse & the wife of Francis Barnard to be divided between them"; to "my loving friend & nurse Goodwife Ward," moveables, including "a book whose author was Mr. John Rogers"; to "my maid Jane William," clothing and 50s.; to "my maid that was Elizabeth Ingram," clothing; to "Goodman Nicholls," his debts forgiven; to "Goodman Gardiner ... all that he oweth me, & to his wife" clothing and "my old Bible"; to "Francis Barnard" moveables and to "his wife" moveables; to "his son Thomas ten pounds to be improved in bringing him up at school" and "my new Bible"; residue to "the children of my brother[s] Daniell & William Stace (living in old England at Burnam near Maldon in Essex) to be equally divided between them," according to certain conditions, but if the conditions are not met, then to "the aforesaid Thomas Barnard"; "what of my household goods is to be set to sale ... my nurse & the wife of Francis Barnard may have the said refusal thereof"; "my friends Richard Goodman & Francis Barnard to be my executors and overseers"; "my friends Goody Ward & Goody Barnard" to help them in distributing the linen and woollen goods; a "postscript" (apparently written by the executors after the death of Mary Barnard) recorded further small legacies to "her cousin Henry Hayward & his wife"; to "G[oody] Hopkins"; and to "Goody Wasley at Hartford" [HamCCR 1:48-50].

The inventory of the estate of "Mary Barnard late deceased in Hadley," taken 15 February 1664/5, totalled £184 18s. 5d. (as well as £215 13s. 6d. in debts owed to the estate, and £81 18s. 10d. owed by the estate), with no real estate included [HamCCR 1:50-51].

BIRTH: About 1598 (aged 36 in 1634 [Hotten 279]).
DEATH: Buried at Hadley 23 May 1664 [Pynchon VR 237].
MARRIAGE: By 1634 Mary Stace. She died by 28 March 1665 [HamCCR 1:51]. (The parish register of Burnam, Essex, includes the burial of "Daniel Stace" on 3 March 1648/9 and of William Stace on 3 December 1660. The will of Daniel Stace, dated 4 February 1648/9, makes bequests to his

children, and does not name any other relatives [Archdeaconry of Essex Wills 20:200].)

CHILDREN: None recorded.

ASSOCIATIONS: The larger bequests in the will of John Barnard were to his sister Mary Bedient and her children, and to his kinsman Henry Hayward and his children. Henry Hayward was a generation younger than John Barnard (aged 7 in 1635 [Hotten 278]), so if this pattern of bequests was intended to indicate an equal degree of kinship, then we would expect that Henry Hayward was a nephew of John Barnard or of John Barnard's wife.

In the middle of the record of Hadley births for 1666 is the following entry: "Morgan Bedient son of Morgan Bedient of Staynes in England was born June 25, 1651, and Tho[mas] Bedient son of the aforesaid Morgan was born July 22, 1654, which to oath was made before Mr. Henry Clark & Lt. Smith of Hadly by Laurance Carter & Mary Bedient mother of the said two sons" [Pynchon VR 178; HamVR 40]. (The parish register of Staines, Middlesex, England, includes some baptisms for children of a Robert Bedient in the 1660s and 1670s, but no entries for the family of Morgan Bedient [*The Parish Registers of Staines, Middlesex. 1644-1694* (n.p., 1886)].

The Francis Barnard who is named in the will, and also later became an administrator of the estate, was presumably also a close kinsman of John Barnard.

The identity of "cousin Steele" is not certain, although it may be Samuel Steele (son of *JOHN STEELE*), who had daughters Mary and Sarah by the date of this will. This may be an excellent clue to the English origin of John Barnard, as the origin of the Steele brothers is known [GMB 3:1754-59].

COMMENTS: "John Bernard," aged 36, and "Mary his wife," aged 38, sailed for New England on "the last of April 1634" on the *Francis* of Ipswich; with them were "Fayth Newell," aged 14, and "Henry Haward," aged 7 [Hotten 278-79].

JOHN BARNARD

ORIGIN: Unknown
MIGRATION: 1634 on the *Elizabeth*
FIRST RESIDENCE: Watertown

CHURCH MEMBERSHIP: Admission to Watertown church prior to 3 September 1634 implied by freemanship.

FREEMAN: 3 September 1634 (as "John Bernard," fourth in a sequence of eleven Watertown men) [MBCR 1:369].

OFFICES: Watertown selectman, 28 November 1643 [WaTR 9]

ESTATE: On 25 July 1636, granted sixty acres at Watertown as a Great Dividend [WaBOP 3]. Granted ten acres in the Beaverbrook Plowlands, 28 February 1636/7 [WaBOP 7]. Granted ten acres in the Remote Meadows, 26 June 1637 [WaBOP 10]. Granted a Farm of two hundred eighty-seven acres, 10 May 1642 [WaBOP 12].

In the Watertown Inventory of Grants "John Bernard" held eleven parcels: homestall of thirteen acres; three acres of meadow; two acres of swamp; another two acres of swamp; six acres of upland in Dorchester Field; three acres of meadow; five acres of meadow in West Meadow; ten acres of plowland in the Further Field; ten acres of meadow in the Remote Meadows; sixty acres of upland in a Great Dividend; and thirty-one acres and a half of upland beyond the Further Plain [WaBOP 80]. In the Inventory of Possessions he held two parcels: two acres of meadow and six acres of upland [WaBOP 118]. In the Composite Inventory "John Bernard" held thirteen parcels: homestall of seven acres; five acres of meadow ("two acres bought of William Potter & three acres granted to him"); two acres of swamp; another two acres of swamp; six acres of upland in Dorchester Field; three acres of meadow; six acres of upland ("bought of William Jenison"); five acres of meadow in West Meadow; ten acres of plowland in the Further Plain; ten acres of meadow in the Remote Meadows; sixty acres of upland in a Great Dividend; thirty-one acres and a half of upland beyond the Further Plain; and a Farm of two hundred eighty-seven acres [WaBOP 24].

On 30 November 1647, "whereas there is a difference between Joseph Tayntor and widow Barnad [*sic*] about a piece of land, lying at the end of widow Barnad's swamp behind Joseph Tayntor's house (he purchased of old Peirce), it is determined at present, that the land is the Town's" [WaTR 1:11].

On 31 August 1666, "Edmund Bloy [i.e., Blois] complaining that widow Barnad had taken in the town land & the highway, lying between her house & Abraham Browne's ... goodman Tayntor was appointed to warn widow Barnad to appear at the next meeting of the selectmen to answer the complaint" [WaTR 1:87]. On 27 September 1666, "Widow Barnad appearing & upon the hearing of the case respecting the complaint brought against her ... as also considering the grants in the Town Book, the selectmen saw cause to view the land & the highway, & accordingly did, & upon the place determined that the land was granted to Mr. Tho[mas] Cartor & the highway to run as it is now fenced" [WaTR 1:88].

On 19 December 1673, "Widow Barnad coming to us the selectmen to help her to a highway to a parcel of land lying against the river which she saith she or her husband bought of one Jacob, we not finding that this land was any of the town grants given out to their inhabitants we answer her that we can do nothing in it till she makes it appear that it was granted to Jacob as his proportion in some of the divisions of land given out by the town to her inhabitants" [WaTR 1:118].

The inventory of the estate of "Pheby Barnard of Watertowne," taken 5 October 1685, totalled £293 16s. 8d., of which £220 10s. was real estate: "the dwelling house, barn, orchard and about 20 acres of land adjoining," £110; "60 acres of dividend land," £30; "30 acres of land in lieu of township," £31 10s.; "20 acres of land upon the great plain which is doubtful as yet," unvalued; "about 4 acres of swampland lying near Chester's Brook," £12; "7 acres of remote meadow," £7; and "about 256 acres of farm land," £30 [MPR Case #1080].

BIRTH: By about 1607 based on estimated date of marriage.
DEATH: Buried at Watertown 23 June 1646 [WaVR 12].
MARRIAGE: By about 1632 Phebe Whiting, daughter of Anthony and Anne (Sherman) Whiting of Dedham, Essex. She died at Watertown 1 August 1685 [WaVR 57].
CHILDREN:

    i   JOHN, b. about 1632 (aged two in 1634 [Hotten 282]); m. 15 November 1654 Sarah Fleming [WaVR 17], daughter of John Fleming [Bond 225].

    ii   SAMUEL, b. about 1633 (aged one in 1634 [Hotten 282]); "Sam[ue]ll Barnard" took the oath of fidelity at Watertown in 1652 [NEHGR 3:401]; d. Watertown 8 September 1683 [WaVR 54]. The "inventory of the estate of Sam[ue]ll Bernard deceased at Watertowne," undated but entered between other estates which were brought into court on 6 October 1685, consisted of "His part in John Bernard's estate, about a 7th or 8th part," not valued, "three acres of meadow in Watertowne," not valued, and "four pounds due by bill from Tho[mas] Loverun" [MPR 6:259 (does not include the first item), Case #1086].

  iii   HANNAH, b. say 1635; m. Cambridge 25 June 1656 Samuel
        Goffe.
   iv   MARY, b. Watertown 7 November 1639 [WaVR 7]; m.
        Cambridge 16 June 1662 William Barrett.
    v   JOSEPH, b. Watertown 12 November 1642 [WaVR 10];
        apparently died unmarried by 1708, when three of his
        siblings sold his land in Kittery [GDMNH 77]. (On 20
        October 1676, "John Crafford now of Portsmouth in the
        County of Dover & Portsmouth, now in the Massatusetts
        Jurisdiction in New England, & Elizabeth his wife" sold
        to "Joseph Barnard of Water Town, in the County of
        Middlesex," twenty acres in Kittery [YLR 3:21]. On 9
        October 1708, John Barnard Sr. and John Dix Sr. both of
        Watertown ... and James Barnard of Sudbury" sold to
        Biall Hambleton of Berwick twenty acres in Kittery [with
        same description as land of YLR 3:21] [YLR 7:114-15].
   vi   JAMES, b. say 1644; m. Watertown 8 October 1666 Abiel
        Phillips [WaVR 28], daughter of Rev. *GEORGE PHILLIPS*
        [GMB 3:1449].
  vii   ELIZABETH, b. say 1648; m. Watertown 7 January 1670/1 John
        Dix [WaVR 33], son of *EDWARD DIX* [GMB 1:552].
 viii   BENJAMIN, b. about 1650 (aged 26 in 1676 [GDMNH 76, citing
        an unknown source]); m. by 1687 Sarah Wentworth,
        daughter of William Wentworth (Benjamin and wife
        Sarah sold land on 24 August 1687 [YLR 6:29-30]; on 19
        December 1705, "Paul Wentworth of Rowley, ...
        husbandman," was "appointed guardian unto Sarah
        Barnard a minor in the fifteenth year of her age, and to
        Benja[min] Barnard a minor in the thirteenth year of his
        age, children of Benja[min] Barnard late of Watertown ...
        deceased" [MPR Case #1050]; on 30 April 1706, "Sarah
        Barnard, daughter of Benj[amin] Barnard late of
        Watertown ... deceased, a minor in the fifteenth year of
        her age, have nominated and chosen ... my honored
        uncle Mr. Paul Wentworth of Rowley ..., husbandman, to
        be my guardian" [MPR 11:43]) [GDMNH 76, 739;
        Wentworth Gen 1:109-11].

ASSOCIATIONS: On 15 September 1638, Anne Wilson of Dedham, Essex,
widow, bequeathed to "my daughter Phebe Barnard of New England ten
pounds, and to her two children born here before she went over, vizt.

John and Samuel, to each of them twenty shillings apiece" [Waters 1177, citing Commissary of London for Essex and Herts., original will in file for 1638-9, Number 152].

In her will, dated 1 March 1686/7 and proved 20 January 1689/90, "Anne Browne, widow & relict of Edmund Browne, clerk, deceased, of Sudbury," bequeathed to "my loving kinsman John Barnard of Watertowne the one-half part of that twenty & five pounds in money which he hath of mine in his hands, provided he without any trouble do pay the other half part of the said money unto my adopted son & heir hereafter named"; to "my cousin John Deekes of Watertowne the fifteen pounds in money he hath of mine in his hands"; to "my loving kinsman James Barnard of Sudbury, whom I do hereby make, ordain & appoint & adopt to be my only son & heir, all whatsoever my estate of what kind soever not hereby before disposed of" [MPR Case #2952].

Anne Wilson was Anne (Sherman) (Whiting) Wilson, daughter of Henry Sherman and widow of Anthony Whiting and Thomas Wilson [Waters 1174-75]. One of her daughters was Phebe, wife of John Barnard, and another was Anne, wife first of John Lovering of Watertown and then of Edmund Brown of Sudbury. One of her brothers, Samuel Sherman, was father of Samuel Sherman of Boston and of *PHILIP SHERMAN* of Portsmouth, Rhode Island, and another of her brothers, John, was father of Capt. John Sherman of Watertown. Anne's uncle Edmund Sherman was father of Edmund Sherman of Wethersfield and of Richard Sherman of Boston [NEHGR 51:309-15].

COMMENTS: "John Bernard," aged 30, and "Phebe his wife," aged 27, sailed for New England on "the last of Aprill 1634" on the *Elizabeth* of Ipswich; with them were "John Bernard," aged 2, "Samuell Bernard," aged 1, and "Tho[mas] King," aged 15 [Hotten 280, 282].

There is no document which names all the children of John Barnard, so some justification must be supplied for the list given above. The passenger list entry and the will of Anne (Sherman) (Whiting) Wilson provide a solid anchor at the head of the list, telling us that two and only two children, John and Samuel, were born in England, by 1634. Mary and Joseph are provided by the vital records of Watertown. The will of Anne (Whiting) (Lovering) Browne ties together John Barnard, James Barnard and Elizabeth (Barnard) Dix, wife of John Dix.

The inclusion of Benjamin in this family is proved by deeds from York County. On 20 December 1675, Humphrey Spencer of Kittery sold to "Beniame[n] Barnard of Water Town in the County of Middlesex" thirty acres in Kittery [YLR 4:55]. On 1 January 1685/6, "Joseph Barnard of the parish of Barwicke, in the Town of Kittery, in the Province of Mayne," sold to "my brother Benjam[in] Barnard, of Dover in the Province of New Hampshire," fifty acres in Berwick "as it was bought of Benoni Hogsden, & by the deed of sale bearing date June 30th 1681" [YLR 4:65-66]. On 24 August 1687, "Benjamin Bernard of Dover ..., yeoman, and Sarah his wife" sold to "Joseph Bernard of Barwick in the Township of Kittery ... fifty acres situate and being in the Township of Kittery, that land which I bought of Joseph Bernard" [YLR 6:29-30].

No direct evidence ties Hannah (Barnard) Goffe to this family, but at the time she married Samuel Goffe in Cambridge there was no other Barnard family in this part of Massachusetts, and on 1 June 1685, Samuel Goffe, as executor to Edmund Browne of Sudbury, sold land to James Barnard of Sudbury.

A slight problem appears with the lack of Watertown birth records for this family before 1639. We know that all the children except for John and Samuel must have been born in New England. To marry in 1656, Hannah was probably born about 1636, and certainly earlier than 1639. James might also have been born in this gap prior to 1639, but we have placed him after the birth of Joseph in 1642, thus making him only 22 at marriage. We know that the immigrant John Barnard was living in Watertown by 1636 when he received a grant of land. If the order of birth of the children is given as above, there is a slight possibility that Barnard resided in some town other than Watertown for a year or two after his arrival in New England, and that Hannah was born there. The more likely alternative is that the Watertown records are simply defective at this point. If this is so, then we might rearrange the birth order, and suggest that Hannah was born about 1635 and James about 1637.

RICHARD BARNARD

On 14 November 1635, "Richard Bernard" was appointed to a Watertown committee to lay out land [WaTR 2].

COMMENTS: This record is the only appearance of this name in Watertown records, or elsewhere in New England, in the early years. It may be an error for some Richard of another surname, or it may be intended for JOHN BARNARD, who had arrived in Watertown in 1634.

If the record is really meant for a Richard Barnard, he must have died soon or returned to England.

THOMAS BARRETT

On 15 April 1635, "Tho[mas] Barret," aged 16, was enrolled at London as a passenger for New England on the *Increase* [Hotten 66].

COMMENTS: Savage thought this passenger might be the settler at Braintree, later of Chelmsford, but this cannot be, as the latter had children born in the early 1630s, and must have been born by about 1605 [NEHGR 42:258].

There was a Thomas Barrett who died in Concord in 1652, having married in about 1647 [TAG 11:28]. Although the chronological fit is better in this case, there is nothing to connect him back to the passenger of 1635.

GEORGE BARSTOW

ORIGIN: Halifax, Yorkshire
MIGRATION: 1635
FIRST RESIDENCE: Watertown
REMOVES: Dedham 1637, Scituate by 1649, Cambridge by 1652

CHURCH MEMBERSHIP: Either George Barstow or his wife had joined the second church at Scituate by 24 February 1649/50, when they had a child baptized [NEHGR 57:83]. He attempted to join the church at Cambridge, but this was apparently blocked by Rev. Charles Chauncy [see *DEATH* below].

OFFICES: Dedham highway surveyor, 30 March 1640 [DeTR 1:66].

Admitted to the Ancient and Honorable Artillery Company in 1644 [HAHAC 1:137-38].

ESTATE: On 11 August 1637, the town of Dedham allowed "Will[ia]m Bearstowe" to "lay out some part of his lot ... for his brother George Bearstowe" and that the town "shall confer on him some more ground for an addition thereunto" [DeTR 1:34]. On 30 January 1642/3, "granted to Georg[e] Bearstowe a parcel or parcels of swamp to be laid out to his eight-acre lot proportionable to other like lots acoording to a former grant to them" [DeTR 1:93]. Granted one acre and two roods "of upland ground fit for improvement with the plow," 6 February 1642/3 [DeTR 1:96]. Granted one acre and a half of woodland, 4 February 1644/5 [DeTR 1:110].

On 26 December 1646, "Georg[e] Bearstow granted to the town of Dedham that parcel of his house lot that lyeth at the west end thereof where clay is accustomed to be digged ... for & in consideration whereof the town of Dedham aforesaid granteth to the said George Bearstow & to his heirs forever 4 acres of swamp" [DeTR 1:112-13].

In the Dedham country rate of 4 September 1648, "Geo[rge] Bearstoe" was assessed 3s. 10d. [DeTR 1:152]; in the "valuation of the houses in Dedham as they were estimated for the country rate 1648," the name of "Geo[rge] Bearstoe" is entered, but with no valuation [DeTR 1:154].

In his will, dated 10 March 1652/3 and probated on an unknown date, "George Barstow of Cambridge" requested that "my goods shall be equally divided into 3 parts, my wife and two children having each of them an equal share therein"; George Barstow did not sign or make his mark to this will, but "Thomas Marrett" signed and "Susan Barstow" made her mark [MPR Case #1330].

The inventory of the estate of "Georg[e] Barstow of Cambridge ... who departed this life the 18 day of the first month Anno Domini 1652," taken 3 October 1653, totalled £85 14s. 6d. (against which were debts of £6 5s.), with no real estate included [MPR Case #1330].

The inventory of the estate of "Susan Barstow, lately deceased at Cambridge," taken 4 May 1654, totalled £66 2s. 5d., against which there were debts of £5 16s. The court granted "administration of this estate of Susan Bearstow to Tho[mas] Marrit her father" and ordered "that the estate be thus divided: There being two children surviving the one a daughter, called Margaret, about 4 years old, and upward, the other a son called George, about 2 year old & 2 month," they are to be brought up by their grandfather, who is to pay to Margaret £14 at age 18 or at marriage and to George £28 at age 21 [MPR Case #1334].

BIRTH: About 1614 (aged 21 in 1635 [Hotten 131]).
DEATH: Cambridge 18 March 1652/3. On 9 June 1653 "William Barstow, of Scituate," acknowledged that whereas "a suit hath been commenced against me, the said Will[i]am Barstow, by Mr. Charles Chauncy, pastor of the church of Christ at Scittuate, for slandering him, the said Mr. Chauncy, in saying that he was the cause of the death of my brother,

G[e]orge Barstow, late deceased; and also in saying that he, the said Mr. Chauncy, sent his bulls abroad to the church at Cambridge, whereby my said brother was hindered from communion with the said church, which was the cause of my brother's death, through excessive grief; in all which expressions and sayings I do humbly and freely acknowledge that I have done the said Mr. Chauncy manifest wrong" [PCR 3:35-36].

MARRIAGE: By 1649 Susanna Marriott, daughter of Thomas Marriott. She died at Cambridge on 17 April 1654.

CHILDREN:

i   MARGARET, bp. Scituate 24 February 1649/50 [NEHGR 57:83]; m. in November 1670 or shortly thereafter Simon Gates (on 9 November 1670, John Woods of Marlborough sued "Symon Gates dwelling in Cambridge" for "making suit in way of marriage to his daughter Frances Woods & drawing away her affection, without first obtaining liberty of her father, and after he had obtained liberty to proceed from her parents, & promises of marriage was made by the said Symon & Frances one to another, yet the said Symon hath deserted her & hath published his purpose of marriage with another person to the great wrong & damage of the said Frances his daughter," and on the same day "Symon Gates and John Marrett" posted bond for the appearance of Gates [MCF Folio #35] [John Marrett was brother of Susanna (Marriott) Barstow, the mother of Margaret]; Simon and Margaret named a son George, b. at Cambridge 6 April 1678; in 1684 Simon Gates and George Barstow, Margaret's brother, were tenants in Brookline of John Hull [SLR 13:93]; on 24 September 1705, Samuel Sewall reported that he went to "George Bairsto's, where saw him, his wife, sister Gates" [Sewall 529; see also Sewall 164, 268, 294-95, 297, 388, 394, 549]). (Clarence A. Torrey stated in various places that this couple married, but without giving his reasoning [TAG 24:145; NEHGR 120:164]; his conclusions were presumably based on the evidence given above.)

ii   GEORGE, bp. Scituate 12 June 1653 ("George the son of George Bastow (deceased at Cambridge)") [NEHGR 57:84]; m. by 1684 Mercy Clark (eldest child b. Boston 2 November 1684 [BVR 162]), daughter of James Clark ("Mercy the daughter of James Clarke" bp. Roxbury 2

September 1660 [RChR 123]; Martha Clark, daughter of
James Clark, married on 19 June 1677 Samuel Gary
[Lawrence Brainerd, *Gary Genealogy: The Descendants of
Arthur Gary* ... (Boston 1918), p. 37, citing "Superior Court
Files, Suffolk County, Vol. 49, Page 83"]; in her will of 23
June 1720, "Martha Gary of Roxbury" included bequests
to "my cousins Susanna Steiner, Martha Reed, Mary
Bastow & Margret Bastow" [SPR 28:158]; George and
Mercy (Clark) Barstow had four daughters
corresponding to these four cousins of Martha (Clark)
Gary [Barstow Gen 1:226-27]).

ASSOCIATIONS: George Barstow was brother of MICHAEL BARSTOW,
WILLIAM BARSTOW and John Barstow. (See sketch of Michael Barstow
for further details.)

COMMENTS: On 19 September 1635, "W[illia]m Beeresto," aged 23, and
"Geo[rge] Beeresto," aged 21, were enrolled at London on the *Truelove* as
passengers for New England [Hotten 131].

Since George Barstow arrived in New England with his elder brother
William in 1635, and appeared with him in Dedham in 1637, we assume
that George also resided in Watertown during the intervening two years.
He signed the Dedham town covenant, probably in 1637 [DeTR 1:3].

On 4 November 1648, in the account of "the rate made for & concerning
the hunting of wolves, ... Geo[rge] Bearstoe for charge & time expended
about the hounds" was to receive £1 10s. [DeTR 1:132]. On 8 June 1649,
Dedham selectmen ordered "the constable ... to pay unto George Bearstoe
or his assigns out of the town rate £1 10s. [DeTR 159-60]. (The wording of
this entry indicates that George Barstow was at this date no longer a
resident of Dedham.)

On 11 January 1666/7, the town of Dedham made an order regarding
the clay ground, that "all [is] to be done according to that contract with
George Bearstow as it is recorded in the town book" [DeTR 2:125].

BIBLIOGRAPHIC NOTE: In 1964 Arthur Hitchcock Radasch published
the *Barstow-Bestor Genealogy: Descendants of John[1] and George[1] Barstow*,
which, in addition to its coverage of the two named brothers, also
contains a copy of the will of Michael Barstow.

MICHAEL BARSTOW

ORIGIN: Halifax, Yorkshire
MIGRATION: 1635
FIRST RESIDENCE: Charlestown
REMOVES: Watertown by 1642

OCCUPATION: Yeoman. Shopkeeper (on 3 March 1636/7, "Goodman Micaell Bairstow desired a place for a shop which was granted him by the side of Goodman Nashe's" [ChTR 26]).

CHURCH MEMBERSHIP: On 5 December 1635 "Miles Bastow with Marcia his wife" were admitted to Charlestown church [ChChR 8].

FREEMAN: 3 March 1635/6 (as "Michaell Bastowe," third in a sequence of three Charlestown men) [MBCR 1:371].

EDUCATION: Signed his deeds. His inventory included "one great Bible" valued at 10s. and "several divine books, small one and 3 books of a lar[g]er volume" valued at 10s.

OFFICES: Deputy for Watertown to Massachusetts Bay General Court, 18 May 1653 [MBCR 3:297, 4:1:120].

Watertown selectman, 28 November 1643, 8 November 1648, 20 December 1651, 22 December 1652, 8 December 1656, 16 December 1657, 10 January 1658/9, 9 January 1659/60, 31 December 1660, 6 [January?] 1661/2, 4 January 1663/4, 7 November 1664, 1 November 1666 [WaTR 1:9, 16, 26, 31, 48, 54, 59, 64, 70, 74, 78, 84, 88]. Watertown commissioner to end small causes, 4 April 1659 [WaTR 1:61]. Committee "chosen & empowered by the proprietors of the Cowpen Farm, where Henry Cuttris lives, to sell the said Farm, housing & land thereto belonging," 7 November 1664 [WaTR 1:84].

ESTATE: In 1635 "Mich[ae]ll Bastow" had one hayground allotment, which was soon increased to two [ChTR 19, 20]. Had five acres Mystic Side on 6 March 1636/7 [ChTR 27]. Had 2½ cow commons in 1637 [ChTR 32]. In the 23 April 1638 allotment of Mystic Side land, had parcels of ten, twenty-five and five acres [ChTR 37]. Had 2½ cow commons in the stinted common on 30 December 1638 [ChTR 42].

In the 1638 Charlestown Book of Possessions, "Micheall Bastow" held seven parcels: "four acres of arable land ... in the East Field ... with a dwelling house and other appurtenances (one acre of these 4 was sold to Thomas Carter, senior)"; "two acres of meadow ... in the South Mead"; "two acres of meadow ... in Mystic Marshes"; two and a half milch cow commons; "five acres of woodland ... in Mystic Field"; "ten acres of woodland ... in Mystic Field, in two parcels" of five acres apiece; and "twenty and five acres of land ... in West Rockfield" [ChBOP 41, 69].

On 18 April 1646, "Michael Bairstow of Watertowne, yeoman," sold to Stephen Fosdick of Charlestown, carpenter, five acres of woodland on Mystic Side in Charlestown [MLR 12:607]. On 13 June 1655, George Parkhurst of Boston sold to "Michael Beirstow of Watertowne ... yeoman" one-half of a twelve-acre parcel of land in Watertown [MLR 1:115]. On 14 July 1655, "Michall Bastowe of Wattertowne" sold to "Steeven Fosdik of Charletowne ... five acres of land" on Mystic Side [ChBOP 138-39; MLR 12:607]. On 29 March 1671, "Michael Bairstow of Watertowne," with the consent of "Grace Barstow my loving wife," deeded to "my loving kinswoman Deborah the wife of Philip Shattucke of the same place" six acres of land in Watertown [MLR 4:183].

On 2 February 1671, "Michaell Bairstow of Watertown ... yeoman" sold to John Train of Watertown, planter, "one dwelling house with barns, cowhouses, dyehouse and other outhouses, gardens, orchards, yards, backside, with planting land, pasture land, enclosures adjoining, containing by estimation about eighteen acres ... also forty-one acres of upland called Great Dividend, being the ninth lot in the fourth division ... also eleven acres of meadow called Remote or West Pine Meadow lying in three parcels, one part in Warrin's dividend, ... two other parcels lyeth in the dividend of John Wincoll" [MLR 4:362-64].

In his will, dated 23 June 1674 and proved 20 June 1676 [MCR 3:141], "Michael Barstow of Watertown" bequeathed to "my dear pastor Mr. John Shearman, pastor of the church in Watertown, my farm lying & being in Watertown & granted unto me by the inhabitants of the said town ... & is accounted the 40th lot in the land known by the name of farm land"; to "Hannah Barstow, *alias* Prince, one great Bible and the debt due to me in my book which her first husband William Barstow was indebted to me"; to "the Church of Christ in Watertown" £16; to "Elizabeth Randall the wife of William Randall of Scittuate in Plimouth Colony" £5; to "Susan Perry the wife of William Perry (in Marshfield Colony [*sic*])" £5; to "Michael Barstow (the son of John Barstow deceased ...) my lot of upland & meadow lying & being in Watertowne near the dwelling house of John Trayne ... also I give him my lot at Barehill lying in Watertowne & known by the name of land in lieu of township"; to "John & Jeremiah the children of the aforesaid John Barstow deceased to each of them" £15; to "Deacon Thomas Hastings of Watertowne" £10; to "Deacon Henry Bright of Watertowne" 40s.; residue to "be equally divided into ten parts or shares, two of which parts or shares I give unto the children of my brother George Barstow deceased and eight of the said shares I give to the children of my brother William Barstow deceased that is to each child a single share of the ten shares or parts"; Deacon Thomas Hastings to be sole executor; Deacon Henry Bright to be overseer [MPR 4:168-69; NEHGR 8:169-70]. (The Middlesex probate file for Michael Barstow does not include the original of this will. The verbatim transcript which was published in the *Register* in 1854 does not give the source from which the transcript was made. The Middlesex record book copy does not include the bequest to Susan Perry, which is found in the *Register* transcript. The *Register* transcript very likely represents a copy of the original, which in 1854 was probably in private hands; the current location of this will is unknown.)

The inventory of "the goods of Michaell Bairstow late of Wattertown ... being all that was found in the house of John Traine [of Watertown]," taken 13 May 1676, totalled £57 15s. 10d., of which £45 was real estate: "six acres of meadow and upland," £30; "a lot at Bare Hill, 30 acres," £5; and "a farm the 40th lot of a hundred acres," £10 [MPR 4:170, Case #1332]. The inventory of "the goods of Michaell Bairstow late of Wattertown that were found in the house of Willyam Dady of Charlstown" totalled £203 12s. 7d., with no real estate included [MPR 4:170-72, Case #1332].

On 25 September 1676, "Thomas Hastings of Watertowne, executor to the last will & testament of Michael Barstow late of the same place deceased," sold to Thomas Welch of Charlestown one acre and three-quarters of meadow in Charlestown [MLR 6:163].

BIRTH: About 1600. (Bond found the baptism at Shelf, Halifax, Yorkshire, 17 November 1600, of Michael Barstow, son of Matthew Barstow [Bond 677]; Matthew Wood found the baptism at Halifax, 6 January 1600/1, of Michael Barstow, son of Michael Barstow of Northowram [NYGBR 121:98]. Given the size of this parish and the multiplicity of Barstow families therein, further research needs to be undertaken before we can identify the parents of Michael Barstow and his brothers.)

DEATH: Between 30 October 1674 [WaTR 1:120] and 13 May 1676 (date of inventory) (and probably closer to the latter date).

MARRIAGE: (1) Halifax, Yorkshire, 15 February 1624/5 Grace Halstead [Bond 677]; she died by 1635.

(2) By 1635 Mercy _____ [ChChR 8]. She died by 1642.

(3) By 1642 Grace (Walker) Carver, widow of Richard Carver [NEHGR 146:230-34]. She died at Watertown on 20 July 1671 [WaVR 33].

CHILDREN: None recorded.

ASSOCIATIONS: Brother of GEORGE BARSTOW, WILLIAM BARSTOW and John Barstow.

We know that George and William Barstow came to New England in 1635 because of their appearance on a passenger list of that year. Michael Barstow is first seen in New England in 1635 when he was admitted to Charlestown church, so he presumably came in that year as well, though he does not appear in any of the surviving passengers lists. The fourth brother, John, who would have been about ten in 1635, may have come with his brother Michael in 1635, but as we have no record of him in New England until 1652 [Bond 678], we do not assume that he came in 1635, and so do not treat him here. He and his progeny are well-treated in the volume prepared by Arthur Hitchcock Radasch which also covers his elder brother George.

Grace Halstead, first wife of Michael Barstow, was daughter of Abraham Halstead of Halifax, Yorkshire; her sister SUSANNA HALSTEAD accompanied Michael Barstow to New England and her brother Jonas Halstead followed some years later [NYGBR 120:145-47].

COMMENTS: On 27 October 1647, "Mr. Bryan Pendleton & Michaell Bairstow are allowed to take so much out of the house of Thom[as] Philpot, upon the sale thereof, as to discharge their engagement of about £6 to the keeper for him" [MBCR 2:200].

On 17 November 1656, it was "agreed that Captain Mason, Lieutenant Beeres, Ensign Shearman, Michaell Bearsto, with the three deacons, should have the ordering of the sitting of persons in the meeting house, Old Goodman Hammond & Goodman Stratton are joined to the same business & the rules are 1. office. 2. age. 3. state. 4. gifts" [WaTR 1:47].

BIBLIOGRAPHIC NOTE: In 1992 Robert Charles Anderson presented the evidence that Michael Barstow had three wives [NEHGR 146:230-34].

WILLIAM BARSTOW

ORIGIN: Halifax, Yorkshire
MIGRATION: 1635 on the *Truelove*
FIRST RESIDENCE: Watertown

REMOVES: Dedham 1637, Hingham by 1645, Scituate by 1650

OCCUPATION: Carpenter. On 31 October 1666, "Mr. Josepth Tilden and Will[i]am Barstow [complained] against John Palmer, Junior, for purloining and pilfering of a parcel of boards from the saw mill" [PCR 4:137-38].

Innkeeper. On 5 June 1666, "[w]hereas there is a great neglect in both Will[i]am Barstow and Robert Barker in not keeping of an ordinary fit for the entertaining of strangers, the Court have ordered, that Will[i]am Barstow shall make competent provision for strangers for their entertainment and refreshment for this year" [PCR 4:129].

CHURCH MEMBERSHIP: William Barstow's first three children were baptized at Dedham on the basis of his wife's membership in the church; the baptisms of his children in Hingham and Scituate may well have been on the same basis, so there is no evidence that he was ever a church member in New England.

FREEMAN: Admitted to Plymouth Colony freemanship on 1 June 1658 [PCR 3:137] and included in Scituate section of Plymouth Colony list of 1658 [PCR 8:199].

EDUCATION: Signed his deed of 16 May 1666 [PCLR 3:115].

OFFICES: Committee to provide timber for a shed for swine, 23 March 1636/7 [DeTR 1:28]. Committee to lay out the bounds of the town of Dedham, 14 July 1641 [DeTR 1:79].

Plymouth grand jury, 1 June 1658, 3 June 1668 [PCR 3:135, 4:187]. Committee to lay out land, 5 October 1663 [PCR 4:46, 99]. Petit jury, 4 June 1657, 1 March 1663/4 [PCR 4:50, 7:83]. Assisted in "the running of the line betwixt the jurisdiction of the Massachusetts" and Plymouth, for which he was reimbursed on 8 June 1664 [PCR 4:63]. Scituate highway surveyor, 5 June 1666, 2 June 1667 [PCR 4:123, 149].

ESTATE: On 11 May 1637, "W[illia]m Berstowe" was granted three acres of swamp at Dedham [DeTR 1:31]. Granted six acres of meadow, 28 July 1638 [DeTR 1:46].

On 10 July 1642, "Will[ia]m Bearestowe complaining of his 8 acre houselot, it was viewed and found to be very defective in the one half of the same by a multitude of stones, wherefore we order & grant unto the said Will[ia]m eight acres of upland between the corners of the great Naponset Swamp about southwest from our town" [DeTR 1:86].

Granted eight acres and one rood of upland, 6 February 1642/3 [DeTR 1:96]. Granted three acres of woodland, 4 February 1644/5 [DeTR 1:110].

On the 23rd of an unknown month in 1648, "Rich[ard] Wheeler & Joh[n] Farington, having bought Will[iam] Bearstow's grant of 8 acres, request an addition thereto from the town" [DeTR 1:151, 177].

On 16 May 1666, "William Barstow" of Scituate, planter, deeded to "Josepth Barstow my eldest son ... a part of my upland and a part of my meadow which I have in the township of Scittuate which I lately purchased of Robert Stetson, that part or parcel of upland which I the said William Barstow had given to my said son Joseph Barstow upon which he the said Joseph Barstow have already built a dwelling house" [PCLR 3:115].

On 2 July 1667, Plymouth Court "granted unto Will[i]am Barstow, that he shall have a parcel of land ordered and laid out unto him lying to the westwards of Cornet Studson's grant, in reference to satisfaction for his pains, &c., in the country business"; on 7 July 1668, this grant was ordered to be "forty acres of arable land, or at the utmost but fifty" [PCR 4:160, 188].

On 2 March 1668/9, "letters of administration was granted unto Anna Barstow to administer on the estate of Will[i]am Barstow, late deceased" [PCR 5:13]. The inventory of the estate of "Willam Berstow," presented at court on 5 April 1669 by "the widow Barstow," was untotalled and included no real estate [PCPR 2:2:56].

On 5 April 1669, "Joseph Barstow of Scituate ..., planter & son & heir of William Barstow of Scituate aforesaid deceased," confirmed to Joseph Silvester of Scituate "two parcels of upland being by estimation fourteen acres" in Scituate, inasmuch as "my honored father William Berstow lately deceased did in his lifetime ... for & in consideration of the natural affection & fatherly love & goodwill which he had & did bear unto his son-in-law Joseph Silvester of Scituate aforesaid, tailor, ... give & bequeath ... unto him the said Joseph Silvester" the two parcels of land [PCLR 6:82-83]. On [blank] June 1669, "Joseph Barstow of Scittuate ... planter," noting that "whereas my honored father Will[i]am Barstow, deceased, in his lifetime did declare and manifest himself, that the said Joseph Barstow and my brother Will[i]am Barstow should after his decease have and enjoy and possess the land which he then was seized of & in his own possession, but dying suddenly was prevented of settling the same in so particular a manner as he intended, nevertheless I the said Joseph Barstow do not intend or desire to infringe my said brother Will[i]am Barstow, of the least right or interest of what my father ever to my knowledge intended him," therefore "I the said Joseph Barstow" grant to "the said Will[i]am Barstow ... all that dwelling house, barn and outhousing, which my father Will[i]am Barstow was possessed of at the time of his decease lying and being in Scittuate aforesaid, and near unto the third herring brook, with twenty acres of upland ... belonging to the said house ..., and one other parcel of upland containing ten acres ..., and one parcel of marsh or meadow land being nine acres," with the reservation "of the aforesaid housing, orcharding and lands for the sole use and benefit and behoof of Anna Berstow, mother of the said Joseph and William, until the said Will[i]am shall attain to the age of twenty and one years," and of her dower rights for her natural life [PCLR 4:97-99].

BIRTH: About 1612 (aged 23 in 1635 [Hotten 131]).
DEATH: Dedham 1 January 1668/9 [DeVR 11].
MARRIAGE: Dedham 8 July 1638 Ann Hubbard [DeVR 126]. She was admitted to Dedham church on 16 April 1641 [DeChR 25]. She married (2) JOHN PRINCE of Hingham (in his will of 23 June 1674, Michael Barstow made a bequest to "Hannah Barstow *alias* Prince, one great Bible and the debt due to me in my book which her first husband William Barstow was indebted to me" [MLR 4:168-69]).
CHILDREN:

 i JOSEPH, b. 6 June 1639 [DeVR 1], bp. Dedham 25 April 1641 [DeChR 25]; m. Hingham 16 May 1666 "Susanah Lincolne the daughter of Thomas Lincolne" [HiVR 8], husbandman [Hingham Hist 3:16].

 ii MARY, b. 28 December 1641 [DeVR 2], bp. Dedham 2 January 1641/2 [DeChR 26]; m. by 1664 Joseph Silvester, son of *RICHARD SILVESTER* (eldest child b. Scituate 11 November 1664) [PCLR 6:82-83; NEHGR 85:261-63; GMB 3:1680]. ("Mary Bairstow" who m. Boston 14 May 1656 William Ingram [BVR 57] has not been placed in any of these Barstow families; the surname may have been corrupted in transcription.)

 iii PATIENCE, b. 3 December 1643 [DeVR 2], bp. Dedham 9 June 1644 [DeChR 28]; m. (1) by 1664 Moses Simonson, son of *MOSES SIMONSON* (by 27 July 1664 William Barstow had given "a small tract" of land "unto my son Moses Simons" [PCR 4:68-69; GMB 3:1683]); m. (2) Marshfield 21 February [1677/8] Samuel Baker ("Samuel Baker [*worn*] Simmons were m[*worn*] 21 of February [*worn*]" [MarVR 9 (just after marriages for mid-1677)]; "Elenor the daughter

of Samuel Baker & Patience his wife" b. Marshfield 10
April 1679 [MarVR 19]).

iv   SARAH, bp. Hingham [blank] December 1645 [NEHGR
121:18]; m. 1666 Nathaniel Church, son of *RICHARD
CHURCH* [GMB 1:362, citing PCR 8:116-17]. (In the
published version of Rev. Peter Hobart's record Sarah's
surname is given as "Boston," but this surname is not
found in New England at this date, and examination of
the original shows that the surname should be read as
"Bestow.")

v   REBECCA, bp. Hingham 5 March 1647/8 [NEHGR 121:20];
living 23 June 1674, when her uncle MICHAEL
BARSTOW bequeathed to eight children of his brother
William; no further record (but she may well have been
married by 1674). (This child is assigned to this family for
several reasons: she does not fit into the family of any of
William's brothers; there is an appropriate gap in the list
of known children; the will of Michael Barstow requires
eight children in this family. William was last seen in
Dedham on 4 February 1644/5, and had certainly left
before 1648 [DeTR 1:100, 151, 177], so these baptisms for
Sarah and Rebecca nicely cover the period between
William's residences in Dedham and Scituate;
furthermore, William's widow married a Hingham man.)

vi   DEBORAH, bp. Scituate 18 August 1650 [NEHGR 57:83]; m.
Watertown 9 November 1670 Philip Shattuck [WaVR 33].

vii   WILLIAM, bp. Scituate 3 October 1652 [NEHGR 57:84]; m. by
1676 Martha _____ (eldest child b. Scituate 12 March
1676[/7?]). "Martha Bestow" was a member in full
communion of the Second Church of Scituate by 1704
[NEHGR 57:321]. Martha, wife of William Barstow Sr.,
died at Scituate 13 August 1711. (Some sources claim that
William Barstow had a wife named Sarah [Barstow Gen
2:6], but we only have evidence for Martha. Note that
William did not name a daughter Sarah, but his second
child was Martha, baptized at the Second Church at
Scituate 16 June 1678 [NEHGR 57:182], and that William,
son of this William, had wife Sarah.)

viii MARTHA, bp. Scituate 22 April 1655 [NEHGR 57:85]; m. 9
December 1674 Samuel Prince [NEHGR 5:379, 383 (the

full date is given in the chart pedigree on the latter of these two pages; the source is not explicitly stated, but may perhaps be from the papers of Rev. Thomas Prince)] (her stepbrother).

ASSOCIATIONS: William Barstow was brother of MICHAEL BARSTOW, GEORGE BARSTOW and John Barstow. (See sketch of Michael Barstow for further details.)

COMMENTS: On 19 September 1635, "W[illia]m Beeresto," aged 23, was enrolled at London on the *Truelove* as a passenger for New England [Hotten 131]. (The next entry on the list was for "Geo[rge] Beeresto," aged 21.)

On 7 June 1636, "Willi[am] Bayrstow" was one of three men "censured to be whipped 6 strokes apiece for drunkenness" [MBCR 1:176].

On 29 August 1636, "Will[ia]m Bearstow" began attending Dedham town meetings, during that period when they were still held in Watertown [DeTR 1:21]; it was probably at this meeting that he signed the town covenant [DeTR 1:3]. For this reason we assume that he resided in Watertown for the two years after his arrival in New England and before his settlement at Dedham.

On 18 October 1639, "Will[ia]m Bearestowe & Will[ia]m Hudson" were presented for "felling trees in our town near unto Mr. Stoughton's farm," and on 29 November 1639 Dedham selectmen determined that it "was done by misunderstanding of some things & the men poor & confessing their fault. It is ordered that they shall lose only their labor & so the rails & posts with the residue of the trees whatsoever so felled shall rest in the power of the town to be otherwise disposed of" [DeTR 1:60, 62].

On 5 October 1656, "Will[i]am Barstow, of Scittuate, covenanteth and engageth to make a good and sufficient bridge over the North River, a little above the third herring brook" [PCR 3:108]. On 3 June 1657, "Will[i]am Barstow is allowed by the Court to draw and sell wine, beer, and strong waters for passengers that come and go over the bridge he hath lately made" [PCR 3:118]. In later years he was hired to make repairs to the bridge [PCR 3:123, 192, 4:41, 68-69].

On 2 October 1650, John Turner the elder unsuccessfully sued "Will[i]am Besto ... for the carrying away of hay" [PCR 7:51]. Barstow was also plaintiff on several occasions [PCR 7:80, 107].

On 9 June 1653, Mr. Charles Chauncy sued "Will[i]am Bastow" for £1000 for slander; the court awarded the plaintiff £100 and costs, but the plaintiff retained only the costs [PCR 7:65]. (This suit derives from the complaint made against Chauncy with regard to the death of GEORGE BARSTOW.)

BIBLIOGRAPHIC NOTE: In 1966 Arthur Hitchcock Radasch published *The William Barstow Family: Genealogy of the Descendants of William[1] Barstow, 1635-1965*, which covers this immigrant and his descendants comprehensively.

WILLIAM BARTHOLOMEW

ORIGIN: London
MIGRATION: 1634 on the *Griffin*
FIRST RESIDENCE: Ipswich
REMOVES: Boston by 1666, Charlestown by 1680

OCCUPATION: Merchant [SLR 5:226-28]. Licensed to sell strong waters for one year, 1658 [EQC 1:116]. Fined ten shillings in September 1658 for "selling dear" [EQC 1:119].
CHURCH MEMBERSHIP: Admission to Ipswich church prior to 4 March 1634/5 implied by freemanship. On 11 May 1662, "Mr Willyam Bartholmew and his wife" were admitted members of Boston church [BChR 58].
FREEMAN: 4 March 1634/5 (seventh in a sequence of nine Ipswich men) [MBCR 1:370].
EDUCATION: Signed the bill of presentments, 10 October 1650 [EQC 1:225]. William signed his name and Anna made her mark to a 1676 deed [ELR 4:159]. His inventory included "books viz: a Bible in quarto, *Clarks Martyrologie*, &c.," valued at 16s. 3d. (See Bartholomew Gen 33 for a sample of his handwriting.)
OFFICES: Deputy to Massachusetts Bay General Court for Ipswich, 6 May 1635, 3 September 1635, 3 March 1635/6, 2 November 1637, 12 March 1637/8, 2 May 1638, 13 March 1638/9, 7 October 1641, 26 May 1647, 22 May 1650 [MBCR 1:145, 156, 164, 205, 220, 227, 250, 336, 2:186, 3:105, 4:1:2]. Committee to succour neccessitous captives from St Christophers, 23 May 1666 [MBCR 4:2:310].

Essex grand jury, 24 September 1650 (as "Mr."), 27 September 1653 [EQC 1:197, 289]. Essex petit jury, 31 March 1646, 29 February 1649/50, 30 March 1652 [EQC 1:93, 186, 247]. Elected treasurer by the Essex commissioners,

28 June 1654 [EQC 1:351]. Arbiter with Maj. Daniel Denison in the matter of Mr. John Spencer vs. Henry Dow, October 1649 [EQC 1:176], and the matter of Francis Bates and the daughter of Thomas Moulton, March 1652 [EQC 1:250]. Court of Assistants petit jury (as "Mr."), 11 March 1674/5 [RCA 1:32]; grand jury, 6 March 1676/7, 6 September 1678 [RCA 1:78, 119].

On 29 March 1659, William Bartholomew was released from training, paying 10s. yearly to the company [EQC 2:150]. On 15 October 1679, the fines of "Mr. W[illia]m Bartholomew & those that petitioned with him" "for their not appearance in their arm at the time of the late alarm" were remitted [MBCR 5:251].

ESTATE: On 15 February 1649[/50?], Joseph Armitage of Lynn gave security in the form of a bay mare to William Bartholomew [ELR 1:7]. On 22 October 1653, William Evans of Topsfield acknowledged a debt to William Bartholomew of Ipswich [ILR 2:21].

On 15 January 1653[/4], Martin Stebbins of Boston, brewer, sold to William Bartholomew of Ipswich all the copper and all the "brewing vessels" owned by Stebbins in his brewhouses in Boston [SLR 1:330]. On 1 November 1655, it was determined that although both Nathaniel Rogers of Ipswich and William Bartholomew had taken possession of the dwelling house formerly owned by Joshua Hews of Roxbury, and "since belonging to Joshua Foote deceased," a deed of sale given by Joshua Foote for the use of Mr. Robert Crane of Coggeshall in Essex, dated 20 October 1653, was in force and all the property actually belonged to Nathaniel Rogers and his brethren Samuel, Ezekiel and Timothy Rogers of Ipswich [SLR 2:210]. On 20 July 1659, Robert Nash of Boston, butcher, sold to "William Bartholmew" of Ipswich a parcel of land with buildings in Boston [SLR 3:438-39].

On 24 May 1666, Joseph Bowd of Marblehead, "liquor stiller," mortgaged to William Bartholomew of Boston, merchant, one dwelling house and lands in the occupation of Robert Sweete, and one dwelling house, still house, garden and lands in Marblehead [ELR 2:121]. On 20 May 1671, Joseph Bowd of Marblehead, yeoman, sold to William Bartholomew of Boston, merchant, a dwelling house and land in Marblehead [ELR 3:120-21]. On 9 October 1676, William Bartholomew of Boston sold to John Williams of Boston, butcher, "his dwelling house and land" in Marblehead, formerly purchased of Joseph Bowd [ELR 4:159].

On 14 August 1666, William Bartholomew paid off a mortgage on behalf of John Sunderland of Boston and received a parcel of land in Boston with two tenements on it [SLR 5:49-51].

On 16 August 1667, William Bartholomew of Boston, merchant, and Ann his wife sold, for £4, to Joseph Bartholomew of Boston, mariner, a 115 foot by 60 foot parcel of land with a dwelling house, leanto, cellar, and outhouse, with the new warehouse in Boston [SLR 5:226-28]. On 26 May 1693, "Joseph Bartholmew late of Boston ... now of London, mariner," sold, for £165, to Edward Gouge of Boston, merchant, "all that his piece or parcel of land lying situate on the southwesterly side of the Mill Creek in Boston aforesaid, measuring in length one hundred and fifteen foot or thereabouts ... and in breadth sixty foot or thereabouts" [SLR 17:18-20].

On 12 March 1669/70, "Samuel Benet of Rumney Marsh" sold to William Bartholomew of Boston, merchant, "all that his the said Samuell Bennett his farm, being a tract or parcel of land, meadow & marsh ground thereto belonging, with the messuage, tenement or farmhouse & other buildings on part thereof standing, now in the possession or occupation of John Greene & Henry Greene ... together also with a parcel of upland being six acres ... also a moiety or an equal half part of a meadow called or known by the name of Squire's Meadow, lying & being within Maulden bounds, and also fourteen acres of salt marsh lying in Rumney Marsh, formerly purchased of Capt. Rob[er]t Bridges, commonly called the fourteen-acre lot" [ELR 3:103-4].

On 25 November 1679, "William Bartholmew of Boston ... and Ann his wife" deeded to "our dear and wellbeloved nephew Henry Bartholomew of Boston ... all that our piece or parcel of land situate on the southwest side of the Mill Dock in Boston aforesaid together with all & all manner of house, houses, wharf, wharves, buildings, tenements, ways, entries, easements, commodities, privileges & appurtenances thereunto belonging or appertaining and all our right, title and interest to all and every part thereof and also all & singular our goods, chattles, leases, debts, ready money, plate, jewels, rings, household stuff (apparel only excepted), utensils, brass, pewter, bedding and all other our substance whatsoever moveable & immoveable, quick and dead of what nature, kind, quality and condition soever ... and that without any money or annuity or other thing therefore to be yielded, paid or done unto us the said William Bartholmew and Ann his wife" [SLR 11:254-55].

The inventory of the estate of William Bartholomew, exhibited at Charlestown on 17 June 1681, totalled £21 17s. 3d., and included no real estate [MPR Case #1335].

BIRTH: About 1603 (based on age at death), son of William and Friswide (Metcalfe) Bartholomew of Burford, Oxfordshire [Bartholomew Gen 16].

DEATH: Charlestown 18 January 1680/1 ("Mr. William Bartholomew, late of Boston, now sojourning with Mr. Greene in Charlstowne" [ChVR 1:65-66]), aged 78 [Wyman 64, citing gravestone].

MARRIAGE: By 1653 Ann _____ (and much earlier if she is the mother of all his children [SLR 5:226-28]). On 2 May 1669, "the wife of Wm. Barthol" was summoned in the case of Jeffery Thistle charged with abusing William Lightfoot's wife [EQC 4:159-60]. She died at Charlestown on 29 January 1682/3 ("Mrs. Anna Bartholomue, relict of Mr. Wm. Bartholme" [ChVR 1:113]).

CHILDREN:

i   MARY, b. say 1637; m. (1) Gloucester 24 December 1657 Matthew Whipple; m. (2) by 1661 Jacob Green (on 23 February 1661/2, "Mrs. Mary Green (the wife of brother Jacob Green)" was admitted to Charlestown church [ChChR 13]; on 24 March 1667/8, "Jacob Greene of Charlestowne with Mary my wife have made and constituted our father W[illia]m Bartholmew of Boston our true & lawful attorney" to attend to "the right and interest of Mary my said wife in and concerning the estate left her by her former husband Mathew Whipple" [ILR 4:79; Putnam's Mag 2:8]).

ii JOSEPH, b. about 1638 (deposed aged twenty-four years 23 June 1662 [EQC 2:402]); of London on 26 May 1693 [SLR 17:18-20]; no further record. (See Bartholomew Gen 55-56.)

iii Child, b. by 1645 (in his will of 6 January 1645/6, Richard Bartholomew bequeathed to "my bro[ther] Will[ia]m's 3 children £20 apiece" [EQC 1:102]); no further record. (The William Bartholomew who married at Roxbury on 17 December 1663 Mary Johnson has been identified as this third child [Bartholomew Gen 56-64; SLR 13:33], but nothing other than identity of name argues in favor of this conjecture.)

iv Child, b. about November 1658 ("Wm. Bartholomew of Ipswich requested the court to appoint his friend Edmund Batter of Salem his attorney, he not being able to attend court, as his wife was near confinement" [EQC 2:131]).

ASSOCIATIONS: On 14 June 1661, William Bartholomew appointed his "loving brother, Henry Bartholomew," his attorney in a small action brought by John Hathorne [EQC 2:285]. William was brother of Henry Bartholomew (in New England 1645) and Richard, Thomas, Abraham and a sister Sarah (as named in Richard's 1645 letter/will, at which time their mother may have been living [EPR 1:51-52; EQC 1:102]). In this will Richard made a bequest to "my brother William's 3 children."

In his will of 9 February 1659[/60?], Edward Brown of Ipswich mentioned "my eight acres of land within the common field which I bought of my Brother Bartholomew" [EPR 1:307]. This may be a clue to the identity of William Bartholomew's wife, or to some other relationship between Bartholomew and Brown. (Raymon Meyers Tingley thought that Brown's wife was Faith Lord, a sister of Robert Lord of Ipswich, and that Bartholomew's wife was therefore Anna Lord, another sibling [Tingley-Meyers 61, 205]. As usual, Tingley does not supply any evidence for these claims, and they should not be accepted without further research.)

COMMENTS: The evidence for the origin of William Bartholomew is somewhat out of the ordinary, deriving from the coincidence of names in the wills of William Bartholomew of Burford, Oxfordshire, and Richard Bartholomew of Boston and London, and from an unusual feature in the will of the former. The will of William Bartholomew of Burford, dated 25 April 1634, named eldest son John, third son Henry, fourth son Richard, fifth son Francis, sixth son Thomas, seventh son Abraham, and daughters Mary and Sarah [Bartholomew Gen 17-21, citing PCC 66 Seger], whereas the testamentary letter of Richard Bartholomew, dated 6 January 1645[/6], named brothers Henry, William, Thomas, Abraham and sister Sarah [Bartholomew Gen 53-54 (with facsimile copy); EPR 1:51-52]. Assuming that these pertain to the same set of siblings, William Bartholomew omitted his son William, while Richard Bartholomew omitted brothers John and Francis and sister Mary. John died in 1639 [Bartholomew Gen 22], and Francis and Mary may also have died before Richard wrote his letter.

The peculiar feature of the will of William Bartholomew of Burford which clinches the identification is his careful enumeration of the birth sequence of his sons, with no second son mentioned. The gap in the list of children of William where the immigrant William would fit comes at just about the correct time. The author of the Bartholomew genealogy argues that William was omitted from his father's will because of his religious beliefs [Bartholomew Gen 27], but this was rarely the case, despite the mythology frequently erected around such circumstances. The more likely explanation is that shortly before the will was written in April 1634, the senior William Bartholomew had settled an estate upon his son William, in preparation for the latter's departure for New England that same year. In this regard, note that the father in his will described himself as a mercer, which would place him in the same economic class as that occupied by his immigrant son.

William Bartholomew's passage to New England on the *Griffin* is demonstrated by his testimony in the trial of Ann Hutchinson, who is known to have come in that ship. Evidences that Bartholomew knew Ann Hutchinson in London include his comments at court in 1637:

> I would remember one word to Mrs. Hutchinson among many others. She knowing that I did know her opinions, being she was at my house at London, she was afraid I conceive or loth to impart herself unto me, but when she came within sight of Boston and looking upon the meanness of the place, I conceive, she uttered these words, if she had not a sure word that England should be destroyed her heart would shake.... Only I remember her eldest daughter said in the ship that she had a revelation that a young man in the ship should be saved, but he must walk in the ways of her mother [Hutchinson 2:385].

Throughout his life, William was public-spirited. He served the courts as an appraiser [EQC 1:196, SLR 5:ix], and frequently deposed for his neighbors [EQC 1:259]. In March 1653, he acted as an attorney for several fishermen, and also served as trustee to others over the years [EQC 1:278; SLR 2:211, 3:483-85]. On 19 June 1650, Mr. William Bartholomew of Ipswich and Mr. Henry Bartholomew of Salem each contributed 50s. toward the charge of the Commissioners of the Colonies, which was soon repaid them by a county rate [MBCR 3:202]. William Paine of Ipswich appointed his "friend" Robert Lord of Ipswich his attorney 14 June 1654, witnessed by William Bartholomew and John Safford [EQC 1:368].

In a 1658 deposition, William Bartholomew staunchly defended Mr. John Giffard regarding a trial in General Court over Gifford's conveying away £900 of the company's estate [EQC 2:80-81].

He was not often in the courts for his own benefit, although in September 1647 he did sue Edward Colcord for "defamation, charging Richard Bulgar and himself with cheating" [EQC 1:127], and, with his company, sued Mr. Robert Knight for £220 14s. for fish to be made good in London [EQC 1:127]. On 30 September 1656, Mr. William Bartholmew sued Daniel Clark for "a heifer promised to his wife."

In September 1652, William Bartholomew of Ipswich witnessed against John Broadstreet, who was charged for having familiarity with the devil [EQC 1:265].

The extent of his wealth and numerous servants is amply seen in his 1659 altercation with Zaccheus Curtis [EQC 2:131-34].

BIBLIOGRAPHIC NOTE: In 1885 George Wells Bartholomew Jr. published a genealogy of the descendants of William Bartholomew, including an extensive account of his English ancestry [*Record of the Bartholomew Family. Historical, Genealogical and Biographical* (Austin, Texas, 1885), cited above as Bartholomew Gen]. The section on the immigrant contains considerable biographical detail not included in the sketch above [pp. 27-43].

THOMAS BASCOM

ORIGIN: Unknown
MIGRATION: 1634 on the *Recovery*
FIRST RESIDENCE: Dorchester
REMOVES: Windsor 1635, Northampton by 1659

FREEMAN: Massachusetts Bay oath of fidelity, 26 March 1661 [HamCCR 1:5].
EDUCATION: His inventory included "a Bible" valued at 4s. and "other books" valued at 4s.
OFFICES: Hampshire County juror, 27 March 1660, 25 March 1662, 29 March 1664 [HamCCR 1:1, 10, 30]. Northampton constable (as "Thomas Bascomb Sen[io]r"), 26 March 1667 [HamCCR 1:83].
ESTATE: On 22 November 1634, "Thom[as] Baskecomb" was granted four acres at Dorchester [DTR 8].

In the Windsor land inventory on 4 February 1640, "Thomas Bascombe" held seven parcels of land (one or more of these may have been granted as late as 3 May 1653, as that date is also associated with this list): "an homelot six acres and half" (annotated "sold to John Moses"); "in W[illia]m Phelpes meadow two acres" (annotated "sold to Robart Hayward"); "in Long Meadow four acres"; "for upland thirty-two acres"; "a parcel lying betwixt John Heller and Nicolas Palmer's homelots two rod in breadth" (annotated "this made on ex[ecution] to John Hiller Senior"); "of woodland twenty-four acres"; and "a parcel of ground three-quarters of an acre" [WiLR 1:70].

On 9 October 1646, William Trall of Windsor sold to "Thomas Bascombe of Winsor ... one parcel of land containing five acres three-quarters" [WiLR 1:70]. By an unknown date, Thomas Bascomb had sold to James Enno two acres of swamp in the Long Meadow in Windsor [WiLR 1A:139]. By 9 July 1656, "John Mooses" had "by purchase of Thomas Bascomb his dwelling house and homelot, containing six acres and half," "one parcel of five acres and three-quarters," "one parcel three-quarters of an acre," "of woodland twenty-four acres," "thirty-two acres of woodland," and "four acres of meadow (this last parcel John Mooses purchased of Daniel Clark, and he of Thomas Bascomb, but being not passed in record Thomas Bascomb passed it over to John with the rest)" [WiLR 1A:166]. By 5 December 1669, "Thomas Bascon Senior of Northampton" had sold to John Heller Senior the "two rod in breadth that he had of the [illegible] for a bricklot" [WiLR 1:54].

In his will, dated 8 July 1679 and proved 26 September 1682, "Thomas Bascom Sen[io]r of Northampton" bequeathed to "my son Thomas all my lands of all sorts together with my house, orchard & barn," also "my cartwheels, plough, chains & all other husbandry implements & mason tools" and other moveables; to "my son William Janes ... my cloth suit"; to "my son Robert Lymon my serge coat"; residue to be divided equally "between my children, viz: my son Thomas Bascom, Hannah Janes & Hephzibah Limon"; "my son Thomas Bascom" to be executor and "my wellbeloved & trusty friends Deacon William Holton & Deacon Medad Pumry" to be overseers [HamCCR 2:10].

The "inventory of the estate of Thomas Bascom Sen[io]r who deceased May 9th, 1682," taken 15 May 1682, totalled £112 17s. 4d., of which £92 10s. was real estate: "half the homestead," £40; "five acres of land that lyeth at Munhan Bridge," £20; "two acres & half in the second square," £12 10s.; and "three acres & half of land in young rainbow," £20 [HamCCR 2:11].

BIRTH: By about 1605 based on estimated date of marriage.
DEATH: Northampton 9 May 1682 (from inventory).
MARRIAGE: By about 1630 Avis_____ (assuming she was the mother of all his children). "Advice Bascombe, wife of Thomas Bascombe Senior," died at Northampton 3 Febuary 1676 [Pynchon VR 158]. (Since we don't know the date of birth of the child who died in 1647, there may have been

a gap of as many as ten years between the first and second children of Thomas Bascom; if this were true, we would suggest that Avis may have been a second wife, and that a possible earlier wife was the mother of Hannah.)

CHILDREN:

   i   HANNAH, b. say 1630; m. (1) Windsor 15 November 1650 John Broughton [WiVR 1:53] (on 25 March 1662, "Hannah his wife" was appointed administratrix on the estate of "John Broughton who died intestate," and "Thomas Bascum is desired to assist his daughter with his counsel & advice" [HamCCR 1:13]); m. (2) Northampton 20 November 1662 William Janes [Pynchon VR 141].

   ii   Child, d. Windsor in 1647 [Grant 80].

   iii ABIGAIL, b. Windsor 7 June 1640 [Grant 27]; m. Northampton 12 September or December 1657 John Ingersoll [Pynchon VR 141; Northampton VR 1:95; for more information on this family, see NEHGR 151:153-65].

   iv   THOMAS, b. Windsor 20 February 1641/2 [Grant 27]; m. Northampton 20 March 166[6/]7 "Mary Newell, daughter of Tho[mas] Newell of Farmington" [Pynchon VR 148].

   v   HEPZIBAH, b. Windsor 14 April 1644 [Grant 28]; m. Northampton 5 November 1662 Robert Lyman [Pynchon VR 141], son of *RICHARD LYMAN* [GMB 2:1219].

COMMENTS: "Thomas Biscomb" appears as a passenger for New England on the *Recovery* in 1634 [Coldham 107; NGSQ 77:250].

   In his list of "what children has been born in Windsor from our beginning," Grant credited Thomas Bascom with three children [Grant 90]. From this we conclude that the child of Thomas Bascom who died in Windsor in 1647 must have been born before the move to Windsor.

THOMAS BASSETT

ORIGIN: Unknown
MIGRATION: 1635 on the *Christian*
FIRST RESIDENCE: Windsor
REMOVES: Stratford by 1651, Fairfield by 1653

OCCUPATION: Carpenter (carpentry tools appraised separately from rest of estate [Fairfield PR 2:41]).

FREEMAN: On 9 April 1640, "Tho[mas] Bassette" was one of eleven Windsor men made free at a Connecticut Court of Election [CCCR 1:46].

OFFICES: On 19 May 1659, "Thomas Basset of Fairfield is freed from watching, warding and training" [CCCR 1:336].

ESTATE: On 9 February 1640[/1], "Thomas Bassett of Winsor" deeded to Francis Gibbs of Windsor "one parcel of land on the north side of the rivulet in the pallisado containing one acre and quarter" [WiLR 1:86].

In the Windsor land inventory, on 28 February 1640[/1], "Thomas Bassett" held 4 parcels: "a parcel of ground in the pallisado an acre and quarter"; "also bought of Walter Fyler six acres"; "over the Great River in breadth next the same fourteen rods, the length to the east three miles"; and "northeast from the mill six acres" [WiLR 1:95]. (The first of these parcels is the same deeded to Francis Gibbs on 9 February 1640[/1]; the discrepancy in dates is not explained.)

On 18 August 1653, the town of Fairfield "granted unto Thomas Basset one homelot containing in quantity two acres & half" [Fairfield LR A:43]. On 25 November 1661, Thomas Bassett sold to Richard Vowells "Thomas Beardsly deceased his dwelling house & homelot ... in quantity two acres & half"; Bassett acknowledged the sale as "the successor of the said Beardsly" [Fairfield LR A:105]. On 24 May 1664, Thomas Bassett sold to "Robert Beechem ... one dwelling house with three acres of land adjoining" [Fairfield LR A:162].

The inventory of "the estate of Thomas Bassett deceased in Fairfeild," presented at court 14 January 1669/70, totalled £58[?] 5s. in household goods and cattle and £5 15s. 6d. in carpentry tools; the widow was appointed administratrix, and was ordered to sell the tools, sheep and hogs to pay the debts, and then report to the next court, which would "proceed to a final settlement of the estate & children"; the court of 11 March 1669/70 ordered the administration to be continued [Fairfield PR 2:41]. (The total for the column of household goods and cattle does not seem to match the individual figures in the column, even if the amount for the carpentry tools is added in.)

On 26 July 1679, whereas "the administrators of Thomas Basset deceased did formerly sell unto Samuell Moorhouse an acre of land in Concord Field, the said Samuell having received a record of the said land, the record bearing date the 4 of May 1678, Thomas Dickerson doth acknowledge that his father Dickerson did give to Thomas Bass[ett] the said acre of land" [Fairfield LR A:366].

BIRTH: About 1598 (aged 37 in 1635 [Hotten 42]; aged 68 in May 1666 [Connecticut Archives, Crimes & Misdemeanors, 1:17b]).

DEATH: Before 14 January 1669/70 (date of presentation of inventory).

MARRIAGE: (1) On 15 May 1651 the "Governor, Mr. Cullick and Mr. Clarke are desired to go down to Stratford to keep Court upon the trial of Goody Bassett for her life, and if the Governor cannot go, then Mr. Wells is to go in his room" [CCCR 1:220].

(2) After July 1656 Joanna (_____) Beardsley, widow of Thomas Beardsley of Fairfield (when the 5 July 1656 inventory of Thomas Beardsley was brought to court, his widow acknowledged it, and, although the record book was damaged by fire, "Johanna Be---" can still be read [Fairfield PR 1:92-93]).

CHILDREN:

With second wife

    i   (probably) THOMAS, b. say 1660; m. by about 1690 Sarah, possibly daughter of Josiah and Mercy (Camp) Baldwin (as argued by Donald Lines Jacobus [Ackley-Bosworth 244-46, 250]).

    ii   Child (implied by court order which speaks of "settlement of the estate and children").

COMMENTS: "Tho[mas] Bassett," aged 37, was enrolled on 16 March 1634/5 at London as a passenger for New England on the *Christian* [Hotten 42].

Early in 1644 Mr. William Whiting sued Thomas Bassett [CCCR 1:102].

BIBLIOGRAPHIC NOTE: In 1960 Donald Lines Jacobus prepared an account of Thomas Basset, including the argument for assigning to him a son Thomas [Ackley-Bosworth 244-46; see also FOOF 1:34-35].

WILLIAM BASSETT

ORIGIN: Dorking, Surrey
MIGRATION: 1635 on the *Abigail*
FIRST RESIDENCE: Lynn

OCCUPATION: Husbandman. In 1682, the account of work done on a bridge in Lynn included payment to William Bassett Sr. for "his boat one day" [EQC 8:438].

FREEMAN: Oath of fidelity, 1677, 1678 [EQC 6:400, 7:158].

EDUCATION: He signed as a witness to the 1673 will of Hugh Alley [EQC 5:367] and signed his own will. His inventory included "books" valued at £1.

OFFICES: Essex grand jury, 28 November 1671, 25 June 1672, 28 November 1682 (as "Ensign William Basset"), 25 November 1684 (as "William Bassett Sr."), 30 June 1685 (as "William Bassett Sr.") [EQC 4:429, 5:41, 8:440, 9:337, 457]. Petit jury, 24 June 1662, 29 November 1664, 24 November 1668, 28 June 1670, 30 November 1675 (as "Sgt. William Bassett"), 25 June 1678 (as "Sgt. William Bassett"), 28 November 1682 [EQC 2:385, 3:203, 4:66, 251, 6:73, 7:1, 8:394]. Coroner's jury, 4 December 1680 [EQC 8:60].

Lynn selectman, June 1673, June 1674, June 1675, September 1677, November 1678, June 1679, November 1679, June 1681 [EQC 5:198, 356, 6:51, 325, 7:124, 222, 319, 8:148]. Constable, June 1666 [EQC 3:335]. Committee to lay out a cartway (as "Sgt. William Bassett"), June 1678 [EQC 7:39].

Sergeant by 20 October 1675 [EQC 6:111]. Sergeant in Capt. Joseph Gardner's company on the expedition against Narragansett, December 1675 - February 1676 [Bodge 164-66]. Quartermaster by 29 June 1682 [EQC 8:365]. Ensign by 28 November 1682 [EQC 8:440]. "He was probably the Capt. William Bassett who was of a council of war with Maj. Benjamin Church at Scarborough, Me., Nov. 11, 1689" [Essex Ant 7:77, citing an unknown source].

ESTATE: On 1 June 1660, William Bassett of Lynn, husbandman, with the consent of Sarah his "now wife," sold to Andrew Mansfield, husbandman, three acres of meadow in Lynn [ELR 3:39].

In the 7 October 1661 will of his stepfather, Hugh Burt, "my son Will[iam] Bassitt" received 2 acres of salt marsh, 5 acres of upland, and "my wearing apparel" [EQC 2:239-30].

On 23 February 1664/5, William Bassett of Lynn, husbandman, and Sarah his wife sold to Allen Bread of Lynn, husbandman, two acres of salt marsh in Rumney Marsh [ELR 2:106-07]. On 29 October 1667, Edward Richards of Lynn, joiner, and Ann his wife sold to William Bassett of Lynn, husbandman, twelve acres [ELR 3:45]. On 20 February 1668[/9?], Richard Richardson of Lynn, wood cutter, sold to William Bassett of Lynn, husbandman, three acres in Lynn [ELR 3:51]. On 15 April 1675, Benjamin Chadwell of Lynn, husbandman, with the consent of Elizabeth his wife, sold to William Bassett of Lynn, husbandman, eight acres of salt marsh in Rumney Marsh [ELR 4:113]. On 28 June 1680, Thomas Wheeler of Stonington, yeoman, sold to William Bassett, Sr. of Lynn, yeoman, nine acres of fresh marsh [ELR 5:81-82].

On 4 June 1685, the General Court answered a petition by William Bassett and others of Lynn, Reading, Beverly and Hingham, by granting a tract of land "in the Nipmug country, of eight miles square, for their encouragement & others that were serviceable to the country in the late Indian War" [MBCR 5:487; Bodge 406]. (No settlement was made on this grant, but in 1728 many of these petitioners were among those granted land at Narragansett Township No. 3, now Amherst, New Hampshire; William Bassett's grant was claimed by "William Bassett, grandson" [Bodge 422].)

On 10 July 1690, William and Sarah Bassett of Lynn sold to John Bancroft of Lynn two and a quarter acres of meadow in Lynn [ELR 9:59-60]. On 10 July 1690, William and Sarah Bassett of Lynn sold to Thomas Bancraft of Lynn three acres of meadow [ELR 9:172-73]. In a deed recorded 9 July 1691, William Bassett Sr. of Lynn, yeoman, and Sarah his wife sold to William Bassett Jr. of Lynn, "his son," ten acres of land in two parcels in Lynn [ELR 9:11].

In his will, dated 10 February 1701[/2] and proved 22 May 1703, "William Basset" of Lynn, being "of good old age," bequeathed to "my dear and loving wife" the improvement of the whole estate during her natural life, all moveables to be to her absolute disposal; to "my eldest son William Bassett" all real estate in Lynn, he to pay legacies; to "my son John Bassett," £5; to "my son Elisha Bassett," 50s.; to "my son Samuell Bassett," 50s.; to "my daughter Elizabeth Bassett *alias* Richards," 40s.; to "my daughter Sarah Ellwell," 40s.; to "my daughter Merriam Sandy," 40s.; to "my daughter Mary Rich," 40s.; to "my daughter Rachel Silsbe," 40s.; to "my daughter Rebecca Bassett," 40s.; to " my daughter Hannah Lille," 40s.; "my son William Bassett" sole executor [EPR 308:58-60, Case #2048].

The inventory of the estate of "William Basset of Lyn," taken 23 April 1703, totalled £110 14s., of which £74 was real estate: "one old house, half a barn & seven acres & half of land," £67 10s.; and "one piece of salt marsh lying by the beach," £6 10s. [EPR Case #2048].

BIRTH: Baptized Dorking, Surrey, 30 May 1624, son of Roger and Ann (Holland) Bassett. (Roger Bassett and Ann Holland were married at Dorking on 27 April 1623.)
DEATH: Lynn 31 March 1703.
MARRIAGE: By about 1647 Sarah _____ (assuming she was the mother of all his children).

CHILDREN:

i   ELIZABETH, b. say 1647; m. (1) Salem 1 April 1674 John Procter; m. (2) (int.) Lynn 22 September 1699 Daniel Richards.

ii   SARAH, b. say 1649; m. Gloucester 23 November 1675 Thomas Elwell.

iii   WILLIAM, b. say 1651 (his father called Sr. in November 1672 [EQC 5:107]; eldest son [EPR Case #2048]); m. Lynn 25 October 1675 Sarah Hood.

iv   JOHN, b. Lynn [blank] November 1653; m. by about 1687 [Mary?] _____ (daughter Sarah m. in 1707 [TEG 18:33]). (The wife's forename is given as Mary in published sources, but evidence for this name has not been found.)

v   MIRIAM, b. Lynn [blank] September 1655; m. by 1681 Ephraim Sandin (eight children bp. at Marblehead 28 April 1695 to Ephraim and Miriam Sandin; estimated date of marriage obtained by assuming two-year intervals between births, and last of the eight children born in 1695).

vi   MARY, b. Lynn [blank] March 1657[/8?]; m. by about 1676 Michael Derich (or Derrick or Rich).

vii   HANNAH, b. Lynn 25 February 1659/60; probably d. by about 1670.

viii   ELISHA, b. say 1662; m. by 1689 Elizabeth _____ (eldest known child b. Lynn 15 December 1689).

ix   SAMUEL, b. Lynn 18 March 1663/4; named in the 1673 will of Ann Burt [EQC 5:204]; living 1701/2, unm.

x   RACHEL, b. Lynn 13 March [1666]; m. Salem 23 January 1693[/4] Ephraim Silsby.

xi   REBECCA, b. say 1668; living 10 February 1701/2 (named in father's will); no further record.

xii   HANNAH, b. say 1670; m. by 1691 John Lille (eldest known child b. Woburn 3 June 1691 [WoVR 1:151]).

ASSOCIATIONS: Hugh Burt made extensive provision for "my son Will: Bassitt" in his 1661 will [EQC 2:329]. In June 1673 William Bassett was appointed administrator of Ann Burt's estate [EQC 5:203]. William served as guardian of Sarah Burt [ELR 4:202]. These evidences, combined with William's position in the port book entry for the Burt family and the parish register entries from Dorking, Surrey, are more than sufficient evidence that William's mother remarried to HUGH BURT.

COMMENTS: On 17 June 1635, "W[illia]m Bassett," aged 9 years, was enrolled at London for passage to New England on the *Abigail*, as part of the group headed by Hugh Burt, aged 35, Ann Burt, aged 32, and Edward Burt, aged 8 [Hotten 93].

Aside from the dates of birth, sometimes imperfect, for six of the children, the sequence of birth of the children is based on the assumption that William Bassett in his will first named all his sons from eldest to youngest, and then all his daughters in the same manner. This is the principal reason for assuming that the daughter Hannah born early in 1660 died young, to be replaced by a second; this makes the second Hannah a more likely age if her marriage to John Lille really did take place as late as 1691.

Much of the civil and military service cited above occurred after William Bassett, son of the immigrant, was an adult. There is good reason, however, to believe that all of these offices were held by the immigrant. The first appearances as juror and selectman occur when the son was about twenty or perhaps even younger. The records of service are then continuous for about twenty years, with no indication that the younger man had moved into the positions held by the older man. By the 1680s, the officeholder was sometimes designated as "William Bassett Sr.," but never does an officeholder appear as "William Bassett Jr." The holding of military office shows a steady progression from Sergeant to Ensign, and apparently to Captain. The most telling evidence is that for payment by the county for use of a boat: on 29 June 1682, "Quartermaster Bassett's boat [was] hired 2 days" [EQC 8:365], and on 28 November 1682, "Will[iam] Bassett Sr." was paid "for his boat one day" [EQC 8:438]. This indicates that the immigrant was the military man. There is no evidence that William, the son of the immigrant, performed any public service while in his twenties and thirties.

William Bassett was named overseer in the will of Christopher Linsy of Lynn, 9 April 1669 [EQC 4:158]. On 25 June 1672, William Bassett and eleven other Lynn men petitioned against their neighbor John Hawthorne, for serving too much strong drink despite the "advice of his friends to the contrary" [EQC 5:61].

Two members of this family were accused in the 1692 witchcraft hysteria, but both survived. Sarah (Hood) Bassett, wife of William, son of the immigrant, was complained against on 21 May 1692, and Mary (Bassett) Derich, daughter of the immigrant, was accused on 23 May 1692 [Enders A. Robinson, *The Devil Discovered: Salem Witchcraft, 1692* (New York 1991), pp. 290-91; Paul Boyer and Stephen Nissenbaum, eds., *The*

Salem Witchcraft Papers, 3 vols. (New York 1977), 77, 245, 269, 482-83, 486, 490, 655-56, 691-92, 1022].

BIBLIOGRAPHIC NOTE: In 1903 Sidney Perley published a very brief, undocumented genealogy of William Bassett and the first few generations of his descendants [Essex Ant 7:77]. In 1939 Nora E. Snow compiled an account of the immigrant and of his son William [Snow-Estes 2:57-60]. In 1998 Marcia Wiswall Lindberg prepared a more extensive study of William Bassett and his early descendants [TEG 18:28-39].

CLEMENT BATE

ORIGIN: Biddenden, Kent
MIGRATION: 1635 on the *Elizabeth*
FIRST RESIDENCE: Hingham

OCCUPATION: Tailor.
CHURCH MEMBERSHIP: Admission to Hingham church prior to 3 March 1635/6 implied by freemanship.
FREEMAN: 3 March 1635/6 (third in a sequence of three Hingham men) [MBCR 1:371].
EDUCATION: Signed his deed.
OFFICES: Hingham selectman, 20 March 1642/3, 14 February 1647/8, 1 January 1649/50, 1 January 1651/2 [HiTR, 1642-1651, pp. 3, 12, 18, 27].
ESTATE: "The several parcels of land and meadow legally given unto Clement Bates by the town of Hingham": 3 July 1636, "for a houselot five acres"; 1635, "for a planting lot ten acres"; 4 June 1636, "for a great lot twenty acres," in two pieces, one of eighteen acres and one of two acres; 5 June 1635, three acres of meadow; 20 November 1637, "for a small planting lot two acres"; 5 March 1637[/8], "one acre and a quarter of fresh meadow," which Clement Bate relinquished to James Buck; [no date], one acre of salt marsh; 1647, "one acre of salt marsh at Conyehassett ... the 21 lot in the first division ... which acre of meadow was given in satisfaction for meadow given him at Nantascus"; 1647, "one acre and half of salt marsh at Conyehassett ... the 19th lot in the third division"; and 1647, "liberty to set a barn upon the common over against his house" [HiBOP 59].

On 2 March 1640[/1], "Clement Bates of Hingham" sold to John Stoddar Sr. of Hingham "one house lot in Hingham aforesaid containing by estimation two acres ... which said house lot was formerly Jonathan Bozward of Hingham ..., and also one great lot containing ten acres of land ... which said great lot was given to the aforesaid Bozward by the town of Hingham" [SLR 6:40-41].

In his will, dated 12 October 1669 and proved 2 November 1671, "Clement Bate of Hingham" bequeathed to "James Bate my eldest son my house lot next adjoining to my son Joseph Bate containing five acres more or less given unto me by the town of Hingham," also "one half of my planting lot lying upon Pleasant Hill containing ten acres ... only he shall have but one quarter of the swamp that lies at the southernmost end of the planting land the other quarter to Benjamin Bate my son," also "one half of my meadow lying at the upper end of Broadcove Meadow except about three-quarters of an acre joining to Nicolas Baker's meadow ... the which parcel I give unto my son Joseph Bate," also "a little piece of meadow lying at Conyhassett being about one acre," also "all my apparel" and one ox; to "my son Joseph Bate" £10 to be paid by "my son Samuell Bate," also "one piece of salt meadow lying at Conihassett in the first division"; to "Benjamin Bate my son" £10 to be paid by "James Bate his brother"; to "Samuell Bate my son one half of my planting lot lying on Pleasant Hill, together with one half of the swamp lying beneath the planting hill," also "one half of my meadow lying at the upper end of Broadcove Meadows," also "my now dwelling house with all other outhouses thereunto belonging with that lot of five acres the house stands upon," also one ox; to "my four sons James, Joseph, Benjamin & Samuell all my household stuff"; James Bate to be executor and to pay to "Mr. Hubbard our pastor" 20s. [SPR 7:159-60].

The inventory of the estate of Clement Bate, taken 24 September 1671, totalled £215 12s., of which £192 was real estate: "one house lot, orchard and barn," £40; "one house lot," £20; "one piece of salt meadow at Broadcove," £60; "two acres and half of salt meadow at Conihassett," £12; and "one planting lot at Pleasant Hill," £60 [SPR 7:160-1].

BIRTH: Baptized Lydd, Kent, 26 January 1594/5, son of James and Mary (Martine?) Bate [NEHGR 51:269]. (The baptismal date given here is from the Lydd Bishop's Transcripts, and differs slightly from the version published in 1897.)
DEATH: Hingham 17 September 1671 "aged 81 years died Sabbath Day night" [NEHGR 121:126].

MARRIAGE: By about 1621 Ann _____. On 1 October 1669 "Clement Bates wife died" at Hingham [NEHGR 121:124].

CHILDREN:

  i JAMES, b. about 1621 (aged 14 in 1635 [Hotten 48]); m. Hingham 19 April 1643 Ruth Lyford [NEHGR 121:15], daughter of *JOHN LYFORD* [GMB 2:1215].

  ii CLEMENT, b. about 1623 (aged 12 in 1635 [Hotten 48]); drowned at Hingham in November 1639 [NEHGR 121:12].

  iii JOHN, bp. Biddenden, Kent, 18 October 1624; bur. there 18 December 1624 [NEHGR 66:54].

  iv RACHEL, bp. Biddenden 22 October 1626 [NEHGR 66:54]; "Rachell Bate died the daughter of Clement Bate" at Hingham in June 1647 [NEHGR 121:20].

  v JOSEPH, bp. Biddenden 28 September 1628 [NEHGR 66:54]; m. Hingham [blank] January 1657/8 Esther Hilliard (this marriage immediately follows a marriage dated 8 January 1657/8, and so may have occurred on that day or later in the month [NEHGR 121:107]).

  vi Child, bur. Biddenden 2 April 1631, unbaptized [NEHGR 66:54].

  vii BENJAMIN, bp. Biddenden 24 June 1632 [NEHGR 66:54]; m. by an unknown date Jane Weeks, daughter of George Weeks (in her will of 29 January 1666, Jane Humphrey [widow successively of George Weeks and Jonas Humphrey] bequeathed to "my son-in-law Benjamin Bate Mr. Taylor's book on the 32 psalm" [Stevens-Miller Anc 1:271-73, citing SPR 5:108]).

  viii SAMUEL, bp. Hingham 24 March 1638/9 [NEHGR 121:11]; m. Hingham 20 February 1666/7 Lydia Lapham, daughter of Thomas Lapham [HiVR 11]. (Hobart takes notice of the marriage, but without providing the bride's name [NEHGR 121:119].)

ASSOCIATIONS: Brother of JAMES BATE of Dorchester.

COMMENTS: On 6 April 1635, "Clement Bates," aged 40, tailor, "Ann Bates," aged 40, with five children: "James Bates," aged 14, "Clement Bates," aged 12, "Rachell Bates," aged 8, "Joseph Bates," aged 5, and "Ben[jamin] Bates," aged 2, and two servants "Jo[hn] Wynchester," aged

19, and "Jarvice Gold," aged 30, were enrolled at London as passengers for New England on the *Elizabeth* [Hotten 48].

On 6 May 1657, the General Court answered the petition of Anne Bate regarding Lydia Buck [MBCR 3:434, 4:1:293].

JAMES BATE

ORIGIN: Lydd, Kent
MIGRATION: 1635 on the *Elizabeth*
FIRST RESIDENCE: Dorchester
RETURN TRIPS: England 1648

OCCUPATION: Husbandman.
CHURCH MEMBERSHIP: Admitted to Dorchester church late in 1636 [DChR 2].
FREEMAN: 7 December 1636 (first in a sequence of seven Dorchester men) [MBCR 1:372].
EDUCATION: Signed his name to his will, but made his mark four days later when entering his codicil. His inventory included "books" valued at 12s.
OFFICES: Dorchester selectman, 8 November 1637, 30 October 1638, 3 August 1642 [DTR 24, 35, 50]. Assessor, 30 October 1638 [DTR 35]. Fenceviewer, 9 March 1641/2 [DTR 48].

Deputy to General Court for Dorchester, 13 May 1640 [MBCR 1:288].
ESTATE: Granted two acres of meadow at Dorchester, 18 February 1635/6 (as "Mr. [blank] Bates") [DTR 15]. Granted two acres "in the marsh next Goodman Grenwayes," 27 June 1636 [DTR 17]. Granted six acres of marsh "in lieu of 2 acres due to him in the Calves Pasture and other acres taken from his predecessors," 2 January 1637/8 [DTR 27]. Granted two lots of eight and three-quarters acres each, 18 March 1637/8 [DTR 29].

In his will, dated 22 November 1655 and proved 14 January 1655/6, "James Bate Elder of Dorchester" bequeathed to "my son Mr. Richard Bate of Lid Towne in Kent in Old England" his entire estate in old England and New England "to be disposed of by him according to his discretion, yet desirous that he would attend unto such directions thereabout as I shall send in writing," and to be sole executor; in a codicil of 26 November 1655, "James Bate the elder" declared that "upon further thoughts my will & mind is that my son James Bate shall be joined executor with him my said son Richard," only for the purpose of collecting debts and selling land and goods in New England "excepting what is mentioned in my directions to be given unto my grandchild James Foster" [SPR 1:82].

The inventory of the estate of "Mr. James Bate of Dorchester," taken 8 January 1655/6, totalled £413 9d., of which £100 was real estate: "his dwelling house, homelot & meadow," £30; and "in land 28 acres at the Great Neck," £70. There were several debts owing to the estate, including one "to be paid in Barbadoes"; in addition, "there is more land valued unto 16 pounds we leave to the determination of the court whether to put it in this inventory or no" [SPR 3:36].

BIRTH: Baptized Lydd, Kent, 2 December 1582, son of James and Mary (Martine?) Bate [NEHGR 51:269].
DEATH: Between 26 November 1655 (date of codicil) and 8 January 1655/6 (date of inventory).
MARRIAGE: Saltwood, Kent, 16 September 1603 Alice Glover. (On 13 September 1603, a license was issued for the marriage of "Jacobum Bate de Lyd, yeoman, and Aliciam Glover de Saltwood virg[in]," to be performed at Saltwood [Archdiocese of Canterbury Marriage Licences, Book 6, 1603-1607; NEHGR 51:270].) She was admitted to Dorchester church about 1638, along with her daughters Lydia and Mary [DChR 3]. She died at Dorchester on 14 August 1657 [DVR 25].
CHILDREN:

i   THOMAZINE, bp. Lydd, Kent, 26 May 1605; bur. there 6 April 1606 [NEHGR 51:270].

ii WILLIAM, bp. Lydd 9 July 1607; bur. Lydd 29 September 1625 [Lydd Bishop's Transcripts].

iii RICHARD, bp. Lydd 12 November 1609; m. (1) 3 June 1633 (license) Susan Isham; m. (2) 18 April 1637 (license) Ellen Wallis. (Richard remained in England and died there in 1657 [NEHGR 51:268, 270].)

iv THOMAZINE, b. by 1614 ("Thomasine, daughter of son James," named in will of James Bate of Lydd, proved 31 March 1614 [NEHGR 51:272]); bur. Lydd 16 April 1624 [NEHGR 51:270].

v   LYDIA, bp. Lydd 22 October 1615 [NEHGR 51:270]; m. by 1649 *ROGER WILLIAMS* of Dorchester [GMB 3:2007].

vi MARY, bp. Lydd 21 November 1619 [NEHGR 51:270]; m. by 1640 HOPESTILL FOSTER (eldest known child bp. Dorchester 7 December 1640 [DChR 153]; James, son of

Hopestill and Mary Foster, was b. at Dorchester 13 April 1651 [DChR 161] and was named in the 22 November 1655 will of his grandfather [see *ESTATE* above]).

vii   MARGARET, bp. Lydd 16 September 1621 [NEHGR 51:270]; m. by 1655 *CHRISTOPHER GIBSON* [GMB 2:763].

viii   JOHN, bp. Lydd 4 May 1623; bur. there 15 September 1625 [NEHGR 51:270].

ix   JAMES, bp. Lydd 19 December 1624 [NEHGR 51:270]; m. by 1648 Hannah Withington (eldest known child bp. Dorchester 19 June 1648 [DChR 159]; in early March 1654/5 "Mary Bates daughter of James Bates [was] baptized, her father being then [from] home gone for England by way of Virg[inia], her grandfather - Elder Withington gave her a name" [DChR 166]).

ASSOCIATIONS: Brother of CLEMENT BATE of Hingham.

COMMENTS: On 17 April 1635, "James Bate," aged 53, husbandman, "Alice Bate," aged 52, "Lyddia Bate," aged 20, "Marie Bate," aged 17, "Margaret Bate," aged 12, and "James Bates," aged 9, were enrolled at London as passengers for New England on the *Elizabeth* [Hotten 68].

"James Bates" signed an agreement on 2 February 1646/7 regarding fencing, and on 23 February 1646/7 the length of fence for which "Mr. Bates" was responsible was entered [DTR 76, 78].

James Bate is sometimed referred to in secondary sources as "Elder Bate," implying that he held that church office. No evidence for this can be found. The misunderstanding apparently arises from a misinterpretation of his will, in which he is referred to as "James Bate Elder," while in the codicil he is called "James Bate the elder"; both of these instances most likely are meant only to distinguish him from his son of the same name.

NICHOLAS BATT

ORIGIN: The Devizes, Wiltshire
MIGRATION: 1635 on the *James* of London
FIRST RESIDENCE: Newbury

OCCUPATION: Linen weaver.

CHURCH MEMBERSHIP: Nicholas Batt's name appears on a 1671 list of church members at Newbury who supported Edward Woodman against Rev. Thomas Parker; he was fined 13s. 4d. for his troubles [EQC 4:359, 361, 367].

EDUCATION: He signed his name to deeds and to his will.

ESTATE: On 4 April 1649, Nicholas Batt of Newbury, weaver, sold to John Bartlett of Newbury, shoemaker, three acres of meadow [ELR 114:21].

In "1663" [date incomplete], Nicholas Batt of Newbury, weaver, "for diverse good causes ... but especially in consideration of part of a portion with my daughter Ann, in marriage with John Webster," blacksmith, granted the said John Webster and Ann his wife four acres of upland and meadow formerly granted to him by the town of Newbury for his house-lot in Newbury, his wife, Lucy Batt, making her mark [ILR 2:317-18].

On 29 February 1669[/70?], Richard and Hannah Dole of Newbury sold to Nicholas Batter of Newbury a four acre lot in Newbury [ELR 18:9-10]. On 3 February 1670/1, Edward Richardson of Newbury sold to "Nicholas Batt of the aforesaid town" "half an acre of land ... that I lately bought of John Merrill that lyeth in Newbury at [the] lower end of the Ox Common" [ILR 4:313].

In his will, dated 18 June 1674 and proved 26 March 1678, Nicholas Batt of Newbury, "being aged and weak of body," bequeathed to "my daughter Marey Elithorp," moveables; to "Sarah Mighill," moveables; to "my two grandchildren Nicholas Webster and Nicolas Mighill," livestock; to "my three granddaughters, Sarah Webster, Mary Elithorp and Sarah Mighill ... each of them a pewter platter"; residue to "my wife during her lifetime provided that she continue a widow, except a lot of meadow which I gave to John Webster at his marriage," she to be sole executrix; after her decease, residue to "be equally divided into five equal parts," two parts to "my daughter Ann Webster," and "the other three parts shall be equally divided between my two daughters, Mary and Sarah, always provided that John Webster, or his heirs, being my daughter Ann's children, shall have liberty to buy the land of both my other children"; "my loving friends Richard Dole & Benjamin Rolfe" to be overseers [EPR 3:187-88, Case #2134; ILR 4:151-52].

The inventory of the estate of Nicholas Batt, taken 12 December 1677, totalled £242 11s. 6d., of which £155 was real estate: "housing & orchard with the land the trees stand on," £40; "about two acres & half of land called Coleman's Lot," £20; "a lot of meadow called Silver's Lot, about 5 acres," £25; "another lot of meadow, about 5 acres of land below Ilslye's,"

£30; "a lot & half of meadow at Plum Island," £18; "a freehold," £20; and "half an acre of meadow at Pine Island Bridge," £2 [EPR 3:188-89, Case #2134; ILR 4:152].

On 6 November 1677, "[w]hereas Nicolas Batt of Newbury is lately deceased and the law gives liberty to prove a will before two magistrates, the clerk John Webster, who married the eldest daughter of said Batt, came to the Worshipful Major General Denison, Esq., and desired that no such will might be proved in private without his or his wife's knowledge, as they had something to say. They were so advised by the Honored Major General to have this caution entered" [EQC 6:345]. When the will was proved on 26 March 1678, "objection was made by John Webster" [EQC 6:425].

On 28 February 1677/8, "John Emery Jr., aged about 50 years," deposed "that in the year 1653 on the day that John Webster was contracted to Ann Batt, eldest daughter of Nicolas Batt of Newbury, I being at my father Emrye's house, where the said Jo[hn] Webster was contracted to the aforesaid Ann, Goodman Batt & his wife being then & there present, my father Emery say Brother Batt what will you give John Webster with your daughter as her portion, the said Batt replied and said whilst I live I cannot do much for her but I will weave her cloth and after my decease & my wife's she as my heir shall have all my housing & lands and ... the said Batt affirmed that the aforesaid was his eldest daughter and should have a double portion and the said Batt said that he accounted the housing and land would amount to such a value; the said Batt did further say that in case he had his life and health, he would give the other children their portions as he could in his lifetime as he was able, and in case he should die the other two daughters should have their portions out of his other estate" [ILR 4:150; EPR 3:189-90]. "John Emery Sr. and Maray his wife" deposed similarly [ILR 4:150; EPR 3:189]. On 27 February 1677/8, "John Webster Junior aged 22 years" deposed "that about four or five months before the death of my grandfather Batt I heard my father and my grandfather discoursing about building a room to my grandfather Batt's house, my father said if I should build a room you had need give under your hand to secure me from damage, my grandfather answered, you need not to fear coming to lose for I have made my will already and in that will all my land is given to you after my death and your mother's; this deponent further saith, that ever since I took notice of things my father hath enjoyed the orchard behind my grandfather's house as his own, and I have heard both my grandfather [and] my grandmother say that the aforesaid orchard was my father's orchard & that after their death my father was to have all the rest of the lands" [ILR 4:150; EPR 3:190].

On 30 April 1678, "John Webster of Newbury" petitioned that "whereas Nicolas Batt late of Newbury deceased did before the contraction of your petitioner to his daughter Ann, voluntarily & fully promise and engage his house and land ... after his own & his wife's decease, as a portion to his said daughter ... yet the said Nicolas Batt afterward ... did (as is affirmed) make his will & testament and thereby disposed of his land as his other estate (which petitioner humbly conceives was not bequeathable, being before disposed of & conveyed to him on the marriage of his said daughter which was duly confirmated)" and whereas "the relict of the said Nicolas Batt, who, being made executrix by the will of the said Nicolas Batt, offereth the said land to sale, whereby your petitioner is endangered to be defeated of his just right," the court should debar the sale, or at least record this petition as Webster's continued claim on the land [ILR 4:155; EPR 3:190]. The resolution of this dispute is not entered in the probate or land records.

BIRTH: By about 1608 based on estimated date of marriage.
DEATH: Newbury 6 December 1677.
MARRIAGE: By about 1633 Lucy _____, who died at Newbury 26 January 1678[/9].
CHILDREN:

  i ANN, b. say 1633; m. Newbury 13 June 1653 John Webster.
  ii MARY, b. say 1637; m. Rowley 16 December 1657 Nathaniel Elithorp.
  iii SARAH, b. Newbury 2 June 1640; m. Rowley 6 July 1659 John Mighill.

ASSOCIATIONS: Christopher Batt, who settled later at Newbury, was of no known relationship to Nicholas Batt. In 1897 and 1898 J. Henry Lea presented much solid English research on the Christopher Batt family, with material on the Batts of The Devizes [NEHGR 51:181-88, 348-57, 52:44-51, 321-22], which provides three generations of Christopher Batt's English antecedents. No marriage was found for Nicholas, nor were the baptismal records located of his children who were born in England. Lea had not, however, seen the marriages from St John the Baptist, The Devizes, after 14 October 1601, nor had he seen any burial records for that parish. Examination of those records has not uncovered any information on Nicholas Batt.

COMMENTS: Nicholas Batt appears in the list of those who departed from Southampton on the *James* of London about 5 April 1635 [Drake's Founders 56].

In September 1654, Nicholas Batt signed the petition in favor of Lt. Robert Pike of Salisbury, for which he was later sorry [EQC 1:366-67]. On 9 April 1657, Batt also signed a petition in support of his neighbor, William Titcomb [EQC 2:41].

There is a record of a Nicholas Batter, in a list of known Lynn names, being admitted as a freeman on 14 March 1638/9 [MBCR 1:375], which has been misinterpreted by writers as relating to Nicholas Batt of Ipswich. Pope claims that Nicholas Batt, as "Nicholas Battye," was a proprietor at Lynn in 1638, and Savage states that "Nicholas Batter" had a grant of sixty acres there, having been made a freeman on 14 December 1638 (a misreading of the date given above) [Savage 1:141]. The Lynn land grant of 1638 shows a "Nicholas Battye" who received sixty acres [EQC 2:270], and this is what Pope and Savage are referring to. "Nicholas Battie" of Lynn also appears in court records of 1645 and 1647 [EQC 1:84, 131]. Nicholas Battey of Lynn was the freeman of 14 March 1638/9, and was clearly not Nicholas Batt of Ipswich.

EDMUND BATTER

ORIGIN: Salisbury, Wiltshire
MIGRATION: 1635 on the *James* from Southampton
FIRST RESIDENCE: Salem

OCCUPATION: Merchant. Maltster. Licensed to sell strong water at retail at Salem, 1651, 1662-1670, 1673-1680 [EQC 1:243, 2:370, 3:18, 109, 294, 378, 463, 4:199, 311, 5:255, 429, 6:92, 228, 370, 8:48].
CHURCH MEMBERSHIP: Admission to Salem church prior to 3 March 1635/6 implied by freemanship. "Edmond Batter" and "Sarah Batter" were in the list of Salem church members compiled in late 1636 [SChR 5, 6].
FREEMAN: 3 March 1635/6 [MBCR 1:371].
EDUCATION: Edmund ciphered well enough to be Salem town clerk and county treasurer [STR 1:151, 185; EQC 2:49], and copied documents for the local courts [EQC 4:111]. Sarah, his first wife, signed as witness to a 1658 will [EQC 2:192]. Mary, his second wife, and her adult son signed a 2 September 1695 agreement and affixed to the document a seal featuring

a rooster [EPR Case #2137]. Mary bequeathed "all my books" to son Daniel.

OFFICES: Deputy for Salem to the Massachusetts Bay General Court, 17 May 1637, 12 March 1637/8, 2 May 1638, 8 September 1642, 10 May 1643, 23 May 1655, 22 May 1661-64, 29 April 1668, 11 May 1670, 31 May 1671, 1675, 1677-79, 24 May 1682, 7 November 1683, 27 May 1685 [MBCR 1:194, 220, 227, 2:22, 33, 3:373, 4:1:221, 449, 4:2:1, 30, 71, 100, 116, 142, 362, 448, 484, 5:41, 43, 132, 184, 350, 420, 475; STR 1:183, 185, 2:29, 37, 46, 87, 112, 200, 221, 259]. Commissioner to seize coin, 19 May 1669 [MBCR 4:2:421].

Treasurer of Essex County, July 1657 [EQC 2:49, 180]. Committee to lay out a highway, by December 1661, June 1671, July 1674 [EQC 2:342, 4:397, 5:383]. Committee to place a fence, June 1641 [EQC 1:28, 30]. Commissioner to end small causes at Salem, 13 June 1644, 27 November 1655, November 1656, March 1661, November 1677, 16 November 1678 [STR 1:130, 186, 2:275; EQC 1:410, 2:6, 278, 6:369, 7:134]. Committee to audit accounts, June 1665, November 1666, June 1670 [EQC 3:262, 376, 4:268]. Committee to settle bounds, 22 December 1663, May 1682 [STR 2:40; EQC 8:312]. Appointed to carry in the votes at the Commissioners' meeting, 11 March 1666/7 [STR 2:78]. Arbiter, March 1647, 18 November 1661, 22 December 1663, January 1666/7, June 1667, March 1669, June 1678 [STR 1:153, 2:17, 20, 40, 77; EQC 3:416, 4:108, 7:6].

Essex grand jury, 25 January 1641[/2], 26 December 1648 (foreman), 26 June 1649, 25 December 1649 (foreman), December 1650, 24 June 1651, 25 November 1651, June 1653, 28 November 1654, 26 June 1655, 30 November 1658, 28 June 1659 [EQC 1:33, 153, 169, 181, 204, 228, 238, 282, 373, 390, 2:123, 157]. Petit jury, 3 October 1637, 25 December 1638, 31 December 1639, 31 March 1640, 30 June 1640, 29 December 1640, 28 December 1646, 27 June 1654, 10 November 1662, November 1666, 29 June 1669 [EQC 1:6, 10, 14, 17, 19, 246, 347, 3:366, 4:143; STR 2:29]. Coroner's jury, November 1664, November 1669 [EQC 3:223, 4:211].

Salem selectman, 16 February 1635/6, 15 May 1637, 1647-50, 1654-57, 1659-70, 1672-73, 1676-77 [STR 1:13, 49, 104, 148, 157-59, 161-64, 175-82, 184-85, 187-90, 192-96, 206, 231, 2:2, 4-9, 11-16, 21, 23, 31-32, 35, 38, 41, 43, 47, 49, 53-54, 56, 58, 60-61, 64-66, 68, 74-75, 79-81, 84, 86-91, 94-95, 99-101, 110, 140, 158, 207, 221; EQC 4:252]. Treasurer, 1659-66, 1673 [STR 2:2, 32, 41, 61, 66, 68 *et passim*]. Auditor, 19 February 1666/7 [STR 2:76]. Rater, 11 September 1637, 7 May 1638 [STR 1:57, 95]. Clerk, 1667-70 [STR 2:87, 90, 102, 110]. Overseer of church construction, 1670 [STR 2:111]. Committee to treat with Rev. Higginson, 17 July 1671 [STR 2:128]. Tithingman, 7 July 1644 [STR 1:131]. Committee to finish highway, 24 September 1673 [STR 2:173].

Fence viewer, 7 May 1656 [STR 1:192]. Committee to lay out land, 28 March 1674 [STR 2:195].

In 1647, Edmund Batter was directed to go to Capt. Trask for a barrel of powder [STR 1:147]. On 17 May 1655, Edmond Batter and Lt. Lathrop were ordered to work about the fort [STR 1:183]. In July 1657, "Mr. Edmond Batter" was freed from "the troop, but to bear arms in the foot company of Salem, as formerly" [EQC 2:49]. On 13 August 1679, six men, including "Mr. Edmo[nd] Batter," were ordered to lay in one barrel of powder in readiness for the town's use [STR 2:305].

ESTATE: On 6 April 1635, "Mr. Batter" and his "brother-in-law" were granted a two-acre houselot in Salem [STR 1:9]. In the 1636 Salem land grant "Mr. E. Batter" received 200 acres [STR 1:21]. In the 25 December 1637 grant of meadow and marsh "Mr. Batter" received three-quarters of an acre based on five persons in his household [STR 1:101]. On 3 April 1637, Mr. Batter was granted ten acres of marsh "in lieu of 20 acres w[hi]ch he should surrender out of his farm for his brother Antram" [STR 1:43].

On 12 July 1637, "Mr. Edmund Batter" made his request for a farm with twenty acres of meadow "if it be next to Mr. Sharp" [STR 1:51]. On 30 July 1637, he was granted a farm "next to our brother Ray" [STR 1:52].

On 9 October 1637, Mr. Batter was allowed 100 acres of upland and 12 acres of meadow "provided the town at their next meeting do agree thereunto as we do, provided that if Mr. Batter shall remove out of town then the town do reserve the land to themselves" [STR 1:58].

On 25 December 1637, meadow at "Brookeby" formerly granted to Edmond Batter was confirmed with the consent of Mr. Thorndike, the original grantee [STR 1:62]. Further, Edmond Batter was granted another thirty acres of land adjoining his farm [STR 1:62]. On 27 February 1642/3, Mr. Batter was granted half an acre of land so that he might set his fencing straight [STR 1:117].

On 11 January 1652[/3?], John Rowden of Salem mortgaged his dwelling house and five acres of land to Edmond Batter [ELR 1:16]. On 19 January 1652/3, Edmond Batter of Salem sold to Richard Way fourteen acres of upland [ELR 1:15]. On 5 April 1653, Edmond Batter of Salem sold to "Thomas Anthrop" his farm at Brooksby excepting what was sold to Richard Way and excepting a parcel of meadow called Cranbery Pond [ELR 1:25].

On 2 May 1661, Edmond Batter was granted 35 feet of land to build warehouses [STR 2:22]. On 28 May 1661, Edmond Batter's petition to the General Court produced a grant of two hundred and fifty acres, located "in the wilderness on the north side of Merremacke River" [MBCR 4:2:17, 57].

On 24 May 1662, Samuel Condey of Marblehead, fisherman, acknowledged that he was under execution to Edmond Batter and that all Condey's land in Marblehead was under attachment, "together with my person to be at the said Edmond Batter's service & him faithfully to serve till the said debt be satisfied." If he failed to so pay the debt, the house and lands became Batter's [ELR 2:59]. On 23 October 1665, Edmond Batter purchased two acres in Marblehead from John Clements and Apphia his wife of Marblehead [ELR 2:112].

On 17 December 1665, Edmond and Sarah Batter sold a two acre parcel in Salem to Michael Shaplin of Salem [ELR 3:8]. On 29 April 1667, Edmond Batter of Salem, merchant, sold to Thomas Goldthwaite of Salem, cooper, "thirty or forty acres" in Salem [ELR 3:11]. On 9 March 1667[/8?], Edmond Batter of Salem, merchant, took a mortgage on the dwelling house and land of John Northy of Marblehead [ELR 3:35]. On 22 June 1669, "Mr. Ed[mund] Batter" of Salem, merchant, took a mortgage on fifteen acres of land at Plum Island in Newbury belonging to James Browne of Newbury, glazier [ELR 3:65-66]. On 13 December 1669, Edmond Batter of Salem, merchant, sold to Daniel Andrews of Salem, bricklayer, thirty rods of ground in the town of Salem [ELR 3:73]. On 31 December 1669, Edmond Batter of Salem, merchant, sold to John Martin of Salem, fisherman, a dwelling house and land received from John Clements [ELR 3:79]. On 18 January 1669[/70?], Edmond Batter of Salem, merchant, sold for natural affection to Hilliard Veren Sr., "my brother-in-law" of Salem, and Dorcas and Sarah his daughters "my two cousins" fifty rods of land in Salem [ELR 6:76]. On 7 June 1670, Edmond Batter of Salem, merchant, sold to Henry West of Salem, saddler, twenty rods of land in Salem adjoining Batter's dwelling house [ELR 6:108]. On 17 June 1670, Edmond Batter of Salem, merchant, sold to Henry West of Salem, saddler, twenty rods of land in Salem town [ELR 3:86]. On 22 February 1670[/1?], Edmond and Mary Batter of Salem sold to Thomas Baker of Topsfield, yeoman, two acres of meadow taken in an execution against William Prichett [ELR 3:108].

On 15 May 1674, Edmond Batter of Salem, merchant, sold to Jacob Pudeater of Salem, blacksmith, one quarter of an acre in Salem [ELR 4:62]. On 20 April 1679, Edmond Batter of Salem took the mortgage of John Alford of Salem, seaman, on a dwelling house and the adjoining thirty poles of land [ELR 5:40]. On 19 May 1679, Edmond Batter of Salem sold to Stephen Small of Salem two acres of upland in the North Field, formerly John Robinson's, deceased [ELR 5:35]. On 20 August 1679, Edward Norris of Salem, schoolmaster, sold to Edmond Batter of Salem, merchant, one quarter of an acre of land in Salem behind Norris's dwelling house [ELR 5:44].

In October 1681, Edmond Batter of Salem, merchant, and Mary Batter his wife sold to Stephen Sewall of Salem, merchant, 28 rods of land in Salem [ELR 6:39]. On 5 August 1682, Edmond Batter of Salem, merchant, recorded a deed selling twelve rods of land to Daniel Epes of Salem, schoolmaster [ELR 6:58].

In his will, dated 11 February 1684 and proved 14 August 1685, Edmond Batter, wishing to be buried "in the grave where my first wife lyeth," bequeathed to "my present dear wife" one-third according to law, and a third of the debts owed; residue to "my four children" except for specific legacies; to "my son Edmond" a double portion; "to my other three children Mary, Elizabeth and Daniel" equal portions, to the sons "when they come to twenty one years" and "to the daughters at eighteen years"; "my wife to breed up the children at her own cost and charge with the help of the use of their several portions"; if "my son Edmond shall be thought fit to enter the college two or three years I do desire it"; "my honored father Gookin and my dear wife" executors; Mr. William Brown Jr., Capt. John Higginson and Stephen Sewall, overseers, to be paid £5 [EQC 9:507].

On 30 March 1686, the will was set aside when Daniel Gookin, Esq., Mrs. Mary Batter, Capt. William Browne, Capt. John Higginson and Mr. Stephen Sewall all came forward and relinquished their appointments. "The widow declared that she would do the best she could for the estate in getting in the payment of debts for her own and four children's good, there being no other children that Mr. Batter left by any former wife." The Court appointed her administratrix, "she having declared that the paper left for a will did not grant her what was intended for her. She was to have the estate for her maintenance." She petitioned 30 March 1686 "the estate as chiefly in old vessels and housing much out of repair; that there are four small children to be brought up; that her husband upon his death bed forbade her to put some articles into the inventory, etc." Daniel Gookin Sr. of Cambridge, "father-in-law of Mr. Edmund Batter, late of Salem, renounced his executorship to which he was appointed without his knowledge, as did also his daughter Mary Batter, widow of said Edmund" [ECQ 9:596].

Subsequently an agreement, dated 2 September 1695, was filed with the court, dividing the estate into eight parts, the widow to receive three parts, eldest son Edmond two parts, and the other children one part each. The widow received the "new end of dwellinghouse and new leanto, old bake house," £50; "ground the house stands on and so much more of the garden" 28½ poles, £30 17s. 8d.; "warehouse and wharf by the South River, about 5 acres of land at Buffington's," £40; "1½ acre of land by Skerrye's," £9; "also a parcel of land by Leache's," £6. Son Edmond received the "old end of the houses and shop ... the milk kitchen or old Hall and the barn," £45; "land the said housing stands on [blot]" and other lands, his share totalling £252. Mary received two parcels of land valued at £31 1s. 6d. and £13 5s., her share totalling £126 1s. 9d.; Elizabeth received one parcel of land valued at £31 1s. 6d., her share totalling £126 1s. 9d. Daniel received two parcels of land valued at £65 and "a piece of land by Newhall's" valued at £2 10s., his share totalling £126 10s. [EPR Case #2137].

In her will, dated 4 June 1702 and proved 9 March 1702/3, "Mary Batter of Salem, ... widow, being in bodily health" bequeathed to "my son Edmund Batter ... my dwelling house with the land which it stands upon, also the land between said house and my shop" provided he give "his brother Daniel" liberty to pass between the house and shop; to "my son Daniel" the use of a room in the house as long as he is single; to "my son Edmund" half a parcel of land and household items; to "my son Daniel Batter" the shops and land on which they stand and "all the rest of my lands"; to "my son Daniel my warehouses with the land it stands upon and the wharf belonging to it" and household items, silver and "all my books"; to "my daughter Mary Emerson half a parcel of land" or money, "which my son Edmund shall choose"; to "my cousin Mary Gookin" many expensive household items; to "my daughter Emerson" furniture, clothing and silver, to go to her children at her death; to "my granddaughter Ruth" household goods; to "my granddaughter Elizabeth Batter" household goods; to "my cousin Mary Gookins" £5; residue of bonds and money, a double share to "my son Daniel" and a single share to "my daughter Emerson"; residue of estate to be equally divided between "my three children"; £5 to some poor persons in need; if son Daniel die without issue, his estate to go to "my daughter Emerson or to her child or children"; "my son Daniel Batter" sole executor; "my respected friends Major Steven Sewall and Mrs. Mary Lyndell," executors in trust [EPR 308:27-28].

The inventory of the estate of Mrs. Mary Batter late of Salem, deceased, widow, taken 15 June 1705, totalled £107 14s., to which were appended "housing & lands, unvalued" [EPR 308:391].

BIRTH: About 1609 (deposed aged "about fifty years" November 1658 and 30 March 1659 [EQC 2:128, 134, 148]; deposed September 1665 aged "about fifty-seven years" [EQC 3:276]; deposed June 1667 aged "about fifty-eight years" [EQC 3:419]; deposed with Jeffery Massey 26 March 1669 "both more than sixty years of age" [EQC 4:103]; deposed June 1670 "aged about sixty-one years" [EQC 4:266]; deposed 27 June 1673 aged about sixty-four [EQC 5:211]; deposed June 1681 "aged about seventy-two years" [EQC 8:120]; deposed 11 October 1683 aged "about seventy-two years" [EQC 49-18-1]).

DEATH: Salem 29 July 1685 ("Cousin Dummer returns, and brings word of Mr. Batter's death this morn. He went from court, as Mr. Addington the Speaker remembers, last Thursday" [Sewall 1:72]).

MARRIAGE: (1) By about 1630 Sarah Verin. Sarah was baptized at St Thomas, Salisbury, 17 November 1609, daughter of Philip and Dorcas (_____) Verin [NEHGR 131:102] (also deposed "aged about forty-eight years" on 3 December 1658 [EQC 2:134]). She died at Salem on 20 November 1669.

(2) Salem 8 June 1670 Mary Gookin, daughter of Daniel Gookin. She died between 4 June 1702 (date of will) and 9 March 1702/3 (date of probate).

CHILDREN:

With first wife

    i   EDMUND, b. say 1630 (called jr. as witness at court November 1651 [EQC 1:244]); predeceased his father, unmarried [EQC 9:596].

With second wife

    ii   EDMUND, b. Salem 8 January 1673/4; m. (1) Salem 26 October 1699 Martha Pickman; m. (2) Salem 25 May 1714 Barbara (Weld) Hide; m. (3) Salem 25 September 1724 Hannah Higginson.

    iii   MARY, bp. Salem [blank] February 1676/7 [SChR 31]; m. Salem 14 May 1696 John Emerson Jr.

    iv   ELIZABETH, bp. Salem 7 April 1679 (where she is called "Sarah" [SChR 33]); d. before 9 May 1701 (date Mrs. Mary Batter of Salem, widow, took letters of administration on the estate of "your daughter Elizabeth Batter late of Salem" [EPR 307:161]), unmarried.

    v   DANIEL, bp. Salem [blank] January 1682/3 [SChR 35] (came of age on 25 January 1703/4 [EPR 308:391]); m. Salem 12 February 1704[/5] Mrs. Sarah Hunloke.

ASSOCIATIONS: Through his first wife, Edmund Batter was in-law to the numerous Verin clan [NEHGR 131:100-12]. Edmund was called "brother" in the will of Richard Alwood of New Sarum (i.e., Salisbury), whose first wife was Dorcas Verin and whose second wife was Elizabeth Batt, sister of Christopher Batt of Newbury [Abel Lunt Anc 182, citing PCC 54 Rivers].

THOMAS ANTRUM married at St Edmunds, Salisbury, on 24 May 1630 Jane Batter, certainly a sister of Edmund Batter [EQC 3:321]. In the settlement of Obadiah Antrum's estate, the Bakers came to court to depose that Obadiah had feared his "Uncle Batter would cozen his wife of all that he had" [EPR 2:14].

John Phelps (born about 1643 based on depositions [EQC 7:90, 9:21]), son of Henry Phelps, was ordered to be given "over to his uncle, Mr. Edmond Batter, to take care of him and place him out to some religious family as an apprentice" [EQC 2:262]. This suggests that Henry's wife was another sister of Batter's.

The Batter family was sparsely represented in the Salisbury, Wiltshire, parish registers. John Batter and Elinor Oliver were married at St Thomas, Salisbury, on 26 April 1609. Thomas Batter and John Batter were having children baptized in St Edmunds, Salisbury, before and after 1609, but no record of Edmund's baptism appears. In his 1649 will, Thomas Batter of New Sarum, innholder, named wife Eleanor, daughters Mary Batter, Dorothy Batter, Anne Clavell, Margaret Jole, son Thomas Batter and kinsman Thomas Palmer [Consistory Court of Salisbury, 29 Aug 1650]. Baptisms in St Edmunds included only Dorothy and Anne.

COMMENTS: On 5 April 1635, "Edmund Batter, maulter," was enrolled at Southampton for passage to New England on the *James.* He and eight other men were called "late of New England," which is probably a scribal error for "New Sarum," since none of them left prior records in New England and all were demonstrably from in and around Salisbury [Drake's Founders 56].

In 1629/30, Edmund Batter paid 1s. for a pew in St Edmunds, Salisbury, Wiltshire [*Churchwardens' Accounts of St Edmund & St Thomas, Sarum, 1443-1702,* Wiltshire Records Society, Salisbury, 1896, 1:189].

Savage incorrectly suggested that son Daniel Batter married Mary Trask [NEHGR 55:323-24].

On 26 December 1637, Margaret Weston challenged three of the jurymen of Salem, including Edmund Batter, but we are not told on what grounds [EQC 1:7].

We know a number of curious details about Edmund Batter. He owned a "great dog" that killed Mr. William Brown's goat [EQC 1:18]. He never shied away from violent arguments, but took his complaints to court, as he did in January 1641/2, when he complained of Mr. William Paine who claimed he "but struck him with the back of his hand" [EQC 1:34].

Batter was an implacable foe of Quakers [EQC 2:105-06, 151]. In June 1660, he was admonished for saying that Elizabeth Kitchin had been "apawawing," and calling her "base quaking slut." He confessed to calling her "a quaking slut, meeting of her betimes in the morning coming as he supposed from a quaking meeting" [EQC 2:219].

From the early 1640s until the year before his death, Edmund Batter was a major player in the probate court, serving as administrator, executor, overseer, or appraiser for a large number of his neighbors [EQC 1:246, 255, 324, 358, 379, 426-27, 2:7, *et passim*, 9:407]. Perhaps his most complicated service was begun in 1643 as commissioner of Mr. Humphrey's estate, duties for which he was well paid [EQC 1:55, 2:304, 3:109]. His immediate relatives were cautious in letting him touch their interests [EQC 2:14].

In a statement to the court in July 1675, Edmund Batter described how he cared for the estate of "Elinor Robinson," that

> about ten years after her husband's death, the house fell down
> and said Batter at his own cost gave her 30li. to build another
> house to live in, which was seven or eight years before she died;
> that when she grew old, he supplied her with all necessities; that
> in her last sickness, he took care to get Mr. Wells to look after her
> and paid him 39li. for his services; that when she died, he paid for
> her coffin, the administrator refusing to do it [EQC 6:39].

In November 1655, John Legg of Marblehead was fined for slandering Edmond Batter, saying that he carried a false account to Ipswich court [EQC 1:414]. In June 1677, Mr. Batter was presented for "rescuing his horse after it was impressed," probably in King Philip's War [EQC 6:316].

In June 1678 the court returned a verdict for Mr. Edmond Batter, who had been sued by Edmond Bridges. Bridges claimed Batter defamed him by calling him the leader of a factious company in Salem and that it was their design to overthrow all order and government in Salem, also for saying Bridges was the cause of all the mischief in Salem. The court did not agree [EQC 7:32].

In November 1679 Mr. Ives called Mr. Batter "a very passionate man" and not fit to arbitrate [EQC 7:309]. In summer 1685, William Pynson stood in the street and declaimed to Thomas Robbins that "old Batters [is] an old bawling knave I cannot pass the streets for him for his bawling after me for thy debts" [EQC 9:481].

BIBLIOGRAPHIC NOTE: In 1977 John B. Threlfall identified the English origin of the Verin family and explained Edmund Batter's relationship to "brother-in-law" Hilliard Verin by the marriage of Hilliard's sister Sarah to Batter [NEHGR 131:102].

ROBERT BAYLIE

On 11 September 1635, "Robert Baylie," aged 23, was enrolled at London as a passenger for New England on the *Hopewell* [Hotten 130].

COMMENTS: This man has not been found in any New England record.

SARAH BEAL

On 19 June 1635, "Sara Beale," aged 28, was enrolled at London as a passenger for New England on the *James* [Hotten 88].

COMMENTS: Pope thinks that this was the wife of THOMAS BEAL of Cambridge [Pope 41], but this is not necessarily so. That the 1635 passenger was not the wife of Thomas is indicated by her assocation in the ship list with the family of THOMAS EWER, who settled in Charlestown, and the admission to Charlestown church on 30 November 1642 of "Sarah Beel" [ChChR 10].

She may be the Sarah Beale who married at Woburn on 10 August 1649 Edward Winn and is called in the will of THOMAS BEAL "sister Wenn." In October 1668, "Sarah Win" gave her age as "about 60" [MCF Folio #48; Pope 507], which is in close agreement with the age given by the passenger of 1635.

THOMAS BEAL

ORIGIN: Unknown
MIGRATION: 1634
FIRST RESIDENCE: Cambridge

CHURCH MEMBERSHIP: Admission to Cambridge church prior to 8 December 1636 implied by freemanship. In 1658 "Thomas Beale & Sarah his wife" were members in full communion of Cambridge church [CaChR 8].
FREEMAN: 8 December 1636 [MBCR 1:372].
EDUCATION: Thomas Beal signed his will, and his widow signed hers by mark. His inventory included "a parcel of books" valued at £1 10s. Her inventory included "a Bible" valued at 2s. 5d. and "books" valued at 5s.
OFFICES: Cambridge selectman, 12 November 1645, 8 November 1647, 13 November 1653 [CaTR 51, 70, 101]. Constable, 10 November 1651 [CaTR 93]. Hogreeve, 8 May 1647, 14 April 1651 [CaTR 61, 92]. Fenceviewer, 13 March 1647/8, 13 January 1650/1 [CaTR 73, 90]. Lotlayer, 9 April 1648 [CaTR 75]. Clerk of the market, 11 September 1648 [CaTR 77].
ESTATE: Granted three acres in Westend Field in Cambridge, 4 August 1634 [CaTR 9]. Granted a proportional share of one in the undivided meadow, 20 August 1635 [CaTR 13].

In the Cambridge land inventory on 5 September 1635, "Thomas Beale" held two parcels: "in the town one house with backside about half a rood"; and "in Westend Field about three acres" [CaBOP 16]. In the inventory of 1639 he held three parcels: "in the town one dwelling house with garden"; "bought of Captain Patricke at the hither end of Wigwam Neck two acres"; and "in the new lots next to Manotomie given by the town three acres of upland" [CaBOP 63]. By 1639 Edmond Angier had "bought of Thomas Beale five acres of marsh on the west side of Charles River" [CaBOP 50]. In the inventory of 6 September 1642, "Thomas Beale" held five parcels: "in the town one dwelling house with about half a rood of ground"; "within the neck of land two acres"; "on the plain towards Menotamye three acres"; "on the southside of Charles River four acres"; and "in the upper division there four acres" [CaBOP 102].

On 8 February 1635/6, Cambridge selectmen "granted Tho[mas] Beale a lot in the town" [CaTR 16]. In the 8 February 1635/6 list of the "names of those men who have houses in the town," "Tho[mas] Beale" is credited with one [CaTR 18].

Granted three acres and a half "on the west side of Monotamye River," 1645 [CaBOP 127]. In an undated distribution, Thomas Beale was granted two lots on the south side of Charles River, four acres in the lower division and four acres in the upper division [CaBOP 332].

In the Shawsheen division of 9 June 1652, "Tho[mas] Beal" received Lot #77, of 100 acres [CaTR 98].

In his will, dated 24 August 1661 and proved 27 October 1661, "Thomas Beal of Cambridge ... aged about sixty three years" bequeathed to "my dear & loving wife Sarah Beale, during the time of her widowhood, ... all my estate, in houses, lands, goods, chattels, & debts &c." and "upon her marriage or her death, which shall first happen, my will then is, that the one moiety or half part ... be disposed of in manner following, vizt. to the Reverend President of the College Mr. Chauncey fifty shillings & to the Reverend Pastor of this Church of Cambridge Mr. Mitchell fifty shillings (leaving my executrix to add thereto, out of her moiety as God shall guide her) and the remainder of the aforesaid half part, my will is that it be divided equally between my kinsman Richard Post, & my sister Sarah Wenn" (with further provisions if either of them should die); "also my will is that immediately after my decease, my sister Sarah be paid by my executrix three pounds out of such of my apparel as will suit her husband, also I do give her my best great Bible to be delivered her after the decease of my executrix, the which £3 & Bible I do give her over & above her share abovementioned"; Captain Daniel Gookin to have first option on buying the real estate; residue to "my loving wife Sarah Beals," she to be executrix [MPR Case #1423].

The "inventory of the estate of Thomas Beall late of Cambridge who deceased the 7th of the 7th month [September] 1661" totalled £208 4s., of which £95 was real estate: "one dwelling house and barn with the privileges thereof, the yard about it and a woodlot," £75; and "four acres of broke up land," £20. There were also £41 11s. 5d. in debts owed to the estate, and £10 3s. 5d. owed by the estate [MPR Case #1423].

In 1662 "Widow Beale" was granted two acres in the first division on the south side of Charles River [CaBOP 142]. On 27 March 1665, "Widow Beale" was granted twenty acres and two cow commons [CaBOP 147].

On 10 March 1666/7, "Elijah Corlet of Cambridge ..., schoolmaster, and Sarah Beale of the same place, widow," with the consent of Barbara Corlet, wife of Elijah, sold to Walter Hastings, canner, "our several lots of land ... in the Great Swamp near to the Fresh Pond, that is to say Elijah Corlet one acre and a half ... and the said widow Beale her lot containing also one acre and a half" [MLR 5:219]. On 1 October 1671, "Sarah Beale of

Cambridge ... widow" sold to Andrew Belcher of Hartford, mariner, "one barn" in Cambridge "near my dwelling house with the land whereon it stands ... containing by estimation one rood" [MLR 4:519]. On 20 December 1671, "Sarah Beale of Cambridge ... widow" sold to Edmund Angier of Cambridge, woollendraper, "two acres ... lately laid out to me on the south side Charles River near Boston line, & is a part of the first dividend" [MLR 4:360].

In her will, dated 29 June 1677 and proved 1 April 1679, "Sarah Beale relict widow & executrix of the last will of Thomas Beale late of Cambridge in New England deceased" bequeathed to "my loving kinsman Henery Frencham of Boston," £5; to "my loving kinsman Richard Frencham," £5; to "Daniel Gookin Esq., or in case of his death before me I give it to his wife and children," £10; to "the children of my late dear pastor Mr. Mitchel deceased," 20s. apiece; to "my loving friend Edward Mitchison," 20s.; to "Mrs. Mary Gookin," clothes; to "my sister Wing I give my serge petticoat & a piece of the same & one of my books which she shall choose"; to "Mr. Corlet I give twenty shillings and to his wife a pair of green worsted stockings"; to "Thomas Danforth Esq. & to his wife & to his two daughters Sarah & Mary," 10s. apiece; to "Mr. John Pincheon Junior & his wife," 20s. apiece; to "the wife of Marshall Mitcheson," clothes; to "my cousin Thomas Post," moveables; to "Elizabeth Post, his daughter," moveables; "my loving friends Daniel Gookin Senior Esq., Thomas Danforth Esq. & Edward Mitcheson" to be executors; if there is any residue, it should be "laid out in a piece of plate for the use of the church of Cambridge (whereof I am a member)"; "all my wearing apparel not above given I bequeath to Ruth the wife of John Greene & to Sarah the wife of James Broadish equally to be divided between them" [MPR Case #1422].

The inventory of the estate of "Sarah Beale deceased," taken 12 December 1678, totalled £138 5s. 1d., of which £63 was real estate: "a dwelling house and yard and town rights," £55; and "twenty acres of land beyond the village," £8 [MPR Case #1422].

BIRTH: Baptized Biddenden, Kent, 25 March 1599, son of Thomas and Joan (Beale) Beale [NEHGR 66:347, 349-50]. (He deposed aged "about sixty-three years" on 24 August 1661 [MPR Case #1423].)
DEATH: Cambridge 7 September 1661 (from inventory).
MARRIAGE: By an unknown date (but probably in England before migration) Sarah _____. (See sketch of SARAH BEALE.) She died after 29 June 1677 (date of will) and before 12 December 1678 (date of inventory).

CHILDREN: None recorded.

ASSOCIATIONS: Thomas Beale made bequests to "my kinsman Richard Post & my sister Sarah Wenn," and his widow, Sarah Beale, made bequests to "my sister Wing" and "my cousin Thomas Post" and "Elizabeth Post, his daughter." SARAH BEALE, probably the 1635 passenger to New England, was baptized at Biddenden, Kent, on 15 January 1603/4 [NEHGR 66:347, 350], and married at Woburn on 10 August 1649 Edward Winn [WoVR 3:20, 304]. Another sister of Thomas Beale, Elizabeth, married in England Richard Post and had with him sons Richard and Thomas, who came to New England [NEHGR 66:345, 350-52].

Widow Sarah Beale made bequests to "kinsman Henery Frencham" and "kinsman Richard Frencham." As they are not named in her husband's will, these are likely her kinsmen and not his. Although Henry Frencham is said to be of Boston, he has left little if any record in New England. This surname does occur, however, in the part of Kent from which the Beale family came [NEHGR 66:344]; this is the reason for suggesting that Thomas Beale had married Sarah in England before migration.

BIBLIOGRAPHIC NOTE: In 1912 Elizabeth French published English probate and parish register entries which established the English origin of Thomas Beale, and his connection to the Post family [NEHGR 66:344-52].

GAMALIEL BEAMON

ORIGIN: Unknown
MIGRATION: 1635 on the *Elizabeth & Ann*
FIRST RESIDENCE: Dorchester
REMOVES: Lancaster 1661, Dorchester 1675

CHURCH MEMBERSHIP: Gamaliel Beamon was not a member of Dorchester church, but his wife was [DChR 168].

ESTATE: On 14 May 1649, Gamaliel Beaman requested "a little land by his house" in Dorchester [DTR 1:305].

On 8 February 1657[/8], "Gamaleel Beman" requested a plot of land "to set a barn" [DTR 1:90]; his request was granted at the next meeting [DTR 1:92].

As a result of his death, the rate for Gamaliel Beaman's Dorchester estate for 1679 was abated [DTR 1:241].

On 18 April 1694, Nathaniel Wilson of Charlestown sold to William Sheafe of Charlestown "all that my housing and lands lying and being in the township of Lancaster ... viz: nine acres more or less as it was given to me by my honored father-in-law Gamaliel Beman of said Lancaster it being part of his second division as appears by said town records and lyeth at a place called Cold Spring" [MLR 10:290].

BIRTH: About 1623 (aged 12 in 1635 [Hotten 76]).
DEATH: Dorchester 23 March 1678/9 [LanVR 20; DTR 29]. (The Lancaster record clearly states "Sr." but the Dorchester record calls him "Jr."; if this death record does apply to the immigrant, then the original or the transcript of the Dorchester record is in error on this point.)
MARRIAGE: By about 1649 Sarah _____. She was alive on 24 May 1668 [DChR 10].

On 1 February 1656[/7], "goody Beaman" was admitted to Dorchester church [DChR 21]. On 14 June 1657, "were baptized four of Gamalliell Beamond['s] children presented by their mother who only is member in whose right they were baptized, 3 of them being grown up were very backward, especially the eldest" [DChR 168]. On 24 May 1668, "[blank] the wife of Gamalliell Beaman" was dismissed to the church at Lancaster [DChR 10].

CHILDREN:

i   THOMAS, b. about 1649; bp. Dorchester 14 June 1657 ("Thomas Beamond 8 year old" [DChR 168]); m. Marlborough 26 July 1678 Elizabeth Williams.

ii   JOSEPH, b. about 1651; bp. Dorchester 14 June 1657 ("John Beamond 6 year old" [DChR 168]); no further record.

iii   GAMALIEL, b. about 1653; bp. Dorchester 14 June 1657 ("Gamalliell Beamond 4 year old" [DChR 168]); no further record.

iv   MARY, b. about 1656; bp. Dorchester 14 June 1657 ("Mary Beamond she sucked on her mother not weaned" [DChR 168]); m. Charlestown 22 or 23 January 1688/9 Henry Cookery [ChVR 1:186].

v   SARAH, b. Dorchester 19 January 1658/9 [DVR 6]; m. Dorchester 28 December 1680 Ebenezer Williams [DVR 24].

vi   NOAH, b. Lancaster 3 April 1661 [LanVR 10]; m. Dorchester 1 January 1684/5 Patience Trescott [DTR 100].

vii   THANKFUL, b. Lancaster 18 April 1663 [LanVR 12]; m. Charlestown 27 September 1683 Nathaniel Wilson [ChVR 1:119].

viii   MEHITABLE, b. Lancaster 26 May 1667 [LanVR 12]; no further record.

ASSOCIATIONS: On April 1680, John Beamon was dismissed from Dorchester to the church at Taunton [DChR 12]. His son John was baptized at Dorchester on 1 April 1677 as "son of John Beaman of Lancaster ... his wife [Priscilla Thornton] being a member of that church before the wars dissipated them," and in August 1681 "Jno. Beaman not in full communion [was] dismissed to the church at Taunton" [DChR 186, 190]. Since this John was married by the mid-1670s, he would have been born no later than the early 1650s. This would make him about the same age as the older children of Gamaliel Beamon, but there is no evidence that he belongs in this immediate family. His presence in both Dorchester and Lancaster does suggest a connection with Gamaliel Beamon, however, and if John is not an elder son of Gamaliel, he is very likely a kinsman of some degree.

COMMENTS: On 8 May 1635, "Gamaliell Beomont," aged 12 years, was enrolled at London as a passenger for New England on the *Elizabeth & Ann* [Hotten 76].

Savage missed the birth of the last child, Mehitable, and Pope missed both Thankful and Mehitable.

JOHN BEAMON

ORIGIN: Bridgenorth, Shropshire
MIGRATION: 1635 on the *Elizabeth*
FIRST RESIDENCE: Salem

ESTATE: On 30 March 1640, "John Beaumont" was granted five acres of planting ground to be laid out by the town of Salem [STR 1:105].

On 6 July 1647, "John Beamont, son of John Beamont, deceased, being son-in-law of John Tucker, is placed in the care of Daniell Ray as an apprentice until he is 18 years old" [EQC 1:118].

BIRTH: About 1612 (aged 23 in 1635 [Hotten 60]).

DEATH: By July 1647 (when his son was apprenticed [EQC 1:118], and his widow had remarried).
MARRIAGE: By about 1640 _____ _____. She married (2) by July 1647 John Tucker of Salem [EQC 1:118].
CHILD:

　　　i　JOHN, b. about 1640 (assuming he was at least seven when he was apprenticed [EQC 1:118]).

ASSOCIATIONS: Perhaps brother of "William Beamond," aged 27, a passenger on the same ship [Hotten 60].

COMMENTS: On 15 April 1635, "Jon Beamond," aged 23 years, was enrolled at London for passage to New England on the *Elizabeth* [Hotten 60]. Like William Beamon, John took the oath from two magistrates of Bridgenorth, Shropshire [Dawes-Gates 2:114].

　　A "John Beamont" appears in the Scituate section of the 1643 Plymouth Colony list of men able to bear arms [PCR 8:191], but it is unlikely that he is the same as the Salem man.

WILLIAM BEAMON

ORIGIN: Bridgenorth, Shropshire
MIGRATION: 1635 on the *Elizabeth*
FIRST RESIDENCE: Salem
REMOVES: Saybrook by 1643

FREEMAN: Connecticut 20 May 1652 [CCCR 1:231]. In list of freemen at Saybrook, 4 October 1669 [CCCR 2:523].
ESTATE: On 8 November 1637, the Salem selectmen heard "William Beman's" request for a lot, "and is promised to have a lot in due time" [STR 1:59].

　　In the inventory of his Saybrook lands, "Will Beaman" owned his house and home lot of five acres; six acres of upland; seven acres and a half of meadow; four acres of upland; three acres of land in the planting field; a right in the town commons "belonging to an estate of two hundred pounds"; and a right in the ox pasture "belonging to an estate of one hundred and fifty pounds" [SayLR 1:3].

　　On 7 March 1681/2, William Beaman appeared on the list of men entitled to land in the ox pasture based on an estate of 150 pounds [SayLR

1:117]. In the Pataconke lands laid out to Saybrook inhabitants, "William Beament" received fourteen acres [SayLR 1:86].

On 27 January 1687[/8], "William Beamont" of Saybrook deeded to his "beloved son Samuell Beamen of Saybrook" half "my now dwelling house and the one half of my barn and the one half of my orchard and homestead," as well as half his other lands, two steers, and one feather bed and bolster "given him by my wife before her decease" [SayLR 1:210]. "William Beamont" acknowledged this deed 18 March 1688, and in a deed dated 25 November 1691, further clarified it to mean that at his death Samuel was to receive the other half of the dwelling house and all other real estate, as well as one yoke of oxen, all utensils, "his great table in the parlor and also one rug, two blankets and two pair of sheets," and no responsibilities for William's debts [SayLR 1:211].

BIRTH: About 1608 (aged 27 in 1635 [Hotten 60]).
DEATH: Saybrook 4 February 1698/9 [SayVR 3].
MARRIAGE: Saybrook 9 December 1643 Lydia Danforth [SayVR 3], daughter of NICHOLAS DANFORTH. On 23 May 1667, John Winthrop Jr. treated "Beamond Lydia 40 y[ears] wife of Willia[m] Beamond of Saybrooke ... *gravida est* [pregnant] within 6 weeks of her time" [WMJ 727]. She died at Saybrook 16 August 1686 [SayVR 3].
CHILDREN:

i   LYDIA, b. Saybrook 9 March 1644/5 [SayVR 3]; m. (1) Saybrook 3 February 1667/8 Samuel Boyes [SayVR 7]; m. (2) Saybrook 15 April 1684 Alexander Pygan [SayVR 15].

ii   MARY, b. Saybrook 12 November 1647 [SayVR 3]; m. Saybrook 3 January 1671/2 John Tully [SayVR 11].

iii   ELIZABETH, b. Saybrook 2 March [1650]; m. Saybrook 26 March 1677 John Chapman [SayVR 13].

iv   DEBORAH, b. Saybrook 29 November [1652] [SayVR 3]; m. Saybrook 27 September 1681 Thomas Gilbert [SayVR 3].

v   ABIGAIL, b. Saybrook 20 February 1654/5 [SayVR 3]; d. Saybrook 29 September 1683 [SayVR 3], unmarried.

vi   SAMUEL, b. Saybrook 28 February 1656/7 [SayVR 3]; m. by about 1690 Hester Buckingham, daughter of Thomas Buckingham (in his will of 14 March 1708/9, Thomas Buckingham bequeathed £20 to "my granddaughter Hester Beamont" at age eighteen [New London PD Case #814]).

vii   REBECCA, b. Saybrook 7 September 1659 [SayVR 3]; m.
        Saybrook 17 December 1684 John Clarke [SayVR 6].
viii   (possibly) SARAH, b. say 1661 (or perhaps 1667 [WMJ 727]); m.
        Saybrook 2 May 1688 Nathaniel Pratt [SayVR 21]. (Ferris
        suggests this placement, noting that there was no other
        Beamon family in Saybrook [Dawes-Gates 2:119].)

ASSOCIATIONS: Perhaps brother of "Jon Beamond" who came on the
same ship in 1635 (see JOHN BEAMON) [Hotten 60].

COMMENTS: On 15 April 1635, "W[illia]m Beamond," aged 27, was
enrolled at London as a passenger to New England on the *Elizabeth*
[Hotten 60]. Mary Walton Ferris identified the magistrates who
administered this oath, indicating that William had come most recently
from Bridgenorth, Shropshire [Dawes-Gates 2:117].

Wife Lydia (Danforth) Beamon was the only woman named among the
grantees of Saybrook in the will of Joshua, son of Uncas. In 1941,
Winifred Lovering Holman pointed out that the transcription of the will
published in 1859 was faulty, incorrectly reading "Lydia Beamon" as
"Lydia Raymond" [NEHGR 13:235; TAG 17:225].

Pope states that William Beamon "[deposed] in Court to R. Saltonstall's
acct. 25 (5) 1644" [Pope 41]. The source for this has not been found.

BIBLIOGRAPHIC NOTE: In 1931 Mary Walton Ferris published an
account of William Beamon [Dawes-Gates 2:116-21].

ELIZABETH BEARDS

On 15 April 1635, "Elizabeth Beards," aged 24, was enrolled at London as a
passenger for New England on the *Increase* [Hotten 66].

COMMENTS: There is no evidence that Elizabeth Beards arrived in New
England.

WILLIAM BEARDSLEY

ORIGIN: Ilkeston, Derbyshire
MIGRATION: 1635 on the *Planter*
FIRST RESIDENCE: Concord

REMOVES: Stratford by 1645

OCCUPATION: Mason.

CHURCH MEMBERSHIP: Admission to Concord church prior to 7 December 1636 implied by freemanship.

FREEMAN: 7 December 1636 (as "Will[iam] Beadseley," third in a sequence of five Concord men) [MBCR 1:372].

EDUCATION: Signed his will. His inventory included "books" valued at £2.

OFFICES: Deputy for Stratford to Connecticut Court, 11 September 1645, 13 September 1649 (absent), 16 May 1650, 11 September 1651, 6 October 1651, 20 May 1652, 29 October 1653, 26 February 1656/7, 20 May 1658 [CCCR 1:130, 195, 207, 224, 225, 231, 248, 288, 315]. On 6 October 1651, William Beardsley was one of three men "propounded for Assistants to join with the magistrates for the execution of justice in the towns by the seaside" [CCCR 1:226]. Committee to provision soldiers, 18 September 1649 [CCCR 1:198]. Committee to answer petition of Arthur Bostick (as "Goodman Beardsley"), 6 October 1659 [CCCR 1:340].

ESTATE: In his deed dated 29 July 1648, Robert Blott of Boston recorded the fact that the property he sold in Concord to Samuel Stratton of Concord was bounded on the south by "Goodman Bearsley" [SLR 1:94].

In 1659 the town of Stratford recorded "certain lands given, bought & granted to Wil[lia]m Beardsly by the town": "one acre & half granted by the town & three acres & a half bought that was Goodman Knowls lying all in one parcel"; "one acre in the Old Field"; "four acres upon the neck"; "six acres and a half ... lying on the neck"; "eleven acres & three quarters of upland & meadow lying together in the New Field"; "twenty & one acres of meadow & upland lying together in the field called Mr. Waklin's Neck"; and "four acres & a half of meadow" [StrLR 1:64].

This inventory is supplemented with records of other landholding by William Beardsley and his immediate family: "three quarters of an acre of upland ... in Old Field ... purchased of Mr. Graves and Mr. Stanlye[?]"; "by purchase nine acres of meadow ... lying in the Great Meadow"; "also four acres of meadow ... lying at the ditch"; "Joseph Bearslye by gift from his father William Bearsly as appears in his will in proportion to the equal half of the accommodations"; "Joseph Bearsly by way of division hath two acres and a half of upland in the new pasture ... 15 March 1666.67"; "widow Marie Bearslye hath by way of division two acres and a half of upland in the new pasture ... 27 August 1667"; "widow Mary Beardslee hath four acres and half of meadow lying in the Great Meadow at the wood end ... 18 1month [March] [16]74"; "widow Mary Beardslye hath three acres of upland ... lying in the New Field ... March 28: [16]74"; "widow Mary Beardsly by way of division hath one acre of land & eight rod ... Number 29th lying at the northwest end of the town ... March first 1680/81"; "widow Mary Beardslee by way of division in the woods hath eleven acres & half of land ... 18 1month [16]74"; "widow Mary Beardsly by way of division in the swamp being in the field hath two acres & 16 rod of land ... 18 1month [16]74"; "widow Mary Beardslye by way of division in the woods hath forty acres of land ... lying in a place commonly called the trap falls ... 24 1month 1673 & 74"; "widow Mary & Daniell Beardsly by way of exchange with Isaac Nickalls Junior hath purchased seven acres & half & thirty-two rod of land ... it being swamp division"; "Daniell Beardsley by way of division at the north end of the town hath three-quarters of an acre of land & eight rod ... March first 1680/81"; and "Daniell Beardsley by way of exchange with Mr. Samuell Sherman Senior hath purchased six acres of land lying on both sides of Paquanock River ... this 5th day of January 1681" [StrLR 1:63-64].

On 7 July 1668, Daniel Beardsley acknowledged that for "several years before "Timothy Willcockson [had] by purchase from William Bearsly deceased ... twenty-one acres of upland and meadow be it more or less two acres meadow lying together lying in the New Field on a neck called commonly Wakelyn's" [StrLR 1:158].

In his will, dated 28 September 1660 and proved 6 July 1661, "William Beardsly of Stratford" bequeathed to "all my daughters that are now married I give ten pounds apiece"; to "my son Samuel that red cow which I have now lent him, I only reserve four acres of that land at Pequanocke for my wife to improve if Joseph fall in to help her if she please, the rest is Samuel's, I also give him one of the new white blankets"; to "Joseph my son," should he choose to be "an assistant to my wife" while she lives or until she remarries, "& leaves the sea," half "my accommodations in Stratford" and if not, "I give twenty pounds of my share of the bark to add to his part"; if "my loving wife" pleases to add to the portions of "my daughters" she to add to them equally; residue to wife and children "at the discretion of Mr. Blackman, Philip Groves, John Brimsmayd, John Burdsie and Joseph Hawly," overseers; "Daniell after the decease of my wife that he have her half of the lots"; to "my son John" 10s. [StrLR 1:39; Fairfield PR 1:67-68 (partially burned)].

On 6 July 1661, the widow presented the inventory of William Beardsley, totalling £327 15s. 6d., with real estate valued at £71: "house, barn, and all the rest of the accommodations, meadows & upland" [StrLR 1:37-38; Fairfield PR 1:68-69].

On 23 March 1718/9, distribution was made of "the estate of Captain John Beardslee, late of Stratfield deceased," to the following persons: "Henry Lacy"; "Alexander Fairchild"; "John Beardsle Junior son of Mr. Dan[ie]ll Beardsle of Stratford"; "John Fairchild son to Alexander Fairchild"; "the representatives of Mary Wells of Hatfield [written over Deerfield] deceased sister to said Captain Beardsle"; "the representatives of Hannah Dickerson deceased sister as abovesaid"; "the representatives of Sarah Dickerson deceased sister as abovesaid"; "Ruth Smith of Long Island"; "the representatives of Joseph Beardsle deceased"; "the representatives of Sam[ue]ll Beardsle deceased"; "Mrs. Rebekah Beebee of Danbury"; "Mr. Daniel Beardsle Senior of Stratford"; "the distribution in particular to the children of Joseph Beardslee deceased ... to Joseph Beardsle ... to John Beardsle ... to Ephr[aim] Beardsle ... to Jonathan Beardsle ... to Thomas Beardle [sic] ... to Josiah Beardsle ... to Elisabeth Pulford" [Fairfield PD Case #481]

BIRTH: About 1605 (aged 30 in 1635 [Hotten 45]).

DEATH: After 28 September 1660 (date of will) and before 6 July 1661 (probate of will).

MARRIAGE: Ilkeston, Derbyshire, 26 January 1631/2 Mary Harvey. She was baptized at Ilkeston on 5 June 1605, daughter of Richard and Ellen (Elliot) Harvey [TAG 37:77-79]. (This baptismal date makes Mary four years older than her stated age at immigration. Daughter Mary's age may also be misstated, as she would have been born before the above marriage date if the entry in the passenger list is correct.) She was living on 28 March 1674 [StrLR 1:64].

CHILDREN:

    i   MARY, b. about 1631 (aged four on 2 April 1635 [Hotten 45]); said to have m. by 1651 Thomas Welles (eldest child of Thomas and Mary Welles b. Wethersfield 10 January 1652 [WetVr Barbour 285, citing LR 1:18]). (Secondary sources state this marriage, and claim a Wethersfield marriage record of "[blank] May 1651" [FOOF 1:46], but this record has not been found, and no other evidence supporting this marriage date has been found.)

    ii   JOHN, b. about 1633 (aged two on 2 April 1635 [Hotten 45]); m. about 1656 Hannah _____ (on 25 November 1667, John Winthrop Jr. treated "Beardsly Hanna (29 years old) the wife of John of Stratford nupta pro 11 annos et nunquam concepit" ("... married for 11 years and unable to concieve") [WMJ 884]; he treated her again on 24 June 1668 [WMJ 820]).

iii   JOSEPH, b. about 1634 (aged six months on 2 April 1635 [Hotten 45]); m. by 1666 _____ _____ (eldest child b. Stratford 10 June 1666 [StrVR Barbour 9, citing LR 1:51]). (Jacobus claimed that she was "Phebe Dayton of Brookhaven, L.I." [FOOF 1:47], but this marriage must be for a later Joseph. Stratford vital records do have such a marriage, undated, but nestled in among a group of marriages from the first three decades of the eighteenth century [StrVR Barbour 52, citing StrLR 2:479]; "Phebe, d. Joseph Jr. & Phebe, [was] b. 23 Jan. 1729/30" [StrVR Barbour 52, citing StrLR 5:20].)

iv   RUTH, b. say 1636; m. by 1668 Joseph Smith of Jamaica, Long Island (on 23 March 1668/9, John Winthrop Jr. treated "Smith Ruth wife of Joseph of Jamaica" for hysterical fits [WMJ 883]) [TAG 25:72-74 and evidence discussed there].

v   SAMUEL, b. say 1638; m. by 1664 Abigail Clark, daughter of John Clark of New Haven (on 8 March 1663/4, John Winthrop Jr. treated "Beasly Sam: his wife about 22 y: she was Abigail Clerk daughter of John Clerk of Newhaven" [WMJ 535]).

vi   HANNAH, b. say 1642; m. by about 1662 Nathaniel Dickinson [NEHGR 152:170-71].

vii   DANIEL, b. about 1645 (d. Stratford 7 October 1730 in 86th year [FOOF 1:48, citing gravestone inscription]); m. by 1681 Ruth Goodwin, daughter of Thomas Goodwin (eldest child b. Stratford 18 August 1681 [StrVr Barbour 9, citing StrLR 2:482]; "a conveyance given by Daniel and Ruth Beardsley mentions that Ephraim Stiles married their mother Ruth Wheeler" [FOOF 1:48; McCormick-Hamilton 122-23, 507]).

viii   REBECCA, b. say 1646; m. (1) by 1666 Israel Curtis (eldest known child b. Stratford 18 March 1666/7 [FOOF 1:171]); m. (2) after 1704 James Beebe ("On 31 Mar[ch] 1719, Israel Curtis of Danbury conveyed to William, Daniel and John Beardsley, Jonathan Wakelee, John Parruck, and Nathan Beardsley (later referred to as children of Samuel

Beardsley dec'd), land in Stratfield set out to my mother Rebecca Beebe from the estate of Capt. John Beardsley" [FOOF 1:704-5, citing an unknown source]).

ix   SARAH, b. say 1648; m. Hadley 8 January 1668/9 Obadiah Dickinson [HamVR 70; Pynchon VR 223; NEHGR 152:172].

ASSOCIATIONS: Mary Harvey's siblings included RICHARD HARVEY and ANN HARVEY, both passengers on the *Planter* [TAG 37:77-79].

COMMENTS: "W[illia]m Beardsley," mason, aged 30, "Marie Beadsley [*sic*]," aged 26, "Marie Beadslie," aged 4, "John Beadslie," aged 2, and "Joseph Beadslie," aged six months, were enrolled at London on 2 April 1635 as passengers for New England on the *Planter* [Hotten 45].

BIBLIOGRAPHIC NOTE: In 1961 Donald Lines Jacobus detected the connection between the Harveys and the Beardsleys and published his results [TAG 37:77-79].

The surname was spelled in various ways, and Savage divided this immigrant in half, placing part of him under Beardsley and part under Bearsley.

RICHARD BEATS

In the 8 February 1635/6 Cambridge inventory of houses, "Richard Beats" held two houses [CaTR 18].

COMMENTS: Both Bond and Savage interpret this surname as "Beach," and say that he was "soon after of Watertown." The earliest record for Richard Beach in Watertown is the birth of a child there on 6 August 1639 [WaVR 7]. There is no record for either surname between early 1636 and late 1639 anywhere in New England. Furthermore, "Beats" at this time seems to be a variant of Betts, rather than Beach. For these reasons, we do not identify Richard Beats of Cambridge in 1636 with Richard Beach of Watertown in 1639. The Cambridge record might be a defective record for JOHN BETTS, who was apparently in Cambridge by this time.

No record is seen for a Richard Beats in New England other than the 1636 Cambridge item.

HENRY BECK

ORIGIN: Possibly Warwickshire (see *COMMENTS* below)
MIGRATION: 1635 on the *Blessing*
FIRST RESIDENCE: Dover
REMOVES: Portsmouth 1652

OCCUPATION: Planter.
CHURCH MEMBERSHIP: Subscribed for the support of the Portsmouth minister on 14 February 1658/9 and again on 17 March 1670/1 [NHGR 1:10, 13]. He had a seat allotted to him in the Portsmouth meetinghouse on 13 March 1693/4 [NHGR 3:172].
FREEMAN: Henry Beck is found in the Portsmouth section of the Province Voting List, dated 16 February 1679/80, for electing deputies to the General Assembly (with the annotation "not appeared") [NHPP 19:659].
EDUCATION: Henry Beck sometimes made his mark to deeds, and sometimes made a signature; his wife Ann Beck made her mark.
OFFICES: Grand jury, 8 October 1652, 30 June 1657, 28 June 1659 [NHPP 40:97, 125, 135]. Petit jury, 25 June 1656, 26 June 1660, 25 June 1667 [NHPP 40:118, 144, 220].
ESTATE: In 1642 the town of Dover laid out Lot 21 to Henry Beck, it being a twenty-acre lot, forty by eighty rods, on the west side of Back River [GDMNH 49 (list 352)]. On 19 December 1648, Henry Beck's estate at Dover was assessed at £40 16s., on which he was to pay tax of 13s. 7d. [NHGR 1:179, citing Dover Town Records].

On 13 January 1652[/3], "Henry Becke" was assigned ten acres in the "out lots" in Portsmouth [NHGR 1:9, citing Portsmouth TR 1:11]. His name appeared in the distribution of common lands in Portsmouth on 22 January 1660/1 (as of the year 1657) [GDMNH 46 (list 330b)]. On 31 January 1664/5, granted 60 acres of "dividend lands" at Sagamore Creek by the town of Portsmouth [GDMNH 45 (list 330a)]. He was named a tax-payer of Great Island and Sandy Beach in 1671, of Great Island for support of the Portsmouth minister on 28 November 1677, and of Greenland and Sandy Beach on 25 August 1684 [GDMNH 40 (list 312c); NHPP 18:920; GDMNH 11, citing "London Transcripts iv 89-113" at New Hampshire Historical Society].

On 28 June 1657, "Hener[y] Becke of Sagamore Creek of Piscataway River" sold to Thomas Laiton of Dover "twenty acres of land, upland and marsh being on the western side of the Black River in Dover"; signed by mark [NHPLR 5:127]. On 1 September 1668, "Henry Beck of Sagamore Creek in the Town of Portsmo[uth] on the River of Piscattaqua, planter," sold to Joseph Walker of the same town "one parcel of marsh or meadow ground being about an acre more or less lying in the said creek"; Henry Beck and Ann Beck signed by mark [NHPLR 3:55].

On 6 January 1679[/80?], "Henry Beck Senior of Sagamore Crek belonging to the Town of Portsmo[uth] & in the County of Dover & Portsmo[uth] & Ann his wife" deeded to "Thomas Beck the supposed son of Henry Beck aforesaid" for the maintenance of "his father Henry Beck Senior & his mother Ann Beck ... the farm or tenement which the said Henry Beck Senior as aforesaid is now possessed of," including housing, household goods and cattle; Henry Beck made his signature and Ann Beck made her mark [NHPLR 3:168].

BIRTH: About 1617 (aged 18 in 1635 [Hotten 278]).
DEATH: Last seen on 13 March 1693/4 [NHGR 3:172]. (Noyes, Libby and Davis say that he was "last mentioned in list of church members 1699" [GDMNH 86]. However, the name in this 1699 record is "Mr. Beck" [NHGR 3:55], and Henry does not otherwise have the honorific title. Furthermore, an earlier list includes "Mr. Beck," "H. Beck" and "H. Beck Senior" [NHGR 3:50-51], so there was apparently another man of this surname, but higher social rank, in Portsmouth by the end of the seventeenth century. Coffin claimed that the immigrant "lived to be 110" [NEHGR 11:256], which would require that Henry Beck died about 1727, for which there is no evidence whatsoever.)
MARRIAGE: By about 1640 Anna _____. (There is evidence for only one wife; the apparent large gap between the birth of the first child and the second suggests, however, that Henry Beck may have been married more than once.)
CHILDREN:

i   CALEB, b. by about 1640 ("Caleb Becke" was included in a 1661 land distribution list of "all sons as are of the age of 21 years" or "are married, although under the age of 21" [Rambles 1:27-28; GDMNH 46, citing Portsmouth TR 1:69]); m. by an unknown date (but probably about 1670) Hannah Bolles (b. Wells 25 November 1649 [GDMNH 101]), dau. of Joseph Bolles (in his 18 September 1678 will "Joseph Boolls of Wells" included a bequest to "my daughter Beck" [Maine Wills 83; GDMNH 101]).

    ii   HENRY, b. about 1654 (aged about 19 in 1673 [GDMNH 86,
          citing an unknown source]); m. by 1686 Elizabeth _____
          (administration on estate of Henry Beck granted 26 April
          1686 to widow Elizabeth [NHPP 31:302]).
    iii   THOMAS, b. say 1658; m. by about 1683 Mary _____ (eldest
          known child d. 1 January 1774, aged 91 [GDMNH 86]).
          (Various sources give her surname as Frost, but no
          evidence has been found to support this, and there is no
          apparent place for her in any of the early Frost families
          [GDMNH 246-48].)

COMMENTS: On 13 July 1635, "Henry Beck," aged 18, was enrolled at
London as a passenger for New England on the *Blessing* [Hotten 108].

Henry Beck was said by a grandson of the same name to have been
born in the parish of "geywareck" in Warwickshire [NEHGR 60:299].
Unfortunately, no parish of this or a similar name in Warwickshire has
been located. One Henry Beck, son of Thomas Beck, was baptized at
Alcester, Warwickshire, on 12 October 1615, and is worthy of further
investigation.

Joshua Coffin's claim that Beck came from Hertfordshire on the *Angel
Gabriel* can be dismissed, as we now have the record of the vessel on
which Beck did sail, information not available to Coffin [NEHGR 11:256].
Other statements made by Coffin about the early generations of this
family are unsupported, and should be treated with distrust; the
ascription to Henry Beck of a son Joshua and a daughter Mary who
married Deacon White is apparently a typical case of generation slippage,
for Thomas Beck, son of the immigrant, did have such children; there is
no evidence that the surname of the wife of the immigrant was Frost
[NEHGR 11:256].

On 22 October 1640, Henry Beck signed the Dover Combination [NHPP
10:700-1], and on 4 March 1640[/1], he took part in the petition of settlers
at Northam [Dover] against coming under the government of
Massachusetts before the patentees should be heard from [NHPP 1:128].

BIBLIOGRAPHIC NOTE: In 1907 Catharine T.R. Mathews published a
brief and unsatisfactory account of Henry Beck and his son Caleb
[NYGBR 39:98-100].

STEPHEN BECKET

On 30 April 1634, "Stephen Beckett," aged 11, was enrolled at Ipswich as a passenger for New England on the *Francis*. He was in company with "Mary Pepper," aged 3½, and grouped as a dependent of "Rich[ard] Pepper" [Hotten 278].

COMMENTS: No record of this person has been found in New England.

Savage suggests, without evidence, that he may have been the same as Stephen Beckwith of Norwalk in 1654 and later [Savage 1:151, 152].

JEREMY BELCHER

ORIGIN: Unknown
MIGRATION: 1635 on the *Susan & Ellen*
FIRST RESIDENCE: Ipswich

OCCUPATION: Merchant. Licensed to sell strong waters, March 1658 [EQC 2:69].
CHURCH MEMBERSHIP: Admission to Ipswich church prior to 13 March 1638/9 implied by freemanship.
FREEMAN: 13 March 1638/9 [MBCR 1:375].
EDUCATION: He signed his deeds, while Mary made her mark [ILR 3:292].
OFFICES: Essex petit jury, 31 March 1646, 25 March 1651, 30 March 1658, 26 September 1665, 26 March 1667, 28 September 1669 [EQC 1:93, 210, 2:61, 3:270, 387, 4:175]. Grand jury, 28 September 1647, 26 September 1648 [EQC 1:124, 146].

Ipswich selectman, 1665 [EQC 3:271].

Sergeant by January 1660/1 [ILR 2:19].
ESTATE: On 28 May 1659, "Jerremiah Belchar" was granted three hundred acres by the General Court [MBCR 4:1:378].

On 1 June 1660, Jeremiah Belcher of Ipswich, merchant, mortgaged to George Corwin of Salem, merchant, his one-hundred acre farm with houses, barn and other edifices, and sixteen acres of meadow in Ipswich. In addition to the mortgaged property, Jeremiah sold his oxen, Buck, Golden, Duke and Darby, his cows Black and Pye, and a steer to George Corwin at the same time [ELR 2:93].

On 4 January 1660/1, Jeremy Belcher of Ipswich, sergeant, sold to Thomas Wells of Ipswich eight acres of salt marsh at Hog Island [ILR 2:19].

On 30 November 1664, Jeremiah Belcher acknowledged that he mortgaged to George Corwin of Salem, merchant, "all my farm, containing one hundred acres" and housing, and also sixteen acres of meadow, also "my dwelling houses and ground" in Ipswich [ELR 2:93].

On 12 July 1666, Jeremiah Belcher Sr. with "Mary my wife" sold one house and lot to Joseph Redding of Ipswich [ILR 3:292].

On 16 November 1668, Jeremiah Belcher agreed to pay Mr. Thomas Kellon of Boston, merchant, £24 in fish [ILR 3:226-27].

On 8 April 1674, Jeremiah Belcher of Ipswich, merchant, with the consent of his wife [unnamed], mortgaged to George Corwin his farm and one hundred acres of land in Ipswich, also sixteen acres, all subject to a former mortgage held by Corwin [ELR 4:52-53].

On 28 July 1674, Jeremiah Belcher Sr. of Ipswich acknowledged a debt to Thomas Kellond of Boston, merchant, for £30 [SCC 479].

The Cogswells indicate "debts of my brother John which we found paid on sergent [B]elsher's book," June 1676 [EQC 6:153].

On 3 May 1680, Jeremiah and Mary Belcher of Ipswich sold to Phillip Cromwell of Salem, slaughterer, four hundred and fifty acres of meadow near Haverhill line [ELR 5:85]. On 3 May 1680, Jeremiah and Mary Belcher of Ipswich sold to John Cromwell two hundred and fifty acres of meadow near Haverhill, formerly mortgaged to William Reeves, "but the said debt being discharged the aforesaid land is again in my possession" [ELR 5:85]. On 13 July 1680, Jeremiah Belcher Sr. and Mary Belcher of Ipswich deeded to James Powlen of Salem, gunsmith, two hundred acres of meadow [ELR 5:100-1].

On 30 September 1690, "Samuel Belcher of the Islands of Shoales" attempted to move to the house he had built and paid for, but was denied entrance "by his mother-in-law Mrs. Mary Belcher the widow and relict of his deceased father, whom he out of kindness and respect to the memory of the deceased had left in the said house" [EQC 49-112-1].

On 10 October 1692, Daniel Gould and Dorcas his wife, John Andrews and Judith his wife, Thomas Andrews and Mary his wife, Richard Belcher and Ann Belcher stated that "our father Mr. Jeremiah Belcher late of Ipswich ... deceased, ... before his marriage to our mother gave by way of jointure upon confirmation of said contract his house in Ipswich aforesaid with several lands ... entailed upon such children as should be born of our said mother in the time of their marriage together as appeareth by said jointure upon record being date ... amongst which lands is the house and land about it the grist mill ... and whereas our honored mother by said jointure hath only her natural life in it the reversion belonging to us their children, and our mother the relict of said Jeremiah having need for her support," they decided to sell the land belonging to the dwelling house [ILR 5:539].

On 11 November 1692, widow Mary conveyed a lot to Samuel Belcher [ELR 49:251].

On 31 March 1693, Samuel Belcher, "now resident in Ipswich, clerk," was granted administration on the estate of Jeremiah Belcher, late of Ipswich [EPR Case #2303]. A fragment of his inventory, dated [torn] 1693, and presented [torn]ember 24, 1694, survives in the original probate file. His untotalled inventory contained no real estate, and included a "linen wheel" [EPR Case #2303].

On 1 July 1721, "John Gould of Charlestown, housecarpenter, Walter Russell of Cambridge, yeoman, Daniel Gould of Charlestown, cordwainer, ... and Moses Burnam, laborer, and Thomas Andrews, yeoman, both of Ipswich, ... heirs to Mr. Jer[emiah Belcher late] of Ipswich," sold to "Nathaniel Adams & Samuel Adams, yeomen, both of Ipswich, ... that farm situate, lying and being in said Ipswich which formerly belonged to the aforesaid Mr. Nathaniel Belcher which farm Mr. Nathaniel Adams father of said Nathaniel and Samuel Adams died possessed of ... furthermore we do bind ourselves to defend the said Nathaniel & Samuel Adams and their heirs and assigns in the possession of the said premises from the heirs of Richard Belcher late of Charlestown aforesaid and the heirs of David Belcher son of said Jeremiah Belcher and from the heirs of John Andrews who married one of the daughters of said Jeremiah Belcher and from any person or persons whatsoever who shall claim any right or interest in the abovementioned premises"; signed by John Gould, Walter Russell, Daniel Gould Junior, Moses Burnam, Ann Burnam and Thomas Andrews [ELR 40:9].

BIRTH: About 1614 (aged 22 in 1635 [Hotten 59]; deposed aged "about fifty years" on 23 November 1666 [EQC 3:373]; deposed aged "about fifty-two years" on 20 June 1667 [EQC 3:424]; deposed aged "about fifty-four years" in about 1668 [EQC 4:7]; deposed aged "fifty-nine years" on 21 March 1671/2 [ILR 3:209]).
DEATH: After 28 July 1674 (when he acknowledged a debt [SCC 479]) and before 30 September 1690 (when his son Samuel called him deceased [EQC 49-112-1]). (He may still have been alive as late as 1677, when

Robert Lord finally recorded Belcher's 1652 marriage contract, apparently
with Belcher's current acknowledgement [ILR 4:467].)

MARRIAGE: (1) By about 1639 ___ ___. (It has been noted that on
shipboard "Mary Clifford," aged 25, is listed next to Jeremy [Hotten 59]
and that he had a grandson "Clifford Belcher" [NEHGR 60:249].)

(2) (marriage contract) 30 September 1652 Mary Lockwood [ILR 1:240],
perhaps daughter of Edmund Lockwood. She died at Ipswich [blank]
October 1700 as "widow Belcher." (Mary Lockwood was probably a
previously unidentified daughter of *EDMUND LOCKWOOD* of
Cambridge [GMB 2:1192-94]. With his first wife he had at least two
children, but only a son Edmund has been identified. These children of
the immigrant's first marriage were to be "dispose[d] of." Since the son
Edmund, even though he eventually resided in Stamford, married a
woman from Ipswich, this may be where he was placed, so it would not
be surprising if we found other children in that town as well.)

CHILDREN:

With first wife

i   SAMUEL, b. about 1639 (d. 10 March 1713/4, aged 74 years
     [Sibley 2:43-45, citing gravestone and *Boston News-Letter*
     for 22 March 1713/4; Ipswich VR 2:489, citing a private
     family record, gives the date of death as 14 August 1714,
     but this must be wrong, and may reflect a probate event,
     as administration on his estate was granted 30 August
     1714 (see EPR 311:175)]); Harvard College 1659 [Sibley
     2:42-45]; m. (1) say 1668 Mary Cobbett (in his undated
     will, proved 22 November 1685, "Thomas Cobbett, pastor
     of the Church of Christ at Ipswich," referred to a debt
     due "from my son Belcher for what he oweth us for
     stockings & shoes for Samuel & for the one half of his
     diet since his mother died ... it being now about an year
     and half since my daughter died" and bequeathed to "our
     grandchild Samuel Belcher ... [and] to his sister Elizabeth
     Belcher" [EQC 9:558, 552-3; see also NEHGR 60:250, citing
     EPR Case #5707]); m. (2) Mercy (Wigglesworth)
     Brackenbury, daughter of Rev. Michael Wigglesworth
     and widow of Samuel Brackenbury, son of *WILLIAM
     BRACKENBURY* [GMB 1:202] (in her will of 31 March
     1708, "Sibyl Wigglesworth of Cambridge ... widow" of
     Michael Wigglesworth bequeathed to "my daughter

Mary [*sic*] Belcher, to her son W[illia]m Brackenbury & to her granddaughter Mary Brackenbury" [MLR 12:361]).

ii JEREMY, b. about August 1641 (aged 81 years 6 months at death on 6 February 1722/3 [NEHGR 60:251, citing gravestone, Revere cemetery]); m. (1) by 1668 Sarah (Weeden) Senter (first known child recorded Boston 31 October 1668 [BVR 107]), daughter of Edward and Elizabeth (Cole) Weeden and widow of John Senter [SLR 8:51-52; TAG 20:109-10; GMB 1:432-33]; m. (2) Boston (intention) 20 March 1716/17 Rebecca Nash [BTR 2:97].

iii MARY, b. say 1643; m. Cambridge 23 June 1662 Joseph Russell (eldest surviving son Walter signed the 1721 deed [ELR 40:9]).

iv JOHN, b. about 1649 (deposed aged "about twenty-two years" about 1671 [EQC 4:376]); no further record.

With second wife

v ABIGAIL, b. say 1654; m. by 1671 John Gould (eldest known child b. Reading "28 March 1670-1 [*sic*]").

vi DORCAS, b. about 1656 ("d. 5 June 1730, in 74th year" [Wyman 427, citing Stoneham gravestone]); m. by 1684 Daniel Gould (eldest known child b. Reading 5 March 1684/5).

vii JUDITH, b. Ipswich 19 August 1658; m. by 1684 John Andrews (eldest known child b. Ipswich 7 March 1684/5).

viii MARY, b. Ipswich 12 July 1660; m. Ipswich 9 February 1681/2 Thomas Andrews.

ix DAVID, b. Ipswich [no day or month given] 1662; no further record. (He did not participate in the sale of land for his mother's support in 1692 [ILR 5:539], and he was not a principal in the deed of 1721. The inclusion in the latter instrument of "the heirs of David Belcher" as potential claimants is more likely a lawyerly caution than evidence that there were living descendants of this son; if David did survive until adulthood, and died without widow or issue, his heirs would be his siblings.)

x RICHARD, b. Ipswich 10 September 1665; m. (1) Ipswich 20 May 1689 Mary Simpson; m. (2) Woburn 11 October 1705 Ruth Knight [WoVR 3:22].

xi ANN, b. say 1667; m. by 1699 Moses Burnham (eldest known child b. Ipswich 10 December 1699).

COMMENTS: On 13 April 1635, "Jeremy Belcher," aged 22 years, was enrolled at London for passage to New England on the *Susan & Ellen* [Hotten 59].

On 23 September 1652, Humphrey Griffin sued "Jerime Belcher" for debt and the marshal attached Belcher's orchard [EQC 1:266].

In March 1654, "Jer. Belcher" sued Ned Acockett, an Indian, for debt, but withdrew the suit [EQC 1:336]. This may have been related to the matter which caused Jeremiah Belcher to petition the General Court before 19 October 1658, "craving the remitment of the fine of £52 imposed on him by the last Ipswich Court for selling strong water, powder, & shot, the Court, considering the petitioner is poor & an honest man, not using any such trade, do judge meet to abate the said fine to £5" [MBCR 4:1:352].

Belcher appeared in court to make many depositions in the 1660s, mostly about the financial affairs of his neighbors. He accompanied the contentious John Godfrey to Haverhill in the mid-1660s and witnessed regarding Godfrey's refusal to receive wheat in payment of debt from George Hadlock [EQC 4:72]. On 21 February 1671/2, Jeremiah Belcher, aged 59 years, deposed regarding the grant of a mill [ILR 3:209]. Occassionally Belcher was sued for debt, as in June 1670 [EQC 4:277] and 23 November 1675 [SCC 640].

Proof of much of Jeremiah Belcher's posterity not otherwise seen is found in a deed of 1721, in which several of his heirs quitclaimed land to Samuel and Nathaniel Adams [ELR 40:9]. John Gould of Charlestown, house carpenter, Walter Russell of Cambridge, yeoman, Daniel Gould of Charlestown, cordwainer, Moses Burnam, laborer, Thomas Andrews, yeoman, heirs to Mr. Jeremy Belcher late of Ipswich, quitclaimed to Nathaniel Adams and Samuel Adams, yeomen of Ipswich, a farm in Ipswich "which formerly belonged to the aforesaid Mr. Jeremiah Belcher, which farm Mr. Nathaniel Adams father of said Nathaniel and Samuel Adams, died possessed of." They further bound themselves to defend Nathaniel and Samuel Adams "from the heirs of Richard Belcher, late of Charlestown, and the heirs of David Belcher, son of said Jeremiah Belcher, and from the heirs of John Andrews who married one of the daughters of said Jeremiah Belcher." Ann Burnam, wife of Moses Burnam, joined those signing and acknowledging this deed, although she was not named in it. The signatories quitclaimed the rights of six of the seven children of Jeremiah with his second wife, and one of the children of Jeremiah and his first wife.

BIBLIOGRAPHIC NOTE: In 1906 J. Gardner Bartlett published accounts of all early New England Belcher families, including a treatment of Jeremy Belcher and five generations of his agnate descendants [NEHGR 60:249-56, 358-64].

THOMAS BELL

ORIGIN: Bury St Edmunds, Suffolk
MIGRATION: 1634
FIRST RESIDENCE: Roxbury
RETURN TRIPS: Brief voyages to England about 1640 and 1645; returned to London permanently by 1648

OCCUPATION: Merchant.
CHURCH MEMBERSHIP: Admitted to Roxbury church as member #122, among those who arrived in 1634 [RChR 80]. A later annotation to this entry states that "Mr. Tho[mas] Bell and his wife had letters of dismission granted & sent to England, anno 1654, 7mo. [September]" [RChR 80]. "[blank] Bell the wife of Thomas Bell" was admitted to Roxbury church as member #143, late in 1635 [RChR 81].
FREEMAN: 25 May 1636 [MBCR 1:371].
EDUCATION: Sufficient to conduct a thriving business.
OFFICES: Admitted to Ancient and Honorable Artillery Company in 1643/4 [HAHAC 1:125].
ESTATE: In about 1639, Thomas Bell received 196 acres in Roxbury's 4000 acre grant [RBOP 5] (placing him among the sixteen richest men in the town).

In the Roxbury Book of Possessions, compiled about 1652 or 1653, "Mr. Thomas Bell" owned "his house and barn, and lot, four and twenty acres"; "fourteen acres more or less"; "one acre more or less of meadow"; "four acres more or less" south of Stony River; "two acres and a quarter" of salt marsh; "one house and four acres" by Stony River; "in the division of the Nookes" the twentieth lot; "with the said house bought of John Mathew eighteen acres one quarter and twenty rods"; in the first and third parts of the last division "the four and twentieth lot ... fourscore and eleven acres and three quarters and twenty rods"; in the 4000 acres "one hundred three score and six acres"; "six acres more or less bought of Hugh Thomas"; and "a fourth part of sixteen acres of salt marsh" on the Boston line [RBOP 16].

In an arbitrated agreement of 16 July 1652, "Mr. Thomas Bell of London" received payment from Mr. James Oliver of Boston for sugar sold to William Clough [SLR 1:215].

On 8 January 1652[/3], William Phillips "the younger of Boston," merchant, mortgaged a cottage and small plot of land in Boston to Thomas Bell and Hezekiah Usher [SLR 1:272]. On 4 November 1651, Major General Edward Gibbons of Boston paid his way out of debt by mortgaging and ultimately deeding one-eighth of a watermill in Boston to "Thomas Bell of London, merchant," Anthony Stoddard and Hezekiah Usher [SLR 1:287, 2:341]. On 24 June 1665, Sir Thomas Temple, knight and baronet, of Boston, mortgaged to "Thomas Breden of Boston aforesaid & to Thomas Bell & John Bredon of London, merchants," a dwelling house and land in Boston, a farm house on Deer Island with a lease of years unexpired, a ship called the *Blessing*, four hundred sheep and lambs on "Notley's Island" and sixty head of neat cattle, and his full right in Nova Scotia and "the trade thereof" [SLR 4:308-10].

In his will, dated 29 January 1671/2 and proved 3 May 1672, "Thomas Bell, senior, of London, merchant," bequeathed to "Mr. John Elliott, minister," at Roxbury and "Capt. Isaac Johnson," a church overseer, "and to one such other like Godly person now bearing office in the said church ... all those my messuages or tenements, lands and hereditaments ... at Roxbury in New England aforesaid" in trust "for the maintenance of a schoolmaster and free school for the teaching and instructing of poor men's children at Roxbury"; "whereas my son Thomas Bell did pay unto me the sum of £300 which he received in marriage with his wife, I therefore in consideration thereof and the pains he hath taken in my business do thereby give and bequeath unto the said Thomas Bell my son (over and besides £200 formerly given him in debts and money) the sum of £1200"; if son Thomas be dead, then to "Jane now the wife of my said son Thomas Bell," £500 "in recompense of the £300 my said son received in marriage with her"; to "my grandchild Clement Bell," £300 at twenty-one; to "my grandchild Thomas Bell" £300; to "my grandchild Simon Bell" £150 at twenty-one; having given "in marriage with my daughter Susan to John Wall deceased the sum of £300 and afterwards £400 to Mr. John Bell her now husband" now give to "the said John Bell and the said Susan his wife," £80; to "my grandchild John Wall," £120 at twenty-one; to "Simon Baxter, my son-in-law, and Sarah his wife," £80; to "Edward Baxter my grandchild," £50, and to "Simon Baxter my grandchild," £150, and to "Sarah and Susan Baxter, my grandchildren," £120 apiece at twenty-one or day of marriage; to "my daughter Mary Turpin, wife of John Turpin,"

£300; to "Edward Bell, son of my brother Edward," £10 at age twenty-one; to "Elizabeth and Sarah Bell," £50 apiece at age twenty-one or marriage; to "Susanna [blank], late the wife of Edward Bell, and to her two children which she had by the said Edward," £20 apiece; to the poor of the parish of Allhallows Barking, London, "where I now dwell," £15; to "Thomas Makins, my sister's son, in New England," £20; to "the other child of my said sister, whose name I remember not," £20; to "all the children of my sister Christian ... who married one Chappell or Chapman," £20 apiece; to "my cousin Ann Bugg, widow," an annuity of £3 per year for life; to "my cousin Thomas Wildboare (my cousin Sarah's son)," £10 at twenty-one; to "Susan, the said Sarah's daughter," £10; to "my said cousin Sarah Wildboare," £20, and "her husband to have no power over it"; to "Mr. Isaac Daffron" and his wife, £40; to "poor necessitous men late ministers of the gospel of which number I will that Mr. Knowles and Mr. John Collings both late of New England be accounted," £100 to be distributed among them; to "the said Mr. Knowles, Mr. Samuel Knolls his son, Mr. John Colling and one Mr. Ball," £10 apiece; "whereas my cousin Mr. John Bayley of Little Warmfield in the county of Suffolk is at this present indebted unto me the sum of £435, now I do give and dispose of the same in manner following, that is to say, £40 thereof to him my said cousin John Bayley, £20 more thereof to his wife, £50 more thereof to Martha his daughter and to his other four children"; to "my cousin William Whood," £10; to "my cousin Whood wife of the said William Whood," £3 a year for life; to "my uncle's daughter of St Edmundsbury whose husband's name is John Cason," £3 a year for life; to "Mary Bell, daughter of my brother Bell," £50 at age twenty-one or marriage; to "my maid Mary, that now dwelleth with me," £50; to "Susan my dear and wellbeloved wife" houses lately built in Gracechurch Street, London, for life, then to "son Thomas"; "I omit to give anything to his daughter"; residue to "the said Susan my dear and wellbeloved wife," she to be sole executrix [PCC 56 Eure; see also Waters 23-24].

In her will, dated 10 May 1672 and proved 21 March 1672/3, "Susanne Bell of the parish of All Hallows Barking, London, widow (and relict and executrix of the last will and testament of Thomas Bell late of the same parish, merchant, deceased)," requested to be buried in the said parish "as near to my deceased husband as may be," and bequeathed to "my son-in-law John Bell and Susan his wife," £20, and likewise to "John Wall my grandchild"; to "my said daughter Susan my biggest silver tankard with a foot to it and I give more to John Wall my grandchild my silver beer bowl"; to "my son-in-law Simon Baxter and Sarah his wife," £30 for mourning for themselves and "all their children"; to "the said Sarah Baxter my daughter my large silver caudle cup and porringer that covers it and to her daughter Sarah Baxter my silver sugar chest"; to "Susan Baxter my granddaughter my pair of silver candlesticks"; to "my grandson Edward Baxter a silver sugar dish"; to "my grandson Simon Baxter my silver plate"; to "my grandson Robert Baxter," £50 at twenty-one and if he die before age, then to "my grandson Simon Baxter" at same age, and if he die, then to "my executor"; to "him four silver spoons"; to "my son-in-law John Turpin and Mary his wife," £15; to "my said daughter Mary my silver server and the silver pint cup with a cover, because it was the desire of Mr. Richards, who gave it me that she should have it after my decease"; to "my daughter-in-law Jane Bell my six trencher salts and my best diamond ring, with my great looking glass"; to "my grandson Clement Bell," one silver tankard; silver plate to "my grandson Thomas Bell," to "my grandson Simon Bell," and to "my granddaughter Susan Bell"; to "my loving brother William Brydon," £5 per year for life; to "his daughter Usher," £10; to "my cousin Seale," £5 per year for life towards the bringing up of her two children; to "my cousin Deborah Kerby," £10; to "my cousin Hannah Brydon, daughter of my brother John Brydon, deceased," £10; to "John Collins, son of Mr. John Collins of London," £10; to "Deborah Royston, wife of Peter Royston," silverware; to "Elizabeth the wife of Humphrey South," silverware; to "Mr. Thomas Brooks," £5; to the poor, £5; to "Mrs. Anne Elliot, the wife of John Elliot of Roxbury in New England," clothing; to "Mrs. Martha Sanderson," 20s. per year for life, along with some clothing; to "Mr. John Knowls," 20s. per year; to "Mrs. [blank] Spinnadge widow living in Duke's Place," 20s. per year; to "Mrs. Day widow of Spittlefields in the parish of Stepney," 20s. per year; to "my cousin Mary Bell now living with me," furniture; to "my poor kindred of St Edmond's Bury or thereabouts in the County of Suffolke," 20s. per year; to "my maid Mary (if she be living with me at the time of my decease and behave herself well)," furniture; to "my cousin Elizabeth Bell ... my chest of drawers in my chamber"; to "my granddaughter Susan Bell," £50 at age twenty-one or at marriage; "my son Thomas Bell" sole executor and residuary legatee, and "my sons-in-law John Bell, Simon Baxter and John Turpin" overseers [PCC 32 Pye; see also Waters 1062-63].

BIRTH: By about 1606 based on date of marriage.
DEATH: Buried All Hallows Barking, London, 30 April 1672 as "Mr. Thomas Bell the elder."

MARRIAGE: Bury St Edmunds St James, Suffolk, 15 August 1631 Susanna Brydon. She was baptized there 26 August 1604, daughter of John "Briden," glover, who in his will of 25 February 1616/7 bequeathed to her £6 13s. 4d. at age twenty-four [Archdeaconry of Sudbury Will Book 46:228]. She died 13 March 1672/3 and was buried at All Hallows Barking, London, on 20 March 1672/3 as "Mrs. Susanna Bell, widow."

CHILDREN:

i THOMAS, b. about 1633 (deposed aged twenty-two years, 12 December 1655 [SLR 2:195]); m. by an unknown date Jane ____.

ii Child, b. England 1634 and d. soon [see *COMMENTS* below].

iii SUSAN, b. say 1635 (presumably the child born soon after landing in New England); m. (1) by an unknown date John Wall; m. (2) by an unknown date John Bell.

iv SARAH, b. Roxbury 4 October 1640; m. All Hallows Barking, London, 13 October 1657 Simon Baxter.

v JOHN, bp. Roxbury 9 April 1643 [RChR 114]; "[t]he last of this month [June 1643] John Bell, the son of Thom[as] Bell that was baptized about 2 month before, died" at Roxbury [RChR 171].

vi MARY, bp. Roxbury 28 September 1645 [RChR 116]; m. by an unknown date John Turpin.

ASSOCIATIONS: In his will Thomas Bell made a bequest to "Thomas Makins, my sister's son in New England," and to "the other child of my said sister, whose name I remember not." This sister would be Katherine (Bell) Meakins, wife of *THOMAS MEAKINS* of Boston and Braintree [GMB 2:1246-47].

The suggestion has been made that "my sister Christian ... who married one Chappell or Chapman" was wife of either George Chappell or William Chappell of New London; but given the disparity in social class of Bell and the Chappells, and the fact that Thomas Bell does not explicitly state that his sister was of New England, these suggestions seem unlikely.

COMMENTS: Bell dealt in a variety of commodities from masts to moose skins [Aspinwall 105-6, 143, 396, 418]. He had numerous business dealings with his affluent neighbors the Winthrops, the Bartholomews, the Welds, and others, apparently occasioned by his contacts in England [Aspinwall 9-10, 13, 31, 66-70, 81-82, 92-93, 113].

On 24 August 1647, Thomas Bell was one of the overseers to receive Anthony Stoddard's bond pledging to preserve the estate of Joseph Weld, whose widow Stoddard intended to marry [SLR 1:30]. He was certainly in England in 1648 when he was to receive payment from Ralph Woory of Charlestown at Mr. William Peak's house on Canon Street in London [Aspinwall 85, 182-83], and in 1649 when he appointed Mr. Henry Shrimpton his agent [Aspinwall 250, 255]. Continual references to "Mr. Tho: Bell of London" are evidence that he had returned permanently many years before the Roxbury church sent letters of dismission [Aspinwall 381; SLR 1:260], and there is no evidence of his presence in New England after 1647. He is called of "Seething Lane" in 1651 and 1652 [Aspinwall 388-90; SLR 1:254].

On 19 December 1663, Henry Shrimpton of Boston, merchant, and Mary his wife, late relict and executrix of Robert Fenn of London, made their discharge to Thomas Bell of London, merchant, the other executor named in Robert Fenn's will [SLR 4:221].

Late in her life, Thomas Bell's widow wrote a spiritual memoir, which was published in London in 1673: *The Legacy of a Dying Mother, Being the Experiences of Mrs. Suanna Bell, Who Died March 13, 1672, with an Epistle Dedicatory by Thomas Brooks Minister of the Gospel.* Rev. Brooks addresses his epistle to "his Honored Friends, Mr. T.B., I.B., S.B., I.T. merchants, and to their wives, and to the rest of the children of Mrs. Susanna Bell, deceased" [p. 1]. The four sets of initials indicate son Thomas Bell and sons-in-law John Bell, Simon Baxter and John Turpin.

After a brief description of her earlier spiritual experiences, Susanna Bell reports that "it pleased the Lord to order it so, that I changed my condition, and the Lord provided for me a good husband, one that feared him. And some troubles being here, many of the people of God went for New England, and among them my husband desired to go, but I and my friends were very averse unto it. I having one child, and being big with another, thought it to be very difficult to cross the sea with two small children.... But after this, I being well delivered, and the child well, it pleased the Lord soon after to take my child to himself. Now upon this, so far as it pleased the Lord to help a poor wretch, I begged earnestly of him, to know why he took away a child, and it was given in to me, that it was because I would not go to New England. Upon this the Lord took away all fears from my spirit, and then I told my husband I was willing to go with him" [pp. 45-46]. The voyage took eight weeks, and Susanna thanked "the Lord for his goodness in preserving us upon the sea, I being big with child, and my husband sick almost all the voyage" [p. 47].

Susanna Bell then discoursed at length on her preparations to be admitted to Roxbury church [pp. 48-54], after which she told of a voyage to England made by her husband at about the time the Civil War broke out there [pp. 55-56]. This was soon followed by another voyage to England, and "in a few years after he brought me over to England" [p. 56].

RICHARD BELLINGHAM

ORIGIN: Boston, Lincolnshire
MIGRATION: 1634
FIRST RESIDENCE: Boston
REMOVES: Rowley by 1643, Boston by 1653

OCCUPATION: Magistrate.
CHURCH MEMBERSHIP: On 3 August 1634, "Richard Bellingham and Elizabeth his wife" were admitted to Boston church [BChR 18]. On 25 February 1643[/4], "Our brother Mr. Richard Bellingham and our sister Penelope his wife, before called Penelope Pellham, (with like consent of the church) had letters of recommendation granted to the church at Rowley" [BChR 41].
FREEMAN: 25 May 1636 [MBCR 1:372].
EDUCATION: Brasenose College, Oxford, matriculated 1 December 1609, aged 17 (as son of William, of Bromby Woods, co. Lincoln, esquire); student at Lincoln's Inn [Foster 1:104].
OFFICES: Governor of Massachusetts Bay, 1641, 1654, 1665-72 [MA Civil List 16-17]. Deputy Governor, 1635, 1640, 1653, 1655-65 [MA Civil List 16]. Assistant, 1636-39, 1642-52 [MA Civil List 21-23]. Treasurer, 1637 [MBCR 1:195, 264]. Magistrate at Boston Court, 25 May 1636 [MBCR 1:175]. Commissioner of military affairs, 6 May 1635 [MBCR 1:146].

Boston selectman, 6 October 1634, 16 December 1639 - 20 February 1642/3 [BTR 1:2, 44, 55, 65, 70, 72]. Committee to determine divisions of Boston land, 18 December 1634 [BTR 1:3]. Committee to control use of wood for the poor, 23 March 1634/5 [BTR 1:4]. Hosted a meeting about the free school, 22 December 1670 [BTR 2:57].

Magistrate at Ipswich Court, 2 June 1641 [MBCR 1:328]. Essex magistrate, 27 June 1643, 20 February 1643/4, 9 July 1644, 8 July 1645, 24 June 1662 [EQC 1:52, 60, 61, 77, 2:385].

ESTATE: On 27 February 1634[/5], Richard Bellingham purchased "a messuage called Winesemet" and interest in a ferry from Samuel and Amias Maverick and John Blackleach and his wife [SLR 1:15]. On 12 August 1636, Mr. Richard Bellingham gave 40s. to the support of a free school master, being third on a list of the "richer inhabitants" of Boston tapped to fund the school [BTR 1:160].

On 6 September 1638, Richard Bellingham, Esq., was granted 700 acres of land by the General Court [MBCR 1:240]. On 9 March 1659[/60?], Richard Bellingham of Boston, Esq., and Penelope his wife, registered their ownership of seven hundred acres of land granted by the General Court on 6 September 1638 [ELR 2:17]. On 10 March 1659[/60?], Bray Wilkins of Lynn, husbandman, and John Gingion of Lynn, tailor, purchased from, and then mortgaged to, Richard Bellingham of Boston, Esq., seven hundred acres of land in Salem bounded by "a hill where an Indian plantation sometime had been"; if Wilkins or Gingion discovered minerals on the property and used them so that they made as much as £100 a year from them, they were to pay a portion to Bellingham [ELR 2:1-2].

On 27 January 1644/5, "the remaining part of the said marsh near John Lowe's house not formerly disposed of (except two rods broad next Thomas Marshall his garden pales) is granted unto Richard Bellingham, Esq., for the continuance of peace and love" [BTR 1:83].

In the 1645 Boston Book of Possessions, "Richard Bellingham, Esqr.," held three parcels: one house and quarter-acre lot, a garden plot, and a piece of marsh [BBOP 1].

On 26 February 1648/9, "Mr. Richard Bellingham" was given liberty to wharf in front of his property between Walter Merry and William Winbourne, "provided that it doth not prejudice the battery" [BTR 1:93].

On 16 February 1652[/3], Richard Bellingham of Boston, Esq., sold to John Hart of Boston, shipwright, half a small parcel of land at Merry's Point [SLR 1:281]. On 13 January 1656/7, Richard Bellingham of Boston, Esq., and "Penelope my wife" sold and mortgaged to James Everell of Boston a parcel of marsh in Boston; to this deed Penelope signed only her first name [SLR 2:338-39]. On 23 August 1657, Richard Bellingham of Boston, Esq., and Penelope "his wife" sold to John Viall of Boston, innkeeper, a quarter acre of land at Merry Point [SLR 3:42].

On 14 April 1662, John Pemberton of Wenisimett, planter, "son and heir to James Pemerton of Malden lately deceased," with the consent of Deborah his wife, mortgaged to Richard Bellingham of Boston, Esq., a parcel of woodland in Malden for the payment of rents due to

Bellingham on the farm at "Wenissimett," leaving the two ferry boats as "good as he found them" and the houses and fences the same [SLR 4:12-13].

On 26 September 1664, Richard Bellingham, Esq., was on a list of those to be paid for 33 rods and a quarter for a piece of field near the common to build a highway [BTR 2:23]. The town evidently paid him in kind, by laying out a fenced piece in town for him [BTR 2:27].

On 11 November 1672, Richard Bellingham of Boston, Esq., and Penelope his wife sold to Thomas Walker of Boston, brickmaker, a fenced parcel of eighteen rods in Boston [SLR 8:15]

On 16 February 1673[/4], James Penniman, aged forty-one, John Clough Jr., aged forty-seven, and Meneno Negro, aged about sixty, all deposed that Richard Bellingham had given a fifty-foot square of land to Angola, declaring Angola had been

> the only instrument that under God saved my life coming to me with his boat when I was sunk in the river between Boston & Winisimet several years since & laid hold of me & got me into the boat he came in & saved my life which kindness of him I remember [SLR 8:298]. (See also NEQ 72:119-29.)

In his will, dated 25 November 1672 and proved 19 December 1672, Richard Bellingham bequeathed to "my beloved wife" the rent of a farm, "my dwelling house, with the yard and field adjoining" for her life; to "my only son and his daughter during their natural lives" the farm Lt. John Smith is tenant in; to "the relief of four daughters of Col. William Goodrich" the rents of two farms, the proceeds of which also to be used to "pay my debts and other legacies"; after the death of wife, son and son's daughter, the farm his wife had during her life and the whole estate in Winnisimet to be "an annual encouragement to some godly minister ... faithful to those principles ... practiced in the first Church of Christ in Boston of which I am a member"; Mr. John Oxenbridge, Mr. James Allen, Mr. John Russell and Mr. Anthony Stoddard feofees in trust and executors; that a minister's house and meetinghouse be built at Winnisimet; lots for inhabitants be given out there; four or six young students be brought up for the ministry; a yearly allowance to "any godly congregational minister who shall be willing to settle in that place"; trustees to care for "my beloved wife"; annual support for a godly congregational minister "for his further support"; support for one sermon preached every quarter of the year "to instruct the people in Boston in church discipline" [NEHGR 14:237-38, citing a manuscript copy].

A postscript to the will states that Rev. Mr. James Allen said

The reason the Governor gave me (when he delivered his will to me written with his own hand which was in the year 1670 after his son died [by his last wife] Mr. John Bellingham whom he designed his heir) that his son Samuel had two hundred a year of his estate and fifteen hundred pounds a year befalled him (there being thirteen persons' lives between him and it, which were all deceased without heirs), & he will trust none to take up for him, and never come to take it, if I leave it him, besides he will give it away for a song, therefore I will dedicate it to God, and benefit of this country. He also told me he was persuaded he would not suffer his daughter to marry, so he should have no posterity of his own [NEHGR 14:239, citing manuscript].

Richard Wharton, attorney for Dr. Samuel Bellingham, son and heir of Richard Bellingham, suggested that Rev. James Allen had added a phrase to the end of Bellingham's will, and considerable legal conflict was the result. The will's executors and Wharton competed over leases and the widow's thirds, with the result that Wharton was denied portions of the estate he claimed for Samuel. Charles II, responding to a petition by Samuel Bellingham, suggested that the Massachusetts General Court reopen the matter, and the court accordingly, upon re-examination, declared the will null. James Allen brought the will back to court in 1705, claiming that the General Court had usurped the power of the County Court by ruling on the will in the first place, an argument that, with subsequent elaboration, kept the estate in the courts for more than a century [Chelsea Hist 1:393-634, citing numerous original documents].

The inventory of the estate of the "late Richard Bellingham Esqr., late governor of the Massachusetts Colony," taken 20 December 1672, totalled £3244 3s. 7d., of which £2864 was real estate: "the 4 farms at Winnisimmett," £1920; "a parcel of marsh in the occupation of [blank] Newbarry," £16; "a parcel of marsh in the occupation of [blank] Chamberlin," £48; "a pasture in Boston being about 2½ acres ... at the south end of the town butting upon Angola's house," £250; "the ground upon the hill behind Mr. Davenport's," £30; and "the dwellinghouse and ground belonging to it and shops before it," £600 [SPR 7:303-5].

BIRTH: About 1592, son of William Bellingham, Esq., of Bromby Woods, Lincolnshire (aged 17 on 1 December 1609 [Foster 1:104]; "in the 81st year of his age" on 7 December 1672 [NEHGR 7:206, citing Sewall's Almanacs]).
DEATH: 7 December 1672 ("Ricd. Bellingham, Esq. Govr. of the Mass. Col. and the last Patentee, d. in the 81st year of his age, 7th 10mo [i.e.,

December] 1672" [NEHGR 7:206, citing Sewall's Almanacs]).

MARRIAGE: (1) By 1622 Elizabeth Backhouse, daughter of Samuel and Elizabeth (Borlace) Backhouse of London [NEHGR 36:382, 385-86, citing Close Rolls of Charles I]. She died by 1641.

(2) 9 November 1641 Penelope Pelham, sister of HERBERT PELHAM and *WILLIAM PELHAM*, in a controversial marriage:

> The young gentlewoman was ready to be contracted to a friend of his, who lodged in his house, and by his consent had proceeded so far with her, when on the sudden the governor treated with her, and obtained her for himself. He excused it by the strengh of his affection, and that she was not absolutely promised to the other gentleman. Two errors more he committed upon it. 1. That he would not have his contract published where he dwelt, contrary to an order of court. 2. That he married himself contrary to the constant practice of the country [WJ 2:43].

When called to court on this matter, Bellingham refused to step down off the bench, and the court thinking it unfit that he sit in judgment on himself, let the matter rest [WJ 2:43].

Penelope died at Boston 29 May 1702 ("At 5. p.m. Madam Bellingham dies, a virtuous gentlewoman, *antiquis moribus, prisca fide*, who has lived a widow just about 30 years" [Sewall 1:468]).

CHILDREN:

With first wife

   i   SAMUEL, b. say 1622; Harvard College 1642 [Sibley 1:63-64]; called "Doctor" in New England records [SCC 1:271], possibly University of Leiden, M.D. [Sibley 1:63; Morison 143]; m. (1) by 1650 Lucy _____ (deed dated 23 July 1650 by Samuel Bellingham of Boston, gent., and wife Lucy [EQC 2:399]; a published pedigree of unknown reliability says she was "Lucia, daughter of John Goldesborough" [A.R. Maddison, *Lincolnshire Pedigrees*, Volume I, Harleian Society Volume L (London 1902), p. 118, citing "Harl. MS. 1550"]); m. (2) St James Dukes Place, London, 18 April 1695 Elizabeth (Smith) Savage [NEHGR 36:383; Chelsea Hist 1:496-97, 502-8].

  ii   Child, bur. Boston, Lincolnshire, 27 March 1628, as "the child of Mr. Richard Bellengham recorder" [Boston PR 2:137].

  iii   Child, bur. Boston, Lincolnshire, 7 April 1629, as "the child of Mr. Richard Bellengham recorder" [Boston PR 2:143].

With second wife

    iv   HANNAH, bp. Boston 14 August 1642 [BChR 290]; d. soon.

    v   JOHN, b. say 1644; Harvard College 1661 [Sibley 2:73-74]; d. in 1670 (apparently unmarried) [NEHGR 14:239].

    vi   JAMES, bp. Boston 10 May 1646 "being about 7 days old" [BChR 302]; d. soon.

    vii   SARAH, bp. Boston 30 July 1648 [BChR 312]; d. soon (on 14 August 1648 John Winthrop Sr. wrote to John Winthrop Jr. that "Mrs. Bellingham was delivered of a daughter, which dyed lately" [WP 5:246]).

    viii   ELIZABETH, bp. Boston 9 January 1649[/50] [BChR 318]; d. soon.

    ix   ANN, bp. Boston 26 July 1652 [BChR 323]; d. soon.

    x   GRACE, bp. Boston 13 August 1654 [BChR 328]; d. Boston 3 September 1654 [BVR 47].

ASSOCIATIONS: Richard was brother of William Bellingham, who had arrived in New England by 1640 (freeman, 12 October 1640 [MBCR 1:378]) and who died in Rowley by 24 September 1650 [EQC 2:361]. William called Mr. Thomas Nelson "my loving friend" in his will. Samson Eaton, "kin to Mr. William Bellingham," came over too late to receive the great portion he expected from William's estate, about which estate Richard Bellingham told Richard Longhorne, "my brother gave it to my son Samuel" [EQC 2:362].

William Hibbins married 4 March 1632[/3] Hester Bellingham at Boston, Lincolnshire, where Richard had been recorder [Boston PR 2:163]. It is through this connection that Richard Bellingham was "brother of Mrs. Ann Hibbins, who was executed for witchcraft in June, 1656," Ann being William Hibbins's second wife [NEHGR 14:237, 48:74].

In an undated letter (presumably 1668), directed to "Mr. Bellingam," the writer mentions "your brother Goothwicke['s] daughters I hope they are godly gentlewomen" [NEHGR 7:274]. This refers to the daughters of Col. William Goodrick of Kelby, York, who were favored with support in Bellingham's will [NEHGR 36:383].

COMMENTS: "Mr. Richard Bellengham" served as recorder of Boston, Lincolnshire, in the 1620s [Boston PR 2:137, 143, 163].

In a letter dated Salem 25 October 1638, Hugh Peter gossiped that "Mr. Bellingham is very very greedy for more money" [WP 4:71].

On 16 April 1639, Thomas Wells wrote that "My dear friend Mr. Bellingham sent me word that he paid for his [servant's] passage by water, the which I shall thankfully repay at his coming to Connecticut, which he hath appointed before his return to the Bay" [WP 4:116].

Winthrop remembers a curt and unsatisfactory episode in court where "the treasurer" [Bellingham] snapped at "the governor" [Winthrop] for interupting his examination,

> the defendant having answered upon oath to certain interrogatories ... and the treasurer pressing him again with the same interrogatory, the governor said, he had answered the same directly before. The treasurer thereupon said, (angrily), "Sir, I speak not to you." The governor replied, that time was very precious, and, seeing the thing was already answered, it was fit to proceed. Thereupon the treasurer stood up, and said, if he might not have liberty to speak, he would no longer sit there [WJ 1:320].

The clash of the two egos occurred repeatedly. In 1641 Winthrop states "There had been much laboring to have Mr. Bellingham chosen [governor]" [WJ 2:35]. He shared in the general condemnation of Bellingham for his irregular second marriage [WJ 2:43] and illustrated how Bellingham held a grudge even though "the governor offered himself ready to it [reconciliation], but the other was not forward" [WJ 2:116]. Winthrop mentioned how "Mr. Bellingham and Mr. Saltonstall" were the only two magistrates unable to agree with the majority, time and again [WJ 2:186, 209, 292].

On 28 February 1652/3, Mr. Richard Bellingham "engageth to secure the town from all damage by receiving of him for one whole year" [BTR 1:113].

On 25 March 1662, Richard Bellingham, Esq., sued twelve different people for trespass, but withdrew most of the suits when his case against Samuel Platts was found for Platts and he had to appeal to the Court of Assistants [EQC 2:367].

On 24 June 1662, Richard Bellingham tried to recover his brother William's lands and sued Thomas Wood and James Bayly [EQC 2:395-401]. Mr. Joseph Jewitt had taken the opportunity "when Richard was very sick, to buy this estate in Rowley, of Richard's son Samuell, for an inconsiderable sum, expecting said Richard would die. This was done suddenly upon said Samuell's departure for England" [EQC 2:397]. Richard further stated that Joseph Jewett

> got possession of the farm, but not without some just blemish in meddling betwixt father & son, he well knowing how businesses was betwixt them as most in Rowley did at that time, yet

persuading my son Samuel to sell his father's estate & though Joseph Jewet knew his title was weak & little worth [EQC 2:401].

In his business dealings he was not above taking advantage of his position as governor to benefit himself [EQC 3:322]. Savage had no kind words to say about Bellingham, labelling the terms of Winthrop's successors an "unbroken reign of dismal bigotry" and calling Dudley, Endicot and Bellingham, "hard, harder, hardest" [Savage 1:161]. Hubbard remembered him as "a notable hater of bribes" and Eliot called him "a very learned man, compared with his contemporaries in New England" [WJ 1:173].

BIBLIOGRAPHIC NOTE: In 1882 Charles Hervey Townshend published a treatment of Bellingham's English ancestry [NEHGR 36:381-86].

JOHN BELLOWS

ORIGIN: Unknown
MIGRATION: 1635 on the *Hopewell*
FIRST RESIDENCE: Concord
REMOVES: Marlborough 1663, Concord 1676, Marlborough by 1683

OCCUPATION: Perhaps carpenter, as his inventory included a large number of woodworking tools.
EDUCATION: Signed his will.
ESTATE: In his will, dated 19 June 1683 and proved 2 October 1683, "John Bellows Senior of Marlborough," weak in body, bequeathed to "Mary my loving wife" cattle, including one cow "that I had of Mrs. Mary Rowlandson" and household kettles; "my lands in Marlborough" and other moveable goods to be "disposed of unto my children, namely Isaac, John, Thomas, Eleazar, Nathaneel, Mary and Abigail, when they shall be of the age of one and twenty years, or married"; to "my son Isaac" a double portion and residue "beside what I have given unto his mother"; "I have already bequeathed unto my daughter Abigail Lawrence" her portion in cattle and other items; "Mary my loving wife whole executrix," and maintenance from "my estate for so long as she shall remain my widow"; "loving friends Joseph Rice and Joseph Newton" overseers [MPR Case #1518].

The inventory of the estate of "John Bellows deceased, late of Marlborough," taken the 6th and the 8th of August and exhibited 2 October 1683, totalled £136 18s. 6d., of which £60 was real estate: "The home lot with all the outlands, both uplands & meadows, & cedar swamp pertaining to the home lot, together with the dwelling house & orchard thereon." Along with a large number of wood-working tools, he had also owned "one back sword & two barrels of guns, a sword, the barrels and one hammer" valued at £1 1s. [MPR Case #1518].

BIRTH: About 1624 (aged 12 in 1635 [Hotten 49]; deposed 1669 "aged about 44 years" [MCR Folio #51 & #53]).
DEATH: Marlborough 10 January 1683 [sic]. (This may be intended for 10 July, which would be consistent with the probate records.)
MARRIAGE: Concord 9 May 1655 Mary Wood [CoVR 8], daughter of John Wood (in his will of 26 November 1677, "John Woods Senior of Marlborough" made a bequest to "my son-in-law John Bellows" [MPR 6:82, Case #25456]. She died at Marlborough on 16 September 1707.
CHILDREN:

    i   MARY, b. Concord 26 April 1657 [CoVR 8]; named in father's will, 19 June 1683, unmarried [see COMMENTS below].
    ii   SAMUEL, b. Concord 22 January 1657[/8] [CoVR 8]; d. Marlborough 29 September 1680 (apparently unmarried).
    iii   ABIGAIL, b. Concord 6 May 1661 [CoVR 10]; m. Cambridge 19 April 1682 Isaac Lawrence.
    iv   ISAAC, b. Marlborough 13 September 1663; m. by 1694 Elizabeth Howe (eldest child b. Marlborough 17 March 1694/5; on 26 March 1725, in response to a court order to "John How sole executor of the last will of Isaac How late of Marlbrough," "appeared Isa[ac] Bellows [and] Moses Newton, 2 sisters husbands ..." [MPR Case #12039]).
    v   JOHN, b. Marlborough 13 May 1666; m. by 1695 Hannah Newton, daughter of Moses Newton (eldest child b. Marlborough 12 May 1695; 3 April 1724 will of Moses Newton includes bequests to "son-in-law John Bellows," 5s., and to "the children of my daughters Hannah Bellows & Mercy Leonard deceased, to each of them one shilling" [WPR 1:196-98]).
    vi   THOMAS, b. Marlborough 7 September (or November) 1668; named in father's will, 19 June 1683; no further record.

    vii   ELEAZER, b. Marlborough 13 April 1671; m. Marlborough 11
            October 1692 Esther Barrett.

    viii   DANIEL, b. Marlborough 15 March 1672/3; d. Concord 20 July
            1676 [CoVR 19].

    ix   NATHANIEL, b. Concord 3 April 1676 [CoVR 19]; named in
            father's will, 19 June 1683; no further record.

COMMENTS: On 6 April 1635, "Jo[hn] Bellowes," aged 12, was enrolled at London as a passenger for New England on the *Hopewell* [Hotten 49].

No record of John Bellows appears between 1635, when he was a passenger to New England, and 1655, when he married in Concord. (Savage says that Bellows was of "Concord 1645" [Savage 1:162], but the record supporting this statement has not been found.) However, some of the other young passengers on the *Hopewell* (Alexander Thwaites, John Abbott and (probably) Mary Abbott, and (possibly) John Jones) settled in Concord, and so we assume that John Bellows also settled first in Concord, perhaps as a servant.

The last child of John Bellows was born in Concord early in 1676, and son Daniel died there a few months later, indicating that this family retreated to Concord after the raid on Marlborough early in King Philip's War.

John Bellows in his will listed all his living children, and divided his estate among them at marriage or age twenty-one, but Mary and Abigail were already twenty-one, and Abigail was already married, and had received her portion. His inclusion of Abigail in this list must have been an oversight. Mary was apparently still unmarried at the time of writing of the will.

The 1898 Bellows genealogy gives John Bellows a tenth child, Benjamin, born at Concord 18 January 1676/7, and tells us that this Benjamin was father of Col. Benjamin Bellows, the founder of Walpole, New Hampshire [Bellows Gen 4], but no son Benjamin is named in the will of John Bellows. The full entry for this birth reads "Benjamin Bellowes the son of Mary Bellowes born January the 18th day 1676[/7]" [CoVR 20]. The eldest child of John Bellows was Mary, born in 1657, and this record should be interpreted as the birth of an illegitimate son of Mary, making this Benjamin grandson and not son of the immigrant.

We do not learn who the father of Benjamin was, but five years later Mary was summoned to court, apparently for fornication. On 29 September 1682, Jonathan Johnson, Marlborough constable, informed the court that "I have warned Isaac Woods to appear the next Tuesday at

Cambridge according to the warrant and I went to Goodman Bellowses house to warn Mary Bellows; her father not being at home, her mother told me that she was not at home and she could not tell where she was and that she had been gone from home a week and more and that she thought that Goodman Fox and Isaac Bellows had concealed her away; also I have warned John Mainard and James Woods for to appear for witnesses in the case" [MCF Folio #99]. On 3 October 1682, "Mary Bellows being warned to the court & legally called, made no appearance & an attachment for her appearance at next court is ordered to be sent out against her" [MCR 4:50]. No further records of this case have been found.

BIBLIOGRAPHICAL NOTE: In 1898 Thomas Bellows Peck compiled *The Bellows Genealogy or John Bellows The Boy Emigrant of 1635 and his Descendants, Comprising a Full History of Col. Benjamin Bellows, the Founder of Walpole, N.H., and His Descendants, and a Partial Account of the Families of Isaac, John and Eleazer Bellows of Marlborough, Mass., and of Nathaniel Bellows of Groton Ct.* [Keene, New Hampshire, 1898].

EDWARD BENNETT

ORIGIN: Unknown
MIGRATION: 1635
FIRST RESIDENCE: Weymouth
REMOVES: Rehoboth 1643

CHURCH MEMBERSHIP: Admission to Weymouth church prior to 25 May 1636 implied by freemanship.
FREEMAN: 25 May 1636 [MBCR 1:372]. Propounded as Plymouth Colony freeman, 4 June 1645 [PCR 1:84].
ESTATE: In the Weymouth land inventory, compiled about 1643, Edward Bennett held seven parcels: "five acres in Kingokehill first given to himself"; "twenty and two acres in the westerneck 14 of them given him by the town and eight of them first given to Aingell Hollard"; "five acres in the East Field 2 acres first given him by Town and 3 acres first given to Thomas White"; "six acres at hockley first given to himself"; "one acre of salt marsh at the back river first given to himself"; "one acre and a quarter of salt marsh at hocklie"; and "one acre of fresh marsh" [Weymouth Hist 1:195-96].

BIRTH: By 1615 based on date of freemanship.
DEATH: After 4 June 1645 [PCR 1:84].
MARRIAGE: None recorded.
CHILDREN: None recorded.

COMMENTS: Savage suggests that this man "perhaps was that Edward of Providence 1676, who resided there through Philip's war." However, on 29 November 1686 Edward Bennett of Providence sold to Stephen Arnold of Pawtuxet "a tract of upland: it arising to my father Samuell Bennett, deceased, who was one of the number of the purchasers" [PrTR 14:152-54].

James S. Elston has suggested that the Priscilla Bennett who married at Rehoboth on 5 October 1651 William Carpenter was daughter of Edward [James S. Elston, *Descent from Seventy-Nine (Now Ninety-Two) Early Immigrant Heads of Families*, 2 vols. (Burlington, Vermont, and Middleboro, Massachusetts, 1962-71), 1:16; TAG 70:204], but no evidence is seen for this relation, and she may just as well have been a sister or totally unrelated.

Edward Bennett of Weymouth and Rehoboth is not seen in the records after 1645.

Pope says that Bennett "[r]eceived arms from Mr. Pynchon in 1636 [Pope 45]," but this record has not been found.

RICHARD BENNETT

On 8 February 1635/6, the town of Salem ordered that "Richard Bennet may have a 2 acre lot" [STR 1:12].

COMMENTS: No other record has been found for this man in New England.

Pope and others say that this is the same Richard Bennett who appeared in 1641 in Boston [BTR 1:58]. Given the gap of six years without any records, and the lack of any evidence connecting the Salem and Boston men, we do not make that identification.

SAMUEL BENNETT

ORIGIN: Unknown
MIGRATION: 1635 on the *James*
FIRST RESIDENCE: Lynn
REMOVES: Boston by 1650

OCCUPATION: Carpenter [EQC 1:115; SLR 1:294]. On 23 November 1682, John Paul deposed "that he lived with Mr. Samuell Bennitt upwards of thirty years ago in his house for the term of six years, being most of that time on the farm with him. Bennitt improved it by planting, fencing, plowing and selling timber and wood and carrying coals to the iron works, etc." [EQC 8:403]. In November 1682, Oliver Purchase deposed that he worked as a clerk at the old ironworks at Lynn and "contracted with old Mr. Samuell Bennett of Boston, now surviving, who dwelt upon that farm now called Mr. Green's or Hutchins's farm for thousands of cords of wood and timber" [EQC 8:404].
EDUCATION: He signed his deeds.
OFFICES: Arbiter, November 1652 [EQC 1:273]. Surveyor of highways for Rumney Marsh (Boston), 9 March 1656/7 [BTR 1:134]. One of three men to "go the bound line between Malden and Rumney Marsh, and Lin and Rumney Marsh," 24 April 1657 [BTR 1:136]. Acting "in behalf of Boston selectmen," June 1673 [EQC 5:193].

Admitted to Ancient and Honorable Artillery Company in 1639 [HAHAC 1:85-86].
ESTATE: In the 1638 distribution of land in Lynn, "Samuell Bennitt" received 20 acres [EQC 2:270].

On 16 September 1643, John Elderkin sold to Samuel Bennett "the new built watermill in Linn" [SLR 1:53; ELR 1:3]. On 25 March 1644, Samuel Bennett of Lynn, carpenter, sold to Nicholas Potter of Lynn, bricklayer, sixty acres in Lynn [ELR 1:25]. On 22 May 1645, Samuel Bennet of Lynn mortgaged his purchase of a windmill from the trustees of the children of Mr. Jose Glover, late of Sutton, Sussex [SLR 1:66, 77]. (This may be the "mill of Samuel Bennett" from which William Ivory stole corn in 1649 [EQC 1:174].)

On 1 October 1649, Valentine Hill and John Leveret of Boston sold to Samuel Bennet of Lynn a six hundred acre farm bordered by Boston, Lynn and Charlestown [SLR 1:110]. On 29 November 1649, Valentine Hill of Boston sold to Samuel Bennet of Lynn "Walker's plain" [SLR 1:110].

On 26 October 1649, Thomas Erington of Lynn sold a thirty-five acre farm in Charlestown to Samuel Bennet of Lynn [SLR 1:110]. On 15 March 1649[/50?], William Hooke of Salisbury sold to "Samuel Benet of Lin ... all that upland which was given to him by an arbitration betwixt Tho[mas] Dexter & him or his father Humfrey Hook" [SLR 1:117]. On 20 May 1650, Samuel Bennett, carpenter, sold to Robert Mansfield four acres of salt marsh in Lynn [ELR 1:7].

On 25 March 1653, Mr. John Coggan of Boston, merchant, and Martha his wife sold to "Samuell Bennit of Linne ... carpenter" one dwelling house and land "the said John Coggan sometime since purchased of Mr. John Cockshall then of Boston aforesaid, merchant, lying upon the outside of the lands belonging to the Township of Boston which were granted unto the said John Cogshall about the year one thousand six hundred thirty and seven as by the town book will appear" [SLR 1:294]. On 1 April 1653, Samuel Bennett of Lynn, carpenter, sold to Thomas Wheeler of Lynn, miller, a watermill in Lynn, the lands belonging to it, and two dwelling houses with eleven acres and five acres of marsh [ELR 1:21].

On 3 December 1656, Samuel Bennet of Lynn and his wife Sarah sold to George Wallis, gent., "now resident in New England," a farm house at Rumney Marsh called "Rumly Hall" [SLR 2:310]; on 2 April 1657 this sale was nullified [SLR 3:14].

On 10 November 1657, Samuel Bennet of Boston, yeoman, sold to John Otway of Boston, husbandman, a small parcel partly in Boston and partly in Lynn [SLR 3:161]. On 20 December 1658, Samuel and Sarah Bennet of Boston, in consideration of debts owed to William Franklin "in the time of his life" and now due to Phebe Franklin of Boston, widow of William Franklin, deceased, sold to her their farmhouse and three hundred acres of land, on the border of Malden [SLR 3:290]; this land was turned over to Phebe Franklin "and her daughter."

On 14 May 1660, Hope and Rachel Allen of Boston mortgaged to Samuel Bennet "inhabiting within the bounds of the said Boston" their dwelling house "newly erected with the workhouse garden and grass plot enclosed" in Boston [SLR 3:369], and Samuel Bennett deeded it back to them on 3 May 1666 [SLR 5:40].

In early December 1665, John Gifford and Samuel Maverick both deposed that Samuel Bennett had pledged that if his son, Samuel Bennett Jr., married the daughter of Capt. William Hargrave of Horsley Downe near London, the elder Samuel would settle on his son the "house he now lives in with barns, stables and all other outhouses, orchards, gardens, and all the upland and meadow fenced in ... with several acres of woodland and 80 pounds of stock" if Samuel Jr. paid his father £20 a year during his natural life "if he needed it" [SLR 4:328]. On 16 October 1666, Samuel Bennett of Boston, gentleman, made it official by drawing up a formal deed to that effect, entailing the property to the male heirs of Samuel Jr.'s body lawfully begotten, or failing them to "his wife Sarah Bennet Daughter unto Capt. William Hargrave of London" for her natural life. If Samuel Jr. died without male heirs, then after the death of his wife Sarah Bennett, the premises were to return to Samuel Bennett Sr. and his male heirs, "vizt: John Bennet & Elisha Bennett and their male heirs" [SLR 7:76-77].

On 10 December 1665, Samuel and Sarah Bennett of Lynn sold to William Browne of Salem, merchant, half the land against Mill Creek on which a new warehouse stood and a fourth part of the drawbridge [SLR 5:37-38]. On 1 May 1666, Samuel Bennett of Lynn and Sarah his wife sold to Capt. George Corwin of Salem, merchant, half the land against the Mill Creek and the fourth part of the drawbridge [SLR 5:41].

On 12 March 1669/70, "Samuell Benett of Rumney Marsh" sold to William Bartholomew one farm house and out houses, with all his farm, also "the moiety or one-half part of a meadow called or known by the name Squire's Meadow lying & being within the bounds & limits of Molden," also "a parcel of salt marsh lying & being in Rumley Marsh formerly purchased of Captain Robert Bridges called by the name of the fourteen-acre lot" [EQC 8:396-404, at 398-400].

On 20 May 1670, Richard Blood of Groton sold to Samuel Bennett of Boston, gentleman, ten acres of meadow and pasture in Lynn [EQC 8:64]. On 27 February 1671, Samuel Bennett of Rumney Marsh, Boston, house carpenter, and Sarah Bennett his wife sold to Benjamin Muzzey and Hudson Leverett of Boston ten acres of meadow and pasture in Lynn [EQC 8:196]. On 6 May 1672, Samuel Bennet of Rumney Marsh, yeoman, sold to Benjamin Muzzey of Rumney Marsh, a parcel in the further pasture; Samuel's wife Sarah released her thirds in the land [SLR 9:420]. On 16 July 1672, Samuel Bennet of Rumney Marsh sold a parcel at "Written Trees" to Benjamin Muzzey of Rumney Marsh [SLR 9:422].

On 1 March 1672[/3?], Samuel Bennett of Boston, carpenter, sold to Joseph Jenckes Jr. of Lynn, smith, twenty acres of land in Lynn [ELR 4:18-19].

On 25 August 1674, Samuel Bennet of Rumney Marsh, Boston, gentleman, sold to "my son John Bennet" a two-hundred acre parcel of land in Boston on the Malden line, in return for an annual payment of £6 10s. "to be paid if living in New England" [SLR 9:225].

BIRTH: About 1610 (aged 24 in 1635 [Hotten 107]; deposed "aged about forty-eight years" 29 October 1653 [EQC 2:92]).

DEATH: After 18 January 1682/3 (when Sarah was called "wife to Samuel Bennit"). Perhaps the Samuel Bennett who died at Lynn 28 March 1691.

MARRIAGE: By 3 December 1656 (and by about 1640 if she was the mother of all his children) Sarah _____ [SLR 2:310]. She died at Boston 18 January 1682/3 (buried at Copp's Hill as "Sarah Bennit, wife to Samuel Bennit, aged 75 years" [Copp's Hill 195]). She was a niece of BONIFACE BURTON, as seen in his will; he left her 1s., her husband 4d., and "everyone of his children" 4d. [SPR 6:35].

CHILDREN:

    i   SAMUEL, b. by about 1640; m. by 1665 Sarah Hargrave, daughter of Capt. William Hargrave of Horsleydown, in Bermondsey, Surrey [SLR 4:328, 7:76-77].

    ii   JOHN, b. about 1645 (aged "about thirty-seven years" in November 1682 [EQC 8:403]); m. by 1677 Aphra (_____) Adams, widow of _____ Adams (eldest known child b. Boston 13 June 1677 [BVR 140]; on 1 April 1678, "John Bennett of Boston ... mariner ... in consideration of his duty and fatherly affection towards his now wife Aphra Bennett and their two children John Addams & Sarah Bennet" made a deed of gift to the two children of "his half part of a farm ... in joint possession of the said John Bennett and Mr. Elisha Bennett mariner and also brother to the said John Bennett" [SLR 12:177-79; see also SLR 13:314-15]). "Aphra Bennet" deposed "aged about thirty-five years" on 29 December 1676 [SCC 761].

    iii   (probably) Daughter, b. say 1650; m. by 1670 Joseph Holloway. (On 18 July 1670, "Joseph Holloway, aged about thirty-five years, testified that he was at his father Bennett's house the day that Post was sick" and that Joseph Armitage "stumbled and fell upon my mother and a skillet that was before the fire" [EQC 4:304]. This might mean that Joseph Holloway had married a daughter of Samuel Bennet, or that Bennett's wife was mother by an earlier husband of Holloway or of Holloway's wife. In 1673 the Lynn presentment included "Joseph Holloway, for saying that he recorded his marriage and had not, whereby we vehemently suspect that he committed fornication before marriage" [EQC 5:222, 259]. Whether this was the same Joseph Holloway, and, if so, whether this was the same wife, is not evident. On 27 March 1677, "Joseph Holoua, aged thirty years," testified about events at Lynn [EQC 6:258], indicating that there may have been two men of the name in that town.)

   iv   ELISHA, b. before 1658 [EQC 2:223; SLR 7:77-78]; m. by 1690 Dorothy _____ (eldest known child of "Elisha & Dorothy Bennett" b. Boston 4 April 1690).

   iv   (possibly) LYDIA, d. Lynn 2 September 1661.

ASSOCIATIONS: On 18 July 1670, Joseph Holloway, aged about 35, deposed he was "at his father Bennett's house" [EQC 4:304].

COMMENTS: On 13 July 1635, "Samuel Bennet," aged 24, was enrolled at London for passage to New England in the *James* [Hotten 107].

In July 1645 Samuel Bennett was presented for "saying scornfully that he cared neither for the town nor its order" [EQC 1:82]. (This item is incorrectly identified as a Marblehead presentment, but the two "witnesses" were Allen Bread and John Fuller, both Lynn residents.) On 4 August 1646, Samuel Bennett was admonished for sleeping in church [EQC 1:101]. On 6 July 1647, Samuel Bennett of Lynn was sued by John Gillo for not setting up the frame of a house and for not fulfilling a covenant about a ten-acre lot [EQC 1:115].

In February 1650/1, Samuel Bennett was ordered to repair his defective highway in the lane by Anthony Newell's house [EQC 1:208].

Evidently Samuel Bennett had his son Elisha living with Robert Barges, for Barges sued Bennett at court June 1660 "for about two years' diet for his son Elisha" [EQC 2:223].

When in 1653 the Hammersmith (Lynn) and Braintree iron works were found insolvent, the accounts produced evidence of Samuel Bennett's work, including "carting 64 loads," "wood granted by Samuell Benit ... [and] the frame at Samuell Benit's land bought of Mr. Knolls" [EQC 1:292-93]. In a letter dated 28 September 1652, the ironworks investors discussed poor management by Mr. J. Gifford, complaining, among other things, that "he built [a house] for the Scots cost £35 and he built it upon Samuell Bennet's ground which was very unadvisedly done" [EQC 2:89]. Further, "the measure of coal is neglected and must be looked after. Samuel Bennit ought not to have any carriage for the company unless he is complying to the commissioners he having had above £100 this last year, which makes him so stout and insolent with the company" [EQC 2:90]. The question of whether Samuel Bennett owed the company money was put to arbitrators in 1657 [EQC 2:127], but the case was withdrawn in June 1659 [EQC 2:159]. Bennett was still suing the company for his payment as late as 1671 [EQC 4:339].

On 24 November 1663, Benjamin Muzzey and John Fuller deposed that they heard Henry Greenland say that Samuel Bennett was "the veriest rascal in New England and that he would not take his word for a groat" [EQC 3:106]. On 21 July 1674, Samuel Mower deposed that "at the latter end of November, 1673, he saw Mr. Sam[ue]ll Bennitt with another on the road near John Moors at Lynn, & Mr. Bennitt fell down, & the other man called me to help him up and I went, & asked the other man what Mr. Bennit ailed & he laughed, but said nothing but we helped him up: & I led him a little way up the hill, & he could not speak, or did not speak rationally, but faltered: & when I let him go he fell down turning round he had a very high color I judged he had drunk too much" [EQC 5:379]. In January 1676/7, Isaac Waldron sued Thomas Marshall over cattle that passed through the hands of Samuel Bennett. Waldron swore that "Mr. Sam[ue]l Bennet would sell anything for a pint of liquor, and that I suppose most of his chapmen that use to deal with him, knows it to be true, if they do not, his poor wife, and children do" [SCC 763]. This calumny had a serious repercussion when, on 30 January 1676/7, Samuel Bennet was convicted of "denying by writing or acknowledgment under his hand what he had formerly given his oath unto & not being careful of what he swears unto" and barred forever from giving testimony in any case whatever [SCC 786].

BIBLIOGRAPHIC NOTE: In 1908 Mellen Chamberlain published a lengthy acccount of "The Farm of Samuel Bennett," following well into the eighteenth century the conveyances which subdivided Bennett's extensive landholdings in Rumney Marsh [Chelsea Hist 1:267-92].

MARY BENTLEY

On 18 July 1635 "Mary Bentley," aged 20, was enrolled at London as a passenger for New England on the *Defence* [Hotten 107].

COMMENTS: There is no evidence that Mary Bentley arrived in New England.

WILLIAM BENTLEY

On 19 September 1635, "William Bentley," aged 47, was enrolled at London as a passenger for New England on the *Truelove*. On the same ship were "Alice Bentley," aged 15, and "Jo[hn] Bentley," aged 17 [Hotten 131-32].

COMMENTS: This family does not appear in New England records. Savage thought he resided at Boston, but this is probably a confusion with *WILLIAM BEAMSLEY*, whose record of freemanship calls him "Will: Benseley" [GMB 1:139, citing MBCR 1:372].

MUSACHIELL BERNARD

ORIGIN: Batcombe, Somerset
MIGRATION: 1635
FIRST RESIDENCE: Weymouth
RETURN TRIPS: Probably returned to England soon after 1643.

OCCUPATION: Clothier (in England) [Hotten 283].
ESTATE: In the Weymouth land inventory of about 1643, "Masachel Barnard" held three parcels: "six acres in the plain first given to Richard Longe"; "three acres in the plain first given to Thomas Baylie"; and "eight acres in the Mill Field first given to himself" [Weymouth Hist 1:194]. By the date of this inventory he had passed to John Burge "two acres in Harrises Range first granted to Mesechill Barnard," to Richard Webb "in Harrises Range 3 acres ... first given to Masachiell Barnard," to John Staple "in the plain three acres ... first given to Mr. Barnard" and to Andrew Ford "seven acres of land in the East Field first given to Masachill Barnard" [Weymouth Hist 1:185, 188, 191, 194; see also NEHGR 119:8-9].
"Mr. Barnard" was in a 2 February 1651/2 list of "great lots named in the old town book and formerly granted to be laid out on the east side of Fresh Pond" [Weymouth Hist 1:199]. (As this refers to an earlier grant, and as others in this list were known to have left Weymouth prior to the

date of the list, Musachiell Bernard need not have been in Weymouth at this date.)

BIRTH: Baptized Worksop, Nottinghamshire, 27 September 1607, son of Rev. Richard Bernard [NEHGR 113:191]. (Musachiell Bernard's stated age at immigration suggests that he was born about 1611. There is a gap in 1611 in the list of children recorded to Rev. Richard Bernard at Worksop [NEHGR 113:191-92], but examination of the published register shows that the records were apparently complete for this and surrounding years, and there is no hint that Bernard had any children between 1609 and 1613 [George W. Marshall, ed., *The Registers of Worksop, co. Nottingham, 1558-1771* (Guildford 1894)]. This is probably an instance in which the passenger list is in error.)
DEATH: Living 1666 (on 14 November 1666 William Harris of Providence, writing to London, stated in his letter that he was leaving it with "Mr. Barnard, who, as you know, is Mr. William's wife's brother" [NEHGR 113:190, citing RIHSC 8:68]).
MARRIAGE: By about 1632 Mary _____, born about 1607 (aged 28 years in 1635 [Hotten 283]).
CHILDREN:

  i   JOHN, b. about 1632 (aged 3 in 1635 [Hotten 283]); no further record.
  ii   NATHANIEL, b. about 1634 (aged 1 in 1635 [Hotten 283]); no further record.
  iii MARY, b. Weymouth 27 September 1637 [NEHGR 8:348]; no further record.
  iv   SARAH, b. Weymouth 5 April 1639 [NEHGR 8:348]; no further record.

ASSOCIATIONS: Musachiell Bernard and his sister Mary Barnard, wife of *ROGER WILLIAMS* of Providence, were children of Rev. Richard Bernard of Batcombe, Somerset [NEHGR 113:191-92]. Richard Bernard was significant in New England history beyond this genealogical contribution, as several of his communicants at Batcombe joined Rev. Joseph Hull in the migration to New England in 1635 [Hotten 283-86]. In addition, Bernard, as a convinced non-separating Puritan, engaged in a pamphlet war with Rev. *JOHN COTTON* over the issue of the church government.

COMMENTS: On 20 March 1635, "Musachiell Bernard of Batcombe, clothier, in the County of Somersett," aged 24, with "Mary Bernard his wife," aged 28 years, "John Bernard his son," aged 3 years, and "Nathaniell his son," aged 1 year, enrolled at Weymouth for passage to New England on an unnamed vessel [Hotten 283]. On the same vessel, "Rich[ard] Persons salter," aged 30, may or may not have been Musachiell's servant [Hotten 283].

In his article describing the Barnard families of Epworth, Lincolnshire, Moriarty gives the date of Musachiell's brother Benjamin's baptism and burial first as 1615, and then as 1613 [NEHGR 113:191-92]; examination of the published Worksop register shows that 1613 is the correct year [George W. Marshall, ed., *The Registers of Worksop, co. Nottingham, 1558-1771* (Guildford 1894)].

BIBLIOGRAPHIC NOTE: In 1959 George Andrews Moriarty published an article "Bernard of Epworth, co. Lincoln," collecting information on John of Epworth, his son Rev. Richard of Worksop, Nottinghamshire, and Batcombe, Somerset, and the latter's two children who came to New England [NEHGR 113:189-92]. Rev. Richard Bernard, a prominent Puritan controversialist, is treated in DNB.

THOMAS BESBEECH

ORIGIN: Ashford, Kent
MIGRATION: 1635 on the *Hercules*
FIRST RESIDENCE: Cambridge
REMOVES: Scituate 1637, Duxbury 1639, Sudbury by 1647, Marshfield by 1658, Sudbury by 1672

CHURCH MEMBERSHIP: "Goodman Besbitch" joined Scituate church on 30 April 1637 [NEHGR 9:280]. "Brother Besbetch" was invested as deacon at Scituate on 22 February 1637/8 [NEHGR 10:37].
FREEMAN: On 2 January 1637/8, "Mr. Thomas Besbidge" was admitted a freeman of Plymouth Colony (and therefore added to the end of the Plymouth list of freemen of 7 March 1636/7) [PCR 1:53, 74]. "Mr. Thom[as] Besbeech" appears in the Scituate section of the 1639 Plymouth Colony list of freemen, where his name is crossed out, and also in the Duxbury section of the same list, where his name is again crossed out [PCR 8:175]. "Mr. Thomas Besbech" appears in the Marshfield section of the 1658 and the 29 May 1670 Plymouth Colony lists of freemen [PCR 5:277, 8:201].
EDUCATION: His inventory included "his books" valued at £2 10s.

OFFICES: Deputy for Duxbury to Plymouth General Court, 6 June 1643 [PCR 2:57].

Plymouth petit jury, 2 January 1637/8, 6 March 1637/8 [PCR 1:74, 7:8]. Grand jury, 4 September 1638, 1 March 1641/2 (as "Mr. Thomas Besbeech," for Duxbury) [PCR 1:87, 96, 2:34]. On 7 June 1642, "Mr. Thomas Beesbeach, for departing the Court without license, being warned to serve on the grand inquest, is fined 5s." [PCR 2:42].

ESTATE: In the 8 February 1635/6 Cambridge list of houses, "[blank] Besbeth" had one house in town [CaTR 19]. By 6 March 1636/7, "Mr. Besbeche" had sold to John Page of Watertown ten acres of meadow in Rocky Meadow [CaTR 27, 43]. By 1639 "Thomas Besbidge" had sold to William Cutter "one house in the town with backside about half a rood ... which he bought of William Lewes" [CaBOP 54].

On 19 July 1639, "Mr. Thomas Besbeech of Duxborrow" sold to "Edmond Chaundlor of the same one acre of land lying to the north side of the lands of the said Thomas Besbeech" [PCR 12:46].

On 3 May 1642, Plymouth Court appointed a committee to "set the ancient bounds right betwixt the lands of Mr. Thomas Beesbeach and John Washbourne" [PCR 2:39, 52].

On 2 April 1647, "Thomas Besbeech of Sudbery" sold to "Mr. John Reiner of Plymouth ... all that his house and housing and sixty acres of upland ... excepting one acre sold unto Edmound Chandeler of Duxbery, three acres of meadow more or less adjacent" [PCR 12:141].

In his will, dated 25 November 1672 and proved 7 April 1674, "Thomas Beesbeech of Sudbury" bequeathed to "my grandchild & adopted son Thomas Beesbeech (alias) Thomas Browne the eldest son of my daughter Mary wife to William Browne of the said Sudbury and to his heirs lawfully begotten all my house & lands lying & being in Old England in the parishes of Hetcorne & Frittenden in the County of Kent," he "paying forty shillings per annum unto my daughter Mary wife to the said William Browne after the decease of her said husband William & not before, nor after if she marry again, and the like said sum of forty shillings per annum unto my daughter Alice the wife of John Bourne of Marshfeild" under the same conditions; daughters Mary and Alice were also to receive the goods of the testator which were in the hands of their husbands, and neither they nor their husbands were to challenge the bequest made to his adopted son; to "William Browne son of my said daughter Mary the twenty acres of meadow given me by the said town of Sudbury"; to "Edmund Browne son of my said daughter Mary the forty acres of upland joining to the brook which was given me by the said town of Sudbury"; to "Hopestill Browne son of my said daughter Mary and to his three sisters vizt: Suzanna, Elizabeth & Sarah all my lands in the new grants in the said Sudbury"; to "Mary Rice wife of Benjamin Rice, daughter of my said daughter Mary, two oxen & two cows"; to "Thomas Bourne son of my said daughter Alice all my marsh ground which I bought of George Sole in Marshfeild"; to "Sarah Bourne daughter of my said daughter Alice (as formerly I have given to each of her sisters) a cow"; to "Mary the daughter of the abovesaid Thomas Beesbeech (alias) Thomas Browne and to Experience the son of Elizabeth Bent wife of Joseph Bent of the said Sudbury" 5s. apiece; residue to "the abovesaid Thomas Beesbeech (alias) Thomas Browne & to the abovesaid Edmund Browne," they to be executors; "Capt. Hopestill Foster of Dorchester" to be overseer; to "Thankfull & Patience daughters of the abovesaid Thomas Beesbeech (alias) Thomas Browne" 5s. apiece; to "Ebenezer son of the abovesaid Mary Rice" 5s.; to "my daughter Mary Browne wife of the abovesaid William Browne my plate beerbowl" [MPR Case #1476].

The "inventory of the estate of Mr. Thomas Besb[eech] of Sudbury ... who deceased this life March the 9th 1673/74," taken "25 March 1673/74 [*sic*]," was untotalled; the real estate was valued at £450: "a parcel of land in Sudbury, called by the name of the new grant," £20; "his lands in England in Kent in Hetcorne and Frettenden," £400; and "a parcel of marshland lying in Marshfield in Plimouth Collony," £30; there was "also a considerable estate in the hands of John Bourne his son-in-law living in Marshfeld in Plimouth Collony the value whereof we know not which is disposed of by will" [MPR Case #1476].

BIRTH: Baptized at Biddenden, Kent, on 3 March 1589/90, son of John and Dorothy (Austin) (Foster) Besbeech [NEHGR 67:34].
DEATH: Sudbury 9 March 1673/4.
MARRIAGE: Biddenden, Kent, 14 January 1618/9 Anne Baseden [NEHGR 67:34]; she was buried at Frittenden, Kent, on 21 April 1634 [NEHGR 67:34].
CHILDREN (all baptized Frittenden):
  i   MARY, bp. 23 January 1619/20 [Frittenden Bishop's Transcripts]; m. Sudbury 15 November 1641 William Browne.
  ii   SARAH, bp. 6 January 1621/2 [NEHGR 67:34]; bur. Frittenden 16 June 1628 [Frittenden Bishop's Transcripts].
  ii   ALICE, bp. 29 June 1624 [NEHGR 67:34]; m. Marshfield 18 July 1645 John Bourne [MarVR 1].

ASSOCIATIONS: Thomas Besbeech was uncle of the half-blood of HOPESTILL FOSTER, who came to Dorchester in 1635 [NEHGR 67:36].

COMMENTS: "Tho[ma]s Besbeech of Ashford," Kent, was given a certificate of conformity in March 1634/5 by Thomas Warren of Sandwich and Thomas Harmon, vicar of Headcorn, in preparation for sailing to New England on the *Hercules*; with him were children "Mary, Alice, El[i]zab[eth] Egelden, Jane Egelden, Sara Egelden, John Egelden," and servants "Tho[ma]s Neuley, Joseph Pacheury, Agnes Love" [NEHGR 75:220].

On 4 September 1638, "Nathaniell Tilden [was] presented for denying a land way that formerly Mr. Besbeech & others had used by grant from the town of Scituate" [PCR 1:98].

On 22 January 1638/9, "Mr. Thomas Besbeech" was at the head of a list of eight Scituate men who received from Plymouth Court a "grant of a plantation called Seppekann, and the lands thereabouts, for the seating of a township for a congregation there" [PCR 1:108]. (This is apparently the source for Pope's claim that Thomas Besbeech was "Proprietor at Barnstable, 1638-9." Although Besbeech may have been involved in the preparations for the move from Scituate to Barnstable in 1639, the records make it clear that he went to Duxbury in 1639.)

An "Elisha Beesbeach" appears at Scituate in 1642 [PCR 2:45, 167, 168], and had a full life in that town; the surname is later more commonly Bisbee or Bisbey. He has frequently been included as a son of Thomas Bisbeech. The will of Thomas Besbeech and the chronology make this impossible.

Pope says that the immigrant "sold land at Sudbury 13 October 1664" [Pope 47], but no record for this transaction has been found.

BIBLIOGRAPHIC NOTE: In 1913 Elizabeth French published the English wills for the immigrant's parents, as well as entries from two Kent parish registers [NEHGR 67:33-34].

ANTHONY BESSEY

ORIGIN: London
MIGRATION: 1635 on the *James*
FIRST RESIDENCE: Lynn
REMOVES: Sandwich 1637

OCCUPATION: Husbandman.

FREEMAN: Oath of fidelity at Sandwich, 1639 [PCR 8:184]. (He is not in the equivalent list for 1657, indicating that this list was compiled after Bessey's death in the first half of that year.)

EDUCATION: On 22 September 1651, "Anthony Besse" wrote a letter to an unknown correspondent, "Concerning the Indians" and their religious practices [Florence Besse Ballantine, *Descendants of Anthony Besse, 1609-1656* (n.p. 1965), p. 9; no indication of the location of the original]. He signed his will. His inventory included "his books and some other small things" valued at £1 16s. Her inventory included "a Bible and some sheep's wool and feathers" valued at 8s.

OFFICES: Sandwich highway surveyor, 6 June 1654 [PCR 3:49].

In the Sandwich section of the 1643 Plymouth Colony list of men able to bear arms [PCR 8:192].

ESTATE: On 16 April 1640, "Anthony Bessy" received one acre in the division of meadow land at Sandwich [PCR 1:149].

In his will, dated 10 February 1656/7 and proved 3 June 1657, "Anthony Bessey of Sandwidge" bequeathed to "Jane my wife" three cows, three yearlings, two heifers, one bull, a cow, "one yearling steer that Dorkas my daughter hath given unto Jane my wife," and "my bed"; to "Dorcas my daughter" two heifers previously given and one more; to "Ann my daughter" one heifer; to "Nehemiah my son" one heifer previously given; "the house and land now possessed by me unto my two sons viz: Nehemiah and David and two steers likewise to them both"; to "Nehemiah my gun and my cutlass and my boots," apparel and all the meadow to be equally divided between "my two sons"; to "my daughter Mary" one heifer; to "my daughter Jane" one heifer; to "my daughter Elizabeth" one ewe lamb in Mr. Edward Dillingham's hands; debts owing to others for "my wife" to discharge; "in case my mother send anything over to me as formerly she hath done, that it be disposed of among my family in general"; residue "amongst the family until my wife shall marry and then to be divided amongst my children"; if she marry, the five "biggest" children to be "put forth and their cattle with them"; "the little one my wife goeth with that my wife give to it a portion if god give it life"; wife executrix, "loving friends James Skiffe and Richard Bourne" overseers [Plymouth Wills 1:328, citing PCPR 2:51; see also MD 14:152-53].

The inventory of his estate, taken 21 May 1657, was untotalled [about £70], and like most Plymouth inventories included no real estate [Plymouth Wills 1:329, citing PCPR 2:52].

In her will, dated 6 August 1693 and proved 5 October 1693, "Jane Barlow of Sandwich" bequeathed to "my son John Barlow ... my dwelling house and all my land on which it stands and land adjacent ... together with my great iron kettle and the money that he owes me"; to "my son Nathan Barlow forty shillings in money and my featherbed and the iron kettle that he now hath of mine"; to "my son Nehemiah Bessie one cow"; to "Alce Hunter and Rebeckah Hunter the daughters of my daughter Rebeckah Hunter one cow apiece"; to "my three daughters viz: Anna Hallett, Elizabeth Bodfish and Rebeckah Hunter all my wearing clothes and the rest of my estate to be divided between them"; "Stephen Skeffe Esq." to be executor [PPR 1:86; MD 19:44-45].

The inventory of "the estate of Jane Barlow late of Sandwich who deceased the 22 day of August 1693," taken "this 4th [*sic*] day of August 1693," totalled £38, with no real estate included [PPR 1:86; MD 19:45].

BIRTH: About 1609 (aged 26 in 1635 [Hotten 107]).
DEATH: Between 10 February 1656/7 (date of will) and 21 May 1657 (date of inventory).
MARRIAGE: By about 1639 Jane _____. She married (2) before 10 January or February 1661/2 George Barlow [PCR 4:7], and died 22 August 1693 (assuming that the date of the inventory was correctly 24 August).
CHILDREN:

    i   DORCAS, b. say 1639; living 4 March 1661/2, unmarried [PCR 4:10]; no further record.
    ii   ANN, b. say 1641; m. by 1662 Andrew Hallett, son of ANDREW HALLETT [TAG 26:193-95].
    iii NEHEMIAH, b. about 1643 (of full age on 2 August 1664 [PCR 4:17]); m. by 1680 Mary Ransom, daughter of Robert Ransom (eldest known child b. Sandwich [blank] November 1680 [SandVR 1:61]; son Nehemiah b. Sandwich [blank] July 1682/3 [*sic*] [SandVR 1:62]; the 14 December 1697 inventory of Robert Ransom Senior included "a hores & saddle & arms he gave to his grandson Nehemiah Bessey before he died" [PPR 1:280]).
    iv   MARY, b. say 1645; living 4 March 1661/2, unmarried [PCR 4:10]; no further record.
    v   JANE, b. say 1647; on 3 June 1662, "concerning a cow belonging to Jane, the daughter of Anthony Bessey, of Sandwich, the Court have ordered G[e]orge Barlow, in whose hands the said cow hath been for some time, to

return her to the overseers of the estate of the said
Anthony Bessey, to be disposed of by them for the use
and good of the said Jane Bessey" [PCR 4:17]; no further
record.

vi   DAVID, b. Sandwich 23 May 1649 [SandVR 1:4; PCR 8:9];
named in his father's will, 10 February 1656/7; no further
record.

vii   ELIZABETH, b. say 1654; m. by 1674 Joseph Botfish, son of
ROBERT BOTFISH.

viii REBECCA (posthumous), b. about summer 1657; m.
Barnstable 17 February 1670[/1?] William Hunter [MD
6:137].

COMMENTS: On 13 July 1635, "Anto Bessy," aged 26, was enrolled at
London for passage to New England on the *James* [Hotten 107].

Although there is no record of the presence of Anthony Bessey in Lynn,
we assume he resided there briefly, since several of his fellow passengers
on the *James* made that their first residence.

On 5 March 1638/9, "Anthonie Bessie [was] presented for living alone
disorderly, and afterwards for taking in an inmate without order" [PCR
1:118]. (Anthony Bessey was probably married about the time of this
presentment.)

On 10 January or February 1661/2, Anna Bessey, Dorcas Bessey and
Mary Bessey posted bond, promising "to appear at the Court to be holden
at Plymouth the first Tuesday in March next, to answer for her unnatural
and cruel carriages towards George Barlow, [their] father-in-law" [PCR
4:7]. On 4 March 1661/2, "Anna Bessey, for her cruel and unnatural
practices towards her father-in-law, George Barlow, in chopping of him
in the back, notwithstanding the odiousness of her fact, the Court,
considering of some circumstances, viz:, her ingenious confession,
together with her present condition, being with child, and some other
particulars, have sentenced her to pay a fine of ten pounds, or to be
publicly whipped at some other convenient time when her condition will
admit thereof"; "Dorcas Bessey and Mary Bessey, for carriages of like
nature towards their father-in-law, though not in so high a degreee, were
both sentenced to sit in the stocks during the pleasure of the Court, which
accordingly was performed"; "the younger, viz:, Mary Bessey, was
sharply reproved by the Court, as being by her disobedience the
occasioner of the evil abovementioned"; "G[e]org[e] Barlow and his wife

were both severly reproved for their most ungodly living in contention with the other, and admonished to live otherwise" [PCR 4:10].

BIBLIOGRAPHIC NOTE: In 1950 Mrs. John E. Barclay published an account of the family of Anthony Bessey; we have followed her judgment on the birth order of the children of the immigrant [TAG 26:193-95].

In 1965 Mrs. Florence Besse Ballantine compiled and edited *Descendants of Anthony Besse, 1609-1656.*

JOHN BEST

ORIGIN: St George, Canterbury, Kent
MIGRATION: 1635 on the *Hercules*
FIRST RESIDENCE: Salem

OCCUPATION: Tailor (in England). (Perley calls him a currier [Perley 2:62], but he apparently confused the 1635 immigrant with a later John Best who lived in Salem from 1669 to 1711 [Perley 3:47].)
EDUCATION: Presumably at least the minimum afforded a tailor's apprentice.
ESTATE: On 18 February 1638/9, John Best was admitted an inhabitant of Salem and requested accommodation [STR 1:84].

COMMENTS: With a certificate of conformity from Thomas Jackson, minister of St George's, dated 28 February 1634/5, "Jno. Best, of St George's, Canterbury, tailor," was enrolled as a passenger for New England on the *Hercules* of Sandwich [Drake's Founders 84].

Perhaps he was the John Best baptized at St Mary Magdalen, Canterbury, Kent, on 3 March 1611[/2], son of Nicholas Best.

Savage credits John Best with a son John, who married in 1670 (and purchased land in Salem in 1674 [ELR 4:97]), but since no mention of John Best is found in the thirty intervening years, we must conclude that the immigrant died or departed not long after being admitted as an inhabitant of Salem.

RICHARD BETSCOMBE

ORIGIN: Bridport, Dorset
MIGRATION: 1635
FIRST RESIDENCE: Hingham
RETURN TRIPS: To England in 1647

OCCUPATION: Haberdasher.
CHURCH MEMBERSHIP: Admission to Hingham church prior to 9 March 1636/7 implied by freemanship.
FREEMAN: 9 March 1636/7 (as "Rich[a]rd Betsham," first in a sequence of five Hingham men) [MBCR 1:372].
OFFICES: Massachusetts Bay petit jury, 19 September 1637 [MBCR 1:203].
    Hingham selectman, 20 March 1642[/3?] [HiTR, 1642-1651, p. 3]. Appointed to assist constable in collecting rate, 1646 [HiTR, 1642-1651, p. 9].
ESTATE: "The several parcels of land and meadow legally given unto Richard Betscome by the town of Hingham": 16 September 1635, "for a houselot five acres," in two pieces, one of two acres and one of three acres; 18 September 1635, "for a great lot sixteen acres," in two pieces, one of fourteen acres and one of two acres; 1 June 1635, "for a planting lot six acres"; 10 November 1637, "for a small planting lot one acre and half"; 1635, "two acres of salt marsh lying in the home meadow"; 12 June 1637, "another parcel of salt marsh at Layford's in the plain neck lying for one acre"; and 5 March 1637[8], "three parts of an acre of meadow lying in crooked meadow" [HiBOP 22].

BIRTH: Baptized Symondsbury, Dorset, 3 April 1601, son of John and Grace (Coade) Battiscombe [M&JCH 17:17-18; NEHGR 63:161-62].
DEATH: After 1647, probably in England.
MARRIAGE: St Mary the Virgin, The Devizes, Wiltshire, 24 August 1630 Mary Strong, daughter of Philip Strong (see COMMENTS below). "Mrs. Betscombe" died at Hingham on 6 June 1646 and was buried there the next day [NEHGR 121:19].
CHILDREN:
  i   MARY, bp. Symondsbury, Dorset, 27 August 1631 [M&JCH 17:18]; no further record.
  ii   MARTHA, b. say 1633; no further record.
  iii ANNA, bp. Hingham [blank] August 1639 [NEHGR 121:12]; no further record.

    iv   EXPERIENCE, bp. Hingham 24 October 1641 [NEHGR 121:14]; no further record.

COMMENTS: One of the appraisers of the estate of Anthony Cooper of Hingham, on 26 February 1635[/6], was "Richard Betscombe" [SPR NS 1:2].

    On 25 August 1640, "Richard Betscombe of Hingham in New England late of Bridporte in the County of Dorset haberdasher in behalf of Mary & Martha his daughters makes a letter of attorney to Andrew, Robert & Christofer his brothers to receive two legacies of 50s. apiece given by Philip Strong late of the Devizes in the County of Wiltes gent. deceased to the said Mary & Martha of Philip Strong brewer his son & executor" [Lechford 289]. (In his will of 14 July 1635, "Phillip Strong the elder of the Borough of the Devises in the County of Wilt[shire] gent.," among other bequests, bequeathed to "my three daughters Ruth, Abigaill and Mary all my books to be equally divided amongst them" and to "the children of my son-in-law and daughter Richard Bescombe and Mary Bescombe five pounds of lawful English money to be equally divided amongst them and to be paid unto them within five years next after my decease" [PCC 104 Sadler].)

    On 18 November 1645, "Richard Betscomb of Hingham, haberdasher, acknowledged before me the notary public the receipt of six pounds for the use of Leonell Browne of Bredport in Dorsetshire, woolen draper, & empowered himself to procure a release from him" [Aspinwall 10].

    On 6 October 1647, "James Wyton of Hingham, mariner, granted a letter of attorney irrevocable to Richard Betscomb of Hingham to ask &c. of the executors of the last will &c. of Thomas Wyton of Hooke Norton in Oxfordshire, yeoman, deceased a certain legacy or legacies given him by the said last will & of the receipt to give acquittance &c." [Aspinwall 88].

    This letter of attorney would appear to have been granted in anticipation of a trip to England by Richard Betscombe. There is no further record for him or any other member of his family in New England, and their fate should be searched in England.

BIBLIOGRAPHIC NOTE: In 1909 Henry F. Waters published abstracts of the wills of the parents of the immigrant [NEHGR 63:161-62]. Burton Spear and Martha Strong have proposed five-generations of agnate ancestry for the immigrant [M&JCH 17:16-18, 26:86-88].

JOHN BETTS

ORIGIN: Unknown
MIGRATION: 1634 on the *Francis*
FIRST RESIDENCE: Cambridge

OCCUPATION: Yeoman.

EDUCATION: John Betts signed all his deeds, except for his last two, made not long before his death. His wife, Elizabeth Betts, signed all her deeds and other documents. His inventory included "two Bibles and some small books" valued at £1. Her inventory included "two Bibles" valued at 16s. and "some small books" valued at 4s. She bequeathed to "brother Bridge my demicaster hat and my great Bible," to "John Merrett my old great Bible," to "Abigall Fisher of Dedham my little new Bible," and to "sister Gibson the practical catechism."

ESTATE: In the 8 February 1635/6 accounting of houses in Cambridge, "Richard Beats" was credited with two in the town (see *COMMENTS* below for the argument for believing that this record is for John Betts) [CaTR 18].

Granted seven acres and two roods in the Old Ox Pasture, 11 May 1638 [CaTR 33, 76].

In the Cambridge land inventory of 1642, "John Betts" held eight parcels: "in the town one dwelling house with about half a rood of land"; "in the town one dwelling house"; "by the town one acre of land"; "in the Ox Pasture seven acres & a half"; "in the West Field ten acres"; "in the Wigwam Neck two acres"; "in the Long Marsh six acres & half"; and "in the Alewife Meadow four and twenty acres" [CaBOP 108].

Granted nine acres "for small farms," "for two houses" (this base amount to be multiplied by eight or nine, depending on location), 1645 [CaTR 67]. Granted "six acres of the nearest common meadow for what he came short of his purchased meadow," 1645 [CaTR 68]. Granted one acre "on the west side of Monotamye River," 1645 [CaBOP 126]. Granted eight acres "on the other side Menotime Bridge," 1646 [CaTR 66]. Granted seventy-two acres "out of the waste land towards Dedham on the west side of the highway," 1648 [CaBOP 136]. Granted ninety acres in the Shawsheen division, 4 June 1652 [CaTR 97].

By late 1646, John Betts had sold to Edward Winship twenty acres of the land in Alewife Meadow [CaBOP 132].

On 21 December 1649, John Betts of Cambridge, yeoman, sold to John Swan of Cambridge, planter, "eight acres of land granted him by the town for a woodlot ... with the privileges for two cows on the common" [MLR 1:207]. On 6 December 1652, John Betts of Cambridge sold to Thomas Fanning of Cambridge "all that my interest in the Shaw Shine lands ... my lot upon record in the town books, being ninety acre"; "John Betts as also Elizabeth my wife" acknowledged [MLR 1:211]. On 23 January 1656[/7?], John Betts of Cambridge, yeoman, sold to John Stedman of Cambridge "two acres of land ... in a place commonly called Wigwam Neck"; acknowledged and signed by John Betts and Elizabeth Betts [MLR 13:212-13].

On 24 April 1661, John Betts of Cambridge, yeoman, sold to Thomas Danforth of Cambridge, treasurer of Harvard College (as agent for the President and Fellows of Harvard College), "one parcel of land" in Cambridge containing "one acre and one rood"; John Betts made his mark and Elizabeth Betts acknowledged and made her signature [MLR 13:424-25; NEHGR 96:278-81; Morison 206]. On 6 December 1662, John Betts of Cambridge, yeoman, sold to John Shepard of Cambridge, cooper, "one parcel of land situate, lying & being in the abovenamed town, and is by estimation twenty poles"; John Betts made his mark and Elizabeth Betts signed [MLR 3:373].

The inventory of "the estate of John Beets late of Cambridge who deceased the 21 of the 12th month 1662," presented at court 2 April 1663, totalled £67 4s. 8d., of which £26 was real estate: "a dwelling house and garden plot" [MPR Case #1660].

In her will, dated 16 December 1663 and proved 14 March 1663/4, "Eliz[abeth] Beets of Cambridge" bequeathed to "John Bridge Senior my dwelling house with the privileges thereunto belonging, with that part of the pump that stands before my door, with the loose things about the house and in the cellar and yards, upon this consideration, that he is now to put the said house into good reparation and to uphold the same and the yards during my natural life without any trouble to me and to pay out such legacies as shall be hereafter expressed"; there then follow small bequests, mostly of household goods, to about fifty residents of Cambridge and some neighboring towns, without relationships being stated (the few references to "brother" and "sister" apparently indicate a church relationship); "my trusty and wellbeloved friends John Bridge and Thomas Chesholm to be my executors" [MPR 2:200-3, Case #1659].

The inventory of "the estate of Elez[abeth] Beets of Cambridge deceased the 2th of the 11th 63," taken 6 January 1663/4, totalled £71 14s. 4d., of which £26 was real estate: "a dwelling house and garden plot" [MPR 2:203-7, Case #1659].

BIRTH: About 1594 (aged 40 in 1635 [Hotten 279]).
DEATH: 21 February 1662/3 (from inventory).
MARRIAGE: By an unknown date Elizabeth Bridge, sister of JOHN BRIDGE of Cambridge. She was born about 1599 ("Elizabeth Betts aged about 54 years" deposed on 21 June 1653 [MCF Folio #7]). "Elizabeth Betts, wife of John and sister of Deacon John Bridge," died at Cambridge 2 January 1663/4.
CHILDREN: None recorded.

COMMENTS: On 30 April 1634, "John Beetes," aged 40, was in the list of passengers sailing from Ipswich to New England on the *Francis* [Hotten 279].

As there are no records for John Betts in New England between this entry on a passenger list and some Cambridge records for 1638, there might be some question whether the immigrant of 1634 is the later resident in Cambridge. However, careful examination of the 8 February 1635/6 record for "Richard Beats" helps the identification. In this record, "Richard Beats" is said to hold two houses in town [CaTR 18]. There is no other record for this name in early Cambridge.

Examination of the later landholdings of John Betts shows that he had acquired much of his land from WILLIAM WESTWOOD. The house lot held by William Westwood on 4 June 1635 matches in description the house lot held by John Betts in 1642, and the parcels held by Westwood in Wigwam Neck and in Long Marsh also went to Betts [CaBOP 7-8, 108].

William Westwood was one of those who moved from Cambridge to Hartford, probably late in 1635 or early in 1636. His name does not appear in the 8 February 1635/6 list of those holding houses in Cambridge, so he had apparently already sold his Cambridge land before that date, in preparation for his move to Connecticut.

Since we have no evidence that anyone else held these lands between William Westwood and John Betts, we suggest that the record for "Richard Beats" is defective, and was intended for John Betts.

John Betts was a man of some education and sufficient estate to have at least two servants at one time. Yet he apparently did not become a member of the church, he did not become a freeman, and he performed no civil service. As the records below demonstrate, he must have been a cantankerous man, for he was before the authorities frequently for a number of minor offenses. Then in 1652 he severely mistreated one of his servants, who soon died, at which point Betts was charged and tried for murder. The depositions entered in this case give a very clear picture of the character of John Betts. He was not the sort of man the leaders of the Massachusetts Bay Colony wanted in their settlements.

On 4 December 1638, "John Bets appeared, & was discharged, there being not evidence sufficient to prove his overselling" [MBCR 1:247].

On 8 November 1642, "John Betts was fined ... 19s. 6d. for his haystacks & cow houses and dunghills that he annoyed the street before his door with & though often warned to clear the street yet denied to do it" [CaTR 48]. On 13 November 1643, "John Betts was reckoned with, about harms done in his corn by the town's herd of cows to the value of £3 which sum is clearly paid," and the payment acknowledged by John Betts [CaTR 49]. On 9 September 1650, John Betts sued "Mr. Josepth Cooke, for detaining his 2 oxen and three cows" [CaTR 87]. On 13 January 1650/1, "the townsmen do consent that one of the elders and two of the deacons at the request of John Betts shall determine whether in equity any satisfaction ought to be rendered by the town unto the said John Betts for the land on which the new meeting house standeth and with their determination the said John Betts promiseth to set down satisfied" [CaTR 89].

At a General Court which began on 18 May 1653 and was continued to 2 June 1653,

> Jno. Betts, of Cambridge, being at a Court of Assistants, on his trial for his life, for the cruelty he exercised on Rob[er]t Knight, his servant, striking him with a plowstaff, &c., who died shortly after it, the jury brought in their verdict, which the magistrates not receiving, came, in course, to be tried by the General Court. Jno. Betts, the prisoner, came accordingly to his trial, submitted himself for trial to God and the country, & pleaded not guilty to his indictment. The evidence against him being examined & heard, the Court proceeded to censure him, viz:-
>
> The General Court do not find Jno. Betts legally guilty of the murdering of his late servant, Robert Knight; but forasmuch as the evidence brought in against him holds forth unto this Court strong presumptions and great probability of his guilt of so bloody a fact, and that he exercised and multiplied inhumane cruelties upon the said Knight, this Court doth therefore think meet, that the said Jno. Betts be sentenced, viz.: 1. That the next lecture day at Boston (a convenient time before the lecture begin),

the said Betts have a rope put about his neck by the executioner, and that from the prison he be carried to the gallows, there to stand upon the ladder one hour, by the glass, with the end of his rope thrown over the gallows; 2ly, That he be brought back to prison, and, immediately after the lecture, to be severely whipped; 3ly, That the said Betts shall pay all the witnesses brought in against him 2s. per day for so many days as they have attended upon the Court of Assistants and the General Court upon his trial; 4ly, That he shall pay fifteen pounds into the country treasury for and towards the charge the Courts have been at upon his trial; 5ly, That the said Betts be bound to the good behavior for one whole year in the sum of twenty pounds [MBCR 4:1:145, 3:309; RCA 3:24-34 (which includes many depositions); NEHGR 96:278-81].

The General Court then ordered that "the fifteen pounds due to the country from John Betts be paid to the surveyor general to purchase powder withal" [MBCR 4:1:147, 3:300].

On 21 June 1653, "Elizabeth Betts aged about 54 years" deposed that she had witnessed Thomas Abbott and Anne Williamson in the act of fornication on or about 1 June 1653 [MCF Folio #7]. (Note that the event described in the deposition occurred within days of the trial of John Betts for murder, and that Thomas Abbott, a servant of John Betts, and Anne Williamson, a servant of Reana (_____) (James) Andrews [RCA 3:28; GMB 2:1071], had both deposed in the murder trial, giving testimony that was not particularly damaging to Betts.)

On 29 July 1629, the Massachusetts Bay Company, while still in London, took "note of diverse propositions offered to the consideration of this company by one John Betts ..., pretending that he is able to discover diverse things for the good & advancement of the plantation, & the benefit of this Company; whereupon some of those here present were desired to enquire further of him, not only of his ability, but of his deportment in his life & conversation, and then the Company to treat with him as they shall think fit" [MBCR 1:48-49]. Nothing further is heard of these propositions, but Savage thought this man might be the same as the immigrant of 1634 [Savage 1:172]. This conclusion is not impossible, but there is no evidence specifically supporting the identification.

WILLIAM BETTS

ORIGIN: Unknown
MIGRATION: 1635
FIRST RESIDENCE: Scituate
REMOVES: Barnstable 1639, Dorchester by 1651, Westchester by 1662

OCCUPATION: Dishturner.
CHURCH MEMBERSHIP: Admitted to Scituate church on 25 October 1635 [NEHGR 9:280].
FREEMAN: On 1 June 1641, "W[illia]m Betts, of Barnestable," was propounded for freemanship in Plymouth Colony (but there is no record that he was ever admitted) [PCR 2:17].
EDUCATION: Signed his deed of 9 March 1651/2 (as "William Beets").
OFFICES: In Barnstable section of 1643 Plymouth Colony list of men able to bear arms (as "Will[ia]m Beetes") [PCR 8:193].

Magistrate at Westchester Court of Sessions, 13 September 1662, 30 September 1662 [Westchester Court 30, 34].
ESTATE: On 8 February 1638[/9?], William Betts of Scituate sold to Thomas Ensign of Scituate four acres of upland in Scituate [PCR 12:194]. (Note that this sale took place just three weeks before Betts married Ensign's maid, and also not long before Betts moved to Barnstable.)

On 9 March 1651/2, "William Betts of Dorchester ... dishturner" sold to Sampson Mason of Dorchester, shoemaker, "all that his dwelling ... in Dorchester with all other buildings, gardens, orchards, yards thereunto belonging and also his homelot containing by estimation six acres ... and also all other accommodations and common right unto the said house and homelot and all the appurtenances thereunto belonging" [SLR 1:187-88].

In his will, dated 12 February 1673 and proved 2 January 1675/6 [27 Charles II], "Will[ia]m Betts of the Youngers Plantation, in the jurisdiction now of New Orange so called," bequeathed to "my wife Alice Betts, after my decease, my house and houselot, with the barn and all the meadow that is lying by my houselot now in possession, also one third part of my land in the planting field, within fence, all which are situate on the Younckers Plantation, for and during her natural life," along with all his cattle, moveables and debts, to be at her disposal; to "my son Samuell, after the decease of his mother, my house and homelot, whereon the house standeth, also the barn and four acres of meadow," also "one third part of my lands within fence and without lying at the Younckers Plantation, excepting what I have herein bequeathed to John Barrett," also "a homelot, next adjoining to the homelot of Goodman Newman's, lying situate in the Town of Westchester," also "all my turning tools and lasts, six acres of meadow"; to "my son Hopestill one third part of all the rest of my land in the Younckers Plantation, excepting what I have herein bequeathed," also "eight acres of fresh meadow"; to "my son John, after the decease of his mother, one third of my land in the planting field, within fence, and one third part of the rest of my land in the Younckers Plantation, excepting what I have here bequeathed," also "two six acre lots of meadow," also "I will that my son John do live with his mother during her life, and to manage her land and stock," also "my house and orchard and two homelots next adjoining to the orchard, and eleven acres of upland by the west meadow, and one acre quarter and thirteen rods of salt meadow," also "I will that my son John pay all my debts that I am justly indebted"; to "my daughter Hittabell Tibbott," 20s.; to "John Barrett, son to Sam[ue]ll Barrett, twenty acres of upland ... also one small lot of fresh meadow, containing one acre & half"; "I will that my meadow at Younckers Plantation, which hath been wrongfully taken away from me, if recovered, to be equally divided between my three sons"; "my wife Alice Betts to be my sole executrix" [New York Wills 1:218-23].

On 2 December 1679, "Hopestill Betts of the Younghers Plantation" sold to Jonathan Whelply of Westchester "one moiety of my homelot within fence next adjoining to my brother Samuell Betts lot lying situate in the Younghers Plantation aforesaid together with the one moiety of all my lands and four acres of land more lying situate at the Younghers Plantation bequeathed to me by my father's will (excepting my dwelling house and my garden plot) together with all the apple trees, firewood trees, runs, springs thereon ... as also common privileges, profits and commodities belonging unto the said land" [Westchester TR 1:134].

BIRTH: By about 1614 based on date of marriage.
DEATH: Between 12 February 1673[/4?] (date of will) and 2 January 1675/6 (probate of will).
MARRIAGE: 27 or 28 February 1638/9 Alice _____ ("William Betts and Alice - Goodman Ensygne's maid [married] in the Bay" [NEHGR 9:286]).
CHILDREN:

    i   HANNAH, bp. Barnstable 26 January 1639/40 [NEHGR 9:282]; m. by an unknown date Samuel Barrett (William Betts made a bequest to "John Barrett, son of Samuel Barrett"

(without stating a relationship); the nuncupative will of
John Betts was attested by John and Mary Barrett; John
Barrett and his family are listed immediately after the
rest of the Betts clan in the 1698 Fordham census).

ii   SAMUEL, bp. Barnstable 12 February 1642/3 [NEHGR 9:282];
m. by an unknown date Ruth _____ (this name given in
secondary sources, but no record evidence found to
support this marriage).

iii   HOPE[STILL] (son), bp. Barnstable 16 March 1644/5 [NEHGR
9:283]; d. after 2 December 1679 (date of will [Westchester
TR 1:134]), apparently unmarried.

iv   JOHN, b. say 1648; m. by an unknown date Susanna _____ (in
a nuncupative will "declared about the middle of March
1692" and attested "the 28th of February 1692/3," John
Betts made allowance for his wife, two sons and two
daughters [Westchester TR 1:269-72]; "widow Susana
Bets and two children: Hanna, Else" are included in the
1698 Fordham census [NYGBR 38:218]).

v   MEHITABLE, b. say 1650; m. (1) by about 1670 George Tippett
(William Betts bequeathed to "my daughter Hittabell
Tibbott"; the inventory of the estate of "George Tippitts
of Yonckers" was taken 29 September 1675 [Westchester
TR 1:234-35]); m. (2) in late 1675 or early 1676 Lewis
Vittrey (on 25 March 1676, administration on the estate of
"Lewis Vittrey, late of the Younckers Plantation, near
Eastchester," was granted to "Mehittabell, his widow and
relict" [Westchester TR 1:236]); m. (3) Samuel Hitchcock
("Samuell Hichkocks and his wife Mahetabel" and "Joarge
Tippit" (son of Mehitabel with her first husband) appear
at the head of the sequence of Betts family households in
the 1698 Fordham census [NYGBR 38:218]).

COMMENTS: Walter Kendall Watkins suggested that this immigrant
was the "W[illia]m Bett," aged twenty, who sailed for Virginia on the
Thomas & John in June 1635 [NEHGR 55:300; Hotten 84], but as with
virtually all other such claims, there is no evidence that this 1635
passenger to Virginia later came to New England.

On 2 November 1652, the town of Dorchester paid one shilling to
"W[illia]m Betts for stoples for the great guns" [DTR 311].

The earmark of William Betts was recorded at Westchester on 11 June 1665 [Westchester TR 1:15].

In a document recorded on 3 August 1681, "We whose names are here underwritten are fully satisfied that we do properly belong to the Town of WestChester according to the laws of this government and do belong to the North Riding of Long Island & now are fully satisfied we are not in John Archer's Patent & do desire our names may be recorded in WestChester records"; signed by William Chadderton, Samuel Hitchcock, John Betts, Alice Betts and Charles Vincent [Westchester TR 1:80].

The 1698 census of the "Inhabitants of Fordham and Adjacent Places" contains a sequence of seven households, six of which appear to represent children, grandchildren and greatgrandchildren of William Betts [NYGBR 38:218]:

> Samuell Hichkocks and his wife Mahetabel and two children: Marce, Mary.
>
> Joarge Tippit and his wife Joane and one child: Joarge and one slave Adum.
>
> Johannis van Cherreck and his wife Mary and two children: Johannis, Mary; four negroes: Hetter, Tone, Marce, Ester.
>
> Widow Susana Bets and two children: Hanna, Else.
>
> Samuell Betts and his wife Ruth and three children: John, Ruth, Elesabeth.
>
> Hopestill Bets.
>
> John Bearret and his wife Mary and three children: Samuel, Hanna, Anna and Mary Sqier.

Samuel Hitchcock was the third husband of Mehitable Betts, daughter of William Betts, and George Tippett was her son with her first husband.

Johannis van Cherreck is not known to be related to William Betts in any way (but his position in the midst of these other entries would indicate that research directed at establishing such a relation might be worthwhile).

Susanna Betts was widow of John Betts, son of William Betts.

Samuel Betts was son of Samuel Betts, son of William Betts.

Hopestill Betts was the unmarried son of William Betts.

John Barrett was son of Hannah (Betts) Barrett, daughter of William Betts.

ZACHARY BICKNELL

ORIGIN: Unknown
MIGRATION: 1635
FIRST RESIDENCE: Weymouth

ESTATE: On 9 March 1636/7, "William Reade, having bought the house & 20 acres of land at Weymouth, unfenced, for £7 13s. 4d., which was Zachary Bicknel's (after Bicknel's death) of Rich[a]rd Rocket & his wife, is to have the same sale confirmed by the child when he cometh to age, or else the child to allow all such costs as the Court shall think meet" [MBCR 1:189].

In the Weymouth land inventory of about 1643, Robert Martin held "ten acres in the East Field first given to Zakry Bicknell" [Weymouth Hist 1:198].

"Zach[ar]y Bicknell" appears in the 2 February 1651/2 list of "great lots named in the old town book and formerly granted to be laid out on the east side of Fresh Pond" (as Bicknell had been long dead by this date, this was a confirmation to his heirs of an earlier grant [Weymouth Hist 1:199]).

BIRTH: About 1590 (aged 45 in 1635 [Hotten 284]).
DEATH: Before 9 March 1636/7 [MBCR 1:189].
MARRIAGE: By about 1624 Agnes _____, who was born about 1608 (aged 27 in 1635 [Hotten 284]). She married (2) by 9 March 1636/7 Richard Rocket [MBCR 1:189] and died at Braintree 9 July 1643 [NEHGR 3:247].
CHILD:

> i   JOHN, b. about 1624 (aged 11 in 1635 [Hotten 284]); m. (1) by about 1654 Mary _____ (eldest child d. Weymouth 4 August 1737 "in his 84th year" [Weymouth Hist 3:79]); m. (2) Weymouth 2 December 1658 Mary Porter.

COMMENTS: "Zachary Bickewell [*sic*]," aged 45, "Agnis Bickwell his wife," aged 27, "Jno. Bickwell, his son," aged 11, and "Jno. Kitchin his servant," aged 23, sailed to New England in 1635 on the unnamed ship from Weymouth, Dorsetshire [Hotten 284].

Various secondary sources make claims about this family which are not supported by the evidence. First, the place of origin is sometimes given as Barrington, Somerset, but this is based merely on the appearance of the name "Zacary Bicknell" in a muster roll of 1569, and should be considered no more than a clue [Weymouth Hist 3:78]. Second, the maiden surname of the wife of the immigrant is sometimes given as Lovell, but no evidence for this is seen. Third, the first wife of John Bicknell, son of the immigrant, is sometimes said to be a daughter of Abraham Shaw, but again, no evidence for this is seen.

JOSEPH BIDDLE

ORIGIN: Unknown
MIGRATION: 1635
FIRST RESIDENCE: Plymouth
REMOVES: Duxbury by 1639, Marshfield by 1643

OCCUPATION: Carpenter [MD 2:95-96, citing PCLR 2:1:47].
FREEMAN: Oath of fidelity at Duxbury, 1639 [PCR 8:182].
EDUCATION: Signed his will by mark. His inventory included "books" valued at £1 10s.
OFFICES: Duxbury highway surveyor, 2 March 1640/1 [PCR 2:9]. Plymouth grand jury, 2 June 1646 [PCR 2:102]. Marshfield tax collector, 1 June 1647, 7 June 1648 [PCR 2:116, 125]. Marshfield constable, 4 June 1650 [PCR 2:153]. Marshfield highway surveyor, 7 June 1652, 3 June 1668, 1 June 1669, 5 June 1672 [PCR 3:9, 4:181, 5:19, 93]. Coroner's jury, 3 May 1653, 31 January 1654/5, 14 February 1654/5, 7 February 1660/1 [PCR 3:28, 70-72, 208]. Petit jury, 3 March 1662/3, 1 March 1663/4 [PCR 4:50, 7:108].

On 7 June 1637, "Joseph Biddle" volunteered to serve in the Pequot War [PCR 1:61]. In Marshfield section of 1643 Plymouth Colony list of men able to bear arms [PCR 8:196].

ESTATE: On 4 July 1635, Isaac Robinson acknowledged that he had sold to "Joseph Bidle half a lot of ground lying above the island creek, which the said Isaac bought of Edmond Chanler, and he of John Barnes" [PCR 1:34]. On 20 March 1636/7, Joseph Biddle was assigned hayground for one cow [PCR 1:56]. On 2 November 1640, "Joseph Biddle" was granted "thirty acres, with some meadow to it" [PCR 1:165].

On 4 May 1653, "whereas in the year 1640 or thereabouts there was a parcel of land lying at the North River near Scittuate, granted by the court unto Experience Michell and John Paybody deceased, videlicet fifty acres to the said Experience Michell and thirty acres unto the said John

Paybody," which Mitchell and Paybody "have since sold ... unto Josepth Beedle of Marshfeild, carpenter," who now sells the land to John Hoare of Scituate, planter [MD 2:95-96, citing PCLR 2:1:47].

On 3 June 1662, "Josepth Beedle" was included in the list of "servants and ancient freemen" who were granted land at Saconnet Neck [PCR 4:18].

In his will, dated 17 April 1671 and proved 29 October 1672, "Joseph Biddle of Marshfield" bequeathed to "Mr. Samuell Arnold one of my cows"; to "the poor of this town one of my cows"; to "Jacob Bumpas my late servant one yearling"; to "Edward Bumpas Senior a suit of my wearing apparel"; to "John Branch a suit of my wearing apparel"; residue, including land, to "my loving wife Rachell during her life, and after her decease to her daughter Martha Dean" [PCPR 3:44].

The inventory of the estate of Joseph Biddle, taken 26 September 1672, totalled £225 7s. 10d. The real estate was listed at the beginning of the inventory, but was not valued: "his dwelling house and lands and outhouses or housings in Marshfield," and "his part of lands that is granted to him by the Court as he was a servant of the first comers into the country" [PCPR 3:44-45].

BIRTH: By about 1611 based on date of marriage.
DEATH: Marshfield 1 September 1672 [MarVR 427; NEHGR 8:192].
MARRIAGE: Plymouth 28 October 1636 RACHEL DEANE, widow [PCR 1:45].
CHILDREN: None recorded.

COMMENTS: On 5 January 1635/6, Joseph Biddle was fined 40s. for being drunk [PCR 1:36]. On 5 October 1636, "Joseph Beedle & Edw[ard] Dowty" sued one another, and were instructed to submit to arbitration [PCR 1:44]. On 3 December 1639, "Joseph Beedle" was presented at court, and on 3 March 1639/40, "Joseph Biddle, of Duxborrow, for suffering men to drink drunken in his house, is censured 20s. sterling" [PCR 1:137, 143].

RACHEL BIGG

ORIGIN: Cranbrook, Kent
MIGRATION: 1635 on the *Elizabeth*
FIRST RESIDENCE: Dorchester

CHURCH MEMBERSHIP: "Rachel Bigge" was admitted to the second church at Dorchester about 1638 [DChR 4]. (The next entry in the church admissions was for PATIENCE FOSTER, her daughter.)

EDUCATION: Signed her will by mark "R.B." Bequeathed "my book of Doctor Preston" to one of her granddaughters.

ESTATE: On 2 January 1637/8, it was ordered that "Mrs. Biggs shall have 1 acre of marsh in lieu of Calves' Pasture near her own at the neck" in Dorchester [DTR 28]. On 18 March 1637/8, "Mrs. Biggs" was granted 4 acres, 2 quarters and 20 rods in the neck and 4 acres, 3 quarters and 2 rods of cow pasture [DTR 30].

In her will, dated 17 November 1646 and proved 30 June 1647, "Rachell Bigg of Dorchester ... widow" noted that she had "sold my house and land wherein I now dwell unto my nephew Hopestill Foster for one hundred & twenty pounds to be paid as appeareth under his hand within half one year after my decease according as I shall appoint in writing which I do herein dispose [as] followeth together with the rent hereof if any be then due after my decease ... he shall pay unto Thankfull Stowe threescore pounds ... and I give more unto Thankfull Stowe twenty pounds which is due unto me from the said Hopestill Foster ... and if the said Hopestill Foster do not pay the said threescore pounds so given unto Thankfull Stowe then I give the said house and land unto her the said Thankfull Stowe ... [and] unto Hopestill Foster he performing the payments before given ... threescore pounds the remainder of the said sum of one hundred & twenty pounds & the rest of the said house & lands which shall or may be due at my decease so it amounts not to above eight pounds, out of which legacies ... he shall give three pounds unto his daughter Thankfull to be laid out upon a silver pot for her marked with R.B., twenty shillings to his son Hopestill to buy for him three silver spoons, and also forty shillings to his daughter Patience to be laid out upon six silver spoons for her all the spoons to be marked R.B."; also to "the said Hopestill Foster," bedding; "whereas my son-in-law John Stow oweth unto me one hundred and forty pounds ... out of which I give unto his eldest son Thomas Stow thirty pounds he paying out of it forty shillings to be laid out upon six silver spoons to be marked R.B. of which I give three of them to his daughter Marie & the other three to his son Samuell and ... to his eldest son John a silver cup which I bought of his father"; to "Elizabeth Stow the wife of Henry Archer thirty pounds paying out of it five pounds to be laid out in fifteen spoons marked with R.B. of which I give six unto her daughter Rachel & three to John & three to Isaac & three to Theophilos their three sons"; to "Elizabeth Stow the wife of the said

Henry Archer my silver pot and my book of Doctor Preston"; to "Nathanell Stowe having given him formerly a small tenement & land I give him more twenty pounds"; to "Samuell Stow thirty pounds, all which legacies so given and bequeathed unto them shall be paid unto them by their father as he can make payment either out of his lands or otherwise"; to "Peter Masters my son-in-law now living in England twenty shillings & to his daughter Elizabeth ten shillings and to his wife Katherin my silk kirtle"; to "Mr. Richard Mather forty shillings and to the poor in Dorchester twenty shillings"; to "Mr. Newman & to Mr. John Miller ten shillings apiece"; to "James Batte Senior five shillings & to his son James five shillings"; to "the now wife of Thomas Lyne five shillings and to Clement Batte twenty shillings and his daughter Rachel ten shillings and to the residue of his children five shillings apiece"; to "the now wife of Will[ia]m Batcheller twenty shillings & to every of her children five shillings apiece and to Thomas Beatts twenty shillings"; to "Thomas Beall, John Compton, Goodwife Turner, the wife of Richard Brittainne, Goodman Meade, old Margery & to Goodwife Place to every of them five shillings"; to "poor Goodwife Hill and to Goodwife Patching," 10s. apiece; to Thankfull Stow all my household stuff & plate ungiven"; residue to "my loving son-in-law John Stowe whom I make my whole sole executor" [SPR 1:89-91; NEHGR 5:300-1].

BIRTH: Baptized Lydd, Kent, 17 June 1565, daughter of James and Joan (Adam) Martin [NEHGR 92:397].

DEATH: Dorchester between 17 November 1646 (date of will) and 30 June 1647 (probate of will).

MARRIAGE: Tenterden, Kent, 14 September 1583 "John Bigge" [NEHGR 66:58]. He was buried at Cranbrook 13 August 1605 (as "householder"). (See COMMENTS below for an abstract of his will.)

CHILDREN:

    i   ANNA, bp. Cranbrook 16 August 1584; bur. there 27 August 1584.

    ii   SMALLHOPE, bp. Cranbrook 29 August 1585; m. by an unknown date Ellen _____ (in his will of 3 May 1638 "Smalehope Bigg" bequeathed to "Ellen my loving wife" [Consistory Court of Kent 51:115; Waters 21]; "Ellen Bigge of Cranbrooke, widow of Smalehope Bigge," made her will on 24 November 1638 [Waters 21-22]).

    iii PATIENCE, bp. Cranbrook 5 May 1588; m. by about 1621 Richard Foster (only known child aged fourteen in 1635

[Hotten 68]) [NEHGR 52:194-203; Waters 22].

iv   ELIZABETH, bp. Cranbrook 1 November 1590; m. Biddenden, Kent, 13 September 1608 JOHN STOWE [NEHGR 70:347].

v   JAMES, bp. Cranbrook 28 January 1592/3; bur. there 12 January 1593/4.

vi   RACHEL, bp. Cranbrook 20 October 1594; m. (1) Biddenden, Kent, 4 March 1616/7 Moregift Starr [NEHGR 92:398]; m. (2) Cranbrook, Kent, 9 November 1619 Peter Masters [NEHGR 92:398].

vii   ANNA, bp. Cranbrook 30 January 1596/7; bur. there 16 May 1597.

viii   JOHN, bp. Cranbrook [blank] June 1598; bur. there 18 December 1598.

ix   MARY, bp. Cranbrook 18 May 1600; bur. there 24 April 1610.

x   JOHN, bp. Cranbrook 19 December 1602; m. (1) (lic.) 12 May 1626 Mary Maplisden [NEHGR 92:398]; m. (2) (lic.) 16 September 1634 Sibylla Beacon [NEHGR 92:398].

xi   THANKFUL, bp. Cranbrook 17 February 1604/5; bur. there 14 August 1605 (note that this was just three days after she was named in her father's will).

ASSOCIATIONS: Through her sister, Mary (Martin?) Bate, Rachel was aunt of CLEMENT BATE and JAMES BATE. Through Mary (Bigg?) Betts, apparently sister of her husband, Rachel was aunt (by marriage) of Thomas Betts of Guilford [NEHGR 92:296-301].

COMMENTS: On 17 April 1635, "Rachell Bigg," aged 6 [*sic*], was enrolled at London as a passenger for New England on the *Elizabeth* [Hotten 68; Savage 1:177]. (This must be a clerical error; Rachel would have been sixty-nine at the time of this record.)

In his will, dated 11 August 1605 and proved 30 October 1605, "John Bigge of Cranbrook, co. Kent, clothier," bequeathed to "the poor of Cranbrook," 5s.; to "either of my prentices," 5s. apiece; to "every one of my daughters, Patience, Elizabeth, Rachell, Mary and Thanckful, one hundred pounds apiece at their ages of 20 or days of marriage"; to "my wife, Rachell Bigge, one hundred marks and all my household stuff"; "executors to pay my debts and such money as I owe to my brother Scotchford's executors on the mortgage of my house and land I now dwell in"; to "my wife, £10 a year out of my land in recompense of her title of dower, to be paid quarterly"; "my house and land at Linton and Maidstone to my son Smalehope Bigge and his heirs"; "after my executors have redeemed the house and land I now dwell in, if my son John at his age of 21 release all right thereto to my son Smalehope, then the house in Linton and Maidstone shall remain to my son John, and the bequest to Smalehope shall be void"; "the portions of my daughters to be employed in their bringing up"; "my wife to bring up my youngest son John"; "Rachell my wife and Smalehope my son to be joint executors"; inventory of estate totalled £690 8s. 6d. [NEHGR 92:396, citing Consistory Court of Canterbury 39:196].

On 26 November 1646, Thomas Lechford recorded an "attestation unto an acquittance from Hopestill Foster, Thomas Stow, Nathaniel Stow & Samuel Stowe unto Elisabeth Ayerst of Maidstone, widow, for £60 by them received by a deed dated 8 May 1646, as also to a release from the said persons unto John Marshall of Speildherst in the County of Kent, clerk, & Sibill his wife, late the wife of John Bigg late of Maidstone, gent., & to John Ayerst, son & heir of W[illia]m Ayerst late of Maidstone deceased, salter, for & concerning certain messuages &c. given by the said John Bigg & this was by deed 8 May 1646" [Aspinwall 43].

BIBLIOGRAPHIC NOTE: Several articles relating to Rachel (Martin) Bigg and her connections have appeared in the *Register*. In 1875 E.W.N. Starr and W.H. Whitmore presented a transcript of the will of Rachel's son John Bigg [NEHGR 29:253-60]. In 1884 Henry F. Waters published a number of English wills for the Bigg family [NEHGR 38:60-62; Waters 21-23]. In 1898 William H. Whitmore compiled an account of Hopestill Foster, Rachel's grandson [NEHGR 52:194-203]. In 1912 Elizabeth French collected a number of additional English wills along with some parish register entries, and compiled an account of one Bigg family of Kent, not necessarily ancestral to the immigrants of this sketch [NEHGR 66:54-61]. In 1916 Elizabeth French presented parish register entries for the Stowe family, and created a pedigree of the family, a member of which married one of Rachel's daughters [NEHGR 70:347-49]. In 1938 John Insley Coddington published wills and parish register entries for a Betts family of Kent, from whom descended Thomas Betts of Guilford, Connecticut; Coddington argued that the mother of Thomas Betts was sister of Rachel's husband [NEHGR 92:296-301]. Later the same year Coddington added two English wills and more parish register entries which add much to our knowledge of Rachel's family [NEHGR 92:395-98].

In 1948 Mary Lovering Holman prepared an account of John and Rachel (Martin) Bigg [Stevens-Miller Anc 1:459-64].

In 1990 John Brooks Threlfall published a brief account of John and Rachel along five generations of proposed agnate ancestry for John Bigg [GMC50:37-62].

The last three sources vary widely between one another on the data from the Cranbrook parish register, so the register has been reexamined, and the dates given above are from that reexamination.

THOMAS BIGGS

On 13 July 1635, "Tho[mas] Biggs," aged 13, was enrolled at London as a passenger for New England on the *Blessing* [Hotten 108].

COMMENTS: There is no evidence that he arrived in New England. (See JOHN BRIGGS.)

JOHN BILL

On 3 April 1635, "Jo[hn] Bill," aged 13, was enrolled at London as a passenger for New England on the *Hopewell* [Hotten 46].

COMMENTS: He is not found in any New England record. (Savage thinks this may be the John Bill who died in Boston in December of 1638, but John L. Cobb and Vada Tuttle Larson (aided by William H. Schoeffler) think it more likely that this record is for James Bill who died at that time [TAG 60:195-96].)

MARY BILL

On 6 April 1635, "Marie Bill," aged 11, was enrolled at London as a passenger for New England on the *Planter* [Hotten 49].

COMMENTS: She is not found in any New England record, but as she was in the family of William Tuttle in the passenger list, and as the Tuttles and Bills were related and from the same part of England, Mary Bill is likely a member of the Bill family of Ringstead, Northamptonshire [TAG 60:195].

JOHN BILLINGS

ORIGIN: Unknown
MIGRATION: 1635 on the *Speedwell*
FIRST RESIDENCE: Richmond Island
REMOVES: Piscataqua (Kittery Point) by 1639

OCCUPATION: Fisherman [MPCR 1:113-14].
EDUCATION: Signed his name to a deed [MPCR 1:113-14].
ESTATE: On 10 January 1639[/40] [recorded a second time with the year altered to 1649/50], "John Lander of Pascataquacke, sailor," and "John Billine of the same place, fisherman," entered into an agreement whereupon "John Billine is to have the house which hath the chimney in it being the western end of the house & the loft over it, and John Lander is to have the chamber being the eastern end of the house & the loft over it, and John Billine is to have half the land that is cleared & already fenced and his part is to be bounded to the south and John Lander is to have the other half bounded to the north, & John Lander is to have one-half of the shallop & all things thereunto belonging, and the said John Lander is to have the starboard side & John Billine to have the larboard side & the other half thereunto belonging, and the said John Lander is to have free egress & regress to come to the fire for his uses so often as occasion shall need, and John Billine is to have one-half of all the land that is uncleared that does belong unto the house, & it is bounded to the south, and John Lander is to have the other bounded to the north, and John Billine has the old sow & two young shoats, and John Lander is to have the little sow & two young shoats, all which house, land, and goods are equally divided and delivered to both parties" [YLR 1:10, 15].

On the "last day of February 1639[/40]," "John Lander and John Billin of Pascataquack, fishermen," sold to "Joseph Milles of the said place, planter, eight acres of land ... which land is marked out from the land that is cleared by the said John Lander and John Billin ... and twenty acres more of land thereunto adjoining" [MPCR 1:113-14]. (On 11 November 1647, Joseph Milles sold this parcel to Thomas Crockett, and in December 1647, Crockett sold it to "Rise Thomas" [MPCR 1:114-15].)

On 16 May 1645, there was "granted unto John Billine in the behalf of Sir Ferd[inando] Gorges a parcel of marsh ground at Brabote Harbor lying betwixt the house lately Steven Craford's and the great rock containing by estimation 4 acres" [YLR 1:10, 16]. On 26 March 1647,

"Goodwife Thomas ... doth affirm that her late husband John Billings gave unto William Wormewood ii acres of ground, and that John Lander gave him ii more" [MPCR 1:104].

On 21 June 1662, "John Billing of Kittery" deeded to "my mother Elizabeth Thomasse during her life, & after her decease to return unto the above named John Billing," livestock and "my marsh lying & being in Braveboate Harbour" [YLR 1:121].

BIRTH: By about 1616 based on estimated date of marriage.
DEATH: Before 6 July 1646 when his widow sued Robert Mendam [MPCR 1:95; GMB 2:1254].
MARRIAGE: By about 1641 Elizabeth _____. She married (2) before 26 March 1647 Rice Thomas [YLR 1:121].
CHILD:

i   JOHN, b. by 1641 (assuming he was 21 when he conveyed land to his mother [YLR 1:121]); m. by 1671 Ann Andrews (on 4 July 1671, the court at York took notice of "several complaints ... concerning Ann Billine's misbehavior towards her husband by frequent absenting of herself from her home & husband," and ordered that if she continued in this way "she shall be forthwith sent to the House of Correction" [MPCR 2:217]), daughter of John Andrews of Kittery (so stated by Noyes, Libby and Davis [GDMNH 65, 93]; John Billings was seen several times in the company of the children of John Andrews [MPCR 2:284, 456-57, 3:265]).

ASSOCIATIONS: John Billings sailed to New England on the same ship with JOHN LANDER [Trelawny Papers 93, 97] and was for several years closely associated with him, sharing house and real estate, and also working with him [YLR 1:10, 15; MPCR 1:113-14].

COMMENTS: On 28 June 1636, John Winter wrote to Robert Trelawny about six men, under the leadership of JOHN LANDER, who had come to Richmond Island in 1635 on the *Speedwell*, but had since then left the Trelawny plantation; one of the six was "John Bellin" [Trelawny Papers 93]. A day later Narias Hawkins, master of the *Speedwell*, also wrote to Trelawny about the same incident, listing the same six men, including "Billin" [Trelawny Papers 97].

On 25 May 1640, John Billings joined the other inhabitants of the "Lower End of Pascataquack" in granting the glebe, most of the signers living on the west side of the river [NHPP 1:113; GDMNH 43, citing Portsmouth Town Book, p. 99]. On 8 September 1640, "John Billin" sued John Winter in an action of debt [MPCR 1:58].

ROBERT BILLS

ORIGIN: Unknown
MIGRATION: 1635 on the *Pied Cow*
FIRST RESIDENCE: Charlestown

OCCUPATION: Husbandman.
EDUCATION: His inventory included "one Bible" valued at 5s. and "3 books" valued at 4s. 6d., as well as a pair of spectacles, an inkhorn, and a sealing wax.
ESTATE: On 4 September 1638, "John Knowles (having married the widow of Ephraim Davies, who was sister to Rob[e]rt Bills) was granted administration of the estate of Rob[e]rt Bills" [MBCR 1:235]. The "inventory of the household stuff & goods pertaining to Robert Bills, who deceased about December 15, 1635," was untotalled; on 1 October 1638, "Samuell Peirce affirms ... that John Knowls married the widow of Ephraim Davis & to her was allowed to administer the estate of Robert Bills marrying his sister"; the appraisers were Jabez Sprague and Robert Hale [SPR NS 1:16-18].

BIRTH: About 1603 (aged 32 in 1635 [Hotten 110]).
DEATH: About 15 December 1635 "in the house of Edward Carington, in Charlestown" [MBCR 1:182].
MARRIAGE: None recorded.
CHILDREN: None recorded.
ASSOCIATIONS: On 31 December 1634, "George Bills, brother-in-law to Mr. Ephraim Davis," was buried at St Nicholas Acons, London [St Nicholas Acons PR 107]. On 26 November 1636, administration on the estate of Ephraim Davis of St Nicholas Acon, citizen of London, deceased, was granted to Elizabeth Davis, his widow [PCC Admon Act Book 1636-1638, p. 29]. On 11 February 1637/8, "John Knoles of the parish of St Giles Crippellgate and Elizabeth Davis widow of this parish" were married at St Nicholas Acons [St Nicholas Acons PR 70].

COMMENTS: On 23 July 1635, "Robert Bills," husbandman, aged 32, was enrolled at London as a passenger for New England on the *Pied Cow* [Hotten 110].

THOMAS BIRCHARD

ORIGIN: Terling, Essex
MIGRATION: 1635 on the *Truelove*
FIRST RESIDENCE: Roxbury
REMOVES: Hartford by 1639, Saybrook by 1648, Edgartown by 1653, Norwich 1682

OCCUPATION: Laborer [Hotten 131]. (Given his later prominence in New England, this occupational designation entered in the London port book must be regarded with some skepticism; however, no other evidence of his occupation has been found.)
CHURCH MEMBERSHIP: "Thomas Bircharde" was admitted in 1635 to the Roxbury Church as member #137 [RChR 81].
FREEMAN: 17 May 1637 (as "Thom[as] Bircher," first in a sequence of three Roxbury men) [MBCR 1:373].
EDUCATION: Thomas Birchard and his second wife signed their deed of 6 June 1667.
OFFICES: Connecticut juror, sometime between 11 April and 1 August 1639 [CCCR 1:29]. Deputy for Saybrook to Connecticut General Court, 16 May 1650 (marked "absent"), 15 May 1651 [CCCR 1:207, 218, 220].

Edgartown committee to divide lands [Edgartown TR 1:131]. Town clerk (as "Thomas Burchard the elder"), 8 June 1653 [Edgartown TR 1:121]. Commissioner to end small causes, 1654, 1655, 1656 [Edgartown TR 1:119, 120, 121].
ESTATE: In the Hartford land inventory in February 1639[/40], "Thomas Birchwo[od]" held five parcels, along with a sixth parcel acquired at a later date: "one parcel on which his dwelling house now standeth with other outhouses, yards or gardens therein being part whereof is lying in the Westfield & containeth by estimation five acres"; "one parcel lying in the North Meadow of meadow & swamp containing by estimation five acres one rood & eleven perches (more or less) viz: two acres three roods & thirty-five perches of meadow & two acres one rood & thirty-six perches of swamp"; "one parcel more lying in the North Meadow

containing by estimation eight acres"; "one parcel lying in the Cowpasture containing by estimation nine acres"; "one parcel lying in the little oxpasture containing by estimation eight acres"; and "one parcel of land with a messuage or tenement standing thereon which he bought of Zachariah Field containing by estimation four acres" (annotated "October the 4th 1650, it was when this parcel of land was bought but not recorded before the 21th of February 1652") [HaBOP 124-25].

In 1640 "Thomas Birchwood" was granted twenty-six acres of "upland on the east side of the Great River" [HaTR 23, 52].

On 4 January 1648[/9], Thomas Birchard held a £300 interest in the Eight Mile Meadow in Saybrook [Goodwin Anc 1:56, citing Potopogue Proprietors' Records 1:1]. On 31 October 1656, "Thomas Birchard of Martins Vinyard" sold to William Pratt of Saybrook his interest, and that of his son, John, in the upland and meadow in "Potopouge Quarter" [SayLR 2:99]. On 1 November 1656, Thomas Birchard sold to John Clark Sr. of Saybrook "two pieces of land in that town, one of nine acres in the planting field, and the other of six acres in the North Meadow which belonged to his son John" [Goodwin Anc 1:58, citing a deed in private hands].

In 1663 Thomas Birchard deeded "to my cousin Thomas Trapp" certain lands on Martha's Vineyard, the deed being signed by Thomas Birchard and also by "Katiren Burchard" [Edgartown TR 1:19]. On 6 June 1667, "Thomas Birchard of Martha's Vineyard" sold to Robert Codman of Martha's Vineyard "my ten-acre lot, more or less, which I bought of Richard Smith ... and also half a share of fish and whales which was my son John Birchard's"; "Tho[mas] Birchard" and "Katrine Birchard" signed the deed [Dukes LR 1:320].

A 1669 list of Thomas Birchard's lands on Martha's Vineyard comprised "my houselot with addition the town gave me in changing some of my lots and five acres I had of John Pease in all I judge eighteen acres"; "my dividend lot with my pond lot lying together, my pond lot 1 part of it of old John Folger and part of it I changed with Bland and his wife, a third part I took out of my dividend lot, both parcels I judge to be about thirty acres"; "thirdly at Crackatuxett two lots the third and fifteen with my thatch lot without side the fence that was containing three acres"; "my land [at] Mashakett containing I judge sixty-three acres"; "fifthly one ten-acre lot within the general fence"; "sixthly my meadow two acres more or less which I bought of Richard Smith lying at Poche on Chappaquidick Island"; and share in the fishweirs, whales and grazing rights" [Edgartown TR 1:74-75]. On 13 June 1676, "Thomas Burchard" deeded to "my kinsman Thomas Trapp ... my thatch lot lying in Mr. Mayhew's dividend near Cracketuxett being in the number of thatch lots the ninth and also my two lots lying in a place called Cracketuxett one being in number the third, the other the fifteenth" [Edgartown TR 1:7].

On 2 May 1682, "Thomas Birchard of Edgartown upon Martha's Vineyard" sold to Joseph Norton of Edgartown "all my right, title & interest in the neck which is called Aquampacher Neck near Pahoggannot" [Dukes LR 4:36]. On 24 March 1682/3, "Thomas Birchard of Norwich" sold to "Nicolas Marson of Say-Brook ... a hundred-pound right in the Oxpasture of Say-Brook" [SayLR 2:237]. On 9 May 1683, "Thomas Birchard late inhabitant upon Martha's Vineyard" sold to "Thomas Wollin resident upon Martha's Vineyard ... one share and half share of land lately purchased by Mr. Sarson lying and being near Sanchacantackitt" [Dukes LR 1:209].

On 16 September 1684, "[t]here being presented unto this Court a writing of Mr. Thomas Birchard deceased as an addition to his will this Court approves the same & orders it to be recorded. And that the executor or administrator to that estate pay those legacies according to the true meaning & intent of the deceased as is expressed in the said writing under his hand and witnessed by Morgan Bowers & John Reed" [NLCR 4:87].

On 25 November 1684, "John Birchard petitioning this Court and presenting some reasons against the probation of the Court of the addition to Mr. Thomas Birchard's addition to his last will although John Birchard had notice that the codicil was to be presented & the said John Birchard would not appear in the season to make his objections and this Court seeing it their duty & could do no otherwise but approve the said addition to Thomas Birchard's will yet this Court grants liberty to John Birchard to appear to the next Court of Assistants in May next or else that John Birchard pay the ten pounds given by Mr. Thomas Birchard to some of his children" [NLCR 4:96].

BIRTH: Baptized Fairsted, Essex, 12 October 1595, son of "W[illia]m Byrcharde."

DEATH: Between 9 May 1683 [Dukes LR 1:209] and 16 September 1684 (court order on codicil to will).

MARRIAGE: (1) Fairsted, Essex, 23 October 1620, Mary Robinson [TAG 51:18]. "[blank] Birchard, the wife of Thomas Birchard," was admitted in late 1635 or early 1636 to the Roxbury Church as member number #146

[RChR 81], and it was presumably she who died in Roxbury as "Goodwife Birchard" on 24 March 1654/5 [RChR 176; see also TAG 16:162-63].

(2) By 1659, widow Catherine Andrews (on 22 September 1659, "administration to the estate of Lewis Martine was given 21th July 59 to Thomas Trapp in behalf of Mr. John Andrewes, to whom it was given, & the said Thomas Trapp failing in giving security to the recorder who understanding & finding the said Thomas Trapp to be conveying himself & the said goods out of this jurisdiction to Martin's Vineyard to Thomas Burchard who married the said Thomas [*sic*] Andrewes mother" [SPR 3:192-93; TAG 64:88-89]), living on 6 June 1667 [Dukes LR 1:320].

(3) By 1680 Deborah _____ ("Deborah, wife of Thomas Burcham of Martin's Viniarde, d. in Charlestowne, May 10, 1680" [ChVR 1:110]).

CHILDREN:

i   ELIZABETH, bp. Terling, Essex, 1 November 1621 [Terling PR]; no further record.

ii MARY, bp. Terling, Essex, 2 April 1623 [Terling PR]; no further record.

iii SARAH, bp. Terling, Essex, 22 August 1624 [Terling PR]; m. Hartford 25 October 1647 Bartholomew Barnard [HaVR 608].

iv SUSANNAH, bp. Terling, Essex, 22 June 1626 [Terling PR]; no further record.

v   JOHN, bp. Terling, Essex, 31 January 1627/8 [Terling PR]; m. (1) (recorded at Norwich but probably at Hartford or Saybrook) 22 July 1653 Christian Andrews [NoVR 22-23; TAG 64:85, 89]; m. (2) by 1680 Jane (Lee) Hyde, daughter of Thomas Lee and widow of Samuel Hyde [TAG 16:227-28, and sources cited there].

vi THOMAS, bp. Terling, Essex, 24 September 1629 [Terling PR]; bur. there 19 February 1630/1 [Terling PR].

vii DEBORAH, bp. Terling, Essex, 18 April 1632 [Terling PR]; bur. there 6 April 1633 [Terling PR].

viii HANNAH, bp. Terling, Essex, 17 October 1633 [Terling PR]; m. (as "Hanna Burchet") Guilford 12 April 1653 John Baldwin "both of Guilford" [GuilVR Barbour 4; see also TAG 64:86].

ASSOCIATIONS: On 14 March 1681, in an order relating to the disposition of the estates of Richard Webb and his wife Elizabeth, "Mr. Bartholemu Barnard in the right of his wife and in the right of all that are related to his father Burcher [claimed] a right to a proportion out of the estate of both the above deceased by virtue of kindred" [Fairfield PR 3:86-87]. "Attempts to prove how Birchard and Webb were related have proved unavailing" [Goodwin Anc 61-62].

Thomas Birchard and his second wife, "Katherine," were witnesses on 4 March 1674 to the will of John Pease of Martha's Vineyard who, in his will, gave to his son, John Pease, all the land that had been given to him at Mohegan [now Norwich, Connecticut]. This was the place to which John Birchard, Thomas's son, had removed. Thomas Trapp, the relative of Mrs. Birchard, also witnessed the will. Perhaps this indicates some connection between John Pease, or his wife, and either Thomas Birchard or his wife.

COMMENTS: On 19 September 1635, "Thomas Burchard," aged 40 years, "laboring man," "Mary Burchard," aged 38, "Elizabeth Burchard," aged 13, "Marie Burchard," aged 12, "Sara Burchard," aged 9, "Suzan Burchard," aged 8, "Jo[hn] Burchard," aged 7, and "Ann Burchard," aged 18 months, were enrolled at London for passage to New England on the *Truelove* [Hotten 131].

A suggestion has been made that Thomas Birchard lived briefly at Guilford, Connecticut, because his daughter Hannah was described as being of Guilford at the time she married [Goodwin Anc 1:57]. This suggestion is not supported by other evidence, and Hannah was probably there on her own.

"Tho[mas] Birchard" was apparently a principal instigator of the "rebellion" of some of the inhabitants of Martha's Vineyard who favored annexation to the government of the Massachusetts Bay Colony, and was the first signatory on the petition dated 15 October 1673, which petition also contained the signature of "Thomas Trappe" [Goodwin Anc 1:59-60; MA Arch 48:138].

The claim has been made for some years in various secondary sources that Mary Birchard, daughter of Thomas Birchard, was the famous, unnamed "bride of Bride's Brook." John Winthrop Jr., magistrate of New London, was called upon to marry Jonathan Rudd of Saybrook to an unnamed bride, but Saybrook not being within Winthrop's jurisdiction, and there having fallen a heavy snow, the young couple and their attendants met Winthrop part way at his suggestion, and the marriage was performed in the forest on the New London side of the brook which served as the boundary line between New London and the Colony of Connecticut. Winthrop deposed some years later concerning this event, but gave neither the date nor the name of the bride. However, he affirmed that this event was the source of the name Bride's Brook for this particular stream [CCCR 2:558-59]. Unfortunately, without some evidence that the bride was Mary Birchard, we cannot expediently assume that it was she who married Jonathan Rudd. Those who have made this claim say that only Thomas Birchard was influential enough to cause Winthrop to travel out in the snow to perform this marriage. Winthrop says nothing about this courtesy, and says that he himself suggested such a meeting; moreover, the suggestion that only Birchard was prominent enough to cause Winthrop to leave home is absurd since there were many men in the area more prominent and influential than Thomas Birchard.

Suggestions have also been made in secondary sources of marriages made by two other daughters of Thomas Birchard, Elizabeth and Susanna, but no evidence supports these suggestions.

BIBLIOGRAPHIC NOTE: In 1915 Frank Farnsworth Starr prepared a good treatment of Thomas Birchard and his family, utilizing primary sources [Goodwin Anc 1:55-62]. While not every item of biographical information appeared therein, valuable verbatim quotations from original documents, and footnotes showing full references, make this a critical and reliable source.

Though she did not know the English home of Thomas Birchard and his family, or have data from the parish registers there, Edna M. Rogers compiled a comprehensive genealogy of Thomas Birchard and his descendants to the children of the third generation [TAG 16:157-63, 221-28, 17:35-49, 177-90]. While this has details not mentioned by Starr, both have to be used together to provide a full picture of Thomas Birchard's peregrinations.

Prentiss Glazier discovered the English origin of Thomas and Mary (Robinson) Birchard and a full list of their children which, with additional data from the parish registers and wills concerning the Robinson ancestry, was published in 1975 [TAG 51:17-21].

SIMON BIRD

ORIGIN: Unknown
MIGRATION: 1635 on the *Susan & Ellen*
FIRST RESIDENCE: Boston
REMOVES: Billerica

OCCUPATION: Laborer.

CHURCH MEMBERSHIP: On 24 February 1643/4, "Simon Birde of Rumley Marsh laborer" was admitted to Boston church [BChR 40]. On 5 July 1646, "[o]ur brother Simon Bird was in the name of our Lord Jesus with the consent of the church excommunicated out of the church by our Elder Leveritt for filthy unclean dalliances with his maid servant" [BChR 46], and on 30 April 1648, "[o]ur brother Simon Bird upon his openly professed repentance for his unclean dalliances for which he was excommunicated out of the Church was now by our Elder Oliver in the name of Christ and with the consent of the Church by their silence restored unto the fellowship thereof" [BChR 49].

FREEMAN: 29 May 1644 [MBCR 2:293].

EDUCATION: Signed his will. His inventory included "two Bibles & other books" valued at £1 2s. The joint inventory of 1680 included "one pike and one Bible & six other books" valued at 6s.

OFFICES: Boston constable (for Rumney Marsh), 12 March 1654/5 [BTR 1:122].

ESTATE: In his will, dated 4 January 1665[/6] and proved 2 October 1666, "Simon Bird of Billerica" bequeathed all to "my beloved wife," and at her decease: to "Mr. John Wilson Junior my esteemed cousin," £40, and to "my cousin Mrs. Mary Danforth of Roxbury," £20; to "our reverend pastor Mr. Samuell Whiting Junior," £10; to "the Church of Christ at Billerica," £10; to "my landlady Buttolph," £5; to "Mary Bruer of Lynne, daughter of Crispuse Bruer," £5; to "Mary Danforth of Billerica, daughter of Jonath[an] Danforth," 40s.; "my wife Mary Bird my sole executrix" [MPR Case #1791].

The inventory of the estate of "Simon Bird of Billerica deceased," taken 13 July 1660, totalled £206 7s. 6d., of which £125 was real estate: "one house [and] houselot with 13 acres of meadow & the appurtenances & privileges appertaining thereto," £125 [MPR Case #1791].

On 16 December 1679, "upon the death of Mary Jeffs executrix to Simon Bird this Court doth appoint Henry Jeffs & Sam[ue]ll Manning to be administrators to the estate of Simon Bird abovesaid" [MCF Folio #87; MCR 3:317]. On 26 December 1679, "Hen[ry] Jeffs" posted bond of £200 "on the estate of Simon Bird, whose relict widow & executrix the said Jeffs did marry & she is now deceased" [MCF Folio #87; MCR 3:321].

The inventory of the estate of "Simon Bird & Mary Bird," attested on 6 April 1680, totalled £200 12s., of which about £190 was real estate: "several pieces of broken up land and several pieces of English pasture we judge at four pounds an acre without any housing or fruit trees"; "the rest of the land that is wilderness, grass and woodlands belonging to the house we judge is worth fifty shillings an acre"; "the dwelling house and the well of water near the house with free passage out of the highway to the house and from the house to the well we judge at six pounds"; "one acre of meadow in the furthest great meadow we prize at fifty shillings an acre"; "seven acres in the great meadow we prize at three pounds an acre"; "four acres at Shawshin we prize at four pounds an acre"; and "two acres and a quarter fifty shillings an acre before the fencing be up" [MPR Case #1792; MPR 5:188-89].

On 11 August 1680, a series of executions against the estate of "Henry Jeffs administrator of the estate of Simon Bird deceased" divided the land of Simon Bird to the legatees named in his will [MPR 8:182-93; MCR 3:339].

BIRTH: About 1615 (aged 20 on 13 April 1635 [Hotten 59]).
DEATH: Billerica 7 July 1666.
MARRIAGE: By 1643 Mary _____. On 11 June 1643, "Mary Bird the wife of one Simon Bird" was admitted to Boston church [BChR 38]. She married (2) at Billerica on 3 October 1666 Henry Jefts, and she died at Billerica on 1 April 1679.
CHILDREN: None recorded.
ASSOCIATIONS: The two largest bequests in Simon Bird's will were to "Mr. John Wilson Junior my esteemed cousin" and to "my cousin Mrs. Mary Danforth of Roxbury." These two legatees are the children of Rev. John and Elizabeth (Mansfield) Wilson of Boston. In the passenger list of the *Susan & Ellen*, Simon Bird appeared immediately preceding JOHN MANSFIELD, aged 34, who was brother of Wilson's wife. Immediately after John Mansfield on the same list was CLEMENT COLE, who was a servant of Capt. ROBERT KEAYNE, whose wife was Ann Mansfield, a sibling to Elizabeth and John. Clement Cole was another of the six men who ran from their masters and were dealt with on 6 October 1635 [MBCR 1:162]. Extensive research in the Bird, Mansfield, Wilson and Keayne families has failed to uncover the genealogical connection between Simon Bird and the children of John Wilson.

COMMENTS: "Symon Burd," aged 20, was enrolled at London on 13 April 1635 as a passenger for New England on the *Susan & Ellen* [Hotten 59]. (On 28 April 1616, "Symon Byrde the son of Thomas Byrde and Faith his wife" was baptized at Wood Ditton, Cambridge, but there is no evidence to connect this baptism to the immigrant.)

On 6 October 1635, Simon Bird was one of six men who "shall be whipped for running from their masters, & for stealing a boat & diverse other things with them, as also shall give satisfaction to the country for their charges in sending to fetch them home, & likewise shall serve their said masters twice so long at the end of their time, as they have been absent from their master's service, by reason of their running away" [MBCR 1:162].

HENRY BIRDSALL

ORIGIN: Unknown
MIGRATION: 1635
FIRST RESIDENCE: Boston
REMOVES: Salem

CHURCH MEMBERSHIP: "Henry Burdsall" was admitted to Salem church on 25 February 1637/8 (with a later annotation "dead") [SChR 7].
FREEMAN: 2 May 1638 [MBCR 1:374].
EDUCATION: His inventory included "books" valued at 5s. [EPR 1:144].
OFFICES: Essex petit jury, 25 March 1639 [EQC 1:10].
ESTATE: As the result of a 14 December 1635 order allotting land to Boston's "then inhabitants," "Henry Burchall" was granted fifteen acres [BTR 1:22, 26].

On 10 December 1649, Henry Cooke of Salem, butcher, mortgaged his house, shop and one acre of land to Henry Birdsall [ELR 1:7].

The will of Henry Birdsall was proved 28 November 1651, but has not survived [EPR 1:143].

The inventory of the estate of Henry Birdsall, taken 17 November 1651, totalled £47 19s. 10d., of which £14 10s. was real estate: "one dwelling house, outhouses & 1 acre & quar[ter] land," £10; and "5 acres of upland in the Northfield & half acre of salt marsh in the Southfield," £4 10s. He had "1 old sword, musket & halberd" valued at 9s. "Tools for his trade" were valued at £2, but we are not told the nature of that trade [EPR 1:143-44].

BIRTH: By about 1585 based on date of marriage.
DEATH: By 17 November 1651 (date of inventory).
MARRIAGE: St Stephen, Norwich, Norfolk, 9 April 1610 Agnes Kempe.
CHILDREN:

i   JUDITH, bp. St Stephen, Norwich, 2 June 1611; m. Salem [blank] June 1639 Henry Cooke.

ii   ANNE, bp. St John Timberhill, Norwich, 24 May 1616; no further record.

iii NATHAN, bp. St Andrew, Norwich, 3 September 1620; on 16 February 1654[/5] "Nathan Birdsall of Salem" sold to Henry Cooke of Salem five acres of land in Salem [ELR 1:26]; probably the Nathan Birdsall who was granted land at Easthampton on 5 July 1653 [Easthampton TR 1:37], and who later resided at Oyster Bay, where he had a son Henry [Oyster Bay TR 1:684] and a granddaughter Judith (see *COMMENTS* below).

COMMENTS: On 28 October 1643, Henry Birdsall witnessed the partially nuncupative will of John Sanders of Salem [EPR 1:26]. On 20 February 1643/4, "Henry Burdsell" was a witness in the case of Randall Houlden vs. Goody Oliver [EQC 1:61]. On 3 February 1644/5, Henry "Burtsoll" was chosen to "keep the meeting house to sweep it & keep it clean upon all occasions of public meeting & is to have yearly, three pounds & 15s. to be paid proportionably every half year" [STR 1:135]. He was duly paid in 1647 [STR 1:151].

Son Nathan is said to have resided at New Haven. A "Nathan Burchall" appeared in New Haven records from late 1643 until early 1645 [NHCR 1:109, 120, 139, 152]. This may or may not have been Nathan Birdsall, son of Henry. Contrary to statements in secondary sources, Henry Birdsall did not reside in New Haven.

NATHANIEL BISHOP

ORIGIN: Unknown
MIGRATION: 1634
FIRST RESIDENCE: Boston

OCCUPATION: Currier [BChR 40]. Innholder [SLR 9:262].

CHURCH MEMBERSHIP: "Nathaniell Bushopp a currier" was admitted to Boston church on 24 February 1643/4 [BChR 40]. On 21 April 1672, "the wife of Nathaniell Bishope was admitted member [of Boston First Church] upon a letter of dismission from the Church of Ipswich under the hands of William Hubbard, Thomas Cobbet, Robert Payne" [BChR 68].

FREEMAN: May 1645 [MBCR 2:294].

EDUCATION: Signed his deeds and his will. He witnessed several of his neighbors' wills, and always signed his name. His inventory included "a parcel of books" valued at 27s. His wife Alice made her mark to their 1652/3 deed.

OFFICES: Boston leathersealer, 11 March 1649/50 [BTR 1:99].

ESTATE: In the 1645 Boston Book of Possessions Nathaniel Bishop held "one house and garden" [BBOP 28, 76].

On 10 March 1652[/3], Nathaniel Bishop of Boston, currier, sold to John Wiate of Ipswich "that his house wherein the said John Wiate now dwelleth" in Ipswich, and the land about it [ILR 1:160].

On 9 November 1674, "Nathaniel Bishop of Boston in New England innholder & Alice his wife" mortgaged to Mary Fletcher of Boston, widow, "all that our mansion house with the ground whereon it standeth with the yard & garden place & all other our land adjoining with the brewhouse standing upon part thereof which housing & ground are situate, standing & being near the South Meetinghouse in Boston aforesaid"; this mortgage was cleared on 29 November 1678 [SLR 9:262].

In his will, dated 10 June 1687 and proved 24 June 1687, "Nathaniell Bishopp of Boston," currier, "sick and weak," bequeathed to "my loving daughter Ruth Fuller, wife of William Fuller of Boston, victualler," for her natural life, benefit of a tenement in Boston occupied by William Evans, situated on the lane leading to the third meetinghouse, also a small garden plot; after said Ruth's decease the property to be divided equally between "Ruth's children ... Ruth Katland the wife of Phillipp Katland, Hannah Smith the wife of William Smith and Rebecca Pierce"; to "my loving daughter Rebecca Holland wife of Adam Holland" for her natural life, benefit of the tenement "wherein I now live" in Boston, including land, yard, garden, orchard, housing, stables and buildings; after Rebecca's decease, the property to go equally to the above three grandchildren; residue two-thirds to "my said daughters Ruth and Rebecca" equally, one third to "my three grandchildren" equally; daughters Ruth and Rebecca executors; "loving friends Mr. Joseph

Bridgham and Mr. James Hill both of Boston" overseers [SPR Case #1573, 10:47-50, NS 2:433].

The inventory of the estate of Nathaniel Bishop, taken 15 June 1687, totalled £260 9s. 8d., of which £200 was real estate: "lands and all the housing," £200 [SPR 10:50-51]. The inventory also included "an old musket and two old swords" valued at 10s. [SPR 10:51].

BIRTH: About 1607 (deposed aged 75 years on 28 November 1682 [SPR 6:396]).
DEATH: Between 10 June 1687 (date of will) and 15 June 1687 (probate of will).
MARRIAGE: By 1634 Alice _____.   Alice was living on 9 November 1674, but was not mentioned in the 1687 will of her husband [SLR 9:262]. (In his will of 21 January 1666/7, James Mattocks bequeathed 20s. to his daughter Alice, the wife of John Lewis. "Alice Bishop, widow," and John Lewis, were married at Boston 22 November 1659 [BVR 71]. Savage and others have concluded that Alice (Mattocks) (Bishop) Lewis was the widow of Nathaniel Bishop [Savage 1:185; NEHGR 66:356], but since Nathaniel was clearly alive until almost twenty years after that date, the wife of John Lewis was certainly the widow of some other Bishop, as yet unidentified [TAG 68:27-28].)
CHILDREN:

  i   SARAH, b. Boston 20 March 1634[/5] [BVR 2]; m. Boston 18 September 1654 Samuel Bucknell ("Samuel Bucknell & Sarah Bishop daughter of Nath Bishopp of Boston" [BVR 48]).

  ii   SAMUEL, b. say 1637; d. Boston 7 March 1646[/7?] [BVR 24] (see *COMMENTS* below).

  iii   RUTH, b. Boston 14 April 1639 [BVR 7]; m. (1) Boston 15 April 1656 John Peirce [BVR 57]; m. (2) by 1684 William Fuller [TAG 26:162-63, citing MA Arch 16:336].

  iv   JOSEPH, b. Boston 14 July 1642 [BVR 12]; witnessed a deed on 20 January 1658 [SLR 13:152]; no further record.

  v   BENJAMIN, b. Boston 31 May 1644 [BVR 17], bp. Boston 2 June 1644 "being about 3 days old" [BChR 296]; no further record.

  vi   JOHN, b. Boston 31 [*sic*] January 1646 [BVR 23], bp. Boston 31 January 1646/7 "being about 2 days old" [BChR 304]; d. soon.

vii HANNAH, bp. Boston 11 February 1648/9 "being about 7 days old" [BChR 314]; no further record.

viii JOHN, bp. Boston 26 January 1650/1 [BChR 320]; no further record.

ix REBECCA, b. Boston 8 April 1652 [BVR 36], bp. Boston 11 April 1652 [BChR 322]; m. by 1687 Adam Holland [SPR 10:47-50].

ASSOCIATIONS: On 6 November 1665, Nathaniel Bishop deposed to the accuracy of the inventory of the estate of "the late Henry Bishop, his brother"; property from Henry's estate was found in New Haven and Barbados, as well as Boston [SPR 4:260; see also Putnam's Mag 6:6-8, SLR 5:471]. Among the interesting inventory items were: "3 months' service done by me for my sister, £12," and "charges for one year's diet and a suit of clothes for the child my brother took, £8 10s." [SPR 5:145]. "Sister" was no doubt Henry's widow, Elizabeth, who died shortly after Henry, but we are not told the identity of the child [SPR Case #391].

A third brother was James Bishop of New Haven. On 6 February 1648/9, when he was in legal difficulties in New Haven, "Henry Bishop was asked if he had any witness, he produced his brother James Bishop" [NHCR 1:434].

Jacobus further suggests that Nathaniel, Henry and James were brothers "perhaps also of Thomas (d 1671/2) of Ipswich, Mass." [FANH 201]. In support of this, we note that Thomas named a son Nathaniel, and, like Henry, had mercantile interests in other colonies.

On 19 November 1651, George Harwood of Boston, carpenter, gave power of attorney to his wife, Jane, and to Nathaniel Bishop, to sell his house and land in Boston [Aspinwall 355]. Unfortunately, Harwood did not describe his relationship to Nathaniel Bishop, and we are left wondering if he was more than a trusted friend.

COMMENTS: In his list of the children of Nathaniel Bishop, Savage includes "Samuel, whose death by the more ancient copy of our record (for we have no original for very many years) 7 March 1647, is made the day of his birth by the absurdity of more recent copy; in his room was born another Samuel, perhaps the same year" [Savage 1:185]. This seems to imply that there were two sons named Samuel, but we have record for only one, who died on 7 March 1646/7.

We have placed this child where we have because there is no later time gap of sufficient size; however, if the child was born in Boston in 1637, his birth should appear in the Boston records. Other solutions are possible:

the child was the oldest in the family, born in England before migration; the child was born in some New England town other than Boston; or the record is defective, and was actually intended for the son John born about two months before this death.

In 1641, William Whitred sued Nathaniel Bishop in Ipswich Court [EQC 1:38].

On 14 October 1656, Nathaniel Bishop prepared his first of several inventories for the Suffolk Court. That year he appraised the estate of Thomas Wyborn of Boston, followed by the estate of Robert Reynolds presented 27 July 1659, the estate of William Blantine on 2 July 1662, and then the estate of Nathaniel Robinson in summer 1667 [SPR Cases #972, #213, #306, #457]. On 1 July 1659, he witnessed the will of Richard Webb and, on 21 August 1666, the will of Elizabeth Robinson [SPR Case #212; SPR 6:9].

On 31 May 1658, "John Peirce is admitted an inhabitant [of Boston], and Nat[haniel] Bishop acknowledged himself ... bound to the town treasurer ... to secure the town from any charge that may arise by the foresaid Pierce or his family to the said town" [BTR 1:143]. (This is most likely Bishop's son-in-law, the husband of his daughter Ruth.)

On 11 March 1685/6, Sewall recounts the stampede at the old meetinghouse on the occasion of the sermon preceding James Morgan's execution for killing Joseph Johnson. It was caused by a "madwoman" hitting the women next to her and screaming that the gallery was falling:

> Persons crowd much into the Old Meetinghouse by reason of James Morgan; and before I got thither a crazed woman cried the Gallery or Meetinghouse broke, which made the people rush out with great consternation.... Know not whether the mad woman said the House fell, or whether her beating women made them scream, and so those afar off, not knowing the cause, took it to be that.... [*The mad woman was*] the daughter of Goodman Bishop, master of Morgan. She went in at the southwest door, beat the women, they fled from her: they above supposed they fled from under the falling gallery [Sewall 99-100].

Which of Goodman Bishop's daughters this might have been is uncertain.

Pope states that Nathaniel Bishop "sold Ipswich land 25 May 1643," but no record of this transaction has been found.

RICHARD BISHOP

ORIGIN: Unknown
MIGRATION: 1635
FIRST RESIDENCE: Salem

OCCUPATION: Husbandman.
CHURCH MEMBERSHIP: Admitted to Salem church 25 August 1639 [SChR 8].
FREEMAN: 18 May 1642 [MBCR 2:291].
EDUCATION: Signed his name to a 1670 petition [EQC 4:315]. His inventory included books valued at 7s. [EQC 6:104].
OFFICES: Essex grand jury, 25 December 1649, 25 June 1650, 29 November 1653, 27 June 1654, 15 August 1659, 29 November 1659 [EQC 1:180, 191, 313, 347, 2:182; STR 1:222]. Essex petit jury, 9 July 1644, 28 December 1646, 26 December 1648, 31 December 1650, 25 November 1651, 20 October 1653, 24 June 1662, 28 June 1664 [EQC 1:64, 153, 204, 238, 309, 2:6, 385, 3:154; STR 1:104, 131, 146, 2:28, 47]. Coroner's jury, 27 August 1644 [EQC 1:71].

Salem constable, June 1636, 31 December 1644, 28 December 1647 [EQC 1:2, 129; STR 1:133]. Committee to mend the causeway, 3 September 1656 [STR 1:194]. Surveyor, 22 April 1657/8, 14 March 1659/60 [STR 1:214, 2:4].
ESTATE: Received 20 acres in Salem, but not in the freeman's land, 1636 [STR 1:22]. In the 25 December 1637 division of marsh and meadow, received one acre, for a household of six persons [STR 1:103]. Prior to the spring of 1639, Richard Bishop surrendered part of his ten-acre lot and took up land elsewhere in Salem [STR 1:82]. On 20 November 1639, Richard Bishop received a grant of 1½ acres "by his other five acres" [STR 1:92].

On 27 April 1654, he was granted four acres of meadow at the further end of Salem "provided it lie within Salem bounds," otherwise he could not have it [STR 1:176]. In 1658 he was granted four acres of meadow and swamp [STR 1:220]. On 7 April 1659, Richard Bishop of Salem, husbandman, sold to Samuel Eborne of Salem four acres of upland in Salem, "being the remaining part of a ten acre lot, six acres of which was lately sold to John Pease" [ELR 1:57]. In 1659 he was charged for the keep of one cow [STR 1:207].

On 2 March 1667[/8], Richard Bishop of Salem, husbandman, sold to Josiah Southwick of Salem, husbandman, half of an acre of meadow and salt marsh [ELR 3:39]. On 30 December 1670, Richard Bishop of Salem, husbandman, sold to Josiah Southwick of Salem, husbandman, ten acres in the north field [ELR 4:85].

Administration on the estate of Richard Bishop was granted on 30 March 1675 "to his son Thomas Bishop and his son-in-law John Durlan" [EPR 2:431]. Both a prenuptial contract and an imperfect nuncupative will were presented to the court. By the terms of the 12 July 1660 prenuptial contract, if "Marie Gault" survived Richard, then she should "enjoy the dwelling house of the said Richard Bishop with garden and orchard and the remainder of the two acre lot the said house standeth upon with a lot of upland opposite ... with all timber and fire wood ... also one half acre of salt marsh ... and half the estate he dies possessed of." "The house wherein the said Marie Goult at present liveth" was to be sold to pay the debts of Gault's estate, and Richard Bishop was to have "the best bed she [Marie] now hath with all the furniture thereunto belonging" [EPR 2:433].

The nuncupative will of Richard Bishop was presented in the 29 March 1675 deposition of Richard Croade, who said, "... being in the chamber with Goodman Bishop the night before he died, the latter [Richard] asked for Goodman Robbins and deponent to witness how he disposed of his estate": to "his son Thomas all except what John Durland had purchased"; to "his grandchild Mary Durland" half an acre at the upper end of the lot "because he said she might marry a tradesman or a seaman and would want a piece of ground to set a house upon"; "his grandson Richard to inherit from Thomas on account of his name"; "for his son Nathaniel if he had not been a churl he might have sent him something" [EPR 2:434-35].

Mary Bishop, widow of Richard Bishop, further added her witness to his nuncupative will, saying "that she often heard her husband Richard Bishop say during the time that she lived with him, that after her decease he desired his son Thomas Bishop to enjoy his dwelling house, orchard and ground in Salem, about two acres, only he would reserve half an acre of it to dispose of as he should afterward wish, also that his said son should have all his upland, half an acre of salt marsh in the north field, all of which the said son should not dispose of but should leave it for his son Richard after him." To his sons at Long Island "he replied that he would give them nothing, that they had been very unkind to him" [EPR 2:434].

The will notwithstanding, the court decreed on 21 December 1675 that "twenty-two acres in the north field and half an acre of meadow that is undisposed of, be divided between three of the children, viz., John,

Nathaniel, and the wife of John Durland, only to John, the eldest, a double portion" [EQC 6:104].

The inventory of the estate of Richard Bishop, taken 8 March 1674/5, totalled £143 19s. 11d., of which £100 was real estate: "his dwelling house and out housing with the garden plot, orchard and the land thereunto adjoining," £60; 22 acres of upland in the north field, £35; and one-half acre of salt marsh, £5 [EQC 6:105].

BIRTH: By about 1603 based on estimated date of first marriage.
DEATH: Salem 30 December 1674.
MARRIAGE: (1) By about 1628 _____ _____.

(2) By June 1635 Dulsabel (_____) King [MBCR 1:151]. She was born about 1604 (deposed "aged about 50 years" on 30 June 1654 [EQC 1:361]) and died "old" at Salem on 23 or 24 August 1658. She was widow of Richard King, whose administration was granted to Richard Bishop on behalf of his wife on 2 June 1635 [MBCR 1:151; EPR 1:1].

(3) Salem 22 July 1660 (marriage contract 12 July 1660) Mary (_____) Gault, widow of William Gault, who died Salem 1 April 1659 [EPR 2:433]. She was born about 1611 (deposed aged about 64 years on 29 March 1675 in the matter of her marriage contract and her late husband's nuncupative will [EQC 6:106]; deposed aged about seventy-five years for court of June 1685 [EQC 9:484]). Widow Mary married (3) Salem 11 March 1674/5 Thomas Robbins.
CHILDREN:
With first wife

    i   JOHN, b. say 1628; m. by 1686 Mary _____ (on 7 September 1686, John Bishop and Mary his wife, of Southampton, sold land inherited from father Richard Bishop [ELR 7:84-85]).

    ii   NATHANIEL, b. say 1630; m. by about 1665 _____ _____ (their son Daniel, of Easthampton, adult by 8 September 1686 when he sold land inherited through his deceased grandfather Richard and deceased father Nathaniel [ELR 7:84]).

    iii   THOMAS, b. about 1632 (deposed aged about fifty-two years for November 1684 court [EQC 9:343]; deposed "aged 54 or thereabouts" on 27 March 1685 [SJC Case #2285]); m. by 1661 Lydia Norman, daughter of John Norman and granddaughter of *RICHARD NORMAN* (eldest known child b. Salem 14 March 1661/2; on 27 March 1685

"Thomas Bishop aged 54 or thereabouts" deposed regarding land which "John Norman Senior my father-in-law" gave to "my brother John Norman" [SJC Case #2285]) [Sarah Stone Anc 49].

iv   MARY, b. about 1634 (deposed aged about twenty years, 30 June 1654 [EQC 1:361]); m. (1) Salem 14 June 1661 John Barnett *alias* Barbant; m. (2) by 1674 John Durlan/Darling [EPR 2:434; ELR 6:29].

ASSOCIATIONS: John Bligh deposed calling Richard "father Bishop," in the matter of his nuncupative will. Bligh married Salem 11 November 1663 Rebecca Gault, daughter of Richard's last wife, Mary [EQC 6:107]. The Blighs and their children were primary witnesses in Thomas Robbins's suit against William Pynchon, charging that Pynchon abused Thomas and his wife Mary, starving them and consuming both Robbins' estate and that left to Mary by her husband Bishop (depositions for June court 1684 [EQC 9:480-485]).

COMMENTS: In 1636, part of Richard Bishop's lot was to be used by Salem for firewood. Since he had already planted upon parts of it, the town agreed to allow him a proportionately sized piece of arable land elsewhere [STR 1:15].

On 18 October 1654, Richard Bishop and Elias Stileman Jr. took the inventory of the estate of George Williams of Salem [EQC 1:375]. In November 1654, Richard Bishop and Thomas Robins proved the will of Mary Williams [EQC 1:377].

On 25 December 1655, Richard Bishop's "bill for the highways" of £1 7s. was offerred for payment, suggesting that he was in charge of some portion of the highway work [STR 1:188]. On 18 January 1660/1, Robert Temple was fined for "railing speeches against Mary Bishop" [EQC 2:318]. On 7 January 1661/2, perhaps in his capacity of constable, Richard Bishop complained to the selectmen about the disorder in "sitting at meeting house" [STR 2:20].

TOWNSEND BISHOP

ORIGIN: Unknown
MIGRATION: 1634
FIRST RESIDENCE: Salem
RETURN TRIPS: Left New England in late 1645

CHURCH MEMBERSHIP: Townsend Bishop is in the list of Salem church members compiled late in 1636 [SChR 5], but was undoubtedly a member by 2 September 1635, based on his date of freemanship.

FREEMAN: 2 September 1635 [MBCR 1:371].

EDUCATION: Wrote an elegant, educated hand [STR 1:46]. He kept the minutes of the 28 August 1637 Salem meeting [STR 1:56].

OFFICES: Deputy for Salem to Massachusetts Bay General Court, 3 March 1635/6, 25 May 1636, 8 September 1636, 2 November 1637, 13 May 1640 [MBCR 1:164, 174, 178, 205, 288]. Commissioner to end small causes, 1644 [STR 1:130]. Committee to value towns, 8 September 1636 [MBCR 1:180]. Arbiter, 7 March 1643/4 [MBCR 2:58].

Essex magistrate, 27 September 1636-28 March 1637, 10 July 1644 [EQC 1:2-5, 64; MBCR 1:175]. Petit jury, 26 December 1643 (foreman) [EQC 1:55; STR 1:121].

Salem selectman, by February 1635/6-1637, 1643 [STR 1:13, 38, 50, 121]. Tithingman, 1644 [STR 1:131].

ESTATE: On 6 April 1635, "Mr. Townsend Bishop" received "2 acres the 2nd lot from the lane's end" among the Salem houselots [STR 1:9]. On 11 January 1635/6, he was granted a farm of three hundred acres, probably the same grant mentioned in the freemen's land [STR 1:14, 20; EQC 1:323]. In the 25 December 1637 distribution of marsh and meadow he received one acre, with a household of ten persons [STR 1:103].

On 26 February 1638/9, Mr. Bishop received a grant of 150 acres, including 40 acres of meadow [STR 1:85].

On 6 October 1641, Townsend Bishop of Salem deeded to Henry Chickering of Dedham the three hundred acre farm granted to Bishop by the town of Salem in 1635 [EQC 9:53].

On 11 March 1645/6, Robert Moulton and Michael Shafflin, agents for Mr. Townsend Bishop, sold to Mr. Ralph Fogg of Salem "the new messuage or dwelling house of the said Mr. Bishop's standing by the rocks near Captain Hawthorne's house in Salem" [ELR 1:2-3].

By 29 June 1648, "the farm which was Mr. Bishop's containing about one hundred and four score acres of upland and meadow" is mentioned in a Simon Bradstreet deed [ELR 1:4].

BIRTH: By 1612 based on estimated date of marriage.

DEATH: After 9 July 1645 [EQC 1:81].

MARRIAGE: By 1637 _____ _____.

CHILDREN:

    i   LEAH, bp. Salem 19 June 1637 [SChR 16]; no further record.

ii   JOHN, bp. Salem 31 July 1642 [SChR 19]; no further record.
ASSOCIATIONS: A friend and neighbor, at least, of John Endicott [WP 4:72].

COMMENTS: In a 29 October 1638 letter to John Winthrop, John Endicott writes of his neighbor:

> At present I am bold to entreat your favor in a case of Mr. Bishop's, the bearer hereof. It is a case of conscience. I have labored to give him the best satisfaction I can but it seems he is not satisfied. I hope that he is one truly fearing God and therefore I desire much (if God see it good) he may be satisfied in his scruples and fears: It concerns chiefly the magistracy, concerning their power in matters of God's worship. I leave him to state the question, that you may the better satisfy him and the better understand him [WP 4:72].

On 21 July 1644, Townsend Bishop witnessed the will of Richard Ingersoll of Salem [EQC 1:76].

On 9 July 1645, "Mr. Townshend Bishop" was presented for "turning his back on baptism, and detaining his child." He was referred to the Elders "to be convinced by them" [EQC 1:81]. Whatever solution was reached, it caused Bishop to offer no children for baptism at Salem church after this date. He also disappeared from New England records, no longer serving as magistrate or in any other public function. As Robert Moulton and Michael Shafflin were acting as agents for Townsend Bishop on 11 March 1645/6 [ELR 1:2-3], we conclude that Bishop left New England in the latter part of 1645.

An extensive controversy ensued over subsequent sales of Bishop's three-hundred-acre farm, which kept his name alive in the Essex records long after his departure [EQC 7:10-20, 8:116-21, 9:52-56].

JAMES BITTON

"James Bitton," aged 27, was enrolled at London on 15 April 1635 as a passenger for New England on the *Increase* [Hotten 66].

COMMENTS: Not seen in any New England record. Savage suggests that this entry in the London Port Book is defective, and that the name might be "Britton," so that this could be the record of departure of James Britton of Weymouth, or James Britton of Woburn [Savage 1:257].

MARTHA BLACKETT

On 20 July 1634, "Martha Blackett maid servant to our teacher John Cotton" was admitted to Boston church [BChR 18].

COMMENTS: No evidence whether she died, married or returned to England. A very small family of this name appears in the Boston, Lincolnshire, parish register, but no daughter Martha is recorded there.

JOHN BLACKLEACH

ORIGIN: London
MIGRATION: 1634
FIRST RESIDENCE: Winnisimmett
REMOVES: Salem by 1635, Boston by 1645, New Haven by 1658, Hartford by 1660, Wethersfield by 1665

OCCUPATION: Merchant. Innkeeper (on 10 October 1667, the "Court grants Mr. John Blackleach liberty to retail wine and liquors to his neighbors that are honest, sober householders, and those only, till the last of November next" [CCCR 1:76]).
CHURCH MEMBERSHIP: Admission to a Massachusetts Bay church (presumably Salem) prior to 6 May 1635 implied by freemanship. In the list of Salem church members compiled in late 1636 (with later annotation "recommended") [SChR 6]. "Mr. Blackleach and his wife being removed to live at Hartford desired their dismission unto that church, which was consented unto by the church here and sent unto them by the elders" about the end of October 1661 [SChR 92].
FREEMAN: 6 May 1635 [MBCR 1:371]. Admitted freeman of Connecticut, 13 May 1669 (said to be of Stratford) [CCCR 1:105]; on the "list of freemen on the south side Hartford," October 1669 [CCCR 1:518].
EDUCATION: Signed his will. His inventory included "several books" valued at £1 6s.
OFFICES: Deputy for Salem to Massachusetts Bay General Court, 25 May 1636 [MBCR 1:174].

Salem assessor, 11 September 1637 [STR 1:57]. Essex petit jury, 27 September 1636 (foreman), 26 December 1643 [EQC 1:3, 55; STR 1:121].

Connecticut committee on fortifications, 11 October 1675 [CCCR 2:375].

ESTATE: On 27 February 1634[/5], "Samuell Maverick and Amias his wife, John Blackleach [blank] his wife" sold to Richard Bellingham "a messuage called Winesemet" [SLR 1:15].

On 16 February 1635/6, "the freemen of Salem" granted to "Mr. John Blacklech of the same ... one farm containing three hundred acres ... provided always that if the said Mr. Blackleech shall at any time make sale of it, that the town shall have the first proffer of it before any other" [STR 1:13, 20]. In the 25 December 1637 division of marsh and meadow, "Mr. Blackleach" received one acre, for a household of nine persons [STR 1:103]. On 14 August 1637, "Mr. Blacklech [is] appointed the piece of meadow that was appointed our brother Gott that lyeth near to Mr. Blaklech's farm" [STR 1:54].

On 21 January 1638/9, "[w]hereas Mr. John Blackleech desireth 50 acres of land to be granted him as an addition to his former grant of 300 acres, upon exchange of 50 acres of his rock ground for it, alleging that he hath not sufficient ground to maintain a plow, the town therefore for the furthering of his endeavors in plowing & for his encouragement therein hath freely granted unto him without exchange such land as was formerly granted to Mr. Gott upon the plain near adjoining to his said farm conditionally that he will be at the charge of plowing of it or the greatest part of it" [STR 1:78].

On 22 April 1638, "Mr. John Blackleech of Salem agreed not to dispose of his farm, 3 cows, 1 heifer, 23 ewe goats, 7 weather goats, and his house at Salem, also his 10 acre lot, without the consent of his wife Eliz[abeth]; and that after their lives it shall be for the use of their children" [EQC 1:55]. On 15 May 1662 at Hartford, "Elizabeth Blackleach" confirmed that "John Blackleach Senior formerly of Bostown now of Hartford did sell unto John West his then tenant all the farm formerly granted by the town of Salem & given unto him by them with all the housing & all other benefits thereupon which farm aforesaid was formerly in the occupation of Lawrence Leech" [HaBOP 513-14].

In an undated entry in the Hartford land records, "Mr. Blackletch" was credited with two parcels of land: "one parcel which he bought of Mr. W[illia]m Goodwin on which his dwelling house now standeth together with several outhouses, barns, stables, easements, orchards, gardens therein being, containing by estimation three acres" (annotated "sold Jno. Blackleach his son"); and "one parcel of land lying on the west side of the Little River & containeth by estimation twenty & eight acres, three roods & twenty and eight perches" (annotated "sold his son Jno. Blackleach") [HaBOP 513].

In a will, dated 16 August 1671, John Blackleach of Wethersfield bequeathed "to my now wife Elizabeth all my estate either lands goods or chattels ... during her natural life, entreating her as she is able to help them most which are and shall be most dutiful to her and please her best"; "Solomon and Mary have had least yet, therefore consider them the more in cause they be dutiful"; "whereas I purchased lands of Mr. John Russell & of John Hubbard formerly lying and being within Wethersfield ... which I also recorded at Hartford & made it over to my wife during her natural life, and to our children after our death ... I bequeath to my son, John, a double portion ... because my son, Benoni and my daughter Elizabeth have had a portion each of them already, and Solomon and Mary but little, therefore to Solomon and Mary my children, in case they outlive me and my wife, I give twice so much as to Benoni and Elizabeth;" if any of the children die without issue, then his or her part should be the inheritance of those remaining [NEHGR 36:190-91, citing "Mass. Not. Rec. Book, 4:91"]. (This will was apparently never submitted for probate, and may be related to the 1675 action below.)

On 9 November 1674, James Wells and John Clarke "laid out to Mr. John Blackleach, of Hartford, his grant of land on the east end of Midleton bounds," two hundred rods by one hundred and sixty rods [CCCR 1:251].

On 13 May 1675, in "answer to Mr. John Blackleach Senior his petition, this Court declares that they cannot approve or allow of Mr. Blackleach his deed of gift therein mentioned, in so making over the reversional distribution of his estate to posterity as that his present necessities cannot be relieved, which the revenue can in no measure supply suitable to their old age; therefore do order that whoever of his children hath or shall relieve the said father and mother shall be duly repaid out of the said lands after their decease, notwithstanding the said imprudent act of so setting it over to be distributed amongst their children" [CCCR 1:250-51].

The inventory of "Mr. John Blackleach," taken 3 September 1683, totalled £373 16s. 6d., of which £355 was real estate: "house, homelot, orchard, old barn," £100; "6 acres 3 roods of meadow the long lot of Mr. Russell's," £65; "2 acres of beaver meadow," £10; "ten acres meadow at the crossway bought of Mr. Russell," £90; and "ten acres of dry swamp cleared," £90 [HaPR 4:132].

On 29 October 1683, a "Special Court held at Hartford" ordered that the remainder of the estate of John Blackleach "be distributed amongst Mr. John Blackleach his children that were alive at his decease according to his deed of gift upon record, the children known to be alive are Mr. John

Blackleach, Exercise Hodges & Mary Jefferies. It is also thought Benony may be alive" [HaPR 4(court side):74].

BIRTH: By about 1605 based on estimated date of marriage.
DEATH: Wethersfield 23 August 1683 [WetVR Barbour 28, citing WetVR 1:74].
MARRIAGE: By 1630 Elizabeth Bacon, baptized at Stepney, Middlesex, 6 August 1609, daughter of Robert and Christian (Locksonne) Bacon [NEHGR 148:9]. She was admitted to the Salem church on 17 May 1638 (with later annotation "removed") [SChR 7]. She died at Wethersfield 20 July 1683 [WetVR Barbour 28, citing WetVR 1:74].
CHILDREN:

  i   ELIZABETH, bp. St Gregory by St Paul, London, 5 December 1630 [NEHGR 148:17]; d. before 1641.

  ii   JOHN, bp. St Gregory by St Paul, London, 10 January 1631/2 [NEHGR 148:17]; m. (1) before 5 May 1659 Elizabeth [Sheafe?]; (2) Elizabeth Harbert. (The difficult problem of this man's marital career is discussed in detail by Gale Ion Harris [NEHGR 148:21-24].)

  iii   MARY, bp. St Gregory by St Paul, London, 11 April 1633 [NEHGR 148:17]; d. before 1651.

  iv   DESIRE, b. Salem 13 April 1636 [EQC 1:74]; living in 1644, but not named among her mother's children at Hartford in 1662.

  v   EXERCISE, b. Salem [blank] January 163[6/]7 [EQC 1:74], bp. 24 January 1636[/7] (where the father is called *Jonathan* in error) [SChR 16]; m. (1) Boston 24 August 1660 Richard Raser [BVR 76]; m. (2) by 1663 Thomas Hodges (only known child b. Boston 1 February 1663/4 [BVR 88]).

  vi   JOSEPH, b. Salem 8 January 163[8/]9 [EQC 1:74], bp. there (as "Joshua") 3 February 1638[/9] [SChR 17]; living in 1644 but not named with his mother's children in 1662.

  vii   ELIZA[BETH], b. Salem [blank] December 1641 [EQC 1:74], bp. 12 December 1641 [SChR 18]; d. Salem in 1642 [EQC 1:74].

  viii BENONI, b. Salem 1 May 1643 [EQC 1:74], bp. 14 May 1643 [SChR 19]; m. by 1665 Dorcas Bowman, daughter of *NATHANIEL BOWMAN* [NEHGR 148:30-33, and sources cited there; GMB 1:195].

  ix   ELIZABETH, b. Salem 12 August 1644 [EQC 1:74], bp. Salem 4 August 1644 [SChR 20]; on 25 February 1660/1 at

Hartford, John Winthrop Jr. treated "Blacleech Eliz: 16
yr:" [WMJ 249]; m. (1) by 1664 John Stedman (on 6 March
1664/5, John Winthrop Junior treated "Stedman John his
wife" [WMJ 588]); m. (2) Saybrook 10 July 1677 Thomas
Dunk [SayVR 11].

x   SOLOMON, bp. Boston 18 October 1646 ("from the Church of
Salem") [BVR 1:25]; d. soon.

xi   SOLOMON, bp. Boston 3 September 1648 ("from the Church
of Salem aged about 2 days") [BVR 1:28]; m. by 1678
Sindeniah _____ (on 13 September 1678, "Solomon
Blackleich, commander of the James Friggett, being by
the disposing and all ordering hand of God's providence
arrived in the harbor of the town of New Plymouth,"
bequeathed his estate to "my dear and loving wife
Sindeniah" [PCR 5:267-68]).

xii   MARY, bp. Boston 7 September 1651 ("of [blank] Blacklech of
Salem") [BVR 1:35]; m. by 1673 Aaron Jeffries (eldest
known child b. Boston 4 December 1673 [BVR 128]).

COMMENTS: Among other commodities which he must have bought
and sold, John Blackleach evidently traded in wine, for on 12 March
1637/8 it was found that "[t]here is due to the country, for wine bought &
sold by him, thirty-three shillings & four pence" [MBCR 1:224].

"John Blackleath" of Salem received Matthew Dove as a servant from
George Luxon for the term of four years from 1 June 1640 [Lechford 254].
On 8 November 1654, he was discharged from all debts and demands by
Hezekiah Usher [SLR 2:104-5].

In December 1644 "John and Elizabeth Blackleach certified that their
children were as follows: Desire, born 13: 2: 1636, aged eight years;
Exercise, born 11 mo: 1637, aged seven years; Joseph, born 8: 11 mo: 1639,
aged five years; Elizabeth, born 10 mo: 1641, died in 1642; Benony, born
the prime of the 3 mo: 1643; and Elizabeth, born 12: 6: 1644" [EQC 1:74].
(Based on this record, we conclude that the word "prime" was missed or
misunderstood in the entry for Benoni.)

On 13 March 1661/2, "[t]his Court duly and with serious deliberation,
having weighed and considered the nature of the offence of Mr. John
Blackleich in his contemptuous expressions against several persons in
authority in this Colony, do declare, that though the heinousness of the
transgression deserves a fine of an hundred pounds, yet also considering
some weakness that too evidently appears that he is incident unto, this

Court doth impose the fine of thirty pounds to be paid by the said Mr. Blackleich to the public treasury" [CCCR 1:376]. On the same day, "[t]his Court, upon further consideration of the frame of the matter respecting Mr. John Blackleich, and observing that there is too much appearance of prejudice in the testimonies that have been presented, and how indirect the course was whereby anything was discovered, i.e. by lying in wait, cannot but see just cause to acquit Mr. Jo[hn] Blackleich of that fine imposed, there appearing reason to suspect that both Loveridge and Burnam are guilty of the crime they testify against Mr. Blackleich" [CCCR 1:377-78].

On 13 May 1669, "Mr. John Blackleach Senior moving this Court for their approbation that he might use his endeavors to make known to the Indians (in the best way he can) something of the knowledge of God according as he shall have opportunity, this Court grants his desire therein, with their desires that he may through the blessing of God be an advantageous instrument to the end proposed" [CCCR 2:111].

John Blackleech, especially in his Connecticut years, moved very frequently, and the list given under *REMOVES* is not complete. On 14 March 1665/6, John Winthrop Junior treated "Mr. Blackleach John Senior of Wethersfield" [NEHGR 148:14, citing WMJ 634]. In 1669 he was made a freeman, as of Stratford, but just months later he is in the list of Hartford freemen.

John Blackleech was a frequent speculator in lands, and the material under *ESTATE* above represents only a portion of his transactions.

BIBLIOGRAPHIC NOTE: In 1994 Gale Ion Harris published an exhaustive account of John Blackleach and his family [NEHGR 148:7-44]. Harris makes the interesting suggestion that Richard Blackleach of Stratford, Connecticut, with obvious ties to the family of John Blackleach, may have been the latter's illegitimate son [NEHGR 148:38-40].

THOMAS BLACKLEY

On 28 July 1635, "Tho[mas] Blackly," aged 20, was enrolled at London as a passenger for New England on the *Hopewell*, with a certificate of conformity from the minister of St Giles Cripplegate, London [Hotten 110].

COMMENTS: Pope makes this man the same as the Boston testator of 1673, Thomas Blatchley [Pope 52-53; SPR Case #673], but this latter man is Thomas Blatchley of New Haven, who first appears in Hartford in 1640, so there is no apparent connection with the passenger of 1635. There is no evidence that the passenger of 1635 arrived in New England.

JEREMY BLACKWELL

"Jeremy Blackwell," aged 18, was enrolled on 19 September 1635 at London as a passenger for New England on the *Truelove* [Hotten 131].

On 23 April 1641, George Burcham of London, merchant, laid down conditions for the settlement of a debt owed to him by Jeremy Blackwell, at the conclusion of which Burcham would pay £8 10s. to "the said Jeremy his executors"; one of the actions to be taken was a payment by "his [Jeremy's] brother John Blackwell unto Jonathan Newcomen mercer dwelling on London Bridge" [Lechford 387].

COMMENTS: The terms of the settlement of the debt indicate that Jeremy Blackwell had died by April 1641. Assuming that this is the same as the passenger of 1635, he was otherwise unrecorded in New England during the intervening six years.

RALPH BLAISDELL

ORIGIN: Unknown
MIGRATION: 1635
FIRST RESIDENCE: York
REMOVES: Salisbury 1640

OCCUPATION: Tailor. Innkeeper (on 4 November 1645, "Ralfe Blasdell [was] licensed to keep an ordinary at Salsbery and to draw wine till the next General Court" [EQC 1:87]; on 30 March 1647, "Ralph Blassdell of Salsbery and John Baker of Ipswich had their licenses for drawing wine renewed" [EQC 1:112]).
EDUCATION: Elizabeth Blaisdell made her mark to several deeds.
OFFICES: Deputy for York to Saco Court, 25 June 1640 [MPCR 1:54].
   Petit jury, 28 September 1647, 26 September 1648 [EQC 1:124, 149].

ESTATE: On 22 July 1642, "Ralph Blasedell of Sawlsbury, in the County of Norfocke, tailor," sold to Robert Knight, mason, "one dwelling house being situated in Agamenticus ... with all lands, as uplands, meadows, gardens, fences, timber, commonage & all appurtenances whatsoever thereunto belonging" [YLR 3:42].

Ralph Blaisdell received grants of land in Salisbury in 1640, 1641, 1644 and 1645 [Nicholas Davis Anc 60, apparently citing Salisbury Town Records].

On 25 March 1645, "John Harison Sr. of Boston, cordish maker," sold to "Ralf Blasdale of Salisbury my accommodation of house and 2-acre lot in Salisbury ...; also, my planting lot of 6 acres ...; also, 4 acres of meadow adjoining my houselot ...; also, 30-acre lot of upland on west side of Pawwaus River ...; also, my cove of meadow in the great meadows" [Essex Ant 6:171, abstracting NLR 2:98]. On 9 March 1648[/9?], "Ralfe Blasdall of Salisbury, tailor," mortgaged to "John Severance of Salisbury, husbandman, his now dwelling house and houselot and a little piece of upland bought of Tho[mas] Bradbury (formerly belonging to Mr. John Hodges, where his house stood) ...; also, 4 acres of meadow before his house; also, a division of upland towards the ferry; excepting the glass of the chamber window, three locks, two spring locks and the house-door lock and the shop board" [Essex Ant 6:44, abstracting NLR 2:70].

On 24 June 1651, administration on the estate of "Ralfe Blasdell, intestate," was granted to "his widow, Elizabeth Blasdell" [EPR 1:130].

On 19 October 1654, "Elizabeth Blaisdale of Salisbury, widow," sold to "John Severans of Salisbury, victualler, 6 acres of meadow in Salisbury in two lots" [Essex Ant 6:174, abstracting NLR 2:108]. On 20 March 1655, "Elizabeth Blaisdall of Salisbury, widow," sold to "Wymond Bradbury of Salisbury right of commonage connected with house and land my deceased husband Ralfe Blasdall bought of Mr. Bradbury as attorney of Mr. John Hodges, the deed having been delivered to Capt. Robert Pike, and not now appearing" [Essex Ant 6:42, abstracting NLR 2:61].

On 19 February 1661[/2], "Elizabeth Blesdale of Salisbury, widow," sold to Abraham Morrill of Salisbury, blacksmith, "4 acres of marsh in higgledy-piggledy lots in Salisbury towards Hampton" [Essex Ant 3:140, abstracting NLR 1:148].

On 14 July 1667, "Elizabeth Blasdale of Salisbury, widow, for love, conveyed to her daughter Mary Blasdale, now wife of Joseph Stowers, the right of commonage Ralf Blasdale, my husband, did in his lifetime bought of Jno. Harizon in Salisbury, and 4 acres of marsh in cow common, ... being No. 3 on town record"; on 24 February 1667[/8], "Henry

Blasdale, son of Ralfe and Elizabeth Blasdale, consents to this grant" [Essex Ant 6:174, abstracting NLR 2:106].

On 8 October 1667, administration on the estate of "Elizabeth Blasdale" was granted to Joseph Stowers [EPR 2:102]. The inventory of the estate of "Elizabeth Blaesdell of Salisbury," attested in court 8 October 1667, totalled £15 4d. and included no real estate [Essex Ant 6: 171, 175, abstracting NLR 2:98, 109; EPR 2:102].

On 14 April 1668, Joseph Stowers unsuccessfully sued John Severans for "mowing or causing to be mowed a certain parcel of marsh belonging to plaintiff, thereby claiming propriety thereof, said marsh lying in the cow common in the old town of Salisbury, and formerly belonging to the common right of Jno. Harison and by him sold to Ralf Blasdale and by his successors conveyed to said Stowers, being the third lot as recorded and laid out" [EQC 4:21-22].

On 12 September 1698, whereas administration on the estate of "Ralph Blaisdell late of Almsbury deceased intestate was granted unto Elizabeth Blaisdell relict widow of the said deceased she dying" before administration was completed, administration is now granted to "Ebenezer Blaisdell grandson to the said Ralph Blaisdell deceased" [EPR 306:68].

The inventory of the estate of "Ralph Blaisdell of Salsbury deceased," taken 22 December 1698, totalled £95, of which £93 was real estate: "twenty acres of upland in Almsbury at a place commonly called Cobbet Hill," £20; "thirty acres of land abutting upon Merrimack River in Almsbury," £30; "three acres of fresh meadow at the new meadow in Salsbury," £3; "six acres of meadow at the points in Salsbury," £12; "four acres of meadow in the cow common in Salsbury," £8; "thirty acres of land in the division above the mills in Salsbury," £6; "twenty-five acres of land in the last division on the north side of Cane's Creek in Salsbury," £4; and "two common rights in the town of Salisbury," £10 [EPR 306:118].

BIRTH: By about 1607 based on estimated date of marriage.
DEATH: By 24 June 1651 (grant of administration).
MARRIAGE: By about 1632 Elizabeth _____ (assuming she was the mother of all his children). She died at Salisbury [blank] August 1667.
CHILDREN:

    i   HENRY, b. about 1632 [Nicholas Davis Anc 64-65]; m. (1) by 1657 Mary Haddon, daughter of *GARRETT HADDON* [GMB 2:832-33]; m. (2) by an unknown date Elizabeth _____ [Nicholas Davis Anc 65 (evidence not shown)].

ii   MARTHA, b. say 1640; m. (1) by 1661 Richard Bowden (only
      known child b. Boston 18 May 1661 [BVR 78]); m. (2) by
      an unknown date (Thomas?) Sealey; m. (3) Dover 15
      January 1686/7 JOHN CLOUGH [DoVR 109]. (The
      identity of Martha as a daughter of Ralph Blaisdell and
      the delineation of her marital career are the result of
      detailed research carried out by Charles Thornton Libby
      and published by Walter Goodwin Davis in 1956
      [Nicholas Davis Anc 8-9, 55-56, 62-64, and the evidence
      cited there].)

iii   MARY, b. Salisbury 5 March 1641[/2?] (daughter of "Ralph and
      Elisabeth"); m. (1) by about 1661 Joseph Stowers, son of
      NICHOLAS STOWERS [GMB 3:1782]; m. (2) Haverhill 19
      December 1676 William Sterling.

iv   SARAH, d. Salisbury 17 January 1646[/7] ("daughter [of]
      Ralfe").

COMMENTS: The records of the Saco Court on 25 March 1636 include
the following garbled entry: "Also to [missing] goods and chattels of
Tho[mas] Joanes & Ralfe [missing] Hooke which they should make by the
[missing]" [MPCR 1:1]. The index to these published records includes an
entry for Ralph Blaisdell on page one, which can only refer to this
mutilated entry.

   On 18 March 1639[/40], "William Hooke" and "Ralph Blasdell" witnessed
a deed of GEORGE BURDETT [YLR 4:20]. WILLIAM HOOKE and Ralph
Blaisdell both moved to Salisbury in 1640. No other man with the
forename Ralph is known to have resided in York in these early years.
For all these reasons, we believe that the above damaged entry refers to
Ralph Blaisdell.

   Relying on one of our basic guidelines in this study, that anyone present
in New England by the date of the May election court must have arrived
in New England during the previous calendar year, we must conclude
that Ralph Blaisdell came to New England no later than 1635.

   Although the English origin of Ralph Blaisdell has not been uncovered,
the surname is found almost exclusively in Lancashire [Nicholas Davis
Anc 59]. Partly because of this, there is a longstanding tradition that
Blaisdell came to New England on the *Angel Gabriel,* sailing from Bristol in
1635. Although this is possible, there is no evidence pointing in that
direction. A number of Lancashire families did sail from Bristol in 1635,
accompanying Rev. RICHARD MATHER on the *James.* There was a third

vessel known to have come to New England from Bristol with passengers in 1635, the *George*. So even if we had reason to believe that Ralph Blaisdell sailed from Bristol, we could not say which ship he was on. And we don't know even that much.

On 13 December 1649, "Joseph Armitage of Lin did constitute Raph Blazdale of Lin in New England & John Herbert of Salem" his attorney to collect a debt [Aspinwall 265]. This record may be in error as to the residence of Blaisdell at the time; if it is correct, his residence in Lynn cannot have been very lengthy.

The 1698 probate record of Ralph Blaisdell indicates that most of his land, and probably his residence, were in that part of Salisbury that was set off as Amesbury.

There is no evidence for a son Ralph, as claimed in some secondary sources [GDMNH 95; Hoyt 63], but doubted in others [Nicholas Davis Anc 64].

BIBLIOGRAPHIC NOTE: The account of the ancestry and other genealogical connections of Ralph Blaisdell compiled by Gustave Anjou is one of his most egregious concoctions, and should be consulted only for its entertainment value.

In 1897 and later years David W. Hoyt compiled a serviceable treatment of Ralph Blaisdell and his descendants, although it is weak on documentation [Hoyt 63-66, 618-42, 880-82].

The best study of Ralph Blaisdell in print was compiled in 1956 by Walter Goodwin Davis [Nicholas Davis Anc 59-66].

Since 1936, The Blaisdell Family National Association has published *Blaisdell Papers*, which appears twice a year and contains a variety of articles on all aspects of the Blaisdell family.

ANNE BLASON

On 18 April 1635, "Ann Blason," aged 27, was enrolled at London as a passenger for New England on the *Susan & Ellen* [Hotten 63].

COMMENTS: There is no evidence in any New England record that she arrived.

THOMAS BLODGETT

ORIGIN: Stowmarket, Suffolk
MIGRATION: 1635 on the *Increase*
FIRST RESIDENCE: Cambridge

OCCUPATION: Glover (in England).
CHURCH MEMBERSHIP: Admission to Cambridge church prior to 3 March 1635/6 implied by freemanship.
FREEMAN: 3 March 1635/6 (as "Thomas Bloyett," twelfth in a sequence of fourteen Cambridge men) [MBCR 1:371].
EDUCATION: Signed his will. His inventory included "a Bible and other books" valued at £1 5s.
ESTATE: Thomas Blodgett purchased the house and other land of JONAS AUSTIN, probably including the propriety, at about the time of Austin's move to Hingham in 1636 [CaBOP 26, 34, 48]. On 6 February 1636/7, "Thomas Blogget" was granted two acres of swamp [CaTR 26].

In 1639 "Thomas Blogget" held three parcels of land in Cambridge: "given by the town in the West Field two acres of planting ground"; "given by the town one houselot upon the Cow Common"; and "bought of Jonas Austen two acres of planting ground in the West End" [CaBOP 59]. By 1639 "Thomas Blogget" sold to Edmund Frost "one house [with] garden [and] backside in Water Street" [CaBOP 48]; this was the house Blodgett had acquired from Jonas Austin. By 1639 "Thomas Blogget" sold to Robert Daniel "one house upon the common with garden and backside about half an acre" [CaBOP 61].

On an unknown date, "Thomas Bloged" received eight acres in the lower division on the south side of Charles River and eight acres in the upper division [CaBOP 331] Also on an unknown date, "Thomas Bloggitt" held parcels of two acres and one acre in Fresh Pond Meadow [CaBOP 333].

In his will, dated 10 August 1641 and proved 8 March 1642/3, "Thomas Blogget" bequeathed to "my present wife Susan Blogget my whole estate after my decease as well within doors as without," she to pay to "my eldest son Daniel" £15 at age 21 or one month after her decease, to "my second son Samuel" £15 at age 21 or two months after her decease, and to "my daughter Susan" £15 at her decease; if "my children should come into the hands of a father-in-law" who did not "deal by them as is meet," then "the deacons & our brother Fessington & our brother Edward Winchship" should resolve the matter [SPR 1:21].

The inventory of the estate of "Thomas Blogget, late deceased, appraised the 28 of the 10 month [December, year not given, but apparently 1642]" and presented at court 8 March 1642/3 was untotalled; the real estate was valued at £47 10s.: "four acres planting ground," £14; "five acres meadow & marsh," £3 10s.; and "the house & yards," £30 [SPR 2:15].

On 6 January 1642/3, "Susan Bloget" held five parcels in Cambridge: "on the Common one dwelling house and outhouse with about half an acre of ground"; "in the New West Field two acres"; "in the West End two acres"; "on the south side of Charles River two acres and half of marsh"; and "in the Fresh Pond Meadow two acres & half" [CaBOP 101-2]. In 1645 "Susan Blogett" (by then married to James Thomson) was granted "three acres & half" on the west side of Menotomy River [CaBOP 130].

BIRTH: About 1605 (aged 30 in 1635 [Hotten 61]).
DEATH: Cambridge between 10 August 1641 (date of will) and 10 December 1642 (date of inventory).
MARRIAGE: By about 1627 Susanna ____. She married (2) Woburn 15 February 1643/4 *JAMES THOMSON* [GMB 3:1809-11]. She died at Woburn on 10 February 1660/1.
CHILDREN:
  i   JOHN, b. say 1627; bur. Stowmarket, Suffolk, 4 May 1632 [Blodgett Gen 1:2].
  ii   NATHANIEL, bp. Stowmarket 28 February 1628/9 [Blodgett Gen 1:2]; bur. there 8 May 1630 [Blodgett Gen 1:2].
  iii DANIEL, bp. Stowmarket 14 May 1631 [Blodgett Gen 1:2] (aged four in 1635 [Hotten 61]); m. (1) Chelmsford 15 September 1653 Mary Butterfield; m. (2) Chelmsford 10 March 1669[/70] Sarah Underwood.
  iv   SAMUEL, bp. Stowmarket 12 July 1633 [Blodgett Gen 1:2] (aged 1½ on 8 April 1635 [Hotten 61]); m. Woburn 13 December 1655 Ruth Eggleton [Dawes-Gates 1:285-86].
  v   SUSANNA, b. Cambridge [blank] June 1637 [NEHGR 3:248]; m. Woburn 28 November 1655 Jonathan Thomson (her stepbrother), son of *JAMES THOMSON*.
  vi   THOMAS, d. Cambridge 7 August 1639 [NEHGR 3:248].

COMMENTS: On 18 April 1635, "Tho[mas] Blogget," glover, aged 30, "uxor Suzan Bloggett," aged 37, and two children "Daniell Blogget," aged

4, and "Samuell Blogget," aged 1½, were enrolled as passengers for New England on the *Increase* [Hotten 61].

BIBLIOGRAPHIC NOTE: In 1943 Mary Walton Ferris prepared an account of Thomas Blodgett and of his son Samuel [Dawes-Gates 1:91-92].

In 1955 Bradley DeForest Thompson and Franklin Condit Thompson published a multi-volume typescript genealogy of the Blodgett family, the first volume of which contains the information on the English origin of the immigrant [Bradley DeForest Thompson and Franklin Condit Thompson, *Blodget-Blodgett Descendants of Thomas of Cambridge*, 6 vols. and index vol. (Concord, New Hampshire, 1955), cited above as Blodgett Gen].

EDMUND BLOIS

ORIGIN: Unknown (but see COMMENTS below)
MIGRATION: 1634
FIRST RESIDENCE: Watertown

OCCUPATION: Planter.
CHURCH MEMBERSHIP: Admission to Watertown church prior to 22 May 1639 implied by freemanship.
FREEMAN: 22 May 1639 [MBCR 1:376].
EDUCATION: Signed his deeds and his will by mark. His inventory included "2 sieves, 2 books, a peck, 5 small vessels," valued at 5s.
OFFICES: Watertown hogreeve, 6 February 1648/9 [WaTR 1:17].
ESTATE: Granted six acres in the Town Plot at Watertown, 9 April 1638 [WaBOP 11]. Granted a Farm of forty-three acres, 10 May 1642 [WaBOP 13].

In the Watertown Inventory of Possessions Edmund Blois held three parcels: homestall of six acres; one acre of meadow; and four acres of upland in the Hither Plain [WaBOP 92]. In the Composite Inventory he held four parcels, comprising the three listed above plus the Farm [WaBOP 38].

On 13 April 1650, Watertown selectmen "ordered that John Sherman shall lay out to Edmund Bloys four acres of land near the meeting house as shall be most convenient, which land was granted to the said Bloys the last General Town Meeting" [WaTR 1:20].

On 6 April 1671, "Edmund Bloyce of Watertown ... planter, with Mary my wife," sold to Joseph Taynter of Watertown "one parcel of land ... near the dwelling house of William Hagar in Watertowne abovenamed being by estimation about three acres ... all which the aforesaid Edmund Bloyce was possessed of in that place by grant from the town of Watertowne"; Edmund and Mary both signed by mark [MLR 4:173]. On 10 June 1672, "Edmund Bloyes of Watertowne ... planter" sold to Nathaniel Coolidge of Watertown, tailor, "the reversion of a parcel of land (after my decease) in Watertowne containing by estimation seven acres and a half ... (the barn upon the said land or any addition I the said Edward Bloyes shall make to it during my life is excepted out of this sale) with what dwelling house for habitation I the said Edmund Bloyes shall build or cause to be built during my life the reversion of that as well ... the land lying and being near the meeting house in Watertowne and is at present in two parcels"; signed by mark [MLR 4:386].

On 18 November 1679, "in reference to the necessity of old Goodman Bloyse it was voted [by the selectmen] that Deacon Bright and Deacon Hastings are appointed and desired to take care in all respects for a suitable supply for the said Bloyse and the charge to be discharged by the Town Rate" [WaTR 1:143].

In his will, dated 5 December 1676 and proved 5 April 1681, "Edmund Bloyse of Watertown" bequeathed "all my household stuff & moveables, a cow & 40 acres of land which was given me for a farm by the inhabitants of Watertowne which is mine to dispose of the gift of it is upon the town book there and anything that is mine to dispose of I give to my loving & dear wife & do make her my sole executrix of all that I leave when God take me away as a barn & a hovel that stand upon the land where I now dwell & a couple of swine" [MPR 5:190, Case #2110].

The inventory of the estate of "Edmond Bloyse deceased," taken 1 March 1680/1, was untotalled; the only real estate listed was "a farm in the woods of forty acres," valued at £4 10s. [MPR 5:191, Case #2110].

On 5 April 1681, "Ruth Bloyce the relict widow of Edm[und] Bloyce deceased" chose Corporal William Bond and Mr. John Biscoe as overseers of her husband's estate [MCR 4:5].

On 12 June 1681, "Ruth Bloyes widow of Watertown" sold to Henry Godden of Watertown "all that parcel of land that was late in the possession of my father Hugh Parsons deceased lying & being in Watertown abovesaid, containing by estimation four acres"; she made her signature [MLR 7:381]. On 8 February 1698/9, "Ruth Bloss of Watertowne ... widow woman and sole executrix of Edmund Bloss late of Watertowne deceased" sold to Joseph Child of Watertown, carpenter, "a farm situate, lying and being within the limits & bounds of the abovesaid town containing by estimation forty acres"; signed by mark and acknowledged 13 February 1698/9 [MLR 12:288].

BIRTH: About 1588 (deposed 7 April 1663 "aged about 75 years" [MCF Folio #35]; deposed 17 December 1671 "aged about ninety years" (clearly exaggerated by a few years) [MCF Folio #77]).
DEATH: Between 18 November 1679 (when Watertown selectmen provided for his care [WaTR 1:143]) and 1 March 1680/1 (date of inventory).
MARRIAGE: (1) By about 1623 Mary _____. She died at Watertown on 29 May 1672 [WaVR 35].

(2) Cambridge 27 September 1675 Ruth Parsons (the groom's name given as "Edm[und] Bloyce"), daughter of Hugh Parsons [MLR 7:381]. On 3 April 1677, administration was granted to "Edm[un]d Bloyce & Ruth his wife, upon the estate of their mother, the widow Parsons deceased" [MCR 3:167]. She died after 13 February 1698/9 [MLR 12:288].
CHILD:

i   RICHARD, b. about 1623 (aged 11 in 1634 [Hotten 278]); m. Watertown 10 February 1657[/8] Micaell Jennison [WaVR 19], daughter of Robert Jennison (on 3 April 1666, "Michall Blosse, widow of the late deceased Richard Blosse of Watertowne who died intestate leaving three young children," and administratrix of his estate, petitioned that "her father-in-law Edmund Blosse and her brother Samuel Jeneson may be joined administrators with her" [MPR Misc 87, citing "Box 1666-1667" (not found in MCF Folios); see also Bond 307 and MPR Case #2108].

ASSOCIATIONS: Francis Blosse, admitted as a freeman on 2 June 1641 [MBCR 1:379] and buried at Cambridge 29 September 1646, may have been a relative. Pope has an entry for a John Blois, supposed to have been buried at Cambridge on 23 April 1646 [Pope 55], but this is a completely imaginary person, Pope having misread the account of the family prepared by James O. Bloss [NEHGR 41:298].

COMMENTS: On 30 April 1634, "Mary Blosse," aged 40, and "Richard Blosse," aged 11, were on the passenger list of the *Francis* of Ipswich, about to sail for New England [Hotten 278-79].

Although nothing connects them directly with the immigrant, men named "Edmond Bloss" and "Edmund Bloyse" appear in the parishes of Bentley and Holbrook in southeastern county Suffolk in the early seventeenth century. This is a highly likely area of origin for passengers on the *Francis* in 1634, so the origin of the immigrant should be sought there.

Although Mary and Richard Blois apparently arrived in New England in 1634, it may be that Edmund did not come until as late as 1637, as the earliest record for him in New England is the grant of land in April of 1638.

Both Pope and Savage have Edmund's first wife dying in 1675, but the record of her death in Watertown is for 1672.

Edmund Blois appears frequently between 1651 and 1679 as a creditor in the Watertown town accounts, the reason not always stated [WaTR 1:28, 29, 32, 34, 40, 43, 53, 55, 59, 64, 71, 73, 78, 97, 99, 100, 108, 111, 116, 120, 123, 132, 139]. On 3 February 1656/7, the town paid £5 to "Sergeant Bloyse for the pound" [WaTR 1:51]. On 22 January 1657/8, "ordered that brother Bloyse shall have for his salary of looking to the meeting house per year" £3 [WaTR 1:55]; many of the payments to him in later years were for this same service, with the salary eventually raised to £4 10s.

BIBLIOGRAPHIC NOTE: In 1887 James O. Bloss published a brief account of the "Descendants of Edmund and Mary Bloss," to the birth of the fifth generation [NEHGR 41:298-99].

WILLIAM BLOOMFIELD

ORIGIN: Unknown
MIGRATION: 1634 on the *Elizabeth*
FIRST RESIDENCE: Cambridge
REMOVES: Hartford 1636, New London 1659, Newtown 1662

CHURCH MEMBERSHIP: Admission to Cambridge church prior to 2 September 1635 implied by freemanship.
FREEMAN: 2 September 1635 (as "Will[ia]m Blumfeild") [MBCR 1:371].
EDUCATION: Signed his deeds.
OFFICES: On 11 March 1657/8, "William Blumfield" is freed from training [CCCR 1:311].
Newtown selectman, 9 January 1663 [Newtown Town Minutes 1:50].

ESTATE: On 8 February 1635/6, "William Blunfeld" was granted "six acres on the south side of the river" in Cambridge [CaTR 17]. By the time of the 1639 Cambridge land inventory Robert Stedman had "bought of William Blomfield one house with backside about half a rood" [CaBOP 59].

In the Hartford land inventory in February 1639[/40], "Will[ia]m Blumfeild" held fourteen parcels, of which the last four (at least) had been acquired after the date of the inventory: "one parcel on which his dwelling house now standeth with other outhouses, yards & gardens therein being containing by estimation one acre & three roods"; "one parcel of upland containing by estimation twelve acres"; "one parcel lying in the soldiers' field containing by estimation two roods"; "one parcel lying on the east side of the Great River containing by estimation one acre & two roods"; "one parcel lying in the South Meadow containing by estimation one acre & two roods"; "one parcel in the Great Swamp containing by estimation three roods & eight perches which lyeth in a greater parcel containing by estimation five acres & belongeth to James Cole & Thomas Bunse & Arthur Smith & Rob[ert] Bartlett & to the said Will[ia]m Blumfeild which greater parcel abutteth on the Indians' land"; "one parcel of upland lying near to Hockanum which he bought of Thomas Bliss Senior containing by estimation six acres"; "one parcel of land continuing to the east end of Hartford bounds containing by estimation twenty & five acres ... which he bought of Thomas Bless Senior"; "one parcel lying near Hockanum containing by estimation four acres"; "one parcel lying near Hockanum which he bought of Gylles Smith containing by estimation three acres"; "one parcel of boggy meadow lying in the North Meadow containing by estimation two acres" (annotated in margin "May 20th 1652"); "one parcel lying in the Great Swamp at the upper end of it next the South Meadow which he bought formerly of John Hopkins deceased, & now confirmed to him by Jane Hopkins, executrix & late wife of the aforesaid John" (annotated in margin "June:1:1654" and "passed to S:Tho:Watts"); "one parcel being the homelot which he bought of Richard Fellowes containing by estimation [blank] with all the houses thereon with an orchard & all the trees therein" (annotated in the margin "April the 3: 1656"); and "one parcel lying in Forty Acres which he bought of Nath[aniel] Warde containing by estimation one acre" (annotated in margin "passed to Benj: Harbor") [HaBOP 285-88].

On 24 March 1640/1, the town of Hartford ordered that "William Blumfielld shall have the ground whereon the pound standeth and to be made up of ground about it four acres to be laid out by a committee to be chosen to that purpose which ground shall be allowed over and above the ground that he shall have for his division" [HaTR 47].

On 10 February 1655[/6?], "the lands of William Blomfield recorded" at Middletown were: "one piece of upland whereon his house standeth containing three acres"; "one piece of meadow land lying in the Long Meadow containing 5 acres"; "one piece of meadow land lying at Wongonke containing one acre"; "another piece lying at Wongonke containing two acres"; "another piece lying at Wongonke containing one acre"; "one piece of upland lying at Pistol Point containing four acres"; and "another piece of upland lying to the North Field," "all the land above written being sold to Nathaniel Dickinson Senior" [Middletown LR 1:20].

On 3 August 1659, "Thomas Baylie of New London" sold to "Will[iam] Blomfeild of Hartford my house and land lying by it, about six acres ... being my whole right that I have in that place ... with all other conveniences and privileges belonging both to the house and land ... also two acres of land lying upon the west end of Goodman Redfin's lot" [NLLR 3:168].

On 25 February 1660[/1?], "William Blumfeild of New London" appointed "my loving friend Mr. James Rogers of New London to be my lawful attorney," with power of substitution, to collect all debts and "to take into his possession any horse, mares, cattle or other goods that I leave in New England" [NLLR 1B:44].

On 1 May 1661 [NS], "Francis Doughty of the Manadus in the Newnether Lands" sold to "William Blumfelld of New London in Newengland the housing and lands which I bought of Richard Gelldersleeve of Hempsted the said housing and lands being situated and being ... in Medlborough on Longe Iland in the New Netherlands" [Newtown Town Minutes 1:35]. (The settlement of Middleborough was renamed Newtown after the English conquest.)

In a tax list dated "Midleburrough March 16th 1662," "William Blumfield" was assessed 18s. 9d. [Newtown Town Minutes 1:47].

On 30 November 1662, "William Blumfeild late inhabitant in the town of New London" appointed "my trusted and wellbeloved friend Peter Bletchford my true and lawful attorney," with power of substitution, to collect any debts due to Bloomfield [NLLR 1B:80].

On 23 July 1663, "William Blumfeild of Newtowne upon Long Island" deeded to "my daughter Sarah Woodward of the town of New London ... my homestead lot lying in New London which I bought of Thomas Baylie ... also I make over unto her another piece of land which I bought of the said Thomas Baylie ... further I make over unto her one cow ... for the necessary support of herself and children" and then "to her eldest child Joseph Sacket ... when he shall come to age," with further provisions "in case my son-in-law Woodward do not so far provide for my daughter's comfortable subsistence" [NLLR 3:287].

On 27 July 1663, "William Blomfeild of Newtowne On Long Iland" sold to "Georg[e] Tong of New London my dwelling house with the homelot and orchard six acres more or less" [NLLR 3:288].

On 24 February 1664, "William Blomfield in Newtowne" deeded to "Danell Blomfield my son dwelling in the aforesaid town the house & barn and homelot which I bought of Frances Doughtie with the third part privileges and accommodations belonging to the said lot [which is] thirty-three acres of upland & a third ... likewise a third part of my meadow which ... is sixteen more or less acres" and some livestock [Newtown Town Minutes 1:17-18].

In her will of 1 April 1682, "Isbell Blomfeild of Newtowne in the West Riding of Yorksheere upon Long Island" bequeathed to "my loving son Daniell Blomfield ... all the share of the housings & lands which was left me by my deceased husband William Blomfeild with all other things that do belong or appertain to myself except wearing apparel" [Newtown Town Minutes 2:260].

BIRTH: About 1605 (aged 30 in 1635 [Hotten 280]).
DEATH: After 1 March 1666/7 [Newtown Town Minutes 1:82] and probably before 26 February 1667[/8?] (when he does not appear in "a rate made ... for a sessions house" [Newtown Town Minutes 1:19-20]).
MARRIAGE: (1) By 1633 Sarah _____ .
  (2) By 1639 Isabel (Pearce) Sackett, widow of *SIMON SACKETT* [GMB 3:1615]; she died after 1 April 1682 (date of will).
CHILDREN:
  With first wife
      i   SARAH, b. about 1633 (aged 1 in 1634 [Hotten 282]); m. (1) about 1652 her stepbrother Simon Sackett, son of *SIMON SACKETT* [GMB 3:1615]; m. (2) by 1663 Lambert Woodward [NLLR 3:287].
  With second wife
      ii   DANIEL, b. about 1639 (deposed 2 or 3 February 1668/9 "aged 30" [Newtown Court Minutes, 1656-1690, p. 204]); d. intestate and apparently unmarried before 23 September 1703 (date of inventory), administration granted to

> Joseph Sackett, next of kin [NYGBR 65:249, citing Queens County, New York, Will Book A].
iii JOHN, bp. Hartford 23 August 1645 [HaVR 575]; no further record.
iv SAMUEL, b. Hartford 12 July 1647 [HaVR 578]; "Daniell & Sameuell Blomfield" granted twenty acres in Newtown, 31 March 1669 [Newtown Town Minutes 2:84]; not in mother's will, 1 April 1682.

COMMENTS: The passenger list of the *Elizabeth*, dated 30 April 1634, included "William Blomfield," aged 30, "Sarah his wife," aged 25, and "Sarah Blomfield," aged 1 [Hotten 280, 282].

William Bloomfield may have resided briefly at Middletown about 1655, but he appears in Hartford on both sides of this date.

On 19 August 1663, "W[illia]m Blumfield appeals from the sentence or judgment of the Court held at Hartford, June 15, [16]63, to the judgment and determination of this Assembly" [CCCR 1:408]. The court ordered "that Mr. Rogers shall pay unto Blumfeild the sum [torn] pounds in current pay, and Mr. Rogers to keep the mare and bull and [torn] as his proper estate, and discharge Mr. Loveland's debt and pay the cost [*of this*] Court, and the first Court his case was in trial. Blumfeild is to pay the char[ges of] the special Court" [CCCR 1:409].

On 12 August 1665, Francis Kidfield successfully sued William Bloomfield for damage done to Kidfield's corn by Bloomfield's swine. In the several depositions recorded there are repeated references to "Goodman Blumfield" and "Goodwife Blumfield" [Newtown Court Minutes, 1656-1690, pp. 50-53]. The suit was renewed on 23 October 1665, with "Daniell Whithead being employed by William Blumfield an attorney"; as there was "an agreement made & acknowledged by William Blomfield & not performed further the court finding no further evidence appears but the man proving troublesome the court fines him five shillings to the use of the town" [Newtown Court Minutes, 1656-1690, p. 54].

"William Blomfield" appears twice in a list of those required to maintain fencing, the apparent date of which was 1 March 1666/7 [Newtown Town Minutes 1:82].

ROBERT BLOTT

ORIGIN: Puddington, Bedfordshire
MIGRATION: 1634
FIRST RESIDENCE: Charlestown
REMOVES: Concord about 1640, Boston 1642

CHURCH MEMBERSHIP: "John Blacke [*sic*] and Susanna his wife" were admitted to Charlestown church on 4 January 1634/5 [ChChR 8; TAG 67:68]. On 28 December 1644, "Robert Blott and Susan his wife upon letters of dismission from the Church at CharleTowne having declared their spiritual condition to the Elders in private at their private meeting" were admitted to Boston church [BChR 43].
FREEMAN: 4 March 1634/5 (second in a sequence of five Charlestown men) [MBCR 1:370].
EDUCATION: Signed his deed of 1648. Signed his will by mark.
OFFICES: On 5 June 1643, "Thomas [*sic*] Blott" was appointed swineherd at Boston [BTR 1:74]. On 29 March 1658, "Robert Blott is appointed to keep the sheep for this year" [BTR 1:144]. On 5 May 1659, "Tho[mas] [*sic*] Blott is chosen cowkeeper for this year" [BTR 1:152]. On 30 April 1660, "Robert Blott is chosen cowkeeper" [BTR 1:155].
ESTATE: On 2 April 1634, the town of Charlestown ordered "that Robert Blott have a garden plot between his house and Mr. Walford's the smith" [ChTR 11]. In January 1635 "John Black," corrected to "Rob[er]t Blott," was granted five acres of planting ground [ChTR 15]. In the 1635 allotment of hayground, "Tho[mas] [*sic*] Blott" received two, which was then increased to three [ChTR 19, 20]. In 1637 "Rob[er]t Blott" held four cow commons [ChTR 32]. In the Mystic Side allotments on 23 April 1638, "Rob[er]t Blott" received parcels of fifteen, thirty-five and zero acres [ChTR 36]. By the time of the 1638 Charlestown land inventory, Robert Blott was not shown as holding any land, and several of the parcels of land which had been granted to him were in the hands of William Stitson [ChBOP 49].

On 21 March 1635/6, "Thomas [*sic*] Blott" was one of several men "former[ly] granted allotments that were not built upon according to a former order made the 30th of the 9th month last, and therefore that they are free to be otherwise disposed of" [BTR 1:9]. (This grant to Blott may have been made in 1634, at the time of his arrival in New England, after which Blott moved to Charlestown and left this lot unattended.)

In the 1645 Boston land inventory, "Robert Blott" held one parcel of land: "one house and garden" [BBOP 32].

On 29 July 1648, "Robert Blott of Boston" sold to "Samuel Stretton of Concord his house & land in Concord granted by the town to the same forty acres more or less with all the appurtenances & privileges thereto belonging" [SLR 1:94].

On 9 April 1649, "Rob[er]t Blote" was one of a large number of men who bound themselves to pay an annual rent for their land on Long Island [BTR 1:95].

In his will, dated 27 May 1662 (with codicil dated 27 March 1665) and proved 2 February 1665/6, Robert Blott made "Edward Ellis my son-in-law husband to Sarah my daughter my executor" and bequeathed to him "my house & the lot belonging thereunto, with all the appurtenances, also my will is that he shall pay to my eldest daughter's children, whose name was Woodford of Conniticott, three pounds"; Edward Ellis also to "give my daughter Tosior's children seven pounds and three bushels of wheat & two of Indian corn, besides to her eldest son John Green Cloth to make him a coat," and to "give to my daughter Lovett's children of Braintree seven pound and three bushels of wheat and two bushels of Indian, also to my son-in-law Danil Turin's children eight pounds"; "my daughter Tosior & my daughter Lovet shall have half the household stuff equally divided between them, and the other half to my daughter Ellis and also three bushels of malt to be divided between my three daughters"; "also to Daniell Lovett my son-in-law I give my best coat." In the codicil of 27 March 1665, Robert Blott reported that he had consumed all the corn mentioned as bequests, and that the relevant portions of his will were null and void, bequeathed to "Daniel Lovett's eldest son ... a remnant of cloth," affirmed that his bequest of his house and ground to "my son Ellis" was only for the benefit "of my daughter Sara & the children of my son Ellis," and made "my son & daughter Ellis" his executors [SPR 1:456].

The inventory of the estate of Robert Blott, taken 22 August 1665, totalled £112 5s., of which £100 was real estate: "the dwelling house & land adjoining" [SPR 4:262].

BIRTH: By about 1584 based on date of marriage.
DEATH: Between 27 March 1665 (codicil to will) and 22 August 1665 (date of inventory).
MARRIAGE: Harrold, Bedfordshire, 31 August 1609 Susanna Selbee [TAG 67:65]. She died at Boston 20 January 1659[/60] [BVR 71].
CHILDREN [TAG 67:67]:

     i   MARY, bp. Harrold, Bedfordshire, 24 December 1609; m. by about 1636 *THOMAS WOODFORD* [GMB 3:2057-60].

ii JOHN, bp. Harrold 27 October 1611; bur. there 21 September 1617.

iii ELIZABETH, bp. Harrold 8 March 1613/4; possibly m. (1) Ralph Green and (2) _____ Tozier [see COMMENTS below].

iv ANN, bp. Harrold 12 January 1616/7; probably d. soon.

v GEORGE, bp. Harrold 3 October 1619; bur. there 22 October 1620.

vi JOANNA, bp. Harrold 1 October 1620; m. in late 1644 or early 1645 Daniel Lovett (on 7 September 1644, "Johannah Blott a maid servant to our Deacon Mr. Valentine Hill" was admitted to Boston church [BChR 41]; on 8 June 1645, "our sister Johanna Blott now the wife of one Daniel Lovitt of Braintree, at her desire had letters of recommendation granted by the silence of the Church unto the Church at Braintree" [BChR 44]).

vii ROBERT, bp. Puddington, Bedfordshire, 22 May 1623; no further record.

viii ANNA, bp. Puddington 9 January 1624/5; possibly m. (1) Ralph Green and (2) _____ Tozier [see COMMENTS below].

ix LYDIA, bp. Puddington 1 July 1627; m. by 1646 Daniel Turell (or Turin) (eldest known child b. Boston 16 August 1646 [BVR 23]).

x SARAH, bp. Puddington 2 October 1631; m. Boston 6 October 1652 Edward Ellis [BVR 38].

ASSOCIATIONS: In her will of 18 February 1649/50, *ELIZABETH PURTON* bequeathed a Bible and 40s. to Robert Blott, and also left him in control of some of her estate [GMB 3:1535-36]. In his will of 30 April 1656, *SAMUEL WILBORE* bequeathed to Robert Blott 20s. [GMB 3:1987]. Whether these bequests indicate kinship relations has not been determined.

COMMENTS: The recordkeepers of early New England had a hard time with Robert Blott's name. He appears several times in Charlestown records as "John Black" [TAG 67:67-68], "John Blott" and "Thomas Blott," and in Boston as "Thomas Blott" [Goodwin Anc 2:197-98]. These various records are consistent with the existence of one New England resident named Robert Blott, and we have proceeded under that assumption.

"John [*sic*] Blott" was admitted as an inhabitant of Charlestown in 1634 [ChTR 11], and the January 1634/5 list of Charlestown inhabitants included "Jno. Black," corrected to "Rob[er]t Blott" [ChTR 15]. On 10 February 1634/5, "Rob[er]t Blott" signed the Charlestown petition initiating the office of selectman [ChTR 13].

On 28 March 1642, "Tho[mas] [*sic*] Blott" was admitted to be a townsman at Boston [BTR 1:68].

Given the limited number of early records for Concord, there is difficulty in determining when Robert Blott resided in that town in order to be granted the piece of land that he sold in 1648. We suggest that he resided there briefly between his departure from Charlestown and his arrival in Boston, and so place this residence roughly about 1640.

In his will Robert Blott bequeathed to "my daughter Tosior's children seven pounds and three bushels of wheat & two of Indian corn, besides to her eldest son John Green Cloth to make him a coat." We know nothing more for certain about this daughter. Most authors have concluded that this daughter had two husbands, first Green and then Tosior (or Tozier). There may be some doubt about the first husband, inasmuch as the bequest to the eldest son is subject to two interpretations: a son named John Green is given cloth; or a son named John is given green cloth. For the purposes of the present discussion, we will assume as others have that the first of these two interpretations is the correct one.

The only potential Green husband who has been suggested is Ralph of Boston, who had a son John born there on 22 December 1642 [BVR 13]. Some attempts have been made to identify the second husband of this daughter as Richard Tozier of Kittery, but, as Jacobus and Noyes, Libby and Davis have noted, "that is impossible" [Hale, House 482; GDMNH 689]. Finally, given our recently acquired knowledge of the baptisms of the children of Robert Blott, there are two daughters, not otherwise assigned, who might be the subject of this bequest. Additional evidence on this daughter would be welcome.

BIBLIOGRAPHIC NOTE: Robert Blott and his family have been treated many times by some of the best genealogists of the past. The most complete treatment was by Frank Farnsworth Starr in 1915 [Goodwin Anc 2:193-201]. Other, briefer, compilations of value are those of Mary Lovering Holman in 1948 [Stevens-Miller Anc 1:411-13] and Donald Lines Jacobus in 1952 [Hale, House 480-82].

In 1992 Penny G. Douglass published the records which demonstrate the English origin of Robert Blott [TAG 67:65-67]. Robert Charles Anderson appended to this article an argument that all records in early Charlestown for a John Black were really intended for Robert Blott [TAG 67:67-68].

THOMAS BLOWER

ORIGIN: Sudbury, Suffolk
MIGRATION: 1635 on the *Truelove*
FIRST RESIDENCE: Boston

ESTATE: On 9 September 1639, "Capt. Keayne was ordered to pay the £12 10s. which he received of Mr. Saltonstall for part of Mrs. Blower's mo[ney?]" [MBCR 1:273].

On 1 April 1640, Nathaniel Lufkin of Hitcham, Suffolk, wrote to John Winthrop regarding "one Thomas Blower who now liveth (as I hear) at Boston in New England.... This Thomas Blower oweth me twenty-four pounds of current English money.... There is one Edmund Rice and Henry Bruning whom this bearer knows well who can tell of this debt as well as myself" [WP 4:222-23].

BIRTH: Baptized Stanstead, Suffolk, 23 April 1587, son of Thomas and Susan (Vincent) Blower [TAG 52:73-74].
DEATH: By 9 September 1639 [MBCR 1:273].
MARRIAGE: Stanstead, Suffolk, 19 November 1612 Alice Frost [TAG 52:67], baptized Stanstead 1 December 1594, daughter of Edward and Thomasine (Belgrave) Frost [TAG 10:135]. She married (2) probably at Barnstable soon after 6 July 1640 William Tilly [WP 4:262; TAG 71:113].
CHILDREN:
    i   HANNAH, b. say 1613; bur. All Saints, Sudbury, Suffolk, 7 May 1630 [TAG 56:99].
    ii   ALICE, bp. St Gregory's, Sudbury, 30 June 1615 [TAG 56:99]; m. St Katherine by the Tower, London, 6 January 1633/4 *RICHARD BRACKETT* [NEHGR 127:17; GMB 1:203-6].
    iii JOSHUA, bp. All Saints, Sudbury, 15 December 1621, and bur. there 22 August 1623 [TAG 56:99].
    iv   THOMAS, bp. All Saints, Sudbury, 22 February 1623/4, and bur. there 25 April 1625 [TAG 56:100].

v   MARY, bp. All Saints 13 February 1625/6 [TAG 56:100]; no
       further record.
vi   JOHN, bp. All Saints 23 February 1627/8 [TAG 56:100]; m. by
       1654 Tabitha _____ (eldest known child b. Boston 12
       February 1654/5 [BVR 46]) [TAG 21:238-43]. (The
       knowledge that John's mother married secondly a
       Barnstable man makes it virtually certain that this John
       was the one in the Barnstable section of the 1643
       Plymouth Colony list of men able to bear arms [PCR
       8:194].)
vii   THOMAS, bp. All Saints 16 May 1630 [TAG 56:100]; no further
       record.
viii (probably) PYAM, b. about 1638 (d. Cambridge 1 June 1709,
       aged 71); m. Cambridge 31 March 1668 Elizabeth Belcher.
       (Pyam is placed tentatively as a child of this couple for
       three reasons: there is no other Blower family in early
       New England; Alice (Frost) Blower would have been
       about forty-four years old at the time this child was born;
       and Pyam named a son Thomas [MPR Case #2109].)

ASSOCIATIONS: Alice (Frost) (Blower) Tilly was sister of Thomasine
Frost, who married Edmund Rice, immigrant to Sudbury, and also of
Elizabeth Frost, who married first Henry Rice and then Philemon Whale,
the latter also an immigrant to Sudbury [TAG 15:227, 26:10-11; TG 6:131-
41; Stevens-Miller Anc 143-44].

COMMENTS: On 19 September 1635, "Tho[mas] Blower," aged 50, was
enrolled at London as a passenger for New England on the *Truelove*
[Hotten 132].

BIBLIOGRAPHIC NOTE: In 1976 John Brooks Threlfall wrote an article
on *RICHARD BRACKETT*, which also included fundamental material on
the Blower family and the Vincent family [TAG 52:65-75; see also 50GMC
63-116, especially 77-78], and additional material on the Vincent family
was published by the same author in 1985 [NEHGR 139:148-49]. In 1980
John Brooks Threlfall presented additional material on the Blower family,
including an account of legal difficulties encountered by Alice just before
she left England [TAG 56:99-100]. In 1996 Robert Charles Anderson
discussed Alice's second marriage [TAG 71:113].
   In 1998 Mary Beth Norton published a detailed study of the legal
difficulties of Alice (Frost) (Blower) Tilly resulting from her midwife

activities ("`The Ablest Midwife That Wee Knowe in the Land': Mistress Alice Tilly and the Women of Boston and Dorchester, 1649-1650" [*William and Mary Quarterly*, 3rd Series, 55:105-34]).

ELIZABETH BOANEO

On 2 August 1635, "Elizabeth Boaneo one of our brother Richard Bellingham's maid servants" was admitted to Boston church [BChR 20].

COMMENTS: There is no evidence whether she died, married or returned to England.

MARY BONNER

On 3 August 1634, "Marie Bonner maid servant to our teacher John Cotton" was admitted to Boston church [BChR 1:19].
    On 18 August 1644, "Our sister Mary Bonner now the wife of Mr. Daniel Mawd, teacher of the church at Dover, at her desire hath letters of dismission granted her unto that church of Dover" [BChR 1:41].

COMMENTS: See sketch of DANIEL MAUDE for further details.

THOMAS BONNEY

ORIGIN: Sandwich, Kent
MIGRATION: 1635 on the *Hercules*
FIRST RESIDENCE: Charlestown
REMOVES: Duxbury 1637

OCCUPATION: Shoemaker.
FREEMAN: Propounded for Plymouth freemanship 5 March 1638/9 [PCR 1:117], but not admitted. Oath of fidelity at Duxbury, 1639 and 1657 [PCR 8:181, 182].
EDUCATION: Signed his will by mark.
OFFICES: Duxbury constable, 7 March 1642/3, 5 June 1644 [PCR 2:53, 72]. Surveyor of highways, 7 June 1653 [PCR 3:32]. Coroner's jury, 23 July 1661 [PCR 3:223].

In Duxbury section of 1643 Plymouth Colony list of men able to bear arms [PCR 8:190].

ESTATE: On 2 July 1635, "Faintnot Wines & Tho[mas] Bonny were granted a houseplot about the hill & to have ground at Wenotomie's River" in Charlestown [ChTR 14], and on 11 July 1635, "Isaack Cole, John Lewis, Faintnot Wines & Tho[mas] Bonny to have houseplots laid out by 3 or 4 about the hill" [ChTR 14]. (This grant did not carry with it proprietary rights, as Bonney did not share in the town grants of 1635, 1636 and 1637.) On 6 March 1636/7, "Rob[er]t Cutler was admitted a townsman, & bought the house & houseplot which was granted to Tho[mas] Bonny" [ChTR 26].

On 6 April 1640, Thomas Bonney, with others, was granted the lands lying on the northwestern side of the North Hill in Duxbury, with the lands by Christopher Wadsworth's farm, and the meadow there, to be divided amongst them [PCR 1:144]. Bonney was also granted 30 acres in Duxbury at Namassacuset River on 31 August 1640 [PCR 1:160-61].

In his will, dated 2 January 1688/9 and proved 1 May 1693, "Thomas Boney Senior, shoemaker, living in Duxborough," bequeathed to "my beloved wife Mary Boney all my houses and land in Duxbury as also all my cattle and all my household stuff ... during her natural life and if anything remains of the moveables my will is that they be disposed of by her amongst my children as she thinks fit"; to "my son Thomas Boney all my houses and lands in Duxbury after his mother's decease"; "my beloved wife Mary Boney sole executrix and administratrix" [PPR 1:146; MD 34:182].

BIRTH: By 1614 (admitted inhabitant of Charlestown in 1635).

DEATH: Between 2 January 1688/9 (date of will) and 1 May 1693 (probate of will).

MARRIAGE: By about 1655 Mary _____ (see *COMMENTS* below). She died after 2 January 1688/9, when she was named in her husband's will.

CHILDREN:

i   MARY, b. say 1655; m. Duxbury 14 December 1675 John Mitchell, son of *EXPERIENCE MITCHELL* [GMB 2:1272].

ii   THOMAS, b. say 1659; m. (1) by 1684 Dorcas Samson, daughter of *HENRY SAMSON* [MFIP Samson 8-9; GMB 3:1623]; m. (2) Duxbury 18 July 1695 Sarah Studley.

iii (possibly) SARAH, b. about 1660; m. by 1680 Nathaniel Cole (eldest known child b. Duxbury 21 September 1680; this connection is apparently found only in the "chronicle" of Perez Bonney).

iv   HANNAH, b. say 1663; on 27 October 1685, "Hannah Bonny convict for fornication with John Michell, & also with Nimrod, negro, & having a bastard child by said Nimrod, is sentenced to be well whipped" [PCR 6:176-77]; no further record.

v   JOHN, b. about 1664 (d. Pembroke 16 November 1745, aged 81; the precise birthdate of 25 February 1664, seen in some secondary sources, is probably taken from the "chronicle" of his son, Perez); m. by 1690 Elizabeth Bishop, daughter of James Bishop (eldest child b. Pembroke 27 June 1690; in her will of 3 August 1732, "Mary Bishop of Pembroke ... widow and relict of James Bishop late of Pembroke deceased" included bequests to "the children of my deceased daughters Abigail Bonney and Mary Lasthley" and to "my two daughters Elizabeth Bonney and Hannah Simmons" [PPR 8:217-18]).

vi   WILLIAM, b. say 1668; m. (1) by 1693 Ann _____ (eldest child b. Plympton 4 January 1693/4 [MD 3:166]; her surname given as May in some sources, again probably based on the "chronicle" of Perez Bonney, but no other evidence seen); m. (2) Plymouth 11 July 1700 Mehitable King [PVR 87].

vii JAMES, b. about 1672 (d. Pembroke 24 January 1723/4, aged 52); m. (1) Duxbury 12 June 1695 Abigail Bishop, daughter of James Bishop; m. (2) after 1714 Desire Billington [MF 5:60].

viii JOSEPH, b. say 1674 (or later); m. Plymouth 14 November 1707 Margaret Phillips [PVR 89].

COMMENTS: On 14 March 1634[/5], "Tho[ma]s Boney & Edw[ar]d [*recte* Henry] Ewell shoemakers of Sandwich" received their certificates from Mr. Thomas Warren, rector of St Peters, Sandwich, for their passage to New England on the *Hercules* [NEHGR 75:219].

In 1898 Charles L. Bonney transcribed a portion of "Perez Bonney's chronicle of his predecessors and likewise his own posterity"; Perez Bonney, a grandson of the immigrant, was born in 1710 and compiled his "chronicle" in 1758. Perez Bonney spoke of "my grandfather, Thomas Bonney, who came from Dover, in England, and was born about the year

1604, and married Mary Terry, but she died, and then he married Mary Hunt, being as I have been told about 50 years old" [Charles L. Bonney, *The Bonney Family* (Chicago 1898), pp. 6-7]. Unfortunately, none of this can be confirmed. Writing in 1935, Howard Dakin French stated that he had "not yet been able to determine just what dependence may be placed" on the account of Perez Bonney [NEHGR 89:223].

Thomas Bonney was presented to the court on 3 March 1645/6 for "uncivil carriages and lascivious actions toward women and maids" [PCR 2:96]. Mr. John Farnyseede and Elizabeth, his wife, brought an action against Thomas Bonney for defamation and slander, Bonney having said that "Mistress Farniseede did justle him in her house, and that he took it as a temptation of him unto lust," but he admitted that it was his own "base heart" that made him conclude these things from her words and deeds, and begged for forgiveness [PCR 2:97-98].

On 2 August 1646, following a controversy between Thomas Bonney of the first part and John Willis and Mr. John Farneseede of the second part, for damage done in the corn and garden of Thomas Bonney, the court ordered all three parties to share the cost of the damages, and Thomas Bonney was to pay the costs of court [PCR 2:107-8].

Christopher Wadsworth complained that Thomas Bonney had wounded a mare belonging to Wadsworth [PCR 4:7]. Thomas Bonney was in court again on 6 June 1650 complaining about Jonathan Brewster the younger, the court finding for the defendant [PCR 7:48], and on 5 March 1655/6, Roger Glasse complained against Thomas Bonney for denying to pay him for carrying some things "into the bay," the jury finding for the plaintiff [PCR 7:76].

BIBLIOGRAPHIC NOTE: In 1935 Howard Dakin French published an article on Thomas Bonney and his children, which corrected some earlier printed errors, but which lacked documentation and left many points unresolved [NEHGR 89:220-23].

RICHARD BONYTHON

ORIGIN: St Breage, Cornwall
MIGRATION: 1635
FIRST RESIDENCE: Saco

OCCUPATION: Magistrate.

CHURCH MEMBERSHIP: "Captain Richard Bonython" was assessed £3 for the minister's rate at Saco, 17 September 1636 [MPCR 1:lxii].

EDUCATION: Sufficient to serve as a magistrate.

OFFICES: Magistrate, 25 March 1636, 21 October 1645 [MPCR 1:1, 83]. Councillor under Gorges, 1639, 1640 [MPCR 1:31, 36, 42, 55-56, 76]. Assistant, 6 July 1646 [MPCR 1:93].

ESTATE: On 29 February 1629/30, the Council for New England, "in consideration that Thomas Lewis, gentleman, hath already been at the charge to transport himself & others to take a view of New England in America, aforesaid, for the bettering of his experiences in advancing of a plantation, & doth now wholly intend by God's assistance with his associates to plant there," granted to "Thomas Lewis & Capt. Ric[hard] Bonighton ... all that part of the mainland in New England in America aforesaid, commonly called or known by the name of Swanckadocke, ... lying & being between the cape or bay commonly called Cape Elizabeth & the cape or bay commonly called Cape Porpus"; livery of seizin was performed on 28 June 1631, to Lewis but not to Bonython, indicating that the latter was not yet in New England [YLR 2:110-11].

On 14 July 1647, "[w]hereas Rich[ard] Bonighton of Saco, gentleman, desired one hundred acres of land for Rich[ard] Comeman his son-in-law, betwixt the River of Saco & Thomas Williams his house, ... Robert Child, gent.," and Richard Bonython exchanged land, Child receiving "the like proportion of upland & marsh, on the northeast side of the River of Saco, in my patent not broken up"; "Eliza[beth] Bonighton" and "Lucretia Bonighton" witnessed [YLR 1:1:40].

On 1 July 1661, "Richard Commings father of Tho[mas] Cumings is plaintiff as executor to Capt. Richard Bonighton in an action of the case for a debt due to the said Ric[hard] Bonighton contra Mr. John Bonighton defendant"; annotated "withdrawn" [MPCR 2:99]. (This record was inaccurately reported by Noyes, Libby and Davis [GDMNH 99], and, given the imprecise usage of the terms "executor" and "administrator" at the time, does not necessarily imply the existence of a will.)

On 23 September 1681, "John Wincoll, John Penwill, & Abraham Preble, being chosen by mutual consent of James Gibbines, John Bonighton, Phillip Foxwell & John Harmon, heirs & proprietors of that patent land, granted to Mr. Lewis & Capt. Rich[ar]d Bonighton, as by their agreement obligatory bearing date the twelfth day of November one-thousand six-hundred and eighty may appear, for equally dividing the said land between the said proprietors," proceeded to divide the patent into eight parts, four of which went to James Gibbons, two to John Bonython and two to Philip Foxwell and John Harmon jointly [YLR 3:102-3]. (In this division, James Gibbons was the only representative of Thomas Lewis; John Bonython as the eldest and only son received a double share of Richard Bonython's half of the patent, while the shares intended for Richard Bonython's two daughters came into the hands of his grandsons Philip Foxwell and John Harmon [Charity Haley Anc 58; see also YLR 1:1:152-53, 4:22, 8:30-31, 242-43, 12:160, 173, 13:137-38].)

BIRTH: Baptized at St Columb Major, Cornwall, 8 April 1580, son of John and Eleanor (Myleinton) Bonython [Arthur J. Jewers, ed., *The Registers of the Parish of St Columb Major, Cornwall, from the Year 1539 to 1780* (London 1881), p. 10; Bonython Gen 40, citing St Breage parish register].

DEATH: Before 29 June 1654 (when "Mr. Richard Foxwell & Mr. Comings [were] plaintiffs in an action of trespass upon the case for pulling down their house & laying claim to their lands, contra Mr. John Bonighton defendant" [MPCR 2:24]).

MARRIAGE: By about 1607 Lucretia Leigh, daughter of William and Phillippa (Prest) Leigh of St Thomas by Launceston, Cornwall [Bonython Gen 203-4 and sources cited there, especially "Chancery Proceedings. 6 Charles I. T. 14/3"].

CHILDREN:

   i   JOHN, b. say 1607 [see COMMENTS below]; m. by about 1650 Agnes _____ (in his nuncupative will of 17 February 1676[/7], John Bonython bequeathed a double portion to "the eldest son John" and "declared that his three sons should according to their proportion of estate afford to his wife Agnes Bonighton their own mother a comfortable maintenance" [NEHGR 34:99, citing "County Registers of York"]; eldest son John seems to have been born about 1650 [GDMNH 98-99; NEHGR 38:55]).

   ii   FRANCIS, bur. St Breage, Cornwall, 22 January 1609/10.

   iii   GRACE, bp. St Breage 19 April 1610; no further record.

   iv   ELIZABETH, bp. St Breage 20 September 1612; m. about 1647 Richard Cummings [YLR 1:1:40].

   v   SUSANNAH, bp. St Breage 5 February 1614/5; m. by 1635 *RICHARD FOXWELL* [GMB 1:695].

ASSOCIATIONS: Richard Bonython and *THOMAS LEWIS* had formed a close association some years before either had arrived in New England [Bonython Gen 203-4].

COMMENTS: On 25 March 1636, "Mr. Richard Bonithon for incontinency with Ane [blank] his father's servant is fined forty shillings, & the said Ane 20s. he to keep the child" [MPCR 1:1]. Based on the baptismal dates of his siblings, John Bonython must have been born before 1610 or after 1615. Although he could well have had an illegitimate child at age nineteen or twenty, we think it more likely that he was older than this in 1636, and so place his birth about 1607. (Based on circumstantial evidence, Philip Howard Gray thought that "Ane [blank]" of 1636 was the same as John's wife Agnes, and that she could be identified with Susanna Lewis, daughter of Richard Bonython's partner *THOMAS LEWIS* [Penobscot Pioneers 2:34-37]. The evidence presented by Gray is slight and unconvincing.)

Savage thought that a daughter of Richard Bonython "married Richard Codman," and has an entry for Richard Codman, the totality of which is "York 1653, son-in-law of Richard Bonython" [Savage 1:211, 416]. Richard Cummings, who married Elizabeth Bonython, had his name garbled frequently, and from this Savage was enticed to create Richard Codman, a man who did not exist.

BIBLIOGRAPHIC NOTE: In 1884 Charles E. Banks published an account of the Bonython family, including three generations of the agnate ancestry of the immigrant [NEHGR 38:50-56]. The documentation supplied by Banks was quite good by the standards of his time, but from our perspective is inadequate, and this research should be replicated. We are reliant on this source for the identification of the mother of the immigrant.

Walter Goodwin Davis, although he did not descend from Richard Bonython, had occasion to discuss the family three times in the course of his writings on other families; his treatment of the landholdings of Bonython is more extensive than what we have supplied in this sketch [Lydia Harmon Anc 9; Charity Haley Anc 56-59; Nicholas Davis Anc 99, 118-20].

In 1966 Eric Glenie Bonython published a comprehensive account of many branches of the Bonython family throughout the world [*History of the families of Bonython of Bonython and Bonython of Carclew in the Duchy of Cornwall; to which is added an account of the Bonythons who settled in South Australia, the small branch at Newlyn East and St. Columb Minor, Cornwall, and those who settled in what is now Maine, U.S.A., in 1630* (n.p. 1966), cited above as Bonython Gen].

In 1992 Philip Howard Gray prepared an account of the immigrant, the most prominent feature of which is an speculative and idiosyncratic suggestion for the identity of the wife of John Bonython, son of Richard, a suggestion which we do not accept [Penobscot Pioneers 2:33-38].

JAMES BOOSEY

ORIGIN: Colchester, Essex, or vicinity
MIGRATION: 1635
FIRST RESIDENCE: Wethersfield

OCCUPATION: Joiner and wheelwright (his inventory included "his joiner's & wheelwright's tools" valued at £10).
OFFICES: Deputy to Connecticut Court for Wethersfield, 1639-49 [CCCR 1:27, 29, 34, 41, 46, 50, 58, 64, 71, 93, 96, 99, 103, 111, 116, 117, 124, 128, 130, 132, 133, 138, 145, 146, 149, 155, 157, 159, 161, 163, 166, 170, 174, 178, 185, 188]. Surveyor of arms for Wethersfield, 8 August 1639 [CCCR 1:30]. Committee to view lands, 16 January 1639/40 [CCCR 1:42]. Committee to erect house of correction, 10 April 1640 [CCCR 1:47]. Committee to survey the line between Hartford and Wethersfield, 9 November 1641 [CCCR 1:69].
    Clerk of the Wethersfield train band, 10 April 1645 [CCCR 1:125]. Lieutenant by 9 September 1647 [CCCR 1:157].
ESTATE: In the Wethersfield land inventory on 10 March 1641[/2?], "the lands of James Boosye lying in Wethersfield" were as follows: "one piece whereon his house and barn standeth containing three acres one rood"; "one piece lying in the Great Meadow containing twelve acres"; "one piece lying in Beaver Meadow called Dams containing two acres"; "one piece lying in the Wet Swamp containing fourteen acres"; "one piece lying in the West Field containing forty & two acres"; and "one piece on the east side of Conectt. River containing eighty-four acres" [WetLR 1:142].
    In the Wethersfield land inventory on 11 May 1644, "the lands of James Boosye which he bought of Ro[bert] Cooe lying in Wethersfield" are as follows: "one piece whereon his house standeth containing three acres"; "one piece in the Great Meadow containing seven acres"; "one piece lying in Beaver Meadow containing five acres"; "one piece in long row in the Dry Swamp containing thirteen acres"; "one piece in the West Field containing thirty and nine acres"; and "one piece on the east side of Conecticutt River containing threescore & eighteen acres" [WetLR 1:34].

In his will, dated 21 June 1649 and proved on an unknown date, "James Boosey late of Wethersfield upon the River on Conecticoat who died the 22th of this instant month" bequeathed to "my eldest son Joseph Boosey" £200 at age twenty-one and also "my homelot with a barn standing upon it which I bought of Mr. Olcot which was Thomas Sherwood's the younger containing six acres ..., 17 acres of my plain that is to say the little plain running to the great plain ... and seven acres in the Great Meadow which I bought of Rob[er]t Coe ... and five acres in Beaver Meadow ... and all my upland which I bought of Rob[er]t Coe ... and twenty-nine pounds in such pay as his mother can conveniently pay him in, when my son Joseph comes to the enjoyment of this land according to this my will he shall repay back again the hundred pounds unless he take this hundred pound in land"; to "my daughter Mary Boosey" £50 at age twenty-one or marriage; to "my daughter Hanah Boosey" £50 at age twenty-one or marriage; to "my daughter Sarah Boosey" £50 at age twenty-one or marriage; "my two sons Joseph & James shall have all my lands after the death of their mother, Joseph shall have all my purchased land, except four acres in Beaver Meadow, which is twenty acres on the Great Plain and four acres in the Great Meadow which was John Simonses & Jarimiah Jagers, this with that before mentioned is the whole purchased land except the four acres in Beaver Meadow before expressed, my son James shall have my now dwelling house & houselot and barns & houses standing thereon with all the lands which was given me by the town that is now in my possession which is twelve acres in the Great Meadow, 56 acres of upland & swamp with four acres in Beaver Meadow which was named before"; residue of land to be divided among children, with Joseph receiving four shares, James two shares, and each of the three daughters, Mary, Hannah and Sarah, one share apiece; residue to "my wife," she to be sole executrix; "Mister Wells, Brother Smith Senior & Brother Dickinson" to be supervisors [HaPD Case #695].

The inventory of the estate of James Boosey, taken 4 August 1649, totalled £983 8s., of which £400 was real estate: "his house and lands"; "his joiner's and wheelwright's tools" were valued at £10 [HaPD Case #695].

On 15 May 1668, "[u]pon the petition of Ensign Steele, John Pratt and Nath[aniel] Standley &c. This Court do hereby order that the children of James Boosey or their heirs shall not be prejudiced or disenabled, by the law for claim of land and prosecution within twelve month & a day, to sue for or recover any right or title they may have or ought to have in any land in reversion after the death of their mother, either by will or heirship at common law" [CCCR 2:85; see also Connecticut Archives, Private Controversies, Series One, 1:62].

The inventory of the estate of "Alice Wakely deceased," taken 6 September 1683, totalled £348 19s., of which £233 was real estate: "homelot 7 acres with dwelling house, barn, outhouses, orchard, cider press," £150; and "11 acres of land in the Great Meadow," £83 [HaPR 4:131].

Within a few months of Alice's decease, her sons-in-law Samuel Steel and Nathaniel Stanley instituted legal proceedings to recover the land which they believed Alice had illegally sold prior to 1668. This legal action generated a large number of informative documents, including copies of James Boosey's will and of the inventories of his Wethersfield landholdings, copies which are generally more legible than the originals [Connecticut Archives, Private Controversies, Series One, 2:172-189b].

BIRTH: By about 1604 based on estimated date of marriage.

DEATH: Wethersfield 22 June 1649 (from will).

MARRIAGE: By 1629 Alice _____ [WP 2:184, 195]. She married (2) Hartford 5 October 1652 James Wakeley [HaVR 608]. On 23 February 1652/3, Connecticut Court judged the account of the deputies "in marrying Jeames Wakely & the widow Boosy to be legal" [CCCR 1:238]. She died at Wethersfield 30 August 1683 [WetVr Barbour 265, citing WetVR 1:58; FOOF 1:627].

CHILDREN:

i   JOSEPH, b. say 1630; m. by 1655 Esther, probably daughter of *ANDREW WARD* [FOOF 1:118-20; GMB 3:1920]. She m. (2) Jehu Burr, son of *JEHU BURR* [FOOF 1:118-20; GMB 1:279].

ii MARY, b. Wethersfield 10 September 1635 [TAG 9:30, citing WetLR 1:22]; m. by 1652 Samuel Steele, son of *JOHN STEELE* [GMB 3:1759].

iii HANNAH, b. Wethersfield 10 February 1641/2 [TAG 9:30, citing WetLR 1:22]; m. by 1658 John Pratt, son of *JOHN PRATT* [GMB 3:1509].

iv SARAH, b. Wethersfield 12 November 1643 [TAG 9:30, citing WetLR 1:22]; m. Hartford 2 June 1659 Nathaniel Stanley [HaVR 621].

v   JAMES, b. Wethersfield 1 February 1645/6 [TAG 9:30, citing WetLR 1:22]; named in father's will, 21 June 1649; no further record.

COMMENTS: On 6 January 1629/30, Samuel Borrowes wrote to John Winthrop from Colchester, Essex, "that there is a friend of mine which is willing to go this voyage for New England, he hath been inclined to that voyage a great while but he came not to me with a resolution for to go till this morning after my father's letter was writ and he desired me to write to you for to enter his name and his wife's and if it please you to undertake for them in their passage over and send word I pray whether you will undertake for them or no and for the half of the money for their charge going over and for half the money for carrying over the goods he means to carry.... His name is James Boosye and alleso his wife" [WP 2:184]. On 20 January 1629/30, Borrowes wrote further with reference to "Jhemes Boseye and his wife which I am very sorry that I did meddle in the business about sending to your worship for them, had I thought that he would have proved so inconstant he should have writ himself; he tells me the reason he cannot go this voyage is that he had sold his commodities and the party tells him since that he will not have them except he will stay for his money till after Michaelmas so he desired me to write to you to have him excused for this voyage" [WP 1:195]. Boosey and his wife apparently waited five more years before coming to New England.

BIBLIOGRAPHIC NOTE: In 1915 Frank Farnsworth Starr published a typically comprehensive account of this immigrant [Goodwin Anc 263-71]. In 1960 Donald Lines Jacobus prepared a briefer account [Ackley-Bosworth 258-59].

JOHN BORDEN

ORIGIN: Kent
MIGRATION: 1635 on the *Elizabeth & Ann*
FIRST RESIDENCE: Watertown

BIRTH: Baptized Headcorn, Kent, 22 February 1606/7, son of Matthew and Joan (_____) Borden [NEHGR 84:227].
DEATH: Soon after arrival in New England, probably late 1635 or early 1636.
MARRIAGE: By 1627 Joanna _____. She married (2) by 1638 JOHN GAY and died at Dedham on 14 August 1691 [DeVR 21].

CHILDREN:
   i   MATTHEW, b. about 1627 (aged 8 in 1635 [Hotten 78]); came
       to New England in 1635; no further record.
   ii ELIZABETH, b. about 1632 (aged 3 in 1635 [Hotten 78]); m. (as
       "Elizabeth Gay") Salem 1660 Richard Martin (recorded
       Boston, day and month of marriage not given [BVR 76;
       NEHGR 130:38-39]).
   iii JOHN, b. 24 June 1635 (or 1636?) (recorded at Dedham, but
       born at sea if the 1635 date is correct, or in Watertown if
       the date is correctly 1636 [DeVR 1; NEHGR 130:36]); m.
       New London 11 February 1661[/2?] Hannah Hough
       [NLLR 4:327].

ASSOCIATIONS: Brother of Richard Borden who settled in Portsmouth,
Rhode Island, by 1638.

COMMENTS: "John Borden," aged 28, his wife "Joan," aged 23, "Mathew
Borden," aged 8, and "Eliz[abeth] Borden," aged 5, were enrolled at
London on 12 May 1635 as passengers for New England on the *Elizabeth
& Ann* [Hotten 78].

   Savage says that "in 1650 one of the name is found at Stonington,
whence he perhaps removed 1660, to Lyme," and Pope says that the
immigrant "took oath of fidelity in 1652." This was John Borden, the son
of the immigrant.

BIBLIOGRAPHIC NOTE: In 1930 G. Andrews Moriarty published a
lengthy account of "The Bordens of Headcorn, co. Kent," which was
aimed mostly at presenting the paternal ancestry of Richard Borden, who
came to New England by 1638, but also includes the ancestry of John
Borden [NEHGR 84:70-84, 225-29, especially 227].

   In 1976 Robert Charles Anderson published an article on JOHN GAY of
Dedham, demonstrating that Gay had married the widow of John
Borden, that Borden's daughter Elizabeth appeared in her marriage
record as "Elizabeth Gay," and that Borden had a son John born soon
after the family arrived in New England [NEHGR 130:35-39].

THOMAS BOREMAN

ORIGIN: London
MIGRATION: 1634
FIRST RESIDENCE: Ipswich

OCCUPATION: Cooper [EQC 7:86].
CHURCH MEMBERSHIP: Admission to Ipswich church prior to 4 March 1634/5 implied by freemanship.
FREEMAN: 4 March 1634/5 [MBCR 1:370].
EDUCATION: He could sign his name, as could his youngest daughter, Joanna [ILR 3:293-94]. His inventory included "books" valued at £1. His widow signed her will by mark.
OFFICES: Deputy for Ipswich to Massachusetts Bay General Court (as "Mr. Boreman"), 8 September 1636 [MBCR 1:178].
   Essex petit jury, 31 March 1646, 27 September 1649, 27 September 1653, 27 March 1655 [EQC 1:93, 175, 289, 381].
   On 29 March 1664, "Thomas Boreman, having been formerly released from training, paying something yearly to the use of the company and being behind several years, upon his wife's petition, court granted one-half of what was in arrears remitted, if he paid to the clerk of the company the other half. Also that he be released from training for time to come" [EQC 3:142].
ESTATE: In 1635 "Thomas Boreman" held three parcels of land in Ipswich: fifty-five acres; "a six-acre lot on the northeast side the hill by the town"; and "an houselot in the town upon which he hath built an house" [Boardman Gen 104-5, citing ITR]. On 7 May 1639, he was recorded as holding six parcels in Ipswich: "one houselot about two acres"; "an island about fifty and five acres of land, meadow and upland"; six acres of planting ground; "two acres for a houselot lying on the south side the Town River"; and "a small parcel about a rood of ground on the street called the East End" [Boardman Gen 105, citing ITR].
   On 27 December 1647, "Thomas Boreman" of Ipswich sold to Philip Longe of Ipswich "my house and house lot" containing two acres, together with the commonage belonging to it, also a parcel of seven acres [ILR 1:123-24]. On 22 March 1650/1, Mathias Button of Ipswich deeded 9 3/4 acres near Labor-in-vain Creek to "Thomas Borman of Ipswich, cooper," in exchange for Boreman's eleven acres [EQC 7:86]. [A map of this land, which was later the subject of a suit, appears facing EQC 7:86].

On 7 October 1652, John and Mary Emery sold to "Thomas Boreman" of Ipswich a twenty acre island in Ipswich [ILR 1:115].

On 27 September 1665, "Daniel Borman" quitclaimed to "his father Thomas Borman" all his right and interest in Thomas's farm, in return for £225 paid in installments; this arrangement was approved by "Mr. Thomas Borman Senior with his two sons, that is Robert Kinsman and Thomas Low," who gave bond on the agreement [ILR 3:39, 293-94].

In the 1666 division of Plum Island, he received a double share, as did other wealthy men whose country rate exceeded 6s. 8d. [TopsHC 8:105].

On 9 December 1667, Thomas and Margaret Boreman of Ipswich sold to Thomas Perring of Ipswich a six-acre lot of marsh at Plumb Island [ILR 3:137].

On 17 December 1670, the same day he signed his will, Thomas Boreman Senior of Ipswich sold to Robert Kinsman of Ipswich a ten acre piece of saltmarsh called "the Nookes" [ILR 3:182-83].

In his will, dated 17 December 1670 and proved 19 June 1673, "Thomas Borman Senior" of Ipswich, weak in body, bequeathed to "my wife" the use and benefit of the entire farm during her life, also cattle and household stuff; after wife's death, land was to return to "my son Thomas"; to "my daughter Joanna" on the day of her marriage or at age 22 years, her portion to the value of £100; to "my son Daniel" six acres leaving Thomas right of first refusal should Daniel wish to sell; to "my daughter Mary, the wife of Robert Kinsman that is to say to her children," £20; to "my daughter Martha the wife of Thomas Loe to her children" £20; to "my son Daniel" £8 for the use of "his two sons at the age of one and twenty years"; to "my son Kinsman" the right to a footpath to go to his land "he bought of me"; to "my son Daniel and Robert Kinsman" ten acres more or less; "my brother Daniel" to live "with my wife while she lives" and after her death "my son Thomas" to maintain him; wife sole executor; "my well beloved friends" Simon Tomson and Thomas Burnam, overseers [EPR 2:349-51]. A codicil dated 3 May 1673 allowed "my wife" the right to dispose of cattle, household goods and land "as need shall require" [EPR 2:351].

The inventory of the estate, taken 26 May 1673, totalled £553 6s. 6d., of which £350 was real estate: "the dwelling house, barn & outhousing with all the lands adjoining," about 42 and a half acres, £280; and "ten acres of planting land" at Button's Point, £70 [EPR 2:351].

In her will, dated 8 August 1679 and proved 30 March 1680, "Margret Borman" bequeathed to "my daughter Kinsman" household goods; to "my daughter Loe" pewter and household goods; to "my daughter

Fellowes" linen and clothing; to "my son Daniel" furniture and debts "he owes me" and to "his wife" a new hat; to "my son Thomas" livestock and furniture; residue of livestock: three parts to "my daughter Kindsman" and one part to "Martha and Johana"; son Thomas sole executor; to "Dinah my son's maid" household goods [EPR 3:350-51].

The inventory of the estate of "Mrs. Margerit Borman" of Ipswich, taken 19 March 1679/80, totalled £84 8s., with no real estate included [EPR 3:350].

BIRTH: Baptized Claydon, Oxfordshire, 18 October 1601, son of Thomas and Elizabeth (Carter) Boreman [Boardman Gen 77, 93-99].
DEATH: After 3 May 1673 (date of codicil) and before 19 June 1673 (probate of will).
MARRIAGE: St Helen's Bishopgate, London, 17 August 1630 Margaret Offing (the entry for this marriage in the original parish register did not include the words "and Cordwayner of London" [NEHGR 62:303]), for whom Thomas provided in a deed dated 26 February 1661/2 [EQC 3:271]. She was living 30 June 1676 when she made her mark to an agreement [EQC 5:85], and she was probably the "Mrs. Borman" who died at Ipswich 25 November 1679.
CHILDREN:
  i   DANIEL, b. say 1633; m. Ipswich 12 April 1662 (with an awkward marriage contract [EQC 3:270-71; ILR 2:177-78]) Hannah Hutchinson, daughter of Richard Hutchinson [EQC 3:270, 8:434].
  ii   MARY, b. say 1635; m. before 1657 Robert Kinsman (eldest known child b. Ipswich 21 December 1657).
  iii   MARTHA, b. about 1641 (deposed "aged about twenty-seven years" for September 1668 court [EQC 4:50]; deposed "aged twenty-eight years" for March 1669 court [EQC 4:125]; d. 22 January 1720/1 in her 79th year [TopsHC 8:105, citing Essex cemetery gravestone]); m. Ipswich 4 July 1660 Thomas Low.
  iv   THOMAS, b. about 1644 (deposed "aged twenty-four years" 29 June 1674 [EQC 5:321]; "aged thirty-four years" in a deposition for 1679 court [EQC 7:187]; d. Ipswich 3 October 1719 "in his 76th year"); m. Ipswich 1 January 1667/8 Elizabeth Perkins.
  v   JOANNA, b. say 1650 (under age 22 in 1670 when her father made his will); m. Ipswich 29 January 1672/3 Isaac Fellows.

ASSOCIATIONS: In her will of 27 April 1631, "Elizabeth Borman of Cleyden," Oxfordshire, directed that "my son Daniell shall stay & have his being with my son John Boreman and allow unto my said son Daniell meat, drink and apparel and ten shillings a year" and bequeathed to "my son Thomas Boreman forty shillings" [Boardman Gen 97]. In his will of 17 December 1670, "Thomas Boreman Senior of Ipswich" ordered that "my brother Daniell shall abide with my wife while she lives, and after her decease that he shall continue while he lives with my son Thomas to be maintained by him" [EPR 2:350]. The circumstance of Daniel Boreman who is clearly incompetent in both these documents is the most important clue to the identity of the immigrant Thomas Boreman [Boardman Gen 43, 114].

Samuel Boreman, immigrant to Ipswich by 1638 and later a resident of Wethersfield, was first cousin of Thomas Boreman [Boardman Gen 101-2]. The presence of Thomas and Samuel Boreman in Ipswich simultaneously in the late 1630s further supports the proposed identification.

On 17 March 1628/9, the Massachusetts Bay Company purchased from "Felix Boreman, dwelling in Fleete Lane" in London, twenty-five swords valued at £4 12s. [MBCR 1:36]. This was an elder brother of the immigrant Thomas Boreman.

COMMENTS: Thomas led a relatively quiet life, although he was sued by both Mathias Button and Henry Walker in December 1641 [EQC 1:38], and Walker continued the suit to the next court [EQC 1:41].

In an entry for "Thomas Boreman or Bordman," Savage began with early records of Thomas of Ipswich, and then switched over to the records of one of the men named *THOMAS BOREMAN* of Plymouth Colony [Savage 1:215; GMB 1:185-86]; these were two different men.

BIBLIOGRAPHIC NOTE: In 1895 Charlotte Goldthwaite compiled *Boardman Genealogy, 1525-1895: The English Home and Ancestry of Samuel Boreman, Wethersfield, Conn. [and] Thomas Boreman, Ipswich, Mass., with Some Account of Their Descendants (Now Called Boardman) in America* (Hartford 1895), cited above as Boardman Gen. This comprehensive volume contains transcripts of the wills, parish registers and private letters upon which our knowledge of the English origin and ancestry of these two immigrants is based.

EDWARD BOSWORTH

ORIGIN: Unknown
MIGRATION: 1634 on the *Elizabeth Dorcas*
FIRST RESIDENCE: Boston

ESTATE: On 5 August 1634, it was "ordered, that such monies as shall be laid out for the maintenance of Widow Bosworth & her family, shall be paid again by the Treasurer" [MBCR 1:123]. On 7 July 1635, in "consideration of money disbursed by Mr. Henry Seawall for the transportation of Edward Bosworth & his family, it is ordered, that Jonathan Bosworth shall pay to Mr. Seawall the sum of £5 upon the 29th of September next; Will[ia]m Buckland £5 on the said 29th of September; Nathanaell Bosworth 50s. at the said day, & 50s. more that day twelve month; & Beniamyn Bosworth 30s. on the said 29th of September, and £3 10s. at midsummer next; all these sums to be paid to the said Mr. Seawall" [MBCR 1:152].

BIRTH: By about 1586 based on estimated date of marriage.
DEATH: 1634 in Boston Harbor.
MARRIAGE: By about 1611 Mary _____. She died at Hingham 18 May 1648 [NEHGR 121:21].
CHILDREN:

  i   MARY, b. say 1611; m. by about 1632 WILLIAM BUCKLAND.
  ii   JONATHAN, b. about 1613 (deposed in June 1639 "aged about 26 years" [Lechford 84]); m. by 1636 Elizabeth _____. (Since *JONATHAN BOSWORTH* had arrived by 1633, he was treated separately in an earlier volume in this series [GMB 1:187-91].)
  iii BENJAMIN, b. about 1615 (deposed in June 1639 "aged about 24 years" [Lechford 84]); m. (1) by about 1645 _____ _____ (only known two children, not necessarily twins, bp. Hingham 6 April 1647 [NEHGR 121:19]); m. (2) Lancaster 16 November 1671 Beatrice (Hampson) Josselyn [LanVR 14], widow of Abraham Josselyn [TAG 53:100].
  iv   NATHANIEL, b. say 1619; m. by about 1644 Bridget Bellamy (eldest known child m. Hingham 21 February 1664/5 John Lobdell [NEHGR 121:117; Bosworth Gen 109, 112]), daughter of Jeremiah Bellamy [Bosworth Gen 112-13, and sources cited there].

ASSOCIATIONS: The transatlantic passage of the Bosworth family was paid by Henry Sewall [MBCR 1:152]. This would indicate that the Bosworth family came on the *Elizabeth & Dorcas*, and that they may have been from Coventry, Warwickshire, or vicinity [Sewall 1073-74].

COMMENTS: In the sketch of *JONATHAN BOSWORTH* in an earlier volume in this series, the statement was made that "WILLIAM BUCKLAND, who was in New England as early as 1631, had married Jonathan's sister, Mary Bosworth, apparently very soon after the family arrived" [GMB 1:190]. This conclusion is not correct, for there must have been two William Bucklands in early New England, as noted only a few pages later in the same volume [GMB 267-68].

In September 1640 "Benjamin and Nathaniell Bosworth charge bills upon Joseph Bosworth of Coventry in the County of War[wickshire], shoemaker, for ten pounds to be paid by Thomas Lund of London, leatherdresser, or his assigns upon 20 days sight" [Lechford 306].

BIBLIOGRAPHIC NOTE: In 1926 Mary Bosworth Clarke published an excellent and detailed genealogy of Edward Bosworth and his descendants [*Bosworth Genealogy: A History of the Descendants of Edward Bosworth Who Arrived in America in the Year 1634*, cited here as Bosworth Gen].

ROBERT BOTFISH

ORIGIN: Unknown
MIGRATION: 1634
FIRST RESIDENCE: Lynn
REMOVES: Sandwich 1638

OCCUPATION: On 20 August 1644, "Rob[er]te Boatfish" was "licensed to draw wine" at Sandwich [PCR 2:75].
FREEMAN: 6 May 1635 (as "Rob[er]te Bootefishe," second in a sequence of nine Lynn men) [MBCR 1:371]. On 7 January 1638/9, "Rob[er]te Badfish" of Sandwich desired his freedom [PCR 1:108]. Sandwich oath of fidelity 1639 [PCR 8:184].
EDUCATION: Signed his name as "Robert Botfish" to articles of agreement as a member of a Sandwich committee on 26 February 1647[/8?] [PCR 12:211].

OFFICES: Essex jury, 27 September 1636, 28 March 1637 (as "Rob[er]t Bottfish ... of Saugus"), 27 June 1637 [EQC 1:3, 5, 6]. Sandwich surveyor of highways (as "Rob[er]te Botefish"), 2 March 1640/1 [PCR 2:9]. Plymouth petit jury (as "Rob[er]te Boatefish"), 17 June 1641, 6 June 1650 [PCR 7:21, 49]. Grand jury (as "Rob[er]te Boatfish"), 5 June 1644 [PCR 2:71].

"Rob[er]te Botefish" is in the Sandwich section of the 1643 Plymouth Colony list of men able to bear arms [PCR 8:192].

ESTATE: On 16 April 1640, "Rob[er]t Botfish" was one of the townsmen of Sandwich involved in dividing some upland and meadow among the townsmen of Sandwich and the Indians, from which division he received five acres [PCR 1:147, 149].

BIRTH: By about 1614 based on estimated date of marriage.
DEATH: Sandwich 19 November 165_ [SandVR 1:22].
MARRIAGE: By about 1639 Bridget _____. "Bridget Bodfish widow" married (2) Barnstable "about the 15 of December 1657" SAMUEL HINCKLEY [MD 6:98; NEHGR 65:318].
CHILDREN:

    i   MARY, b. say 1639; m. Barnstable [blank] November 1659 John Crocker [PCR 8:43; MD 3:150].

    ii   SARAH, b. say 1643; m. Barnstable 21 June 1663 Peter Blossom [MD 3:53], son of *THOMAS BLOSSOM* [TAG 63:239-41].

    iii JOSEPH, b. Sandwich 3 April 1651 [SandVR 1:6, 16]; m. by 1674 Elizabeth Bessey, daughter of ANTHONY BESSEY [TAG 26:194].

COMMENTS: "Rob[er]t Bodfish" was fined on 4 December 1638 by Plymouth court for keeping two swine unringed [PCR 1:107]. On 2 October 1650, he testified in the matter of Benjamin Nye versus Thomas Dexter Jr. [PCR 7:51-52].

HENRY BOURNE

ORIGIN: Unknown
MIGRATION: 1634
FIRST RESIDENCE: Scituate
REMOVES: Barnstable 1639

CHURCH MEMBERSHIP: "Hennery Borne" was admitted to Scituate church on 25 January 1634/5 [NEHGR 9:279].

FREEMAN: Admitted freeman of Plymouth Colony on 2 January 1637/8, and then added to 7 March 1636/7 list of freemen [PCR 1:53, 74]. In Scituate section of Plymouth Colony list of 1639 (where the name is crossed out) and in Barnstable section of same list [PCR 8:175, 177]. In Barnstable section of Plymouth Colony lists of 1658 and 20 May 1670 [PCR 5:277, 8:200].

OFFICES: Plymouth grand jury, 5 June 1638, 4 September 1638, 1 March 1641/2, 7 June 1642, 2 June 1646, 3 June 1656, 1 June 1658, 4 June 1661, 8 June 1664 [PCR 1:87, 96, 2:34, 41, 102, 3:100, 135, 215, 4:61]. Petit jury, 1 March 1641/2 [PCR 7:29]. Barnstable deputy to Plymouth General Court, 29 August 1643, 5 March 1643/4, 5 June 1644, 20 August 1644 [PCR 2:59, 68, 72, 75]. Barnstable highway surveyor, 8 June 1655 [PCR 3:79]. Barnstable constable, 3 June 1668 [PCR 4:181].

In Barnstable section of 1643 Plymouth Colony list of men able to bear arms [PCR 8:193].

ESTATE: Sometime after October 1636 Henry Bourne bought the Scituate house of Richard Foxwell [NEHGR 10:42].

On 6 March 1643[/4?], "Henry Bourne of Barnestable" sold to William Wills of Scituate "all that his marsh meadow lying in New Harbour marshes in Scittuate and near adjoining unto Long Iland containing by estimation twelve acres" [PCR 12:99-100].

Plymouth Colony probate records contain an undated, unproved and incomplete will for "Sarah Bourn, relict of Henry Bourne late of Sandwich deceased"; this is entered between a will proved on 31 October 1684 and another proved on 4 March 1684/5. In the surviving portion of the will are two bequests: moveables to John Hamlin, and "all the rest of my estate" to John Phinny Junior [PCPR 4:2:84]. (These are clearly the first two bequests in the will, and perhaps the only bequests.)

BIRTH: By about 1613 based on estimated date of marriage.

DEATH: After 20 May 1670 [PCR 5:277].

MARRIAGE: By 1638 Sarah _____. On 11 November 1638, "Sister Bourne dismissed from the church at Hingham" was admitted to Scituate church [NEHGR 9:280]. She died late in 1684 [PCPR 4:2:84].

CHILD:

     i   Son, stillborn and bur. Barnstable 28 May 1642 [NEHGR 9:285].

ASSOCIATIONS: In his will of 14 November 1648, Thomas Rickard of Scituate bequeathed "unto my cousin Henery Borne my best coat" [Plymouth Wills 167].

COMMENTS: Pope lists among the children of Henry "Ezra, (parent not given,) b. in Sandwich May 12, 1648." Henry Bourne did not reside in Sandwich, but Richard and Thomas Bourne did, and Ezra was most likely a son of Richard Bourne. Savage claims that Henry Bourne had at Barnstable "Dorcas, bapt. 26 Aug. 1649" [Savage 1:218], but no such record is found at Barnstable; there was a Dorcas, daughter of John Smith, baptized at Barnstable on 18 August 1650 [NEHGR 9:284], but there seems little room for confusion here. From all appearances, Henry Bourne and his wife had no children who survived childhood.

JARED BOURNE

ORIGIN: Unknown
MIGRATION: 1634
FIRST RESIDENCE: Boston
REMOVES: Portsmouth [RI] 1654, Swansea by 1672

CHURCH MEMBERSHIP: "Jarrard Bourne [servant] to our brother Willyam Coulborne" was admitted to Boston church on 22 June 1634 [BChR 18]. "Jarrod Bourne upon rumors of his incontinency departed from the fellowship of the congregation to Road Iland. The church sent letters to advise him to return to them and clear himself; instead of coming to the church he sent a letter full of proud expressions and railing accusations against civil government and others for which he was by joint consent excommunicate from the fellowship of the church on the 13th day 3d month [May] 1655" [BChR 55].
FREEMAN: 6 May 1635 (as "Jarrett Bourne," sixth in a sequence of ten Boston men) [MBCR 1:370]. "Jerit Borne is received an inhabitant" of Portsmouth, Rhode Island, on 23 January 1654/5 [PoTR 66].
EDUCATION: Signed his deeds.
OFFICES: Fenceviewer at Muddy River, 26 October 1640 [BTR 1:56]. On 23 February 1651/2 (and again on 26 April 1652), "William Beamsley and Jarratt Borne are chosen to see the general fence at Muddy River to be put into repair according to order" [BTR 1:108, 110]. Constable at Muddy

River, 12 March 1653/4 [BTR 1:118]; on 28 November 1654, "Edward Devotyon is chosen constable for Muddy River in the room of Jaratt Bourne" [BTR 1:121].

Rhode Island petit jury, 4 June 1655, 7 March 1659/60, 27 April 1670 [PoTR 68, 91, 152]. Coroner's jury (published as "Jariard Borden"), August 1661 [PoTR 107]. Grand jury, 19 October 1666 [PoTR 136]. Deputy for Portsmouth to Rhode Island General Court, 17 October 1667 [PoTR 139].

ESTATE: On 8 January 1637/8 (based on an order of 14 December 1635), "Jarrett Bourne" was granted eight acres at Muddy River [BTR 1:23]. On 23 February 1651/2, "Jarratt Borne complaining that Raphe Roott makes use of his marsh at Muddy River which was formerly granted to Jacob Eliatt as appears by the record of the 1st of the 5th month [July], 1637, for the deciding the bounds thereof Deacon Marshall, Ensign Oliver, and Peter Oliver, are chosen to view the ground and to make return of their issue" [BTR 1:107]. By 13 June 1651, *JACOB ELIOT* had purchased "one house ... with the yard to it" from "Jarat Bourne" [GMB 1:627, citing SPR Case #113].

In the Boston Book of Possessions in 1645, "Garret Bourne" held "one house and garden" [BBOP 34, 87].

On 23 November 1649, "Jared Bourne of Muddy River" mortgaged to Thomas Dudley "all those my two houses situate on the northwesterly side of Muddy River in the bounds of Boston near together in one of which the said Jared now dwelleth together with seven acres near adjoining to the said houses, two acres whereof is already in the sea, & all that barn being about a mile from the said houses & eight acres of upland ground near the said barn & twelve acres of marsh near the mouth of Charles River" [SLR 1:109].

On 25 October 1664, "Jarred Bourne late of Muddy River" sold to Theophilus Frary and Jacob Eliot "all that my parcel of land formerly purchased of Samuell Andrewes of Cambridge being eight acres ... & two small parcels of meadows" [SLR 5:29-30]. On 27 October 1665, "Jared Bourne late of Muddy River ... but now inhabitant of Road Island" sold to John Hull of Boston, goldsmith, "six acres & a quarter of land ... at Muddy River" [SLR 6:228-29].

His earmark for cattle was entered at Portsmouth on 18 October 1667 [PoTR 268].

On 9 February 1673/4, when *WILLIAM BRENTON* made his will, "Jared Bourne senior" was tenant on Brenton's "farm and houses at Mattapoisett" [GMB 1:220-21, citing MD 34:75-79, citing PCPR 3:1:143-45].

BIRTH: By 1614 based on date of freemanship.

DEATH: After 9 February 1673/4.

MARRIAGE: (1) By 1643 Mary ____; "Mary wife of Garret Bourne" died at Boston on 30 May 1644 [BVR 17].

(2) By 1651 ____ ____.

CHILDREN:

With first wife

    i   JARED, b. about 11 July 1643; bp. Roxbury 6 August 1643 ("Jarratt the son of our brother Jarratt Burne being about 26 days old was baptized at Roxbury," 6 August 1643 [BChR 293]; "Gerrard Bourne the son of Gerrard Bourne a member of Boston, & living at Muddy River was here [i.e., Roxbury] received by communion of churches," 6 August 1643 [RChR 115]); d. Boston 30 August 1643 (Boston vital records includes "John of Garret & Mary Bourne born 30th 5th month & died 30th 6th month" [BVR 15]; the name of the child and date of birth conflict with the information of the baptism, and are clearly wrong, but we take the date of death given here, lacking any other evidence on this point).

With second wife

    ii   JARED, bp. Boston 7 March 1651/2 [BChR 323]; m. by 1690 Elizabeth Brayton (in his will of 17 October 1690 Francis Brayton of Portsmouth made a bequest to his daughter Elizabeth Bourne [Austin 250]).

COMMENTS: Although he was not a member of the Baptist church at Swansea, Jared Bourne did appear in the records of that church in 1672, in a manner in keeping with his prideful remarks to the Boston Church nearly twenty years earlier:

> 11th of 2d mo [April 1672] Whereas bro Cole hath been charged by Jared Bowen of lying and false witness bearing and unfitness for com[munion] in the lords supper with the church It is ordered that bro Luther and bro Edey desire the said Jared Bowen to come before this church this day month either to charge or vindicate our said bro: and the brethren are to require our said bro Cole to appear then to answer the said charge.

> 9 of 3d mo [May 1672] Whereas bro: Cole was accused by Jared Bowen as is abovesaid the whole charge was upon examination found false and Jared Bowen hath acknowledged the same and

taken the whole blame of so reporting on himself as fully appears by a paper under his hand and fixed on the doorpost of this meeting house [NEHGR 139:34-35].

ELIZABETH BOWIS

"Elizabeth Bowis" is 134th on the list of Roxbury church members (which would be in mid-1635), listed by Eliot without comment [RChR 81].

COMMENTS: She is seen in no other New England record and may have died soon, married or returned to England.

WILLIAM BOWNE

ORIGIN: Unknown
MIGRATION: 1635 on the *Recovery*
FIRST RESIDENCE: Salem
REMOVES: Gravesend by 1646, Middletown [NJ] by about 1669

CHURCH MEMBERSHIP: "William Bownd" and "Anne Bound" were in the list of Salem church members compiled late in 1636, each with the later annotation "excommunicated" [SChR 6]. On 15 December 1642, "William Bound and wife, for holding the baptism of infants to be no ordinance of God," were presented at Salem court; "W[illia]m Bound was dispensed with, being in a way of conviction before elders" [EQC 1:52].
FREEMAN: 17 May 1637 (as "Willi[am] Bounde," fourth in a sequence of eight Salem men) [MBCR 1:373].
OFFICES: Elected magistrate at Gravesend, 20 March 1656, 20 March 1657 [Gravesend TR 3:2, 7] (and apparently in other years [Stillwell 3:31]).

On 2 November 1669, "William Bowne and James Bowne of the Town of Middletown, on Newasink Neck, are appointed to act as Patentees" of Middletown [Old Monmouth 201, citing Book A, p. 19].
ESTATE: Granted 40 acres at Salem in the division of 1636, in the "freeman's" section [STR 1:20, 26]. (By 13 January 1651/2, he had sold this to Robert Goodale [STR 1:171; EQC 7:294].) Granted three-quarters of an acre in the 25 December 1637 division of swamp and meadow, with a household of five [STR 1:103].

William Bowne was granted a planter's lot at Gravesend, Long Island, 18 March[?] 1646 [Gravesend TR 1:4].

In a "list of what land every man hath in tillage the year in Gravesend, viz: 1657," "W[illia]m Bowne" was credited with twelve acres [Gravesend TR 3:5].

On an undated list (but apparently of 1670) of "the names of the purchasers of Newasink, Narumsunk and Pootapeck" in Middletown, "W[illia]m Bowne" held one share [Old Monmouth 207, citing Book A, pp. 33-34].

On 21 January 1677[/8], "[w]hereas William Bowne, heretofore of Gravesend, in the West Riding of Yorkshire, upon Long Island, and late of Middletown, in New Jersey, died intestate, and John Bowne, of Middletown, aforesaid, his eldest son, having made his application that he may have letters of administration on the estate of his father deceased, within this province, it being likewise with the consent and good liking of the rest of his brothers," administration on the estate was granted [Stillwell 3:31, abstracting an unknown source].

BIRTH: By about 1609 based on estimated date of marriage.
DEATH: By 21 January 1677[/8] (date of administration).
MARRIAGE: By about 1634 Anne _____.
CHILDREN:

i   JOHN, b. say 1634; m. by 1664 Lydia Holmes, daughter of Obadiah Holmes (eldest known child b. Gravesend 1 April 1664 [NS] [NYGBR 4:40]; in his will of 9 April 1682, Obadiah Holmes bequeathed to his daughter Lydia Bowne [Brady Anc 234]).

ii   JAMES, bp. Salem 25 December 1636 [SChR 16]; m. Gravesend 26 December 1665 [NS] Mary Stoute [NYGBR 4:199].

iii ANDREW, bp. Salem 12 August 1638 [SChR 16]; by about 1667 Elizabeth _____ (only known child m. New York 9 November 1687 John Haines [NYChR 63]; in his will of 6 May 1707 Andrew Bowne named "my loving wife sole executrix," and on 28 June 1708, administration was "granted unto Elizabeth Bowne sole executrix" [New Jersey Wills 1:209-10]). (Andrew's wife has been identified as Elizabeth Haines, because of an abstract of the 24 August 1689 will of John Haines which makes "his brother-in-law Mr. Andrew Bowne" one of his executors [*Collections of the New-York Historical Society*, Abstracts of

Wills, Vol. 1, 1665-1707 (New York 1893), p. 187], but in
the first volume of corrections to these abstracts, we learn
that the correct reading is "his father-in-law Mr. Andrew
Bowne," which is in accord with the marriage cited above
[*Collections of the New-York Historical Society* (New York
1908), Vol. 16, p. 20].

iv   PETER, bp. Salem 7 June 1640 [SChR 18]; no further record.

v   (probably) GERSHOM, who appears (as "Gresham Bowne")
along with Andrew Bowne as one of four men
appraising a vessel on 23 July 1685 [Peter R. Christoph
and Florence A. Christoph, eds., *Books of General Entries of
the Colony of New York, 1674-1688* (Baltimore 1982), p. 414;
see also Stillwell 3:41-42], although he may be related in
some other way.

COMMENTS: "William Bowne" is on the passenger list of the *Recovery*,
sailing from Weymouth in England, dated 31 March 1635 [Coldham 107;
NGSQ 77:250]. Most of the passengers on this ship settled in Dorchester
or Weymouth, but a few went to Salem. His presence on this list would
indicate an origin in the West Country. Since this list includes only heads
of household, we cannot tell whether his wife or any children came with
him at this time.

The 1637 Salem land grant credited William Bownd with a household of
five, of whom we know only William, his wife Anne and sons John and
James. He may well have had another child born before his arrival in
New England.

Savage has incorrect dates of baptism for sons James and Peter, and
misnames Peter, calling him Philip. Pope's entry for "William Knowne" of
Salem in 1642 is an error for this William Bowne, presumably misreading
the court appearance of that year [Pope 275].

The absence of any records for this family after 1642 indicates that they
left New England about this time, perhaps because of the disagreements
of William and Anne with the church and civil authorities over infant
baptism. His residence between 1642 and 1646 is unknown.

The name William Bound appears again in Essex County in the 1660s.
On 27 December 1665, William Bound was one of those who swore to an
agreement between two Marblehead men. On 12 July 1669, William
Bound married Mary Haverlad at Lynn (a marriage ascribed by Savage to
the immigrant of 1635). Given the gap of more than twenty years

without any appearance in the record, there is little likelihood that these two records apply to the subject of this sketch.

BIBLIOGRAPHIC NOTE: In 1873 J.T. Bowne published an article entitled "The Bowne Family," which consisted mostly of brief, unsourced extracts from records [NYGBR 4:24-26]. In 1914 John E. Stillwell compiled a competent account of the immigrant and his family [Stillwell 3:29-108]. In 1943 John Insley Coddington prepared an article on "A Bowne Problem," which focussed on an unplaced John Bowne, and in passing briefly discussed the immigrant William Bowne and his family [TAG 19:166-67; see also NEHGR 55:300-1].

THOMAS BOYDEN

ORIGIN: Unknown
MIGRATION: 1634 on the *Francis*
FIRST RESIDENCE: Scituate
REMOVES: Watertown by 1639, Boston by 1650, Medfield by 1662

OCCUPATION: Planter [SLR 5:192-94]. Carter [SLR 3:390].
CHURCH MEMBERSHIP: "Thomas Boiden, Brother Gilson's servant," joined the Scituate church on 17 May 1635 [NEHGR 9:279]. Thomas Boyden was called "a member of the church of Watertowne" when son John was baptized at Boston on 21 April 1650 [BChR 318]; his admission to that church would have preceded his admission to freemanship.
FREEMAN: 26 May 1647 [MBCR 2:295].
EDUCATION: Both Thomas and second wife, Hannah, signed their 1659 deed [SLR 3:390-92]. Thomas signed their 1662 deed, but Hannah made her "H" mark [SLR 4:61-62].
OFFICES: Suffolk petit jury, 30 April 1678, 29 April 1679 [SCC 898, 999].
   Boston surveyor of highways, 12 March 1659/60 [BTR 1:154].
ESTATE: In the Watertown Inventory of Possessions, Thomas Boyden held two parcels: "an homestall of ten acres"; and "three acres of meadow" [WaBOP 33, 122].
   On 21 November 1644, Thomas Boyden of Watertown purchased two acres of meadow in Watertown from George Parkhurst of Watertown [SLR 1:54]. On 27 March 1651, Thomas Boyden of Boston sold to William Clarke of Watertown a thirty-acre lot in the Watertown great dividend, being the first lot of the third squadron [SLR 1:135].

On 24 February 1653/4, Thomas Boyden of Boston, planter, and Frances his wife exchanged two acres of land and £5 for three acres of land in Boston owned by Theodore Atkinson of Boston, feltmaker, and Abigail his wife [SLR 5:192-94].

On 14 February 1659/60, Thomas Boyden of Boston, carter, and Hannah his wife sold to Joshua Scottow of Boston, merchant, seven acres of upland and meadow in Boston, once purchased from Thomas Bell [SLR 3:390-92].

On 12 September 1662, Thomas Boyden of Medfield and Hannah his wife sold to Mr. Simon Lynde of Boston, merchant, "all that their dwelling house & barn with the yard backyards & garden & orchard ground thereunto belonging the which the said Thomas Boyden lately possessed & dwelt in as it now is, situate in or at the entrance of the lane called Sudbury Lane in Boston" [SLR 4:61-62].

In her will, dated 3 October 1676 and proved 25 October 1676, "Hannah Boydon wife of Thomas Boydon of Meadfield being now in Boston & in a sick and weak condition" bequeathed "unto my eight children which I had by my husband Joseph Morse deceased ... Samuel Morse, Joseph Morse, Jeremiah Morse, Hannah Flood, Sarah Lawrence, Dorcas Clarke, Elizabeth Lawrence and Mary Plimpton" the estate at her disposal to be equally divided among them, only "in consideration of the much trouble and charge that my daughter Flood is at now in my sickness, I do give her 40s. more"; "my three sons Samuel, Joseph and Jeremiah Morse" executors [SPR 6:132].

On 15 April 1678, Thomas Boyden of Medfield contributed one bushel of wheat toward the rebuilding of Harvard College [NEHGR 10:49].

BIRTH: About 1613 (aged 21 in 1634 [Hotten 279]).

DEATH: After 15 April 1678 [NEHGR 10:49].

MARRIAGE: (1) By 1639 Frances _____. She died as "Francis wife of Thomas Boyden" at Boston 17 March 1657/8 [BVR 66].

(2) Boston 3 November 1658 Hannah (Phillips) Morse, widow of Joseph Morse [BVR 67]. She died at Medfield 3 October 1676.

CHILDREN:

With first wife

i   THOMAS, b. Watertown 26 September 1639 [WaVR 1:7]; m. by 1667 Martha Holden (eldest child b. Watertown 14 July 1667 [WaVR 1:29]), daughter of Richard Holden (on 25 July 1679, "Thomas Boyden & Martha his wife" were among the "children of Ri[chard] Holden of Watertown"

who deeded land to "John Holden our brother" [MLR
7:154]).

ii   MARY, b. Watertown 15 October 1641 [WaVR 1:9]; no further
record.

iii   JOHN, bp. Boston 21 April 1650 [BChR 318]; no further record.

iv   JONATHAN, b. Boston 20 February 1651/2 [BVR 33]; bp.
Boston 22 February 1651/2 (baptismal record shows
Jonathan as son of "our brother William Boyden" [BChR
323]); m. Medfield 26 September 1673 Mary Clark.

v   SARAH, b. Boston 12 October 1654 [BVR 46]; no further
record.

COMMENTS: "Thomas Boyden," aged 21, sailed from Ipswich on "the
last of April 1634" for New England as a passenger on the *Francis* [Hotten
279].

The evidence identifying the Thomas Boyden of Scituate as the Thomas
Boyden of Watertown is indirect. On the same ship with Thomas
Boyden were several members of the family of *WILLIAM HAMMOND* of
Watertown, including his daughter Elizabeth Hammond, who married in
Scituate in 1636 Samuel House [Hotten 279; GMB 2:852-54]. Insofar as
this supports the connection of Thomas Boyden with both Scituate and
Watertown, it also suggests that his place of origin in England was in
northern Essex or southern Suffolk.

Savage, Pope and Bond all credit Thomas with children Rebecca and
Nathaniel, with a precise date of birth given for Rebecca, but no original
record is found for either of them, in Watertown vital records or
elsewhere. Given the gap of nearly nine years between the second and
third children listed above, however, there may well have been other
children.

THOMAS BOYLSTON

ORIGIN: London
MIGRATION: 1635 on the *Defence*
FIRST RESIDENCE: Watertown

OCCUPATION: Planter.

ESTATE: On 30 September 1639, Gregory Stone of Cambridge granted to Nathaniel Sparhawke, agent for Thomas Boylston of London, clothworker, use of "Boilston's" house and ground in Watertown, with sixteen acres by it, and three acres by Fresh Pond, and two acres in Rocky Meadow, and forty acres in the great dividend and nine acres of plow land, as well as future allotments [SLR 1:67].

On 10 May 1642, "Thomas Boyson" was granted a Farm of seventy-three acres at Watertown" [WaBOP 14].

In the Watertown Inventory of Grants of about 1643, "Thomas Boyson" held one parcel: "six acres of upland beyond the Further Plain & the fifty-third lot" [WaBOP 86]. In the Inventory of Possessions of about 1643, he held six parcels: "an homestall of sixteen acres"; "forty acres of upland ... being a Great Dividend in the first division & eighteen[th] lot"; "three acres of upland"; "two acres of meadow"; "ten acres of plowland in the Further Plain"; and "ten acres of Remote Meadow ... & the seventy-eighth lot" [WaBOP 121]. In the Composite Inventory of about 1644, he held eight parcels: "an homestall of sixteen acres"; "forty acres of upland being a Great Dividend in the 1 division & the 18 lot"; "three acres of upland"; "two acres of meadow in Rock Meadow"; "ten acres of plowland in the Further Plain & the 60 lot"; "ten acres of meadow in the Remote Meadow & the 78 lot"; "six acres of upland lying beyond the Further Plain & the 55 lot"; and "a Farm of seventy-three acres upland in the 9 division" [WaBOP 30].

On 24 November 1648, "Nicholas Phillips of Waymouth in New England sealed a receipt of £16 from Hezekiah Usher & Henry Shrimpton by order of Mr. Tho[mas] Boylston merchant for the use of Tho[mas] Boylston late of Waymouth his wife & children" [Aspinwall 172, 183, 199-200]. (The designation of the immigrant as "late of Waymouth" is presumably a scribal error for "late of Watertown," induced by the residence of Nicholas Phillips in Weymouth.)

On 26 July 1652, "Thomas Boyson" of Watertown, planter, for "love and affection which he beareth towards his wife and children," appointed Lt. Hugh Mason of Watertown and John Steadman of Cambridge feoffees in trust to manage the "one half of forty pounds per annum" paid in the hands of "Richard Boyson citizen and clothworker of London, kinsman of the said Thomas Boyson," together with half the houseland and orchard in Watertown and half the household stuff, also one half of the neat cattle "and all the wages due for his boys keeping cattle this year in

Watertown." These funds were to go to the "maintenance and education of his wife and children" [SLR 1:247-48].

On 21 February 1668/9, Thomas Boylston's heirs agreed that the widow Sarah, "now Chinery," had given general satisfaction in the settlement of his estate, and "hath not wronged any person," but "the time is long since the party deceased," and she was freed of any accounting of her administration [MCF Folio #56].

On 18 March 1670/1, a division of the land of Thomas Boylston was made, allowing Thomas Boylston his double portion, being the homestall and sixteen acres belonging to it, also two acres at Rock Meadow; "Thomas Smith in the behalf of Sarah his wife" received twelve acres in Lieu of Township and ten acres of meadow; "the two children of John Fisher by Elisabeth Boilson" received "forty acres of [Great] Dividend and seventy-five acres of farmland"; to the widow "her third part out of them all during her natural life" [MCF Folio #56].

On 27 March 1671, Thomas Smith of Charlestown, butcher, sold to "John Chinery, my father-in-law, & to Thomas Boylston, my brother-in-law, ... as feoffees of trust for & in the behalf of Sarah Boylston my wife & children that I have by her" "all that house in Charlestowne wherein I now dwell, with all the land adjoining thereunto and outhouses that are or shall be erected thereon and all the household goods & furniture therein, as also all my lands, rights & interests in Watertowne" [MLR 4:171-72].

On 20 June 1679, "Thomas Smith of Charlestown ... butcher" for "natural good will, love and affection which I have & bear unto my wellbeloved wife Sarah Smith & my children which I have had by her" to "my brother Thomas Boylston of Muddy River, chirurgeon, & John Chinnery of Waertown, yeoman, as feoffees in trust in behalf & to the use of my said wife & children the sum of ninety-four pounds ... which I have lying in the hands of Mr. Spencer Piggott of London, apothecary, being the remainder of one hundred pounds ... which said Piggott received of Mr. W[illia]m Andrews executor of the last will & testament of Mr. Thomas Boylston (in right of his wife) my said wife's uncle as a legacy given to her" [MLR 7:130].

BIRTH: About 1615 (aged 20 in 1635 [Hotten 99]).
DEATH: After 26 July 1652 [SLR 1:247-48] and before 12 March 1654/5 [WaVR 1:17].

MARRIAGE: By 1640 Sarah _____. She married (2) Watertown 12 March 1654/5 John Chenery [WaVR 1:17] and died Watertown 14 September 1704 [WaVR 2:28].

CHILDREN:

i ELIZABETH, b. Watertown 21 September 1640 [WaVR 1:8]; m. Medfield 6 April 1658 John Fisher.

ii SARAH, b. Watertown 30 September 1642 [WaVR 1:10]; m. by 1664 Thomas Smith of Charlestown (eldest known child b. Charlestown 22 July 1664 [ChVR 1:47]).

iii THOMAS, b. Watertown 26 January 1644/5 [WaVR 1:26]; m. Charlestown 13 December 1665 Mary Gardner [ChVR 1:51].

COMMENTS: On 2 July 1635, "Tho[mas] Boylson," aged 20, with a certificate of conformity from the minister at "Fenchurch, London," was enrolled as a passenger for New England on the *Defence* [Hotten 99]. (The minister was probably from the parish of St Gabriel Fenchurch, although there were other churches along Fenchurch Street, including St Dionis Backchurch, the parish where the immigrant was probably baptized.)

On 2 April 1650, "Thomas Boidson" brought suit against Thomas Pratt for "withholding money due that was sent him by his uncle"; John Sawin deposed that in 1648 "he spoke with Mr. Boidson the old man and he fell aspeaking with him about young Boidson his wife, & children, and he said he had assigned his house and land in New England to Thomas Pratt, to improve for the use of Boidson, and his children, also that he received £20 more of him for the same use, that in case young Boidson and children were in want, the said Tho[mas] Pratt should be helpful unto him" [MCR 1:10].

On 5 October 1652, the Middlesex Court "committed Thomas Boylstone to the marshal's custody for abusing of his wife" [MCR 1:22].

Don C. Stone has demonstrated that the immigrant was that Thomas Boylston baptized 12 February 1614/5 at St Dionis Backchurch, London, son of Edward and Anne (Bastian) Boylston [Don C. Stone, "The Boylston Family in England and Their Connection with the Pipe Family" (unpublished manuscript 1997), p. 15].

Thomas Boylston of London, clothworker, who acted in behalf of the immigrant was brother of this Edward Boylston [SLR 1:67; Aspinwall 172, 183, 199-200]. In his will of 1 July 1648, "Thomas Boylson citizen and clothworker of London" bequeathed to "Thomas Boylson, son of my brother Edward Boylson deceased, and to his wife and children (the said

Thomas being a bad husband) eight hundred pounds, to remain in my executor's hands, to be paid &c. in his good discretion" [Waters 806, citing PCC 128 Essex].

Bond comments that he "was not a very exemplary husband or Christian, and that his friends in England had not full confidence in his prudence and discretion; as an agent was employed to purchase an estate for him in Watertown. It is not improbable that he had been a gay young gentleman of London, whose habits were not formed after the puritanical model, and, not being a member of the church, he was never admitted freeman" [Bond 702].

THOMAS BRACY

ORIGIN: London
MIGRATION: 1634
FIRST RESIDENCE: Ipswich
REMOVES: Newport 1640, New Haven 1647

OCCUPATION: Linen draper (London Fishmongers' guild reports "Thomas Brasey in New England a linen draper by trade" [NEHGR 61:92, citing 1641 Lay Subsidy Roll]).
CHURCH MEMBERSHIP: Thomas Bracy or his second wife was a member of New Haven church by 5 September 1647, when two of their children were baptized there.
FREEMAN: "Mr. Brace" admitted as a freeman of Newport, 14 September 1640, and included in the list of freemen of 16 March 1640/1 [RICR 1:108, 110].
EDUCATION: In December 1619 "Thomas Bressey son of Edmond Bressey late of Wootton in the county of Bedford deceased" was apprenticed to John Abbott of the Fishmongers' Company for six years, and on 2 January 1626/7 he was made free of the company [Fishmongers' Company Records, Freemen & Apprentices, 1614 to 1650]. Signed the marriage allegation book at the time of his first marriage.
ESTATE: While there are no deeds or grants to Thomas Bracy, his lands at Ipswich are mentioned as bounds for the property of William White on 20 April 1635 [ITR]. In a 12 April 1638 deed to John Norton, the lands are described as bounded by a lot "formerly granted to Mr. John Fawne and by him sold unto Mr. Thomas Brecey and now in his possession" [ITR].

BIRTH: Baptized Maulden, Bedfordshire, 8 November 1601, son of Edmund Bressey [Sarah Stone Anc 103].

DEATH: By 1649 based on remarriage of his widow.

MARRIAGE: (1) London 30 January 1626/7 [license] Hannah Hart ("Thomas Bracy of the parish of St Michael the Querne, linendraper and a bachelor, aged about 24 years ... with Hanna Hart of the parish of Christchurch, maiden, aged about 18 years, the daughter-in-law of John Abbot of the same parish, linendraper ... to be married in the parish church of Christchurch London" [Bishop of London Marriage Allegations 11:78]). She died within a few years.

(2) St Lawrence Jewry, London, 4 August 1631 Phebe Bisby, daughter of William Bisby. She married (2) prior to 12 February 1649[/50?] Samuel Martin (when her father wrote his will [PCC 19 Bowyer]). Phebe was living 6 December 1683 when she was appointed administratrix and sole beneficiary of her late husband Martin's estate [Manwaring 1:334].

CHILDREN:

With second wife

i   PHEBE, b. say 1634; m. (1) by about 1658 Joseph Dickinson (daughter Phebe m. Stephen Hurlbut on 12 December 1678 [TAG 20:168]) [NEHGR 152:171]; m. (2) John Rose [Robert Rose Gen 13]; m. (3) Samuel Hale [Hale, House 3-8]. (In 1944 Donald Lines Jacobus marshalled the evidence and the arguments for these three marriages [TAG 20:166-71].)

ii CONSTANCE, b. say 1636; m. by 1660 John Morey (on 22 March 1660/1, John Winthrop Jr. treated "[blank] Murry his wife of Wethersfield, Mrs. Martin's daughter, being within two months of her time had a fall backward by a chair being pulled away as she was sitting down & feareth miscarrying" [WMJ 1:502]; on 26 April 1661, "Thomas Bracey, John Bracey, Constance, wife of John Morray, and Phebe, wife of Joseph Dickinson, sold their interest in the estate of their grandfather, William Bisby of London, to their stepfather, Samuel Martin" [NEHGR 152:171, citing WetLR 2:43-53]).

iii THOMAS, b. say 1638; m. in or soon after 1672 Mary Osborn, daughter of James Osburn (in a letter to John Winthrop Jr. dated 14 November 1672, "James Ozburn" of Hatfield stated that "I have given leave to Thomas Bracy to speak with my daughter Mary, he having a desire to make affinity with her by marriage" [Sarah Stone Anc 106, citing "Winthrop Papers, XVI:40, Mass. Historical Society MSS."]).

iv   JOHN, b. about 1640 (deposed 24 August 1664 aged "twenty-four years or thereabouts" [SJC Case #746]; d. Wethersfield 19 January 1708/9, "aged about 70 as thought" [Sarah Stone Anc 108]), bp. New Haven 5 September 1647 [NHChR 14]; m. after 1677 Anne (Pearce) Carmichael, daughter of John Pearce and widow of John Carmichael [Sarah Stone Anc 107, 125-26; GDMNH 104, 129, 553; YPR 1:39-40].

v   HANNAH, b. about 1640 (on 13 March 1657/8, John Winthrop Jr. treated "Hanna Bracey 18 years" [WMJ 1:93]), probably the "Susannah" bp. New Haven 5 September 1647 [NHChR 14]; m. Boston 25 August 1659 Thomas Paine ("Thomas Paine & Hannah Bray [sic], daughter of Thomas Bray [sic] of Newhaven" [BVR 71]; on 3 January 1659/60, John Winthrop Jr. treated "[blank] Paine his wife (Hannah Bracy formerly)," and on 13 May 1661, he treated "Hanna Paine of Wethersfield daughter to Mrs. Martin" [WMJ 356, 507; see also WMJ 101, 103, 335, 343]).

COMMENTS: Cotton Mather included in his "First Classis" of ministers "[blank] Brucy of Brainford," and later says of him "I say nothing, because I know nothing of Mr. Brecy; but this, he also returned into England" [Magnalia 1:235, 588]. Walter Goodwin Davis suggested that this was John Bressey, younger brother of Thomas [NEHGR 112:41-42].

William Bisby, father of Thomas Bracy's second wife, corresponded with George Wyllys of Hartford and his second wife, who had earlier been the wife of Alexander Bisby, William's brother [Wyllys Papers 11]. On 11 May 1646, writing to Mary Wyllys, William Bisby observed that "I had no letter from my son & daughter [Samuel and Phebe (Bisby) (Bracy) Martin] near you this year, one told me they were purposed to come over, but I hope they are not so foolish to spend £40 or £50 upon a slender occasion nor so flush of money, a great part of my estate is lost & I am unfit for employment, and her sisters unprovided for yet, and matters very unsettled & uncertain here, & I shall be likelier to do as much for them there, as coming over if not more, especially if they bring a trouble upon me in my old days; I have writ my mind briefly to them, she was rash in her first marriage, & so in her second, I know not how the case is with them, I hoped that help I afforded them would have set them aforehand in their estate; I doubt he was in debt, I hear still they are thought to be very poor, if she had taken her friends' advice & married with one that had had some means to maintain them, I would have strained myself to do what I could for her, if she smart for her rashness let her thank herself, I wish she may make a good use of all occurrences & repent for her rashness and folly" [Wyllys Papers 88-89].

Writing again to Mary Wyllys on 21 August 1646, William Bisby directed "that money which is in your hands keep till I demand it myself by special order; if my daughter had stayed & matched by advice of her friends to one that had been likely to maintain her I would have done my utmost, though it may be I should have wronged her sisters, but she must reap the fruits of her rashness; I had formerly a better conceit of her for her spiritual estate; I pray you be as helpful to her that way as you can whenever you see her" [Wyllys Papers 97].

The evidence for the ages of John and Hannah/Susannah would indicate that they may have been twins, born in 1639 or 1640. The other three children are deemed to be older, as the daughters at least must have been born before 1647, and so should have been baptized at New Haven along with John and Hannah/Susannah if they were younger. They are listed here in the order of their first marriages.

BIBLIOGRAPHIC NOTE: Walter Goodwin Davis treated this family in 1930, including extensive information on the ancestry of the immigrant's second wife [Sarah Stone Anc 103-22]. In 1958 he published evidence for four generations of the immigrant's agnate ancestry [NEHGR 112:27-44].

THOMAS BRADBURY

ORIGIN: London
MIGRATION: 1635
FIRST RESIDENCE: York
REMOVES: Salisbury by 1640

OCCUPATION: Planter.
CHURCH MEMBERSHIP: Admission to Salisbury church prior to 13 May 1640 implied by freemanship.
FREEMAN: 13 May 1640 (fourth in a list of four Salisbury men) [MBCR 1:376].

EDUCATION: Many examples of documents in his fine hand, and numerous examples of his signature, survive to attest to an excellent education. The inventory of Thomas Bradbury's estate included "6 books," not individually appraised [EPR 305:18].

OFFICES: Deputy for Salisbury to the Massachusetts Bay General Court, 7 May 1651, 26 May 1652, 14 May 1656, 6 May 1657, 30 May 1660, 22 May 1661 (as "Capt. Tho[mas] Bradbury"), 23 May 1666 [MBCR 3:220, 259, 422, 4:1:37, 77, 255, 286, 416, 4:2:2, 294].

Ipswich grand jury, 4 November 1645 [EQC 1:86]. Clerk of courts, 24 April 1649 [EQC 1:167].

Salisbury magistrate, 8 April 1662, 14 November 1676, 10 April 1677, 9 April 1678, 11 November 1679 [EQC 6:208, 261, 427, 7:272]. Commissioner to end small causes for Salisbury, 8 April 1662, 13 April 1669, 30 May 1676, 9 October 1677, 11 November 1679, 27 September 1681 [EQC 2:383, 4:131, 6:141, 341, 7:277, 8:186].

Salisbury clerk of the writs, 10 December 1641 [MBCR 1:345]. Constable, 29 January 1641/2 (as "John Bradbury") [EQC 1:41]. Selectman, 1674, 1682 [Essex Ant 12:83-84; EQC 8:318].

Clerk of Salisbury train band, 4 November 1645 [EQC 1:87]. Elected ensign at Salisbury, March 1647/8 [MBCR 2:231]. Captain by 22 May 1661 [MBCR 4:2:2].

ESTATE: On 8 October 1647, John Harison of Boston, attorney for Mr. John Hodges of London, sold to "Mr. Tho[mas] Bradbury of Salisbury" one dwelling-house and three-acre house-lot, as well as a planting lot of twelve acres, two six-acre meadow lots, and 40 acres of upland, all in Salisbury [Essex Ant 1:24, 7:136, abstracting NLR 1:12, 2:161]. On 23 October 1647, Thomas Bradbury of Salisbury, planter, sold to Valentine Rowell six acres of meadow, formerly belonging to Mr. John Hodges [Essex Ant 3:11, abstracting NLR 1:110]. On 21 December 1647, John Severans of Salisbury, with consent of his wife, Abigail, sold to "Thomas Bradbury of Salisbury, planter, my dwelling house and old house and the houselots adjoyning on both sides of the street" in Salisbury [Essex Ant 1:24, 7:136-37, abstracting NLR 1:14, 2:162].

On 20 February 1651/2, Thomas Bradbury of Salisbury, planter, for 35s., sold to Edward French of Salisbury, tailor, some meadow land, with Mary Bradbury, wife of the grantor releasing her dower on 1 June 1668 [Essex Ant 1:24, 6:177, abstracting NLR 1:13, 2:115]. On 15 January 1654[/5], Henry Ambross of Boston, with consent of his wife, Susannah, sold to Mr. Thomas Bradbury and John Stevens, both of Salisbury, ten acres of fresh meadow and six acres of salt marsh, together with his commonage, all in

Salisbury [Essex Ant 7:90-91, abstracting NLR 2:159]. On 24 April 1657, Major Robert Pike of Salisbury exchanged land with "Tho[mas] Bradbury of Salisbury," Pike receiving a three-acre lot of meadow and Bradbury a four-acre lot of meadow in the great meadows toward beach point in Salisbury [Essex Ant 9:140, abstracting NLR 2:231]. On 6 January 1657/8, Anthony Stanian of Hampton, and his wife Anne, sold to "Mr. Tho[mas] Bradbury and John Stevens Sr., both of Salisbury, 36 acres of upland, being 3 10-acre lots, and one 6-acre lot formerly purchased by William Partridg of Salisbury, deceased, the former husband of the said Anne, the land being in Salisbury" [Essex Ant 7:136, abstracting NLR 2:162].

On 25 March 1660, John Ilsly of Salisbury, barber, sold to "Mr. Tho[mas] Bradbury of Salisbury four divisions of upland in Salisbury" [Essex Ant 9:138, abstracting NLR 2:225-26]. On 18 May 1661, Samuel Winsley Jr., as attorney for his father, Samuel Winsley, sold to Mr. Thomas Bradbury ten acres of land in Salisbury, formerly "old Goodale's rye lot," and also certain upland, Samuel Winsley Sr. and his wife, Ann, consenting to the transaction [Essex Ant 5:179, 7:137, abstracting NLR 2:20, 162-63]. On 25 June 1662, John Gill of Salisbury, planter, and Phebe, his wife, sold to "Tho[mas] Bradbury a dwelling house, house-lot, orchard, etc., in Salisbury; also one-half of that island called William Barns' island; also, a division of land on ferry neck, being a four-acre planting lot which I bought of Anthony Sadler" [Essex Ant 9:138, abstracting NLR 2:225].

On 20 May 1663, John Ilsly of Salisbury, barber, sold to "Mr. Tho[mas] Bradbury of Salisbury a division of upland" in Salisbury [Essex Ant 9:138, abstracting NLR 2:225-26]. On 26 September 1663, Georg Martyn of Salisbury, blacksmith, sold to Mr. Thomas Bradbury of Salisbury four acres of salt marsh in the Higgledy Piggledy in Salisbury, and two acres of salt marsh in lieu of a division in Mr. Hale's farm [Essex Ant 5:138, abstracting NLR 2:18]. On 25 March 1664, Isaac Colby of Salisbury, planter, sold to "Mr. Tho[mas] Bradbury Senior of Salisbury 3 acres of upland and meadow in Salisbury I bought of John Clough of Salisbury, house carpenter, being a part of the planting lot of Josiah Cobham, and meadow (½ of the first division of meadow granted to Cobham by Salisbury)" [Essex Ant 10:109, abstracting NLR 2:251]. On 13 October 1664, Thomas Bradbury Sr. of Salisbury, planter, "in consideration of a marriage consummated between J[ohn] Stanian of Hampton and my daughter Mary Bradbury, as part of her portion, conveyed to my said son-in-law my share of land and marsh of Mr. Hall's farm in Salisbury, and my part of the addition of land laid out by Salisbury to the said farm" [Essex Ant 9:141, abstracting NLR 2:234]. On 23 April 1666, Robert Ring of

Salisbury, cooper, sold to "Mr. Tho[mas] Bradbury of Salisbury interest in 6 acres of land situated upon a place called Robert Ring's island in Salisbury" [Essex Ant 9:137-38, abstracting NLR 2:224]. On 4 May 1668, Major Robert Pike of Salisbury, planter, "for land," sold to "Mr. Tho[mas] Bradbury of Salisbury my ten-acre lot of upland in Salisbury" [Essex Ant 9:139-40, abstracting NLR 2:231].

On 14 July 1669 (but almost certainly 1670, based on the next two deeds), Onesiphorus Page of Salisbury, weaver, and his wife, Mary, sold to "Mr. Tho[mas] of Salisbury, planter, 2 acres of upland, being an addition to the planting lot of Tho[mas] Hauxworth sometime of Salisbury, deceased" [Essex Ant 8:127,9:140, abstracting NLR 2:188-89, 232]. On 14 July 1670, "Thomas Bradbury of Salisbury, planter, in consideration of 2 acres of marsh in Salisbury in Mr. Hooke's farm ..., formerly belonging to Thomas Hauxworth of Salisbury, deceased, now made sure to me by Onezephorus Page of Salisbury who married Mary, daughter of said Thomas Hauxworth," conveyed to Page "my four-acre marsh granted to me by Salisbury in reference to the common right of Mr. Henry Bylie sometime of Salisbury, deceased," Mary Bradbury, Thomas's wife, releasing her dower [Essex Ant 8:127, abstracting NLR 2:188-89]. On the same date, 14 July 1670, Onesephorus Page of Salisbury and his wife, Mary, sold to "Capt. Tho[mas] Bradbury 2 acres of marsh in Mr. Hook's farm alias the hog house farm," and also certain upland belonging to said farm [Essex Ant 8:127, citing NLR 2:188-89].

On 11 March 1671/2, for "natural love & affection," Thomas Bradbury of Salisbury, planter, sold to "my beloved son," William Bradbury of Salisbury, all his dwelling house lately erected, with all other housing on the same house lot, with the orchards and other uplands adjoining thereunto, as well as "my six-score acre lot at Beach Hill," and his division of swamp land toward the ferry, specifying that, during the natural life of Thomas and his wife, William was to have the use of only half of the pasture towards the ferry, and one half of the "grass Ambres [i.e. Ambrose] marsh," if either Thomas or his wife requires it [ILR 4:337; EPR 3:301; Essex Ant 10:90-91, abstracting NLR 2:245]. At the time of the inventory of the estate of William Bradbury, son of Thomas and Mary (Perkins) Bradbury, the property transferred in the above deed was valued at £300, and a statement to this effect was recorded at the end of the foregoing deed.

On 7 July 1673, Mr. Thomas Bradbury and John Stevens Sr. divided "land they had bought of Mr. Anthony Stanian in the 500 acres granted by Salisbury to the inhabitants" [Essex Ant 11:176, abstracting NLR 2:300].

On 23 June 1674, "Thomas Bradbury of Salisbury, gentleman, for love, conveyed to my daughter, Judith, wife of Caleb Moudie of Newbury, maltster, 6 acres of land at the east end of Ring's Island in Salisbury, which I bought of Robert Ring April 23, 1666 ... after my and my wife's decease" [Essex Ant 12:179-80, abstracting NLR 2:233].

In his will, dated 14 February 1693/4 and proved 26 March 1695, Thomas Bradbury bequeathed "unto my grandchildren Thomas Bradbury & Jacob Bradbury" all his housing and lands in Salisbury, and they were to pay their "Aunt True" £15 each, and discharge their "brother William Bradbury" from all orders of courts concerning the division of their father's estate; the said grandchildren, Thomas and Jacob, were to provide for their grandmother and she to have the use of half of his housing; to "my grandchild Thomas Bradbury" farming implements; to "my daughter Mary Stanian" 20s., she having had her portion upon marriage; to "my daughter Jane True" £10; to "my grandchild Elizabeth Buss" £5; £10 to the selectmen of Salisbury for the poor of the town; and he appointed his wife, Mary Bradbury, and his daughter, Judith Moodie, his executrixes [EPR 305:17-18].

The inventory of his estate totalled £463 16s. 10d., of which at least £250 was real estate: "housing & upland of all sorts, meadows, marsh," £250; and "common rights in Salisbury," no value assigned [EPR 305:18].

BIRTH: Baptized Wicken Bonhunt, Essex, 28 February 1610/1, son of Wymond Bradbury [TAG 18:224-26].
DEATH: Salisbury 16 March 1694/5.
MARRIAGE: By 1637 Mary Perkins, baptized at Hillmorton, Warwickshire, 3 September 1615, daughter of *JOHN PERKINS* [GMB 3:1432]. She died at Salisbury 20 December 1700.
CHILDREN:

 i WYMOND, b. 1 April 1637 (probably in York but recorded in Salisbury); m. Salisbury 7 May 1661 Sarah Pike. She m. (2) Salisbury 10 May 1671 John Stockman.
 ii JUDITH, b. 2 October 1638 (probably in York but recorded in Salisbury); m. Newbury 9 November 1665 Caleb Moody [EQC 3:293] (also recorded Salisbury 9 October 1665).
 iii THOMAS, b. Salisbury 28 January 1640/1; d. unmarried.
 iv MARY, b. Salisbury 17 March 1642/3; m. Hampton 15 December 1663 John Stanyan [HampVR 1:75, 556] (also recorded Salisbury 17 December 1663).

    v   JANE, b. Salisbury 11 May 1645; m. Hampton 16 March 1667/8 Henry True [HampVR 1:75] (also recorded Salisbury 15 March 1667/8).

   vi   JACOB, b. Salisbury 17 June 1647; d. Barbados 12 March 1669 [GDMNH 104 (evidence not shown)].

  vii   WILLIAM, b. Salisbury 15 September 1649; m. Salisbury 12 March 1671/2 Rebecca (Wheelwright) Maverick, daughter of Rev. John Wheelwright and widow of Samuel Maverick [NEHGR 69:159, 96:238]. (On 5 March 1671/2, "William Bradbury of Salisbury, intending to marry Mrs. Rebecca Maverick, widow of Sam[ue]ll Maverick, late of Boston, deceased, do renounce all claim to the estate of Samuel Maverick" [Essex Ant 10:90, citing NLR 2:241].)

 viii   ELIZABETH, b. Salisbury 7 November 1651; m. Salisbury 12 May 1673 Rev. John Buss.

   ix   JOHN, b. Salisbury 20 April 1654; d. Salisbury 24 November 1678, apparently unmarried.

    x   ANN, b. Salisbury 16 April 1656; d. Salisbury "1659."

   xi   JABEZ, b. Salisbury 27 June 1658; d. Salisbury 28 April 1677.

COMMENTS: On 5 May 1636, Thomas Bradbury served as agent at York for Sir Ferdinando Gorges [YLR 1:1:11]; since this event preceded the Massachusetts Bay election court of 1636, we assume, relying on our usual rule, that Bradbury was in New England no later than 1635.

On 13 September 1637, Thomas Bradbury and WILLIAM HOOKE wrote to Governor John Winthrop expressing the need for a minister at York [WP 3:497-98].

On 14 April 1663, Thomas Bradbury sued George Goldwyer unsuccessfully for trespass, accusing him of mowing part of his "higlede piglede" [i.e. Higgledy Piggledy Marsh] lot (in Salisbury) toward Hampton and for carrying away the hay from it, and going about to alter the title of his land [EQC 3:57]. In a similar case, on 28 November 1671, Thomas Bradbury successfully sued John Davis Sr. for trespass in cutting Thomas's grass and fodder on the eastern end of Ring's Island, the writ being dated 24 June 1671 [EQC 4:452]. Occasional appearances in court on other matters have been noted.

In 1665 Thomas Bradbury served as a trustee, or guardian, for Hepsibah Morrill, daughter of the late Abraham Morrill and widow Sarah Merrill [Essex Ant 6:41, citing NLR 2:53]. On 10 April 1677, Capt. Thomas

Bradbury was appointed guardian of his grandson, Wymond Bradbury [EQC 6:264; EPR 3:132].

BIBLIOGRAPHIC NOTE: In 1890 William Berry Lapham compiled a genealogy of the Bradbury family which traced some of the descendants of Thomas Bradbury and also contained records of English Bradburys [*Bradbury Memorial* (Portland, Maine, 1890)]. In 1942 Mary Lovering Holman published an account of the Bradbury English ancestry, together with the lineage of one branch of Thomas Bradbury's descendants [TAG 18:220-26, 19:36-43].

F.L. Weis suggested two royal descents for Thomas Bradbury in early editions of his work, *Ancestral Roots of Sixty Colonists.* The fourth edition of that work, edited by Walter Lee Sheppard, Jr., appeared in 1969 and pointed out that one of the suggested royal descents was invalid. A carefully-prepared typescript at the New England Historic Genealogical Society analyzed a number of difficult points in the Bradbury ancestry, relying on fresh and thorough English research and a clear evaluation of the evidence ["Thomas Bradbury of Salisbury, Massachusetts, and Bradbury of Hertfordshire and Essex, England" (Albuquerque, New Mexico, 1972)]. A series of articles by Robert Charles Anderson and/or John Brooks Threlfall appeared in response to the suggested remaining royal descent and other English ancestry of Thomas Bradbury [TAG 52:176-77, 247; 55:1-16, 151-55, 233-35; 56:13-23; 57:35-44, 55-56, 97-99].

In 1988 John Brooks Threlfall published an extensive treatment of the English ancestry of Thomas Bradbury in numerous lines of ascent, as well as a short treatment of the known ancestry of Thomas Bradbury's wife, Mary Perkins [*The Ancestry of Thomas Bradbury (1611-1695) and His Wife, Mary (Perkins) Bradbury (1615-1700) of Salisbury, Massachusetts* (Madison, Wisconsin, 1988)], and a revised edition of this with additional material appeared in 1995.

ROBERT BRADISH

ORIGIN: Unknown
MIGRATION: 1635
FIRST RESIDENCE: Cambridge
REMOVES: Boston by 1657

OCCUPATION: Dyer (his inventory included "a piece of serge at the mill estimated to be 30 yards," "things belonging to the trade as 5 pair of shears, pair of tainters & other implements" and "two furnaces & some old vessels to dye").

EDUCATION: Signed his will.

OFFICES: Cambridge fenceviewer, 13 March 1653/4 [CaTR 104].

ESTATE: On 28 August 1635, "John Steele of the New towne" sold to Robert Bradish "all that right, title and interest which he hath in all his parcels of land lying and being in Newtowne aforesaid" [CaBOP 15-16].

In the 8 February 1635/6 list of those with houses in Cambridge, "Rob[er]t Bradish" was credited with two [CaTR 18].

In the Cambridge land inventory of 6 September 1642, "Robert Brodish" held seven parcels: "within the town one dwelling house with outhouses and about one rood of ground"; "within the neck of land, three roods of land"; "in Smalllot Hill, seven acres & half"; "within the neck of land ten acres & half"; "in the Long Marsh three acres & half"; "in the Oxmarsh one acre"; and "in the Great Marsh twelve acres" [CaBOP 91-92].

In 1645 "Rob[er]t Broadish" was granted twelve acres for a small farm [CaTR 67]. In 1646 "Robert Broadish" was granted nine acres for a woodlot [CaTR 66]. On 4 June 1652, "Robert Brodish" received Lot #113 at Shawsheen, eighty acres [CaTR 98]. On 23 December 1653, "Rob[er]t Broadish" was granted 2¼ acres in the first squadron of woodlots in Cambridge [CaTR 64].

In his will, dated 12 May 1657 and proved 29 October 1659, Robert Bradish named "my loving wife" executor and bequeathed to "my loving wife Vastie Bradish my whole estate, both that estate which I have in Boston & all my estate in Cambridge ... so long as she liveth"; after her decease, to "my son James Bradish," 20s.; to "my son John Bradish," £40 and furniture; to "my son-in-law Ezekiell Morrell," £10 and furniture; to "my son Joseph," furniture; to "my daughter Mary Gibbs," furniture; residue to "be equally divided amongst four of my children, that is to say James Bradish a part & Joseph Bradish a part & my daughter Mary a part & my daughter Hannah a part"; "if John Bradish die without heirs then his forty pounds to be equally divided between these four of my children last mentioned ... and if Ezekiell Morrell die without heirs then his ten pounds & the bed to be equally divided between these four last mentioned or their children"; "my loving brother Isaac Morrell" to be overseer [SPR 1:335].

The inventory of the estate of Robert Bradish, taken 8 September 1659, totalled £207 2s. 2d., of which £125 was real estate: "a farm at Cambridge rented ten pounds per annum" [SPR 3:161].

In March 1672/3, administration "on the estate of the late widow Vashti Bradish deceased is granted to Joseph & John Bradish her two sons" [SPR 7:282]; on 8 March 1672/3, the brothers posted their administrators' bond [SPR NS 2:531]. The inventory of the estate of "the widow Bradish," taken 10 March 1672/3, totalled £4 11s. 8d., all household goods [SPR 7:302].

BIRTH: By about 1607 based on estimated date of marriage.

DEATH: Between 12 May 1657 (date of will) and 8 September 1659 (date of inventory).

MARRIAGE: (1) By about 1630 Mary _____. She died at Cambridge [blank] September 1638.

(2) By 1639 Vashti (_____) Morrill, widow of _____ Morrill. She died by 8 March 1672/3 (administrators' bond).

CHILDREN:

With first wife

    i   HANNAH, b. say 1630; about January 1640/1 "Robert Braddish of Cambridge [placed] Hannah his daughter apprentice unto Thomas Hawkins for 4 years from this till the end of 4 years from 25 March next or to Hannah his wife meat drink & clothes & double apparel in the end" [Lechford 363]; living 12 May 1657, when named in father's will; no further record.

    ii   MARY, b. say 1632: m. by 1652 Matthew Gibbs ("Mary Gibbs" admitted to Charlestown church, 23 September 1652 [ChChR 11; see also Wyman 406]).

    iii JAMES, b. say 1634; living 12 May 1657, when named in father's will; probably dead by March 1672/3, when his brothers Joseph and John administered the estate of his stepmother.

    iv JOSEPH, b. Cambridge [blank] May 1638; m. Sudbury 10 April 1664 Mary Frost (surnames reversed in marriage record [Sudbury VR 175, 197, citing Middlesex County record]; eldest known child b. Sudbury 10 April 1665 [Sudbury VR 25]), daughter of EDMUND FROST.

With second wife

    v   SAMUEL, b. Cambridge 13 February 1639[/40?]; d. Cambridge 6 July 1642.

   vi   JOHN, b. Cambridge 3 December 1645; m. by 1674 Susanna
        _____ (eldest known child b. Boston 28 September 1674
        [BVR 131]).
   vii   SAMUEL, b. Cambridge 29 November 1648; bur. Cambridge 9
        December 1648.

COMMENTS: In his will, Robert Bradish made a bequest to "my son-in-law Ezekiel Morrell" and named "my loving brother Isaac Morrell" as overseer. Since Isaac Morrill did not have a son Ezekiel [GMB 3:1911], and Isaac's brother Abraham also did not have a son Ezekiel, we conclude that a third Morrill brother, given name unknown, also came to New England, with wife Vashti and son Ezekiel, and died by 1639, when his widow married Robert Bradish.

BIBLIOGRAPHIC NOTE: In 1948 Donald Lines Jacobus compiled a brief account of Robert Bradish and his daughter Mary [Brainerd Anc 57-59]. Jacobus included a brief reference to Joseph Bradish, a grandson of the immigrant who became a pirate; George Francis Dow and John Henry Edmonds provide more detail on this individual [*The Pirates of the New England Coast, 1630-1730* (Salem 1923), pp. 40-43].

HUMPHREY BRADSTREET

ORIGIN: Unknown (but see *BIBLIOGRAPHIC NOTE* below)
MIGRATION: 1634 on the *Elizabeth*
FIRST RESIDENCE: Ipswich

CHURCH MEMBERSHIP: Admission to Ipswich church prior to 6 May 1635 implied by freemanship.
FREEMAN: 6 May 1635 [MBCR 1:370].
EDUCATION: Wife Bridget had several books to bequeath, but signed her will with her initials.
OFFICES: Deputy for Ipswich to Massachusetts Bay General Court, 2 September 1635 [MBCR 1:156]. Committee to consider Mr. Endicott's defacing of the colors, 6 May 1635 [MBCR 1:145]. Essex County jury, 28 December 1641, 26 September 1648 [EQC 1:37, 146].
ESTATE: On 1 March 1641[/2?], Humphrey Bradstreet of Ipswich, yeoman, sold to Thomas Knowlton of Ipswich, shoemaker, "all that my

dwelling house and house lot" in Ipswich [ILR 1:21]. On 20 November 1645, Humphrey Bradstreet exchanged with Richard Hutley ten acres of upland and marsh in Ipswich for eighteen acres in the common field [ILR 1:9].

On 25 February 1648[/9], Philip Fowler of Ipswich deposed that "Humphrey Bradstreete of Ipswich, having 100 acres of land granted unto him by the freemen of the town of Ipswich," did exchange 20 acres of it for 20 acres at Muddy River. This transaction occurred at the house of Goodman Andrews, and Andrews claimed that the 20 acres in question had been granted to him, "whereupon the said Humphrey Bradstreete said to the freemen, `Satisfy me first for my 30 acres at Redy marsh,'" an accommodation he had made to the town some years earlier. The selectmen's committee consulted and granted him 20 acres at his farm [ILR 1:45].

In his will, dated 21 July 1655 and proved 25 September 1655, "Umphrah Brodstreate" of Ipswich, being weak in body, ordered "my body to be buried in the burying place of Rowley" and bequeathed to "my beloved wife" the farm during her lifetime if she does not remarry, if she does remarry half the farm to be for the bringing up of "my son Moses" and in case she die before Moses reached 21, then the benefit equally divided among "my five daughters"; if Moses lived, then the whole farm to him at 21 or at the death of "my wife"; to "my wife Bridget" livestock; to "my son John" all the farm at Muddy River now in the occupation of "Richard Camball" of Ipswich with one half of "my commons from Ipswich"; to "my daughter Hannah Rofe" £20; to "my daughter Martha Beale" £1 and more, £15 in the hand of her mother to be given her or her child at her discretion; to "my daughter Mary Brodstreete" £40; to "my daughter Sarah Brodstreete" £30; to "my daughter Rebeccah Brodstreet" £40; to "my two grandchildren Daniell and Hannah Rofe" each £5 at 21; to "Sammuell Beale" £5 at 21; to the poor of Ipswich £1; to the poor of Rowley £1; "beloved friends Mr. Samuell Phillips, Matthew Boyes and John Harris to join with my wife for the disposing of my children in marriage or otherwise"; "my wife Bridget Brodstreete" sole executrix [EPR 1:217-18].

The inventory of the estate of Humphrey Bradstreet, taken 6 September 1655, totalled £146 10s., of which £230 was real estate: "the farm where he lived," £160; and "the farm at Muddy River," £70 [EPR 1:218-19].

In her will, dated 16 October 1665 and proved 28 March 1666, "Bregit Brodstret widow of Ipswich" bequeathed to "my son Moses" a barn and household goods; to "my eldest daughter Martha Kimball [sic]" a gown, a pewter dish and "Mr. Norton's Book," a sheet and a pillowbear; to "my daughter Mary Kimball my old Bible" and other goods; to "my daughter Kimball and my daughter Wallis" a "skep" of bees, they to give the first swarm to their other two sisters; to "my daughter Wallis Mr. Cobbet's Book" and other goods; to "my daughter Rebecka Bondfeld" clothing and goods; to "my grandchild Hanah Roph" clothing and goods and a cow; residue equally to "my four daughters above written"; "my loving friend Samuel Plats" executor; "my loving friends Samuell Appleton and Joseph Whipple" overseers [EPR 3:31-32].

The inventory of the estate of Bridget Bradstreet, presented on 27 March 1666, totalled £80 24s. 11d. and included no real estate [EPR 3:32].

BIRTH: About 1594 (aged 40 in 1634 [Hotten 280]).

DEATH: Between 21 July 1655 (date of will) and 6 September 1655 (date of inventory).

MARRIAGE: By about 1625 Bridget ____, born about 1604 (aged 30 in 1634 [Hotten 282]); she died at Ipswich [blank] November 1665. She signed with a mark when bound to pay the legacies in Humphrey's will, September 1655 [EQC 1:404].

CHILDREN:

    i   HANNAH, b. about 1625 (aged 9 in 1634 [Hotten 282]); m. (1) by 1655 Daniel Rolfe (father's will); m. (2) Ipswich 20 June 1658 Nicholas Holt.

    ii   JOHN, b. about 1630 (aged 3 in 1634 [Hotten 282]; aged 24 in deposition of 28 March 1654 [EQC 1:332]); m. by 1660 Hannah Peach, daughter of John Peach Jr. of Marblehead (on 26 June 1660, "Hana Bradstreet was granted administration upon the estate of her husband, John Bradstreet, deceased" [EQC 2:215]; on 2 July 1694, "William Waters, Thomas Waters, Elias Staddin & Robert Gifford the legal representatives of Hannah Waters deceased who was one of the daughters of the abovesaid John Peach" were among the "children & grandchildren" who joined in a settlement of the estate of John Peach [EPR 305:1a]); she m. (2) by 1664 William Waters (on 27 September 1664, the siblings of John Bradstreet sued "Will[ia]m Waters and Hanah, his wife, late wife of John Bradstreet and administratrix of his estate" [EQC 3:183, 191, 290]).

    iii   MARTHA, b. about 1632 (aged 2 in 1634 [Hotten 282]); m. (1) by March 1648 Thomas Rowlandson (he fined 10s. for marrying without being published three times [EQC 1:142]); divorced about March 1651 (when "Thomas Rolinson, proven impotent, on complaint of his wife, was to take counsel of physicians forthwith, follow their advice, and report to court" [EQC 1:221]); m. (2) by 1655 William Beale (father's will).

iv   MARY, b. about 1633 (aged 1 in 1634 [Hotten 282]); m. between 1655 and 1665 John Kimball (parents' wills).

v   SARAH, b. about 1638 (deposed aged sixteen years for March Term 1654 [EQC 1:330]); m. Ipswich 13 April 1657 Nicholas Wallis.

vi   REBECCA, b. between 1636 and 1643 (as a minor over fourteen, chose Joseph Jewett as her guardian September 1657 [EQC 1:53]); m. by October 1665 George Bonfield (mother's will).

vii   MOSES, b. about 1643 (deposed aged "about thirty-six years" for November court 1679 [EQC 7:291]); m. Ipswich 11 March 1661/2 Elizabeth Harris.

ASSOCIATIONS: JOHN CROSS and wife Anne were passengers on the *Elizabeth* with the Bradstreets. Humphrey was frequently in conflict with Cross in New England, which, if it was not instant enmity, might indicate a common origin and a long acquaintance.

COMMENTS: "Humphry Bradstreet," aged 40 years, "Bridgett his wife," aged 30 years, "Anna Bradstreet," aged 9, "John Bradstreet," aged 3, "Martha Bradstreet," aged 2, and "Mary Bradstreet," aged 1," were enrolled at Ipswich on the last of April 1634 as passengers for New England on the *Elizabeth* [Hotten 280, 282].

Humphrey Bradstreet sued John Cross at court 27 March 1649, but the case was nonsuited [EQC 1:161]. John Cross returned the favor and sued Humphry Broadstreet, Richard Jacob and John Gage for trespass on 25 September 1649 [EQC 1:176]. Cross also sued John Bradstreet that day. The family was again entangled with Cross in November 1649 when Cross was fined for slanderous speeches against Mr. Rogers of Rowley, and John Bradstreet was fined, evidently for the same thing, and Humphrey served as his surety [EQC 1:179].

A later court case, 26 December 1649, showed that the trespass in question dealt with a gray colt. Bradstreet claimed that the colt was not his, "he never had a colt in his life" [EQC 1:182]. At September Term 1650,

Humphrey Bradstreet and John Bradstreet had their bond of good behavior discharged [EQC 1:200].

On 29 March 1653, Humphrey took Stephen Kent to court "for taking away, using and abusing and not returning a boar, and for suspicion of taking away other swine." The case was withdrawn [EQC 1:277].

BIBLIOGRAPHIC NOTE: In 1899 a series of notes were published that showed the sequence of events leading up to and following the divorce of Humphrey's daughter, Martha, from Thomas Rowlandson. Rowlandson subsequently married again and had nine children recorded at Salisbury [Putnam's Mag 7:123-24].

In 1911 Elizabeth French published several wills and parish register extracts from Gislingham and Capel in Suffolk, and suggested that the "nephew Humfrey Bradstreete" named in the 25 February 1609/10 will of John Bradstreete of Capel was the immigrant; she noted that ISAAC MIXER, who sailed to New England with Humphrey Bradstreet, was from this same parish [NEHGR 65:69-74]. Although this may or may not be the precise connection, Humphrey Bradstreet's presence on the *Elizabeth* makes it almost certain that he came from southern Suffolk or northern Essex.

In her mother's will, Martha is called "my eldest daughter Martha Kimball" [EPR 2:31], but since her second husband, William Beale, appeared in bonds and receipts following Bridget's will, we assume that the "Kimball" is a clerical error for "Beale."

THOMAS BRANE

On 1 July 1635, "Thomas Brane," aged 40, husbandman, was enrolled at London as a passenger for New England on the *Abigail* [Hotten 97].

In his will of 10 December 1635, Dennis Geere of Saugus included among his bequests £3 to "Thomas Braines" [Waters 7-8, citing PCC 79 Campbell].

COMMENTS: DENNIS GEERE also sailed on the *Abigail*, and made a bequest to THOMAS LAUNDER, another passenger. These bequests do not necessarily imply kinship.

Pope included an entry for "Agnes [Brane], widow, Salem, 1637, may be his widow" [Pope 66]. In April 1637 "Agnes Brayne: wid." was admitted to

Salem church [SChR 6]. There is no further record of her in Salem town or church records or in Essex County court records, and there is no indication of a connection with Thomas Brane.

EDMUND BRIDGES

ORIGIN: Unknown
MIGRATION: 1635 on the *James*
FIRST RESIDENCE: Lynn
REMOVES: Rowley by 1641, Ipswich by 1660, Salem by 1670, Ipswich by 1684

OCCUPATION: Blacksmith [EPR Case #3295].
CHURCH MEMBERSHIP: Admission to Lynn church prior to 7 September 1639 implied by freemanship.
FREEMAN: 7 September 1639 [MBCR 1:376].
EDUCATION: Signed his deed of 1682 and his will.
OFFICES: Essex County grand jury, 30 September 1651, 26 September 1654, 25 September 1660 [EQC 1:232, 362, 2:225]. Petit jury, 30 September 1662, 30 September 1673, 28 November 1676, 27 September 1681 [EQC 2:434, 5:224, 6:215, 8:150]. Replacement juror, 30 November 1675 [EQC 6:73].
ESTATE: "Edward Bridges" received ten acres in the Lynn land division of 1638 [EQC 2:271].

On 14 April 1660, Edmond Bridges of Ipswich, smith, and Anthony Potter sold to Elder John Whipple of Ipswich part of a six-acre lot that had previously been Henry Kingsbury's [ILR 1:247-248].

On 26 June 1663, Zacheus Gould of Topsfield sold a small parcel of land to Edmond Bridges and Daniel Black. Bridges and Black immediately mortgaged the property back to Gould, with Bridges accepting one-third of the responsibility for the mortgage and Black two-thirds [ILR 2:162-64].

On 22 February 1663/4, Edmond Bridges of Ipswich, smith, sold to Nicholas Wallis six acres of meadow in Ipswich [ILR 3:204-5].

On 9 December 1670, Edmond Bridges of Salem, blacksmith, sold to Ensign John Gould of Topsfield, yeoman, an eight-acre parcel of land with a dwelling house and barn in Topsfield, also a parcel of ten acres of meadow, swamp and upland in Topsfield [ELR 3:101].

On 12 April 1682, Edmund Bridges Sr. of Salem, blacksmith, made a one year mortgage with Mrs. Eliza[beth] Turner of Salem, widow, for his "dwelling house & shop & wharf, with sixty poles of ground with it" [ELR 6:49].

In his will, dated 6 January 1684[/5] and proved 31 March 1685, Edmond Bridges Sr. of Ipswich, blacksmith, in "weakness of body and many infirmities often prevailing," stated that "I have already given unto all my children but Mary [their] portions as was suitable and convenient to my estate," but in addition bequeathed to "John Bridges my rapier"; to "Josiah Bridges ... my musket"; to "Fayth Bridges" a pewter platter marked with an "EBA"; to "Bethiah Bridges, the fellow or other pewter platter with the same marks"; to "my daughter Mary," £20 in goods; to "my beloved wife Mary Bridges" use of the whole estate during her life unless she marry, then £10; residue of estate at death of wife or her remarriage to be equally divided among "John Bridges my son, my son Josiah Bridges, my daughter Faith Bridges *alias* Black, Bethiah Bridges *alias* Peabodie, and Mary Bridges"; "my beloved wife Mary Bridges & my son John Bridges" executors; "Daniel Epps" with "Lieut. John Appleton" overseers [EPR Case #3295].

The inventory of the estate of Edmond Bridges, taken 16 January 1684[/5], totalled £215 6s. 6d., of which £90 was real estate: "the homestead with all the housing belonging to it," £70; and "9 acres of land," £20 [EPR Case #3295].

An undated account of debts showed £175 12s. 2½d. in sums owed by Bridges, including amounts to settle the entitlements of the Littlehale heirs [EPR Case #3295].

BIRTH: About 1612 (aged 23 in 1635 [Hotten 107]; deposed "aged about forty-six years" in September 1658 [EQC 2:117]). In May 1661 he was released from training "except twice a year" [EQC 2:281].
DEATH: Ipswich 13 January 1684/5.
MARRIAGE: (1) By about 1636 Elizabeth _____. She died at Ipswich 31 December 1664. (Some secondary sources, including Savage, propose an earlier wife Alice, but no supporting evidence for this has been found, so we assume here two wives only for Edmund Bridges.)

(2) Ipswich 6 April 1665 Mary (Langton) Littlehale, widow of Richard [EQC 6:118], born about 1625 (deposed 24 November 1685 "aged sixty years" [EQC 9:545]); she died at Ipswich 24 October 1691. (On 15 March 1664/5, Edmond Bridges of Ipswich acknowledged that "I have nothing to do directly nor indirectly anyways to dispose of or having any interest at

all of Mary Litelhale['s] accommodation at Haverhill notwithstanding she is to be my wife, but leaveth it wholly to the said Mary to dispose of for her own use and her four children which she hath by Rich[ar]d Litelhale" [ILR 5:108]).

CHILDREN:

With first wife

i   EDMUND, b. about 1636 (deposed June 1664 "aged about twenty-seven years" [EQC 3:160, 183]; deposed for 27 March 1666 court "aged twenty-nine years" [EQC 3:312]; deposed in June 1674 "aged about thirty-nine years" [EQC 5:354]); m. Topsfield 11 January 1659/60 Sarah Towne, daughter of William Towne [Amos Towne Anc 4-6].

ii HACKALIAH, b. say 1638 (fined for running away from his father September 1655 [EQC 1:404]); accused by Sarah French for getting her with child September 1656, case discharged [EQC 2:2]; whipped for fornication and ordered to discharge the town about bringing up the child of Mary Quilter, September 1657 [EQC 2:54]; "Hackoliah Bridges drowned at the Gay Head December the 23rd 1671 his estate being inventoried and prized amounted to the just sum of twenty-eight pounds eighteen shillings and eight pence, the said estate was committed into the hand of Mr. Richard Sarson as administrator upon the said estate," who presented the inventory on 25 January 1671/2 [Dukes LR 1:311]; "Hackaliah Bridges being cast away and dying intestate," Essex administration was granted on 8 February 1671/2 "to Obadiah Bridges, his brother, who was to bring in an inventory" [EQC 5:1; EPR 2:253]; apparently unmarried.

iii MEHITABLE, b. Rowley 26 March 1641; no further record.

iv JOHN, b. say 1643; m. (1) Ipswich 5 December 1666 Sarah How; m. (2) Andover 1 March 1677/8 Mary (Tyler) Post, widow of Richard.

v   FAITH, b. about 1645 (deposed at court June 1674 "aged twenty-nine years" [EQC 5:354]); m. after 1660 and by March 1664 Daniel Black [EQC 3:130, 192-94].

vi OBADIAH, b. about 1647 (deposed at court September 1667 "aged about twenty years" [EQC 3:444]; deposed at court November 1669 "aged about twenty-four years" [EQC

4:195]); m. (1) Ipswich 25 October 1671 Mary Smith; m. (2)
by 1677 Elizabeth _____ (his administratrix [EQC 6:344]).

vii   BETHIA, b. say 1649; m. Boxford or Topsfield 26 October 1668
       Joseph Peabody (marriage recorded in both towns).

viii   JOSIAH, b. about 1654 (deposed 2 March 1676 "aged about
       twenty-two years" [EQC 6:239]); m. (1) Ipswich 13
       November 1676 Elizabeth Norton; m. (2) Ipswich 19
       September 1677 Ruth Greenslip.

With second wife

ix   MARY, b. Ipswich 14 April 1667; living 1684/5.

ASSOCIATIONS: The inventory of Roger Lancton of Haverhill was taken
24 January 1671[/2] at the request of "Mr. Edmon Bridges and Samewall
Varnum related to the said Rodger who deceased without a will" [EPR
2:260]. The relationship was evidently through Edmund's second wife.

COMMENTS: On 13 July 1635, "Edmond Bridges," aged 23, was enrolled
at London for passage to New England on the *James* [Hotten 107].

   Edmund Bridges was excused for neglect of public service, at his
request, July 1647 [EQC 1:119]. He did take some responsibilities, since he
was named executor of the will of Thomas Scott of Ipswich, written 8
March 1653/4 [EPR 1:169; ILR 1:190]. He also deposed as attorney to John
Caldwell in November 1653, saying that, "being in Goodman Bridges'
shop, Goodman _____ being present, he heard him say that a woman
and her daughter, gathering berries, saw four women, Mrs. Perkins,
Goody Evens, Goody Dutch, etc. As they approached them, the four
women sat upon the ground, but when they came near, the women had
vanished. He could not say that they were witches" [EQC 1:325].

   In September 1660 Faith Bridges and Daniel Black were in court over his
unlawful seduction of her without her father's permission [EQC 2:243].

   While still minors Edward and Hackaliah were in trouble for things like
lying, fornicating and getting drunk [EQC 2:3, 40-42, 52-54, 68]. Edmund's
children kept unsavory company and were often called to depose in court
about unlawful events they witnessed. Sometimes they were more than
witnesses. Andrew Mansfield of Lynn deposed in September 1667 that
"in hay time, two or three of Goodman Bridges' sons of Ipswich overtook
him on this side of Lynn bridge and stayed there to light their pipes." The
youngest, Hackaliah, was charged with feloniously assaulting a man
upon the highway that night, but the court found for Bridges [EQC 3:444-
45].

JOHN BRIDGE

ORIGIN: Unknown
MIGRATION: 1634
FIRST RESIDENCE: Cambridge

OCCUPATION: Yeoman [MLR 1:93].

CHURCH MEMBERSHIP: Admission to Cambridge church prior to 4 March 1634/5 implied by freemanship. "John Bridge also Deacon of the Church: & Elizabeth his wife, both in full communion," were in the list of Cambridge church members compiled in January 1658/9 [CaChR 4].

FREEMAN: 4 March 1634/5 [MBCR 1:370].

EDUCATION: Signed his marriage contract and all his deeds. His inventory included "a Bible" valued at 5s. and "several old books" valued at £1 4s.

OFFICES: Deputy, 1637-41 [MBCR 1:205, 227, 236, 271, 318, 336]. Committee to set the bounds between Watertown, Concord, Dedham and Cambridge, 2 May 1638, 2 June 1641, 7 October 1641 [MBCR 1:228, 330, 342]. Committee to lay out "Mr. Gurlings" land at Cambridge, 6 September 1638 [MBCR 1:238]. Committee to settle Mr. Nathaniel Eaton's estate, 5 November 1639 [MBCR 1:277]. Committee to settle with Richard Sergent's grandchildren, 12 November 1644 [MBCR 2:80]. Arbiter between Thomas White and Widow Swift, 6 May 1646 [MBCR 3:66]. Committee to lay out land to the Governor and Deputy Governor, 19 October 1652 [MBCR 3:290].

Cambridge selectman, 23 November 1635, 26 October 1638, 1 October 1639, 8 November 1641, 8 November 1642, 13 November 1643, 9 November 1646 [CaTR 1:13, 34, 36, 45, 46, 49, 57]. Ordered to build a house for the cow keep, 23 April 1636 [CaTR 1:22]. Lot layer, 6 March 1636/7 [CaTR 27].

ESTATE: On 4 August 1634, John Bridge received a grant of 75 acres on the west side of the river [CaTR 1:8]. In 1635/6, John Bridge was enumerated as having two houses in Cambridge [CaTR 1:18].

In the Cambridge land inventory on 4 June 1635, "John Bridg" held five parcels: one house and backside of half a rood; one long marsh of one acre and a rood; four acres and three roods in the great marsh; six acres in the neck; and seventy five acres on the west side of the Charles River [CaBOP 10].

On 25 August 1635, John Bridge sold the seventy five acres on the west side of the Charles River to Richard Girling, mariner [CaBOP 15].

In the Cambridge land inventory on 6 January 1642/3, John Bridge held one dwelling house and barn with twelve acres, five acres in the west end, one dwelling house in town with half a rood of land, fifteen acres in the neck, fifteen acres in Rock meadow, ten acres more in Rock meadow, and seven and a half acres in Alewife meadow [CaBOP 85-86].

On 20 October 1635, John Bridge sold to Mr. Roger Harlackinden, and Joseph and George Cooke, "my dwelling house in Newtowne standing by the creek" with the land and marsh belonging to it [CaBOP 41].

On 14 August 1637, John Bridge was granted liberty to set the porch of his barn six feet into the highway [CaTR 1:29].

By 29 September 1639, John Bridge had bought one house and eight acres in the west field from John Barnard, and one house and four acres in the west field from Thomas Judd [CaBOP 55]. Bridge soon sold Judd's old land and house to Thomas White [CaBOP 60].

In 1639, John Bridge purchased five acres of marsh and upland from Nicholas Danford, bought half an acre of upland from Carey Latham, bought one house in town from Sebastian Brigham and was granted fifteen acres of upland in the neck [CaBOP 65].

On 1 September 1643, John Bridge bought six and a half acres in the neck from Richard Champnyes [CaBOP 117]. On 1 May 1644, Richard Jackson bought six acres in Alewife meadow from John Bridge [CaBOP 116]. On 20 July 1645, John Bridge bought two acres in the west field from Abraham Morrill [CaBOP 118].

On 15 January 1645/6, John Bridge was granted twenty acres of plow land "near unto the place where his stacks of hay did stand, in lieu of a lot of unbroken land in the neck" [CaBOP 131]. On 18 October 1647, Thomas Danforth purchased seven acres of land in the neck from John Bridge [CaBOP 134]. On 28 December 1653, John Bridge received a grant of three and a half acres in the woodlots [CaTR 1:64]. On 8 February 1649/50, John Bridge of Cambridge, yeoman, sold to John Wincoll of Watertown fifteen acres in Rocky Meadow [MLR 1:93].

In 1662 in the Strawberry Hill division, "Deacon Bridge" received six acres [CaBOP 144]. In the division of 27 February 1664/5, John Bridge received lot number 93 containing thirty-five acres and four commons [CaBOP 147].

In his undated will, proved in 1665, John Bridge bequeathed to "my wife her covenant made with her before marriage, provided that she take the house that was John Bettes with six acres of land upon Strabery Hill"; to "my grandchild Dorkis Bridge" household goods "that was her mother's ... according to her mother's inventory" and "four pounds which sister

Bettes gave to her"; to "Mathew Bridge all my lands & houses" for the term of his life and at his decease, to be disposed of for the use of "the children that now are" and to the eldest a double portion; to "my son Mathew all my goods & cattle & household stuff whatsoever"; Mathew Bridge executor [MPR Case #2580].

The inventory of Deacon John Bridges, taken 11 April 1665, totalled £372 3s. 6d., of which £198 was real estate: "a house & barn with [worn] orchard, wood lots & town priviledges," £60; "15 acres of land," £60; "12 acres of marsh," £36; "a division of land on the South side of the river," £6; "6 acres of land on the south side of the river," £6; and "a dwelling house in the town," £30 [MPR Case #2580].

BIRTH: By about 1593 based on estimated date of marriage.
DEATH: Cambridge 15 April 1665.
MARRIAGE: (1) By about 1618 _____ _____. She was living 1 May 1654, when she acknowledged a deed, "this deed acknowledged by John Bridge & his wife," but her name was not used and her signature not required [MLR 1:93].

(2) (marriage contract) 29 November 1658 [MLR 2:77] Elizabeth ____, widow of Roger Bancroft and Martin Saunders. She married (4) Reading 29 July 1673 Edward Taylor and died there 22 January 1686[/7?]. On 29 November 1658, "Jno. Bridge of Cambridge ... yeoman" and "John Stedman of Cambridge aforesaid, feoffee in trust in the behalf of Elizabeth Sanders the relict widow of Martin Sanders lately deceased at Brantrey," entered into a marriage contract, whereby John Bridge promised that if Elizabeth died first, she had the right to make a last will and testament in which she could dispose of an amount "not exceeding the full value of sixty pounds, whereof thirty pounds to be of the choicest of that household stuff she the said Elizabeth brings with her, the other thirty pounds to be in corn & cattle," but if John were to die first, his heirs and executors were to "deliver unto the said Elizabeth in household stuff which she now bringeth with her to the said Jno. Bridge forty pounds (inevitable loss by fire excepted) ... and also pay or cause to be paid unto the said Elizabeth Sanders or her assigns thirty pounds in corn or cattle ... and shall also duly & truly & faithfully pay or cause to be paid unto the said Elizabeth or her assigns annually during the term of her widowhood & until she shall again be married unto another husband, the full & just sum of five pounds per annum"; neither John Bridge nor his heirs will "claim any interest in that annuity payable to the said Elizabeth during her life out of the estate of Martin Sanders her said former husband

deceased"; John Bridge posts as bond "his house in Cambridge wherein he now dwells & appurtenances thereof, & ten acres of land thereunto belonging, next adjoining to the said house"; on 23 December 1685, "Timothy Pratt of Boston, tailor, attorney & by order of Edw[ard] Taylor & Elizabeth his wife, the relict of John Bridge Senior withinnamed," receipted to "Matthew Bridge, administrator to the estate of said John Bridge," for "five pounds in leather ... in full satisfaction for the whole of the payment due by virtue of the marriage covenant within expressed" [MLR 2:77-79].

CHILDREN:

With first wife

i   MATTHEW, b. say 1618; m. by 1645 Anne Danforth, daughter of Nicholas Danforth (eldest known child b. Cambridge 15 June 1645; the January 1658/9 list of Cambridge church members included "Anne Bridge the wife of Matthew Bridge daughter also of Mr. Nicholas Danforth" [CaChR 9]).

ii   THOMAS, b. say 1620; m. by 1648 Dorcas _____ (birth of daughter Dorcas at Cambridge 16 February 1648/9; church membership of mother [CaChR 5]).

ASSOCIATIONS: Savage says perhaps brother of Edmund of Roxbury, but we see no support for this.

"Sister Betts," named in John's will, was Elizabeth Betts, wife of Goodman John Betts of Cambridge. She left a will, written 13 December 1663 and proved 14 March 1663/4, which named over fifty persons [MPR Case #1659]. John Bridges was a major legatee of this will, receiving her house and land in return for maintaining it during her lifetime and fulfilling many small legacies at her death. Tempting as it might be to assume that "Sister Betts" had a blood relationship to John Bridges, it is much more likely that the childless Elizabeth was naming her many well-loved friends, neighbors and fellow church members in this will.

Probably in his capacity as deacon, John Bridge had "under his care also" Joseph Lampson, the son of Barnabas Lampson, deceased" [CaChR 4].

COMMENTS: On 6 June 1637, the General Court bound Mathew Bridge and John Bridge "his father" for Mathew's appearance at the next court to answer the charge of causing the "untimely death of John Abbot" [MBCR 1:198]. When Mathew appeared in court on 19 September 1637, no evidence was brought against him, and "he was quit by proclamation" [MBCR 1:203].

Savage includes in this family a daughter Sarah, born at Cambridge on 16 February 1648/9. No such birth appears in Cambridge records. The date given by Savage is the same as that for the birth of Dorcas, eldest child of Thomas, son of the immigrant, suggesting that Savage's notes on this family were in error.

The county court ordered that John Bridge make a bond for £38 to cover his responsibility for money used for the two children of the late John Champney [MLR 1:19]. On 25 March 1657, Richard Champney and John Bridge sold the land belonging to the late John Champney to Mathew Bridge [MLR 2:152-54].

THOMAS BRIGDEN

ORIGIN: Faversham, Kent
MIGRATION: 1635 on the *Hercules*
FIRST RESIDENCE: Charlestown

OCCUPATION: Cooper.
CHURCH MEMBERSHIP: On 5 December 1635, "Thomas Bridgen with Tomazin his wife" were admitted to Charlestown church [ChCR 8].
FREEMAN: 3 March 1635/6 (as "Tho[mas] Brigden," second in a sequence of three Charlestown men) [MBCR 1:371].
EDUCATION: His inventory included "2 Bibles & sundry other old books" valued at £1 5s. Signed his will, but made his mark to the codicil.
ESTATE: On 22 June 1635, "Goodman Brigden was granted to buy Goodman Converse his old house & 2 acres of ground" [ChTR 14].

In 1635 "Goodman Brigden" had one unit of hayground, which was increased to two [ChTr 19, 20]. In 1637 and on 30 December 1638 he had 2½ cow commons [ChTR 32, 42]. In the 23 April 1638 Mystic Side allotments, Thomas Brigden had parcels of fifteen, twenty-five and zero acres [ChTR 37].

In the Charlestown land inventory of 1638, Thomas Brigden held eleven parcels: a dwelling house and garden plot; another garden plot; half an acre in the south field; three acres of meadow; two acres in the line field; two acres more in the line field; two and a half "milch cow commons"; two acres of meadow at Mistick Marshes; fifteen acres of woodland;

twenty-five acres in "West Rockfeilde"; and half an acre of meadow at Mistick Meadow [ChBOP 61]. In the 3 February 1656/7 confirmation of possessions in the stinted pasture, Thomas Bridgen, Senior, had two and a half commons [ChBOP 75]. In the woodlots laid out in March 1657/8, Thomas Brigden, Senior, held eighteen acres and three commons [ChBOP 77].

On 21 January 1647/8, Thomas Bridgen sold to Samuel Richison of Woburn twenty-five acres in Woburn [ChBOP 99].

On 28 April 1651, Richard Russell of Charlestown, inhabitant, sold to Thomas Brigden of Charlestown "a garden plot of ground lying in Charlestowne south of the mill hill ... taking in a slip of ground over against the warehouse eastward of it" [MLR 2:117]. On 28 January 1666[/7], "Thomas Brigdane Senior of Charlestowne ... planter, with the assent and consent of Tamsin my wife," sold to Samuel Peirce of Malden, planter, " a certain parcel of land, containing two acres and three-quarters" on Mystic Side in Charlestown; Thomas signed the deed and Thomasine made her mark [MLR 3:185].

In his will, dated 1 May [or June] 1665 and proved 9 July 1669, "Thomas Brigdine Senior of Charlestowne" bequeathed to "my beloved wife Tamsine Brigdine my whole estate (after my decease) during the time that she doth remain a widow, that is to say my now dwelling house with all the out housing & wharfing thereunto belonging with all the land thereunto adjoining, viz: the little orchard and the great orchard with my piece of land fenced in next Thomas Lines, with my hayground lying on the creek & my lot in the little field with my woodlot on Mystic Side with two and an half cow commons & three acres land lying near the north spring with all my moveables & household stuff," but if she remarries "then only to enjoy and possess the house & the little orchard with one cow common only"; to "my son Thomas Brigdine after the widowhood of my now wife his mother all that land which by this my will she may be deprived of by marrying a second husband, that is to say the great orchard, the piece of land next Tho[mas] Lynes, the hayground in the creek, my lot in the little field, my woodlot on Mystic Side & three acres land lying by the north spring with one & half cow commons ... and at the time of his mother's decease I give unto him my son Thomas Brigdine the dwelling house, wharfing & outhousing and the cow common and all such moveables as are left undisposed of by his mother"; to "my daughter Marie now wife unto Henry Kemball," 40s., also to "her three children Zacharie, Marie & Sarah," 20s. apiece, and also to "Sarah Brigdine, daughter of Thomas Brigdine," 40s.; to "my grandchild Thomas Brigdine the son of Thomas Brigdine ... part of that land which abovesaid is given unto his father"; to "my grandchild Zacharie Brigdine ... the great orchard behind Thomas Jener's house, with that three acres of upland ground on Mystic Side and that one cow's common formerly given to him," the land to be enjoyed by "his father my son Thomas Brigden" until Zachary is 21, but if Zachary dies before age 21, then the land is to go to "John Brigden son of Thomas Brigden," and if John dies before age 21, then the land is to go to "Michael Brigden my grandchild"; "beloved wife Thomazin Brigden" to be sole executrix; "my loving brethren and friend Richard Kettle & John Cutler" to be overseers [MPR 3:87-89].

In a codicil dated 16 June 1668, Thomas Brigden Senior bequeathed to "Henry Kemble's wife Mary," £10 (instead of the 40s. given to her earlier); to "Henry Kemble, the son of Henry Kemble, at the time of the date of my will then unborn," 20s.; redistributed land granted to Thomas, Zachary, John and Michael, sons of his son Thomas; and to "Sarah Brigden, daughter of Thomas Brigden," 20s. additional [MPR 3:89-90].

The inventory of "the estate of Thomas Brigden Senior," taken 1 July 1668, totalled £244, of which £181 was real estate: "the dwelling house & orchard, ground behind it with the barn, & wharfing before it," £80; "the great orchard behind Mr. Jenner's house," £30; "the haylot abutting on Mr. Haugh's farm, with the hayground in the little field," £35; "three acres of upland on Mystic Side," £10; "the woodlot on Mystic Side," £2; "one acre of land at Cold Harbor," £12; and "two cow commons & a half," £12 [MPR 3:90-92].

BIRTH: By about 1604 based on estimated date of marriage.
DEATH: Charlestown 20 June 1668 [ChVR 1:57].
MARRIAGE: By about 1629 Thomasine _____ (assuming she was the mother of all his children). "Tamsine Brigdine, widow of Tho. Brigdine [Senir.], d. in Boston & buried in Charlstown, Mar. 12, 1669" [ChVR 1:71].
CHILDREN:
i THOMAS, b. about 1629 (deposed 22 June 1653 aged "twenty-four years" [MCF Folio #7]); m. by 1655 Mildred Carthrick (eldest known child b. Charlestown 3 January 1655[/6] [ChVR 1:15]), daughter of MICHAEL CARTHRICK of Ipswich.
ii MARY, b. say 1632; m. by about 1660 Henry Kemble (their daughter and eldest known child Sarah (Kemble) Bass d. Boston "April 26, 1746, ae. 86" [Wyman 66]).

iii ZACHARY, bp. Charlestown 2 August 1639 [ChChR 48]; Harvard College 1657 [Sibley 1:494-95]; d. Stonington 24 April 1662, apparently unmarried [Minor Diary 50].

COMMENTS: "Tho[ma]s Bridgen of the same town husbandman & [blank] his wife [and] two children" presented certificates from "John Phillips, minister of Faversham, John Knowler, mayor, and W[illia]m Thurston, jurat.," dated 5 March 1634/5, and enrolled at Sandwich for passage to New England on the *Hercules* [NEHGR 75:221].

JOHN BRIGGS

On 13 July 1635 "Jo[hn] Briggs," aged 20, was enrolled at London as a passenger for New England on the *Blessing* [Hotten 108].

COMMENTS: The entry immediately before this is for THOMAS BIGGS; in both cases the names as published have been read correctly from the original port book, but it may be that the clerk at London erred, and these are two brothers, either Biggs or Briggs.

Savage claims that this John Briggs was first of Lynn and then of Sandwich, where he died leaving widow Katherine and children Samuel and Sarah. Pope has a similar entry, except that he has Briggs first in Watertown rather than Lynn.

The Watertown claim may be disposed of the most easily. On 26 June 1637, "John Brigs" was granted one acre in the Remote Meadows at Watertown [WaBOP 10]. This is the only occurrence of the name in the early Watertown records, and close examination of other Watertown land grants shows a number of parcels allocated to a John Grigs, and the most likely explanation is that the Remote Meadows lot was actually intended for Grigs, and there was no John Briggs of early Watertown.

There is no record for a John Briggs in Lynn in the 1630s, and the claim by Savage is just another example of the mistaken assumption that all the early settlers of Sandwich had first resided in Lynn.

The records for John Briggs of Sandwich cover only the years 1639, 1640 and 1641 [PCR 1:149, 2:18, 8:184; MD 3:224-25, citing PCPR 1:39]. The passenger of 1635 would be twenty-six years old in 1641, and he could well have married and had two children in the six years after arrival; but there are reasons for suspecting that the two men were not the same.

First, as noted above, we are not even certain if the passenger entry was intended for Biggs or Briggs. Second, the inventory for John Briggs of Sandwich has a large collection of woodworking tools and an entry for "work done about a chest," suggesting that he was an accomplished joiner [MD 3:224-25]. The passenger of 1635 would seem to be too young to have served a full joiner's apprenticeship prior to marrying and having two children by 1641. We do not, therefore, believe that John Briggs of Sandwich was the passenger of 1635.

THOMAS BRIGHAM

ORIGIN: Unknown
MIGRATION: 1635 on *Susan & Ellen*
FIRST RESIDENCE: Cambridge

CHURCH MEMBERSHIP: Admission to Cambridge church prior to 18 April 1637 implied by freemanship.
FREEMAN: 18 April 1637 [MBCR 1:373].
EDUCATION: He made his mark to his will and to town documents [CaBOP 154]. His inventory included "a parcel of old [books] with one Bible and a great bible" valued at £1 [MPR 1:10-17].
OFFICES: Cambridge selectman, 1640, 1647 [CaTR 41, 43, 70]. Constable, October 1639, 8 November 1642 [CaTR 36, 46].
ESTATE: In the Cambridge land inventory on 1 May 1635, Thomas Brigham held one house with three and a half acres of land [CaBOP 64, 100]. In 1645 Thomas Brigham held one acre on the west side of Menotime [CaBOP 127]. In 1645, Thomas Brigham received the first numbered lot at Menotime containing ten acres [CaTR 67]. In 1646, Thomas Brigham received 8 acres in the ox pasture [CaTR 65]. On 11 October 1647, Thomas Brigham was charged 3d. per head, for a total of 7s. 8d., being abated one-third part of what he owed [CaTR 63]. On 17 May 1648, Thomas Brigham purchased ten acres of land in Fresh Pond meadow from William Hamlett [CaBOP 134]. In 1648, Thomas Brigham received seventy two [CaBOP 138]. On 9 June 1652, Thomas Brigham received 180 acres in the Shawshine division [CaTR 98].

In his will, dated 7 October 1653 and proved 3 October 1654, Thomas Brigham of Cambridge, "weak in body," bequeathed to "my wife" one-third part of the estate; to "my eldest son Thomas" one-third part of the remainder; residue to be equally divided between "my other four children, John, Mary, Hannah & Samuel"; "my wife" to have use of the whole estate during her widowhood for the bringing up of the children, should she remarry, their bringing up to be at the discretion of the overseers; "my wife" executrix; "my loving brethren Thomas Danforth, John Cooper, Thomas Fox, John Hastings & William Towne" overseers [MPR Case #2702].

An inventory of the estate of Thomas Brigham, taken 10 February 1653/4, was untotalled; the real estate amounted to £208 10s.: "the dwelling house & barn with 4 acres of land adjoining," £70; "the lot bought of goodman Doggett in Watertown," £40; "the upland & meadow in the hither end of Watertown," £60; "10 acres upon Rocky meadow," £15; "9 acres salt marsh," £13 10s.; and "a small farm at Charlestown line," £10 [MPR 1:10-17]. Two servants, "Daniell Mikenna, a scotchman," and "Anne Ketch 6 years to serve" were also valued in the estate, as were "a pair of horseman pistols" valued at £1 10s. [MPR Case #2702].

On 21 March 1656, twenty acres of land in Watertown which had been the property of Thomas Brigham late of Cambridge, were sold by Edmund Rice and Mercy Brigham, now his wife [MLR 7:447; see also MLR 10:654, 656].

BIRTH: About 1603 (aged 32 in 1635 [Hotten 62]), son of John and Constance (Watson) Brigham of Holme-on-Spalding-Moor, Lancashire [Brigham Gen 2:23-24].
DEATH: Cambridge 8 December 1653.
MARRIAGE: By about 1641 Mercy _____. She married (2) Sudbury 1 March 1655/6 Edmund Rice (with whom she had two children [Stevens-Miller Anc 2:130-31]). He was buried at Sudbury May 1663 (recorded Marlborough). She married (3) Marlborough [blank] October or November 1664 William Hunt. He was buried Marlborough October 1667. She died Marlborough 22 December 1693.
CHILDREN:
    i   THOMAS, b. about 1641 (d. Marlborough 25 November 1717, aged 76 years); m. (1) Marlborough 27 December 1665 Mary Rice; m. (2) Marlborough 30 July 1695 Susannah (Shattuck) (Morse) Fay (Joseph Morse and Susanna Shattuck m. Watertown 12 April 1661 [WaVR 23]; John Fay and Susanna Moss m. Watertown 5 July 1678 [WaVR 44]; Susanna, wife of Thomas Brigham, d. Marlborough 16 March 1716, aged 74).

ii JOHN, b. Cambridge 9 March 1644/5; m. (1) by 1673 Sarah Davis (eldest child b. Marlborough 27 March 1673/4; in his will of 12 March 1675/6, Thomas King made a bequest to "my son John Brigham," who must have been his stepson-in-law, married to the daughter of his second wife, Bridget (Loker) (Davis) King [Stevens-Miller Anc 1:82-85]); m. (2) after 1698 Deborah (Haynes) Brown [Brigham Gen 2:34 (evidence not shown)]; m. (3) Sudbury 22 May 1717 Sarah Bowker.

iii MARY, b. say 1649; m. by 1669 John Fay (eldest known child b. Marlborough 30 November 1669) [Brigham Gen 1:57-58].

iv HANNAH, b. Cambridge 9 March 1650/1; m. (1) by 1671 Gershom Eames (eldest child b. Marlborough 3 February 1671/2); m. (2) Marlborough 4 August 1679 William Ward [the marriage record calls her "Hannah Ward"].

v SAMUEL, b. Cambridge 12 January 1653/4; m. Marlborough [blank] [blank] Elizabeth How.

ASSOCIATIONS: Thomas Brigham was first cousin of Constance (Brigham) Crosby, widow of Robert Crosby, who came to New England about 1640, and of Anne (Brigham) Crosby, wife of SIMON CROSBY, who came to New England in 1635 [Brigham Gen 2:26].

COMMENTS: On 18 April 1635, "Tho[mas] Briggham," aged 32, was enrolled at London as a passenger for New England on the *Susan & Ellen* [Hotten 62].

On 8 June 1646, Thomas Brigham was found delinquent in a breach of the order about ringing his hogs. He was cited for "his wife's rescuing of two hogs from the impounder" who should have driven them to the pound, and several other occasions, and was fined 4s. [CaTR 53-54].

On 8 February 1648/9, Thomas Brigham was granted liberty to fell timber on the common to repair his house and fences [CaTR 79].

In February 1652/3, with Richard Jackson, Thomas Brigham sought the counsel of an arbitrator in the matter of a fence on a neck of land, in difference against Mr. Joseph Cooke, Edward Goffe and Thomas Danforth [CaTR 156].

Regarding the tradition that Thomas's wife, Mercy, was Mercy Hurd, Winifred Lovering Holman remarked that the "names of Hurd and Hunt could be easily confused and without further evidence I do not accept that her maiden name was Hurd" [Stevens-Miller Anc 2:109-31, especially 115]. We concur.

BIBLIOGRAPHIC NOTE: In 1907 W.I. Tyler Brigham and Emma E. Brigham compiled *The History of the Brigham Family: A Record of Several Thousand Descendants of Thomas Brigham The Emigrant, 1603-1653* [New York 1907] (cited above as Brigham Gen 1), a comprehensive account of the family. In 1927 Emma Elisabeth Brigham compiled *The History of the Brigham Family, Second Volume* [Rutland, Vermont, 1927], which included "The English Origin of Thomas Brigham the Emigrant, 1603-1635" by J. Gardner Bartlett (cited above as Brigham Gen 2).

THOMAS BRIGHTON

On 19 September 1635 "Tho[mas] Brighton," aged 31, was enrolled at London as a passenger for New England on the *Truelove* [Hotten 132].

COMMENTS: There is no evidence that this man came to New England. Pope says "see Bright and Broughton" [Pope 69]. Thomas Bright appears in a few records in Watertown in 1640, and there is nothing to connect him with the 1635 immigrant. Thomas Broughton of Boston gave his age as 44 in 1658, which would make him ten years younger than Thomas Brighton.

RICHARD BROCK

On 27 April 1635, "Richard Brocke," a carpenter, aged 31, was enrolled at London, with a "certificate from the minister at Westminster," as a passenger for New England on the *Elizabeth & Ann* [Hotten 70].

COMMENTS: Savage states that this immigrant resided in Watertown and died "24 Oct. 1673 or 4" [Savage 1:257]. Early Watertown records contain no records for a Richard Brock, but "Richard Beech" died there on 24 October 1674 [WaVR 38]; this item must be the basis for Savage's erroneous entry. No New England record has been found for the 1635 passenger.

DANIEL BRODLEY

On 8 April 1635, "Daniell Brodley," tanner, aged 20, was enrolled at London as a passenger for New England on the *Elizabeth*, with a certificate of conformity from the parish of St Alphage Cripplegate, London [Hotten 53].

COMMENTS: Savage, Pope and other writers have stated that this man was the same as the Daniel Bradley who appeared in Ipswich in the 1640s, a decade after the sailing of the *Elizabeth*. The name on the passenger list is definitely "Brodley" and not "Bradley," as confirmed by examination of the original record. There is no reason to connect the Ipswich man with the 1635 record, and there is nothing to show that the 1635 passenger arrived in New England.

RICHARD BROOKE

On 18 April 1635, "Richard Brooke," aged 24, was enrolled at London as a passenger for New England on the *Susan & Ellen*, and on 9 May 1635, he was enrolled again on the same ship [Hotten 62, 77]. (In both of these entries, the following name was "Tho[mas] Brooke.")

COMMENTS: Savage says that "RICHARD, Lynn, came in the Susan and Ellen, 1635, aged 24, removed to Easthampton, L.I., where he was of the first settlers 1650" [Savage 1:261]. Pope says "Richard, ae. 24, came in the Susan and Ellen, April, 1635. Proprietor at Lynn in 1638; agreed to pay to Francis Godsome 9 (6) 1639 [Lechford]. May be the same as Richard, gunsmith, Boston ..." [Pope 71]. Torrey's entry for Richard Brooks indicates Lynn, Southampton and Easthampton as his sequence of residences.

There was a Richard Brooks who resided in Lynn soon after 1635. In the 1638 distribution of land in Lynn, Richard Brooks received ten acres [EQC 2:270]. In August of 1639, "Rich[ard] Brooks of Lynn" was to pay 40s. to John Fuller of Lynn [Lechford 153].

If we then found records of a Richard Brooke in Southampton in the 1640s, followed by the appearance of the same name in Easthampton in the 1650s, we would have a standard sequence of migration, as many families moved from Lynn to Southampton in the early 1640s, and a number of the early settlers of Easthampton had earlier resided in Southampton. But Richard Brooke does not appear in the records of Southampton in its early decades, and so there is no particular reason to believe that the 1635 passenger was the man of the same name who much later appeared in Easthampton.

There is even less reason to connect the 1635 passenger with the Richard Brooke of Boston. The 1635 passenger was probably the Lynn resident of 1638 and 1639, but nothing can be confidently stated about his later history.

ROBERT BROOKE

On 14 March 1634/5, "Rob[er]t Brooke of Maidstone in Kent, mercer, & Anne his wife," along with children "Tho[ma]s Brooke, Sam[ue]l Brooke, Elys Brook, Dorothie Brooke, Abra[ham] Gallant [and] James Gallant," were certified by the mayor and ministers of Maidstone as passengers for New England on the *Hercules* of Sandwich [NEHGR 75:217-18].

COMMENTS: Eben Putnam's lengthy annotation of this entry presents a number of marriages for men named Robert Brooke in Maidstone. He concludes that there "seems to be no proof that he remained in New England" [NEHGR 75:224], and in fact he may never have left England.

Savage says this passenger is perhaps the later resident of New London [Savage 1:261-62] and Pope says he resided at Marblehead, where he had a grant of land in 1657 [Pope 71]. These records are all fifteen years or more after the sailing of the *Hercules* and there is no reason to believe that either was the passenger of 1635.

THOMAS BROOKE

On 18 April 1635, "Tho[mas] Brooke," aged 18, was enrolled at London as a passenger for New England on the *Susan & Ellen*, and, on 9 May 1635, he was again enrolled on the same ship, this time giving his age as 20 [Hotten 62, 77]. (In both of these entries, the succeeding name was "Richard Brooke.")

COMMENTS: Savage suggests that this passenger may have been the man of that name who appeared in New London in 1659 and then moved on to Haddam [Savage 1:262], but the twenty-five year gap is unexplained, and this suggestion seems very unlikely.

Pope has two entries for the name Thomas Brooke, one stating that the passenger of 1635 was the man who resided briefly in Watertown and then in Concord, and the other that Thomas was "before Salem court in 1636; died at sea before 1639 [Lechford]" [Pope 71].

As John Brooks Threlfall demonstrated in 1977, Thomas Brooks of Watertown and Concord had children by the late 1620s, and so "could hardly have been" the passenger of 1635 [TAG 53:94].

At a court held at Salem on 27 September 1636, "Thomas Brooke [was] fined 10s. 'for being overseen in drink'; fine paid by his master, who is to be satisfied by Brooke working out of his time" [EQC 1:3]. This record very likely does pertain to the immigrant of 1635, especially as a fine levied in Salem court could well be for a resident of Lynn, and if this Thomas were a resident of Lynn, then this would be consistent with the evidence that Richard Brooke, also a passenger of 1635, was also a resident of Lynn.

Pope's connection of this Salem court record with the death of a Thomas Brooke in or before 1639 is unlikely, however. A petition of John Long, undated but apparently made in late August or early September 1639, and pertaining to the affairs of Simon Whitcomb, includes a reference to "one Thomas Brooke who made his will nuncupative at sea & gave your petitioner all right in said land & premises & died" [Lechford 176]. Thomas Brooke who was a servant in Essex County in 1636 would hardly be in a position to make such a will less than three years later.

Nothing can be said about the history of the 1635 passenger beyond the court record of 1636.

GILBERT BROOKS

ORIGIN: Unknown
MIGRATION: 1635 on the *Blessing*
FIRST RESIDENCE: Scituate
REMOVES: Marshfield by 1643, Scituate by 1646, Rehoboth by 1662
FREEMAN: Plymouth Colony 1 June 1658 [PCR 3:137]. In Scituate section of 1658 Plymouth Colony list of freemen [PCR 8:199]. In

Rehoboth section of Plymouth Colony lists of freemen of 29 May 1670 and of early 1683/4 [PCR 5:278, 8:209].

EDUCATION: He signed his will and deeds by mark. His inventory included "books" valued at 6s.

OFFICES: Marshfield constable, 4 June 1645 [PCR 2:83]. Plymouth grand jury, 6 June 1654, 6 June 1660, 5 June 1666 [PCR 3:49, 188, 4:123]. Petit jury, 5 June 1666, 5 March 1667/8, 25 October 1668, 28 October 1684 [PCR 4:125, 7:143, 144, 150, 285]. Coroner's jury (as "Sergeant Gilbert Brookes"), 16 February 1655[/6] [PCR 3:92].

Rehoboth deputy to Plymouth General Court, 3 June 1679, 7 June 1681, 3 June 1684, 2 June 1685, [blank] June 1686, 3 June 1690 [PCR 6:10, 61, 128, 164, 186, 240]. Rehoboth selectman, 1 June 1680, 7 June 1681, 6 June 1682, 6 June 1683, 3 June 1684, 2 June 1685, [blank] June 1686, [blank] June 1689 [PCR 6:35, 59, 84, 108, 129, 167, 186, 187, 206]. Rehoboth delegate to Plymouth Colony Council of War, 2 April 1667 [PCR 4:145]. Rehoboth surveyor of highways, 5 June 1672, 7 June 1676 [PCR 5:93, 197]. Rehoboth constable, 3 June 1673 [PCR 5:115]. Committee to seat the meetinghouse, 10 December 1680 [Early Rehoboth 4:31, citing ReTR 2:32]. Committee to "lay out the country roads through the town of Rehoboth," 22 September 1684 [PCR 6:144].

In Marshfield section of 1643 Plymouth Colony list of men able to bear arms [PCR 8:196].

ESTATE: On 26 January 1649[/50?], Thomas Simmons of Scituate sold to "Gilbert Brookes of Scituate ... planter ... all that my dwelling house, barn, outhouses, garden, orchard & yards together with nine acres more or less of upland on which the said dwelling house & barn standeth ... in Scituate ... likewise ten acres more or less of upland lying & being in Scituate aforesaid on that hill commonly called Brushey Hill" [PCR 12:217-18].

Rehoboth taxpayer, 1671, 1674 [Early Rehoboth 1:16 (citing Rehoboth Rate Book 2:13-14), 39 (citing Rehoboth Rate Book 1:2)]. On 28 May 1672, "Gilbert Brookes" was credited with one share in Rehoboth North Purchase [Early Rehoboth 1:41, citing Rehoboth North Purchase Proprietors' Records 1:2-4]. On 26 January 1676/7, "Gilbert Brooke" was recorded as being owed £3 14s. expenditures relating to King Philip's War [Early Rehoboth 2:42, citing Rehoboth Rate Book 2:16].

On 20 March 1694/5, "Gilbert Brookes" of Rehoboth appointed "my well beloved friend and son-in-law Robert Crossman" of Taunton as his attorney to take possession of and sell Gilbert's land in Scituate, and, on

19 April 1695, Robert Crossman deeded the nine acres of upland to Joseph Otis of Scituate [PCR 12:218-20].

In his will, dated 6 June 1695 and probated 5 July 1695, "Gilbert Brook" of Rehoboth bequeathed to "my beloved wife Sarah my dwelling house, orchard & homelot" and some moveables "during the time of her widowhood and bearing my name," as well as some livestock and provisions for her current use; to "Benony Wiggins my grandson [blank] acres of land on the north side ... and a quarter part of my commons on the north side," with some moveables; to "Zachariah Carpenter that lives with me" 40s., some weapons and "an axe that was his father's"; to "my nine daughters an equal share of my estate after my decease only my daughter Rachel's share I give to my grandson Benony Wigen"; "my beloved son[s]-in-law Robert Crosman & William Manle" to be executors and "if either of my executors be taken off by death before he hath fulfilled the whole of his trust in my will what charge & trouble he hath been at shall go out of the estate to his surviving children or widow"; "my children shall not have whole shares till my wife do leave that which I bequeathed unto her"; to "my grandchild Bath[s]eba Walker," 20s.; to "my grandson Brooks Thresher," 20s.; and to "Zachariah Carpenter," a coverlet [BrPR 1:128-29].

The inventory of "Mr. Gilbert Brooks of the town of Rehoboth ... who deceased the thirteenth day of June 1695," taken 4 July 1695, was untotalled, with the real estate amounting to £84: "12 acres of land" £9; "homelot," £43; "7 acres," £3 10s.; "£50 commonage," £2 10s.; "one acre," £6; and "lands & rights on the north side," £20 [BrPR 1:129-30].

The account of "Robert Crosman and William Manley executors of the last will & testament of Mr. Gilbert Brooks who died the 30th day of June 1695" was presented on 15 July 1696 [BrPR 1:153]. At the same time, the executors presented an account of legacies that had been paid according to the will:

    to "the widow," £11 10s. 6d.;

    to "Zachariah Carpenter," £3 14s. 6d.;

    to "Bennoni Wigins," £2 5s.;

    to "Rebecca Haskins," 12s. "with other things not particularly mentioned and therefore no sum to them but all her due by will";

    "an account of what portions we have paid to the children:

        to Bathsheba Walker, £7 18s. 9½d.,

        to Bethiah Thresher with what received upon will, £7 18s. 9½d., to Sarah Lyon, £7 13s.,

to Elizabeth Stevenes' children, £5 9s. 4½d.,

and as to Rachel another daughter being at Long Island we have as yet no opportunity to pay her anything,

Mary Colebond as yet will not receive any portion but rather shows dislike of the will,

And as to the lands we have not yet opportunity to divide them, our mother, the widow, having the house & houselot during her widowhood, by will, the rest of the estate as it is circumstanced is in our hand to be further disposed of according to will" [BrPR 1:154].

BIRTH: About 1621 (aged 14 in 1635 [Hotten 93]).

DEATH: 13 June 1695 (from the inventory).

MARRIAGE: (1) By 1646 Elizabeth _____. She was buried at Rehoboth on 17 July 1687 [ReVR 804].

(2) Rehoboth 18 January 1687[/8] Sarah (Redway) Carpenter [ReVR 59], daughter of James Redway and widow of Samuel Carpenter [NEHGR 98:171-72; Early Rehoboth 1:130-32].

CHILDREN (i-viii baptized at Second Church of Scituate):

With first wife

i   ELIZABETH, bp. 21 June 1646 [NEHGR 57:83]; m. by 1663 Francis Stevens (eldest known child b. Rehoboth 15 March 1663 [ReVR 749]).

ii   SARAH, bp. 21 June 1646 [NEHGR 57:83]; m. (1) by 1668 Thomas Grant (eldest known child b. Rehoboth 2 April 1668 [ReVR 628]); m. (2) Rehoboth 5 December 1692 Samuel Lyon [ReVR 235].

iii   MARY, bp. 15 July 1649 [NEHGR 57:83]; m. Dedham 19 November 1669 Nathaniel Colborn [DeVR 11].

iv   RACHEL, bp. 7 July 1650 [NEHGR 57:83]; m. by 1672 James Wiggin ("Benoni Wigins" b. Rehoboth 16 May 1672 [ReVR 779]).

v   PHEBE, bp. 5 September 1652 [NEHGR 57:84]; m. by 1686 William Manley (eldest known child b. Boston 1 September 1686 [BVR 170]) [see Weymouth Hist 3:413-14].

vi   BATHSHEBA, bp. 8 April 1655 [NEHGR 57:85]; m. Taunton 23 December 1673 James Walker Jr.

vii   REBECCA, bp. 12 April 1657 [NEHGR 57:85]; m. Taunton 12
       May 1692 Samuel Haskins, as his third of four wives
       [TAG 28:253].

viii   HANNAH, bp. 2 October 1659 [NEHGR 57:86]; m. Taunton 21
       July 1679 Robert Crossman Jr.

ix   BETHIA, b. Rehoboth 29 April 1662 [ReVR 555]; m. Taunton 5
       December 1683 Samuel Thresher. (This marriage also
       appears in the Rehoboth records, with the bride's name
       given as "Burnice Brooks" and the date of the marriage as
       4 December [ReVR 59].)

ASSOCIATIONS: Almost certainly brother of WILLIAM BROOKS who
also sailed on the *Blessing*, and who appears immediately before Gilbert
on the 1643 list of men able to bear arms, at his admission to freemanship
in 1658, and on the 1658 list of freemen.

His early associations with WILLIAM VASSALL may indicate that
Gilbert Brooks was from Essex in England [NGSQ 74:111].

COMMENTS: "Gilbert Brooke," aged 14, was enrolled at London on 17
June 1635 as a passenger for New England on the *Blessing* [Hotten 93].
His entry followed that of "Will[ia]m Brooke," aged 20.

On 5 March 1638/9, "Gilbert Brookes, the servant of Mr. Will[ia]m
Vassell," was presented at Plymouth Court "for drinking inordinately at
John Emerson's house" [PCR 1:118]. (WILLIAM VASSALL was also a
passenger on the *Blessing* in 1635.)

Deane claimed that Gilbert Brooks "married Elizabeth, the daughter of
Gov. Edward Winslow" [Deane's Scituate 224]. Actually, EDWARD
WINSLOW's daughter Elizabeth married Robert Brooks [MD 1:238-40;
GMB 3:2025]. Deane also said that Gilbert Brooks had "sons Gilbert and
John, probably born in Marshfield" [Deane's Scituate 224-25], but no sons
of this immigrant are found in the records.

On 1 March 1658/9, "Gilbert Brookes" was granted 12s. by Plymouth
Court, apparently for assisting Humphrey Johnson in his role as
"attorney in the behalf of the country about Josepth Tilden's business"
[PCR 7:90].

In 1935 Raymon Meyers Tingley proposed an identification for the first
wife of Gilbert Brooks [Tingley-Meyers 58, 371]. This identification
derives from Tingley's most outrageous fabrication, and should be
consulted for its entertainment value only [GMB 3:1683].

WILLIAM BROOKS

ORIGIN: Unknown
MIGRATION: 1635 on the *Blessing*
FIRST RESIDENCE: Scituate
REMOVES: Marshfield by 1643, Scituate by 1657

OCCUPATION: Husbandman.
CHURCH MEMBERSHIP: He or his wife had become a member of the Second Church at Scituate by 14 September 1645 (even though they were residents of Marshfield at this time), when their first child was baptized.
FREEMAN: Oath of fidelity at Scituate in 1657 [PCR 8:180]. Admitted freeman of Plymouth Colony, 1 June 1658 [PCR 3:137]. In Scituate section of 1658 and 29 May 1670 Plymouth Colony lists of freemen [PCR 5:275, 8:199].
EDUCATION: Signed his will by mark. His inventory included "his apparel and books" valued at £6 6s. 6d.
OFFICES: Plymouth grand jury, 5 June 1644, 1 June 1675 [PCR 2:71, 5:166]. Plymouth petit jury, 1 June 1675 [PCR 5:168]. On 3 March 1645/6, "Will[ia]m Brookes, of the town of Marshfeild," was presented "for the breach of his oath, in disclosing of his fellows' counsel and his own, which he through weakness confesseth he did, and is released" [PCR 2:96]. Marshfield surveyor of highways, 2 June 1646, 6 June 1649 [PCR 2:102, 139]. Scituate constable, 5 June 1667 [PCR 4:148].

In Marshfield section of 1643 Plymouth Colony list of men able to bear arms [PCR 8:196].
ESTATE: On 2 April 1649, "William Brookes of Marshfield, husbandman," sold to John Bryant of Scituate, wheelwright, land which "the said William Brookes hath lately bought and purchased of William Randall of Scittuate, being part of two lots which the said William Randall did formerly buy and purchase of George Kenerick once of Scittuate" [PCLR 3:94].

Granted "a certain island of upland lying in the marsh on the northerly side of the creek commonly called and known by the name of Till's Creek" in Scituate, 31 May 1659 [ScitTR 1:253]. Granted five acres "in a swamp near the land called Spring Swamp," 1673 [ScitTR 1:331].

On 18 February 1666[/7], "William Brookes and Susannah wife of the said William of Scittuate" gave a receipt to Joseph Tilden, administrator of the estate of Mr. Timothy Hatherley for their share of Hatherley's estate [PCLR 4:94].

"Will[i]am Brookes" appears in an undated list recording two tax assessments at Scituate, once with a rate of 1s. 10d., and the second time with no assessment [PCR 7:130]. "William Brooks" had a proportional share of eight in a list of "allowed and approved inhabitants of the Town of Sittuate ... to whom division of land and a common privilege does appertain," apparently dated 1673 [ScitTR 1:326].

In his undated will, proved 6 March 1682/3, "William Brookes" of Scituate bequeathed to "my son Nathaniell Brooks half my upland and half my meadow land ... also half the upland which is on the island within the meadow" and "half the fruit of my orchard forever"; to "my son Thomas Brooks" "the other half of my land & meadow with the housing thereon," with instructions for providing for the testator during his life, but if Thomas die without issue, this land "to return to Nathaniell Brook ... and the said Nathaniell Brook shall pay ... to his six sisters twelve pounds forty shillings to each of them or their children"; "my wife Sussannah Brooks shall live in my house during her widowhood," with provision for her maintenance by Nathaniel and Thomas Brooks, and with a bequest of some moveables and of "all those things which she brought with her when she became my wife"; "my grandchild Beriah shall be at my wife's dispose"; to "my wife's youngest daughter Bathshebath Dunham forty shillings"; the residue of the estate "to be divided amongst my six daughters, only my grandchild Beriah, my daughter Hannah and my daughter Mary forty shillings apiece more than the rest"; "my eldest son Nathaniell Brooks" to be executor; "Cornet Robert Studson and Charles Stockbridge Sr." to be overseers [PCPR 4:2:21].

The inventory of the estate of William Brooks, taken 24 January 1682[/3], totalled £59 19s. 8d., to which were added some items not valued, among which was the only real estate listed: "1 tenement of one house & barn with 60 acres of upland & eight acres of marsh belonging to it" [PCPR 4:2:22].

On 14 March 1693/4, "Nathanell Brooks of Sittuate being true heir to William Brooks deceased having certain knowledge that my father William Brooks in the time of his life did really sell to John Wheston now deceased eight acres of land" confirmed that sale [ScitTR 1:378].

BIRTH: About 1615 (aged 20 in 1635 [Hotten 93]).
DEATH: After 7 July 1680 [PCR 6:47] and before 24 January 1682[/3] (date of inventory).
MARRIAGE: (1) By 1644 _____ _____; she died after 1659 and by 1665.

(2) By 1665 Susanna (Hanford) Whiston, daughter of Jeffrey and Eglin (Hatherly) (Downe) Hanford and widow of *JOHN WHISTON* [Stevens-Miller Anc 1:485-86; GMB 3:1975]; she was named in her husband's will on 6 March 1682/3.

CHILDREN (all baptized at Scituate Second Church):

With first wife

    i   HANNAH, b. say 1644, bp. 14 September 1645 [NEHGR 57:82]; living at the date of her father's will, presumably unmarried, as she is bequeathed more than her married sisters.

    ii   NATHANIEL, bp. 29 March 1646 [NEHGR 57:82]; m. Scituate 24 December 1678 Elizabeth Curtis.

    iii MARY, bp. 28 November 1647 [NEHGR 57:83]; living at the date of her father's will, presumably unmarried, as she is bequeathed more than her married sisters. (The Torrey entry for the younger Thomas Lapham of Scituate suggests that his wife might have been this Mary Brooks, but none of the sources listed by Torrey includes any evidence relating to this suggestion.)

    iv   SARAH, bp. 26 May 1650 [NEHGR 57:83]; probably married by the time of her father's will, and said to have married Joseph Studley, but evidence for this marriage has not been found.

    v   MIRIAM, bp. 6 June 1652 [NEHGR 57:84]; m. Scituate 4 April 1678 John Curtis.

    vi   DEBORAH, bp. 18 March 1654/5 [NEHGR 57:84]; probably married by the time of her father's will, and said to have married Robert Stetson, but evidence for this marriage has not been found. (Robert Stetson was not married in 1675-6, when he had an illegitimate child with Elizabeth Woodworth, daughter of *WALTER WOODWORTH* [GMB 3:2066].)

    vii THOMAS, bp. 28 June 1657 [NEHGR 57:85]; m. Scituate 6 June 1687 Hannah Bisby.

    viii JOANNA, bp. 16 October 1659 [NEHGR 57:86]; m. Marshfield 13 September 1687 John Bisby [PCR 8:89].

ASSOCIATIONS: Probably brother of GILBERT BROOKS, also a passenger on the *Blessing*. William's son Nathaniel named a son Gilbert, born at Scituate 9 November 1690.

COMMENTS: "W[illia]m Brooke," aged 20, was enrolled at London on 17 June 1635 as a passenger for New England on the *Blessing* [Hotten 93]. The next entry on this list is for Gilbert Brooks.

Pope claims that this William resided at Salem in 1639 [see STR 1:93], and that another William Brook resided at Marshfield and Scituate, but the continued co-residence of Gilbert and William in Marshfield and Scituate leads to the conclusion that the Salem resident was not the 1635 passenger.

Savage makes a curious error in saying that William Brook "m. wid. Susanna Dunham of Plymouth" [Savage 1:263], evidently deriving from a misreading of William's will [TAG 30:154].

On 3 March 1644[/5?], "Will[ia]m Brookes" acted as agent for Manasseh Kempton in the sale of land in Scituate; "Gilbert Brooke" was a witness [PCR 12:106]. On 7 July 1680, "Will[i]am Brookes" testified in Plymouth Court in a case involving Zachariah Damon and his mother [PCR 6:47].

ROGER BROOME

On 19 September 1635, "Roger Broome," aged 17, was enrolled as a passenger for New England on the *Truelove* [Hotten 132].

COMMENTS: There is no record for this man in New England.

JOAN BROOMER

On 18 April 1635, "Joan Broomer," aged 13, was enrolled as a passenger for New England on the *Susan & Ellen* [Hotten 62].

COMMENTS: There is no evidence that she arrived in New England.

MARY BROOMER

On 13 April 1635, "Marie Broomer," aged 10, was enrolled at London as a passenger for New England on the *Elizabeth & Ann* [Hotten 58].

COMMENTS: There is no evidence that she arrived in New England.

EDMUND BROWN

ORIGIN: Sawbridgeworth, Essex
MIGRATION: 1634
FIRST RESIDENCE: Boston
REMOVES: Surinam

OCCUPATION: Ship master, merchant [SJC Case #746].
CHURCH MEMBERSHIP: On 22 June 1635, Edmund Browne and Jared Bourne, both "servants to our brother Willyam Coulborne," were admitted to Boston Church [BChR 1:18].
FREEMAN: 6 May 1635 [MBCR 1:370].
EDUCATION: He made his mark to a document in 1662 [SJC Case #746]. His inventory included "a Bible, one Great Book and seven small books" valued with other things at £1 10s. [SPR Case #410].
ESTATE: In the Boston Book of Possessions in 1645, Edward Browne owned "one house and garden" [BBOP 38]. His neighbors included Nicholas Baxter and brother-in-law Mathew Innes. In the allotment authorized 14 December 1635 and executed 8 January 1637/8, Edward Browne was granted eight acres [BTR 1:22].

On 11 October 1666, administration of the estate of Edmond Browne was granted to his relict, Elizabeth, she saying he had died "without issue" and that "he gave all his estate to her to pay his debts and for her livelihood." She reported that he had estate in New England and in Old England [SPR Case #410].

On 28 January 1666/7, an inventory of the estate of "Eadmon Browne of Boston" was taken, totalling £216 3s., of which £114 15s. was real estate: "a dwelling house and orchard" £50; "a piece of ground lying next Nicolas Baxter" £10; "a piece of ground lying next the house and orchard of the said Baxter" £35; "eight acres of land at Mudiriver" £16; "two acres and a half of land at Long Island" £3 15s. [SPR Case #410].

BIRTH: Baptized Sawbridgeworth, Essex, 4 May 1600, son of Edmund and Mary (Cramphorne) Browne.
DEATH: "Edmond Browne departed this life in the country of Serrenam [Surinam] about Mihillmas [Michaelmas] last being in the year of our Lord 1665" [SPR Case #410].
MARRIAGE: Boston 14 February 1653/4 Elizabeth Oklye [BVR 1:43] (see *COMMENTS* below). An ambiguous statement in Suffolk Probate court

suggests that she may have died as early as 2 November 1666. If she was alive on 30 October 1669 when her land is mentioned [SLR 6:135], then she died between that date and 1 January 1672/3 when she is not mentioned in Edmund's nephew's deed [SLR 8:43-44].

CHILDREN:

　　i　MARY, b. Boston 15 December 1656 [BVR 55]; no further record, and apparently died soon.

　　ii　JOHN, b. Boston 9 October 1660 [BVR 73]; no further record and apparently died soon.

ASSOCIATIONS: Brother of *ABRAHAM BROWN* and *JOHN BROWN* of Watertown and of Anna (Browne) Ines, wife of *MATTHEW INES* of Boston [GMB 1:244-46, 255-57, 2:1057-59].

COMMENTS: We gather from church records that Edmund came by 1634, in the employment of William Colbron [BChR 1:18]. Following his period of service to Colbron, Edmond received the houselot covenanted to him and began business as a ship master.

In 1662, Browne shared a barrel of rum at his house in Boston with the other men holding an interest in the ketch *Hope*. The *Hope* sailed for Connecticut in March of 1662/3, but met such violent storms that they were forced into the Carribean, where they stopped at Nevis. Rather than return home, Edmond stayed the last few years of his life in the islands, eventually moving to Surinam, where he died [SJC Case #746].

When the *Hope* returned, the owners came to the wharf to claim their shares. While Mr. Ward's men were busy taking the anchor and the mast, "the wife of Mr. Edmond Browne came aboard when the main sail was cut from the yard, and said, 'half the ketch is mine,' and took away the compasses out of the cabin" [SJC Case #746].

Despite her clear affirmation in probate court that Edmond left no children, a month later, on 2 November 1666, we learned that "whereas Elizabeth the wife of Edmond Browne of Boston lately deceased hath left two children," the court "judged it meet to order and impower Mary the relict of the late Robert Bouchier, *alias* Garret, grandmother to the said children, and Benjamin Ward, shipwright, feoffees in trust" [SPR Case #410]. Edmund's inventory included "a child's coat" valued at 10s. and plenty of pewter dishes, supporting the idea that there were children in the family.

On 1 January 1672/3, Jonathan Browne, "cousin and next heir of Edmund Browne formerly of Boston ... deceased without issue of his body," supports the statement that Edmond had no children [SLR 8:43-

44]. He claimed the reversion of "a house lot in Boston ... formerly granted to ... uncle Edmund Browne, by the said town of Boston" [SLR 8:43-44].

Although Edmund's own mother was Mary, she would have been well over 100 years old by this date; therefore, Mary (_____) Bouchier *alias* Garret must have been mother of Edmund's wife. Furthermore, Elizabeth Oakley, when she married Edmund Browne, must have been a widow with two children of her own, and the two children born to Edmund and Elizabeth must have died soon.

Savage suggests that Edmond moved to Newport in 1639, but it is more likely that his presence there had something to do with shipping interests rather than settlement.

BIBLIOGRAPHIC NOTE: In 1996 Dean Crawford Smith and Melinde Lutz Sanborn published a detailed account of Edmund Brown and his connections [Kempton Anc 174-78].

GEORGE BROWN

ORIGIN: Unknown
MIGRATION: 1634 on the *Mary & John*
FIRST RESIDENCE: Newbury

OCCUPATION: Carpenter.
CHURCH MEMBERSHIP: Admission to Newbury church prior to 13 May 1640 implied by freemanship.
FREEMAN: 13 May 1640 [MBCR 1:377].
EDUCATION: His inventory included "a Bible" valued at 5s. He signed his will.
ESTATE: In his will, dated 26 May 1642 and proved 28 March 1643, George Browne bequeathed to "my beloved wife my house and land with all my household goods" and a cow; to "my brother Richard Browne my wearing clothes and tools"; to "Richard Littleale" 20s. out of the rent of the mill; to "my father and to my brother Michael" 20s. apiece paid out of the mill, "but if god by his providence bring them into this land" then they to have £6 apiece, or if only one comes, then "he shall receive twelve pounds and if afterward the other come then he shall repay to him six pounds"; to "all my brethren and sisters besides" 12d. out of the mill; to "Joseph

Browne son of my brother Richard Browne my share in the Mill [at] Salisbury with the land belonging to it" at age eighteen; "my brother Richard Browne" executor; "my two friends Richard Knight and Thomas Macye" overseers; "if my wife be with child, that then my former will shall be void" and then she to receive house, land and all the rest and to give it to "my child" when it come to eighteen years old; to "my wife the swine and my shirts except one and my bands except three and a hat and a pair of shoes," she to pay debts "which I owe to Richard Littleale and John Bishopp and to Henry Fay and to John Lowle and Mrs. Goodale and Mrs. Oliver"; to "my wife my Bible"; if "my father and my brother Michael come not, then my two nephews [*sic*] Margery and Josua shall have that which my father and brother should have" [ILR 1:5; EPR 1:22-23].

The inventory of the estate of George Browne of Newbury, taken 1 August 1642, totalled £52 6s. 10d., of which £32 was real estate: "a house and four acres of ground with an acre & half of corn on it," £12; and "his share in a mill at Salisbury," £20 [ILR 1:6; EPR 1:23].

BIRTH: By 1613 (adult when he took the oath of allegiance at Southampton in early 1634 [NEHGR 9:267]).

DEATH: After 26 May 1642 (date of will) and before 1 August 1642 (date of inventory). (Savage gives a death date of 1 April 1642 [Savage 1:266], but this is not found in the published Newbury vital records, and also contradicts the date of the will. Apparently Savage had a garbled date for the inventory, and took it for the death date.)

MARRIAGE: By 1642 _____ _____. (Although she is frequently mentioned in his will, he never called her by name. There is no marriage of a woman surnamed Browne in the Newbury records soon after August 1642 who might have been George's widow.)

CHILDREN: None recorded.

ASSOCIATIONS: George Brown was brother of RICHARD BROWN of Newbury.

COMMENTS: On 24 March 1633[/4], "George Browne" took the oath of supremacy and allegiance at Southampton, preparatory to taking passage to New England on the *Mary & John* [Drake's Founders 70].

George's will, in addition to referring to his brother Richard of Newbury, also makes mention of "my father and my brother Michael," if they come. As most of the passengers on the *Mary & John* were from Wiltshire and neighboring counties, this Brown family is probably from that area as well. In the parish register of Calne, Wiltshire, appear the baptisms of George Brown, son of William, in September 1611, and of Richard Brown, son of William, on 31 October 1613. These dates are consistent with what we know of the brothers who came to New England, but we have no reason beyond this for believing that these parish register entries pertain to the immigrants.

JAMES BROWN

On 5 April 1635, at Southampton, "James Browne" and "Lawrence Seager," described as "youths of Hampton of about 17 yeares old," were enrolled for passage to New England on the *James* of London [Drake 55].

COMMENTS: This James Brown was too young to be either the minister of Portsmouth or the freeman of 1637. There is no evidence that he actually arrived in New England.

JOHN BROWN

On 22 June 1635, "Jo[h]n Browne," aged 27, tailor, with a certificate of conformity from the minister of "Baddow in Essex," and with "his 3 servants, Tho[mas] Hart, 24, Mary Denny, 24, [and] Anne Leake, 19," was enrolled at London as a passenger for New England on the *Defence* [Hotten 91].

COMMENTS: Despite various suggestions in the secondary literature, and despite the clues of age, occupation and associated servants, it has not been possible to connect this John Brown with any one of the New England settlers of that name.

JOHN BROWN

ORIGIN: London
MIGRATION: 1635 on the *Elizabeth*
FIRST RESIDENCE: Plymouth
REMOVES: Taunton by 1643, Rehoboth by 1647
RETURN TRIPS: England 1656 (probably), and return to New England by 1660

OCCUPATION: Baker (in England). Magistrate.

CHURCH MEMBERSHIP: Morton speaks in general terms of John Brown's religious activities [Morton 171-72].

FREEMAN: 5 January 1635/6 [PCR 1:4]. In lists of 7 March 1636/7 (as "gen.") and of 1639 (as Assisant) of Plymouth Colony freemen [PCR 1:52, 8:173]. In Rehoboth section of 1658 list of Plymouth Colony freemen [PCR 8:201].

EDUCATION: His inventory included "a parcel of books" valued at £4 12s. His wife signed her will by mark. Her inventory included "a parcel of books" as one item in a group of items valued at £7 12s.

OFFICES: Plymouth Colony Assistant, 5 January 1635/6, 6 March 1637/8, 5 March 1638/9, 3 March 1639/40, 2 March 1640/1, 1 March 1641/2, 7 March 1642/3, 5 June 1644, 4 June 1645, 4 August 1646, 1 June 1647, 7 June 1648, 6 June 1649, 4 June 1650, 5 June 1651, 3 June 1652, 7 June 1653, 6 June 1654, 8 June 1655 [PCR 1:36, 79, 116, 140, 2:8, 33, 52, 71, 83, 107, 115, 123, 139, 153, 166, 3:7, 30, 48, 77]. Plymouth Council of War, 27 September 1642, 2 June 1646, 6 April 1653 [PCR 2:47, 100, 3:26]. Commissioner from Plymouth to the United Colonies, 5 June 1644, 4 June 1645, 2 June 1646, 1 June 1647, 7 June 1648, 6 June 1649, 4 June 1650, 5 June 1651, 7 June 1653, 1 August 1654, 8 June 1655 [PCR 2:71, 83, 100, 115, 123, 139, 153, 166, 3:30, 67, 77]. Committee "for the preparing of some present laws for redress of some present abuses, and for preventing of future," 4 June 1645 [PCR 2:85]. Committee "to let the trade at Kenebeck," 8 June 1649 [PCR 2:144].

One of four "viewer[s] of the haygrounds from the town of Plymouth to Island Creek," 20 March 1636/7 [PCR 1:55]. On 2 October 1637, "Mr. John Browne for Joanes River" was added to a committee "to agree upon an equal course for the division" of the "meadow grounds betwixt the Eele River and South River" [PCR 1:67]. With Myles Standish, laid out the bounds of Taunton, 19 June 1640 [PCR 2:99-100].

Plymouth petit jury, 2 January 1637/8 [PCR 1:74, 7:7]. On 2 October 1650, "Mr. Josepth Peck is ordered by the Court to administer the ordinance of marriage at Rehoboth, in case Mr. Browne can not be persuaded thereunto" [PCR 2:164].

Appointed to dispose of "a quantity of marsh lying on the west side of Sowames River" to the inhabitants of Rehoboth," 26 October 1647 [PCR 2:120].

Appointed with "Captain Willett" to "apprehend Henery Hobson, of Road Island, ... to answer for his derision of authority in counterfeiting the solemnizing of the marriage of Robert Whetcom & Mary Cudworth," 5 March 1660/1 [PCR 3:209].

"Mr. John Browne" was at the head of the Taunton section of the 1643 Plymouth Colony list of men able to bear arms [PCR 8:195].

ESTATE: Granted "a proportion of land, according to the same order of former divisions at Island Creek Pond," 1 March 1635/6 [PCR 1:38], but "finding the neighbors to think themselves prejudiced thereby," he was on 7 June 1636 permitted "to make choice of the like quantity in any other part undisposed of" [PCR 1:42], whereupon Brown "made choice of a parcel of land, part whereof was granted formerly to Mr. Tymothy Hatherley, the which the said Mr. Hatherley did relinquish," described as "all that parcel of land lying on the south side of Joanes River, ranging along the said river up to the great swamp called Joanes River Swamp ... and also that marsh ground laid forth to belong to the said parcel of lands ... together with the long marsh adjoining thereunto ... & also one parcel of fresh marsh lying at the head of Joanes River Swamp, containing about four acres," all of which the Court confirmed [PCR 1:123].

With "Mr. Reynor," granted hayground at "the upper end of Jones River, where John & Josias Winslow had the last year," 20 March 1636/7 [PCR 1:55].

On 8 October 1637, "Clement Briggs of Wessaguscus" exchanged land with "John Browne of Plymouth," Brown receiving "four acres of land of the upper end of that lot of land that appertaineth unto me the said Clement Briggs" and Briggs receiving "the like quantity of four acres of land out of the land of the said John Browne lying at the lower end and adjoining to the residue of the land of the aforesaid Clement Briggs at Joanes River" [PCR 12:22].

Granted "a parcel of marsh ground, containing about three or four acres, ... lying at the head of Jones River Swamp," 7 August 1638 [PCR 1:93].

On 15 July 1640, "Mr. John Browne" sold to "Mr. Will[ia]m Hanbury ... all that his messuage or dwelling house situate by Joanes River with all the houses, outhouses, barns & stables thereunto belonging and all that tract of upland and parcel of marsh meadow thereunto adjoining & also four acres of marsh meadow ... lying at the head of Joanes River Swamp" [PCR 12:60].

On 29 December 1645, "Mr. John Browne in a town meeting did promise & undertake to pay the said purchase" ("that land with twelve acres lying at Watchemoquit Cove & so much more land at Wanomoycet as should be thought worth the payment of the same"), upon which Brown was granted a portion of the land purchased [PCR 12:177-78].

On 26 October 1647, "for such pieces of marsh lying within the fence upon the neck of land which the Indians are possessed of, and do inhabit, which doth not belong unto the township of Rehoboth, Mr. Browne is allowed to make use of the same for himself, without molestation from the inhabitants of Rehoboth, until there be a plantation at Sowames, and then to require no further propriety therein" [PCR 2:120].

On 3 November 1653, "Thomas Willett of the town of Plymouth" sold to "Mr. John Browne of the town of Rehoboth ... gent." "all that his part and propriety of land which he lately bought of Experience Mitchell which did before the said sale belong unto him as purchaser at Sowamsett, Mattapoisett & places adjacent both upland and meadow"; on the same day, "John Browne abovementioned do assign, give and bequeath unto my two sons viz: John Browne and James Browne all my right, title and interest which I have bought of my son-in-law Capt. Thomas Willett lying at Sowamsett, Mattapoisett and places adjacent both upland and meadow" [MD 4:83-84, citing PCLR 2:1:85].

On 24 May 1654, "John Browne of Rehoboth" sold to "Peter Hunt of Rehoboth three score and twelve acres of land that is to say six acres on that neck called and known by the name of Manton's Neck and forty-four acres lying on Wachamacott Neck and twelve acres lying on the head of that cove called Wachamacott Cove and ten acres of marsh or meadow viz: eight of it lying near unto a place called Bowin's Bridge, the rest lying on New Meddow River or Palmer's River" [MD 108-9, citing PCLR 2:1:117]. On 12 July 1655, Thomas Prence of Eastham sold to "John Browne of Rehoboth ... all that tract of land called and known by the name of my half-share with other purchasers situate and being near unto the bounds of Rehoboth and Sowamsett" [MD 10:16, citing PCLR 2:1:159].

On 11 April 1655, "[w]hereas Cpt. Thomas Willitt having a tract of land bordering upon the land of Mr. John Browne at Wanamoysett and being minded to make improvement of the same and for the accommodation of him the said Thomas Willett with a convenient place for building and other necessary uses, ... John Browne do hereby give and grant unto the aforesaid Thomas Willett his heirs or assigns forever that tract of land from a little valley where part of the spring ariseth ranging north and south all along the spring brook which runneth into the salt water ... and joineth unto the other lands of the said Thomas Willett all which tract of land being by estimation twelve acres" [MD 13:230-31, citing PCLR 2:2:18].

On 23 November 1655, "I John Browne out of my especial goodwill have heretofore given to my cousin John Tisdall all that dwelling house which I bought of Goodman [blank] with some garden and a lot of land thereunto belonging containing about three acres ... and furthermore I do hereby declare that for diverse good causes and considerations me thereunto moving did bargain and sell that dwelling house which once myself lived in at Taunton with barn and outhousing and all the land thereunto belonging with all such lands as by any way appertaineth unto me the said John Browne, unto my aforesaid cousin John Tisdall and my cousin James Walker his brother-in-law"; "Mr. James Browne came into the court held at Plymouth the 27th day of October 1670 and did ratify and confirm the act and deed above written signed and sealed by Mr. John Browne his father deceased" [PCLR 3:181].

On 1 January 1660[/1?], "John Browne of Wanamoysett" deeded to "Thomas Willett of the same place fourscore acres of land situate and being near unto a place called Annawamscott and commonly called and known by the name of Mr. Prence his great lot"; on the same day, "Thomas Willett of Wanamoysett" deeded to "my father-in-law John Browne of the same place threescore and fifteen acres lying at Wanamoysett aforesaid" [MD 15:246-47, citing PCLR 2:2:60].

On 29 December 1661, "John Brown of Rehoboth ... do give and grant unto my friend Sampson Mason of Rehoboth and unto Zacariah Eedey and Caleb Eedey now resident in my house one hundred acres" of "a share or tract of land as it is now measured out to be one hundred and fifty acres of planting land besides meadow land and commoning appertaining thereunto proportionable to other shares of the like quantity lying in the Narragansett Bay betwixt Quidnisett and the trading house of Mr. Richard Smith commonly called and known by the name of Mr. Browne's share" [MD 17:242, citing PCLR 2:2:108].

In his will, dated 7 April 1662 and proved 3 October 1662, "John Browne of Rehoboth" bequeathed to "Mary my daughter the wife of Thomas Willett" 12d. per year for life "and it shall be in full of all filial portion which she or any in her behalf shall claim"; to "my grandchild Martha Saffin the wife of John Saffin" £20; to "John Browne my grandchild the house that his father died in with six acres of land adjoining to it ... [and] half the lot that Thomas Willett bought of Experience Mitchell for me, and I do give him seven hundred acres of land lying in the Narragansett Country, three-hundred and fifty of it lyeth in the Great Neck and the other three-hundred fifty is to be chosen where they think fit"; to "my grandchild Josepth Browne and Nathaniel each of them five-hundred acres of land lying in the Narragansett Country where my lot shall fall"; to "my grandchild Lydia Browne and Hannah each of them five-hundred acres of land in the Narragansett Country and their uncle James to dispose of it for them"; residue to "my wife and my son James Browne," they to be joint executors [MD 18:18, citing PCPR 2:2:79b]. The court ordered the following endorsement to be added to the will: "Lest anything mentioned in this will in reference to Mistress Mary Willett the wife of Captain Thomas Willett might be by any misconstrued to the prejudice of the said Mistress Willett, we think it meet to declare that out of the long experience of her dutiful and tender respect to her said father from time to time expressed there hath never appeared to us the least ground of any such thing to this present" [MD 18:19, citing PCPR 2:2:79b].

The inventory of the estate of "Mr. John Browne Senior deceased," taken 19 April 1662, totalled £655 1s. 2d., with no real estate included [MD 18:19-22, citing PCPR 2:2:80-81].

In her will, dated 17 December 1668 and proved 29 March 1674, "Dorethy Browne of Swansey ... being of great age" bequeathed to "my daughter Mary Willett my best petticoat and a cow for all her part and portion"; to "every one of my daughter Maryes Willett's children that shall be living at my decease, six shillings and eight pence apiece"; to "Sarah Elliott daughter of Sarah Elliott deceased a cow"; to "James Browne my son all my part of the house he now dwelleth in and also my part of the new barn"; to "James Browne, my grandchild, my part of the two hundred acres of land, lying by Mr. Blackstone's"; to "my grandson John Browne all and every part of upland and meadow that I have or shall have at my decease ... upon the condition that John Browne shall make his two brothers Joseph and Nathaniel equal with him in the land of the Narragansetts, upon the performance of this condition all the land and meadow that I have or shall have ... I give to the said John Browne, except my part of land at Quidnesse, which I give to Dorethy Browne my granddaughter"; to "Lydia Browne my daughter-in-law a silk petticoat"; to "my daughter-in-law Dorethy Browne a silk petticoat"; to "Lydia Browne and Anna Browne my grandchildren all the rest of my wearing clothes"; residue to be "divided into five equal parts, and given unto my five grandchildren, the children of John Browne deceased"; "my son James Browne shall give John Browne ten pound, upon the condition the said James Browne having the house he now dwelleth in"; "my son James Browne" to be sole executor; "John Butterworth and Thomas Eastabrooke of Rehoboth" to be overseers [MD 18:94-96, citing PCPR 3:1:97].

The inventory of the estate "in partnership betwixt Mr. James Browne and Mistress Dorety Browne deceased" totalled £253 14s. 2d., with no real estate included [MD 18:96-98, citing PCPR 3:1:98].

BIRTH: By about 1591 based on estimated date of marriage.

DEATH: Rehoboth 10 April 1662 [ReVR 804].

MARRIAGE: By about 1616 Dorothy _____. She died at Swansea 27 January 1673/4 and was buried there 29 January 1673/4 ("Mrs. Dororthy [*sic*] Brown the wife of Mr. John Brown Senior deceased the twenty seventh day of January 1673 being the ninety and eighth year of her age or thereabouts and was buried upon the 29 of January 1673" [SwVR 26]).

CHILDREN:

   i   MARY, b. say 1616; m. Plymouth 6 July 1636 *THOMAS WILLET* [PCR 1:43], as his first wife [GMB 3:2000].

   ii   JAMES, by 1627 (in Taunton section of 1643 Plymouth Colony list of men able to bear arms [PCR 8:195]); m. by about 1655 Lydia Howland, daughter of *JOHN HOWLAND* [GMB 2:1023].

   iii   JOHN, by 1627 (in Taunton section of 1643 Plymouth Colony list of men able to bear arms [PCR 8:195]); m. (1) by 1650 _____ _____ (eldest known child b. Rehoboth "last Friday of September 1650" [ReVR 555]); m. (2) by 1661 Lydia Buckland, daughter of WILLIAM BUCKLAND. (Martha Brown died at Rehoboth 14 February 1660 [ReVR 804]. If this date is properly 14 February 1659/60, then she may have been John's first wife; but if the date is 14 February 1659/61, this is not possible, given the date of birth of his first child with his second wife.)

ASSOCIATIONS: On 17 April 1635, "Jo[hn] Browne," aged 40, was enrolled at London as a passenger for New England on the *Elizabeth* [Hotten 68]. On 15 April 1635, "James Walker 15 years & Sarra Walker 17 years servants to Jo[h]n Browne a baker & to one W[illia]m Brasey linendraper in Cheapside" were enrolled at London as passengers for New England on the *Elizabeth* [Hotten 61].

The deed of 23 November 1655 tells us that John Brown of Rehoboth was uncle to the above James and Sarah Walker, which makes it likely that he was identical with the "Jo[h]n Browne a baker" who was in 1635 master of James Walker. Furthermore, since we know that John Brown of Rehoboth was not in New England until 1635, the probability is high that the "Jo[h]n Browne," aged 40, who boarded the same ship with James and Sarah Walker on 17 April 1635 is the same man. If this identification is correct, it would appear that John Brown travelled separately from his wife and children.

James and Sarah Walker may have been children of the widow Walker who appeared at Rehoboth with her son Philip Walker some years later [Early Rehoboth 3:26-27], which would make John Brown or his wife sibling to widow Walker or her husband.

COMMENTS: At the end of his account of the year 1662, Nathaniel Morton wrote: "This year Mr. John Brown ended this life; in his younger years travelling into the low countries, became acquainted with, and took good liking to, the reverend pastor of the church of Christ at Leyden, as also to sundry of the brethren of that church; which ancient amity induced him (upon his coming over to New England) to seat himself in the jurisdiction of New Plymouth, in which he was chosen a magistrate; in which place he served God and the country several years; he was well accomplished with abilities to both civil and religious concernments, and attained, through God's grace, unto a confortable persuasion of the love and favor of God to him; he falling sick of a fever, with much serenity and spiritual comfort fell asleep in the Lord, and was honorably buried at Wannamoiset near Rehoboth, in the spring of the year abovesaid" [Morton 171-72].

On 7 March 1636/7, "Frauncis Cooke complains against ... Thomas Lettis, James Walter, John Browne the younger, & Thomas Teley, in the service of the said John Browne the elder & Thomas Willet" for abusing his cattle; the jury found for the plaintiff [PCR 7:5].

On 7 June 1637, "execution is granted against Mr. John Browne, at the suit of Frauncis Cooke, upon the verdict recovered against him" [PCR 1:60]. On 2 March 1640/1, Plymouth Court presented "Georg[e] Bowers, for defamation of the government," and also presented "the aforesaid Georg[e] Bowers, for a defamation against Mr. John Browne, Assistant, the which defamation doth or may appear by letters under his own hand" [PCR 2:11-12].

On 2 March 1646/7, "Mr. John Browne, of Rehoboth, one of the Assistants of this government," was granted custody of Zachary, son of Samuel Eddy [PCR 2:112-13].

On 29 August 1659, Thomas Mayhew wrote to John Winthrop Jr. that "Mr. Browne of Seacunck, ere he went for England, wrote me he would come on purpose to satisfy himself about those Indians, who had, as I perceived, many doubts of these & all the rest" [MHSC 4:7:36]. John Brown was still in New England on 23 November 1655 [PCLR 3:181], so he probably did not depart for New England until the spring of 1656, when he was not reelected to the posts of Plymouth Colony Assistant and

Commissioner to the United Colonies. He had returned to New England by 1660.

On 3 October 1662, Jonathan Briggs deposed that "about six years agone, as I was in the house of James Walker in Taunton, I heard James Walker ask William Browne what he would do with his land if he should not return from England again. William Browne answered, that if he did not return again, then he would give all his land to his little cousin, which was Peter Walker, who then stood before him" [PCR 4:28]. On the basis of this document, Robert L. French has proposed that this William was probably a son or other relation of John Brown [MQ 50:5-6]. What is more likely is that the document is defective, and John Brown was meant where William Brown was entered. French cites other Plymouth Colony records including the name William Brown, but there is no connection between these records and the deposition above. The date of the Briggs deposition would seem to make it part of the settlement of the estate of John Brown, and also supports the argument that John Brown returned to England in 1656.

If the immigrant did return to England as early as 1656, then the "Mr. John Browne" who was on 4 May 1658 a member of a committee to deal with "Ussamequin and his son ... to deliver the said Indian suspected unto him, that so he may come to a legal trial" [PCR 3:133-34] must have been his son of the same name.

On 2 October 1660, "Mr. John Browne, being deposed, testified in Court having heard a printed letter read, that is supposed to be sent from Captain James Cudworth to himself; he testified that he did receive a letter, subscribed James Cudworth, of Scittuate, which was the substance of what he had now heard, but to all particulars his memory would not reach; and further saith that when he received the said letter he did not question but it was his hand" [PCR 3:199].

Many writers in the past have assigned to this immigrant a number of early Plymouth Colony records which actually pertain to *JOHN BROWN*, brother of *PETER BROWN* [GMB 1:257-59]. Colket has assigned to this immigrant an incorrect baptismal date of a John Brown of Hawkedon, Suffolk; this baptismal date has been assigned by many other writers to *JOHN BROWN* of Watertown [GMB 1:255-57], to whom it also does not apply. Part of the confusion arises from the fact that the subject of the present sketch and John Brown of Watertown both married women named Dorothy.

BIBLIOGRAPHIC NOTE: In 1982 George M. Browne published a brief account of "John Browne of the Old Colony. 1634-1662" [NEHGR 36:368-71]. In 1981 Carl Boyer, 3rd, prepared a more extensive account of this immigrant [*New England Colonial Families, Volume 1, Brown Families of Bristol Counties, Massachusetts and Rhode Island* ... (Newhall, California, 1981), pp. 9-14]. In 1983 and 1984 Robert L. French published a series of articles on John Brown [MQ 49:109-14, 161-67, 50:5-9, 57-61]. (All of these accounts fall into the error of connecting John Brown of Rehoboth with the earlier Plymouth records which pertain to another *JOHN BROWN* [GMB 1:255-57].)

LYDIA BROWN

On 19 June 1635, "Liddia Browne," aged 16, was enrolled at London as a passenger for New England on the *Abigail*, with a certificate of conformity from the minister of "the Little Minories" [Holy Trinity Minories, London] [Hotten 88].

COMMENTS: She may have been the Lydia Brown who married first Thomas Parsons and second *ELTWEED POMEROY* [NEHGR 148:226, 229; GMB 3:1488].

NATHANIEL BROWN

ORIGIN: Unknown (but see *COMMENTS* below)
MIGRATION: 1635
FIRST RESIDENCE: Cambridge
REMOVES: Hartford 1636, Springfield 1649, Middletown by 1651
RETURN TRIPS: To England about 1652, and returned to New England by early 1654

FREEMAN: Connecticut freeman from Middletown, 18 May 1654 [CCCR 1:257].
EDUCATION: His inventory included "a chest, two Bibles and hatchet" valued at 19s.
ESTATE: In 1654 and 1656 Nathaniel Brown was defendant in a number of suits for debt [RPCC 132, 165, 167, 168, 170].

The inventory of the estate of "Mr. Nathaniel Browne of Middletown lately deceased," taken 26 August 1658, totalled £96 2s. 4d., none of which was real estate [HaPD Case #798].

BIRTH: By about 1622 (based on date of marriage), son of Percy and _____ (Rich) Brown [TAG 22:29, 158].

DEATH: Shortly before 26 August 1658 (based on date of inventory and date of birth of posthumous child).

MARRIAGE: Hartford 23 December 1647 Eleanor Watts [HaVR 607]. She married (2) in or after 1660 Jasper Clements and (3) by an unknown date Nathaniel Willett [Moore Anc 158, and sources cited there]. She died at Middletown 28 September 1703 (as "Ellenor abovesaid the wife of Mr. Nathan[ie]ll Brown" [MidLR 1:28]).

CHILDREN:

  i   NATHANIEL, b. Springfield 15 April 1649 [Pynchon VR 41]; d. there 9 June 1649 [Pynchon VR 70].

  ii   HANNAH, b. Middletown 15 April 1651 [MidVR Barbour 73, citing MidLR 1:28]; m. Middletown 5 November 1669 Isaac Lane [MidVR Barbour 73, citing MidLR 1:46].

  iii NATHANIEL, b. Middletown 15 July 1654 [MidVR Barbour 74, citing MidLR 1:28]; m. Middletown 2 July 1677 Martha Hughes [MidVR Barbour 74, citing MidLR 1:37].

  iv   THOMAS, b. Middletown 31 October 1655 [MidVR Barbour 74, citing MidLR 1:28]; no further record.

  v   JOHN, b. Middletown 15 April 1657 [MidVR Barbour 73, citing MidLR 1:28]; no further record.

  vi   BENONI, b. Middletown 15 March 1658/9 (posthumously) [MidVR Barbour 72, citing MidLR 1:28]; no further record.

ASSOCIATIONS: Through his mother's family, this immigrant was closely associated with a number of other New England immigrants, and other prominent persons involved in New England colonization; these connections may be worked out from the series of Jacobus articles on the Rich family [TAG 21:234-38, 22:27-37,157-65, 23:101-10].

COMMENTS: Nathaniel Brown was apparently still in England on 28 November 1632 when his aunt, Dame Elizabeth Morgan, bequeathed to "Nathaniel Browne, her sister's son, ... the benefit of two hundred pounds for and towards his maintenance and bringing up until he be of the age of eight and twenty years" [Waters 871, citing PCC 42 Russell]. On 2

December 1635, Sir Nathaniel Rich bequeathed to "Nathaniel Browne, now in New England and with Mr. Hooker, the two hundred pounds which by my sister Morgan's will was bequeathed unto him and fifty pounds more, as my own gift" [Waters 872, citing PCC 123 Pile]. Although it is certainly possible that Nathaniel Brown came to New England in 1633 with Rev. *THOMAS HOOKER*, we only know, from this latter will, that he was certainly here by 1635. Curiously, with all the information we have on this immigrant and his family, we cannot state a place of origin, although it is likely that he was residing in Essex or London just before migration.

In his will of 20 October 1653, Richard Watts of Hartford bequeathed the residue of his estate to "the children of my daughter Hubbard & the child of my daughter Browne," and further bequeathed to "my daughter Browne the whole charge of her board & the board of her child, her husband & servant, from the time that her husband went from her toward England to the day of my death" [Manwaring 1:160]. From this we conclude that Nathaniel Brown left for England after the conception of his daughter Hannah.

On 1 June 1654, "Natha[niel] Browne complains of his servant Will Taylor for disorderly carriage. Will Taylor for his contemptuous carriage in the Court is committed to prison" [RPCC 128].

BIBLIOGRAPHIC NOTE: Henry F. Waters abstracted a few wills relating to the Rich and Brown families, and published them along with a Brown pedigree [Waters 871-74].

In 1938 the deForests prepared an account of Nathaniel Brown, including a line of descent and a brief outline of his agnate ancestry [Moore Anc 155-62].

In 1945 and 1946 Donald Lines Jacobus published a definitive series of articles on "The House of Rich" [TAG 21:234-38, 22:27-37,157-65, 23:101-10]. The second installment covered the branch of the Rich family which included the mother of the immigrant; the third and fourth installments provided detail on the immigrant himself and the first five generations of his descendants.

RICHARD BROWN

ORIGIN: Unknown
MIGRATION: 1634 on the *Mary & John*
FIRST RESIDENCE: Ipswich
REMOVES: Newbury by 1638

CHURCH MEMBERSHIP: Admission to Ipswich church by 6 May 1635 implied by freemanship.
FREEMAN: 6 May 1635 [MBCR 1:371].
EDUCATION: Could sign his name [EQC 2:7]. His inventory included "books and an hourglass" valued at £1 10s.
OFFICES: Essex grand jury, 26 September 1648 [EQC 1:146]. Essex petit jury, 4 November 1645, 25 September 1649, 25 September 1655 [EQC 1:86, 175, 397].

On 30 September 1656, "Robert Long and Rich[ard] Browne, both of Newbury, [were] released from ordinary training, paying eight shillings each year for the use of the company" [EQC 2:2].
ESTATE: On 20 September 1652, "Rich[ar]d Brown of Newbury" sold to Edmund Moones of Newbury "all that his house, barn, orchard & all the land that was his within the fence, containing five & twenty acres ..., as also his upper five acres of marsh as it lyeth in the great marsh ..., as also as much of his common parcel of meadow on the south side of it, acre for acre, as much as contains the full quantity that Edmund Moons hath on the Little River"; the consideration for this sale was £40 and "thirteen acres of upland as it lyeth in two several parcels in Newbury, viz: eight acres which he lately purchased of Mr. Spencer" and five acres [ILR 1:215-16].

On 27 March 1655, Richard Browne gave bond to pay his wife's son, John Badger, £34 at the age of eighteen, besides half the land left by Badger's father [EQC 1:386].

In his undated will, probated 24 June 1661, "Richard Browne of Newbury" desired to be buried in the burying place in Newbury and bequeathed to "my son Joshua Browne when he shall be of the age of one and twenty years, all that parcel of my upland and meadow that lyeth near the little river as it is now enclosed, and my five acres of upland adjoining to Goodman Smith's land, and my share of meadow, which I have equally with George Little, upon the little river" and livestock "and my own freehold for encouragement to live with his mother until he be of the aforesaid age"; to "my son Richard Browne the house and lot I now dwell upon with the lot adjoining to Robert Long's land and that parcel of land adjoining to Richard Pettingall's" and "my eight acres of salt marsh lying in the great marsh" and "my parcel of meadow adjoining to the land that Benjamin Roafe hath now in possession and the freehold which was Gyles Badger's which belongs to me, and he my son Richard shall pay out of his share ten pounds to each of his three sisters within three years"; to "my son Edmund Browne all my share of land that belongs to me which was formerly Joseph Carter's that is to say half the plowland, pasture and meadow, with the house and barn that hath been built by me and half the privilege of freehold"; both Richard and Edmund to have their legacies at their mother's decease, or if she marry again, at age 21; to "my three daughters Elizabeth, Sara, and Mary" £10 in stock at marriage; and "whereas I am bound to leave my wife worth threescore pounds, in lieu of it I give unto her the thirds of my lands during her natural life"; wife sole executrix, she to pay John Badger his portion; "my son Josua" to have only what was bequeathed in this will "so that he shall never desire any more in relation of any thing given to his brother Joseph deceased by his uncle George Browne deceased"; if a son dies before he comes of age, land falls to the other two and if either daughter die before marriage, then her portion to fall to "my other two daughters"; "loving friends" Richard Kente, Nicolas Noyes, Robert Long and "Josef Noyce" overseers [EPR 1:339-40].

The inventory of the estate of "Richard Browne of Newbury," who "deceased April 26, 1661," taken 5 June 1661, totalled £634 3s., of which £400 was real estate: "six and twenty acres of upland & meadow with house & barn and eight and twenty acres of upland and meadow and a house, ½ a barn & six and twenty acres of upland & meadow" [EPR 1:340-42].

On 4 March 1677/8, "John Bager of the one part and Richard Browne, Sarah Browne and Mary Browne, all of Newbury, on the other part with the consent of Elizabeth Browne mother to them all" settled the estates of Giles Badger and Richard Browne on the occasion of the death of Richard's son, Edmond, at Nevis; John Badger recovered the lands that had been his father's and paid his half-siblings a sum to be agreed upon [ILR 4:161; EPR 3:220-21].

BIRTH: By 1613 based on estimated date of marriage (adult when he took the oath of allegiance at Southampton in early 1634).
DEATH: Newbury 26 April 1661.

MARRIAGE: (1) By about 1638 Edith _____. She died Newbury 2 April 1647.

(2) Newbury 1[torn] February 164[7/8] Elizabeth (Greenleaf) Badger, daughter of Edmund Greenleaf and widow of Giles Badger [Badger Gen 24-27].

CHILDREN:

With first wife

    i   JOSEPH, b. say 1638 (living 26 May 1642 when his uncle left him a legacy [EPR 1:22]); predeceased his father, unmarried.

    ii   MARGERY, b. say 1640 (living 26 May 1642 when her uncle left her a legacy [EPR 1:22]); d. Newbury 26 March 1651.

    iii   JOSHUA, b. Newbury 10 April 1642; m. Newbury 15 January 1668[/9?] Sarah Sawyer.

    iv   CALEB, b. Newbury 7 May 1645; no further record.

With second wife

    v   ELIZABETH, b. Newbury 29 May 1649; living 1661 (father's will) but not named in the settlement of the Badger-Browne estate, and so probably deceased without issue by 4 March 1677/8 [EPR 3:220-21]; possibly the wife of Israel Webster, married Newbury 3 January 1665[/6], when she would have been barely seventeen.

    vi   RICHARD, b. Newbury 18 February 1650[/1]; m. Newbury 7 May 1674 Mary Jaques.

    vii   EDMUND, b. Newbury 17 July 1654; died unmarried having lain "sick at Mevis [i.e., Nevis]" in the winter of 1677/8 [EPR 3:221; ILR 4:161-62].

    viii   SARAH, b. Newbury 7 September 1657; living single 4 March 1677/8 [EPR 3:221]; probably she who married Newbury 7 April 1678 Joshua Boynton.

    ix   MARY, b. Newbury 10 April 1660; living unmarried 4 March 1677/8 [EPR 3:221].

ASSOCIATIONS: Richard was brother of GEORGE BROWN of Newbury [EPR 1:22-23].

COMMENTS: On 24 March 1633[/4], "Richard Browne" took the oath of supremacy and allegiance at Southampton, preparatory to taking passage to New England on the *Mary & John* [Drake's Founders 70].

"Rich[ard] Browne" took the inventory of the estate of Henry Somersby in 1652 [EQC 1:271]. On 30 September 1652, Richard Brown was one of the trustees who participated in the marriage agreement between JEREMY BELCHER and Mary Lockwood [ILR 1:240].

Pope erroneously gives the date of Edith's death as 12 April [Pope 74]. Savage gives the date of Elizabeth's birth incorrectly as 20 March [Savage 1:275].

BIBLIOGRAPHIC NOTE: In 1909 Sidney Perley compiled a thumbnail sketch of this family [Essex Ant 13:168-72].

ROBERT BROWN

On 19 September 1635, "Robert Browne," aged 24, was enrolled at London as a passenger for New England on the *Truelove* [Hotten 132].

COMMENTS: Both Savage and Pope make this passenger the same as the Robert Brown who married at Cambridge in 1649 and died there in 1690, aged 70. Savage especially argues that the age at death is wrong, but there is no record of Robert Brown in Cambridge before 1649, so it is far more likely that the 1635 passenger and the Cambridge resident are different men.

SUSAN BROWN

On 9 May 1635, "Suzan Browne," aged 21, maidservant (apparently in the family of ROBERT JEFFRIES) was enrolled at London as a passenger for New England on the *Elizabeth & Ann* [Hotten 77].

COMMENTS: No record of her has been found in New England.

THOMAS BROWN

ORIGIN: Christian Malford, Wiltshire
MIGRATION: 1635 on the *James* of London
FIRST RESIDENCE: Newbury

OCCUPATION: Weaver.

CHURCH MEMBERSHIP: Admission to Newbury church prior to 22 May 1639 implied by freemanship. He appears on a list of church members in Newbury in 1670/1 [EQC 4:361].

FREEMAN: 22 May 1639 [MBCR 1:375]. Oath of allegiance at Newbury, 1678 [EQC 7:156].

EDUCATION: He signed his name when he witnessed John Goff's will of 4 December 1641 [EPR 1:14], and again when he witnessed the nuncupative will of John Davis of Newbury [EPR 3:90].

OFFICES: Essex grand jury, 25 September 1655 [EQC 1:396].

ESTATE: Prior to 1652, Thomas Brown (and others) agreed to surrender land that had been granted to them on the left side of Merrimack Ridge in Newbury, on condition that they be granted elsewhere three acres for every two previously granted [EQC 1:263].

On 26 March 1652, "Henry Short of Newbury ..., yeoman, as agent and in the behalf of Stephen Dumer, late of Newbery aforesaid, gent.," sold to "Thomas Browne & George Little of the aforesaid town and county, yeomen, ... all that farm of upland & meadow which was granted unto the said Stephen Dumer by the town of Newberry, being three hundred acres ..., sixty acres whereof is meadow" [ILR 1:106-7].

On 23 May 1660, Thomas Brown of Newbury, yeoman, sold to Henry Sewall of Newbury, gentleman, eight acres of meadow lately laid out and given to Henry Sewall in the Birchen Meadows in Newbury [ILR 2:15].

On 11 April 1677, whereas "I Thomas Browne of Newbury ... did give unto Peeter Godfry, in marriage with my daughter when they were first married, the possession of the house and barn and eleven acres of arable land adjoining to the said land lying at hither end of Birchen Meadows, next George Little's, with a four-acre lot in Plum Island which was granted to me for my freehold portion with the privilege of commonage ... which premises the said Peeter Godfry has possessed ever since, but having no assurance of it, in writing, I the abovesaid Thomas Browne, do ... give, grant ... unto the said Peeter Godfry his heirs and assigns forever ... provided the said Peeter Godfry his heirs & assigns pay yearly, and from year to year, forty shillings ... unto me ... during my natural life, if it be demanded" [ILR 4:91].

On 6 January 1682[/3], Thomas Browne of Newbury sold to Joseph Richardson a parcel of his four-acre lot on Plum Island, being 1¼ acres [ELR 11:9-10].

"Newbury Feb. 22nd 1686/7 a writing of a kind of a will appears in court made by Thomas Broune of Newbury deceased and it not appearing to be so legal as the law requires no executor being therein nominated therefore there is administratorship granted unto Francis Broune of Newbury son of the said Thomas Broune upon the estate of the said Thomas Broune deceased" [EPR Case #3839].

On 22 February 1686[/7], "an inventory of Thomas Browne Senior estate late deceased (that is) that part of his estate which was not given and formerly possessed the remainder is five acres of meadow in the Burchen Meadows and some old tools," £16 [EPR Case #3839].

On 21 March 1687/8, Thomas Browne of Newbury sold to John Ordway of Newbury one half of Lot 31 in the first division "Over Artechoake" in the open common in Newbury, "which land was formerly my grandfather Thomas Browne's land called by the name of a Freehold Lot," containing 14½ acres [ELR 11:111-12].

BIRTH: About 1606 (aged 72 in 1678 [EQC 7:156]).
DEATH: Newbury 8 January 1686/7 "by a fall."
MARRIAGE: Christian Malford, Wiltshire, 20 August 1632 Mary Healy. She died in Newbury 2 June 1654.
CHILDREN:

 i FRANCIS, bp. Christian Malford, 1 January 1632/3; m. (1) Newbury 21 November 1653 Mary Johnson; m. (2) Newbury 31 December 1679 Mary Morse.

 ii MARY, b. about 1636 ("the first English child born in this town," d. Newbury 15 April 1716 "in her 80th year"); m. Newbury 13 May 1656 Peter Godfrey.

 iii ISAAC, b. about 1638 (d. Newbury 13 May 1674, aged 36); m. Newbury 22 August 1661 Rebecca Bailey, who m. (2) Newbury 22 June 1697 John Doggett of Marshfield.

 iv (probably) NICHOLAS, b. say 1645; m. Haverhill 27 January 1669[/70] Mary Linforth.

ASSOCIATIONS: The name of Thomas Brown of Newbury is often mentioned with that of George Little, another settler of the town, over a period of many years [e.g., ILR 1:106-7, 5:130].

COMMENTS: On or about 5 April 1635, "Thomas Browne, of Malford, weaver," was included in the list of passengers from Southampton on the *James* [Drake's Founders 55].

Nicholas Brown of Newbury has long puzzled genealogists as he was evidently born about 1645 (assuming he was 25 at marriage), and so would be of the right age to be the son or grandson of an early settler.

Nicholas had ten recorded children, the first two of whom were named Mary and Thomas. Ruth Brown of Newbury, great-granddaughter of Thomas Brown through his son Francis and grandson John, was born in Newbury on 1 July 1695, and died there, testate, in 1744, her will being dated 14 September 1744 and proved 7 October 1744, in which she left her Great Bible to "Ruth Brown daughter of my cousin Joshua Brown of Haverhill" [EPR Case #3787]. Ruth, the daughter of Joshua, was born in Haverhill on 2 October 1740. Joshua Brown of Haverhill was the grandson of Nicholas Brown of Newbury through the latter's son, Thomas, from which we conclude that Nicholas Brown of Newbury was also a son of Thomas Brown, weaver. Ruth Brown, the testatrix, and Joshua Brown of Haverhill were, consequently, second cousins exactly, and Ruth, the young heiress, was therefore a second cousin once-removed of the elder Ruth Brown whose will unintentionally connects Nicholas Brown to Thomas Brown the weaver.

Pope has succeeded in rolling three different Thomas Browns into one man of the name [Hotten 74-75]. Thomas Brown the weaver of Newbury was distinct from THOMAS BROWN, Thomas Antram's servant, also aboard the *James* [see sketch below]. Thomas Brown of Lynn, some of whose records were included in this same Pope entry, was a third man of the name, who first appeared in New England some years later.

BIBLIOGRAPHIC NOTE: In 1909 Sidney Perley published an incomplete genealogy of the descendants of Thomas Brown of Newbury [Essex Ant 13:120-26], and a treatment, with some obvious errors, of the descendants of Nicholas Brown of Newbury appeared in the same year [Essex Ant 13:24-25]. In 1938 Mary Lovering Holman compiled a better treatment of Thomas Brown and his children, but does not mention the son Nicholas [Pillsbury Anc 2:749-50]. In 1998 George Freeman Sanborn Jr. prepared an account of Thomas Brown, including information on his English origin and including the son Nicholas [NEHGR 152:347-52].

THOMAS BROWN

"Thomas Browne, his servant," appears immediately below the entry for THOMAS ANTRAM on about 5 April 1635 in the passenger list of the *James* of London, sailing for New England from Southampton [Drake's Founders 56].

COMMENTS: As noted in the sketch above, Pope has succeeded in rolling three distinct Thomas Browns into one man of the name [Pope 74-75]. THOMAS BROWN the weaver of Newbury, Thomas Brown the servant, presumably of Salem and subject of the present sketch, and Thomas Brown of Lynn were three distinct people.

"Thomas Antram, weaver," and "Thomas Browne, his servant," were passengers on the *James* of London, sailing from Southampton in April 1635. They and six other men were called "late of New England" which is probably a scribal error for "New Sarum," since none of them leave prior records in New England and all were demonstrably from in and around Salisbury [Drake's Founders 56].

No record for this immigrant is found in New England.

WILLIAM BROWN

ORIGIN: Unknown
MIGRATION: 1635 on the *Love*
FIRST RESIDENCE: Salem

OCCUPATION: Fisherman [Hotten 109]. On 23 August 1645, Aspinwall recorded a "copy of Will[ia]m Browne of Salem's affidavit touching my Lord Brook's [and] Saye's & Sir Richard Saltonstall's fishing business, the value of 1/6 part £37 that this was committed to Mr. Ballard & had no relation at all to the vessel whereof Mr. White was master" [Aspinwall 6]. Shopkeeper [STR 1:98].
CHURCH MEMBERSHIP: On 26 November 1648, "Mr. William Browne and Sarah his wife" were admitted to Salem church [SChR 13]. On 10 December 1648, "all the children of Mr. William Brown" were baptized, but not named [SChR 22].

On 11 May 1657, Mr. William Brown was seated with Major Hawthorn in "the magistrate seat" [STR 1:201].

On 30 November 1674, Mr. William Brown was one of three men designated messengers from the Salem church to attend the gathering of a church in Lynn and signify their non-approbation [SChR 128]. On 21 April 1679, Mr. William Brown Sr. and Mr. John Brown Sr. were appointed to represent Salem at the synod at Boston [SChR 148].
FREEMAN: 2 May 1649 [MBCR 2:295].
EDUCATION: Sufficient to run an extremely successful fishing and trading business. In his will, he mentioned his English and Latin books.

OFFICES: Deputy for Salem to Massachusetts Bay General Court, 3 May 1654, 3 May 1659, 11 May 1666 [MBCR 2:340, 4:1:181, 364; STR 1:223]. Assistant 1680-83 [RCA 1:149, 160, 169, 179, 377].

Commissioner to end small causes, 10 November 1655, 1657-59 [STR 1:186, 212, 224]. Essex petit jury, 19 December 1648 [STR 1:104].

Salem selectman, 1650, 1655-57, 1659-60 [STR 1:165-67, 190, 192-96, 199-200, 224, 231]. Salem constable, 17 August 1655 [STR 185], but substitute appointed 24 December 1655 [STR 1:187]. Committee to disburse payment to Widow Jackson, 13 July 1657 [STR 1:202].

ESTATE: In the Salem land grant of 1636, "Mr. Wm Browne" received 20 acres [STR 1:22]; ten acres were added to this on 17 April 1637 [STR 1:47]. In the 25 December 1637 division of marsh and meadow, he received half an acre for a household of two persons [STR 1:103].

On 17 February 1636/7, Christopher Yong was received an inhabitant and granted "half an acre with W[illia]m Browne" [STR 1:37]. On 21 January 1639/40, "William Browne shopkeeper" was granted eighty acres of land [STR 1:98].

On 13 April 1655, William Brown of Salem, merchant, sold to Samuel Shattock of Salem, "one dwelling house wherein formerly dwelt John Bourne" and a quarter of an acre of land on which the house stood [ELR 1:55]. On 26 June 1655, Francis Perry, of Barbados, carpenter, acknowledged his debt to William Brown of Salem, merchant, of £7 sterling to be paid at "some convenient storehouse near the Indian Bridge of Barbados" [ELR 1:62]. On 15 February 1658[/9], James Underwood of Salem mortgaged to William Brown of Salem "my now dwelling house in Salem ... with all the ground adjoining" [ELR 1:51].

On 8 September 1659, Samuel Randall, "now of Boston ... but bound for London in the good ship called the *Prudent Marye*," bound himself to pay a £30 debt to "Mr. William Browne of Salem" at London [ELR 1:74]. On 7 May 1661, Peter Palfrey of Reading, yeoman, sold to Mr. William Brown of Salem, merchant, a dwelling house and three quarters of an acre of ground in Salem near the highway to the meetinghouse [ELR 2:13].

On 3 October 1662, Samuel Pickman of Salem, mariner, sold to Mr. William Brown Sr. of Salem, merchant, seven acres of marsh in Salem, a ten-acre lot "with stage point & all my meadow & mowing ground there[un]to belonging," all property given to Pickman by his "father-in-law Peter Palfrey" [ELR 2:60].

On 18 December 1662, Thomas Marshall of Lynn, yeoman, sold to William Brown Sr. and to Walter Price, both of Salem, merchants, one third to Brown and two thirds to Price, nine acres of meadow [ELR 2:61].

On 20 April 1664, William Brown of Salem, merchant, and Sarah his wife, sold to Thomas Cromwell of Salem, tailor, a dwelling house and its lot by Phillip Cromwell's [ELR 6:97]. On 10 December 1666, Mr. William Brown Senior of Salem, merchant, sold to William Flint of Salem, yeoman, fifteen acres recently bought of John Beckett [ELR 3:3-4]. On 26 November 1668, Nathaniel Felton of Salem sold to Mr. William Brown Sr. of Salem land and a house in Salem [ELR 3:45].

On 5 July 1669, Susannah, the late wife of Samuel Archard and now wife of Richard Hutchenson, sold to William Brown Sr. of Salem her dower thirds in her former husband's estate [ELR 3:75]. On 2 May 1670, William Brown of Salem, merchant, sold to William Flint of Salem thirty rods of land in Salem formerly belonging to the house lot of Samuel Archard, deceased [ELR 3:84]. On 2 June 1670, William Brown Sr. of Salem, merchant, sold to William Flint of Salem, husbandman, all his share of a meadow "which has been divided & enjoyed between us of late years" [ELR 3:84-85].

On 30 June 1671, Abraham Allen mortgaged his new house and shop in Marblehead to William Brown [ELR 3:126]. On 20 August 1672, Moses and Eunice Maverick of Marblehead sold to William Brown Sr., merchant, a two acre island called Maverick's Island [ELR 3:162-63]. On 28 March 1672/3, John Paine of Boston, merchant, sold for £500 to Mr. William Brown Sr. of Salem, merchant, two hundred acres of upland, meadow and a dwelling house in Ipswich [ILR 3:229-31].

On 23 November 1674, William Brown Sr. of Salem conveyed his interest in a deed of sale of an island, excepting the "half warehouse," to Richard Reith of Marblehead [ELR 4:91]. On 28 December 1674, William Brown Sr. of Salem, merchant, sold to Joseph Phippen Jr. of Salem, fisherman, a dwelling house with land and orchard, once owned by Samuel Archard [ELR 4:128]. On 19 April 1678, William Brown Sr. sold to Daniel Rumball of Salem about six feet of land along their common fence [ELR 7:12]. On 21 September 1678, William Brown Sr. of Salem, merchant, sold to Robert Follett of Salem, fisherman, two hundred and seven acres granted to Brown by the town of Salem [ELR 6:36].

On 6 February 1678/9, William Brown Sr. took the five year mortgage of Daniel Epps Sr. of Ipswich, gentleman, on sixty acres of upland and forty acres of salt marsh [ELR 5:29]. On 30 March 1681, William Brown Sr. of Salem, Esq., sold to Samuel Phippen, clockmaker, ten poles of land with a dwelling house and fence in Salem [ELR 7:27]. On 21 December 1682, Thomas and Abigail Jeggells of Salem, sold to William Brown of Salem, Esqr., half an acre of land near the townhouse [ELR 6:122]. On 15 April

1684, William Brown of Salem, merchant, sold to Nicholas Noyce of Salem half an acre of land in Salem near the town house [ELR 6:122]. On 31 March 1686, Ann Pudeator of Salem acknowledged a judgment in favor of William Brown Sr. of Salem, and agreed to deliver £43 10½s. to Brown or his attorney, Mr. Benjamin Brown [ILR 5:221].

In his will, dated 19 March 1686/7 and proved 4 February 1687[/8], "William Browne Senior of Salem" requested to be "laid in the tomb with my dear wife" and bequeathed to "my son William Browne" the house that is mortgaged for £1000, also "that money that my warehouse was sold for unto James Russell" £130, also "my farm at Ipswich which I bought of Mr John Pain," also "two thirds of the island that I bought of Mr. Thomas Webber and John Parker" called Riskehegen; to "his [William Jr.'s] four children now living" £100 apiece; to "my son William the land that is at Stage Point and also six of the great silver spoons and all the Latin books that I have and the English books that I have two of a sort"; to "my son Benjamin my house that I now live in with the land belonging to it," also "land and marsh and the warehouse over against my dwelling house and the barn and land belonging to it," also "all my household stuff," and "all my books"; to "my daughter Winthrop ... more than I gave her at her marriage, which was £1000 in money, more I give her the biggest beaker and the biggest silver tankard and six of the silver spoons"; to "the three children" £100 apiece "out of the money I lent to my son Winthrop"; to "my cousin Francis Browne, wine cooper in London," £50; to "Mr Higginson, pastor of the church of Salem," £20; to "[ ] Noyse" £10; to the church £20; to "the poor in the town that are in greatest want" £50 in clothing and provision; to the school in Salem £50; to "the college" the "remainder of my farm that was never laid out to me" £100 of its value for the "bringing up of poor scholars"; to "my daughter Brown" £20 to buy a piece or two of plate; to "my grandchild Sarah Deane" ten pieces of eight to buy a gold ring "for a remembrance of me, having given her" £1000; to "my cousin Thomas Smith" £15; to "Joseph Endicott" the debt "that his father owed me when he died"; to "my maid Mary" £10; to "Wm Redford" £5; "my two sons William and Benja[min] Browne" executors, to receive "all my money and bullion and all my debts"; to "Benjamin all my fishing vessels"; residue of shipping to be divided between them; residue of land at "Prudent Island" to be equally divided between them [SPR 10:218-21].

BIRTH: About 1609 (aged 26 in 1635 [Hotten 109]).
DEATH: Salem 20 January 1687/8, aged 79 [Salem gravestone]. "Today [Sunday, 22 January 1687/8], I hear that Mr. Brown of Salem, the father,

dyed on Friday last in the afternoon" [Sewall 158]. (This was written while Salem was under siege by the measles, but there is no indication that measles carried off Mr. Brown.)

MARRIAGE: (1) By 1635 Mary _____. She was born about 1609 (aged 26 in 1635 [Hotten 109]). She probably died between 25 December 1637 (grant of land based on household of two [STR 1:103]) and late 1638 (when Brown's first known child was conceived).

(2) By 1639 Sarah Smith, daughter of Samuel Smith of Wenham (in his will of 5 October 1642, Samuel Smith bequeathed £50 to "my son William Browne" and to "his two children William and John Browne £50 between them" [EPR 1:18-20]). Sarah predeceased William, who requested in his will to be buried next to her.

CHILDREN:

With second wife

i   WILLIAM, b. 14 April 1639 [Essex Ant 13:159, citing unknown source]; m. (1) Salem 29 December 1664 Hannah Corwin; m. (2) Salem 26 April 1694 Rebecca Bayley.

ii   JOHN, b. October 1641, and d. 1669 [Essex Ant 13:159, citing unknown source].

iii SAMUEL, b. 31 July 1644, and drowned 11 years old [Essex Ant 13:159, citing unknown source].

iv   HANNAH, bp. Salem 28 June 1646 [SChR 21]; no further record.

v   JOSEPH, b. say 1647; Harvard College 1666 [Sibley 2:206-9]; m. between 9 February 1673/4 (date of her father's will [MD 34:75-79, citing PCPR 3:1:143-45]) and 3 October 1675 (admission to Charlestown church [Wyman 139]) Mehetabel Brenton, daughter of *WILLIAM BRENTON* [GMB 1:222].

vi   BENJAMIN, b. by 1648 (witnessed a 1662 deed [ELR 3:8]); m. by an unknown date _____ _____ (in his will of 8 November 1708, he referred to "my dear late wife" [NEHGR 63:361-62]). (Secondary sources claim that Benjamin married at Charlestown in 1686 Mary Hicks, but no record of such a marriage can be found in Charlestown, nor is there a Hicks family there.)

vii SARAH, b. 23 December 1649 [Essex Ant 13:159]; m. by 1666 Thomas Deane (first known child b. Boston 27 October 1666 [BVR 100]).

viii MARY, bp. Salem 4 January 1651/2 [SChR 23]; d. soon.

ix JAMES, bp. Salem 3 July 1653 [SChR 24]; d. soon.

x MARY, bp. Salem 25 January 1656/7 [SChR 25]; m. between 7 May 1678 (her brother Joseph's will where she is called "my dear sister Mary Browne" [SPR 6:237]) and 12 September 1679 (Boston birth of son John [BVR 150]) Waitstill Winthrop [Winthrop Gen 97-111].

xi JAMES, bp. Salem 2 January 1658/9 [SChR 25]; d. Salem August 1659.

COMMENTS: On 13 July 1635, "fisherman Will[ia]m Browne," aged 26, and "Mary Browne," aged 26, were enrolled at London for passage to New England on the *Love* [Hotten 109].

The William Brown designated to keep goats for Salem was probably the man who was dismissed to the Gloucester church in 1642 [STR 1:87; SChR 22].

When the General Court heard Richard Margerum's petition on 23 May 1655, he was directed to take his case against Mr. William Brown of Salem to a lower court. Margerum was suing Brown for the unjust detaining of an estate, described as "a house and ground and all the appurtenances thereunto belonging of Mr. Will Broune of Salem which house is in Boston to the value of one hundred and twenty-five pounds" [MBCR 2:388; RCA 2:39]. From all appearances, Margerum won this suit.

On 22 May 1661, Governor Endicott requested a special court be convened to hear his suit against Mr. William Brown of Salem, "in reference to the ship lately seized at Marblehead" [MBCR 4:2:15].

When the General Court deemed it politic to send a present to the King in 1665, Mr. William Brown was one of the men named to procure "the best commodity" produced by "this his colony" and see that it was shipped at the first opportunity [MBCR 4:2:150]. His performance was appreciated and further commissions were sent his way, including the order of 19 September 1673, when Mr. William Brown Sr. and three other men were ordered to "have their correspondents in Bilboa, and the trade there ... to procure and purchase a [sic] thirty or forty great guns" [MBCR 4:2:562]. On 15 October 1673, this order was followed by one authorizing him to "send abroad to any part of Europe, America, or else to their correspondents, to procure & purchase sixteen demi cannon" [MBCR 4:2:565].

Meanwhile, "William Broune Senr. of Salem, merchant," had his hands full in a series of suits against WILLIAM LEATHERLAND and Capt.

William Hudson, which culminated in Brown's successful appeal to the Court of Assistants [RCA 1:25; SCC 500-04, 515].

In April 1673 Nicholas Durall and John Burrington were convicted for stealing horses and saddles from the stable of Mr. William Brown Sr. of Salem [SCC 1:249-50].

BIBLIOGRAPHIC NOTE: A portrait of a later Hon. William Browne is reproduced in the Brown sketch published in 1909 by Sidney Perley, which sketch also claims that William was the son of Francis Brown of Brandon or Brundish, Suffolk [Essex Ant 13:159]. In light of Brown's later wealth, Savage is anxious to explain his designation as a fisherman in the passenger list as one who held membership in the Fishmongers Company.

JOHN BRUNDISH

ORIGIN: Unknown
MIGRATION: 1634
FIRST RESIDENCE: Watertown
REMOVES: Wethersfield

OCCUPATION: Tanner.
CHURCH MEMBERSHIP: Admission to Watertown church prior to 4 March 1634/5 implied by freemanship.
FREEMAN: 4 March 1634/5 (as "John Brandishe," third in a sequence of six Watertown men) [MBCR 1:370].
EDUCATION: The inventory included "books" valued at £2.
ESTATE: The inventory of the estate of John Brundish of Wethersfield, taken 27 October 1639, totalled £304 6s., of which "her house and land" was valued at £130; at the end of the inventory was an annotation that "[s]he hath 5 children, the 2 eldest girls, the next a boy, the other two girls"; "a note brought in Court since the inventory" stated that "Rachell Brundishe hath 14 acres of meadow, her houselot 3 acres, and what upland belongs thereunto in every division, saving what her husband and she sold, vizt. her share beyond the river and 6 acres in Penny Wise" [CCCR 1:444-45]. Administration on the estate was granted on 7 November 1639 to the widow [CCCR 1:40]. On 2 April 1640, "Rachel Brundish of Weathersfield presented an inventory of her husband's

estate, which amounted (all debts being paid) to £90 5s. 4d. and the house and land was rated at £130. And it was thought fit and ordered that the relict of the said Jno. Brundish shall have to her own use the £90 5s. 4d.; and the land with the house to be for the children's portions, vizt. £30 to the son and £25 apiece to each of the 4 daughters to be paid into the Court for their use when each of them come to the age of sixteen years and in the meantime the widow to have the use of the land for the bringing up of the children"; further provision was made for the widow to sell some of the land if necessary [CCCR 1:45-46]. (See also Manwaring 1:3-4.)

In the Wethersfield land inventory, on 27 April 1641, "Rachell Brundish widow" held eight parcels: "one piece whereon her house standeth containing three acres"; "one piece in the great meadow containing nine acres & twenty poles ... this is part swamp"; "one other piece in the great meadow containing three acres two roods ... this is part swamp also"; "one piece of meadow & swamp in back lots containing three acres & a half & twenty poles"; "one piece in the east side of east field of dry swamp containing six acres one half"; "one piece in the west swamp containing five acres"; "one piece in the west field containing seventeen acres three roods & twenty poles"; and "one other piece in the west field containing seventeen acres three roods & twenty poles" [WetLR 1:193].

The first volume of Fairfield probate records contains the record of the distribution of the estate of the widow of John Brundish, on a page the top third of which has been lost to fire. After a preamble of which only a few words survive, there are three numbered sections. The first of these also contains only a few words, but mentions an "agreement" which "Anthony [burned]" made which was "dated 5 [burned]." The beginning of the second section is partially lost, but gives to "John Brundish" land, including the "house & houselot," "he paying these legacies [burned] out of the land: unto Mary Purdie the wife of Francis Purdie eight pounds ..., unto Bethia Brundish eight pounds and unto Posthume Brundish eight pounds, Posthume is to have her portion at eighteen years of age" or at marriage, Bethia is to have hers immediately. The third section is undamaged: "It is ordered that the said Anthony Wilson shall have the homelot in Fairfield that sometimes was Rachell Brundishes with the small house that was on it to be to him and to his heirs forever in consideration of which & towards the children portions he is to pay as followeth: unto Mary Purdie the wife of Francis Purdie ten pounds presently, unto Bethya Brundish five pounds and unto Posthume Brundish ten pounds; Bethya is to have it presently and Posthume is to have hers at the age of eighteen years or at her marriage if she marry sooner. Also the said Anthony is to let the said John have the young mare according to a composition that they have made before Mr. Ludlowe the said John is to let the son of Francis Purdie have the first colt of the mare according as it was then agreed. John is to have the money that the tools of a tanner were sold for Rachell Brundishe having sold them thereupon the price 16s., those tools he was to have by the agreement in 5 August 1642" [Fairfield PR 1:88].

BIRTH: By about 1604 based on estimated date of marriage.
DEATH: Between 20 May 1639 [FOOF 1:107, citing unrecorded deed] and 27 October 1639 (date of inventory).
MARRIAGE: By about 1629 Rachel _____. She married (2) on or soon after 5 August 1642 Anthony Wilson, and died by 1648 [Fairfield PR 1:88].
CHILDREN:

    i   MARY, b. say 1629; m. (1) by about 1645 Francis Purdy [FOOF 1:495-96]; m. (2) 1659 or soon after John Hoyt, son of *SIMON HOYT* [GMB 2:1030, citing FOOF 1:495-96; Fairfield PR 3:44].

    ii   Daughter, b. say 1632; d. between 1640 and 1648 (four daughters mentioned in probate proceedings of 1639 and 1640, but only three daughters in distribution of 1648).

    iii   JOHN, b. about 1636 (aged 30 years on 25 June 1666 [WMJ 663]); m. by an unknown date Hannah _____ [Fairfield PR 4:141; NYGBR 49:293-94].

    iv   BETHIA, b. about 1638 (deposed 26 April 1654 aged "sixteen or thereabouts" [NHCR 2:83]); may have married Timothy Knapp or Joseph Taylor [see COMMENTS below].

    v   POSTHUME, b. late 1639 or early 1640 (as indicated by given name); possibly m. "John Winter, of Westchester, whose wife in several deeds 1692-94 rejoiced in the unusual name of `Posthumy'" [FOOF 1:108].

COMMENTS: Savage has brief and identical entries for this man under "Brandisly" and "Brundish" [Savage 1:238, 281].

Our knowledge of the marriages of the children of this immigrant remains limited, principally because most of the children moved into Westchester County, and detailed work in the records of that jurisdiction has not been carried out. The existence of two candidates for the husband of Bethia Brundish apparently arises simply because these two men had wives named Bethia. In the case of Timothy Knapp, there is the added bit of evidence of a man named "Brundage Knapp" in the 1800 census of Salem, Westchester County [NYGBR 58:18], suggesting a genealogical connection between Brundish and Knapp, but we don't know enough to tell whether this man derived his name from the suggested marriage of Timothy Knapp.

BIBLIOGRAPHIC NOTE: In 1930 Jacobus published a brief account of John Brundish and his son John, in which he included an abstract of an important unrecorded deed [FOOF 1:107-9].

CHRISTIAN BUCK

On 13 July 1635, "Christian Buck," aged 26, was enrolled at London as a passenger for New England on the *Blessing* [Hotten 108].

COMMENTS: There is no evidence that this passenger arrived in New England.

WILLIAM BUCK

ORIGIN: Unknown
MIGRATION: 1635 on the *Increase*
FIRST RESIDENCE: Cambridge

OCCUPATION: Plowwright (in England).
ESTATE: In the Cambridge land inventory of 1639 William Buck held one parcel: "in the farther end of the West Field one house with four acres of land" [CaBOP 62].

In the Cambridge land inventory of 1642 he held five parcels: "in the West End, one dwelling house with two acres of land"; "on the south side of Charles River, four acres more or less, being the one-and-twentieth lot in the lower division of those lots"; "in the upper division of those lots four acres more or less, being the nine and thirtieth lot"; "in the lower division of lots there eighteen acres more or less, being the three and thirtieth, four and thirtieth and five and thirtieth lots"; and "in the upper division of those lots eighteen acres more or less, being the five and twenty, six and twenty, and seven and twenty lots" [CaBOP 112]. (Of the four parcels of land south of the Charles River, two were originally granted to him [CaBOP 331], and two were created by combining lots which he purchased from Thomas Parish, Mr. Benjamin and John Meane [CaBOP 332].)

In the division of Shawsheen lands on 4 June 1652, "Will[iam] Bucke" received Lot 91, twenty acres [CaTR 98, 321]. (This lot came into the hands of Golden Moore [MLR 4:159].)

By 8 March 1642[/3], Nathaniel Sparhawk had purchased from William Buck "four acres of land more or less on the south side of Charles River, being the one and twentieth lot in the lower division," and "eighteen acres of land more or less on the south side of Charles River in the upper division of those lots, being five and twenty, six & twenty & seven and twentieth lots" [CaBOP 120, 122-23].

In 1645 "William Bucke" was granted three acres and a half on the west side of Menotomy River [CaBOP 128].

The inventory of the estate of William Buck, taken 27 January 1657/8 and presented by the administrator, "Roger Buck, son of ... William Buck," totalled £26 8s. 6d. (against which were debts of £5 15s. 10d.) of which £16 was real estate: "a dwelling house & ½ an acre of ground," £7; and "four acres & half of land," £9 [MPR 1:146-47].

BIRTH: About 1585 (aged 50 in 1635 [Hotten 65]).
DEATH: Cambridge 24 January 1657/8.
MARRIAGE: By about 1617 _____ _____. She apparently died by 1635.
CHILD:

> i ROGER, b. about 1617 (aged 18 in 1635 [Hotten 65]); m. by 1642 Susan _____ (eldest known child, Samuel, b. Cambridge 6 February 1642/3 [NEHGR 3:248 (surname incorrectly read as "Burt")]).

COMMENTS: William Buck, aged 50, plowwright, was enrolled at London on 15 April 1635 as a passenger for New England on the *Increase*, along with Roger Buck, aged 18 [Hotten 65].

William Buck was not fully integrated into the communal life of his town or colony. All of his land was on the periphery of the town. There is no evidence that he was a church member or a freeman, or ever held office. He apparently was a widower when he arrived, and does not seem to have married during his twenty years and more in New England.

Savage says that Roger Buck "had Mary, b. 1638, who d. 31 August 1669" [Savage 1:284]. The year of birth would seem to have been calculated from an age at death, but this death record has not been found. Roger and his wife had a daughter Mary born on 23 June 1648, and this would seem to be the child to whom this death refers.

THOMAS BUCKLAND

ORIGIN: Unknown
MIGRATION: 1634
FIRST RESIDENCE: Dorchester
REMOVES: Windsor

CHURCH MEMBERSHIP: Admission to Dorchester church prior to 6 May 1635 implied by freemanship.
FREEMAN: 6 May 1635 [MBCR 1:371].
EDUCATION: Her inventory included "two old Bibles" valued at 4s.
OFFICES: Connecticut jury, 1 August 1644 [CCCR 1:109]. Windsor rate collector for colony tax, 6 February 1649/50 [CCCR 1:204].
   Served in the Pequot War, 1637 [CCCR 2:161].
ESTATE: In the Windsor land inventory on 4 February 1640[/1?], Thomas Buckland had seven parcels: "an homelot five acres"; "in the Great Meadow two acres" (annotated "Timothy Buckland"); "also in the meadow twelve acres" (annotated "sold to R. Winchell [and] P. Tilton"); "upon the bank ten acres" (annotated "sold to A. Randall"); "over the Great River in breadth thirty rod, length three miles"; "in the northwest field fourteen acres"; and "towards the pine meadow sixteen acres and half" (annotated "Timothy Buckland"). "Also by purchase from George Hull his homelot seven acres more or less with his barn and all appurtenances ... as also in the Great Meadow sixteen acres." "Also twenty acres of woodland that was granted to the said Gorg Hull by the town" (annotated "sold to the town") [WiLR 1:58].
   The inventory of the estate of "Thomas Buckland who died on the 28 of May 1662," taken 20 June 1662, totalled £346 12s. 4d. (against which were debts of £2 16s.), of which £232 was real estate: "his housing, orchard and homelot on the east side of the street, 3 acres and a half," £75; "on the west side of the street enclosed 4 acres," £8; "in meadow 18 acres," £90; "on the east side of the Great River in breadth 30 rods," £50; "a wood lot 14 acres,"

£7; and "8 acres of woodland above the stone pit," £2. At the end of the inventory was a deduction of £25 for a "half lot over the river ... given to Tim[othy] at marriage," bringing the total to £318 16s. 4d. Appended to the inventory was a list of "The next relations to the party deceased:

> Temprance the widow
> of children
> Timothy his eldest son of the age of 24 years married
> Nicolas his son of age 16 years
> Thomas his son of 12 years age
> Elisabeth his daughter married
> Temprance his daughter of 20 years
> Sara his daughter of 14 years
> Hanna his daughter of 8 years" [HaPR 2:160; HaPD Case

#833].

On the reverse of the inventory is a distribution of the estate, dated 10 September 1662: to the widow, £118; to Nicholas, £30; to Thomas, £30; to Elizabeth, £30; to Temperance, £30; to Sarah, £30; to Hannah, £30; and to "Tim[othy] besides what he had at marriage," £20 16s. 4d., for a total of £318 16s. 4d. "[T]he estate that is distributed shall remain to Elizabeth the wife of Edward Adams to her and her heirs and that her husband give security that it shall not be alienated" [HaPR 2:160; HaPD Case #833].

On 12 October 1671, the Court granted land to several men "who were Pequott soldiers," including fifty acres to "the heirs of Thomas Buckland" [CCCR 2:161].

In her will, dated 21 March 1680/1 and proved 1 November 1681, "Temperance Buckland, widow," bequeathed to "my son Nicholas Buckland my now dwelling house & orchard, being my homelot, ... two acres of pasture land below it, & in the Great Meadow six acres of meadowland" and requested that "while I live, that he take the best care he is able for my comfortable maintenance"; to "my daughter Hannah Buckland all my household goods" [HaPR 4:61; HaPD Case #832].

The inventory of the estate of Temperance Buckland, taken 19 August 1681, totalled £99 18s. 4d., of which £84 was real estate: "the house and homestead," £30; "two acres of pasture in the meadow," £12; and "six acres of meadow," £42 [HaPR 4:61; HaPD Case #832].

On an unknown date, Timothy Buckland, Joshua Willes, "James Mielles," and John Phelps petitioned the General Court of Connecticut, arguing that the division of the estate of Thomas Buckland made in 1662 should have been construed to give £118 to the widow for life only. On 17 May 1686, Nicholas Buckland responded to this petition, arguing that it would be contrary to law for the General Court to reconsider the case, and that the Court should allow the estate to stand as distributed (which of course benefited him, since he was the principal legatee in his mother's will, and received most of the estate in dispute). Most of the probate documents above were copied and entered in this dispute, including the distribution of 1662, to which had been added the annotations that daughter Temperance had married John Ponder and daughter Sarah had married John Phelps [Connecticut Archives, Private Controversies, Series One, 3:142-48]. On 19 May 1686, the court found in favor of Nicholas Buckland [CCCR 3:119-20, 192, 200].

BIRTH: By about 1613 based on estimated date of marriage.
DEATH: Windsor 28 May 1662 [CTVR 21; Grant 83 (day and month not given)].
MARRIAGE: By 1638 Temperance Denslow, daughter of NICHOLAS DENSLOW [GMB 1:528]. "The old widow Buckland" died at Windsor 26 July 1681 [Grant 86].
CHILDREN (all born Windsor):
i   TIMOTHY, b. 10 March 1638[/9] [Grant 25]; m. Windsor 27 March 1662 Abigail Vore [Grant 26], daughter of Richard Vore [TAG 26:69].
ii   ELIZABETH, b. 21 February 1640[/1] [Grant 25]; m. (1) Windsor 25 May 1660 Edward Adams [Grant 23]; m. (2) by 1686 James Miles (see COMMENTS below).
iii TEMPERANCE, b. 27 November 1642 [Grant 25]; m. Hartford 26 June 1668 John Ponder [CTVR 11].
iv   MARY, b. 2 October 1644 (annotated "Dead") [Grant 25]; on 8 December 1657 John Winthrop Jr. treated "Buckland, Mary, Tho[mas] Buckl[and] his daughter, 12 years old," who "hath had measles" [WMJ 267]; d. Windsor 13 December 1657 [CTVR 43].
v   NICHOLAS, b. 21 February 1646[/7] [Grant 25]; m. (1) Windsor 14 April or 21 October 1668 Martha Wakefield [CTVR 11; Grant 25]; m. (2) Windsor 3 March 1685/6 Elizabeth Drake [CTVR 52]; m. (3) Windsor 16 June 1698 Hannah (Smith) (Trumbull) Strong [WiVR Barbour, citing 1:54], daughter of Hugh Smith of Rowley and widow successively of Joseph Trumbull and John Strong [TAG 12:76-77, 35:1].
vi   SARAH, b. 24 March 1648[/9] [Grant 25]; m. by 1675 John Phelps (eldest known child b. Windsor 21 January

1675[/6?] [Grant 61]).

vii   THOMAS, b. 2 February 1650[/1] (annotated "Dead") [Grant 25]; m. Windsor 21 October 1675 Hannah Cook, daughter of Nathaniel Cook [CTVR 14; Grant 68].

viii   HANNAH, b. 18 September 1654 (annotated "Dead") [Grant 25]; m. Windsor 11 August 1681 Joshua Welles [Grant 100].

COMMENTS: In the 17 August 1677 list of "what children has been born in Windsor from our beginning to so far as I am able to find out," Grant credited Thomas Buckland Sr. with eight children [Grant 90].

The undated petition of the heirs of Thomas Buckland (probably made in 1686) was signed by Timothy Buckland, Joshua Willes, "James Mielles," and John Phelps; the responding petition from Nicholas Buckland, dated 17 May 1686, begins with the following phrase: "Whereas my brother and brothers-in-law have given the court the trouble of a petition ..." [Connecticut Archives, Private Controversies, Series One, 3:147-48].

Thomas Buckland had four daughters: Elizabeth, married Edward Adams; Temperance, married John Ponder; Sarah, married John Phelps; and Hannah, married Joshua Welles. Sarah and Hannah are accounted for among the three brothers-in-law signing the first petition above. John Ponder did not die until 1712 and his wife until 1732, so Temperance must have chosen not to partake in the family struggle, perhaps because she was living in Westfield by the time of the petition.

This leaves Elizabeth as the presumed wife of "James Mielles." Edward Adams died at Windsor on 15 August 1683, so Elizabeth was certainly available to remarry by 1686. On 3 September 1684, "James Miles, aged 35," deposed regarding the estate of Robert Hayward of Windsor [Manwaring 1:319-20]. No other record for this man has been found, but he was in the right place at the right time to have married the widow Elizabeth (Buckland) Adams.

BIBLIOGRAPHIC NOTE: In his 1946 account of "The Denslow Family in America," George McKenzie Roberts included extensive treatment of Thomas Buckland, his wife and children [NYGBR 77:55-56, 60-64].

WILLIAM BUCKLAND

ORIGIN: Unknown (but see *ASSOCIATIONS* below)
MIGRATION: 1634
FIRST RESIDENCE: Hingham
REMOVES: Rehoboth by 1656

OCCUPATION: Carpenter [SLR 4:132].
CHURCH MEMBERSHIP: Either William Buckland or his wife had become a member of Hingham church by 1640, when their son Benjamin was baptized there.
FREEMAN: Oath of fidelity at Rehoboth in 1657 [PCR 8:178].
EDUCATION: Signed his deeds by mark.
OFFICES: Plymouth grand jury, 3 June 1656 [PCR 3:100]. Rehoboth constable, 3 June 1657 [PCR 3:116]. Plymouth coroner's jury, 16 February 1677[/8?] [PCR 5:209].
ESTATE: "The several parcels of land and meadow legally given unto William Buckland by the town of Hingham": 3 April 1636, "for a houselot five acres"; 8 October 1637, "for a Great Lot twelve acres of land lying upon the Great Plain in the fifth furlong eastward from the center"; 12 June 1636, "for a planting lot four acres of land lying upon the north side of Weriall Hill"; 12 June 1636, "two acres of salt marsh lying in Layford's Liking Meadow"; and 1647, "one acre and three-quarters of an acre of salt marsh at Conyhassett ... the sixth lot in the third division" [HiBOP 50].

On 29 October 1657, Roger Williams of Providence, as attorney for Mr. John Clarke of Newport, sole remaining executor of "John Hazell deceased," gave a receipt to William Buckland for the £72 "which he stood engaged to pay for his land to the executors of John Hazell aforesaid" [PCLR 2:2:1; MD 13:39-40].

On 1 September 1659, whereas "there is a purpose of marriage intended between Josepth Buckland of Rehoboth and Deborah Allin of the same plantation," "William Buckland of Rehoboth" promised to give them "one-third [part] of all my lands both upland and meadow with all the privileges pertaining to it"; to "build the said Josepth a convenient house for his comfortable living with threescore acres of land adjoining to it"; "after me and my wife's decease ... the said Josepth shall have and enjoy so much more lands both upland and meadow as shall make up the full half of what I do now possess in Rehoboth"; and "after the decease of me and my wife half of all my goods and stock that I have both within doors and without to be his forever, only I do reserve in my hands out of Josepth's estate five pounds to be at my dispose" [PCLR 2:2:66; MD 16:82].

On 25 May 1661, "William Buckland of Reoboath in New England, carpenter," sold to Daniel Cushing of Hingham "one great lot containing twelve acres ... in the township of Hingham ... which was given me by the town of Hingham ..., also another great lot containing eight acres ... which I purchased of Jerome Bellaime ..., also one parcel of salt marsh containing one acre and three quarters which was given me by the said town of Hingham ... in Conahasset marshes the sixth lot in the third division" [SLR 4:132-33].

On 18 April 1664, "William Buckland of Rehoboth" deeded to "my son Benjamin Buckland the third part of my land in Rehoboth that is now in being or any that I the said William shall purchase or possess either there or elsewhere," with some reservations and exceptions [PCLR 3:117].

On 1 November 1684, "Joseph Buckland, planter," posted bond "to administer on the estate of Will[i]am Buckland, of Rehoboth, late deceased" [PCR 6:146].

BIRTH: By about 1609 based on estimated date of marriage.
DEATH: Buried Rehoboth 1 September 1683 [PCR 8:88 (year not given); ReVR 805].
MARRIAGE: By about 1634 Mary Bosworth, daughter of EDWARD BOSWORTH. She was buried at Rehoboth 29 July 1687 [ReVR 805].
CHILDREN:

i   JOSEPH, b. say 1634; m. Rehoboth 5 November 1659 Deborah Allen [ReVR 65].

ii   LYDIA, b. say 1637; m. (1) by 1661 John Brown, son of JOHN BROWN of Plymouth (eldest known child b. Rehoboth 9 June 1661 [ReVR 555]); m. (2) on or soon after 3 June 1664 William Lord; m. (3) Thomas Dunk; m. (4) Abraham Post [Manwaring 1:552-53; NEHGR 146:213, 147:62; Kenneth Lord, *Genealogy of the Descendants of Thomas Lord* ... (New York 1946), pp. 71-74; Ackley-Bosworth 282-84].

iii   BENJAMIN, bp. Hingham [2] July 1640 [NEHGR 121:13]; m. by 1663 Rachel Wheatley (eldest known child b. Rehoboth [blank] November 1663 [ReVR 560]; six children by 1676 [PCPR 3:2:80-81]) [NEHGR 66:176-77, 143:137, and the sources cited there].

iv   (possibly) WILLIAM, b. about 1644 (aged 22 years on 15 January 1666/7 [WMJ 662]); m. by 1666 Elizabeth

Williams, daughter of William Williams of Hartford [TAG 69:174-79].

ASSOCIATIONS: If the marriage of William Buckland did take place in England, then he probably came to New England in 1634 with his father-in-law, EDWARD BOSWORTH. This would further indicate an association with HENRY SEWALL, and an origin in or near Manchester, Lancashire.

COMMENTS: In our earlier account of *JONATHAN BOSWORTH*, brother of Mary (Bosworth) Buckland, we failed to discriminate between the subject of the present sketch and the earlier *WILLIAM BUCKLAND* of New England, but less than a hundred pages later this distinction was properly made [GMB 1:190, 267-68].

On 1 September 1640, "Will[ia]m Buckland, carpenter," was a bondsman for Benjamin and Nathaniel Bosworth in a financial transaction [Lechford 306].

BIBLIOGRAPHIC NOTE: In 1926 Mary Bosworth Clarke included in her treatment of the Bosworth family an account of William Buckland and his children [Bosworth Gen 1:51-60, 2:139-49].

In 1929 Mary A. Anderson compiled an account of this immigrant; she included in this sketch records which more likely belong to his son of the same name [Smith-Hale Anc 493-96].

In 1994 Gale Ion Harris published an account of the family of William Williams of Hartford, which included the evidence for including a son William Buckland in this family [TAG 69:87-94, 174-83].

EDWARD BUGBY

ORIGIN: Unknown (but see *MARRIAGE* below)
MIGRATION: 1634 on the *Francis*
FIRST RESIDENCE: Roxbury

OCCUPATION: There was considerable cloth in his inventory, but no occupation is noted.
CHURCH MEMBERSHIP: "Edward Bugbee an old man" was admitted a member of Roxbury church on 20 August 1665 [RChR 89]. Barely a year before his death, "Edward Bugbey [was] admonished by the church," but we are not told why [RChR 206].

EDUCATION: He made his mark to deeds.

ESTATE: On 1 June 1639, it was recorded that Edward Bugby received eight acres for a great lot at Roxbury [RTR 1:1]. In 1640, it was noted that Edward Bugby was responsible for six goats and seven kids [RTR 1:4].

In the Roxbury land inventory, Edward Bugby owned his house, barn and three-acre lot; three acres more; eight acres more; the first lot in the first and third divisions; nineteen acres and three quarters and twenty rods; twelve acres in the Thousand acres; a house and an acre of land purchased of William Gilford; four acres in the upper calves pasture; sixteen acres and a half in the "Nookes, exchanged with my son Richard Chamberlin"; ten acres in the Nookes; eight acres of swamp bought of Richard Pepper; an acre and a half of salt marsh; and two acres of marsh [RBOP 32]. In the same list, it is noted that John Newell purchased four acres of land in the calves pasture from Edward Bugby [RBOP 50].

On 30 March 1648, Richard Pepper of Roxbury sold to Edward Bugby of Roxbury eight acres in Roxbury [SLR 1:89]. On 20 January 1657/8, "Ed. Budgby" held twelve acres in the Thousand acres at Dedham [RTR 1:6]. On 22 April 1661, Edward Bugby of Roxbury sold to "Daniel Einsworth" ten acres in the last lot in the last division with the trees upon it [SLR 3:475].

In his will, dated 26 November 1668 and proved 30 January 1668/9, "Edward Bugby, being stricken in years," bequeathed to "my son Joseph ... my housing and land, barn and orchard, all that is mine, on the right hand of the way" and eight acres of swamp, eleven acres, one acre of fresh meadow, two acres of salt marsh, eight acres of upland, and livestock, as well as "that bedding and household stuff that I have already given him"; to "my daughter Sarah" the ten-acre lot in the first division and sixteen acres lying by it, twelve acres in the Thousand acres, one acre and a half of salt marsh at Gravely Point, bedding and household stuff, and livestock, and also "my money and eveything that is mine which I have not given to my son Joseph"; "out of that which I have given my daughter Sarah, there shall be paid my son-in-law Chamberlin, the husband of my daughter £18 in corn or cattle"; to "two of my grandchildren Mary and Rebecca Chamberlin" the one half of the £18 and the other half to Rebecca; son-in-law Chamberlin executor [SPR 6:35].

The inventory of Edward Bugby of Roxbury, presented 30 January 1668[/9], totalled £366 6s. 6d., of which £262 10s. was real estate: "his home lot, house, barn & orchard that lyeth on the right hand of the way leading to the great lots," £100; "eight acres of swamp & upland," £40; "eleven acres," £15; "the acre of fresh meadow," £5; "two acres of salt marsh at

Gravely Point," £10; "land lying at Pond Hill," £30; "the ten acre lot in the first division & the 16 acres lying by it," £50; "the twelve acres in the Thousand Acres," £5; and "the acre & half of salt marsh" £7 10s. [SLR 5:130].

BIRTH: About 1594 (aged 40 in 1634 [Hotten 279]; age at death is approximate and probably slightly exaggerated).
DEATH: Roxbury 27 January 1668/9 "Edward Bugbey, aged (as is said) above 80" [RChR 179].
MARRIAGE: By 1630 Rebecca _____. She apparently died before the writing of her husband's will.   (An Edward Bugby married at Sandon, Essex, 29 October 1620 Rebecca Jacob, baptized Sandon 28 June 1601, daughter of John Jacob, and this may be the immigrant couple.)
CHILDREN:

 i SARAH, b. about 1630 (aged 4 in 1634 [Hotten 279]); m. by 1665 (and probably by about 1656) Richard Chamberlain ("Sarah wife to Rich[ar]d Chamberline" admitted to full communion, 28 May 1665 [RChR 89]; "Benjamin, Joseph, Mary, Rebecca, Anna, the children of Rich[ar]d Chamberlain," baptized 4 June 1665 [RChR 125]; "Mehetabel daughter to Rich[ar]d Chamberlaine" baptized 28 January 1665/6 [RChR 126]).

 ii JOSEPH, b. Roxbury 6 June 1640 [RVR MS 3]; m. by 1664 Experience Pitcher, daughter of Andrew Pitcher (eldest known child b. Roxbury 17 September 1664; "Experience Pitcher" bp. Dorchester 25 September 1642 [DChR 155]; in his will of 4 December 1660, Andrew Pitcher of Dorchester made a bequest to "my eldest daughter Experience" [SPR 1:366]; on 9 October 1670, "a daughter of Sister Picher who married one Bugbee of Rocksbery was dismissed to join the church at Rocksbery" [DChR 11]; on 15 July 1675, "Experience Bugby the wife of Joseph Bugby was received to take hold on the covenant" at Roxbury [RChR 92]).

 iii Infant, b. Roxbury [blank] August 1642 [RVR MS 4]; bur. Roxbury 31 August 1642 [RVR MS 97] or [blank] November 1642 [NEHGR 5:334; see also RChR 114].

ASSOCIATIONS: There is no demonstrable link to the RICHARD BUGBY listed by Eliot as one of the earliest Roxbury church members [RTR 74]. There was a contemporary Richard Bugby in Sandon, Essex, who married

17 February 1623/4 Mary Harding and had children: John, bp. 8 November 1624, and Mary, bp. 23 May 1626.

Richard Pepper sailed on the same ship, settled in Roxbury, and dealt in land with Bugby.

COMMENTS: On 30 April 1634, "Edward Bugbye," aged 40, "Rebecca his wife," aged 32, and "Sarah Bugbye," aged 4, were listed at Ipswich for passage to New England on the *Francis* [Hotten 278-79].

While the 1620 marriage of Edward and Rebecca in Sandon, Essex, is a promising record, if it pertains to the immigrants, it would imply that they had no children for ten years following their marriage.

In 1930 Edgar J. Bullard claimed that this immigrant had a son Edward "who received the bulk of his father's estate and remained in Roxbury" [*Bullard and Allied Families* (Detroit 1930), p. 177], but no evidence for such a son is found; this is probably meant for Edward Bugby, son of Joseph and grandson of this immigrant. This and other secondary sources also claim a son John for the immigrant; such a person did exist, but he married in Roxbury in 1690, which would be much too late for a son of Edward Bugby. He may have been related in some other way.

PETER BULKELEY

ORIGIN: Odell, Bedfordshire
MIGRATION: 1635 on the *Susan & Ellen*
FIRST RESIDENCE: Cambridge
REMOVES: Concord

OCCUPATION: Minister.
EDUCATION: B.A. 1604-5, St John's College, Cambridge; M.A. 1608; incorporated at Oxford 1610 [Venn 1:250; Morison 369-70]. "A most excellent scholar, a very well-read person.... His education was answerable unto his original; it was learned, it was genteel, and, which was the top of all, it was very pious: at length it made him a Bachelor of Divinity and Fellow of Saint John's College in Cambridge: the college whereinto he had been admitted, about the sixteenth year of his age; and it was while he was but a junior bachelor that he was chosen a fellow" [Magnalia 1:400].

ESTATE: In the 8 February 1635/6 list of "houses" in the town, "Mr. Peter Buckly" held five [CaTR 18]. In 1636 he held land on the south side of the path to Charlestown [CaTR 33]. By 1645, Herbert Pelham had succeeded to thirteen acres "late Mr. Bucklies house" [CaTR 67].

On 1 February 1644[/5], Peter Bulkeley, minister of Concord, sold to Thomas Browne of Concord "the house which I bought of Robert Tomline" with four acres [MLR 4:42]. This deed was sworn by the witnesses on 22 June 1670. On 25 September 1663, Grace Bulkeley of Concord sold to Thomas Browne eighteen acres in Concord near the house [MLR 3:461].

On 1 March 1651/2, Joseph Hills of Malden and Hannah his wife sold twelve acres in Charlestown, "sometime in the possession of Mr. Edward Mellowes of Charlestown lately deceased," to Abraham Smith of Cambridge with the "consent and advice of Mr. Buckley," who was surety on Mellowes's estate [MLR 1:162].

On 22 February 1653[/4], Peter Bulkeley of Concord sold to William Hunt of Concord fifty acres of upland "I formerly bought of William Judson" and twenty acres "I bought of Robert Tomlin" with the second division due, reserving the wood for firewood. Grace Bulkeley acknowledged Hunt's payment on 30 September 1663 [MLR 3:103].

On 6 January 1657/8, "Peter Bulkly minister of the Word of God in Concord" sold to Thomas Dane of Concord, carpenter, the house, barn and land "I bought of George Haywood," as well as an orchard. The payments for this property were to be made in London to "such person ... as said Peter shall appoint" [MLR 2:222].

In his will, dated 14 April 1658 and proved 20 June 1659, "Peter Bulkely, minister of the Word, being now in the seventy-six year of my age," bequeathed to "my son Edward Bulkley (to whom I did at the time of his marriage give such a portion as I was then able to give)" a large list of books, or if he remove back to England then £5 "to be paid him there in England by my son John"; to "my daughter-in-law, the widow of my son Thomas deceased," the value of one cow; to "my son Eliezur" either the farm used by widow Goble and her son Thomas Goble or "my mill here in the town," or the hundred acres at the end of the Great Meadow, and twenty acres more, the choice of which to be left to the executor and overseers; to "my son Peter the next in value of these three things before named ... the third of the three to remain to those that shall inherit mine house in which I do now live"; to "my son John," books; to "my son Joseph," books; to "my Lord Oliver St. John, Lord Chief Justice of the Common Pleas," my great English Bible as a "token of my due love"; to "my cousin Mr. Samuel Haugh," a book; to "my daughter Dorothy the £150 of English money which I have in England, in the hands of my son John, the most part thereof came to me and my wife by the death of one of my wife's sisters" and further "desire my wife when God shall take her to himself, to add something more to the said £150," the profit to be added; residue to "my dear wife & her heirs by me begotten"; should any of the children be disobedient, she to have power to alter their legacies; wife sole executrix; "my loving brethren, Robert Merriam and Luke Potter, the faithful deacons of our church, & William Hunt & Timothy Wheeler" overseers, each to have a treatise [Bulkeley Gen 107-10, citing MPR Case #3420].

In a codicil dated 13 January 1658[/9], Peter Bulkeley bequeathed a sixteenth part of the mill and iron works to "my beloved wife" [Bulkeley Gen 110, citing MPR Case #3420].

In a second codicil, dated 26 February 1658[/9], Peter Bulkeley specifically charged his overseers with seeing that his will not be altered [Bulkeley Gen 110, citing MPR Case #3420]. In the list of books appended to the will, Peter Bulkeley directed that part of them were to go to son Edward and the other part "to my son Gershom" [Bulkeley Gen 110, citing MPR Case #3420].

On 30 September 1663, Grace Bulkeley, relict of Mr. Peter Bulkeley of Concord, sold three quarters to Timothy Wheeler and one quarter to George Wheeler of all her property in Concord, excepting ten acres intended for Mr. Edward Bulkeley. Further provisions of the deed reserved a sufficient water course from the mill and exempted the Wheelers from maintaining fences. The property transferred by this deed included a dwelling house, outhouses, garden, orchard, pasture, a one-hundred-acre great lot, seventy-two acres of meadow, twenty acres of meadow, four acres of meadow, five acres of meadow, eight acres of meadow, four acres of meadow, thirty acres of meadow, two hundred acres in the hog pens, one hundred fifty acres by the cedar swamp, one hundred twelve acres of woodland, and twenty acres of commons [MLR 3:128].

On 2 October 1663, a division was made of the real estate bequeathed by Peter Bulkeley to his sons Eleazer and Peter. Eleazer inherited the seven-hundred-fifty acre farm and Peter received the rest of the lands [MLR 3:19].

BIRTH: Odell, Bedford, 31 January 1582/3, son of the Rev. Edward and Olive (Irby) Bulkeley ("He was descended of an honorable family, in

Bedfordshire; where for many successive generations the names of Edward and Peter were alternatively worn by the heirs of the family. His father was Edward Bulky, D.D., a faithful minister of the gospel; the same whom we find making a supplement unto the last volume of our books of martyrs. He was born at Woodhil (or Odel) in Bedfordshire, January 31st, 1582" [Magnalia 1:400]) [Bulkeley Gen 14-20].

DEATH: Concord 9 March 1658/9 [CoVR 8]. (Anticipating his death, Peter wrote: "Of seventy-two long years this is the last; A new year now begins, the old year passed: Oh may my heart and life be also new" [Magnalia 1:403]. He recovered, to die in his seventy-seventh year.)

MARRIAGE: (1) Goldington, Bedford, 12 April 1613 Jane Allen, daughter of Thomas and Mary (Fairclough) (Haselden) Allen [Bulkeley Gen 42; NEHGR 52:252-53, 257]. She was baptized at Goldington 13 January 1587/8 and buried at Odell 8 December 1626 [Bulkeley Gen 92]. ("His first wife was the daughter of Mr. Thomas Allen, of Goldington: a most virtuous gentlewoman, whose nephew was the Lord Mayor of London, Sir Thomas Allen. By her he had nine sons and two daughters" [Magnalia 1:403].)

(2) In April 1635 Grace Chetwood [Bulkeley Gen 58, citing a contemporary letter of John Blackiston provided by Charles E. Banks (FOOF 1:707)], "a virtuous daughter of Sir Richard Chetwood" and Dorothy Needham [Magnalia 1:403]. She was born about 1602 (aged 33 or 30 in 1635 [Hotten 59, 76]) and died at New London 21 April 1669 ("April 21 [1669]. Mrs Grace Bulkley the widow of Mr. Peter Bulkley sometime Pastor of the ch[urc]h of Concord, deceased. She was a woman of great piety and wisdom & died in good old age. Her sickness was long and very afflictive. She was sick near 3 months before she died. She had not the use of her understanding but by fits, the greatest part of her sickness" [NEHGR 9:45]).

CHILDREN:

With first wife

    i   EDWARD, bp. Odell 12 June 1614; St Catherine's College, Cambridge, 1629 [Venn 1:250]; m. Lucian ____ [NEHGR 58:201-02, citing PCLR 5:293-94].

    ii   MARY, bp. Odell 24 August 1615; bur. there 13 January 1615/6.

    iii THOMAS, bp. Odell 13 April 1617; m. by 1640 Sarah Jones (eldest child b. Concord 12 August 1640 [CoVR 1]), daughter of Rev. John Jones [TAG 71:52-54].

    iv   NATHANIEL, bp. Odell 29 November 1618; bur. there 11 February 1628/9.

v   JOHN, bp. Odell 6 February 1619/20 (aged 15 in 1635 [Hotten 59]); Harvard College 1642 [Sibley 1:52-54]; m. (1) Odell 19 March 1650[/1?] Anne Try; m. (2) (license) Harrow-on-the-Hill, Middlesex, 6 September 1667 Elizabeth (_____) Okes of East Smithfield; m. (3) Avis _____.

vi   MARY, bp. Odell 1 November 1621; no further record.

vii   JOSEPH, bp. Odell 4 May 1623 (aged 11 in 1635, called "Benjamin" in the passenger list [Hotten 63]); living 1658; d.s.p.

viii   DANIEL, bp. Odell 28 August 1625 (aged 9 in 1635 [Hotten 63]); predeceased his father.

ix   JABEZ, bp. Odell 24 December 1626; bur. there 2 December 1629.

With second wife

x   GERSHOM, b. about 1636 (said to have died aged 77 years and 11 months on 1 or 2 December 1713 [Sibley 1:397]); Harvard College 1655 [Sibley 1:389-402]; m. Concord 6 October 1659 Sarah Chauncy.

xi   ELEAZER, b. say 1638; Harvard College class of 1658 but did not graduate [Sibley 1:572]; named in 1663 division of father's land; no further record.

xii   DOROTHY, b. Concord 2 August 1640 [CoVR 1]; living, unm. at the time of her father's 1658 will.

xiii   PETER, b. Concord 12 August 1643 [CoVR 1]; Harvard College class of 1660 but did not graduate [Sibley 1:576]; m. by about 1670 Margaret _____ (estimated year of birth of eldest child [Bulkeley Gen 127-28]).

ASSOCIATIONS: Peter's sister Elizabeth was wife successively of Richard Whittingham and *ATHERTON HOUGH* [GMB 2:1007]. Peter's sister Martha married *ABRAHAM MELLOWES* [GMB 2:1248-50]. Peter was uncle to Oliver St. John (mentioned in his will) and Elizabeth (St. John) Whiting, wife of Rev. Samuel Whiting of Lynn [Bulkeley Gen 31].

COMMENTS: On 13 April 1635, "Grace Bewlie," aged 30, and "Jo[hn] Backley," aged 15, were enrolled at London as passengers for New England on the *Susan & Ellen* [Hotten 59]. On 18 April 1635, "Ben[jamin] Buckley," aged 11, and "Daniell Buckley," aged 9, were enrolled at London on the same ship [Hotten 63].

On 8 May 1635, "Grace Bulkley," aged 33, was enrolled at London as a passenger for New England on the *Elizabeth & Ann* [Hotten 76]. On 9

May 1635, "Peter Bulkley," aged 50, was enrolled on the same ship [Hotten 77].

No doubt the long drawn out enrollments and the lack of effort to standardize spelling of the names were reflections of the family's attempt to board the ship without being apprehended. Son Edward preceded the rest of the family, becoming a member of Boston church on 22 March 1634/5 [BChR 20].

Despite the fact that Mather indicates that Peter had nine sons and two daughters with his first wife, Jacobus found no record of the ninth son [Magnalia 1:403]. Others have added children George, Richard and William to his progeny with his first wife, but offered no evidence [Wethersfield Hist 2:147-51].

Mather does not repeat the tradition seen elsewhere that on the voyage from England, wife Grace appeared to die. Against common practice, but in the absence of decay, her body was not committed to the deep and on the third day, she showed signs of life, and survived over thirty years [Bulkeley Anc 103; Wethersfield Hist 149].

Mather characterized Bulkeley as an exact Sabbath-keeper, who scrupulously avoided all novelties of apparel and cut his hair exceedingly close [Magnalia 1:401]. His early ministerial years were peaceful despite his leanings since "the good Bishop of Lincoln connived at his non-conformity (as he did at his father's), and he lived an unmolested non-conformist until he had been three prentice-ships of years in his ministry" [Magnalia 1:400].

Toward the end of his life there are several mentions of his "infirmities of body" restricting his travel, and in his own words, "A sluggish mass of clay is this my frame" [Magnalia 1:400, 403].

All the sons were offered a college education, but the last two, Eleazer and Peter did not finish, perhaps because of their father's death.

Roger Williams was "long requested to write my grounds against the English preaching, etc." by various divines, including Peter Bulkeley. Williams mentioned him in a letter of 21 July 1637 to Winthrop:

> In the midst of a multitude of barbarous distractions I have fitted some thing to that purpose: and being not able at present to transcribe the whole: yet having been long solicited by Mr. Buckley (from whom I received some objections) and by many others, and of late by my worthy friend Mr. Peters [torn] sight of them, I have thought good to send so much as I have transcribed to the hand of my lo[ving] friend Mr. Buckly [WP 3:455].

His secular appearances were very rare. On 2 June 1640, Peter was granted a judgment against Alexander Thwaite [MBCR 1:296]. In May of 1652, as uncle to Mrs. Hannah (Smith?) (Mellows) Hills, he was surety for the estate of her children with his nephew Edward Mellows [MBCR 3:271].

BIBLIOGRAPHIC NOTE: Mather published a "quaint, yet informative," biography of Bulkeley [Magnalia 1:400-4; Bulkeley Gen 92].

In 1933 Donald Lines Jacobus compiled *The Bulkeley Genealogy: Rev. Peter Bulkeley, Being an account of his career, his ancestry, the ancestry of his two wives, and his relatives in England and New England, together with a genealogy of his descendants through the seventh generation* (New Haven, Connecticut, 1933). As is evident from its subtitle, this genealogical masterpiece should be consulted for all aspects of the multitudinous ramifications of Bulkeley's genealogical connections, and is used in support of many of the claims made above.

Jacobus went on to publish additional material on this family. In 1933 he corrected some errors regarding this immigrant and his family as published in *Records of Littleton* [TAG 9:227], and in 1944 he wrote at length on the connections of Grace Chetwood [TAG 21:69-83].

In 1976 Michael McGiffert addressed an aspect of Bulkeley's theological views [NEHGR 130:107-29].

HENRY BULL

ORIGIN: Unknown
MIGRATION: 1635 on the *James* of London
FIRST RESIDENCE: Roxbury
REMOVES: Boston 1637, Portsmouth [RI] 1638, Newport 1639

CHURCH MEMBERSHIP: Admitted to Roxbury Church as member #141, late in 1635: "Henry Bull a man servant he came to the land; he lived honestly for a good season, but on the sudden (being weak & affectionate) he was taken & transported with the opinion of familism & running in that schism he fell into many & gross sins of lying etc. (as may be seen in the story) for which he was excommunicate, after which he removed to the Island" [RChR 81].
FREEMAN: 17 May 1637 [MBCR 1:373]. Newport 16 March 1640/1 [RICR 1:110]. On the 1655 roll of Newport freemen [RICR 1:300].

EDUCATION: Made his mark to early Portsmouth records, 7 March 163[7/]8 [RICR 1:52]. Signed his will by mark.

OFFICES: Governor of Rhode Island colony, 6 May 1685, 6 May 1690 (and moderator, but refused to serve) [RICR 3:169, 185, 269].

Assistant, 7 May 1674, 28 October 1674, 15 May 1675, 20 October 1675 [RICR 2:518, 522, 528; RICT 3:36, 41, 43].

Deputy from Newport to Rhode Island General Assembly, 22 May 1655, 27 March 1666, 2 May 1666, 30 April 1672, 30 October 1672, 6 May 1673, 29 October 1673, 5 May 1674, 4 May 1680, 3 May 1681, 26 February 1689/90 [RICR 1:304, 2:139, 146, 449, 465, 482, 508, 516, 3:83, 97, 259]. Deputy for Providence to Rhode Island General Assembly, 19 May 1657 [RICR 1:354].

Committee to receive the Charter, 18 May 1674 [RICR 1:519]. Committee to encourage trade and navigation, 6 May 1685 [RICR 3:169]. Conservator of the Peace for Kingstown, 1 March 1689/90 [RICR 3:263].

Grand jury, 15 June 1671, 18 October 1671, 22 October 1673 (foreman) [RICT 3:6, 8, 35]. Chosen for the grand jury by Newport, but exempted for such service by law, May 1679 [RICT 3:84]. Coroner's jury, 12 May 1673 [RICT 3:25]. Arbiter, 7 September 1680 [RICT 3:97].

Newport sergeant attendant, 12 March 1639/40, 16 March 1640/1, 16 March 1641/2 [RICR 1:100, 112, 120]. Rater, 25 May 1655 [RICR 1:311].

Corporal, Portsmouth train band, 27 June 1638 [RICR 1:56]. Sergeant, 24 January 1638/9 [RICR 1:65].

ESTATE: On 4 February 1640[/1][?], the town of Portsmouth granted Henry Bull the "north field" [RICR 1:76; PoTR 19].

On 12 December 1663, with son Jireh, Henry Bull sold 43 acres in Conanicut and Dutch Island to Caleb Carr. On 27 November 1688, Henry Bull deeded to grandchildren Christopher and Elizabeth Allen of Little Compton 26 acres there and seven negroes. On 16 February 1692/3, he bought of Edward Richmond of Little Compton a tract of 120 acres there for the use of Henry and Ann Richmond, the two youngest children of said Edward, reserving to Edward Richmond and wife Amey the whole profits for life. On 29 January 1703/4, widow Ann Bull of Newport, now residing in Portsmouth, deeded to her kinswoman Sarah Borden, wife of Matthew Borden of Portsmouth, all her household stuff in her house at Newport, formerly the dwelling place of deceased husband Henry Bull. (These deed abstracts are taken from Austin's account of Henry Bull, with no citations given [Austin 266].)

In his will, dated 11 December 1693 and proved 5 February 1693/4, "Henry Bull of Newport" bequeathed to "my beloved wife Ann Bull" £100, livestock and other moveables, and also "all my negro servants during her life and after her decease they shall be equally divided between my grandson Jireth Bull & his sister Mary Coggeshall, also I give my now dwelling house and land thereunto belonging ... containing by estimation sixteen acres" for life, she paying annually £6 to "the relict of my grandson Henry Bull deceased towards the bringing up of his children"; to "my grandson Jireth Bull and to the heirs of his body lawfully begotten unto the third generation and from thence to be fee simple all my farm lying and being in the precinct of the said town of Newport ... containing by estimation one hundred & eighty acres," he to pay £100 to "his sister Mary Coggeshall"; to "my greatgrandson Henry Bull son to grandson Henry Bull deceased ... my now dwelling house in Newport after the decease of my said wife Ann together with all the lands thereto belonging ... containing by estimation sixteen acres," he to pay £50 apiece to "his brother Ephraim Bull & sister Ann Bull"; to "my two grandsons Ephraim Bull and Ezekiel Bull and to their heirs forever my house and land in Newport aforesaid commonly called my son Jireth Bull's deceased house and orchard about one acre as it is now fenced in and to be divided into equal parts"; to "my granddaughter Mary Coggeshall" furniture; to "my granddaughter Elizabeth Allen & her heirs forever my house & land in Newport now in possession of John Payne" and livestock; to "my grandchildren Henry Richman & Ann Richman & their heirs forever all that farm & tract of land at Little Compton now in possession of their father Edward Richmond"; to "my said grandson Henry Richman" £30 when he comes of age; to "my said granddaughter Ann Richmand" £30 when she comes of age or at marriage; to "my three grandchildren Jireth Bull, Ephraim Bull, and Ezekiel Bull" all wearing apparel; to "the poor two hundred & fifty pounds of sheep's wool"; to "my trustees hereafter named" £10; residue to be "equally divided amongst my four grandchildren Jireth Bull, Mary Coggeshall, Ephraim Bull, Ezekiel Bull and the children of my grandson Henry deceased as the fifth part"; appointed "my beloved wife Ann my executrix and my trusty and loving friends John Easton Senior Governor, Daniel Gould Senior of the town of Newport aforesaid, Thomas Cornell Senior of the Town of Portsmouth, Benjamin Mewbury of Newport aforesaid" trustees [Newport Gleanings Item #11].

Executors of his will rendered an account showing an inventory of £968 1s. Payments were made to: widow Ann "a legacy and what was owing her for milk, her choice of six cows, fifty sheep, mare, colt, three feather beds, a quarter of the pewter, roan horse given her by children, allowance for a family of four persons for one year according to husband's will, and sundry things challenged by her as her own by agreement before marriage"; legacy to overseers; to Mary Coggeshall, wife of James £50; to Henry and Ann Richmond £60; to Jireh, Ephraim and Ezekiel Bull and Mary Coggeshall £124; the children of Henry Bull in Narragansett, their fifth of money in overseer's hands; Elizabeth Allen's legacy four young cattle and forty sheep; wearing apparell to the three grandsons [Austin 266, citing an unknown source].

BIRTH: About 1610 (aged 25 in 1635 [Hotten 107]; d. 22 January 1693/4 "aged about eighty-four years" [RIVR 7:91]).
DEATH: Newport 22 January 1693/4 ("Henry Bull aged about eighty-four years, he departed this life at his own house in Newport (he being the last man of the first settlers of this Rhode Island)" [RIVR 7:91]).
MARRIAGE: (1) By 1638 Elizabeth _____. She died Newport 1 October 1665 [RIVR 7:91].

(2) Sandwich 14 February 1664 [*sic*] Esther Allen [SandVR 2:1248]. She died Newport 26 March 1676 [RIVR 7:91].

(3) 28 March 1677 Ann (Clayton) Easton, widow of Gov. Nicholas Easton [RIVR 7]. She died Newport 30 January 1707/8 "aged 80 years" [RIVR 7:91].
CHILDREN:
With first wife
  i   JIREH, b. Portsmouth [blank] September 1638 [RIVR 7:48]; m. by about 1659 _____ _____ (eldest known child b. about 1659 [Austin 265]).
  ii   AMY, b. say 1648; m. (1) by 1668 James Leyouge [TAG 57:103-4, and the sources cited there]; m. (2) by about 1680 Edward Richmond [TAG 57:103-4, and the sources cited there].

COMMENTS: On 13 July 1635, "Henry Bull," aged 25 years, was enrolled at London as a passenger to New England on the *James* of London [Hotten 107].

On 20 November 1637, he was among the many Boston men disarmed as supporters of Wheelwright [MBCR 1:212]. On 12 March 1637/8, he was licensed to depart with Mr. William Coddington, Mr. John Coggeshall, and others [MBCR 1:223].

"Henry Bulle" went to Rhode Island with Anne Hutchinson and was the 18th signer of the Portsmouth compact of 7 March 163[7/]8 [RICR 1:52]. On 28 April 1639, he was present at Pocasset for the creating of Newport's government [RICR 1:87]. It is evident from his appearance on these lists that he was a junior member of each group, well through the 1650s.

As the 1650s progressed, however, his status changed and, on 23 May 1656, an honorific appeared before his name when, upon his petition, "Mr. Hen[ry] Bull" had his fine of £10 remitted [RICR 1:340]. By 1685 he had risen to the rank of Governor, but his tenure was singularly unmarked by accomplishments and when re-elected five years later, he adamantly refused to serve.

On Wednesday, 7 May 1690, Samuel Sewall sailed to Point Judith, and "got in about noon, being their Election day. Governor Bull furnished us with beds for the voyage; dined at Mr. Hedge's. Henry Bull chosen Governor" [Sewall 1:258]. Sewall does not mention that Bull refused to serve this term.

A number of secondary sources add a third child of Henry Bull, a daughter who married an Allen [e.g., Austin 266; TAG 30:122]. These claims all derive from a misunderstanding of the identity of Henry Bull's granddaughter Elizabeth Allen. In 1981 Jane Fletcher Fiske demonstrated that this granddaughter was born Elizabeth Leyouge, and that she was granddaughter of Henry through his daughter Amy [TAG 57:103-4].

HENRY BULL

On 13 April 1635, "Henrie Bull," aged 19, was enrolled at London, with a certificate of conformity from St Savior's, Southwark, Surrey, as a passenger for New England on the *Elizabeth* [Hotten 57].

COMMENTS: The difference of six years between the ages of this Henry Bull and of the other HENRY BULL found in the 1635 passenger lists makes it unlikely that they are the same man. If they are not the same, then there is no evidence that the passenger on the *Elizabeth* ever arrived in New England.

THOMAS BULL

ORIGIN: Unknown
MIGRATION: 1635 on the *Hopewell*
FIRST RESIDENCE: Cambridge
REMOVES: Hartford 1636

OCCUPATION: Soldier.

CHURCH MEMBERSHIP: Based on the two surviving baptismal records for their sons, either Thomas Bull or his wife had been admitted to Hartford church by 1649.

FREEMAN: "Lt. Tho[mas] Bull" appears in the October 1669 "list of freemen on the south side of Hartford" [CCCR 2:518].

EDUCATION: He signed his will. His inventory included "6 chairs & 8 cushions [&] 1 Great Bible" valued at £1 17s. and "1 Martyr Book & other books" valued at £3 9s.

OFFICES: Connecticut petit jury, 1 March 1648/9, 6 December 1649, 28 March 1650, 4 December 1651, 3 March 1652/3, 21 May 1653, 2 March 1653/4, 1 March 1654/5, 15 May 1655, 9 October 1658, 5 September 1661, 9 October 1661, 5 March 1662/3 [RPCC 59, 72, 79, 106, 115, 117, 122, 139, 142, 195, 238, 240, 264]. Grand jury, 15 May 1662 [CCCR 1:379].

Committee "for the viewing of Mattatock" as a location for a new plantation," 6-9 April 1674 [CCCR 2:224-25]. Hartford selectman, 23 February 1662/3 [HaTR 140]. Assessor, February 1667/8 [HaTR 155].

Pequot War, 1637 [John Mason, *A Brief History of The Pequot War* (Boston 1736), in Charles Orr, ed., *History of the Pequot War* (Cleveland 1897), pp. 29, 46]. Among his loose notes, Gov. John Winthrop wrote "Bull of Har[t]f[ord] Church filled with faith in entering the Pequot fort, he put off his arms, he was attacked by 3: Indians he laid hold of one of their arrows &c. & cut the other 2:bowstrings, & cleft one of their heads, & broke his sword, & by that occasion rescued a wounded man out of the fire, & used his sword, his piece of hard cheese received an arrow he killed 22" [Richard S. Dunn et al., eds., *The Journal of John Winthrop, 1630-1649* (Cambridge 1996), 769]. In 1639 "Thomas Bull informed the Court that a musket with 2 letters I W was taken up at Pequannocke in pursuit of the Pequatts which was conceived to be Jno. Woods which was killed at the river's mouth" [CCCR 1:29; RPCC 4].

On 7 March 1649/50, "Tho[mas] Bull is confirmed lieutenant" at Hartford [RPCC 78]. On 21 May 1653, "Lieutenant Bull to be their lieutenant," of a company of men to be ready for action against the Dutch [CCCR 1:242]. On 26 November 1673, "Lt. Tho[mas] Bull is chosen captain for such forces as shall be sent from Hartford County" against the Dutch [CCCR 2:218].

On 7 July 1675, "Capt. Tho[mas] Bull" was commissioned "to repair to those plantations [in southeastern Connecticut] ... for the special defense and safety of those places" [CCCR 2:333]. Thomas Bull directed

Connecticut's defense during King Philip's War [CCCR 2:333-34, 337, 344, 369-71, 373, 416, 582-4].

ESTATE: In the inventory of Hartford land in February 1639[/40] Thomas Bull held nineteen parcels (several of which were acquired after the date of compilation of the inventory): three acres "on which his dwelling house now standeth with other outhouses, yards, & gardens"; two acres two roods of upland; six acres one rood of upland; one rood in the Little Meadow; three acres three roods in the South Meadow; four acres in the Great Swamp; three acres in "the swamp next the Great River which he received of John Willcock for a parcel of land next Wethersfield bounds"; twenty acres of upland "on Wethersfield bounds"; "one parcel of swamp lying by the Great River containing by estimation one acre ... which he bought of William Gebbens"; "one parcel in that which is called the Indian Land containing by estimation one acre ... which he bought of William Gebbens"; (again) "one parcel lying in that land that is called the Indian Land containing by estimation one acre ... which he bought of William Gebbens"; "one parcel of swamp lying in the Great Swamp in the South Meadow containing by estimation four acres ... which he received of Joseph Eson for land belonging to the said Thomas Bull lying in that swamp"; "one parcel lying at Hockanum which he bought of Frances Androwes being meadow land, containing by estimation five acres"; "one parcel on which a messuage or tenement now s[tande]th with other outhouses, yards or gardens therein being which he bought of James Wackle containing by estimation two roods"; "one parcel on which a messuage or tenement now standeth with other outhouses, yards or gardens therein being which he bought of James Wackle containing by estimation four acres"; "one parcel of swamp lying in the Great Swamp in the South Meadow which he bought of James Steel containing by estimation one acre two roods"; "one parcel of land given him by the Town which was part of Mr. Goodwin's land," two acres (with marginal annotation "sold John Stedman"); "one parcel of land which he bought of Joseph Bird with a messuage or tenement standing thereon containing by estimation one acre"; "one parcel of upland which he bought of Joseph Bird containing by estimation thirteen acres & a half ... recorded this 11th May: 1663" [HaBOP 231-35].

On 12 September 1650, "this Court desires Mr. Governor, Mr. Deputy and Mr. Webster to consider of the grant of land to Thomas Bull and others, to settle something upon them according to the grant of the Court in May last" [CCCR 1:211]. On 6 October 1651, the "Court hath also spoken with Lieutenant Bull, about the land at Nihantecutt, laid out to him and others with him, who hath promised to confer with Uncas and endeavor to give him reasonable content and satisfaction, in reference to the premises" [CCCR 1:228].

On 2 March 1651/2, "Thomas Bull and others in the behalf of the rest, having resigned up to the court one hundred acres of the grounds laid out at Niantecutt to them, of that part thereof which lies next to Seabrooke, which said hundred acres the Court grants liberty to the Indians that formerly possessed and planted the same, to possess and plant for the future, so long as they carry peacably and justly towards the English. The Court grants to the said Thomas Bull and the rest of the five of Capt. Mason's soldiers, that they shall have two hundred acres of that upland which lies northward, next adjoining to the remainder of land already laid out to them, which they accept in full satisfaction for the hundred acres they have resigned as before" [CCCR 1:230]. On 12 October 1671, the "Court appoints Ensign Waller and James Morgan to lay out to Lt. Bull, &c. that grant of land which, by way of exchange, was granted to them, 2d March 1651/2, by this Court, according to the grant" [CCCR 2:165]. On 17 October 1672, "this Court grants that Lt. Tho[mas] Bull shall have liberty to exchange a hundred acres of land with the Nihantick Indians" [CCCR 2:189]. On 16 May 1673, "this Court grants to Lt. Thomas Bull two hundred acres of land, with the same limitations as is usual to such grants" [CCCR 2:199]. On 13 October 1673, "this Court appoints Mr. Calkin and Mr. John Birchwood to lay out to Lt. Bull, &c. that grant of land which by way of exchange was granted to him, 2d March 1651/2, by this Court, according to the grant" [CCCR 2:211].

In his will, dated 19 and 20 April 1684 and proved 25 November 1684, "Thomas Bull of Hartford" bequeathed to "my son Thomas Bull of Farmington that lot at four-mile hill in Hartford bounds, that about one hundred acres," and £15 and two cows; to "my son David Bull of Saybrook all that I bought of goodwife Towsland in housing and land in Saybrook" and £20 and "two of my best coats"; to "my daughter Ruth Boardman of Cambridge," £10; to "my daughter Bunts in Hartford," £10; to "my grandchild Susannah Bunts," £5; to "my daughter Abigail Bull the sum of £90 besides what she hath received already," part to be paid by "my son Joseph Bull" and part to be paid by "my son Jonathan Bull"; to "my son Jonathan Bull two acres of my six-acre lot in the south meadow in Hartford and ... three acres of meadow out of that eight acres that was Capt. Cullet's ... [and] my two-acre lot lying by the Indian fort by the Great River side ... [and] six acres of my land that I bought of Mr. Hopkins lying next Mr. Hooker's land ... [and] three acres of meadow at

Hockanum that I bought of Mr. Webster and ... that acre of land that is over against my now dwelling house that I bought of Thomas Whaples deceased ... [and] half that lot that I bought of Capt. Cullett of fourteen acres ... [and] my lot and house that I bought of William Warren near the new meetinghouse in Hartford ... [and] my eighteen-acre lot lying at Rocky Hill ... [and] the one-half of my land at Nahantick with half the housing privileges and appurtenances ... [and] half of my land at Cedar Swamp that I received of the country"; to "all my grandchildren £20, to be divided equally amongst them"; to "Mr. John Whiting," £3, he to be overseer; residue to "my son Joseph Bull," who is to be executor, and to "let my daughter Abigail have the use of the chamber she now lodgeth in so long as she shall see cause"; in "a codicil made about 2 days before the death of Capt. Bull, in consideration that his daughter Bunce had deceased, he gave the £10 devised to her to her daughter Susanna Bunce" [Hartford PD Case #89; HaPR 4:196].

On 25 November 1684, Mr. John Whiting and Abigail Bull both testified that two days before his death, Thomas Bull, his "daughter Bunce being dead," wished to give the £10 pounds he had bequeathed to her to "his granddaughter Susanna Bunce," to which Abigail Bull consented [Hartford PD Case #890].

The "inventory of the estate of Thomas Bull," taken 24 October 1684, totalled £972 6s., of which £811 was real estate: "the house and homestead," £160; "6 acres of meadow in the Great Pasture," £72; "8 acres by the Great River," £80; "5 acres in the Indian ground," £50; "17 acres by the great tree," £170; "7 acres over the Great River," £42; "upland over the Great River," £10; "14 acres of upland upon Rocki Hill," £42; "13 acres at the wolfpound," £40; "108 acres at 4 Mile Hill," £15; "1 acre that was Tho[mas] Waples," £20; "that house and lot where Joseph Bull now dwelleth," £100; and "200 acres of land at Cedar Swamp," £10 [Hartford PD Case #890]. A second inventory, undated, totalled £275, of which £240 was real estate: "In Seabrook land that was bought of the widow Tosland," £120; and "land at Nahantick with housing & with other appurtenances," £120 [Hartford PD Case #890; HaPR 4:197].

BIRTH: About 1610 (aged 25 in 1635 [Hotten 130]).
DEATH: Between 20 April 1684 (date of will) and 24 October 1684 (date of inventory).
MARRIAGE: By about 1639 Susanna _____. She died at Hartford 12 August 1680, aged 70 ("Here lyeth the body of Susannah Bull wife of

Capt. Thomas Bull deceased the 12th of Aug. 1680 aged 70 years"
[tombstone, Hartford Ancient Burying Ground]).
CHILDREN:

   i   MARY, b. about 1639 (on 8 March 1657/8, John Winthrop Jr.
        treated "Bull Mary 19 y. servant to G[oodman] Stanley"
        [WMJ 91]); no further record.

   ii   JOSEPH, b. about 1641 (on 6 February 1657/8, John Winthrop
        Jr. treated "Bull Joseph 17 years old son of Lt. Bull" [WMJ
        85]); m. (1) by 1672 Sarah Manning (eldest known child b.
        Hartford 11 July 1672 [HaVR 585]; on 6 October 1672,
        "Joseph Bull and his wife" were admitted to Hartford
        Second Church, having been "dismissed from
        Cambridge" ["Hartford, Connecticut, Records of the
        Second Church of Christ" (Hartford 1914)]; in the 22
        March 1692/3 distribution of the "estate of Mr. W[illia]m
        Manning late of Cambridge deceased," reference was
        made to what "Joseph Bull hath had with his wife Sarah"
        [MPR 8:162]); m. (2) by 1697 Hannah Humphrey (on 14
        April 1697, "Joseph Bull & Hannah his wife" were among
        the heirs of Michael Humphrey [Manwaring 1:566-67]).
        (Some secondary sources give a precise date for Joseph's
        first marriage, but no such record is found in Cambridge
        or Hartford records or elsewhere.)

   iii RUTH, b. about 1643 (in August 1664, John Winthrop Jr.
        treated "Bull Ruth 21 y. daughter of Lt. Bull of Hartford,"
        and on 22 February 1666/7, he treated "Bull Ruth 24 y.
        daughter of Lt." [WMJ 444, 705]); m. Cambridge 15
        October 1669 Andrew Bordman. (According to
        published Cambridge vital records, Ruth Bordman, wife
        of Andrew, d. Cambridge 17 December 1690, in her 40th
        year, the age at death being derived from the tombstone;
        perhaps the tombstone has been misread, and the age is
        correctly in her 48th year.)

   iv SUSANNAH, b. about 1645 (on 5 April 1658, John Winthrop Jr.
        treated "Bull Susan 14 y.," and on 16 November 1659, he
        treated "Bull Susan 15 y." [WMJ 100, 173]); m. by an
        unknown date Thomas Bunce.

   v   THOMAS, b. about 1647 (on 14 July 1663, John Winthrop Jr.
        treated "Bull Tho: 17 y." at Northampton [WMJ 513]); m.
        (1) Farmington 29 April 1669 Esther Cowles [Farm VR

Barbour 25, citing Farmington LR 1:4]; m. (2) Farmington 13 January 1691/2 Mary (Cheever) Lewis [Farm VR Barbour 25, citing Farmington LR 1:5], daughter of Ezekiel Cheever and widow of William Lewis of Farmington [GMB 2:1186].

vi JONATHAN, bp. 25 March 1649 [HaVR 580] (on 11 January 1660/1, John Winthrop Jr. treated "Bull Jonathan 12 y." [WMJ 237]); m. Hartford 19 March 1684/5 Sarah Whiting [HaVR 610].

vii DAVID, bp. 9 February 1650[/1] [HaVR 582] (on 2 January 1660/1, John Winthrop Jr. treated "Bull David 10 y.," on 10 February 1665/6, he treated "Bull David 15 y. son of Lt. Tho. Bull of Hartford," and on 6 March 1666/7, he treated "Bull David 16 y. son of Lt. Bull of Hartford, servant to J. Richards of Hartford" [WMJ 229, 623, 709]); m. Saybrook 27 December 1677 Hannah Chapman [SayVR 14].

viii ABIGAIL, b. about 1653 (on 11 January 1660/1, John Winthrop Jr. treated "Bull Abigaile 8y.," on 16 November 1665, he treated "Bull Abigalle above 12 y.," and on 3 February 1668/9, he treated "Bull Abigale 16y. daughter of Lt. Bull of Hartford" [WMJ 237, 605, 867]); m. Salem (recorded Andover) 28 April 1696 Rev. Thomas Barnard of Andover [Sibley 3:174-77].

COMMENTS: On 11 September 1635, "Tho[mas] Bull," aged 25, was enrolled at London as a passenger for New England on the *Hopewell* [Hotten 130].

On 10 June 1636, Gov. John Winthrop wrote to his son John Winthrop Jr. at Saybrook that "by Tho[mas] Bull and a man of mine I sent 6 cows, 4 steers and a bull" to Connecticutt [WP 3:268].

The tombstones for Thomas Bull and his wife were examined on a visit to the Ancient Burying Ground at Hartford. The stone for Thomas Bull is a nineteenth-century creation, but the stone for his wife, although heavily restored, dates from the seventeenth century. A published version of the inscriptions from this cemetery misstates the month of her death as April rather than August (William Hosley and Shepherd M. Holcombe Sr., *By Their Markers Ye Shall Know Them: A Chronicle of the History and Restorations of Hartford's Ancient Burying Ground* [Hartford 1994], pp. 63, 133).

BIBLIOGRAPHIC NOTE: In 1981 Mary L. Todd published the results of an inconclusive search for the English origin of Thomas Bull [NEHGR 135:135-37], and in the same year she published *Thomas and Susannah Bull of Hartford, Connecticut, and Some of Their Descendants in the First Five Generations* [typescript, Lake Forest, Illinois, 1981]. In 1988 Alden C. Manchester speculated further on the origin of Thomas Bull [TAG 63:81].

EDWARD BULLOCK

ORIGIN: Barkham, Berkshire
MIGRATION: 1635 on the *Elizabeth*
FIRST RESIDENCE: Dorchester
RETURN TRIPS: 1649

OCCUPATION: Husbandman [Hotten 68]. Mariner [Aspinwall 194].
EDUCATION: Signed his will.
ESTATE: On 18 March 1637/8, in the proportional division on the neck and the cow pasture at Dorchester, "Ed[ward] Bullocke" owned 3 and 3/4 acres and 8 rods in the neck and 2 and 1/4 acres and 8 rods in the cow pasture [DTR 30].

In his will, dated 25 July 1649, "about to go to England," and proved 29 January 1656/7, "Edward Bullock of Dorchester" bequeathed "for my wife's more comfortable maintenance" a yearly allowance managed by "my special good friends and neighbors"; after "my wife's death ... my daughter-in-law Hannah Johnson shall have all my goods, lands and estate that then shall be remaining to be delivered here at time of her marriage or of lawful age"; "my friends Capt. Humphery Atherton, Augustine Clemens, & George Weeks" overseers; will to be void when and if he returns [SPR 1:288-89]. (The will is followed in the probate register by a list of Bullock's debts.)

BIRTH: About 1603 (aged 32 in 1635 [Hotten 68]), son of William Bullock of Barkham, Berkshire [Aspinwall 227].
DEATH: Between 25 July 1649 (date of will) and 29 January 1656/7 (probate of will).
MARRIAGE: By an unknown date _____ (_____) Johnson (presumably a widow with a daughter Hannah Johnson, whom Edward called "my daughter-in-law" in his will).
CHILDREN: None recorded.

ASSOCIATIONS: In the list of debts attached to the end of the will is mentioned "brother Clemens", probably referring to AUGUSTINE CLEMENT as a brother in the church.

COMMENTS: On 17 April 1635, "Husbandman Edward Bullock," aged 32, was enrolled at London for passage to New England on the *Elizabeth* [Hotten 68].

On 6 February 1648/9, John Thompson of Middlesex, England, acknowledged receiving £33 from "Edw[ard] Bullock, mariner," to be adventured in a trip to New England at thirty percent [Aspinwall 195]. He further acknowledged that "Mr Edward Bullock" paid £10 in "good merchantable dry cod fish" to be sold in Bilboa by Thompson to Bullock's best advantage and to pay "unto his brother Wil[lia]m Bullock" the proceeds [Aspinwall 195]. The same day, John Thompson of Boston, mariner, appointed Edward Bullock of Bristol, mariner, his attorney to recover from Mr. Richard Cutt of Piscataqua "and all other person or persons whatsoever inhabiting in N: England all such sums of money as are due unto the aforesaid John Thompson" [Aspinwall 196].

On 12 February 1648/9, John Thompson covenanted with Edward Bullock to support Bullock's diet, etc., if he would proceed to serve with Mr. Lane aboard a ship [Aspinwall 200].

On 26 July 1649, Elisabeth Clements made oath that "Edw[ard] Bullock of Dorchester is the son of Mr. W[illia]m Bullock late of Barkham in Berkshire" [Aspinwall 227].

HENRY BULLOCK

ORIGIN: St Lawrence, Essex
MIGRATION: 1635 on the *Abigail*
FIRST RESIDENCE: Unknown
REMOVES: Charlestown 1638, Salem by 1642

OCCUPATION: Husbandman.
EDUCATION: He signed his will by mark.
OFFICES: Salem fenceviewer, 13 June 1644 [STR 1:129].
ESTATE: In a list dated 1637 "Hen[ry] Bullocke" held three-quarters of a cow common [ChTR 33] (but, as will be seen below, he did not acquire this until a year later, indicating that the list is misdated, or that the list

was revised after its original compilation). On 23 April 1638, "Hen[ry] Bullocke" had Mystic Side allotments of five, twenty-five and zero acres [ChTR 36]. On 26 April 1638, "Hen[ry] Bullock was admitted a townsman [of Charlestown], to buy a houseplot where he can, & to have one cow common if it be to be had; 3/4 of a common being undisposed was granted him" [ChTR 38]. (Land records of other Charlestown inhabitants show that Henry Bullock held a parcel in the High Field [ChBOP 24, 26, 38]; this parcel is found in 1638 in the hands of John Tedd, and is a two-acre lot with a dwelling house [ChBOP 58]. Tedd had clearly purchased the entire estate of Bullock, including the three-quarters of a cow common, and the five and twenty-five acre lots Mystic Side [ChBOP 59].)

Henry Bullock was granted 30 acres by the town of Salem on 23 January 1642/3 [STR 1:115], and another 50 acres on 13 October 1649 [STR 1:160].

On 23 August 1651, Jeffrey Esty sold to Henry Bullock the "herbage or after-feeding of the five-acre lot" [ELR 1:10]. On 19 November 1652, William Towne of Salem sold to Henry Bullock nine and a half acres of land by the Great Cove [ELR 1:15].

In his will, dated 21 December 1663 and proved 29 June 1664, "Henery Bullocke inhabitant in Salem" bequeathed "to Elisabeth my wife, my dwelling house and out houses thereunto belonging with all the land adjoining unto it, which is about eight acres more or less," and "four acres of meadow, lying in the broad meadow that bordereth on the farm that was given to Mr. Bishop, all the which houses and lands she is quietly to enjoy the term of her life," with permission to sell the real estate for her maintenance if necessary; "after the decease of my wife the lands and houses aforesaid be given unto my grandchild John Bullocke the son of my son Henery Bullocke deceased," but if he die before age twenty-one, "then I give the said houses and lands to his sister Elisabeth Bullocke & if she die childless I give the said houses and lands to my son Thomas Bullocke & his heirs"; to "John Bullocke aforesaid after the decease of my wife the bed whereon I do commonly lie & the furniture thereunto belonging"; to "my son Thomas Bullocke ten pound to be paid to him one year after my decease if he come to demand it"; "in case my wife shall sue for her thirds in the land that I gave unto my son Henery & which is sold unto Henery Cooke that then it shall be lawful for the heirs of my son Henery to take possession of the house & land aforesaid given to her"; "I constitute Elisabeth my wife executrix ... & Willyam Flint & Nathaniel Felton overseers of my will & give to each of them 20s." [EPR 1:450-1].

The inventory of the estate of Henry Bullock, taken 4 January 1663/4, totalled £99 15s., of which £45 was real estate: "his dwelling house &

outhouses with the land thereunto belonging," £40; and "4 acres of meadow," £5 [EPR 1:451-52].

BIRTH: About 1595 (aged 40 in 1635 [Hotten 88]).
DEATH: Salem 27 December 1663.
MARRIAGE: (1) By about 1627 Susan _____. She died at Salem 2 November 1644.

(2) After 2 November 1644 (death of first wife), but before 21 December 1663 (date of husband's will), Elizabeth _____, who survived him.
CHILDREN:
With first wife

i   HENRY, b. about 1627 (aged 8 on 20 April 1635 [Hotten 88]); m. by 1654 Alice Flint, daughter of William Flint (eldest known child b. Salem [blank] August 1654, son of "Henry Jr. and Allice"; administration on estate of Henry Bullock granted on 1 July 1657 to "his widow, Alice Bullock" [EPR 1:255]; eldest known child of "John and Ales" Pickering b. Salem 27 September 1660; "Jno. Junior & Al[i]ce Pickering" were executors of the estate of William Flint in 1673 [EPR 2:365]; evidence lacking for connection of Bullock to Flint or Pickering).

ii MARY, b. about 1629 (aged 6 on 20 April 1635 [Hotten 88]); no further record.

iii THOMAS, b. about 1633 (aged 2 on 20 April 1635 [Hotten 88]); living on 23 December 1663 (date of father's will), not near Salem, and probably outside New England.

COMMENTS: "Henry Bullocke," husbandman, aged 40, "Susan his wife," aged 42, and three children, Henry, aged 8, Mary, aged 6, and Thomas, aged 2, were enrolled at London on 20 June 1635, with a certificate from "two justices of peace & minister of St. Lawrence in Essex," as passengers for New England on the *Abigail* [Hotten 88].

Henry Bullock first appears of record in New England when he is admitted a townsman of Charlestown on 26 April 1638 [ChTR 38], and his whereabouts during the preceding two years and a half is unknown.

On 28 February 1642/3, "Sara, wife of Henry Renalds of Salem, [was] presented for pilfering. Now in childbed. Admonished, to sit in stocks one hour next lecture day, and to make restitution to Goodman Bullock" [EQC 1:51].

On 3 November 1645, Salem selectmen "[o]rdered that William Flint & Alice [blank] shall be appointed to come before the Townsmen the next second day to take course for the ten pounds in Mr. Foule's his hand for securing of the town from the charges of keeping the child. And Goodman Bullock to be paid out of it for the charges he hath laid out for the woman & child" [STR 1:138].

Despite his "age and infirmities" which got him excused from training, Henry was "fined for excess in his apparel in boots, ribbons, gold and silver lace, etc." at a court held in Salem in November 1652 [EQC 1:274]. Not stopping there, Henry continued to incur the wrath of the authorities, for at the court held in Ipswich on 31 March 1657 we find a warrant being issued against Henry Bullock of Salem (mistakenly called "Jonath." in one place) "for disorderly meetings in the night at his house by many young persons, when great quantities of wine and strong waters were drunk," which excesses resulted in at least one young person committing two burglaries [EQC 2:38-39].

JOHN BUNDY

ORIGIN: Unknown
MIGRATION: 1635
FIRST RESIDENCE: Plymouth
REMOVES: Boston by 1649, Taunton by 1662

OFFICES: In the Plymouth section of the 1643 Plymouth Colony list of men able to bear arms [PCR 8:187]. John Bundy served seventeen days from Plymouth in the Narragansett campaign of late August 1645 [PCR 2:90].

ESTATE: On 3 June 1662, "John Bundey" was the last name in the list of "sundry ancient freemen of the town of Taunton" who had earlier been granted permission "to look out lands for their accommodation," to whom "some others" had been joined, and who were now granted land on the northern bounds of Taunton [PCR 4:19-20].

On 3 October 1665, "[o]ne hundred and fifty acres of land are granted by the Court unto the three sisters, the daughters of Roger Chandeler, deceased, viz: to each of them fifty acres, lying between the Bay line and the bounds of Taunton, according to the desire of John Bundey" [PCR 4:110].

"The last will and testament nuncupative of John Bundey of Taunton deceased," dated "[torn] of April 1681" and presented at court 29 October 1681: "[torn] Bundy Senior aged sixtyfour years or thereabouts being sick and weak do [torn] my last will and testament; I give and bequeath my house and land that [torn] in to my loving wife during her widowhood; and the land by John Linkorne's; [torn] mind my wife shall be my executrix and enjoy all the moveables within and without & bring up the children; and as for my land in the North Purchase (so-called) it is my will that Mallachy Halloway shall have fifty acres of it paying to my wife the [rent] remaind[er?]; and the rest of my land in the North Purchase to my son James Bundy. It is my will that my loving wife should bring up my sons in the fear of God, and that my wife should enjoy the use of my house and my land about the house, and my land at John [Linkern's] to the sons I have by this wife" [PCPR 4:1:99].

"An inventory of the estate of John Bundey late of Taunton deceased," taken 29 October 1681, totalled £17, of which £16 was real estate: "50 acres of land, being a parcel granted by the Court and ten acres of meadow or meadowish land," £6; "six acres of land near the town," £6; and "the houselot at the town with a little old house on it," £4 [PCPR 4:1:99].

BIRTH: About 1617 ("aged sixty-four years or thereabouts" in April 1681 [PCPR 4:1:99]).
DEATH: Between [torn] April 1681 (date of will) and 29 October 1681 (probate of will).
MARRIAGE: (1) By 1649 Martha Chandler, daughter of *ROGER CHANDLER* [GMB 1:331]. She died at Taunton 1 May 1674 [PCR 8:55].

(2) Taunton 9 January 1676 Ruth Gurney [PCR 8:65 (bride's surname given incorrectly as "Surney")]. She was widow of John Gurney of Mendon, and married as her third husband Guido Bailey [NEHGR 116:18-19; TAG 33:137-41].
CHILDREN:
With first wife
- i   MARTHA, b. Boston 2 November 1649 [BVR 29]; no further record.
- ii   MARY, b. Boston 5 October 1653 [BVR 41]; m. Taunton 5 January 1673 Andrew Smith [PCR 8:58].
- iii   JAMES, b. 29 December 1664 [PCR 8:36]; m. by about 1690 Mary _____ (eldest known child b. about 1690 [MF 15:28]; "Mary Bundy, widow of James Bundy," was named in his

probate papers on 25 November 1721 [MF 15:27, citing "E. Greenwich RI Council Record 1715-1729:20"]).

iv PATIENCE, d. Taunton 27 March 1665 [PCR 8:30, 36].

v SARAH, b. Taunton 4 March 1668 [PCR 8:35]; no further record.

vi SAMUEL, b. Taunton 4 October 1670 [PCR 8:39 (father's name given incorrectly as "Samuel")]; no further record.

With second wife

vii JOHN, b. Taunton 6 October 1677 [PCR 8:70]; in Taunton militia list, 30 May 1700 [Taunton Hist 353]; no further record.

viii JOSEPH, b. Taunton 1 January 1679 [PCR 8:82]; in Taunton militia list, 30 May 1700 [Taunton Hist 353]; in Brookfield militia list, 30 October 1706 [J.H. Temple, *History of North Brookfield, Massachusetts* ... (North Brookfield 1887), p. 171]; no further record.

ix EDWARD, b. Taunton 13 August 1681 [PCR 8:85]; no further record.

ASSOCIATIONS: On 31 May 1671, "John Bundy of Taunton" stated to the Massachusetts Bay General Court that "your poor petitioner diverse years since was an inhabitant in the town of Boston having only one relation in the country viz: one own aunt who was the wife of Mr. Phillip Alley deceased" [MA Arch 15B:240]. Phillip Alley and his wife had facilitated the marriage of John Bundy to Martha Chandler by promising to them their Boston estate; Phillip Alley died first, and his widow in her old age wrote a will which did not include Bundy or his wife, and Bundy was suing for this estate.

COMMENTS: On 6 March 1636/7, "[w]hereas John Bundy stands bound by indenture to serve Griffin Mountegue, carpenter, in New England, the full term of eight years from the 14th of March, 1635, the said John Bundy acknowledged himself conten. to serve out the remainder of his term with Will[iam] Brewster, the Elder, of Plimouth, who hath compounded with the said Mountegue, his master" [PCR 1:51]. On 8 January 1638/9, "Mr. Will[ia]m Brewster hath assigned over to Johnnathan Brewster, his son, all his interest and title into the service of John Bundy for the residue of this term, which is five years from the fourteenth of March next" [PCR 1:107].

The terms of the transfer of apprenticeship from William Brewster to Jonathan Brewster imply that the date of the original indenture with

Mountague was 14 March 1635/6. The question then arises whether the indenture was executed in England or New England, and whether Bundy should properly be accounted an immigrant of 1635 or of 1636. Since Mountague was certainly in New England by 1635, and probably by 1634 [MBCR 1:144], and since the indenture has not been found, we have assumed that John Bundy had arrived in New England by 1635. The possibility remains, however, that Bundy signed his apprenticeship in England and did not arrive in New England until 1636. Furthermore, depending on whether or not he actually se. ed Griffin Montague, he may or may not have resided briefly at Mudd*/* River before moving to Plymouth.

On 21 August 1637, "John Bundy was examined and found guilty of lewd behavior & uncivil carriage towards Elizabeth Haybell, in the house of her master, Mr. Will[ia]m Brewster, and is therefore adjudged to be severely whipped, which was executed upon him accordingly" [PCR 1:65].

BIBLIOGRAPHIC NOTE: The best treatment of this family is in the fifteenth volume of the Mayflower Five Generations series [MF 15:9-10, 26-28].

GEORGE BUNKER

ORIGIN: Odell, Bedfordshire
MIGRATION: 1634
FIRST RESIDENCE: Charlestown

CHURCH MEMBERSHIP: Admitted to Charlestown church on 21 February 1634/5 [ChChR 8].
FREEMAN: 4 March 1634/5 [MBCR 1:370].
EDUCATION: Signed his will as "Georg Buncker." The inventory of his estate included "2 small books," and "One study at the College 3 pounds."
OFFICES: Charlestown constable, 12 February 1637/8, 19 May 1638 [ChTR 34; MBCR 1:229]. Committee "to be at the General Court next to witness in the [matter] concerning Mr. Craddock's bridge," 28 December 1638 [ChTR 41].
ESTATE: Held fourteen hayground commons at Charlestown in 1635, which was increased to fifteen [ChTR 19-20]. Held 10 3/4 cow commons

in 1637 (annotated "This sold to Rice Morris") [ChTR 33]. Held fifteen shares in the stinted common, 30 December 1638 [ChTR 42].

Held five acres of land Mystic Side, 6 March 1636/7 [ChTR 27]. In the 23 December 1638 Mystic Side allotments, held parcels of seventy-five, one-hundred eighty, and five acres [ChTR 37].

George Bunker was granted 50 acres of land by the legislature on 6 September 1638 [MBCR 1:240].

In the 1638 Charlestown Book of Possessions George Bunker held 22 parcels: "two acres of arable land ... situate in the east field"; "three acres of arable land ... in the east field ... one of the 3 acres was sold to Benia Hubbard, who sold it to John March"; "two acres of arable land ... in the east field"; "three acres of arable land ... in the high field ... with a dwelling house and other appurtenances bought by him of the widow Beacher, late wife of Tho[mas] Beacher of Charlestown, deceased"; "two acres of arable land ... situate in the high field"; "four acres of arable land ... situate in the high field"; "one acre of meadow ... situate in the high field"; "one acre of meadow ... situate in the south meadow"; commons for fifteen milch cows; "seven acres of meadow ... situate in the line field"; "ten acres of woodland ... situate in Mystic Field"; "five acres of woodland ... situate in Mystic Field"; "five acres of woodland ... situate in Mystic Field"; "six acres of meadow ... situate in Mystic marshes"; "three acres of meadow ... situate in Mystic marshes"; "ten acres of meadow ... situate in Mystic marshes"; "three acres of meadow ... lying on the west of Mount Prospect"; "four acres of meadow ... situate on the northwest of Mount Prospect"; "seventy acres of woodland ... situate in Mystic Field"; "five acres of woodland situate in Mystic Field"; "one little house with a garden plot ... situate in the middle row"; and "two hundred and seventy acres of land ... situate in water field" [ChBOP 28-29].

On 21 August 1639, George Bunker of Charlestown sold to Abraham Palmer of Charlestown "ten acres of woodland ... situate in Mystic Field" [ChBOP 94]. In 1646, George Bunker sold to Henry Dunster, President of Harvard College, eight acres in "Wenatomie, alias, Menatomie, Field" [MLR 1:104]. On 19 January 1647/8, Thomas Erington of Charlestown mortgaged to George Bunker his house and 20 acres of land there [SLR 1:89]. On 20 May 1648, George Bunker of Charlestown sold to Phineas Pratt of Charlestown "a house or tenement with a garden to it adjoining, which house and garden stands and is situate in Charltowne in the great through fare street which goes from the neck of land into the market place" [ChBOP 99].

On 1 May 1660, "Mr. George Bunker & Margarett his wife on the one party & Nathaniell Tredaway on the other party" concluded a lengthy agreement in which land in Watertown owned by Margaret was leased to Nathaniel; George and Margaret signed by mark [MLR 2:133-35].

On 4 May 1661, "George Bunker of Charlstowne ... in reference to my promise upon the marriage of my son John Bunker, with Hannah his now wife, daughter-in-law of Joseph Hills, and the natural daughter of Mr. Edward Mellowes & Hannah his wife deceased," deeded to "Jno. Bunker my son, and to the said Hannah his wife, their heirs & assigns forever, all that my farm, lying & being in Maulden ... containing two hundred acres, ... together with all my parcel of meadow ground both salt & other, lying at the head of the North River ... containing by estimation ten acres be it more or less, with all & every the particular & parcels of land, houses, outhouses, barns, orchards, gardens & fences whatsoever, formerly letten & set to farm by me unto Thomas Greene commonly called Farmer Greene of Maulden aforesaid" [MLR 2:181-83].

In his will, dated 12 March 1663/4 and proved 4 October 1664, George Bunker "being though in age and much weakness and infirmity of body," stated that "whereas I have already given to my eldest son, John Bunker and to my daughters, Mary, Martha, and Elizabeth, their several portions ... and also have given to my son, Benjamin ... the sum of twenty pounds besides his learning, and to Jonathan my youngest son £75 pounds in part of his portion. I do ... give and bequeath unto my said son Benjamin forty pounds ... I give and bequeath all the remainder of my whole estate ... to my forenamed two sons and to them and their heirs forever to be equally divided betwixt them ... And my will and my mind is that if either of these my said sons shall ... sell his part in these my houses or lands or any part or parcel of them that then the other of them shall have the first tender of the purchase at such price and for such payment as another man would really give or as themselves shall agree ... I nominate ... my said two sons, Benjamin and Jonathan, to be my executors" [MPR Case #3517].

The inventory of the estate of George Bunker, "late of Molden (deceased)," totaled £313 19s. 6d., of which £265 was real estate: "1 house, barn and houses with about 10 acres of land to it in arable & pasture in the neck," £154; six cow commons, £36; "1 cow lot at Ward's Point," £5; and "8 acres meadow (more or less)," £70 [MPR Case #3517].

BIRTH: About 1599 based on date of marriage.

DEATH: Between 12 March 1663/4 (date of will) and 4 October 1664 (probate of will).

MARRIAGE: (1) Odell, Bedfordshire, 8 September 1624 Judith Major. She was admitted to Charlestown church on 17 April 1636 [ChChR 9] and died at Charlestown 10 October 1646 [ChVR 1:10].

(2) After 8 April 1647 (date of her will), Margaret (Welles) Howe, widow of *EDWARD HOWE* of Watertown [GMB 2:1014-16 (which includes a lengthy abstract of her will)]. She was baptized at Boxted, Essex, 31 May 1590, daughter of Richard Welles [TAG 70:177], and died before 18 December 1660, when her will was proved.

CHILDREN (first five baptized Odell, Bedfordshire):

With first wife

  i   MARY, bp. 3 July 1625; m. (1) by 1646 John Gwin ("Mary Gwin" admitted to Charlestown church 7 February 1646[/7] [ChChR 11]); m. (2) by 1662 (and probably earlier) Eleazer Lusher [DeHR 2:130-35, and sources cited there].

  ii   MARTHA, bp. 15 April 1627; m. by about 1652 John Starr, son of Comfort Starr [DeHR 2:130-35, and sources cited there].

  iii ELIZABETH, bp. 17 December 1628; m. by 1657 Edward Burt, son of HUGH BURT (eldest known child b. Charlestown 28 September 1657 [ChVR 1:18]).

  iv JOHN, bp. 28 June 1630; m. Malden [blank] September 1655, Hannah Mellows [Malden VR 211].

  v   JOSEPH, bp. 15 April 1632; no further record.

  vi BENJAMIN, bp. Charlestown 20 September 1635 [ChChR 46]; Harvard College 1658 [Sibley 1:535-38]; m. by an unknown date Mary Chickering, daughter of Francis Chickering (on 12 January 1676/7, "Mary Bunker of Roxbury ..., widow and relict of Mr. Benjamen Bunker late of Maulden," sold to Peter Tufts land at "Pacomptuck, it being the proportion allotted to Francis Chickering of Dedham, in quantity containing seventeen cow commons" [MLR 8:241]). She m. (2) in 1677 or later Capt. William Symmes and m. (3) Braintree 30 July 1695 Rev. Samuel Torrey [TAG 17:70-71].

  vii JONATHAN, bp. Charlestown 8 April 1638 [ChChR 47]; m. Charlestown 30 January 1662/3 Mary Howard [ChVR 1:42].

COMMENTS: "Mr. Geo[rge] Buncker" was admitted an inhabitant of Charlestown in 1634 [ChTR 11], and he appeared on the January 1634/5 list of inhabitants of Charlestown [ChTR 15]. On 10 February 1634/5, "Geo[rge] Buncker" signed the petition to institute the office of selectman [ChTR 13].

George Bunker was among those men disarmed by the legislature on 20 November 1637 for his support of Rev. John Wheelwright and Mrs. Ann Hutchinson [MBCR 1:211-12], but there is no evidence that he ever recanted. Nevertheless, the next year he was made a constable for Charlestown. He was commonly given the title of respect "Mr." The well-known Bunker Hill in Charlestown was named for this man, whose land stretched across the top of the hill.

George Bunker and Edward Burke administered the estate of Augustine Walker of Charlestown on 22 May 1656 [MBCR 3:414].

BIBLIOGRAPHIC NOTE: In 1908 Hosea Starr Ballou published a somewhat romanticized but still useful piece on this immigrant [NEHGR 62:67-69].

JOSEPH BURBANK

On 22 June 1635, "Joseph Borebancke," aged 24, servant to George Hadborne, was enrolled as a passenger for New England on the *Abigail* [Hotten 91].

COMMENTS: No record of this man has been found in New England. There is also no evidence that GEORGE HADBORNE and his family arrived in New England.

GEORGE BURDEN

ORIGIN: Stepney, Middlesex
MIGRATION: 1635 on the *Abigail*
FIRST RESIDENCE: Boston

OCCUPATION: Shoemaker; tanner.
CHURCH MEMBERSHIP: "George Burdon a shoemaker" was admitted to Boston church on 8 January 1636/7 [BChR 21].

FREEMAN: 17 May 1637 [MBCR 1:373].

EDUCATION: He signed his deeds and his will.

OFFICES: He served on a coroner's jury at Boston on 15 September 1640 concerning the death of William Richards [WP 4:285-86].

ESTATE: On 19 February 1637/8, the town of Boston granted "our brother George Burdon" a great lot at Mount Wollaston for five heads, which had not been laid out as of 25 November 1639 when a larger grant was made "now he is increased to eight heads which are now allowed" [BTR 31-32, 43-44]. In the Boston Book of Possessions of 1645, George Burden held three parcels of land: one house and yard; a garden near the common; and 5 1/2 in the new field [BBOP 17]. On 27 April 1640, Burden's lot at Long Island was, with his consent, reassigned to Edmund Jackson [BTR 1:53].

On 13 May 1641, John Crabtree of Boston, for £15, "granted" unto George Burden his then dwelling-house with half an acre of land adjoining and also one acre lying among the garden lots [SLR 1:18]. On 28 June 1641, the town agreed to let "our bro. Everill" and "our bro. Burden" sink a pit at the upper end of the wharf, in front of Burden's house, and put a vessel therein (so that they can cover the same) to water their leather in, and if it be found an annoyance to the town, then they are to fill it up again [BTR 62]. A map showing the approximate location of these sites has been published [BBOP 94-95].

On 31 July 1643, George Burden and others ("partners") were granted all that cove on the northwesterly side of the causeway leading to Charlestown, with all the saltmarsh adjacent, not formerly granted to anyone else, reserving liberty to make use of it from time to time to repair the said causeway [BTR 74]. On 18 December 1651, George Burden of Boston, shoemaker, for £3 sterling, sold Joshua Foote of London, iron monger and Citizen of London, about 80 acres of upland and meadow in Braintree north of the Mannatacut River [SLR 1:153-54]. On 19 February 1651/2, Burden sold for £230 to Aaron Way and William Ireland of Dorchester, all his house, housing, barns, buildings, stables, cowhouses, orchards, tofts, gardens, fold-yards, and all his farm lying at Rumney Marsh, containing 140 acres of of upland and marsh purchased of Nicholas Parker, and also one lot of upland purchased of Mr. George Bunker of Charlestown containing five acres with all the appurtenances thereunto adjoining to the said farm on the west side and five acres of upland purchased of Thomas Call adjoining to the said farm on the west side, and ten acres of upland with all the appurtenances purchased of Thomas Moulton "of Mystic or Malden Planter" lying also on the west side of the said farm, together with fifteen acres of upland purchased of the said Thomas Moulton and Thomas Whitmore lying also on the west side of the said farm, along with all common rights [SLR 1:206-08]. On 14 September 1652, George Burden sold to Mr. John Glover "all that my new cellar, lately had from the town and dwelling-house thereunto adjoining as it was lately divided betwixt me & Mr. Webb," and also the slaughter-house made by William Cotton with all my land on the backside lying betwixt Mr. Webb and that which was lately Hugh Gunnison's [SLR 1:265].

In his will, dated 15 October 1652 and proved 30 April 1657, George Burden named "my loving wife Anne Burden" his executrix, and bequeathed his estate, whether in England or "here in New England," to his wife to manage until "my two children come to the age of eighteen years or marriage ... & then they my two children are to have two parts ... & to my wife the third part, & if my wife shall marry then I will my children shall be at the oversight and disposal of my father Soulsby, if it please God he survive me, with my own brother Timothy, & if my wife & children stay in England but if we return to New England then I make my attorneys the overseers of my will" [SPR 1:291-92].

BIRTH: About 1611 (aged 24 in 1635 [Hotten 97]). (He is probably that "Georg Burden son of Wm Burden carpenter" who was baptized at All Saints, Newcastle upon Tyne, Northumberland, on 22 April 1610, son of William and Cristabell (Bell) Burden, who were married there on 21 May 1609 [parish register].)

DEATH: Between 15 October 1652 (date of will) and 30 April 1657 (probate of will).

MARRIAGE: St Nicholas, Newcastle upon Tyne, Northumberland, 4 February 1634/5, Anne Soulby. (She was possibly that Ann Sowlbe baptized at Dacre, Cumberland, 19 August 1613, daughter of William Sowlbie [IGI], or, less likely, that Ann Soulebie baptized at North Willingham, Lincolnshire, on 30 November 1609, daughter of Jhon [sic] Soulebie [IGI].) On 6 November 1636, "Anne Burdon the wife of George Burdon shoemaker" was admitted to Boston church [BChR 21]. On 8 April 1652, Anne Burden, "dwelling in the City of Bristol in England," gave her husband, of Boston in New England, a power of attorney enabling him "freely to sell & dispose thereof [i.e. of real estate] to any person or persons whatsoever, as if I had never been married to him" [SLR 1:264].

CHILDREN (all b. Boston):

    i   THOMAS, b. and bur. 1 April 1637 [BVR 4].

    ii   ELISHA, b. 4 [*sic*] February 1638[/9] [BVR 6], bp. 3 February 1638/9 [BChR 283]; d. soon.

    iii   EZEKIEL, b. 28 March 1641 [BVR 10], bp. 25 April 1641 [BChR 286]; d. soon (unless this was one of the two children alive at the time of the father's will).

    iv   JOSEPH (twin), b. 1 [*sic*] April 1643 and d. later in the same month [BVR 14], bp. 30 April 1643 "being about 8 days old" [BChR 291].

    v   BENJAMIN (twin), b. 1 April 1643 and d. later in the same month [BVR 14] (but see entry above).

    vi   HANNAH, bp. 4 May 1645 "being about 20 days old" [BChR 298]; d. soon (unless this was one of the two children alive at the time of the father's will).

    vii   ELIZABETH, bp. 28 November 1647, "being about 5 weeks and 4 days old" [BChR 309]; d. soon (unless this was one of the two children alive at the time of the father's will).

    viii   ELISHA, bp. 8 July 1650 [BChR 319]; d. soon (unless this was one of the two children alive at the time of the father's will).

COMMENTS: On 24 July 1635, George Burden, aged 24, was enrolled at London as a passenger for New England on the *Abigail* [Hotten 97].

Rev. Richard Gibson, writing from Richmond Island to Governor John Winthrop on 14 January 1638/9, pleaded with the Governor to intercede to help clear Gibson's wife's name. He asked Winthrop to "please to call before you George Brudett [*sic*] of Boston shoemaker, Anne his wife, and others whom they can name which came over in the ship with her" [WP 4:96]. From this it is clear that Anne, wife of George Burden, came to New England on the same ship as Mary Lewis, who later became the wife of Rev. Richard Gibson, it being "the ship [unnamed] which brought her from England hither some 2 years ago" [WP 4:96]. This would apparently place Anne's arrival in 1636, which indeed is the year we find her joining the church.

On 20 November 1637, George Burden was disarmed for his support of Wheelwright and Hutchinson [MBCR 1:212]. Two days later, on 22 November 1637, he joined a number of other disarmed friends in recanting his decision to sign the petition leading up to this action, and presumably was restored to his former position in the community [WP 3:513].

George Burden was one of twelve men who served on the committee of inquest on the body of William Richards in Boston on 15 September 1640 [WP 4:285-86].

On 30 December 1639, Francis Dowse, "servant to our brother, George Burdon," is allowed an inhabitant [BTR 45]. On 20 June 1640, "Francis Dowse one of our brother Burdon's family" was admitted to Boston church [BChR 30]. On 3 April 1642, "Johanna Andrews our brother George Burdon's maid servant" was admitted to Boston church [BChR 36]. On 15 March 1644/5, "Margery Davisse a widow at our brother Burden's" was admitted to Boston church [BChR 43].

"An Burden our sister in the name of the Lord Jesus and with the consent of the church was excommunicated the 28th day of the 7th month [September] 1651, and the cause thereof arose from her withdrawing from the fellowship of the church at the Lord's table, and being dealt withal by brethren she would give no reason of it, save only she was commanded silence from the Lord and being called before the Church she refused to come, and said she could not join with the Church in any thing. She being called before the Church a second time she refused to come any more to hear the Church, and therefore the Church rejected her" [BChR 53-54].

George Burden and others petitioned the legislature for relief of "unjust molestation" by Sagamore George who laid claim to certain land at Rumney Marsh, in response to which the legislature ordered that the petitioners lay out twenty acres to Sagamore George, and they to have first refusal of it should he ever decide to sell it [MBCR 3:252, 4:1:68-69; MA Arch 30:26].

GEORGE BURDETT

ORIGIN: Great Yarmouth, Norfolk
MIGRATION: 1635
FIRST RESIDENCE: Salem
REMOVES: Dover 1637, York 1639, Pemaquid 1640
RETURN TRIPS: Returned permanently in 1641

OCCUPATION: Minister.
CHURCH MEMBERSHIP: Admission to Salem church prior to 2 September 1635 implied by freemanship.

FREEMAN: 2 September 1635 (as "Mr. George Byrditt," first in a sequence of three Salem men) [MBCR 1:371].

EDUCATION: B.A., Trinity College, Dublin (scholar there 24 April 1619); admitted at Sidney Sussex College, Cambridge, 1623/4 [Venn 1:256; Morison 370].

OFFICES: Governor at Dover, 1637-8 [WJ 1:358-59].

ESTATE: On 22 August 1635, the town of Salem "ordered that Mr. Burdett, shall have a lot upon the rock beyond Mr. Endicott's fence set out by the overseers" [STR 1:9]. On 8 February 1635/6, it was ordered that "Mr. Burdet may have a ten-acre lot at the upper end of Basse River" (annotated "This grant is void") [STR 1:12, 27]. On April 1637, it is ordered that "Mr. Smith [Junior] may purchase that 2 acre lot from Mr. Burditt at £7" [STR 1:45]. On 4 July 1637, "Mr. Burdett is to have a ten-acre lot adjoining to the fort next Marble Head" [STR 1:50].

On 18 March 1639[/40?], "I George Burdett do hereby bind myself, heirs, executors or assigns to pay unto Ann Messant widow, one hundred & twelve pounds of lawful money the last of March which shall be in the year 1641; for the true payment whereof, I bond over to the said widow, my six steers, & three cows, together with the farm I now have in possession of John Allcocke" [YLR 4:20]. On 29 June 1682, "Mr. Edw[ard] Johnson aged about 89 years" deposed that "about forty-two, or 43 years agone, he remembereth that at that time, Mis Ann Messant, alias Godfrey, lived with Mr. Geo[rge] Burdett, then minister of Agamenticus, now called York in the Province of Mayne, & at that time kept said Burdett's house, who had occasion to borrow of said Ann Godfrey a certain parcel of money amounting to the value of seven score pounds or thereabouts, which money remained in the said Burdett's hands, for some years before the said Burdet left the country, a little before which time, the said Ann Godfrey began to consider, how she should have her money, whereupon she desire some assurance for security thereof, upon which he gave Ann Messant, alias Godfrey afterwards, a writing pretending it to be a deed for his farm, but had neither date nor his hand affixed thereunto, as Mr. Vines told her to whom she showed it, whereupon said Ann Messant as then called requested a better assurance of the land of the said Burdett's from him, whereupon he empowered this deponent to deliver unto the aforesaid Ann Messant the legal possession of his farm, land & meadows, lying between Gorgeana as then called, & Brave Boat Harbor, in lieu of her money, for which he the said Johnson, by said Burdett's order delivered to her by turf & twig for her satisfaction" [YLR 3:116; see also GMB 2:778-83, 1096-99].

In a letter probably dated in February 1640/1, Thomas Gorges commented on "how Mr. Burdith's lot and islands are held" [Gorges 30; see also YLR 4:46], and in a letter probably dated in September 1641 wrote of "the islands here at Accomenticus that Mr. Vines gave to Burdith, which as Mr. Godfrey said you would let remain to the benefit of the plantation" [Gorges 83]. In a letter probably dated in September 1641, Thomas Gorges described the estate of "Mr. Burdet ... as it was prized by 4 honest men upon oath amounted not to £20, besides a few cattle that Capt. Wiggins unjustly [torn] Mr. Burdet detains now the value of £30 or £40 all which will nothing near satisfy his creditors" [Gorges 81; see also NHPP 40:26].

BIRTH: About 1602 based on university dates.

DEATH: Ireland 1671 ("After the Restoration this reverend gentleman was made Chancellor and Dean of the diocese of Leighlin, Ireland; and after founding a much respected county family, died in 1671" [Morison 370]).

MARRIAGE: By 1634 Susan _____. (The marriage of George Burditt and Susanna Coocke at St Stephen Coleman Street, London, on 8 November 1627 may possibly be for this couple.)

CHILDREN:

With his own wife

  i   GEORGE, bp. Great Yarmouth, Norfolk, 1 May 1634; remained in England; no further record.

  ii   Child (perhaps more than one), remained in England, no further record. (When he came to New England in 1635, he left his wife and children behind [Gorges 5].)

With other men's wives

  iii SARAH, b. about 1641 (aged about 46 in August 1687 [GDMNH 539]), the mother being Mary, wife of George Puddington [MPCR 1:73-75; Gorges 9, 11-13]; m. after 5 July 1658 (when she was "Sarah Puddington" [GDMNH 571]) John Pennell [GDMNH 539]. (In his will of 25 June 1647, George Puddington did not mention this child, who was of course not his [Maine Wills 99-101].)

  iv   Child, b. 1640 or 1641, the mother being Ruth, wife of John Gooch [MPCR 1:74-75, 80].

COMMENTS: In 1634 George Burdett of Yarmouth, Norfolk, "clerk," was brought before the Court of High Commission charged with "blasphemy, schism, and other crimes of foul nature," described in some detail, for which he was removed from his office at Yarmouth on 5 February 1634/5 [CSPD, Charles I, 1634-1635, 50, 113, 115 (2), 119, 125, 261, 267, 271, 273, 275, 324, 328, 336, 490, 495, 496, 532, 537-39, 543, 547, especially 537-39].

During his few years in New England, George Burdett was continually in trouble with the Massachusetts Bay authorities, both for his ecclesiastical and his domestic activities. Anne Messant, presumably a relative, lived with him without scandal in Dover and in York, and married at the latter place, as his second wife, *EDWARD GODFREY* of York, soon after 1640 [GMB 2:780-81; Gorges 41-43; NEHGR 37:246-50]. On 8 September 1640, "Mr. George Burdett" entered separate suits against John Gouch and Ruth his wife, Daniel Knight and Elizabeth Brady for slander [MPCR 1:58]. Burdett was soon enmeshed in a series of legal proceedings resulting from his dalliances with Mary, wife of George Puddington, and Ruth, wife of John Gooch [MPCR 1:70, 71, 73, 74, 75, 80].

Despite his punishment for radical Puritan activities in New England, Burdett carried on a correspondence with Archbishop William Laud. In 1635 he wrote to Laud attempting to reverse the Court of High Commission action against him; more surprisingly, in 1638 he reported to Laud on actions of Massachusetts Bay "which seems to menace revolt and the erection of a new government" and suggested actions which Laud might take against Massachusetts [Calendar of State Papers Colonial, 1574-1660 (London 1860), pp. 218, 283-84]. Robert Stansby, writing from England to Rev. John Wilson of Boston, on 17 April 1637, complained that in New England "many of the ministers are much slighted with you, insomuch as although you want ministers (as some write) yet some amongst you work with their hands being not called to any place, as Mr. Burdett of Yarmouth etc." [WP 3:390].

Governor John Winthrop took no notice of Burdett until his removal to Dover. His reporting of Burdett's actions was largely a by-product of his concern over the activities of Captain *JOHN UNDERHILL*, who had recently been expelled from Massachusetts Bay for his support of Wheelwright and Hutchinson. In November 1638 Governor John Winthrop wrote that "[b]y order of the last general court, the governor wrote a letter to Mr. Burdet, Mr. Wiggin, and others of the plantation of Pascataquack, to this effect: That, whereas there had been good correspondency between us formerly, we could not but be sensible of their entertaining and countenancing, etc., some that we had cast out, etc., and that our purpose was to survey our utmost limits, and make use of them. Mr. Burdet returned a scornful answer, and would not give the governor his title, etc. This was very ill taken, for that he was one of our body, and sworn to our government, and a member of the church of Salem; so as the governor was purposed to summon him to appear at our court to answer for contempt; but, advising with the deputy about it, he was dissuaded from it, the rather for that, if he should suffer in this cause, it would ingratiate him more with the archbishops (with whom he had intelligence, etc.) but his council was rather to undermine him by making him thoroughly known, etc., to his friends in Pascataquack, and to take them from him. Whereupon the governor wrote to Edward Hilton" [WJ 1:332-33]. About the middle of December 1638, Winthrop noted that "[t]he governor's letter to Mr. Hilton, about Mr. Burdet and Capt. Underhill, was by them intercepted and opened; and thereupon they wrote presently into England against us, discovering what they knew of our combination to resist any authority, that should come out of England against us, etc.; for they were extremely moved at the governor's letter, but could take no advantage by it, for he made account, when he wrote it, that Mr. Hilton would show it them" [WP 1:338]. On 11 December 1638, Thomas Dudley reported to John Winthrop that "I received yesterday a letter from my loving friend Mr. Burdett to excuse himself of the slander laid upon him for baptising any" [WP 4:86].

Winthrop continued the saga in March 1638/9: "The general court, in the 7th month last, gave order to the governor to write to them of Pascataquack, to signify to them, that we looked at is as an unneighborly part, that they should encourage and advance such as we had cast out from us for their offenses, before they had enquired of us the cause, etc. (The occasion of this letter was, that they had aided Mr. Wheelwright to begin a plantation there, and intended to make Capt. Underhill their governor in the room of Mr. Burdett, who had thrust out Capt. Wiggin, set in there by the lords, etc.)" [WJ 1:350]. On or shortly after 6 May 1639, Winthrop told of "[o]ne of Pascataquack, having opportunity to go into Mr. Burdet his study, and finding there the copy of his letter to the archbishops, sent it to the governor, which was to this effect: That he did delay to go into England, because he would fully inform himself of the state of the people here in regard of allegiance; and that it was not discipline that was now so much aimed at, as sovereignty; and that it was accounted perjury and treason in our general courts to speak of appeals to the king" [WJ 1:358-59].

Soon after this Burdett left Dover and moved to York. On 20 February 1639/40, Winthrop wrote of "[o]ne Mr. Hanserd Knolles, a minister in England, who came over the last summer in the company of familistical opinionists, and so being suspected and examined, and found inclining that way, was denied residence in the Massachusetts; whereupon he went to Pascataquack, where he began to preach; but Mr. Burdett, being then there their governor and preacher, inhibited them. But, he being after removed to Acomenticus, the people called Mr. Knolles, and in short time he gathered some of the best minded into a church body, and became their pastor" [WJ 1:392].

In September 1640 Winthrop reported the arrival of Thomas Gorges at York, who "found all out of order, for Mr. Burdett ruled all, and had let loose the reigns of liberty to his lusts, that he grew very notorious for his pride and adultery; and the neighbors now finding Mr. Gorge well inclined to reform things, they complained of him, and produced such foul matters against him, as he was laid hold on, and bound to appear at their court at Sacoe; but he dealt so with some other of the commissioners, that, when the court came, Mr. Vines and two more stood for him, but Mr. Gorge having the greater party on his side, and the jury finding him guilty of adultery and other crimes, with much labor and difficulty he was fined (under £30). He appealed unto England, but Mr. Gorge would not admit his appeal, but seized some of his cattle, etc. Upon this Mr. Burdett went into England, but when he came there he found the state so changed, as his hopes were frustrated, and he, after taking part with the cavaliers, was committed to prison" [WJ 2:11-12].

On 23 February 1640/1, Thomas Gorges wrote to John Winthrop that "Mr. Burdith is at Pemiquid which lies on the borders of this province. He is grown to that height of sin that it is to [be] feared he is given over. His time he spends in drinking, dancing, singing scurrilous songs, and for his companions he selects the wretchedest people of the country. At the spring I hear he is for England" [WP 4:322-23]. On 21 August 1641, Gorges reported that "Burdith, the dishonor of his profession & monster of nature, is now gone for Ingland by way of Spayne" [Gorges 35].

Morison tells us that Burdett died in Ireland in 1671 "after founding a much respected county family" [Morison 370]. We do not know whether this was the same family he had begun before coming to New England, or a new one.

BIBLIOGRAPHIC NOTE: Both Burdett's contemporaries and later historians have been fascinated by him, and a number have penned thumbnail sketches of him. In 1640 Thomas Gorges described him as a man "of singular parts, his praying & preaching to admiration but his life to detestation" [Gorges 17]. Savage comments that both Winthrop and

Hubbard were harshly critical of him, and the criminal proceedings of the courts under the Gorges administration for adultery and other charges "make it plain that N[ew] E[ngland] was not the right place for him" [Savage 1:301]. Noyes, Libby and Davis said of him that he was "a talented exponent of free love, under cover of antinomianism, [and] his children are naturally unknown" [GDMNH 120].

With his usual confessional bias, Charles E. Banks composed a brief biography of Burdett [York Hist 2:113-17].

JAMES BURGESS

ORIGIN: Unknown
MIGRATION: 1635 on the *Hopewell*
FIRST RESIDENCE: Boston

OCCUPATION: His inventory included several woodworking tools.
CHURCH MEMBERSHIP: On 14 July 1661, "Lidya Burgisse" was admitted a member of Boston church [BChR 59]. In a later list of Boston church members, Lydia is not indicated as being "dead, gone" or "excommunicated," implying that she was living as late as 1687 [BChR 84].
ESTATE: On 21 January 1670/1, Lydia Burgess deposed to the accuracy of an inventory of the estate of her "late husband James Burges." The inventory totalled £49 of which £20 was real estate: "a house" [SPR Case #559]. The inventory also included a sword, valued at less than 20s.

BIRTH: About 1621 (aged 14 in 1635 [Hotten 49]).
DEATH: Boston by 21 January 1670/1 (date of inventory).
MARRIAGE: Boston 19 October 1652 Lydia Mead [BVR 38], daughter of Gabriel Mead. She was admitted to Boston church on 14 July 1661 [BChR 59]. She was living 21 January 1670/1 when she swore to the accuracy of the inventory of her late husband.
CHILDREN:

    i   JOHN, b. Boston 21 February 1655[/6?] [BVR 51]; no further record.
    ii JOSEPH, b. Boston 7 January 1658[/9] [BVR 65]; no further record.
    iii MARY, b. Boston 9 June 1664 [BVR 91], bp. Boston 26 June 1664 [BChR 340]; no further record.

iv   MERCY, b. Boston 17 February 1666/7 [BChR 99], bp. Boston
24 February 1666/7 [BChR 345]; no further record.
v   HEZEKIAH, bp. Boston 28 March 1669 [BChR 346]; no further
record.

COMMENTS: On 6 April 1635, "James Burgis," aged 14, was enrolled at
London for passage to New England on the *Hopewell* [Hotten 49].

James was evidently never a church member and did not take a
responsible role in town government. The fate of his entire family after
his death is unknown.

Savage claimed that James Burgess had sons John born in 1654 and
Benjamin in 1655. No records for these supposed sons are found in
Boston, although Francis and Joyce Burgess did have a son Benjamin
born in Boston on 11 October 1654 [BVR 47].

JOHN BURLES

On 13 July 1635, "John Burles," aged 26, was enrolled at London as a
passenger for New England on the *Blessing* [Hotten 108].

On 18 July 1635, "Jo[hn] Burles," aged 27, was enrolled at London as a
passenger for New England on the *Defence* [Hotten 107].

COMMENTS: These two entries are presumably for the same man.
There is no evidence that he ever arrived in New England.

Pope has apparently misread one of these as "John Burt, ae. 29, came in
the Defense in July, 1635," and has the other entered under "BURRELL,
BURRILL, BURWELL," and further misread as "Burules" [Pope 82, 83].

MARGARET BURNS

On 27 July 1634, "Margarett Burnes servant to our teacher John Cotton"
was admitted to Boston church [BChR 18].

COMMENTS: No evidence whether she married, died or returned to
England.

JOHN BURRILL

ORIGIN: Unknown
MIGRATION: 1634
FIRST RESIDENCE: Roxbury
REMOVES Boston by 1644, Roxbury by 1654

OCCUPATION: Shoemaker [SLR 1:287].

CHURCH MEMBERSHIP: About 1634 "Sarah Burrell the wife of [blank] Burrell" was admitted as member #108 at Roxbury church [RChR 80].

ESTATE: In a 1640 Roxbury list, "John Burdwell" was to be paid 12d. apiece for keeping goats and kids [RTR 4].

In the 1642 valuation of Roxbury inhabitants, "John Burwell" was valued at 5s.1d. personal estate, but no valuation of his real estate. He was credited in the same list with 17 acres and 2 half acres [RTR 4].

On 26 February 1648/9, John Burrill and his Boston neighbors, John Baytman, Thomas Hawkins and James Hawkins, were given liberty to tear down the cross work across the mill creek "which hindreth the passage of boats" [BTR 1:94].

In the 1652-3 Roxbury list of possessions, "John Burwell" owned "his dwelling house, barn yard, orchard, two acres and a half, one acre in the calves pasture, four and a half acres, two acres and a half, five acres, nine acres of salt marsh, the one and twentieth lot in the second allotment in the last division containing twenty acres [RBOP 30-31].

In his will, dated 3 August 1654 and proved 15 February 1656/7, "John Burrell of Roxbury, shoemaker, being at this time afflicted by the hand of God with sickness," bequeathed to "wife Sarah & Sarah my daughter, my house wherein I now dwell, the barn & outhouses, my home lot and the orchard and all things belonging thereunto, also five acres of land," also a parcel of land four rods wide and thirty rods long, also seven acres of woodland, also twenty and a half acres of woodland in the middle division, also ten acres of land in the great lot, also one acre of land in the upper calves pasture, also nine acres of salt marsh, all equally divided between "Sarah Burrell my wife and Sarah my daughter"; John Boules and Thomas Weld, overseers [SPR 1:287].

On 19 February 1656/7, administration was granted to "Sarah Burrell, the late wife of the said John," and to "Richard Davis in behalf of his wife late daughter to the said John" [SPR 1:288].

The inventory of John Burrell, taken 23 February 1656/7, totalled £188 17s. 8d., of which £138 10s. was real estate: "in housing, orchard, homelot," £60; "5 acres of land at the Pond," £15; "7 acres of woodland," £3 10s.; "20 acres and ½ of woodland," £10; "one acre in Upper Calf Pasture," £5; "9 acres of salt marsh," £30; and "10 acres in great lots," £15 [SPR 3:79-80].

BIRTH: By about 1609 based on estimated date of marriage.
DEATH: Between 3 August 1654 (date of will) and 15 February 1656/7 (probate of will).
MARRIAGE: By 1634 Sarah _____. She survived her husband and was living 30 July 1657 when she deposed regarding his estate.
CHILD:

    i   SARAH, b. Roxbury [blank] July 1634; m. (1) by 19 February 1656/7 Richard Davis [SPR 1:288]; m. (2) Dorchester 21 December 1664 Samuel Chandler [DVR 21].

ASSOCIATIONS: A George Burrill, cooper, lived in Boston contemporaneously, but there is no evidence that he was related to the subject of this sketch [BTR 1:135].

COMMENTS: Leonard Pitts servant of John Burrell died at Boston 13 February 1644/5 [BVR 20].

    Savage says John's arrival was "1632, or earlier" [Savage 1:309], but no evidence of this is found.

WILLIAM BURROW

On 13 April 1635, "W[illia]m Burrow," aged 19, was enrolled at London as a passenger for New England on the *Susan & Ellen* [Hotten 59].

COMMENTS: There is no evidence that this man arrived in New England. Savage states that he was of Providence in 1641, and was "among freemen 1655, and living 1663, but wife or children are unknown" [Savage 1:312], but this was not necessarily the passenger of 1635, and the name in Providence seems to be Barrows.

HUGH BURT

ORIGIN: Unknown
MIGRATION: 1635 on the *Abigail*
FIRST RESIDENCE: Lynn

OCCUPATION: Husbandman.
EDUCATION: Hugh Burt signed his will. His inventory included "Bibles" valued at 14s. Ann made her mark to her will. Her inventory included "one Bible & one other book" valued at 6s.
OFFICES: Essex grand jury, 25 June 1661 [EQC 2:281]. Petit jury, 1 March 1647/8, 27 November 1660 [EQC 1:135, 2:250].
ESTATE: In the 1638 distribution of Lynn land, Hugh Burt received 60 acres [EQC 2:270].

In his will, dated 7 October 1661 and proved 26 November 1661, Hugh Burt "being very weak of body" bequeathed to "my son Will: Bassitt two acres of salt marsh in the last division in Rumney Marsh which I bought of Timothy Cooper" after "my wife's decease," also five acres of upland "I bought of Robt: Mansfeild," also all wearing apparel; to "my two granddaughters [Mary and Sarah] the daughters of my son Hugh Birt deceased" a cow at twenty-one to be paid to "my son Edward Burtt"; to "my son Edward Burt half my housing, land & meadow undisposed of," also all house and lands at "my wife's decease"; to "my wife one half of my housing lands & meadows" during her lifetime; to "my son Edward Burt half my cattle, sheep & swine"; to "my wife all my goods within doors" at her disposal; "my wife my executrix"; "Mr Nathaniel Handforde & Andrew Mansfield" overseers; "I acquit my son Edward Burt of all the monies that he received of mine in England of all debts whatsoever & also ... all my right & interest in any housing or land in London that came to me by my brother John Burt deceased" [EPR 1:355-56].

The inventory of the estate of Hugh Burt of Lynn, taken 13 November 1661, totalled £143 4s. 9d., of which £75 was real estate: "housing & lands" [EPR 1:356-57].

In her will, dated 8 January 1664[/5?] and proved 26 June 1673, "An Bort" bequeathed to "Willyam Bassit Juner" a cow; to "John Bassit" one cow; to "Elisha Bassit" one cow; to "Samuel Bassit" a steer; these children to have the profit of the cattle and the principal at age 18; to "Elizebeth Basset" a new feather bed, bolster, pillow, pillowbere, blanket and a rug; to "Sarah Bassit" an old feather bed, bolster, pillow, pillowbere, blanket and a tapestry covering; to "Meriam Bassit" a copper kettle, a table cloth, half a dozen napkins, a ewe, and a towel; to "Mary Bassit my biggest iron pot, a long table cloth and four napkins and a hand towel," also a ewe; to "Hannah Bassit" two iron pots, a warming pan, a pair of sheets, a pair of pillowberes, and a ewe; to "Ellin Bartrom" a ewe lamb; to "Hanna Batrom" a ewe lamb; to "the wife of Willyam Bartrom my black broadcloth suit and one pewter basin"; to "Liddi Burrill" 5s. or a ewe lamb; "my brother Francis Burrill and goodman Craft" overseers [EPR 2:361-62].

The inventory of the estate of Anne Burt, taken 18 March 1672/3, totalled £47 2s. 6d., including no real estate [EPR 2:362].

BIRTH: Baptized Dorking, Surrey, 9 August 1590, son of John Burt.
DEATH: Lynn 2 November 1661 [EPR 1:356].
MARRIAGE: (1) By 1614 Ursula _____. She was buried at Dorking 3 October 1628.
(2) By 1635 Ann (Holland) Bassett, widow of Roger Bassett of Dorking, Surrey. She died between 8 January 1664[/5?] (date of will) and 26 June 1673 (probate of will).
CHILDREN (all baptized Dorking, Surrey):
  i   ALICE, bp. 26 December 1614; no further record.
  ii   JOHN, bp. 5 January 1616/7; bur. Dorking 27 January 1637/8. (In the burial record he is explicitly called "John Burte, son of Hughe." He was eighteen when other members of his family sailed for New England, and he apparently chose to remain behind.)
  iii WILLIAM, bp. 2 May 1619; bur. Dorking 16 May 1619.
  iv   HUGH, bp. 21 October 1621; m. by 1647 Sarah Johnson, daughter of *JOHN JOHNSON* of Roxbury (eldest known child b. Lynn 21 July 1647) [GMB 2:1108-9].
  v   URSULA, bp. [12?] December 1623; bur. Dorking 25 October 1628.
  vi   EDWARD, bp. 9 July 1626; m. by 1657 Elizabeth Bunker, daughter of GEORGE BUNKER (eldest known child b. Charlestown 28 September 1657 [ChVR 1:18]; in 1657 "Edw[ard] Burtt aged twenty-eight years or thereabouts" referred in a deposition to "my father Buncker" [MCF Folio #20]).
  vii Stillborn child, bur. Dorking 2 October 1628.

COMMENTS: On 17 June 1635, "Hugh Burt," aged 35, "Ann Burt," aged 32, "Wm Bassett," aged 9, and "Edward Burt," aged 8, were enrolled at London for passage to New England on the *Abigail* [Hotten 93]. On 1 July 1635, "Hugh Burt," aged 15, was registered for passage on the same ship [Hotten 98].

In his will of 30 October 1640, "Thomas Burte of Dorking in the County of Surrey, cordwinder," bequeathed to "Hugh Burte and Edward Burte the sons of my brother Hugh Burte" his houses and land (after the decease of his wife) and £5 apiece; and to "my brother Hugh Burte father of the said Hugh and Edward Burte every year during his natural life" [Archdeaconry of Surrey 231 Harding].

On 19 September 1646, "Hugh Burt of Linne" gave a letter of attorney to James Everill of Boston, shoemaker, to receive of "Susan Burt, the widow relict of Thomas Burt of Darkin in the County of Surrey deceased ... the sum of twenty pounds the annuities of the two years last past" [Aspinwall 29]. On 12 December 1646, Everill substituted John Gwin of Charlestown for this duty [Aspinwall 68]. On 20 September 1647, "James Everill attorney irrevocable of Hugh Burt Senior & Hugh Burt Junior & Thomas Burt" again made a substitution, asking Michael Rainer of Friday Street, London, skinner, to collect the legacies, now described as "the sum of £30 whereof £20 is an annuity for 2 years, due to Hugh Burt Senior, & £10 an annuity due to Hugh Burt Junior & Thomas Burt [*sic - recte* Edward]" [Aspinwall 87].

On 15 February 1648[/9], Hugh Burt of Lynn, "son of Jo[hn] Burt sometimes of Dorkinge in the Count[y] Surrey deceased & elder brother of Thomas Burt late of Dorking aforesaid deceased," constituted "Edward Burt his son" his attorney to recover all debts, sell all houses and lands "at Cowcrosse near London or elsewhere" descending to him from John Burt late of St Clements near London, locksmith [Aspinwall 189-90], and on the same day "W[illia]m Mullings & John Cuddington did upon oath testify that Hugh Burt of Linne was son of John Burt sometimes of Dorking in Surrey deceased & elder brother of Tho[mas] Burt late of Dorking aforesaid deceased" [Aspinwall 190]. Hugh was evidently still trying to secure the bequests in September 1650 when he had Aspinwall affirm that "Hugh Burt the elder of Lynn in New England is living & in health" [Aspinwall 322]. Edward Burt was in London pursuing these matters as late as 1667 [NEHGR 100:218, citing "Chanc. Proc. before 1714; Bridges 54"].

In his will of 31 December 1650, Hugh Burt Jr. gave "to my two children the whole estate that is left me by my uncle in England after my aunt's decease" [EQC 1:209].

On 25 September 1638, Ann Burt was sued by Isaac Disberoe of Lynn. The case was continued, and on 25 December 1638, Ann Burt "was absent, and her husband Hugh Burt answered for her"; the charge and the outcome are unrecorded [EQC 1:9-10]. At the 24 September 1639 court, Hugh Burt of Lynn countersued Isaac Disberoe, and the case was continued to December with no recorded outcome [EQC 1:12, 14].

Ann was in trouble again in December 1643, when "Auld Churchman of Lynn" was presented for living without his wife for seven or eight years, and "for having the wife of Hugh Burt locked with him alone in his house" [EQC 1:56]. On 4 August 1644, Hugh Burt appraised the estate of this same Hugh Churchman, in whose will Burt's son Edward was bequeathed 10s. [EQC 1:63].

On 9 July 1644, John Poole sued Hugh Burt and Robert Mansfield of Lynn for "taking away his arms" [EQC 1:64]. On 4 August 1646, "Hugh Burt the elder" was admonished for "sleeping in time of service" [EQC 1:101].

On 26 March 1661, Hugh Burt, aged 70 years, deposed that he had lived in Lynn about 25 years and well remembered the purchase of land by Richard Longley [EQC 2:269].

In November 1661, Hugh Burt was expected in court to witness against Hugh Dickman for absence from public ordinances, but the court noted that he did not come because "Hugh Burt was dead" [EQC 2:343].

Savage has an entry for George Burt of "Lynn 1635, d. 2 Nov. 1661, leaving George, who went to Sandwich; Hugh; and Edward, before mentioned" [Savage 1:313]. As noted above, Hugh Burt died on 2 November 1661, and Edward was son of Hugh. There is no record for a George Burt, father or son.

BIBLIOGRAPHIC NOTE: In 1939 Nora E. Snow published an account of the family of Hugh Burt [Snow-Estes 2:61-62].

BONIFACE BURTON

ORIGIN: Unknown (but see *ASSOCIATIONS* below)
MIGRATION: 1635
FIRST RESIDENCE: Lynn
REMOVES: Reading by 1644

CHURCH MEMBERSHIP: Admission to Lynn church prior to 6 May 1635 implied by freemanship.

FREEMAN: 6 May 1635 [MBCR 1:371].

EDUCATION: He witnessed a 1656 deed with a large, sweeping "B" [SLR 2:263]. Frances Burton made her mark to her will.

OFFICES: Essex petit jury, 27 June 1636, 24 September 1639, 29 September 1640 [EQC 1:3, 12, 21].

ESTATE: In the 1638 distribution of land in Lynn, Boniface Burton received six acres [EQC 2:270].

In his will, dated 21 February 1666/7 and proved 24 June 1669, Boniface Burton "being in some indisposition of body" bequeathed to "Mr. Increase Mather," 10s.; to "my niece, wife to Samuell Bennett," 1s.; to "her husband, Samuell Bennet and to every one of his children," 4d.; residue to "my wife Francis Burton" [SPR 6:35]. (No file papers for this probate survive and no inventory was recorded.)

In her will, dated 11 February 1669 and proved 17 April 1679, Frances Burton, widow of Boston, "indisposed in body," bequeathed to "Mary Leverett and Hannah Leverett, two of the daughters of Major General John Leverett," two cows at Reading in the hands of "one Pierson and Edwards"; to "Sarah Leverett, wife of Mr. Hudson Leverett," one firkin of butter; to "Goodwife East, Goodwife Tarne, old Goodwife Hurd and Goodwife Ingoldsby," wearing apparel; to "Ann Leverett, Rebecca Leverett, Rebecca Davenport and Sarah Addington," one barrel of pork and a barrel of beef equally divided between them; "Major General Leverett" executor [SPR 6:269-70].

The inventory of Frances Burton, taken 29 April 1679, totalled £48 3s. and included no real estate [SPR 12:298].

John Leverett Esqr. having died about a month prior to the proving of this will, administration was granted to Penn Townsend on 17 April 1679 [SPR 6:270].

BIRTH: Say 1579 (assuming that the age at death stated by Hull and Sewall is greatly inflated).

DEATH: Boston 13 June 1669 ("1st, 3d, 4th. Old Boniface Burton died, being a hundred and fifteen years" [Hull 229 ("1st, 3d" must be a scribal or copying error for "13th")]; "Old Father Boniface Burton, aged 113 years, died 13:4:1669" [NEHGR 7:206]).

MARRIAGE: By February 1666/7 (and probably much earlier) Frances
_____. She died at Boston between 11 February 1669[/70?] (date of will) and 17 April 1679 (probate of will).

CHILDREN: None recorded.

ASSOCIATIONS: In his will, Boniface Burton calls the wife of Samuel Bennett his niece. From other records we know that her first name was Sarah. In her will, Frances does not mention the Bennetts, which suggests that Sarah was related to Boniface rather than Frances.

Edmund Spinckes of Warmington, Northamptonshire, in his 2 October 1669 will, bequeathed to his son Nathaniel "all that estate whatsoever it be that falleth to me or shall fall in New England, as joint heir with John Nayler of Boston in Lincolnshire, clerk, to Boniface Burton, now or late of Boston in New England, my uncle and mother's brother and only brother" [Waters 172].

Frances singled out the children of John Leverett as her heirs and named him her executor, suggesting some connection, perhaps of blood. In 1656, when John Leverett went to England, his wife, Sarah Leverett, sold a house in Boston at his direction and "Bonifas Burton" was the only witness [SLR 2:262-63].

COMMENTS: When William Edward's wife, "a very ignorant sottish and imperious woman," struck a man and scoffed at his church membership, Boniface Burton was one of two witnesses against her in court in December of 1643 [EQC 1:58].

Boniface Burton mentions only one relative in his will, his niece, the wife of Samuel Bennett. The meager nature of the legacies given to her, her husband and their children, may be an indication that these were his only close relatives in the New World and that he wished to prevent their challenging the will, but was displeased with them for some reason (see SAMUEL BENNETT sketch). He made no mention of Edmund Spinckes or John Nayler, both in England, who had expected to become his heirs, Edmund, at least, being the son of Boniface's sister. Boniface evidently felt that his estate was safe from claims from across the water.

On 5 November 1664, Jabesh Hacket of Lynn granted to Susanna Hawkes, daughter of Adam Hawkes of Lynn, "certain monies in the hands of Boniface Burton of Linne Village which are to be paid at the death of the said Boniface," being the sums of £5 30s. and 20s. [SLR 1:54].

RUTH BUSHELL

On 2 July 1635, "Ruth Bushell," aged 23, was enrolled at London as a passenger for New England on the *Abigail*, with a certificate of conformity from the minister of Shoreditch, Stepney, Middlesex.

COMMENTS: She married by 1637 EDWARD MITCHELSON of Cambridge.

EDMUND BUSHNELL

ORIGIN: Horsham, Sussex
MIGRATION: 1635
FIRST RESIDENCE: Boston

OCCUPATION: Steward [WP 3:211].
CHURCH MEMBERSHIP: "Martha Bushnall widow" was admitted to Boston church on 3 February 1638/9 [BChR 1:23].
ESTATE: On 21 March 1635/6, the lands of "____ Bushnall" were viewed by the selectmen of Boston who concluded that they were among those allotments "not built upon according to a former order made the 30th of the 9th month last, and therefore that they are free to be otherwise disposed of" [BTR 1:9].
"I wrote unto you by the *Rebecka* of the death of Bushnell and sent the key of his chest, that you might take out the seeds and inventory his goods" (John Winthrop to his son, 4 April 1636 [WP 3:244]).
On 23 January 1636/7, "____ Bushnall, widow," was to have a house lot and garden "upon the usual condition of inoffensive carriage" [BTR 1:15].
On 19 February 1637/8, "Martha Bushenall, widow," received a great lot "for five heads" [BTR 1:31].

BIRTH: Baptized Horsham, Sussex, 27 April 1606, son of Francis and Ferris (Quenell) Bushnell [Bushnell Anc 2].
DEATH: 28 March 1636 at Ten Hills Farm. On 28 March 1636, Governor John Winthrop wrote to his son John "I went to Tenhils this morning with your mother and your wife to have seen Goodman Bushnell: but the Lord had taken him away half an hour before we came there" [WP 3:240]. On 26 April 1636, the elder John Winthrop again wrote to his son that "I

certified you of the death of goodman Bushnell: one whom you will miss above all the rest: I had him down to Boston to do him what honor I could at his burial" [WP 3:256].

MARRIAGE: Horsham 2 August 1627 Martha Hallor [Bushnell Anc 2]. She married (2) by 1644 *WILLIAM BEAMSLEY* of Boston, whom she survived [GMB 1:141].

CHILDREN (Horsham parish register entries from Bushnell Anc 3-4):

  i   EDMUND, bp. Horsham 16 September 1628; buried Horsham 27 January 1628/9.

  ii   EDWARD, bp. Horsham 10 December 1629; he signed a deed as grantee on 16 November 1668, but failed to acknowledge it, so he may have died soon after the date of the deed [SLR 5:519-21].

  iii ELIZABETH, bp. Horsham 2 April 1632; m. by 1653 Edward Page (eldest known child d. Boston 19 November 1653 [BVR 56]; named in the 14 September 1658 will of her stepfather William Beamsley as "Elizabeth Page" [SPR 1:336]).

  iv   FRANCIS, bp. Horsham 16 March 1633/4; bur. Horsham 5 May 1635.

  v   MARY, b. Ten Hills Farm mid-June 1636 (on 23 June 1636 Governor John Winthrop wrote to his son John that "Goodwife B. is delivered of a daughter and abroad again in a week" [WP 3:275]), bp. Boston 10 February 1638/9 [BChR 1:283]; m. (1) Boston 3 October 1657 George Robinson [BVR 62]; m. (2) between 1658 and 1668 Thomas Dennis (still called Robinson in her stepfather's 14 September 1658 will [SPR 1:336], but made a deed on 16 November 1668 as "Mary Roberson al[ia]s Dennis with Thomas Dennis her present husband" [SLR 5:519-21]).

ASSOCIATIONS: Edmund Bushnell was brother of FRANCIS BUSHNELL and JOHN BUSHNELL, and son of Francis Bushnell, who arrived in New England in 1639, along with other members of the family.

COMMENTS: Edward Hopkins wrote from London on 21 September 1635 to John Winthrop Jr. saying, "I likewise herewith send you a list of the servants names that are now shipped. Edward Bush[n]ell hath all their covenants. They are bound some to Mr. Ny some to myself and some to Edward Bush[n]ell, but we assign them all over to you ... Edward Bush[n]ell was employed by Mr. Ny in buying some things for the servants, and at making up of accounts with him. I find we are indebted to him £3 which he desires to have in the country. More he saith he hath laid out in these occasions, of which he can give no account at present about £4 besides some tools he bought the price whereof he remembers not, but he is honest, and will do no wrong" [WP 3:210].

Philip Nye wrote to John Winthrop Jr. from London on 21 September 1635 saying "You have one Edward Bushnell the bearer hereof a godly man and so is his wife a gracious woman. I would entreat you to take special notice of him as a man you may both for his parts and piety trust in your weightiest affairs, and his fittest employment besides the labor of his hands (to which in many faculties you will find much readiness and forwardness in him) will be to overlook some of the younger sort and train them up according to their capacities ... but of every man's parts and disposition you shall more fully understand of Edward Bushnell who the better you know him the more useful you will judge him" [WP 3:211].

Edmund fell ill at Ten Hills Farm within a few months and, although he was carefully tended, he died, while two others survived. Winthrop wrote to his son, "Your carpenter and the other fellow (who I think truly fears God) are recovering and I hope shall be able to come to you in the *Blessing*. I pray send me some salt peter, for I suppose it was a means through God's blessing to save one of their lives, being far spent in a fever" [WP 3:256].

BIBLIOGRAPHIC NOTES: In 1898 and 1899 William T.R. Marvin and then R.D. Smyth made preliminary, unsatisfactory attempts at organizing the New England data on the Bushnell family [NEHGR 52:446-48, 53:208-14].

In 1918 J. Gardner Bartlett prepared a detailed account of the English origin of the Bushnell family, including Francis Bushnell, his parents and siblings, most of whom came to New England [Bushnell Anc 1-13]. In 1931 Mary Walton Ferris published a line of descent from the elder Francis Bushnell, concentrating on his son William; she was unaware of the work of Bartlett, and so went astray on a number of points [Dawes Gates 2:162-72]. In 1939 Herbert F. Seversmith published entries from the parish register of Horsham, Sussex, pertaining to this Bushnell family; he also was ignorant of Bartlett's earlier work [TAG 16:45-49, 17:31-32]. Seversmith refers to the published version of the Horsham registers, being volume 21 of the publications of the Sussex Record Society, issued in 1915, and this may also have been the source used by Bartlett.

FRANCIS BUSHNELL

ORIGIN: Horsham, Sussex
MIGRATION: 1635 on the *Planter*
FIRST RESIDENCE: Boston
REMOVES: Salem by 1639, Guilford 1639, Saybrook 1660

OCCUPATION: Carpenter [Hotten 49]. Miller [SayLR 1:162].
CHURCH MEMBERSHIP: Deacon at Saybrook [SayLR 1:6].
ESTATE: In the 14 December 1635 division at Boston, "Francis Bushnall" received twenty-four acres in the shape of a triangle [BTR 1:24].

Francis Bushnell was admitted an inhabitant of Salem on 15 April 1639 [STR 1:86].

An undated entry in the Guilford land records contains "A terrier of all the lands belonging to Francis Bushnell in Guilford": "one homelot containing and allowed for two acres"; "one parcel of upland commonly called Bushnell's Point ... containing eighteen acres & a quarter"; "one parcel of meadow ... containing ten acres"; "one parcel of upland with the neck fence containing six acres & three quarters"; "one parcel of upland beyond & without the said fence containing seventeen acres"; and "one parcel of marshland ... one acre" [GuilLR 1:9]. In another undated entry, "[t]he said Francis Bushnell hath assigned & given unto his son-in-law William Johnson of Guilford all his said homelot, housing and land at the point together with the meadow about it & one acre of meadow" [GuilLR 1:9].

An undated entry in the Saybrook land records lists "The lands of Francis Bushnell": "the house and homelot of 3 acres"; "12 acres of meadow in the meadow belonging to the mill being his proportion belonging to a two hundred pound right"; "ten acres of meadow in Oyster River quarter"; "his right in Oyster River quarter belonging to the estate of a hundred and fifty pounds"; and "his right in the oxpasture belonging to the estate of two hundred pounds" [SayLR 1:5].

On 29 July 1685, "[w]hereas it doth appear that there is two parcels of land in Oyster River quarter, the one of meadow about ten acres, and the other of upland about twenty acres belonging to Thomas Norton with a fifty pound commonage in Oyster River quarter, and twenty-five pounds of commonage in the town commons, which lands originally did belong to Francis Bushnell miller in Saybrook deceased and by him disposed to John Norton and from John Norton disposed of to his brother Thomas

Norton and there being no record found of the same, the persons concerned in a loving friendly way viz: John Norton and Samuel Bushnell miller son and executor to the will of his father Francis Bushnell deceased do agree that the abovesaid lands ... shall be and belong to the said Thomas Norton his heirs and successors forever" [SayLR 1:162].

BIRTH: Horsham, Sussex, 8 January 1608/9 (aged 26 in 1635 [Hotten 49]), son of Francis and Ferris (Quenell) Bushnell [Bushnell Anc 2].
DEATH: Saybrook 4 December 1681, aged 72 years [SayVR 3] ("Deacon Francis Bushnell deceased this life December 4th, 1681" [SayLR 1:6]).
MARRIAGE: Horsham 27 June 1631 Mary Grombridge, bp. Horsham 7 January 1605/6, daughter of Thomas and Agnes (Ive) Grombridge (aged 26 in 1635 [Hotten 49]).
CHILDREN:

- i MARY, bp. Horsham 20 April 1632; bur. Horsham 17 June 1634.
- ii ELIZABETH, bp. Horsham 2 February 1633/4 (erroneously called "MARTHA" in the passenger list, aged 1 in 1635 [Hotten 49]); m. by 1654 William Johnson (Hannah Johnson, daughter of William and Elizabeth, b. Guilford "21 1mo. 1654" [TAG 13:89, citing Guilford TR A:60]). (Secondary sources state that this marriage took place at Guilford on 2 July 1651, but the source for this date has not been found.)
- iii SARAH, b. say 1636; m. Saybrook 20 June 1655 Joseph Ingham [SayVR 7; TAG 68:129-38].
- iv JOHN, b. say 1638; m. Guilford "about middle [of] May" 1665 Sarah Scranton [Guilford VR Barbour 36].
- v MARTHA, b. say 1640; m. Saybrook 1 January 1663[/4] Jonathan Smith [SayVR 7].
- vi MARY, b. say 1642; m. Saybrook 1 January 1663[/4] Samuel Jones [SayVR 7].
- vii HANNAH, b. say 1644; m. by June 1668 Stephen Hosmer, son of *THOMAS HOSMER* [GMB 2:1004].
- viii SAMUEL, b. say 1646; m. 17 April 1684 Ruth Sanford [SayVR 12].

ASSOCIATIONS: Francis Bushnell was brother of EDMUND BUSHNELL and JOHN BUSHNELL, and son of Francis Bushnell, who arrived in New England in 1639, along with other members of the family.

COMMENTS: On 6 April 1635, "Franc[i]s Bushnell," carpenter, aged 26, "Marie Bushnell," aged 26, and "Martha Bushnell," aged 1, were enrolled at London as passengers for New England on the *Planter* [Hotten 49].

JOHN BUSHNELL

ORIGIN: Horsham, Sussex
MIGRATION: 1635 on the *Hopewell*
FIRST RESIDENCE: Salem
REMOVES: Boston by 1651

OCCUPATION: Glazier [Hotten 49].
EDUCATION: His inventory included "a Bible & 2 sermon books" valued at 15s. [SPR 5:65]. John Bushnell signed as a witness to the 25 March 1661 deed of William and Anne Hudson and Habbacuck and Hannah Glover [SLR 4:88].
ESTATE: In 1636 received an undisclosed amount of land not in the freemen's land in Salem [STR 1:22]. On 25 December 1637, received half an acre of land in the undivided meadow and swamp, with a household of one [STR 1:103]. At the 15 July 1640 Salem meeting, he requested a "portion of land" [STR 1:106].

On 29 December 1657, the Boston selectmen ordered that liberty be granted to "Mr. Bushnell and Mr. Glover" to set up a pump and to repair the well [BTR 1:141].

On 14 October 1667, administration on the estate of "John Bushnell deceased" was granted to Jane his relict [SPR 5:64-66]. The widow was granted her thirds and the rest was to be "divided amongst the children left by the said John Bushnell" [SPR 5:66].

The inventory of the estate of John Bushnell deceased," taken 18 August 1667, totalled £241 1s. 2d., of which £140 was real estate: "the dwelling house & ground" [SPR 5:64-65]. The inventory also included a considerable amount of glass and "3 diamonds" valued at £5 10s.

On 14 December 1685, a second administration of the estate of John Bushnell deceased was granted to "John Bushnell his son being now come of full age, in right of himself, his surviving sister, and the child of his deceased sister and Deacon Henry Alline, Mr. Edward Wyllys and Mr. John Usher" to make a new appraisement of the house, "Jane ___ relict of the deceased who is removed out of this jurisdiction" having had the previous administration [SPR 9:249].

On 6 March 1685[/6], John Bushnell of Boston, cordwainer, "the only son of John Bushnell once of the said Boston, barber, deceased," and guardian of "Sarah Covel the daughter of Richard Covell by Sarah his wife one of the daughters of my said father, and Richard English of the same place, butcher, and I Jane his wife, daughter of the said John Bushnell," deeded to Sampson Stoddard of Boston, mariner, the house and land near the dock head "in the tenure and occupation of Dorothy Hawkins widow" [SLR 13:455-56].

BIRTH: Baptized Horsham, Sussex, 23 April 1615, son of Francis and Ferris (Quenell) Bushnell [Bushnell Anc 2].

DEATH: Boston 5 August 1667 (as stated in his administration [SPR 5:64]).

MARRIAGE: By 1651 Jane _____. Jane Bushnell married at Saybrook 14 April 1670 John Hill. (This marriage is supported by the 8 September 1670 order to "Goodwife Alexander to deliver the child of the widow Bushnell under her care and custody, to Hope Allen who desired the same that he might dispose thereof & free the town from charge thereby" [BTR 2:55]. The child was undoubtedly the six-year-old John, who, if he accompanied his mother to Connecticut, would have been chargeable to Boston for his maintenance. Also, we know that Jane (____) Bushnell had removed out of the Massachusetts Bay Colony by 14 December 1685 [SPR 9:249], and that her youngest child, William, died at Saybrook on 31 August 1684 [SayVR 7].)

CHILDREN:

i   DOROTHY, b. Boston 19 February 1651[/2?] [BVR 1:33]; presumably d. soon, or without surviving children, since she is not accounted for in the second administration of her father's estate, unless she is the Dorothy Hawkins, widow, living in John Bushnell's house in 1685/6 [SPR 9:249; SLR 13:455-56].

ii SARAH, b. Boston 24 March 1655[/6?] [BVR 1:50]; m. by 5 October 1678 Richard Covell (b. of first child [BVR 1:145; SLR 13:455-56]).

iii ELIZABETH, b. Boston 30 August 1657 [BVR 1:60]; d. Boston 17 April 1662 [BVR 1:86].

iv JOHN, b. Boston 19 January 1659[/60?] [BVR 1:69]; d. Boston 10 April 1662 [BVR 1:86].

v   JANE, b. Boston 18 December 1662 [BVR 1:83]; m. by 27 January 1681[/2?] Richard English (b. of first child [BVR

1:154; SLR 13:455-56]).

vi   JOHN, b. about 1664 (had come of age by 14 December 1685
     [SPR 9:249]); m. by 1687 Sarah (Lovering) Place (eldest
     known child b. Boston 4 August 1687 [BVR 1:172]),
     widow of John Place and sister of William Lovering (on
     28 July 1682, "John Place of Boston ... mariner and Sarah
     his wife" mortgaged land to Elizabeth Winsley, and, on
     21 February 1688/9, Elizabeth Winsley "acknowledged
     full satisfaction for the within mortgage from John
     Bushnell who married the relict of John Place" [SLR
     12:256-57]; on 1 June 1737, "Jane Underwood of lawful
     age" deposed regarding "John Pride who lived in the
     Eastern parts of New England and ... his wife was Jane
     Lovering my mother's own sister" [YLR 18:253]; "Jane
     [daughter] of John and Sarah Place" b. Boston 18 April
     1683 [BVR 160]; on 1 May 1703, Anthony Underwood and
     Jane Place were married at Boston [*Twenty-eighth Report
     of the Record Commissioners* (Boston 1898), p. 16])
     [GDMNH 559, 445].

vii WILLIAM, b. Boston 28 June 1666 [BVR 1:99]; d. Saybrook 31
     August 1684 [SayVR 7].

ASSOCIATIONS: John Bushnell was brother of EDMUND BUSHNELL
and FRANCIS BUSHNELL, and son of Francis Bushnell who came to
New England in 1639, along with other members of the family.

COMMENTS: On 6 April 1635, "Jo[hn] Bushnell," glazier, aged 21, was
enrolled at London for passage to New England on the *Hopewell* [Hotten
49].

    In Samuel Archer's 1637 account to the town of Salem, John Bushnell
was paid 7s. 4d. "towards the glassing of the windows in the meeting
house" [STR 1:64]. He evidently supplied the raters' dinner that year, as
well, and was paid £1 4s. for that service [STR 1:65].

    Although there is no record of him found between 1637 in Salem and
his re-emergence in Boston in 1651, his identity as a glazier makes the
identification reasonably secure.

JAMES BUSKET

On 16 March 1634/5, "James Busket," aged 28, was enrolled at London as a passenger for New England on the *Christian* [Hotten 42].

COMMENTS: There is no evidence that this man arrived in New England.

GILES BUTLER

On or about 5 April 1635, "Gyles Butler" of Marlborough, Wiltshire, laborer or husbandman, embarked at Southampton on the *James* of London [Drake's Founders 56].

COMMENTS: There is no evidence that this man arrived in New England.

WILLIAM BUTLER

ORIGIN: Unknown
MIGRATION: 1634
FIRST RESIDENCE: Cambridge
REMOVES: Hartford

CHURCH MEMBERSHIP: Admission to Cambridge church prior to 6 May 1635 implied by freemanship.
FREEMAN: 6 May 1635 (as "Will[ia]m Butlar," second in a sequence of eight Cambridge men) [MBCR 1:370].
EDUCATION: Signed his will by mark.
OFFICES: Hartford member of Connecticut committee to regulate killing of calves for leather, 29 September 1642 [CCCR 1:75].
ESTATE: On 2 June 1634, the town of Cambridge "ordered that the constable shall pay James Omsted 10s. for making the highway by William Butler's pales" [CaTR 8]. On 20 August 1635, "Will Butler" received a proportional share of 4 in the undivided meadow [CaTR 13].

In the Cambridge land inventory on 4 June 1635, "William Buttler" held four parcels: "in Westend one house and about one acre"; "in Small Lot

Hill about two acres"; "in the Long Marsh about three roods"; and "in the Great Marsh about two acres and a half" [CaBOP 9].

In the Hartford land inventory of February 1639/40, "Will[iam] Butler" held eight parcels: two acres; three roods and twenty-seven perches in the Little Meadow; two acres, two roods and ten perches of meadow and two roods and thirty-five perches of swamp in the North Meadow; fourteen acres and twenty-two perches of meadow and two acres, three roods and thirty-six perches of swamp in the North Meadow; three acres and twenty-four perches on the east side of the Great River; seven acres in the Cow Pasture; fourteen acres in the Little Oxpasture; and one rood in the "Little Meadow which he bought of Nickolas Clarck" [HaBOP 51-52].

In his will, dated 11 May 1648 and proved on an unknown date, "William Butler of Hartford" made "my brother Richard Butler, dwelling in Hartford," sole executor and residuary legatee, and bequeathed to "my sister Weste's children, that are now living in old England," £5 apiece; to "my sister Winter's children, that are now living in old England," £5 apiece; to "my loving friends of Hartford, Mr. Stone and Mr. Goodwyn and Mrs. Hooker and Mr. John Steele" £10 apiece; and to "the church of Hartford, three score pounds"; and made "my two friends Mr. John Cullick and William Gibbens" overseers [CCCR 1:482-83; Manwaring 1:4].

The inventory of the estate of William Butler totalled £369 3s., of which £150 was real estate: "land at Wethersfeild," £60; and "land at Hartford," £30 [CCCR 1:483].

BIRTH: By 1614 based on date of freemanship.
DEATH: After 11 May 1648 (date of will).
MARRIAGE: None recorded.
CHILDREN: None recorded.
ASSOCIATIONS: Brother of *RICHARD BUTLER* of Cambridge and Hartford [GMB 1:285-88].

COMMENTS: The claim has been made repeatedly that William Butler married Eunice, sister of Tristram Coffin [Savage 1:322; NEHGR 24:150; Pillsbury Anc 2:604], but no evidence has been found for this claim. The Coffin family came to New England about 1642 and settled in Salisbury, by which time William Butler had resided in Hartford several years, so it is hard to see how they would even have met. If Eunice did marry someone named William Butler, he was almost certainly someone other than the subject of this sketch.

Pope says that his "inventory [was] brought in to Suffolk Probate by Increase Nowell, admin. about 1652" [Pope 84]. Increase Nowell did administer on the estate of a William Butler in 1652, the only record of which is an undated inventory [SPR 2:59]. Nothing in this document connects with William Butler of Hartford. The inventory amounted to about £10, half of which was for "work at a frame" and for a parcel of shingles, suggesting that this William Butler, whoever he was, was a housewright.

THOMAS BUTTOLPH

ORIGIN: Unknown
MIGRATION: 1635 on the *Abigail*
FIRST RESIDENCE: Boston

OCCUPATION: Leather-dresser, glover [BChR 26].
CHURCH MEMBERSHIP: On 22 September 1639, "Thomas Buttall a glover" was admitted to Boston church [BChR 26]. "Anne the wife of the said Thomas Buttall" was admitted 28 September 1639 [BChR 26].
FREEMAN: 2 June 1641 [MBCR 1:379].
EDUCATION: Thomas signed his deeds. His inventory included "Bibles" valued at £2. Ann made her "A" mark. Ann's inventory included three Bibles valued at 15s.
OFFICES: Boston committee to hire a cow herd, 31 May 1641 [BTR 1:61]. Constable, 18 March 164[6/]7 [BTR 1:90]. Clerk of the market, 14 March 1652/3 [BTR 1:114]. Committee to draw instructions for the selectmen, 11 March 1660/1 [BTR 2:1].
ESTATE: In 1637 "Thomas Buttalph" received [blank] acres of upland and marsh [BTR 1:29]. On 26 April 1641, "our brother Buttoll" and others were granted the use of a rod of land to dress leather [BTR 1:60]. On 26 March 1660, this land was repossessed at the town's pleasure for other development and rented back at 40s. a year [BTR 1:155].

On 30 March 1646, "Tho[mas] Buttolfe" and others were identified as persons with "house plots unbuilt on" who should be warned at the next town meeting [BTR 1:88].

In the Boston Book of Possessions in 1645, "Thomas Buttolph" owned "one house and garden"; "one acre and half (which was first laid out for garden lots)"; "about four acres and half" in the Milne field; "about one acre"; "about half an acre"; "twenty-five acres upland" at Pullin Point; "seven acres of marsh"; "William Hudson of Boston, Sr., granted to Thomas Buttolph five acres of land in the newfield" by deed dated 16 June 1646 [BBOP 15].

On 14 November 164[ ], James Johnson of Boston, glover, sold to Thomas Buttolph of Boston, glover, three and a half acres of land in the "Centry field" [SLR 2:10]. On 18 October 1659, Thomas Buttolph of Boston, glover, and Ann his wife, sold to Deane Winthrop, gentleman, of Pullin Point, "their dwelling house and yard, barn & leanto," also a parcel of thirty-two acres of upland and ten acres of salt marsh at Pullin Point [SLR 3:380].

In his will, dated 25 May 1667 and proved 18 June 1667, "Thomas Butolph of Boston, ... glover," bequeathed to "Anna Butolph my beloved wife the dwelling house wherein I now live together with the yards, stable, barn and other housing belonging to the same" for her life and at her death to "my son Thomas"; to "my wife" all household goods and money, one half the garden for her life, one cow of her choice; to "my son Thomas Buttolph the house where he liveth called the old house," during the life of "my wife his mother" and at her death "I give the old house to my son John Buttolph"; to "my son Thomas" half of Sentry field; to "my son John" half of Sentry field and the other garden, half after my decease and the other half after the death of "his mother"; to "*my daughter Abigail,*" £40; to "my daughter Mehitebell that spot of land that lyeth *front upon the highway*" and "*£50* that is in the hands of John Parker my kinsman"; Ann and Thomas executors; residue in equal shares to wife and children; "loving friends my brother Henry Br[i]gam, Henry Ensign Phillips & Edmond Edendon & John Parker," to be paid 40s. each for being overseers [SPR Case #451, 1:520; NEHGR 16:159-60] (see *COMMENTS* below).

The inventory of the estate of Thomas Buttolph Sr., taken 7 June 1667, totalled £1598 18s., of which £655 was real estate: "the new house with the outhouses, yards, gardens & fences & all appurtenances," £305; "the house called the old house where Tomas Butolph dwelleth," £110; "Sentry field," £130; and "one parcel of meadowland with the fences & appurtenances belonging," £110 [SPR 5:122]. The next item after the list of land is "in the hands of John Parker" £50. The inventory contained considerable leather and leather products in various stages of preparation.

In her will, dated 17 September 1680 and proved 10 November 1680, "Annah Buttolph widow late wife of Thomas Buttolph deceased" bequeathed to "my son Bingley" £30 "with the £10 I formerly lent to my

son Saywell makes the sum of £40 formerly given by my husband's will";
to "my son John's children" 10s. each, John to be paid in a piece of gold; to
"my son Thomas's children," to "Thomas" one cupboard, to "Marah" a pair
of flaxen sheets, to "Abigail" a pair of cotton sheets and linen and "my
great Bible," to "Nicolas" a round table; to "my son Frost's children born
by my daughter Mehitable, to her eldest daughter Mehitable" the best
feather bed and furniture, to "the younger daughter Elizabeth" the other
featherbed and furniture; the residue equally divided between Mehitable
and Betty Frost; "my loving friends Joseph Bridgham and John
Fairweather" executors [SPR 6:344-45].

Her undated codicil, perhaps the same day, bequeathed to "my son
John's wife my best cloak"; to "my daughter Bingley" the best tabby coat,
the best holland apron, the black gown and a green apron and two blue
aprons; to "my daughter Swett" the long scarf and a couple of the best
white aprons; to "Marah Buttolph" the more coat; to "my grandchild
Abigail Buttolph" the stuff gown; to "Goodwife Dinsdale" the muff and a
neck handkerchief; to "Martha Emons" the morning gown; to "Elizabeth
Quick" the red cloth petticoat, a white apron and a neck handkerchief; to
"Ann Bingley" the new cambrick handkerchief; "my old clothes" to be
given to the poor; small linen to be divided between "my daughter
Bingley and my daughter Swett" [SPR 6:345].

The inventory of the estate of Anna Buttolph deceased, taken 5
February 1680[/1], totalled £115 19s. 7d., with no real estate included [SPR
9:33].

On 27 April 1682, John Buttolph of Wethersfield, glover, "son of Thomas
Buttolph Senior late of Boston," to settle the differences over the estate,
agreed with Joseph Bridgham of Boston, tanner, and Joseph Belknap
Senior of Boston, glover, "guardians to and in the name and behalf of
Thomas Buttolph, Nicholas Buttolph, Mary Buttolph, and Abigail
Buttolph, children of Thomas Buttolph Junior late of Boston, deceased,
son of the said Thomas Buttolph Senior deceased, and Mary his wife now
wife of Joseph Swett of Boston, mariner," to deed over one half part of a
parcel of land in Boston called Century Field, given to him in his father's
will [SLR 12:274-76].

BIRTH: About 1603 (aged 32 in 1635 [Hotten 73]).
DEATH: Between 25 May 1667 (date of will) and 18 June 1667 (probate of
will) [SPR 1:520].
MARRIAGE: By 1635 Ann Harding, daughter of John and Mary (____)
Harding of Boreham, Essex [TAG 34:205-8]. Ann died at Boston 10

October 1680 [Granary 52].

CHILDREN:

    i   THOMAS, b. Boston 12 August 1637 [BVR 4], bp. 1 September 1639 [BChR 284]; m. Boston 5 September 1660 Mary Baxter [BVR 76].

    ii   JOHN, b. Boston 28 February 1639[/40] [BVR 7], bp. 1 March 1640[/1] [BChR 285]; m. (1) Salem 16 October 1663 Hannah Gardner, daughter of George Gardner and granddaughter of *THOMAS GARDNER* [TAG 30:162]; m. (2) Wethersfield 27 June 1682 Abigail _____ (probably Abigail (Fitch) Mason, daughter of Rev. James Fitch and widow of John Mason [TAG 40:50-54]); m. (3) between 14 October 1687 and 20 March 1692 Susanna (Clark) (Kelly) Sanford [Manwaring 1:358-60; Ackley-Bosworth 84, 164].

    iii ABIGAIL, b. Boston 18 February 1642[/3] [BVR 12], bp. 19 February 1642[/3] "being about 2 days old" [BChR 291]; m. (1) Boston 15 August 1660 David Saywell [BVR 76]; m. (2) between 1672 and 17 September 1680 Thomas Bingley (Saywell's will [SPR #614] and mother's will).

    iv SAMUEL, bp. 19 July 1646, "about 3 days old" [BChR 303]; d. very soon.

    v   SAMUEL, bp. 15 August 1647, "about 8 days old" [BChR 306]; d. very soon.

    vi SAMUEL, bp. 12 November 1648, "about 10 days old" [BChR 312]; apparently predeceased his father since he is not named in either parent's will.

    vii MEHETABEL, b. Boston 26 October [*sic*] 1651 [BVR 33], bp. 28 September 1651 [BChR 322]; m. 1 June 1668 John Frost (eldest known child b. Boston 9 January 1669[/70?] [BVR 110]), son of *NICHOLAS FROST* [GMB 1:706-8]. (The date of this marriage does not appear in Boston vital records, and has not been found elsewhere; it apparently derives from a family Bible [GMB 1:708].)

ASSOCIATIONS: Ann Harding, wife of Thomas Buttolph, was sister of *ROBERT HARDING* (who came to Boston in 1630 [GMB 2:855-58]), Abraham Harding (who was in New England by 1640 [TAG 34:208-10]), and ELIZABETH HARDING (who came to New England in 1635 and married about 1644 Henry Bridgham [TAG 34:210-11]).

"Leonard Buttall," who wished to make a lime kiln at Fox Hill in 1640, is not demonstrably related to Thomas [BTR 1:56, 59, 97].

COMMENTS: On 4 May 1635, "Tho[mas] Buttolph," aged 32, and "uxor Ann Buttolph," aged 24, were enrolled at London for passage to New England on the *Abigail* [Hotten 73].

On 18 March 1643[/4], "George Clifford servant to our brother Thomas Buttall" was admitted to Boston church [BChR 38]. On 22 September 1663, John White "servant to Thomas Buttoph Sr." died at Boston [BVR 90]. These were probably but a few of the steady supply of servants or apprentices in the Buttolph household.

There are a number of problems with the will of Thomas Buttolph. In his treatment of this immigrant, George E. McCracken makes the point that the will was "personally examined by me in the court house at Boston on 5 June 1976" [TAG 58:130]. He provides us with citations to the original of the will from the file papers, the original of the will register, and the nineteenth-century copy of the will register, but does not tell us whether he examined one, two or three of these. The copy of the will register shows that some parts of the will have been lost because of tears, but it is not clear from the copy whether the tears were in the original of the register or the original of the will. At the time McCracken searched this document, the original of the register was not available to researchers.

We have examined all three versions of the will and find that the original of the will is damaged. The will is written on a single sheet of paper, from which a piece about three inches by one inch is missing from the right center edge, causing the loss of a few words from the ends of about eighteen lines. There exists also what appears to be a complete transcript published in 1862 by W.B. Trask [NEHGR 16:159-60]. He omitted many words and phrases, mostly of a formulaic nature, and he was not the best of transcribers; but in this case, comparison with the surviving sections of the original will shows that his work here is accurate, and that some pieces now lost must have been available to Trask. Therefore, in the abstract of the will given above, those words in italics are from the 1862 transcript and not the surviving original.

On one point we disagree with McCracken. He states that "[i]n previous abstracts of the will the name has been read as 'Parker' which is certainly wrong." He argues that the name is "Purchas" or "Purkas." Although the name, which appears twice, is difficult to read, we see it as "Parker," in the original of the will. This reading is clinched by the original of the inventory, which has an entry for £50 "in the hands of John Parker," and in this case the name is clear and unmistakable. None of this assists us in determining how John Parker and Thomas Buttolph were related.

As an aside, the name of the overseer "Henry Ensign Phillips" does not indicate an early appearance of middle names. The only adult Henry Phillips in Boston at the time of Thomas Buttolph's will was an ensign in the militia. This form of the name may simply be a scribal error, or may be a local usage.

BIBLIOGRAPHIC NOTE: In 1958 George E. McCracken published an account of the family of John Harding of Boreham, Essex, whose daughter Ann married Thomas Buttolph [TAG 34:199-211, especially 205-8]. In 1982 George E. McCracken explored "Thomas Buttolph's Earlier Descendants" [TAG 58:129-140, 231-42].

WILLIAM BUTTRICK

ORIGIN: Unknown
MIGRATION: 1635
FIRST RESIDENCE: Concord

CHURCH MEMBERSHIP: Admission to Concord church prior to 26 May 1647 implied by freemanship.
FREEMAN: 26 May 1647 (as "W[illia]m Butrick") [MBCR 2:295].
EDUCATION: He signed his will. His inventory included "books" valued at 12s.
OFFICES: Attained the rank of sergeant in the local trainband.
ESTATE: In his will, dated 1 March 1687 and proved 28 June 1698, "William Butterick of Concord ... aged about seventy one years" bequeathed to "my eldest son John, I having given him already my houselot in the town of Stowe with the house which I built upon it, it being the fourth lot in number ..., I also have given him my other lot in the town of Stow, being the eighth lot in number ..., also to what I have given him already I do now give and bequeath to him five pounds"; to "my son Samuel ... all my lands that I have in Concord"; to "my daughter Sarah Barrett to what I have given and paid to her at her marriage ... I now give and bequeath to her five pounds"; to "my grandchildren" ten shillings apiece, to "my son John his children, vizt: John, Mary & Hannah, and to my son Samuel his children, vizt: Elizabeth, Samuel, William and

Sarah, and to my daughter Sarah Barrett her children, vizt: Sarah and Samuel"; to "my grandchild William son of my son Samuel Butterick" a feather bed; residue to "my son Samuell," he to be sole executor [MPR 9:194-95].

The inventory of the estate of "Sergeant William Butterick of Concord deceased the 3d of June 1698," taken 8 June 1698, totalled £150 8s. 4d., of which £100 was "housing & lands"; the inventory also included "a Negro man, a cripple," valued at £5 [MPR 3:195-96].

BIRTH: About 1616 (aged 18 or 20 in 1635 [Hotten 53, 59]; deposed 28 March 1659 "aged about 43" [Pope 85, citing Middlesex Court Files]; deposed 7 October 1684 "aged sixty-eight years or thereabouts" [MLR 9:105]; called himself "aged about 71" in his will of 1 March 1687).
DEATH: Concord 3 June 1698 (as "Sergeant William Butterick") [CoVR 57].
MARRIAGE: (1) By 1648 Mary Hastings, daughter of John Hastings; she died by 1653.

(2) By 1653 Sarah _____; she died at Concord 17 July 1664 [CoVR 12].

(3) Concord 21 February 1667[/8] Jane Goodnow [CoVR 13]. (She was probably the widow of Thomas[2] Goodnow (Thomas[1]).)
CHILDREN:
With first wife
    i   MARY, b. Concord 19 September 1648 (daughter of "William and Mary Butricke") [CoVR 5]; d. there 1 November 1648 [CoVR 6].
With second wife
    ii   JOHN, b. Concord 21 September 1653 [CoVR 8]; m. Stow 8 April 1679 Mary Blood, daughter of Robert Blood. (On 10 November 1701 the estate of Robert Blood was divided, and among those who received shares and signed receipts for the same were "Sam[ue]ll Butterick who married Elizabeth, one of the daughters of the said Robert Blood," and "J[oh]n Butterick who married Mary Blood" [MPR 10:176-78].)
    iii   SAMUEL, b. Concord 12 January 1654[/5] [CoVR 8]; m. Concord 21 June 1677 Elizabeth Blood [CoVR 20], daughter of Robert Blood.
    iv   EDWARD, b. Concord 6 January 1656[/7] [CoVR 8]; d. there 15 January 1656[/7] [CoVR 8].

    v   JOSEPH, b. Concord 29 December 1657 [CoVR 8]; no further
         record.
    vi   SARAH, b. Concord 27 July 1662 [CoVR 10]; m. Chelmsford 21
         February 1683[/4?] Samuel Barrett, son of John Barrett.
    vii MARY, b. Concord 17 June 1664 [CoVR 12]; d. there 28 April
         1665 [CoVR 12].

ASSOCIATIONS: William Buttrick may have sailed to New England with
members of the family of the Rev. PETER BULKELEY, moving on with
them to Concord (see *COMMENTS* below).

COMMENTS: On 8 April 1635, "W[illia]m Butterick," aged 20, "an ostler,"
was enrolled at London as a passenger for New England on the *Planter*
[Hotten 53]. On 13 April 1635, "W[illia]m Battrick," aged 18, was enrolled
at London as a passenger for New England on the *Susan & Ellen* [Hotten
59].

   Pope suggests that these two entries are for the same person, but
Savage assigns the second entry to William of Concord, and the first to a
William of Cambridge. The only event which he attributes to this William
of Cambridge is that he "married I think, Elizabeth, daughter of John
Hastings" [Savage 1:325]. There are no records at Cambridge for a
William Buttrick (or any similar spelling).

   In his will of 26 November 1657, John Hastings of Cambridge
bequeathed £10 to "my son-in-law Will[ia]m Buttricke" [MPR 1:127].
(Bond has misread the will, making this son-in-law "William Lakin" [Bond
294].) This bequest appears immediately after that to the testator's eldest
son, and before those to the rest of his children, indicating that Buttrick
had married the eldest daughter of John Hastings, and also suggesting
that this daughter was already dead by 1657, as she herself is not named
in her father's will. Walter Hastings, the eldest son, died at Cambridge 5
August 1705 in his 75th year, and so was born about 1631. The daughter
who married William Buttrick, then, would have been born about 1629 or
1633, and could well have been the mother of the child born in Concord
in 1648. Savage "supposes" that the Concord record blunders, and that
Sarah was intended as mother of the first child as well as the later
children. But there is a gap of five years between the child recorded as
with Mary and the first of the children with Sarah.

   In his will of 29 January 1669[/70], Thomas Bateman of Concord referred
to William Buttrick as "brother," and apparently on this evidence
Buttrick's second wife has been identified as Sarah Bateman. But Thomas
Bateman also calls John Mousall and Thomas Brown "brother," so it is

more likely that this refers to a church relationship than a kinship connection. Furthermore, Thomas Bateman of Concord was son of William Bateman of Concord and Fairfield, and the will of the latter identifies only daughters who married Henry Lyon and Joseph Middlebrook [FOOF 1:38].

We conclude, therefore, that William Buttrick had first wife Mary Hastings, by whom he had one child who died young. He then married Sarah, surname unknown, who was the mother of the rest of his children. However, it is not impossible that Mary and Sarah were one woman; this would require us, however, to overlook the gap in the early births, and the omission of this daughter from her father's will.

Savage apparently placed the supposed second William Buttrick as a resident of Cambridge solely on the basis of the mention in the will of John Hastings of Cambridge. There are other indications of a brief connection with Cambridge. First, in the passenger list of the *Susan & Ellen*, "W[illia]m Battrick" appears as the last entry, immediately following "Jo[hn] Backley," almost certainly John Bulkeley, son of Rev. Peter Bulkeley. If Buttrick was travelling with or in some way connected with the family of the Rev. Peter Bulkeley, then he would almost certainly have resided with or near them in Cambridge during the years before they all moved to Concord. Second, the youngest daughter of John Hastings of Cambridge, Elizabeth, married at Concord on 11 November 1661 John Billings, which may indicate that after her father's death she went to live with relatives in Concord.

These records are all consistent with the hypothesis that there was only one immigrant to New England in 1635 named William Buttrick, and so both of the ship passenger entries are presumably for this one man.

Savage includes a son William in the list of children of the immigrant, but there is no record for such a son. Perhaps he was misled by the bequest to William, son of Samuel, and therefore grandson of the immigrant.

From the notebook of the Rev. John Fiske, we learn that on the "4 of 7th [September] 1654 was dated a letter under the hands of Robert Fletcher, Thomas Adams, William Fletcher, and William Butterick in the name of the rest engaged in the new plantation at Chelmsford" [Fiske Notebook 104]. All four of these men were from Concord. William Buttrick does not appear further in the records of the Chelmsford church, and so he apparently did not follow through on his intention of removing to Chelmsford.

On 7 October 1684, "William Buttrick aged sixty-eight years or thereabouts" deposed regarding the purchase of Concord from the Indians in 1636 [MLR 9:105].

NICHOLAS BUTTRY

ORIGIN: Unknown
MIGRATION: 1635 on the *James*
FIRST RESIDENCE: Cambridge

ESTATE: On 8 September 1636, Massachusetts Bay General Court ordered "William Clements, Samuell Holly, & Martha Buttry shall enjoy their houses & land on the south side of Charles River, without disturbance, till they receive satisfaction for them from the inhabitants of Newe Towne" [MBCR 1:179]. (This land was sold by Miles Ives to John Jackson by 1638 [CaBOP 68, 115].)

BIRTH: About 1602 (aged 33 in 1635 [Hotten 107]).
DEATH: By 8 September 1636 [MBCR 1:179].
MARRIAGE: By about 1634 Martha _____. She m. (2) by 1639 MILES IVES.
CHILD:

> i GRACE, b. about 1634 (aged 1 in 1635 [Hotten 108]); m. (as "Grace Butterice") Cambridge 14 October 1653 William Healey.

COMMENTS: "Nic[h]o[las] Buttry," aged 33, "Martha Buttry," aged 28, and "Grace Buttry," aged 1, were enrolled at London on 13 July 1635 as passengers for New England on the *James* [Hotten 107-8].

NATHANIEL BYAM

On 17 June 1635, "Nathaniell Byham," aged 14, was enrolled at London as a passenger for New England on the *Blessing* [Hotten 93].

On 3 March 1644[/5?], "Nathaniell Byam" witnessed a deed for land at Scituate, and on 20 January 1645[/6?], "Nathaniell Byam" witnessed an agreement regarding the ferry at Marshfield [PCR 12:106, 127].

COMMENTS: Several of the passengers on the *Blessing* in 1635 settled in Scituate, which makes it likely that the Nathaniel Byam seen in that part of Plymouth Colony in 1645 was the passenger of 1635. No further record of him has been found.

INDEX SECTION

This final section contains four indices, three of a familiar variety and one that is experimental. The three that will be familiar are of surnames, places and ships. The unusual index is a rearrangement of the surname index, by first name, instead of last.

INDEX OF SURNAMES

This index lists all persons in this volume who resided in New England in the seventeenth century. Modern authors, historians and genealogists are not indexed. Some of the more prominent inhabitants of New England, most notably John Winthrop and William Bradford, were indexed only if directly involved in the material cited; if they appeared merely because evidence from their writings was cited, their names were not indexed.

INDEX OF FIRST NAMES

While the Index of First Names is derived from the Index of Surnames, there are a number of differences which should be noted. In the first place, this index is intended not for assistance in finding one's place in the text, but for providing clues to further research. As a result this index has been simplified, with each entry including only one of the surnames used by a married woman during her life. All of the surnames are included, but in a different form than in the Index of Surnames.

George Ernest Bowman conceived the idea of an index of first names nearly a century ago, but he never implemented it in print. There are many ways in which such an index might be useful, some of them unexpected. When the first version of this index was printed out, it became obvious that such an arrangement of names would be a useful proofreading tool; all occurrences of "Willaim" instead of "William" would be grouped together and could be corrected at the same time.

Beyond this aid to index production, the index of first names should be helpful to researchers in a number of ways. Anyone searching for an unidentified wife with an unusual first name might want to look at all the entries for "Prudence," for example. Or an onomastic argument for identity, dependent on name usage within a family and on the relative frequency of use of a name, should be assisted by this index. Resourceful genealogists will undoubtedly find more uses for this listing.

INDEX OF PLACES

The index to places includes, but is not limited to, the residences of the early settlers of New England, both in England and New England.

Three features of this index should be noted. First, localities within towns, such as field names and neighborhoods, are generally not indexed. Second, when a town is referred to on the same page by both its native and its English names, the index will usually include only the reference to the English name. Third, many English places are entered in this index under the spelling inflicted upon them in the early New England records; these spellings may in some cases be so bizarre as to be unrecognizable.

INDEX OF SHIPS

Most of the entries in this index are for the ships that brought passengers to New England in 1634 and 1635.

INDEX OF SURNAMES

Bate continued
  Jane (Weeks) 197
  John 197, 200
  Joseph 196, 197
  Lydia 199, 200
  Lydia (Lapham) 197
  Margaret 200
  Mary 199, 200
  Mary (Martin) 125, 196, 199, 287
  Rachel 124-126, 197, 286
  Richard 198, 199
  Ruth (Lyford) 197
  Samuel 196, 197
  Susan (Isham) 199
  Thomazine 199
  William 199
BATEMAN/BAYTMAN
  John 499
  Sarah 524
  Thomas 524, 525
  William 525
BATT
  Ann 201-203
  Christopher 203, 211
  Elizabeth 211
  Lucy (_____) 201, 203
  Mary 203
  Nicholas 200-204
  Sarah 203
BATTE see BATE
BATTER
  Anne 211
  Barbara (Weld) (Hide) 210
  Daniel 205, 208-211
  Dorothy 211
  Edmund 22, 69-71, 183, 204-213
  Eleanor (_____) 211
  Elinor (Oliver) 211
  Elizabeth 208-210
  Hannah (Higginson) 210
  Jane 70, 71, 211
  John 211
  Margaret 211
  Martha (Pickman) 210
  Mary 208-211
  Mary (Gookin) 204, 205, 207-210
  Nicholas 204
  Sarah 210
  Sarah (Hunloke) 210
  Sarah (Verin) 204, 207, 210, 213
  Thomas 211
BATTEY/BATTIE/BATTY/BATTYE
  Nicholas 147, 204
BAVER see BABER

BAXTER
  Edward 238, 240
  Mary 520
  Nicholas 416
  Robert 240
  Sarah 238, 240
  Sarah (Bell) 238-241
  Simon 238-242
  Susan 238, 240
BAYLEY/BAYLIE/BAYLY see BAILEY
BEACH
  Richard 227
BEACON
  Sibylla 287
BEAL/BEEL
  Christian 145
  Elizabeth 217
  Joan (Beale) 216
  John 145
  Nathaniel 145
  Sarah 213, 217
  Sarah (_____) 214-217
  Thomas 213-217, 286
BEALE
  John 107
  Martha (Bradstreet) (Rowlandson) 385, 387
  Samuel 385
  William 387, 388
BEAMON/BEAMAN/BEAMENT/
  /BEAMOND/BEAMONT/BEAUMONT
  /BEMAN
  Abigail 221
  Deborah 221
  Elizabeth 221
  Elizabeth (Williams) 218
  Gamaliel 217-219
  Hester 221
  Hester (Buckingham) 221
  John 218-220, 222
  Joseph 218
  Lydia 221
  Lydia (Danforth) 221, 222
  Mary 218, 221
  Mehitable 219
  Noah 218
  Patience (Trescott) 218
  Priscilla (Thornton) 219
  Rebecca 222
  Samuel 221
  Sarah 218, 222
  Sarah (_____) 218
  Thankful 219
  Thomas 218

Bellamy continued
  Jeremiah 356, 455
BELLINGHAM
  Ann 248
  Elizabeth 248
  Elizabeth (Backhouse) 243, 247
  Elizabeth (Smith) (Savage) 247
  Grace 248
  Hannah 248
  Hester 248
  James 248
  John 246, 248
  Lucy (_____) 247
  Penelope (Pelham) 243-245, 247
  Richard 243-250, 314, 340
  Samuel 246-250
  Sarah 248
  William 243, 246, 248, 249
BELLOWS
  Abigail 250-252
  Benjamin 252
  Daniel 252
  Eleazer 250, 252
  Elizabeth (Howe) 251
  Esther (Barrett) 252
  Hannah (Newton) 251
  Isaac 250, 251, 253
  John 250-253
  Mary 250-253
  Mary (Wood) 250, 251
  Nathaniel 250, 252
  Samuel 251
  Thomas 250, 251
BENJAMIN
  John 67
  Mr. 449
  Widow 460
BENNETT
  Aphra (_____) (Adams) 258
  Dorothy (_____) 259
  Edward 253, 254
  Elisha 257-259
  John 257, 258
  Lydia 259
  Priscilla 254
  Richard 254
  Samuel 182, 254-260, 505, 506
  Sarah 258
  Sarah (_____) 256, 258, 506
  Sarah (Hargrave) 257, 258
BENT
  Elizabeth (_____) 265
  Experience 265
  Joseph 265

BENTLEY
  Alice 261
  Dorothy (Albro) 17, 18
  John 261
  Mary 260, 261
  William 261
BERNARD see BARNARD
BESBEECH
  Alice 265, 266
  Anne (Baseden) 265
  Dorothy (Austin) (Foster) 265
  Elisha 266
  John 265
  Mary 265, 266
  Sarah 265
  Thomas 263-266
BESSEY
  Ann 267, 268
  Anna 269
  Anthony 266-270, 358
  David 267, 269
  Dorcas 267-269
  Elizabeth 267, 269, 358
  Jane 267-269
  Jane (_____) 267, 268
  Mary 267-269
  Mary (Ransom) 268
  Nehemiah 267, 268
  Rebecca 269
BEST
  John 270
  Nicholas 270
BETSCOMBE
  Andrew 272
  Anna 271
  Christopher 272
  Experience 272
  Grace (Coade) 271
  John 271
  Martha 271, 272
  Mary 271, 272
  Mary (Strong) 271, 272
  Richard 61, 271, 272
  Robert 272
BETTS/BEATS/BEATTS/BETTES
  Alice 280, 281
  Alice (_____) 278, 279
  Anna 106
  Elizabeth 281
  Elizabeth (_____) 395, 396
  Elizabeth (Bridge) 273-275
  Hannah 279-281
  Hope/Hopestill 279-281
  John 227, 273-277, 279-281, 394, 396

Brackenbury continued
   Samuel 234
   Sibyl (_____) 234
   William 123, 234, 235
BRACKETT/BRACKET
   Alice (Blower) 338
   Peter 98
   Richard 338
BRACY
   Anne (Pearce) (Carmichael) 374
   Constance 373
   Edmund 372, 373
   Hannah 374, 375
   Hannah (Hart) 373
   John 373-375
   Mary (Osborn) 373
   Phebe 373
   Phebe (Bisby) 373
   Susannah 374, 375
   Thomas 372-375
BRADBURY
   Ann 380
   Elizabeth 380
   Jabez 380
   Jacob 379, 380
   Jane 380
   John 376, 380
   Judith 379
   Mary 377, 379
   Mary (Perkins) 376, 378, 379, 381
   Rebecca (Wheelwright) (Maverick) 380
   Sarah (Pike) 379
   Thomas 320, 375-381
   William 378-380
   Wymond 320, 379, 381
BRADFORD
   Alice 33
BRADING
   James 100
BRADISH/ BROADISH
   Hannah 382, 383
   James 216, 382, 383
   John 382-384
   Joseph 382-384
   Mary 382-384
   Mary (_____) 383
   Mary (Frost) 383
   Robert 381-384
   Samuel 383, 384
   Sarah (_____) 216
   Susanna (_____) 384
   Vashti (_____) (Morrill) 382-384
BRADLEY
   Daniel 405

BRADSTREET/BROADSTREET
   Bridget (_____) 384-387
   Elizabeth (Harris) 387
   Hannah 386, 387
   Hannah (Peach) 386
   Humphrey 384-388
   John 186, 385-388
   Martha 386, 387
   Mary 385, 387
   Moses 385, 387
   Rebecca 385, 387
   Sarah 385, 387
   Simon 311
BRADY
   Elizabeth 494
BRANCH
   John 284
BRANE
   Agnes (_____) 388
   Thomas 388, 389
BRASEY
   William 426
BRAYTON
   Elizabeth 362
   Francis 362
BREAD/BREED
   Allen 148-150, 191, 259
   Elizabeth (Ballard) 149
   Elizabeth (_____) (Ballard) (Knight) 148, 150
BREDEN see also BRYDON
   Capt. 7
   John 238
   Thomas 238
BRENTON
   Mehetabel 443
   William 361, 443
BREWER see BRUER
BREWSTER
   Jonathan 343, 482
   William 482, 483
BRIDGE
   Anne (Danforth) 396
   Dorcas 394, 396, 397
   Dorcas (_____) 396
   Edmund 396
   Elizabeth 275
   Elizabeth (_____) (Bancroft) (Saunders) 393, 395, 396
   John 1, 158, 273-275, 393-397
   Matthew 1, 395-397
   Sarah 397
   Thomas 396, 397

Danforth continued
 Mary 216, 299
 Mary (Wilson) 299, 300
 Nicholas 221, 394, 396
 Sarah 216
 Thomas 98, 216, 274, 394, 402, 403
DANIEL
 Robert 324
DAVENPORT
 Lt. 12
 Mr. 246
 Rebecca 505
DAVIS
 Bridget (Loker) 403
 Elizabeth (Bills) 292
 Ephraim 292
 Isaac 12
 John 380, 436
 Margery (_____) 491
 Richard 499, 500
 Sarah 403
 Sarah (Burrill) 499, 500
 Thomas 98
DAY
 Mrs. 240
 Stephen 152
DAYTON
 Phebe 226
DEAN/DEANE
 Martha 284
 Rachel (_____) 284
 Sarah 442
 Sarah (Brown) 443
 Thomas 443
DEERING/DEARING
 Elizabeth (Mitchelson) (Atkinson) 101, 102
 Henry 101, 102
DENIS
 Widow 21
DENISON
 Daniel 181, 202
DENNIS
 Mary (Bushnell) (Robinson) 508
 Thomas 508
DENNY
 Mary 420
DENSLOW
 Nicholas 452
 Temperance 452
DENTON
 Alice 68
DERICH/DERRICK
 Mary (Bassett) 192-194
 Michael 193

DEVORIX
 John 7
DEVOTION
 Edward 361
DEXTER
 Thomas 256, 358
DICKENS
 Nathaniel 86
DICKERSON
 Thomas 189
DICKINSON
 Hannah (Beardsley) 225, 226
 Joseph 373
 Nathaniel 226, 331
 Obadiah 227
 Phebe 373
 Phebe (Bracy) 373
 Sarah (Beardsley) 225, 227
DICKMAN
 Hugh 504
DILLINGHAM
 Edward 74, 267
DINSDALE
 Goodwife 519
DIPPLE
 Grace 143
 Grace (_____) 143
DISBEROE
 Isaac 504
DIX/DEEKS
 Edward 164
 Elizabeth (Barnard) 164, 165
 John 164, 165
DOGGETT
 Goodman 402
 John 437
 Rebecca (Bailey) (Brown) 437
DOLE
 Hannah 201
 Richard 201
DOTY/DOTEY/DOUGHTY/DOWTY
 Edward 46, 284
 Francis 331, 332
DOVE
 Matthew 317
DOW
 Henry 181
DOWNE
 Eglin (Hatherly) 414
DOWNES
 John 7
 William 157
DOWSE
 Francis 491

Hodges continued
    John 320, 376
    Thomas 316
HOGSDEN
    Benoni 166
HOLDEN/HOULDEN
    John 368
    Martha 367
    Randall 302
    Richard 367
HOLLAND
    Adam 303, 305
    Ann 192, 502
    Rebecca (Bishop) 303, 305
HOLLARD
    Aingell 253
HOLLINGSWORTH
    Richard 22
HOLLOWAY/HOLLAWAY/HOLWAY
    /HOLLOWAY/HOLLEY
    Joseph 29, 258, 259
    Rose (Allen) 29
    William 107
HOLLY
    Samuel 526
HOLMAN
    John 35
    William 92
HOLMES
    Lydia 364
    Obadiah 364
    William 117
HOLT
    Hannah (Bradstreet) (Rolfe) 386
    Nicholas 110, 386
HOLTON
    William 187
HOLWAY/HOLLOWAY/HOLLEY see
HOLLOWAY
HOLYOKE
    Edward 54
    Mr. 149
    Prudence (Stockton) 54
    Sarah 54
HONEYWELL
    William 103, 104
HOOD
    Rebecca 41
    Sarah 193
HOOKE/HOOK
    Humphrey 256
    William 256, 322, 380
HOOKER
    Thomas 431, 472

    Thomas (Mrs.) 516
HOPKINS
    Edward 158, 159
    Goody 160
    Hannah (Andrews) 59, 60
    Jane (_____) 330
    Joan (Arnold) 89, 90
    John 330
    Mr. 472
    Thomas 89, 90
    William 60, 89, 91
HORNE
    John 21
    Sister 114
HOSIER
    Samuel 45, 46
HOSMER
    Hannah(Bushnell) 511
    Stephen 511
    Thomas 511
HOUGH/HAUGH
    Atherton 463
    Elizabeth (Bulkeley) (Whittingham) 463
    Hannah 351
    Mr. 399
    Samuel 461
HOUSE
    Elizabeth (Hammond) 368
    Samuel 368
HOVEY/HOVIE
    Abigail (Andrews) 54, 55
    Daniel 53-55
HOWARD
    Mary 486
HOWE/HOW
    Edward 486
    Elizabeth 251, 403
    John 251
    Margaret (Welles) 486
    Sarah 391
HOWLAND/HOWLANDE
    Arthur 129
    Henry 103, 426
    Lydia 426
    Martha 129
HOWLET
    Thomas 53
HOYT
    John 447
    Mary (Brundish) (Purdy) 447
    Simon 447
HUBBARD/HOBART
    Ann 177
    Benjamin 484

Pepper continued
  Richard 231, 457, 459
PERCON
  John 119
PERKINS
  Elizabeth 354
  John 379
  Mary 379, 381
  Mrs. 392
PERRING
  Thomas 353
PERRY
  Edward 33
  Francis 440
  Susan (Carver) 172, 173
  William 172
PERSALL
  Henry 78
PERSON/PEERSON
  Mary (_____) 86
  Thomas 86
PERSONS
  Richard 263
PETER/PETERS
  Hugh 248, 464
PETTINGALL
  Richard 433
PHELPS/PHELPES
  Henry 71, 211
  John 71, 211, 451-453
  Mary 155
  Sarah (Buckland) 452, 453
  William 155, 186
PHILLIPS
  Abiel 164
  George 164
  Hannah 367
  Henry 518, 522
  John 400
  Margaret 342
  Nicholas 369
  Samuel 385
  William 96, 238
PHILPOT
  Thomas 174
PHINNY
  John 359
PHIPPEN
  Joseph 441
  Samuel 441
PHIPS
  Margaret 57
PICKERING/PICKIRING
  Alice (Flint) (Bullock) 479

  Elizabeth 21
  John 12, 21, 479
  Jonathan 21
PICKMAN
  Martha 210
  Samuel 440
PIERCE/PEARCE/PEIRCE/PEIRSE
  Anne 374
  Anne (_____) (Allen) 38
  Hannah 303
  Isabel 332
  John 119, 304, 306, 374
  Mark 39
  Michael 38, 39
  Rebecca 303
  Ruth 303
  Ruth (Bishop) 304, 306
  Samuel 292, 398
PIGGOTT
  Spencer 370
PIKE
  Elizabeth (Andrews) 58
  Richard 58
  Robert 204, 320, 377, 378
  Sarah 379
PINE
  James 77-79
  Susan 79
PITCHER
  Andrew 458
  Experience 458
PITTLES
  Jonas 37
PITTS
  Leonard 500
PLACE
  Goodwife 286
  Jane 514
  John 514
  Sarah (Lovering) 514
PLASTOWE
  Josias 62
PLATTS/PLATS/PLATT
  Philippa (Andrews) (Felt) 58
  Richard 93
  Samuel 58, 249, 386
PLIMPTON/PLIMTON
  John 118
  Mary (Morse) 367
PLUMB/PLUME
  Elizabeth 153
  Mary (_____) 93
PLUMMER
  Hannah 120

INDEX OF FIRST NAMES

Ann continued
   May 342
   Messant 492, 494
   Prince 172, 177
   Pudeator 442
   Richards 191
   Richmond 466-468
   Soulby/Sowlbe/Sowlbie 489
   Webster 201-203
   Winsley 377
   _____ 15, 25, 60, 183, 191, 197, 342, 346,
   377, 492
ANNA
   Abbott 4
   Atwood 106
   Barrett 281
   Beck 228, 229
   Bessey 269
   Betscombe 271
   Betts 106
   Bigg 286, 287
   Blott 336
   Brown 417, 425
   Chamberlain 458
   Green 336
   Ines 417
   James 39
   Lord 184
   Sanford 4
   Tozier 336, 337
   _____ 229
ANNE
   Allen 36-38
   Armitage 79, 80
   Barrett 79
   Baseden 265
   Bastian 371
   Batter 211
   Besbeech 265
   Birdsall 302
   Blason 323
   Bowne 363-365
   Boylston 371
   Bracy 374
   Bridge 396
   Brigham 403
   Brooke 406
   Brown 165
   Bulkeley 463
   Burden 489-491
   Carmichael 374
   Clavell 211
   Crosby 403
   Cross 387

   Danforth 396
   Elliot 240
   Hermitage 79
   Hudson 512
   Hutchinson 468
   Ketch 402
   Leake 420
   Lillestone 78-80
   Lovering 165
   Partridge 377
   Pearce 374
   Pierce 38
   Sherman 163, 165
   Stanyan 377
   Try 463
   Whiting 163, 165
   Williamson 277
   Wilson 164, 165
   _____ 38, 240, 364, 377, 387, 406
ANNIS
   Almy 43-46
   Green 44, 46
ANTHONY
   Alsop 51
   Bessey 266-270, 358
   Cooper 272
   Newell 259
   Potter 389
   Sadler 377
   Stanyan 377, 378
   Stoddard 24, 238, 242, 245
   Thacher 110-113
   Underwood 514
   Whiting 163, 165
   Wilson 446, 447
   Wright 32
APHRA
   Adams 258
   Bennett 258
   _____ 258
APPHIA
   Clements 207
   _____ 207
ARTHUR
   Bostick 223
   Fenner 86
   Howland 129
   Mackworth 57
   Smith 158, 330
ATHERTON
   Hough 463
AUDREY
   Almy 44, 45
   Barlow 44

Matthew continued
  Barstow 173
  Borden 350, 351, 466
  Boyes 385
  Bridge 1, 396
  Craddock 483
  Dove 317
  Gibbs 383
  Ines 416, 417
  Mitchell 79, 80
  Roe 2
  Rowe 3
  Whipple 183
MEDAD
  Pomeroy 187
MEHITABLE/MEHETABEL
  Beamon 219
  Betts 280
  Bonney 342
  Brenton 443
  Bridges 391
  Brown 443
  Buttolph 518, 520
  Chamberlain 458
  Fien 93
  Frost 519, 520
  Hitchcock 280, 281
  King 342
  Tippett 279, 280
  Vittrey 280
MENENO
  Negro 245
MERCY
  Baker 142
  Baldwin 190
  Barber 155, 156
  Barstow 169, 170, 171, 173
  Belcher 234, 235
  Brackenbury 234
  Brigham 402, 403
  Burgess 498
  Camp 190
  Clark 169
  Gillett 156
  Hitchcock 281
  Hunt 402
  Hurd 403
  Leonard 251
  Newton 251
  Rice 402
  Wigglesworth 234
  No surname 281
  _____ 173, 402

MICAELL
  Blois 328
  Jennison 328
MICHAEL
  Barstow 170-174, 177-179
  Brigden 399
  Brown 418, 419
  Carthrick 399
  Derich 193
  Humphreys 474
  Pierce 38, 39
  Rainer 503
  Shaflin 22, 23, 69, 207, 311, 312
  Wigglesworth 234
MILDRED
  Brigden 399
  Carthrick 399
  Brigden 399
MILES
  Awkley 115
  Ives 526
  Reading 97
MIRIAM
  Bassett 193, 502
  Brooks 414
  Curtis 414
  Sandin 192, 193
MOREGIFT
  Starr 287
MORGAN
  Bedient 159, 161
  Bowers 295
MOSES
  Bradstreet 385, 387
  Burnham 233, 235, 236
  Maverick 441
  Newton 251
  Simonson 177
  Wheeler 52
MUSACHIELL
  Bernard 261-263
MYLES
  Standish 421
NARIAS
  Hawkins 291
NATHAN
  Andrews 3
  Barlow 268
  Beardsley 226
  Birdsall 302
NATHANIEL
  Adams 233, 236
  Alford 24, 25
  Atkinson 102

Susan continued
  Unthank 45
  Vincent 338
  Wall 238, 241
  Wildboare 239
  _____ 12, 449, 479, 493, 503
SUSANNA
  Albro 19
  Allen 28
  Anthony 17-19
  Arnold 82, 83
  Avery 110, 113, 114
  Bachelor 125, 126
  Ballard 150
  Barstow 168-170
  Bell 239, 241-243
  Betts 280, 281
  Blodgett 324, 325
  Blott 334, 335
  Bradish 384
  Brooks 412-414
  Brown 265
  Brydon 241
  Bull 473
  Bunce 472, 473
  Burdett 493
  Buttolph 520
  Clark 520
  Coocke 493
  Dunham 415
  Fuller 150
  Halstead 174
  Hanford 414
  Hawkes 506
  Kelly 520
  Lawrence 124, 125
  Lewis 346
  Marriott 169
  Sanford 520
  Selbee 335
  Steiner 170
  Story 150, 151
  Thomson 325
  Whiston 414
  _____ 28, 83, 114, 280, 325, 384, 473
SUSANNAH
  Ambross 376
  Archard 441
  Bacon 128, 129
  Barstow 177
  Birchard 296-298
  Bonython 345
  Bracy 374, 375
  Brigham 402

  Bull 474
  Bunce 472-474
  Fay 402
  Foxwell 345
  Humphreys 474
  Hutchenson 441
  Lincoln 177
  Morse 402
  Polley 127, 128
  Shattuck 402
  _____ 376, 441
SYLVESTER
  Baldwin 93
TABITHA
  Abdy 6, 7
  Blower 339
  Reynolds 6
  Tankersley 7
  _____ 339
TEMPERANCE
  Baldwin 93
  Buckland 451-453
  Denslow 452
  Ponder 452, 453
THANKFUL
  Beamon 219
  Bigg 287
  Brown 265
  Stowe 285, 286
  Wilson 219
THEODORE
  Atkinson 95-103, 367
THEOPHILUS
  Archer 285
  Frary 361
  Higginson 48
THOMAS
  Abbott 277
  Adams 13, 14, 525
  Allen 462
  Alsop 50-52
  Andrews 52-56, 59-62, 64-66, 71, 232, 233, 235, 236, 296
  Antrum 69-71, 206, 211, 438, 439
  Applegate 31, 72-75
  Armitage 27, 76-81
  Arnold 89
  Arrowsmith 91
  Atkins 104
  Atkinson 102-104
  Avery 113-115
  Bacor 145
  Baker 145, 207
  Bancroft 192

INDEX OF PLACES

INDEX OF SHIPS